Ralph Pat Barrett

SERIES ON

ISSUES IN SECOND LANGUAGE RESEARCH

under the editorship of

Robin C. Scarcella and Michael H. Long

ISSUES IN SECOND LANGUAGE RESEARCH is a series of volumes dealing with empirical issues in second language acquisition research. Each volume gathers significant papers dealing with questions and hypotheses in areas central to second language theory and practice. Papers will be selected from the previously published professional literature as well as from current sources.

OTHER BOOKS IN THIS SERIES

Research in Second Language Acquisition
Robin C. Scarcella and Stephen D. Krashen, Editors

Child-Adult Differences in Second Language Acquisition
Stephen D. Krashen, Robin C. Scarcella, and Michael H. Long, Editors

Second Language Acquisition Studies
Kathleen Bailey, Michael H. Long, and Sabrina Peck, Editors

Sociolinguistics and Language Acquisition
Nessa Wolfson and Elliot Judd, Editors

Language Transfer in Language Learning
Susan Gass and Larry Selinker, Editors

INPUT IN SECOND LANGUAGE ACQUISITION

Edited By

Susan M. Gass and Carolyn G. Madden

NEWBURY HOUSE PUBLISHERS, Cambridge
A division of Harper & Row, Publishers, Inc.
New York, Philadelphia, San Francisco, Washington
London, Mexico City, São Paulo, Singapore, Sydney

1985

Library of Congress Cataloging in Publication Data
Main entry under title:

Input in second language acquisition.

"Selected from papers presented at the Xth University of Michigan Conference on Applied Linguistics . . . held in Ann Arbor on October 28th, 29th, and 30th, 1983"--Pref.

1. Language and languages--Study and teaching--Addresses, essays, lectures. 2. Language acquisition--Addresses, essays, lectures. 3. Interaction analysis in education--Addresses, essays, lectures. I. Gass, Susan M. II. Madden, Carolyn. II. Conference on Applied Linguistics (10th : 1983 : University of Michigan)

P53.I516 1985 418'.007 84-22832
ISBN 0-88377-284-1

NEWBURY HOUSE PUBLISHERS
A division of Harper & Row, Publishers, Inc.

Language Science
Language Teaching
Language Learning

CAMBRIDGE, MASSACHUSETTS

Printed in the U.S.A.

First printing: April 1985
5 4

PREFACE

The papers in this volume were selected from papers presented at the Xth University of Michigan Conference on Applied Linguistics: Language Input: Learners' Use and Integration of Language in Context, held in Ann Arbor on October 28, 29, and 30, 1983. Like the preceding University of Michigan Conference on Applied Linguistics (Language Transfer in Language Learning), this conference was concerned with a topic which until this time had not been the focal point of a scholarly meeting. We wanted to provide a forum in which new perspectives on the study of second language acquisition could be advanced.

The explicit purpose of the conference was to develop a cohesive theoretical framework within which input studies could be conducted. It succeeded in bringing together for fruitful discussions American, Canadian, and European researchers interested in this focus of second language acquisition.

The volume consists of an introduction which provides the reader with background information on the topic of input and relates the papers in the volume to current issues. The introduction is followed by 23 papers divided into four sections. Finally, Diane Larsen-Freeman presents a pre- and postconference view of the issues related to language input.

The conference could not have taken place without the initial encouragement and continued support of Joan Morley and Eric S. Rabkin. We gratefully acknowledge their contribution. In addition, Eleanor Foster and Rosemary Tackabery provided patient administrative and organizational advice and assistance throughout all phases of the conference. We are also grateful to Sandy Fine and Judy Sudak for their assistance with both the conference and this volume. The students of the Linguistics Department and the staff of the English Language Institute deserve special recognition for their constant behind-the-scenes help.

We would like to express our gratitude to the following University of Michigan sources for the funding they provided to run the conference: Rackham School of Graduate Studies, English Language Institute, Department of Linguistics, School of Education, English Composition Board, Departments of Germanic Languages and Literatures, Near Eastern Studies, Romance Languages, and Slavic Languages and Literatures.

Last, but certainly not least, many thanks to our families, Josh, Aaron, Seth, Ethan, Terence, David, and Marcus.

Susan M. Gass
Ann Arbor, Michigan
June 21, 1984

Carolyn G. Madden

Contents

INPUT IN SECOND LANGUAGE ACQUISITION

Section One

INTRODUCTION

1

INTRODUCTION

Susan M. Gass and **Carolyn Madden**
The University of Michigan

Until recently second language researchers have been concerned primarily with such topics as the comparison of syntactic development between first and second language (L2) learners, the universal nature of language acquisition, the influence of a first language (or other languages known) on second language development, the role of language universals in second language acquisition, and social and affective variables which influence the acquisition of an L2. In the past few years, however, the field has begun to broaden its scope of inquiry to include the influence of the learning environment on learners' developing competence in a second language, focusing on input to the learner and the interactions in which learners engage.

Among the important papers contributing to the broadened scope of inquiry is Corder's 1967 paper. In this seminal work he made an important distinction between input and intake. In his words, "The simple fact of presenting a certain linguistic form to a learner . . . does not necessarily qualify it for the status of input, for the reason that input is 'what goes in' not what is available for going in, and we may reasonably suppose that it is the learner who controls this input or more properly his intake." Within the research paradigm of input studies, "input" generally refers to "what is available for going in" and "intake" to what actually does go in. Corder (1973) further distinguishes between 'input' and 'output.' In pedagogical terms, the 'input' is the syllabus taught and the 'output' the learner's grammatical competence at any particular point. The latter is generally inferred directly from what the learner says, or by means of a variety of elicitation tasks.

Another important paper in this area was by Wagner-Gough and Hatch (1975). They pointed out the importance of looking beyond the development of sentence-level syntax and considering the interactions in which learners engage. In other words, they emphasized the fact that we cannot begin to understand acquisition if we limit our research to a consideration of acquisition as a syntactic process, internal to the learner. Rather, they convincingly showed that acquisition is a process which relies on conversational interactions. Thus, syntax is viewed as *developing from* interaction rather than as a *source* of interaction. Central to this view is the role of input to the learner, that is, what kinds of input are accessible to the learner and how the input is integrated and used by the learner.

The studies in this volume highlight the input and intake distinction and further investigate the developing grammars that emerge within the context of learners' interactions and the input they are exposed to.

An important consideration in the investigation of learners' interactions is the nature of the talk to nonnative speakers (NNS), known as foreigner talk (FT). What kind of speech is addressed to the learner? Within the field of acquisition studies, Snow (1972) pointed out that the language of adults to children was not the same as the language adults use with one another. This speech came to be known as "baby-talk," then "motherese" and "caretaker speech." Ferguson (1971) introduced the term "foreigner talk," which he likened to "baby-talk." Some of the salient characteristics of FT are slower rate of speech, louder speech, longer pauses, common vocabulary, few idioms, greater use of gestures, more repetition, more summaries of preceding utterances, shorter utterances, and more deliberate articulation (cf. Hatch 1983b for more detail on these and other features).

The quality of foreigner talk has been the subject of much investigation in recent years. Gass and Varonis (1985) found that the kind of language addressed to NNSs varied as a function of the native speaker's (NS) ongoing assessment and reassessment of a NNS's ability to understand and to be understood. Gaies (1977) similarly found that the language that teachers used when talking to ESL students varied as a function of the proficiency of the learners.

Long (1980) in his seminal work argued that in addition to modified input (FT) one also witnesses modified interaction in conversations with NNSs. Modified interaction refers to the interactional structure of the conversation and not just the language addressed to the learner. For example, there are more instances of comprehension checks, confirmation checks, expansions, requests for clarification, and self and other repetitions in discourse involving NNSs than in discourse involving only two NSs. One also finds a different distribution of question types in foreigner talk discourse (FTD) as opposed to NS discourse (cf. Long 1980 and 1981a for elaboration and exemplification of these features).

In 1980, Krashen proposed the input hypothesis, which states that in order for acquisition to take place learners need to have comprehensible input. He further claims that this input must be at a stage slightly beyond the competence of the learner ($i + 1$). An important point to consider in this regard is: what is the function of modified input and modified interaction for the learner? An obvious response is that it makes language comprehensible so that communication can take place. Within Krashen's framework, if it is not comprehensible, it cannot serve acquisition at all. However, it may also serve to establish an affective bond among speakers which in turn may lead to more cooperative negotiation exchanges in which the NNS feels comfortable asking for clarification, making the input comprehensible. (The ways in which the relationship between input and acquisition can be shown are discussed in Long this volume and 1983c).

Interestingly, some kinds of reduced speech to learners may be culture-bound and if so cannot be considered the sine qua non of acquisition. Ochs (1980) reports on a non-Western society where children do not appear to be addressed in a register different from the one used in adult-adult conversation. While we are not aware of studies of FT in non-Western societies, however, it is clear that if FT and caretaker speech serve a similar function, then Ochs's results should suffice to at least question the claimed essential nature of modified speech.

The chapters in this volume approach the study of input from a variety of perspectives: sociolinguistic, educational, linguistic, and so forth. They are, in general, concerned with input, interaction patterns of learners with native and nonnative speakers, learners' use and integration of input, research methodology, and theory. Sections 2 through 5, the body of the volume, represent important areas of concern within the context of input studies. The sections are not mutually exclusive. Many deal with issues central to more than one section. What we have attempted to highlight by the divisions is a major contribution which we feel each chapter makes, as well as suggesting the interrelatedness of chapters within a section. Section 2 includes six papers on language in the classroom. In Section 3 there are six papers dealing with different aspects of interaction, modification, and negotiation. In Section 4 there are eight papers on the topic of input, intake, and output and the relationship between these concepts. In Section 5 we include four papers which deal with methodological and theoretical issues relating to language input. Finally, Section 6 presents a global look at present, past, and future input studies.

The opening chapter by Wong-Fillmore goes beyond just a consideration of language input as it relates to second language acquisition. Through audio- and video-taped data, as well as personal classroom visits, Wong-Fillmore analyzes the language and structure of classrooms containing nonnative speaking children, specifically attempting to highlight differences between classrooms in which the children were successful in learning English (the target language) and those in which they were not. She includes in her discussion issues other than language factors related to the language situation, such as the pedagogical structure of the classroom (e.g., format, turn-allocation). She finds that consistency and regularity are essential ingredients in the language classroom for the facilitation of language learning. In considering the language input to nonnative speaking children, Wong-Fillmore supports previous research based on immersion programs, finding that the most successful classes are those in which the native and target languages are maintained as separate entities. However, contrary to the commonly held view that the best forum for teaching a language is a relatively free one in which participants can engage in conversation, Wong-Fillmore finds that the most successful classes were those in which the activities were teacher-centered rather than student-centered. Wong-Fillmore's article is rich in detailed information about the structure and language of elementary school classrooms. As such, it provides us with a strong basis for understanding how language learning takes place in a classroom setting.

Saville-Troike's chapter, unique among the contributions to this volume, emphasizes the need to go beyond a consideration of linguistic forms toward a more holistic investigation of the environment children learning a second language experience. Through the use of video- and audio-taped information, Saville-Troike investigates the social milieu Asian kindergarten children are exposed to daily. From this investigation she extracts informative examples of language and cultural development. As might be expected, children at this age are exposed to various socialization rules concerning appropriate behavior in school as well as peer influence on play behavior. Saville-Troike's study highlights some of the effects both channels of socialization have on the communicative and cultural development of non-English-speaking children in a classroom setting and sets the pace for further holistic studies.

Kleifgen's chapter stems from the same data base as that of Saville-Troike. She examines teacher-pupil interactions at three points in time, focusing on the language of a kindergarten teacher to her pupils. Kleifgen specifically considers the nature of the teacher's language as a function of the proficiency of the children she addresses. She considers not only the teacher's speech to NSs as opposed to NNSs, but also how the teacher's speech to an individual child varies as a function of that child's increased proficiency. In particular she examines such variables as length of utterance, frequency of input, grammatical deviations, word type, and word frequency. Kleifgen's chapter is particularly interesting in that it goes beyond pure linguistic adjustments to consider both the instructional and linguistic needs of pupils.

Ellis takes as a point of departure interactions between a teacher and two pupils, a brother and a sister aged 11 and 13, both NSs of Punjabi. Ellis' approach to the analysis of input can be characterized as both quantitative and qualitative. He points out that quantitative analyses fail in at least two important ways: (1) they generally consider input features as stemming from the NSs rather than as a cooperative endeavor involving both interlocutors, and (2) they have not been able to show a direct relationship between input and second language acquisition. As in the chapter by Kleifgen, Ellis is interested in the adjustments made by the teacher and the pupils as a function of increased proficiency. His results were mixed, finding that some features changed while others did not, suggesting that some features are more finely tuned to proficiency level than others. A second important aspect to the chapter by Ellis is his discussion of the relationship between the interactions and the emergence of new target language (TL) forms. He shows with convincing examples how the children incorporate the teacher's utterances to progress to two-, three-, and four-word utterances, which prior to a particular interaction had been only at the "edges" of the learner's competence. He establishes an important link between the interactions in which children engage and the syntactic development of the child.

Wesche and Ready compare the discourse style and content of university professors with those of NNSs and NSs. In an experimental program designed to provide a transition for university-level second language learners, content courses were available in students' first or second language. Wesche and Ready analyzed various factors such as speech rate and pauses, vocabulary choices, syntactic units, and communication devices of two professors, each teaching the same content class to NSs and NNSs. While noted adjustments were made for NNSs, e.g., simplifications and redundancies, the adjustments were not necessarily the same for the two professors. Wesche and Ready look at the shared and individual adjustments and the differential effect on learners. The results of their analysis suggest the need for a dynamic and interactional paradigm for the investigation of FT in a classroom setting.

Pica and Doughty offer an intensive investigation of classroom-centered activities and the differing effects that teacher-directed input and small-group input have on the nature of the developing strategies and language of second language learners. Through an analysis of discourse features and linguistic units in learner classroom interactions, Pica and Doughty add to the growing body of research on language development within a communicative context. Focusing on two classroom styles, teacher-fronted activity and small-group work, the authors substantiate some expected, as well as some unexpected, differences between learners exposed to the two approaches. This research offers a challenging paradigm of investigation for further classroom-centered research.

The chapter by Hirvonen relates to the study by Ellis in that she examines interactions involving children. However, her focus is a different one. She asks interesting and hitherto unexplored questions: How do monolingual and bilingual children differ in their approach to interactions with NNSs? Do these two groups of native-speaking children differ in their awareness of the necessity to modify their speech when addressing children who are not proficient in the language of communication? Her analyses comparing the NNSs in interactions with the two "types" of NSs consist of both sentence-level and discourse-level features. She finds modification in both areas and suggests that it may serve to make meaning more transparent, thus enabling a sustained conversation to take place. Monolingual speakers were surprisingly better able than bilingual speakers to modify their speech. Interestingly, differences were found in the kind of modifications made; bilinguals preferring discourse modification and monolinguals syntactic modification.

In the contribution by Gass and Varonis, the authors continue their research into the negotiation of meaning in NNS–NNS discourse. Based on a model they developed to investigate the ways meaning is negotiated, Gass and Varonis consider negotiation as a function of the context in which it occurs and the social role of the participants. In particular, they are concerned with the effect of different language demands reflected by task types on negotiation. Their data base comes from learners involved in one-way and two-way tasks. Contrary to previous findings in this area, their results do not support the prediction of greater negotiation in two-way information tasks as opposed to one-way. They call into question the familiar distinction between these two task types, suggesting that they are better represented as continuous rather than dichotomous variables. A final point to which the authors allude is possible sex differences in the negotiation of meaning.

The last chapter in this section deals with the comprehension of foreigner talk. Hawkins clearly outlines the importance of modified speech to the learner and then questions the extent to which appropriate responses of NNSs within a conversational setting represent actual comprehension. Her research critically examines a methodology frequently used in the investigation of foreigner talk discourse, presenting challenging results on this issue.

The chapter by Sato is one of three in this volume dealing with interlanguage (IL) phonology. Her study is a longitudinal one examining the speech of a Vietnamese child. The theoretical basis for this study comes from a Labovian sociolinguistic paradigm applied to second language acquisition. Differing speech situations are claimed to evoke different speech styles (ranging from formal to informal) which result in varying phonological forms. The specific phonological feature which Sato investigates is the production of word-final consonants and word-final consonant clusters. Some of her results support the continuum paradigm (based on the amount of attention paid to speech), while others do not. In other words, linguistic features are variably affected. Sato calls into question the defining characteristics of speech style, suggesting that one must consider more than just amount of attention paid to linguistic form.

Zuengler's chapter explores phonological variation within the context of NS–NNS interactions. Basing her research on previous work of NS speech, Zuengler raises some interesting issues concerning the phonological input of

NSs to NNSs. The most salient issue in this research is the notion of status of interlocutors and the effect status has on the phonological forms used by NSs when addressing NNSs. Zuengler's research shifts our attention not only to phonological considerations in examining input but to sociolinguistic ones as well. We will see these issues raised again in the chapter by Beebe.

The approach taken by Avery, Ehrlich, and Yorio differs from the previous two on IL phonology. Their study is unique in that it deals with the relationship between phonological form and discourse function. The discourse framework which they adopt distinguishes between core and noncore propositions. The phonological framework incorporates both segmental and suprasegmental phenomena in the analysis. The authors find that phonological adjustment is not a monolithic phenomenon. Rather, phonological adjustments occur only at certain points in the discourse, dependent on the function of the discourse. Interestingly, the adjustments they find made by NSs to NNSs are also made by NSs to other NSs, suggesting the universal dependence of phonological production on discourse function.

The first chapter in Section 4 is that of Swain. She challenges the by now familiar notion of the importance of comprehensible input by suggesting that what is needed is not comprehensible input but what she calls comprehensible output. The subjects of her analysis are children from grade 6 French immersion programs who were tested on a variety of measures in order to get information on their grammatical, sociolinguistic, and discourse competence. Her approach to the study of input is unlike those in other chapters in this volume. Rather than consider only the input, she is concerned with the relationship of input and output as mediated through aspects of learners' proficiency. Within her framework comprehensible output is the aspect of language use which is essential for acquisition. Without it learners do not have a forum for actively testing and refining their knowledge of the target language.

Related to the notion of comprehensible output is Day's study in which he examines the relationship between learners' use of the target language (in this case English) away from the classroom and their proficiency in English. Day compares the results of standard measurements of proficiency, cloze tests, and learners' self-evaluation of the quantity and type (i.e., TV, newspaper, conversation) of target language and native language used outside the classroom. Counter to expectations, the results indicate little or no support for such a relationship. Day discusses the methodological issue of using self-report data as a means of gathering accurate information about quantity and quality of input.

Brown's study investigates a not too often cited group of learners, i.e., older adults (55 to 75), and compares their requests for specific language input with the requests made by younger adult learners (19 to 23). Searching for differences and/or similarities between the younger and older learners' perceptions of input, in terms of both the quantity and quality of input received, Brown highlights factors which contribute to older learners' success or lack of success in language learning.

Chaudron's study deals with Corder's early distinction between input and intake. In a carefully controlled study involving lecture comprehension, this relationship is investigated. This is clearly an important research area in second language studies, since knowing what of the target language input is integrated by the learner and how it is integrated is necessary to an understanding of the processes of acquisition. Chaudron's chapter goes a long way in setting up a methodology by means of which the input/intake relationship can be understood and through which we can begin to understand the effect a learner's grammar has on the use and integration of target language input.

Olshtain and Blum-Kulka focus our attention on the acculturation process of second language learners. In an experimental task designed to evaluate nonnative speakers' acceptability judgments of apologies and requests, Olshtain and Blum-Kulka investigate whether NNSs shift style preferences toward the target language norms as a function of the length of stay in the target language community. After ascertaining a measure of cultural similarity and difference between the response patterns of American English and Hebrew speakers, the researchers examine the response preferences of L2 learners of Hebrew and compare these with the native Hebrew results. They found that cultural differences in speech act style are best represented as a continuum, with NNSs to some extent following the continuum from native to target language style. Olshtain and Blum-Kulka thus contribute a measure of language development which complements the grammatical acquisition of learners, providing a more complete model of learners' development in a second language environment.

Like Chaudron's study, the chapter by Zobl investigates the effect of controlled input on learners' grammatical competence. As he points out, learners receive only a portion of the TL "data universe" yet they develop grammars which go beyond the immediate input. Input serves as a mediator between the TL grammar and the learner's grammar. He raises an issue which is essential to an understanding of how grammars develop. How is it possible for learners to rely on *and* go beyond the input data? In investigating this question, he considers implicational relationships based on markedness conditions. He claims that markedness conditions relate the input data to the TL data universe, allowing the learner to project from the limited amount of data received to his or her IL grammar.

Kellerman's descriptive analysis of learners' grammatical development first focuses on the concept of learners' "U-shaped behavior." Kellerman provides supporting evidence from other research and examines cross-sectional data of university-level students in a foreign language environment. He investigates the extent to which learners follow the characteristic three stages of U-shaped behavior: first, error-free performance; second, deviant performance; and third, error-free performance. Many issues are dealt with in this chapter in an attempt to account for his data, but most important to the issue at hand is the suggestion that the learner at the second stage is unlikely to be as affected by TL input as in stages 1 and 3, given that the second stage is the only one in which deviant behavior is witnessed. As in Zobl's paper, the importance of input as a unique solution is questioned and the learner's role in generating a grammatical system is emphasized.

The final chapter in Section 4 is that of Liceras. Her concern is with the ways in which second language data reflect linguistic knowledge. Specifically, she deals with the role of intake as a determining factor of a learner's competence. She proposes a model to account for variable intuitions which result from different tasks and claims that it is production mechanisms which result in variability. Her specific object of inquiry is complementizer structures of Spanish learners of English. She focuses on the tripartite relationship of input/intake/output, claiming that intake mediates between input and output. Crucial to a consideration of intake is the knowledge the learner has of the L2, markedness relationships, and metalinguistic abilities. This chapter relates in an interesting way to that of Zobl, who also sees markedness relationships as having a central role in acquisition.

We begin Section 5 with a contribution by Long. His study goes a long way toward filling a lacuna by dealing with a question central to input research: What is the effect of modified input on the learner's ability to comprehend? In a controlled study involving lecture comprehension, Long shows that in fact when lectures display FT features, actual and perceived comprehension is higher than in lectures which lack these features. Importantly, he argues for an indirect causal relationship between adjusted speech and acquisition. Unique to this volume is Long's discussion of the relationship of concepts from philosophy of science to second language acquisition, specifically relating these concepts to studies of input.

Sharwood Smith raises a methodological issue which is basic to research in second language acquisition. What is the nature of argumentation? He points out that single explanations are generally sought when accounting for L2 data. However, in many cases, a more likely explanation stems from interacting factors. Using a broad linguistic base, he examines the placement of adverbs in ILs, finding that a "conspiracy" of factors is necessary to account for the data. Like Zobl, Sharwood Smith claims that theories of L2 acquisition cannot rely exclusively on input as a basis for the formation of grammars. He adds that the concept of input must be broadened to include input from languages other than the L2 (most often the L1).

Beebe's chapter approaches the issue of input and its direct relationship to learners from a sociolinguistic point of view. Beebe provides a review of much of the literature concerning dialect preferences among second language learners, citing many examples of peer influence on language learners as opposed to, for example, the influence of teacher or parent. Other influences, however, are prevalent enough to suggest to Beebe that a sociolinguistic investigation of types of input related to other sociological factors, i.e., status and solidarity within the social environment of the language learner, is warranted. In fact, she importantly points out that such investigations will provide a greater understanding of the choices learners make in determining "what input becomes intake."

The last research contribution in this volume is by Lightbown and d'Anglejan, who make explicit the need to examine more carefully the nature and source of input to language learners. Investigating the interactions of NNSs and NSs of French, Lightbown and d'Anglejan document the unexpected nature of input in these interactions. A first look at learner data suggests that there is a mismatch between input and output, when output is measured against a prescribed notion of input. However, a closer look at input data reveals that many of the input forms are not prescribed forms and are thus perhaps more consistent with the learner's output than the data first suggest. As a result, Lightbown and d'Anglejan suggest a more refined investigation of the actual input to which learners are exposed.

In determining the factors which contribute to the processes involved in second language learning, many of the researchers here have clearly indicated the need to consider a multiplicity of factors along with input in order to determine learner development. In so doing, they have succeeded in increasing our understanding of the nature of input and its relationship to learning. In addition, the volume includes research which has emphasized the need to look at the nature of input more carefully and research which has recommended a closer look at the learner and the internal processes which mediate between what serves as input and the internal grammar which he or she creates, as evidenced most often by the output. While the research has sharpened our vision of the questions and issues, in many cases the results have been tentative. This tentativeness may be due to the difficult situation in which SLA research finds itself: the questions which are being asked as a result of our broadened scope of inquiry and our ever-increasing knowledge of the second language acquisition process are becoming more sophisticated and complex. Yet the methods we have for investigating the questions and the theoretical models which have been developed up to this time are not sufficiently refined to deal with the factors which affect a learner's competence. We anticipate that the focus of future research will address these methodological issues and pave the way for a deeper understanding of the issues discussed in this volume.

We hope that readers of this volume will come to appreciate the complexities involved in the issues of input, in terms of both the processes of acquisition and the tools and theories we have for investigation.

Section Two

LANGUAGE IN AN INSTRUCTIONAL SETTING

On Children

2

WHEN DOES TEACHER TALK WORK AS INPUT?

Lily Wong-Fillmore
University of California, Berkeley

THE PROBLEM

Each year, many hundreds of thousands of non-English speakers enter American schools. Both they and their teachers face formidable challenges. Until they learn English, these students will be unable to take full advantage of the educational and social opportunities that the school offers. Their teachers will have a difficult time teaching them the skills and information that must be taught in school without first helping them learn English. It is frequently assumed that students who are described as "limited in English proficiency" (LEP) will pick up the English they need in a year or two just by being in an environment in which it is spoken. Some instruction in English as a second language is usually provided for them, but there are language-learning specialists who regard it as superfluous: they believe these children will pick up English with or without such instruction. In fact, there is a widely held belief even among second language researchers that for these students true language learning takes place not in the classroom but outside of it as they find occasions to communicate with English-speaking peers in social situations that are more meaningful to them than ones found in the classroom.

Some of these students eventually do pick up enough English to get by in school just by being in an English-speaking environment; but others experience considerable difficulty in doing so. There is substantial evidence showing that many LEP students find it difficult to acquire the level of English proficiency that is needed for school, or they take so long learning English that they are unable to make normal academic progress.

The educational problems of language minority students in this country are well known and need not be recited here. In the past 15 or more years, considerable attention has been given to the special needs of these students, and a great deal of money and effort has been invested in the development of special programs aimed at ameliorating their linguistic and educational problems. The most highly publicized of these has been bilingual education, in which LEP students are educated partly in their L1s and partly in English. In recent years, however, these programs have come under fire, with critics contending that the use of the L1s in school has exacerbated the adjustment problem for language minority students and is responsible for the continued difficulty they have had in learning English. As long as they can get by using their L1s in school, LEP students will not find it necessary to learn English, and they will avoid doing so, the argument goes. Studies of language proficiency in LEP students appear to contradict such views, however.

Several studies that have examined the development of language proficiency in LEP students have shown that between 26.5 percent (Duncan and De Avila 1979) and perhaps 60 percent (Dulay and Burt 1980) of the students identified as LEP students are no more proficient in their L1s than they are in English. In fact, this research indicates that English rather than the L1 is the predominant language for many of these LEP students, suggesting that reliance on the L1 is not responsible for the poorly developed English skills that these students show. Research in bilingual education has shown that the L1 of the students is used far less than English in most bilingual classrooms, including ones that have been identified as successful programs (Tikunoff 1983, Legarreta 1979, Wong-Fillmore et al. 1983). What this all adds up to is the conclusion that many LEP students are getting plenty of exposure to English in school, but they are not learning it very well. At least, the skills they are acquiring in English are less than adequate for dealing with school. The fact that many of these *limited-English-speaking students* appear to be *English-dominant* is especially troubling. What it means is that the limited version of English that they speak is about as complete a language system as they have going for them. That obviously does not bode well for academic development, as educators have discovered. In one large urban school district, over a third of the district's 34,000 *limited-English-speaking* students have been found to be *predominantly English-speaking.* Their linguistic deficiencies are clearly reflected in academic performance: these students reportedly score well below the 23 percentile level in two achievement tests that depend on a knowledge of English.[1] This situation raises some questions that ought to be of as much interest to second language researchers as to educators: What is happening in the process of second language learning for these students such that they are not developing a level of proficiency that allows them to function in school? What kind of language skills do these students need, and how are they acquired? What role do teachers play in the process? To what extent can the language-learning problems of these students be attributed to the kind of programs these students are exposed to? What role do students themselves play in the process? Is there any evidence that what teachers do in their instructional program influences the kind of language their students learn or their ability to learn it? These are issues that my colleagues at the University of California at Berkeley and I have been investigating in several large-scale studies of second language learning in elementary school children, and they are questions that I consider in this chapter. Specifically, I will be discussing research that I have been doing on the part played by teachers in making it possible for LEP students in their classes to learn English, not through ESL instruction but through their teaching of the usual subject matter of school.

BACKGROUND

I became interested in the questions related to the influence of instructional language use and of other teaching practices on language learning several years ago in the course of collecting data for a study of language learning in young children. This study, a 3-year longitudinal investigation of individual differences in second language learning,[2] had me spending the better part of a year in four kindergarten classrooms, an experience which gave me an opportunity to discover the extent to which teachers can influence language learning in their classrooms.

Contrary to the usual assumption that children learn language mainly from peers outside of the classroom and not from teachers, it appears that for many LEP students, the only place in which they come into regular contact with English speakers is at school. Thus, language learning, if it is going to take place at all, is going to have to happen at school. The classroom can be an ideal place to learn English if it allows learners to be in close and continuous contact with teachers and classmates who speak the target language well enough to help in its learning. This, of course, depends on the actual availability of classmates who speak English, and on their willingness to interact with the learners in ways that will help them learn the target language. Unfortunately, in many schools serving LEP students, there are few students who speak the language well enough to provide an adequate model of it for classmates who don't speak it at all. But even where there are English speakers in the student body, the social situation in the school may be such that either by design or by choice, there is little contact between them and the LEP students. The only regular exposure to English that many LEP students can count on getting is in the classroom. There, at least, they can hear their teachers speaking English as they conduct lessons or otherwise direct them in their school work. They can also expect to be given some opportunity to practice speaking the language themselves. Thus, in classrooms serving LEP students, the language used by teachers in instructional events serves at least two major functions. It is the means by which teachers impart to their students the information and skills they are supposed to be learning in school, and it also serves as the linguistic input on which these students can base their learning of English as a second language.

How well their teachers dealt with these two aspects of language use in the classroom made an enormous difference to the subjects whose language learning we were following in a study of individual differences in second language learning. In two of the four classrooms in which my students and I were observing the language-learning behavior of some 60 Cantonese and Spanish-speaking children[3] during the first year of our study, the teachers were the only source of English input. All or very nearly all of the children in these two classes were either non-English speakers or extremely limited in English proficiency. There were, in the other two classes, ample numbers of English speakers to provide additional input for the non-English speakers: one of these was a double class, with a 2 to 1 ratio between English and non-English-speaking students; the other was a normal-size class with a 1 to 1 ratio.

Since we were interested in seeing how individual learner characteristics might affect language-learning behavior, we kept detailed observational records of the daily experiences of our subjects in school. We made observational notes and full-day recordings on audio and video tape of the events in our study classrooms in an effort to discover what kinds of opportunities were available for the subjects to hear and use English in each of the four classrooms. We also made full-day observations periodically of each of our subjects in order to determine how learner characteristics might influence the individual's use of whatever opportunities were available to learn English. We soon discovered that the language used by teachers during instructional activities constituted the only regular contact many of these students had with English. This was especially true in the case of the two classrooms with high concentrations of LEP students, but it was also true in the other two classes for those individuals who were unable or not inclined to interact with English-speaking classmates. About the only time these students had to deal with English at all was when they participated in lessons that were conducted in that language. Our observations of the children outside the classroom, and reports given by parents in home interviews indicate that for many of our subjects, the classroom was the only place where they came into close contact with English speakers. The language used in these lessons comprised their main input for whatever language learning they were to do that year. Our analyses of the data from this study have revealed much about the ways in which individuals differ in their ability to base their learning of a second language on the input available to them. They have also revealed the ways in which classrooms can differ in the extent to which they promote language learning, and in the kind of language skills children can learn in them. The differences we observed in these four kindergarten classrooms had dramatic consequences on language-learning outcomes during that first year of the study. In two of the classrooms, all or nearly all of the children who began school as non-English speakers learned some English by the end of their first year in school. Some learned much more than others, but only two children remained English-free at the end of the year. In the other two classes, a full 40 percent of those who began as non-English speakers remained so after a year in school. Perhaps they were not completely free of English, but they gave us no reason to believe that they could understand or speak more than just a few words of English.

Making sense of the striking differences we found in language-learning outcomes across the four classes was not an easy matter. Two things were clear from the outset, however. The concentration of LEP students in the four classrooms was not a determining factor, since the classroom with the highest concentration of language learners was one of the two classes that worked well for language learning and the other was the class with the smallest proportion of learners. Nor were the differences we found associated with ethnic or linguistic background, since one of the two successful classes was Chinese and the other was Hispanic, meaning, of course, that the same was true for the two less successful classes. One possibility was that by some fluke, there were disproportionately high concentrations of untalented language learners in two of the four classrooms, but an examination of our individual differences data did not reveal any significant differences across classes. Some of the children who learned no English in the two unsuccessful classes were much like the ones who did well in the other two classes.

After eliminating these variables as contributing factors, we turned our attention to the observational data we had collected of instructional events in the classroom to see whether our subjects had had equivalent exposure to the new language. Only then was it possible to see how greatly teachers can influence language learning in their classes by the way they use language in instructional events, and by the opportunities they make available to students during these events to practice the new language. We found that the language-learning outcomes found in this study could be attributed in part to the way these classes were organized for instruction and in part to the way teachers presented the materials they were teaching during lessons. It also turned out that while the composition of these classes was not responsible for the differences we found, it was a factor which influenced the extent to which a given organizational structure promoted language learning across the classes.[4]

Since then, in trying to gain a better understanding of the process by which children learn a second language in school, I have been studying the language used by teachers during instructional events and the practices they follow in their teaching. Looking beyond these four classrooms, I have found that the variable success found in them was not unusual. Considerable variation can be seen across classes in how well they work for language learning. These differences are not always immediately apparent, since once learners know a little of the language it is less easy to tell whether or not they are continuing to make progress. However, if one looks at classes in the early grades where there are many students who have just entered school with no English, it is not hard to see differences. One will find classes in which everyone will have learned some English after a year, and others in which a sizable proportion of the students who begin the year with no English will end it in the same condition.

In an effort to study this problem more directly, my colleagues and I undertook a second study, this one dealing with many more subjects and classrooms.[5] The aim of the second study has been to study the effects of instructional practices followed by teachers of LEP students on second language learning. This study was also a 3-year investigation which took us into 19 third and fifth grade classrooms serving Cantonese- and Spanish-speaking students to see how instructional practices involving matters of language choice and use during instructional activities, organization and structure of lessons, explicit language instruction, and student participation affected language learning.

In all, my colleagues and I have been in some 30 kindergarten through fifth grade classrooms over the past 5 years studying language learning in connection with the several studies I have been doing. Some of these were designated as all-English classes, others as bilingual classes. We have tested, sampled, and observed language learning and teaching in these classes. We also made 4 or 5 full days of video-taped records of the instructional activities our subjects engaged in from all but four of our classrooms. With the aim of figuring out in what ways these classes we were working in differed with respect to the language used by teachers, I have gone into all these classrooms myself and have observed and audio-taped full days of instructional events in each of them. In addition to these classrooms for which I have substantial documentation of language behavior and learning, I have also observed and recorded teachers working with LEP students in another 10 classrooms, giving me data from some 40 classrooms for this investigation.

For the past year or so, I have been been going over my observational records and the video and audio tapes collected in these classes in an effort to characterize the differences between situations that promoted second language learning, and ones that did not. This chapter reports on the picture that has emerged from my observations in these classrooms and from my analyses of the video- and audio-taped materials that were collected in connection with the several studies that have examined language learning in the schools. This is only one aspect of these studies, which are multifaceted investigations of second language learning, and of the effects of instructional practices on language learning. My purpose in doing a separate qualitative analysis of the classroom data has been to generate some hypotheses as to how teachers influence language learning by the way they use language in teaching LEP students. The method that I followed was first to distinguish classes that worked well for language learning from ones that did not based on comparisons of the progress made by LEP students in the learning of English, and then to determine the extent to which these classes differed in the kind of linguistic and instructional experiences they offered students. A fairly clear picture has emerged from this analysis of some of the practices that appear to determine how well classrooms work for language learning. I am now trying to discover by a detailed coding of the data available to me the extent to which the various features and characteristics of instructional language use that are identified here as major variables in these classrooms actually influenced the language learning that took place in them.

CHARACTERISTICS OF CLASSROOMS AS SETTINGS FOR LANGUAGE LEARNING

Two sets of characteristics appear to distinguish classes that work for language learning from those that do not. The first set relates to the way the classes are structured or are organized for instruction, the second to the way language is used in lessons. An explanation of how class structure could possibly figure in language learning might help to put the two types of features into perspective. In organizing classes for instruction, educators seldom consider the effects that different types of structure might have on language learning. The main purpose of structure in the classroom is to facilitate the teaching of subject matter. Classrooms are a complex social environment. Typically, there are some 25 to 30 students representing varying degrees of interest in being there, and willingness in being instructed (Jackson 1968). That many bodies and separate personalities in one room can add up to a chaotic and unpredictable social situation without some sort of structure. Teachers have a curriculum to teach over the course of a year. In order to cover the curriculum in that time, they have to exercise control over the social behavior of the participants in the class. Aspects of this control involve the scheduling of events and the organization of lessons; they also involve the imposition of rules governing movement, behavior, and social interaction among classmates, and between teachers and students during classtime. Verbal behavior is ordinarily tightly controlled during instructional events: teachers regulate the topics of discussion and its pacing and direction; they decide who gets to talk, and for how long; and finally, they judge what the students have to say and how they say it, and correct them when it is deemed necessary (Edwards and Furlong 1978). How classes are organized and how instructional events are structured determine to a large extent the nature of the language that students hear and use in the classroom. There are many ways of organizing and structuring classes, but jargonistically speaking, they can be subsumed under two labels: "teacher-directed" (or "teacher-centered") and "open" (or "student-centered") classes. The first type is on the high end of teacher control; the second is on the low end, with teachers coordinating rather than directing the social and learning behavior of the students. In the first type of structure, many instructional events are organized as whole-class or large-group activities which are directed by the teacher. In the second type, there are fewer teacher-directed activities than individual and group learning activities in which students work cooperatively without much teacher involvement. These two types of structures can add up to quite different language-learning opportunities for LEP students. Let us consider how classes that worked well for language learning differed from those that worked less well, first in the way they were structured and second in the way teachers used the target language during instructional activities.

HOW PARTICIPANT STRUCTURE IN LESSONS AFFECTS LANGUAGE LEARNING

There were, in all the classes studied, some teacher-directed, whole-class or large-group activities, some small-group activities which were either teacher-centered or student-centered (i.e., groups of students working cooperatively on projects), and some seatwork-type activities in which the students were given work assignments to carry out individually. The classes differed considerably, however, in how much each type of activity was used. In a fourth of the classes much of the instruction was carried out as individual seatwork activities. A few classes were at the other extreme, with instruction organized mostly as teacher-directed whole-class or large-group activities. The others were more balanced, making use of both types of activities.

A common belief held by language-learning specialists is that the best situation for language learning is one that is relatively "open" in structure, and in which students can talk freely with one another even during instructional activities. We assume that in such settings students can get maximum contact with classmates who speak the new language, and through this contact get the practice they need in using it. But this seemed not to be the case for the classes that have been studied here. By and large, the most successful classes for language learning were the ones that made the greatest use of teacher-directed activities. In such classes, individual work was assigned mostly as follow-up activities to formal lessons during which teachers led students through the materials that were being taught and directed them in discussions of that material. Indeed, classes that were open in their structure and those that made heavy use of individual work were among those found to be among the least successful for language learning.

In open classrooms where students are given a degree of choice in how they deal with the materials they have to learn and a certain amount of freedom to interact with one another during instructional activities, it seems that how much practice students get with the use of English depends on individual circumstances and on who is in the class. Students who want to interact with English-speaking classmates and teachers, and who have the social skills needed to conduct these interactions in a language that is new to them do quite well in open classes. Those who find it difficult to socialize with others or who feel constrained by the language differences that bar easy communication with classmates and teachers do not learn as much English. Such classes do not work well for anyone at all, however, unless there are sufficient numbers of English-speaking students in the classroom to support the language-learning efforts of the LEP students who are there. In open classrooms with high concentrations of LEP students, there are often not enough English speakers available to provide the input needed by everyone. As noted earlier, the teacher is sometimes the only person in the class who knows English well enough to be of any help to the learners. But since much of the interaction between teacher and students in such classes takes place on an individual basis, the amount of exposure to the new language that students get varies enormously, depending on whether they take advantage of opportunities to interact with the teacher. How well they learn English may well depend on their ability to make the most of limited input. A major problem in such classes is that students do not get enough practice using the language with native speakers. They are free to interact with classmates while they are working, but if no one knows English very well, such interactions do little to further their development of that language. Where the students share a common L1, their interactions are most naturally conducted in the language they know rather than in English, which is new to all of them. If they speak different L1s, they will try to communicate in English to whatever extent they can, but since no one knows it very well, the forms they use are likely to be imperfect ones. The practice they get in trying to communicate with one another in a language they are just learning may result in some of the temporary forms that learners rely on becoming permanent features of their version of the new language. This is a problem in any classroom where learners greatly outnumber fluent speakers of the target language, no matter how the class is organized. Selinker, Swain, and Dumas (1975) have shown that even in immersion classes that were structured in ways that apparently worked well for second language learning, learners developed many permanent interlanguage features through their exposure to the "junky input data" they were providing for one another in their interactions. It is not surprising, then, to learn from Swain (this volume) that after 7 years in school, students in French immersion programs have yet to acquire a fully standard form of their second language. The problem is especially acute in open classrooms, since students generally spend more time interacting with classmates than they do with teachers; under such circumstances, the major source of second language input comes from other language learners, a situation which is hardly conducive to successful language learning.

Classes that make heavy use of individual assignments do not work well for language learning for a somewhat different reason. Like the situation in the open classrooms, students in such classes get neither enough linguistic input to serve their needs nor adequate practice in speaking the language but not necessarily because there are too few English speakers in the class or because they are not inclined to interact with them. The problem instead is that classes that are organized in this manner do not allow for much talk of any type, and thus there are few opportunities to hear and speak the language at all. Teachers spend a certain amount of time each day going over new materials and explaining assignments to students, but for much of the school day, students work independently on the materials that have been assigned to them. Classes that are organized in this manner vary somewhat, but students are often discouraged from talking to one another while they work. Students can consult teachers regarding their assignments, and teachers often spend extra time working with individuals who need help, but much of the time is spent with students engaged in work that is done without interaction. Hence students get little exposure to the language at all except for the short periods during which the teacher explains new materials and assignments, or when there is a need to go to the teacher for individual help with work. The exposure they get to the new language in these ways is all too often insufficient to serve as the basis for learning it. In this case, the learners may be in contact with people who speak the target language, but they are given few opportunities to interact directly with them. In order to learn a new language, learners have to be in a position to engage in interactions with speakers in a variety of social situations, since this is what allows them to figure out what is being said, how the language is structured, and how it is used socially and communicatively by its speakers. In this type of classroom, there is contact with speakers, but too little actual interaction with them to serve the needs of the language learners. Some individuals, namely, those who can make the most of whatever input they get, may acquire the new language nevertheless. Otherwise, it is up to the learners to seek help outside of the classroom. Those who are inclined to seek out English-speaking classmates and who can manage to engage them socially during breaks in the school day will learn some English; those who are not so inclined or who lack the social skills to manage such contacts will learn little.

How were the classes that were successful settings for language learning different? As noted above, the prevailing structural pattern in these classrooms was a balance between teacher-directed activities and individual work activities. But not only were there generally more such activities than in the less successful classes, the events themselves differed in organization from those found in less successful classes. The organization of instructional events is important, since it affects both the delivery and the usability of the language as input, it appears. Since this language constitutes "free input" for the learners, an opportunity to engage in the use of the language without having to seek it out and without the need to play a role in keeping it going, it is an important source of input for all the learners; it is especially so for those who, because of individual circumstances, find it difficult to interact with English speakers on their own. What were the structural characteristics of instructional events or lessons that worked well for language learning? They were, in general, aspects of the structure of events that appear to affect how well the language used in them works as input. Let us consider the characteristics of these lessons in reference to examples drawn from observational records of some of the classrooms that were studied. Excerpts that are referred to here are drawn from lesson transcripts that are included as appendixes to this chapter (see Appendixes A to E). A summary of the structural characteristics discussed here can also be found in Appendix F. It should be noted that the transcripts that are referred to here include both negative and positive instances of the various structural and linguistic features of lessons that work for language learning; *they should not all be regarded as samples of exemplary lessons.* Examples from the transcripts will be referenced by lesson and excerpt numbers.

STRUCTURAL CHARACTERISTICS OF LESSONS THAT WORK FOR LANGUAGE LEARNING

Formal Lessons with Clear Boundaries

First of all, the lessons that appear to work well for language learning were formal, scheduled lessons with clear boundaries. The beginnings of small-group lessons were usually marked by an actual change in the physical location of the students or by some other movement to indicate the formation of the subset of the class involved in the lesson. This sometimes meant moving to the area of the classroom designated as the meeting place for the group, or turning seats around so students face one another. The beginnings of such events were often marked by changes in the teacher's voice quality or volume, or in the teacher's location or posture, these serving to call the group to attention. The teacher in Lesson 1 (Appendix A), for example, marks the beginning of the math lesson she is teaching in all these ways: the students had moved to the front of the classroom where the group that is scheduled for a formal lesson with the teacher usually meets; the teacher had just taken her place in front of the chalkboard where she usually stands at the beginning of the math lesson each day; she straightens her back and lifts her head as she looks out over the group. She pauses for a moment, neither moving nor speaking—a signal to the group that the lesson is about to begin. The students stop their chattering, and she begins. She begins speaking in what is her "public voice," this in contrast to the quieter and softer tone she ordinarily uses when speaking to individual students or when she is talking to the class informally. She had earlier made use of a formulaic starter to get the event going: "Tigers and Bears, take your places." Her use of these math group names had signaled the beginning of the math period to the class, and without further instruction, the students had moved to the parts of the room where they were scheduled to meet. The groups alternate every other day between formal math lessons with the teacher and individual seatwork as assigned at the end of the previous day's formal lesson. The group doing seatwork meets in the back part of the classroom, and the group receiving the formal lesson sits at the front of the room facing the blackboard.

How do such apparently nonlinguistic features of lessons figure in language learning? Features such as boundary markers for lessons frame the event, giving the students an idea of what to expect, both linguistically and instructionally. The events in these classes were clearly scheduled, so students knew what to expect throughout the school day. The formulaic starters used by the teachers helped to signal when these scheduled events were to begin, so the students knew when they should begin paying attention and what they should be listening for. This kind of signaling is similar to that found in studies of "motherese" (Snow and Ferguson 1977), whereby caretakers interacting with babies make use of prosodic cues such as higher pitch, lip rounding, and special intonational patterns to call the learner's attention to language that is meant for them. An impressive consistency in the use of such features was found across lessons in the successful classes. The teachers in these classes tended to follow the same pattern day after day in the way they bracketed their lessons. There was no evidence in these classes of children who appeared not to know where to go, or what to expect at this level, no matter how little English they seemed to know. In the less successful classes, it was often unclear when one event ended and another began. The students frequently appeared uncertain as to what was going on or what they were to do next. In contrast to the successful classes in which little time was wasted getting activities organized, lessons took a great deal longer to get underway in the less successful classes, and teachers had to spend a lot more time informing students as to what was expected of them. Thus, the first type of structural characteristic of successful lessons is consistency in organization: students knew what to expect and what to do procedurally, because the routine was well established.

Lesson Scripts

The next structural characteristic has to do with the format of the lesson itself. In the successful classes, a remarkable consistency was found across the lessons conducted in a given subject area by each teacher. This consistency was in how the lessons were organized, in the activities that were undertaken during each phase of the lesson, and in the language that was used in its conduct. That is, if one were to examine all of the math lessons taught over the period of a month by the teacher in Lesson 1, one would find that she followed essentially the same format each day in what she did and in how she presented the materials in each lesson. Further, she followed essentially the same approach in her math lessons for both math groups. While different materials were covered from group to group, and certainly from day to day for each group, one finds that the lessons in any given subject were framed in very much the same way for everyone. In reading lessons, for example, a teacher might follow a format like this: present new vocabulary items used in the text at hand; elicit discussion on the meanings and uses of the new words and relate them to known words; have the group read the words together from the list; have the group read the text silently; have individuals take turns reading paragraphs in the text; discuss the meaning of the text with the students; and finally, make an assignment for seatwork to be done individually. A lesson format such as this is not very creative and is not presented as an example of fine teaching; however, if a teacher follows even an unimaginative format such as this one day after day, it soon becomes a kind of scenario which is familiar to the students. Once they know what the routine is, they can follow it and play the roles expected of them as participants in the event.

Observations of lessons in the successful classes show that in any subject on a given day, essentially the same lesson format is followed for all groups. The same is true over the period of a month, say, although over the course of the school year, the format may change somewhat as the class progresses through the curriculum. It is almost as if these successful teachers are following "lesson scripts" that they have adopted for each subject that they teach. This is certainly not unique to teachers teaching second language learners, nor is it a surprising practice. Depending on how one looks at it, such a practice might seem commonsensical, or it could be seen as unimaginative, routinized teaching behavior. For the language learners who have to learn from these lessons, however, consistency in presentation serves an important purpose. Once they learn the sequence of subactivities for each subject, they can follow the lesson without having to figure out afresh what is happening each day. They know what they are supposed to do and what they should be getting out of each phase of the lesson; thus they are ahead of the game in figuring out what they are supposed to be learning each day.

The language used by teachers in each phase of these lessons also tends to be routinized, consistent, and therefore familiar. Because of the high degree of regularity in the lesson routines, the students we observed in the successful classes appeared to understand what the objects of the lessons were, and they seemed able to follow what was being presented most of the time. They had to deal with new content each day, but the format in which it was presented was a familiar one. Thus they had a high degree of expectation to aid them in dealing with the new materials being presented. The familiar routines apparently provide a kind of scaffold for the interpretation and learning of the new materials. The children in the successful classes seldom needed help in getting oriented to the content being covered in lessons, and from all appearances they were able to keep up with their teachers in most of these instructional activities whether or not they understood everything that was said. This structural regularity and consistency in presentation added up to a predictability that plays a major role in comprehension, I believe. From day to day, only the specific content being taught was new. Since the activities were familiar, they provided a context within which the language and the subject matter could be understood, all of which adds up to greater comprehensibility for the materials.

Another important aspect of the formatting found in these lessons relates to the use of instructions and signals to guide the learners through the activity. An example of this can be seen in Lesson 1 (Appendix A). In excerpt 1, the teacher tells the students what to do immediately and what they are to expect, and she locates this experience in the context of a prior experience so the students know what they will be doing.

Open your mathbooks . . .
Now we're going to review this page . . .
You did have math on Friday, but we didn't use this book.
Now we are talking about fractional parts . . .
Now look at our problems.

Such formatting statements not only mark the boundaries of the lesson, they also signal movement through the phases of the activities. Notice how pragmatic particles such as "OK" are used to mark movement in the lesson we have been looking at:

OK, now boys and girls, when we . . . (excerpt 2)
OK, let's do another . . . (excerpt 8)

In excerpt 20, the teacher marks the recapitulation phase of her lesson with this:

Everybody remember that? Remember when we did the work on Thursday? OK? It's really easy because your top number is one. So all you have to do is go ahead and divide your second number, the one they want to know the fractional part of, by the denominator of your fraction [she points at the relevant parts of the statements on the board as she says this]. It gets a little more complicated when we are doing it where it had another number on the top half of the fraction, like two-thirds, or two-sixths, but these are easy because you only have to go ahead and do like a division problem, OK?

Such statements help to orient the students during the lesson: they tell them where they are in the lesson and where they are going next. In a sense, these are directions that help students to put what they are learning into a coherent mental framework. Throughout these successful lessons, one finds contextualizing remarks of this sort, which are meant to locate current experiences with respect to prior and future ones so the students have some way of interpreting the new materials being presented to them. By putting the present lesson in the context of previous ones, teachers anchor the new language in things that they have reason to believe the students already know. If the students remember what they did or learned on the earlier occasion, the prior experience becomes a context for interpreting the new experience. In lessons like this, prior experiences serve as the contexts within which the language being used is to be understood.

Turn-Allocation in Lessons

The final type of structural characteristic of lessons in successful classes relates to the way in which turns were allocated to students for participation. This is especially important, since it affects the amount and kind of practice students get in the use of the new language, and the extent to which individuals actually participate in lessons. There were, for each type of lesson, and sometimes in each phase of the lesson, fairly well established ways in which students were to participate. Teachers might begin one phase of a lesson by inviting volunteers to read or to supply instances of whatever is being discussed. They might then call on each student in turn, a more systematic procedure of turn-allocation than that of asking for volunteers since every person gets called on to take a turn. In the next phase, the whole group might be asked to recite in chorus, a procedure which allows everyone to participate, although not individually. Finally, they might call on individuals, ignoring bids for turns by the students themselves.

Here again, teachers in successful classes tended to use a variety of turn-allocation procedures, but they were consistent in following a well-established set of procedures within lessons for any given subject. The students in these classes generally understood what the procedures were, and they knew the rules, although they sometimes ignored them and had to be reminded of them, as we see in the lesson presented in Lesson 4 (Appendix D). In excerpts 18 and 38, we see that students have to be reminded that they have to raise their hands to bid for turns. This excerpt is of the lesson phase during which the teacher calls on individuals of her choosing, but by her rules, students who have an urge to participate before she is ready to call on them can bid for a turn as well, provided they do it by the rules. Although these teachers made use of various turn-allocation procedures, they generally managed to call on everyone at least several times during each lesson. In contrast, in less successful classes, procedures for participation were often unclear, and students engaged in a great deal of competitive bidding for the floor. The ones who were the most eager to be heard, and the most aggressive students got called on frequently; those who were less so got fewer turns to participate and hence less practice in using the new language and less of the feedback that is available through this kind of participation in lessons.

Another problem observed in classes that did not promote successful language learning was reliance on turn-allocation procedures that were inappropriate with respect to the participant structure of the lesson. Systematic turn-allocation, for example, wherein every individual is called on in turn, works well when the group is small, since each individual is likely to get called on more than once. When students know that they will be called on to perform and are able to anticipate when it is going to happen, they prepare themselves and are attentive at least until they have had their turns. This works fairly well even when the group is as large as the one in Lesson 1 (14 students); it would not work, however, in a lesson involving the entire class. In that case, each individual would have to wait for 29 others to be called on between turns. Not only would there be too few turns for each person (usually one per person), but the students would also tend to lose interest in what is going on, since they would no longer have to be attentive once they have had their chance to perform. The worst kind of situation from the language learner's perspective, however, is one in which there are few turns to be had at all, as we see in Lesson 2 (Appendix B). In this lesson, the teacher races through the materials, neither stopping for discussion nor asking students whether they understand what is being presented.

HOW LANGUAGE USE IN LESSONS AFFECTS LANGUAGE LEARNING

Let us consider what prior research suggests are some necessary conditions of language learning: we know from studies of both first and second language acquisition that learners need more than mere exposure to the language to be learned. Language learning is possible when learners are in frequent enough contact with speakers of the language to develop sets of shared experiences and meanings which help them communicate despite the lack of a common language. When speakers interact with learners on a continuing basis, and they have reason to communicate with them, they will find ways of conveying information to them. In the interest of communication, speakers are likely to make substantial modifications in both the form and the content of what they say for the sake of the learners, and some of these adjustments actually help the learners by making it possible for them to figure out what is being talked about, more or less. Learners on their side will try to figure out how to respond and to participate in these interactions, based on the models of the language the speakers have provided for them over time.

Hatch (1983b), in an analysis of discourse data drawn from studies of language learning, has found that the adjustments made by speakers for the sake of learners whether of first or second languages are quite similar: they speak more slowly, enunciate more clearly, make greater use of concrete references than of abstract ones, and use shorter and less complex sentences than they might otherwise. They also make greater use of repetitions and rephrasings than usual, and they accompany their speech with gestures and demonstrations that give learners some extra-linguistic cues to aid in their understanding of what is being said. Others have determined that adjustments in the forms and content of speech to learners are made interactively, with the learners themselves indicating to the speakers when adjustments are needed and when they are not (Cross 1978, Long 1981a). By their attempts to communicate, learners and speakers are said to "negotiate" the form of the messages until they are "comprehensible" to the learner (Hatch 1983b). Krashen (1981a, 1981c) and Long (1981a) have argued that "comprehensibility" is crucial in determining whether the language spoken to learners works as input. Language serves as input, according to this view, when it serves a genuine communicative function and when the learner does not have to know the language in which the message is encoded to figure out what is being said; this is possible when the message can be understood strictly from context. Swain (this volume) contends that comprehensible input is necessary, but in no way a sufficient condition for language learning. She argues that in addition to input that more or less makes sense to the learner, there must also be "comprehensible output," for it is in learners' attempts to construct messages that encode their own communicative intentions in speech that they are in a position to figure out how the language is structured.

CHARACTERISTICS OF TEACHER TALK THAT WORKS AS INPUT

Let us consider the characteristics of the language used in lessons that apparently worked well for language learners, again with reference to examples of lessons taken from the observational records of the classes that were studied. First of all, it should be noted that the students in the classes involved in the lessons found in the appendixes were all quite limited in their knowledge of English. Few of these children had had more than 2 or so years of English, and some had less than that at the time these lessons took place.

At that point, they still needed a great deal of help in order to understand what was being talked about in school. It was a problem for their teachers then to teach anything to them that was complex or which dealt with materials that could not easily be demonstrated. How teachers attempted to communicate what was to be taught in a lesson not only affected how well lessons worked instructionally, it also determined whether the language used in them worked for language learning, as we shall see when we consider the characteristics of language used in successful lessons. (See Appendix F for a summary of these characteristics.)

Clear Separation of Languages

There are various approaches that teachers can take when they believe their students might not understand what they have to say in English. One possibility is simply to ignore the problem, speak normally, and hope for the best. Another is to switch to the student's L1, and teach them what they have to learn in language they know, a solution that is available to teachers who are bilingual. In neither case, however, are the LEP students aided in their efforts to learn the new language. In the first case, the language being used simply does not work for input; in the second, the language being used is not the one that the students are trying to learn. Another solution that is available to bilingual teachers is to repeat what they have to say in English in the students' own language, thereby providing them with translations that they can understand. This was a practice that was observed in classes that were unsuccessful for language learning but never in those that were successful.

In the bilingual classes that worked well for language learning, the two languages of instruction were kept quite separate. This has long been regarded as a crucial element of the immersion approach, according to researchers who have studied its development (Lambert 1984, Cohen and Swain 1976). In these programs the two languages are kept separate in at least two ways: they are used at different times and by different teachers. Like the immersion teachers, the ones in the successful classes in this study did not mix languages but presented what they were teaching directly in the target language. This was not easy, since many of the students in these classes were quite limited in their command of English.

Teachers with students representing a wide range of levels of proficiency in English were especially inclined to resort to language alternation in their teaching. When students range from full proficiency in English to no English at all, teachers find it especially difficult to use language in ways that are suitable for everyone. If they speak in ways that are appropriate for the students who know English, the non-English speakers will be unable to make sense of what they are saying. If they address themselves to the special needs of the LEP students, they do not serve the needs of the English speakers. In these situations, teachers find language alternation (whereby they say everything in both languages) an easy expedient. By switching back and forth between English and the LEP students' language, teachers ensure that everyone understands the materials that are being taught. The problem, however, is that this practice has a decidedly negative effect on language learning.

Language learning occurs when students try to figure out what their teachers and classmates are saying, when teachers through their efforts to communicate with learners provide them with enough extralinguistic cues to allow them to figure out what is being said, and when the situation is one that allows learners to make astute guesses at the meaning of the language being used in the lesson. Translations appear to short-circuit this process from two directions. When translations are used, teachers tend not to make the kinds of modifications in English that they might otherwise make. Modifications are made, as noted earlier, in an effort to give learners access to the meanings of messages that speakers want to communicate to them. But since access to meaning is provided in translation, speakers do not regard it as necessary to make any modifications in the English they are using as well. If we assume that these modifications enable learners to figure out what is being said, then the English that is being used in this way is not usable to them as input. But aside from the fact that the English which is translated fails as input because it is not properly adjusted, it also fails because the learners tend to ignore it. When learners can count on getting the information that is being communicated to them in language they already know, they do not find it necessary to pay attention when the language they do not understand is being used. Observations in classrooms where this method has been used have shown that children tend to tune out when the language they do not know is being spoken (Legarreta 1979, Wong-Fillmore 1982).

An example of this type of language usage in teaching can be seen in Lesson 2 (Appendix B). This lesson is interesting, since the teacher in it is teaching English words through Spanish. The object of the lesson was to teach the students the meanings of these English words so they could use them in sentences that they were to write after the teacher's presentation of the lesson. In many respects, the language found in this excerpt is not greatly different from that found in the other transcripts. The difference is that the students in this class apparently got little out of the experience because they paid attention only to the Spanish. But even if they were listening to the English, it is doubtful that they could have made much sense of it. Consider, for example, excerpts 3 and 4:

[Pointing at the first word on the board:] Number one is "weak." Not the day of the "week." It's when a person is weak. And that means you don't have too much strength. Like, when you get sick, and when you catch the flu. After you get over the flu, you still feel kinda weak. Right? You're not very strong. *Weak.*

Esto quiere decir "débil." Cuando uno está débil, no está fuerte. Por ejemplo, cuando tengamos la gripe, ¿verdad? No tenemos fuerzas. Estamos débil. Es lo que quiere decir esta palabra. [= This means weak. When someone is weak, he's not strong, right? We don't have much strength; we're weak. That's what this word means.]

In order for language like this to work as input, the learners would have had to hold the English they heard in mind until they heard the Spanish; they might then be able to match up pieces of the English text they had heard with the Spanish. They could not have otherwise figured out what the teacher was saying in English, since she did nothing that allowed them to figure out what her words meant. In observing the students during this lesson, it was apparent that few of them understood how the words the teacher was teaching them were to be used. They could, of course, understand her Spanish, but since the words they were supposed to be learning and putting into sentences were in English, they were quite confused. The extent of their confusion was clear from the number of times students had to go to the teacher and to the observer for help with this assignment.

An example of a similar lesson drawn from one of the successful classes can be seen in Lesson 3 (Appendix C). The teacher in this lesson used only English, although she might have alternated between languages as well. It should be noted that the students in this class were no more proficient in English than were those in the previous lesson. The teacher in this class, however, managed to communicate the meaning of the new words she was teaching to the students by connecting them to words they already knew and by getting them to put the new words into their own frame of reference. Consider, for example, the first three excerpts in the transcript:

T: [Points at word "neighborhood" on her chart:] Your *neighborhood.* Who can tell me what that word means? Patricia?

C: Like the place where you live?

T: Um-hum. It's the area where your house is. Your *neighborhood,* boys and girls, is that area, right close by, where your house is.

C: Uh, where it is all the block?

T: Uhm-hum. It *usually* means like within a block or so.

A real problem for teachers in situations such as this is to communicate abstract concepts, ideas that cannot easily be demonstrated but which can be learned only by connecting up words with understandings that can come from real-life experiences. The children involved in the above lesson knew enough English to put things together, but it would be a real problem for teachers to teach labels for concepts such as "neighborhood" at earlier stages of language learning.

Emphasis on Communication and Comprehension

One solution for teachers is to recognize that one can, by using whatever works, e.g., pictures, demonstration, gestures, enactment, to communicate *some* of the information to the students, *but not everything.* Teachers sometimes regard it as essential to teach LEP students everything that is contained in the curriculum at a level that is appropriate for English-speaking students, even when it is clear that they do not have the language skills to deal with instruction at that level. In such situations, the students get little, either of the content or of the language being used in such lessons. The problem is that when students do not understand the language of instruction, something has to give: adjustments must be made both in the content and in the language being used. The immersion programs have provided us with ample evidence that it is possible to develop academic and second language skills simultaneously, but adjustments have to be made, especially in the early stages of school. This is a major way in which language learning in the classroom differs from language learning in other settings. There is a specific content that has to be covered in each lesson, and it has to be communicated well enough for the students to learn it. This is not an easy matter when the students are just learning the language through which the information is being conveyed. But it is possible, as we have learned by observing lessons taught in successful classes.

There was, in the lessons we observed in these classes, an emphasis on communicating directly in English as much of what was to be learned by the students as possible. By making careful modifications in the content itself, by adjusting the language used in the ways that have been described as characteristic of the language used with language learners, by carefully tailoring the language used according to feedback provided by the learners themselves as to whether or not they comprehend what is being said, the teachers in the successful classes made it possible for students to get something out of each lesson, even at the earliest stages of language learning. A point to be made here is that in the lessons we observed, the language being used was in the service of communicating subject matter to students. It was therefore quite different from the language that gets used in, say, typical ESL lessons where the language is used strictly for practice. Aspects of this can be seen in both the way the information was conveyed in the successful lessons, and how language was used in them. Let us consider the math lesson in Lesson 1 again. Notice that the ideas and concepts being discussed and taught in this lesson are quite complex: *fractional parts, equations, division, denominators,* etc. In each case, the meanings of these concepts are conveyed by demonstration. The teacher writes on the board as she speaks, thus relating the words she uses with numbers arranged as problem statements with which the students have some familiarity:

OK, now boys and girls when we talk about one-half of a number [she writes "½"], like one-half of 6 [she writes "× 6" to the right of "½"], that's the same [she writes "=" to the right of the "6"] as dividing 6 [she writes "6/" after the "="] by—, Luis? (excerpt 2)

When Luis supplies the answer "2" (he could hardly get it wrong, since it is clear from her presentation what she is after), she completes the problem statement for all to see, and she repeats the phrase:

Same as dividing 6 by 2! [She writes the problem on the board: 6 over 2. Pointing at the 2, she says:] You use your denominator—that's the bottom number, and you divide this number [points at 6] by the bottom number of the fraction. What is 6 divided by 2? (excerpt 4)

One sees in this transcript how the teacher demonstrates each idea that she is trying to communicate to the students. In this way she gets the information across to the students, even though the language itself was difficult.

What is surprising about this lesson is that it is pitched at a level that is appropriate to the grade level of the class, despite the fact that most of the students in it were quite limited in their English proficiency. They seemed to have no trouble following what she was saying, however, and were apparently able to figure out what they were to do with the problems. By writing the problems as she spoke, she demonstrated how the concepts she was discussing related to the procedures that the students were to learn and put into use. The students could see what they were to do even when they were unable to understand all of what she was saying. By putting the new information she was presenting in the context of work that the students had already completed, she made it possible for them to make use of prior knowledge and experience as contexts for making sense of the new materials. Altogether, the presentation of information in a variety of ways in this lesson added up to a message redundancy that gave the students multiple access to the materials that were taught in it. The students could hardly have missed the point of it.

Grammaticality and Appropriateness of the Language Used in Lessons

An important feature of the lessons that were observed in the successful classes was that ungrammatical or reduced "foreigner-talk" forms were never used in them. The language used by teachers in all of the lesson transcripts which are included in the appendixes was entirely grammatical and appropriate, including the one taken from a not so successful class. The teachers in the successful classes tended to use language which was not only grammatical but registrally appropriate to the activity as well. The register that is used in these lessons is instructional language. Its purpose is to convey information and to teach skills, and thus it tends to be more precise, more expository, and more highly propositional than ordinary talk. Since this is exactly the type of language skills that the students need for school, it is essential for them to be exposed to this level of language by their teachers. At the same time, however, it is clear in examining these transcripts that the language that is being used is not as complex as might be used for this grade level (all of the lesson excerpts are from third grade classes).

Repeated Use of Patterns and Routines

Transcripts of lessons in successful classes show that teachers frequently adopt patterns or routines for their lessons that have the appearance of pattern-substitution drills, the big difference being that the ones found here are used in the teaching of subject matter rather than for practice. This is especially apparent in the math lesson found in Lesson 1. Notice that essentially the same sentence frame is used by the teacher throughout the lesson as she demonstrates the procedure for setting up the problems, and for solving fractional equations:

One half of 6, that's the same as dividing 6 by— . . . Same as dividing 6 by 2. One third of 12. It's the same thing as dividing 12 by what number? . . . It's the same as dividing 12 by 3. (excerpts 2 to 10)

Similarly we find in Lesson 4 (Appendix D) the same routine used repeatedly as the teacher in this lesson elicits from the students definitions of words such as "inventor," "sailor," and "tailor":

What does an inventor do?
They make things. New things.
An inventor made up the first TV.
An inventor made the telephone, the first telephone.
An inventor made the first electric light.
An inventor invents things.
He makes up new things for the first time. (excerpts 29 to 33)

By such means, teachers create situations that not only allow students to interpret the information to be conveyed to them, they also call attention to the way in which sentences pattern in the new language. By this the teachers help the learners to detect the structural regularities in the language used, a first major step in learning a new language. In this way, teachers were able to help students become familiar with some fairly complex structures, as we see in excerpt 53 of the same lesson

Lots of people collect coins. All different kinds of money and coins from all over the world. People who collect coins are called coin collectors.

Since the teacher has been building up a familiarity with these structures throughout the lesson, the students have a frame of reference for dealing with them; thus these sentences can be interpreted by the students, and their structures noticed perhaps, if not learned immediately.

Repetitiveness

An important feature of the language used in these lessons was a fairly high use of repetition. Clear examples of this can be seen in the spelling lesson found in Lesson 4. Not only is this teacher presenting the students with neat paradigm sets of sentence patterns in the lesson, she is also giving them multiple opportunities to hear virtually the same sentences, although with minor modifications. See, for example, excerpt 34 to 36:

T: What does a mayor do?
C: A mayor is the person who own the city?
T: He doesn't own the city.
The mayor doesn't own the city.

We see this again in excerpts 39 to 43, where the teacher provides the students with a timely feminist message in addition to several chances to hear essentially the same sentence:

T: Who is our mayor? [No response.]
T: Ooh! You forgot yesterday! Who is our mayor?
Cs: Mayor Feinstein!
T: Yes! Mayor Feinstein. Is our mayor a man or a woman?
Cs: Woman!
T: Yes, so a woman can be a mayor. A woman can be a governor. A woman can be a president!

What we find in these successful lessons, then, is that repetitions are not necessarily identical, but there are small changes in them which may in fact serve to call the learner's attention to places within such expressions where forms can be substituted. In this way, learners can figure out some of the substitution rules in the language, and they get some clues as to alternative ways of saying the same thing. Paraphrases are also frequently used in such lessons. Teachers seldom say anything in just one way; they say it in several different ways, giving students more than one chance to figure out what has been said. Nice examples of this can be seen in the "inventor" text (Lesson 4, excerpt 33):

An inventor invents things. He makes up new things for the first time.

and in the math lesson (Lesson 1, excerpt 14):

One-sixth of 36 equals, *is the same thing as,* 36 divided by what number? Carlos? Same as 36 divided by—

Tailoring of Student Participation

The manner in which teachers involve students in lessons has been mentioned in connection with the discussion on turn-allocation procedures used in lessons. Let us consider the linguistic characteristics of this aspect of lessons. One way in which turns in successful lessons differ from those in less successful ones is in the kinds of questions that are asked of students. We assume that the questions that give language learners the best practice in speaking are those that invite them to say a lot. Thus questions which elicit one-word answers (e.g., "Is this a compound word?" or "Who is our mayor?") are not as good as open-ended ones (e.g., "What are your views on X?" or "What do you suppose is going to happen if Y?") which call for longer and more complex responses. Constructing such responses, however, calls for perhaps a higher level of control over the structures, forms, and usages of the language than learners may have, especially at the early stages of learning the language. They would find it difficult to respond, even if they understood such questions and had something to say in answer to them.

In lessons taken from less successful classes, one finds several types of unproductive practices in this regard. One of these involves teachers asking questions only of those students who are fairly proficient in the language. The students who are just learning English seldom get called on, and thus they are given little opportunity to practice using the new language in class. Unless they bid for turns to participate in the discussion, their involvement in lessons is mostly passive. Another practice is for teachers to ask only low-level questions requiring simple one-word answers. In such situations, no one gets much practice in speaking the new language except for the teacher. The students learn how to supply one-word answers to questions, but they get little else. A third practice has been discussed in relation to the translation lesson in Lesson 2, in which no questions are asked that require answering. This teacher asks for agreement as in excerpt 3 ("After you get over the flu, you still feel kinda weak. Right?"), or she might use a pseudo-question as a way of moving the topic along as in excerpt 7 ("Number three is 'silk.' Know what that is? It's material.") Neither of these are questions that call for answers, and indeed, the teacher gave no indication that she wanted any response.

In more successful classes, we find a quite different practice. In the lessons observed in them, it appears that teachers do a great deal of tailoring of questions to fit the levels of proficiency of individual students. Those who know the language fairly well get asked open-ended-type questions or ones that call for responses containing complex structures [e.g., "Your *neighborhood.* Who can tell me what that word means? Patricia?" (Lesson 3, excerpt 1)]. Those who are just learning the language are asked questions that require short one-word responses. Similarly, one finds, in lessons where the materials that are being taught are complex, that teachers tend not to ask questions that require complicated answers. In Lesson 1, for example, in which difficult procedures and concepts were being taught, the teacher used only questions that required one-word answers: "What is 6 divided by 2?" "It's the same thing as dividing 6 by (what)?" In this way teachers focus the students' attention on what they are saying rather than on how they should say it. At the same time, however, we see that teachers in these successful classes nearly always repeat the one-word or short responses supplied by the students, and expand them into full sentences by way of confirming their responses. These expansions give the students a chance to hear what their short response represents in their full forms, as we see in this example drawn from Lesson 3 (excerpt 7 to 9):

T: The people who live in your neighborhood are called your what?
Cs: Your neighbors!
T: Yes, the people who live in your neighborhood are your neighbors.

By tailoring the ways students are to participate in lessons according to their ability to use the language and according to the kind of materials being covered in such lessons, teachers lessen the anxiety that language learners are likely to feel when more is expected of them than they can give, or when they have to deal with more than they can easily handle at one time. It is not easy for students to deal with learning a language and learning new materials through that language at the same time, but teachers apparently can make adjustments in their instructional practices that ease the task somewhat.

Richness of Language

The final characteristic of the language used in successful lessons is that of richness and occasional playfulness as well. One might assume that in talking to learners, teachers ought to avoid anything unusual and stick with plain ordinary, unembellished language until the students have gained a degree of mastery over the fundamentals of the new language. In the lessons that we have observed, teachers do try to keep the language simple, but it is in no way the stripped-down, unnaturally plain language featured in many ESL courses. The teachers in successful classes tended to use language in ways that called attention to the language itself. Some especially nice examples of this can be seen in Lesson 5 (Appendix E). The teacher in this lesson was one who took advantage of every available opportunity to impart a feel of the language to his students. We see him offering his students a vocabulary item that is a cut above the ordinary in excerpts 7 through 14:

T: Do you see—have you ever been to a place where there is a bridge?
Cs: Yeah, yes!
C2: And you know—and down—uhm—uh, uh, 14th Street? [Child gestures as he speaks, arching one of his arms high, passing the other arm under it.]
T: Uh, down on East 14th Street? There's a bridge down there?
C: No, uhm, uhm, uh—[He repeats the gesture.]
T: Down by the water?
C: Uhm-hmm.
T: They call that the es-tu-ary, the estuary. That's where the water comes in—from the bay.

Examples of playfulness can also be found in these lessons, especially when the teacher is someone who enjoys verbal play as in Lesson 5:

T: Do you know another animal that looks like a goose?
C: A dock!
T: A duck. But this one here has a looo-ong neck! It begins with—sw—[forms initial sounds of the word]—sw—!
C: I know! I know! Uh, uh, a swan!
T: A swaaaaan! Yes, a swan. Did you ever hear that poem? Swan swam over the sea. Swim, swan, swim! Swan swam back again. Well swum, swan! Did you ever hear that? That's a good poem. An untwistable tongue-twister poem.

There was, throughout these lessons, an emphasis on helping students to develop a greater control of the forms, functions, and uses of the new language. The teachers did it in more ways than by what they taught, however; they also exemplified it in their own use of the language. Teachers vary in their ability to use language creatively, of course, but that, strictly speaking, is not what is required. In these successful classes we find teachers who were not necessarily creative in their use of the language, but they were uniformly able to communicate clearly and effectively. They were effective communicators, I think, because all of them were concerned with communication.

These are just some of the characteristics that appear to differentiate lessons that work for language learning from those that do not. However, it should be noted in closing that they should not be regarded as anything like the truth, the whole truth, and nothing but the truth on the subject, since they were derived from classroom observations and have not been tested to determine the extent to which each of the aspects of classroom structure and language use discussed here actually do contribute to the language-learning outcomes that we find in classrooms serving LEP students. Much work remains before we can say which of these are especially important and which are not. The research reported in this paper is just a beginning.

APPENDIX A

Lesson 1

Teacher with math group made up of about a half of her third grade Spanish-English bilingual class. This group, the "Tigers," consists of the students who know the least English in the class. The students are seated at tables in the front of the room; the teacher stands before them. She straightens herself up, looks out over the class without saying anything for a moment, then speaks up in her "public" voice:

Excerpts

1. T: OK, Tigers. Open your mathbooks to page 226. Now we're going to review this page just for a little while since it's been two days since we have used this book. You did have math on Friday, but we didn't use our books. Now we are talking about fractional parts of something. Now look at our problems.
2. T: OK, now boys and girls, when we talk about one-half of a number, like one-half of 6, that's the same as dividing 6 by—, Luis?
3. C1: 2.
4. T: Same as dividing 6 by 2! [She writes the problem on the board: 6 over 2. Pointing at the 2, she says:] You use your denominator—that's the bottom number, and you divide this number [points at 6] by the bottom number of the fraction. What is 6 divided by 2?
5. Cs: 3!
6. T: Equals 3! [Writes the equation on the board: "$1/2 \times 6 =$"] So one-half of 6 is—
7. Cs: 3!
8. T: 3. OK? Let's do another one. What if I told you I want you to find one-third of—12? [She writes "$1/3 \times 12 =$" on the board as she speaks.] It's the same thing as dividing 12 by what number, Rolando?
9. C2: 3.
10. T: It's the same as dividing 12 by 3. [She writes this as a fraction on the board: 12 over 3.] 12 divided by 3 is—
11. Cs: 4!
12. T: 4! So one-third of 12 is—4!
13. Cs: 4! 4!
14. T: Let's do another. This time, we're going to do one that's a little harder. One-sixth of 36 equals [writes equation on board as she speaks: "$1/6 \times 36 =$"], is the same as, 36 divided by what number? Carlos? Same as 36 divided by—
15. C3: 6.
16. T: 6. What is 36 divided by 6, Yvonne?
17. C4: 6.
18. T: Equals 6! [Pointing at the equation on the board, she asks:] So what is one-sixth of 36?
19. Cs: 6!
20. T: 6. Everybody remember that? Remember when we did the work on Thursday? OK? It's really easy because your top number is one. So all you have to do is go ahead and divide your second number, the one they want to know the fractional part of, by the denominator of your fraction [she points at the relevant parts of the statements on the board as she says this]. It gets a little more complicated when we are doing it where it had another number on the top half of the fraction, like two-thirds, or two-sixths, but these are easy because you only have to do ahead and do like a division problem, OK?

21. T: Do we need to do any more problems to refresh your memory? Oh, Roy! You weren't here. Let's do one more for Roy because he wasn't here last week. These are easy, Roy. We're talking about fractional parts of certain numbers, let's say one-fourth of 24 equals some number. All we do is say 24 divided by the bottom number of the fraction—equals—[She writes the two statements of the problem on the board, with each part written as she refers to it.]
22. T: [To Roy:] OK, what is 24 divided by 4?
23. C5: [No response]
24. T: What number times 4 would give you 24?
25. C5: 6?
26. T: 6. Good. So one-fourth of 24 equals 6. OK, these problems are just like division problems. You divide the second number, the whole number, by the bottom number of the fraction.
27. C7: Do we put down the, this division number—where, the one-third of 6 equals 2?
28. T: OK, no—you don't have to write out the division problem, but I think it's a good idea to do so so you can see exactly how you got the answer. Sometimes we try to do everything in our heads, but then you don't see your mistakes. You can't catch your mistakes. It's all up here [taps forehead], OK? You don't have to write out your division problems, but I think it is a good idea! So that you can check your problems before you go on to next one. So you can make sure you didn't make any mistakes in your division up in your head, OK?

APPENDIX B

Lesson 2

Teacher with third grade Spanish-English bilingual class. She is going over a list of English spelling words written on the chalkboard. The object of the lesson is to teach the children the meaning of these items so they can use them in sentences which they can construct and write out on their own.

Excerpts

1. T: Let me go over these first. Pongan atencion Uds. [= Pay attention.]
2. T: [To a student who seems to be confused:] María puede trabajar contigo. [= María (the TA) can work with you.]
3. T: [Pointing at the first word listed on the board:] Number one is "weak." Not the day of the "week." It's when a person is weak. And that means you don't have too much strength. Like, when you get sick, and when you catch the flu. After you get over the flu, you still feel kinda weak. Right? You're not very strong. *Weak.*
4. T: Esto quiere decir "débil". Cuando uno está débil, no está fuerte. Por ejemplo, cuando tengamos la gripe, ¿verdad? No tenemos fuerzas. Estamos débil. Es lo que quiere decir esta palabra. [= This means weak. When someone is weak, he's not strong, right? We don't have much strength; we're weak. That's what this word means.]
5. T: Number two is "spoke." The past tense. I spoke to my friend yesterday. OK. In the past tense.
6. T: Uh, esto quiere decir "hablar," en el pasado. Yo—ayer hablé con mi amigo. [= This means to speak, in the past. I—yesterday, I spoke with my friend.]
7. T: Number three is "silk." Know what that is? It's material. It's fabric. It's very shiny, and it's very soft. I'm sure you've seen this kind of material.

8. C: [unintelligible] a pillow.
9. T: Yeah, pillows can. The outsides can be made of silk. It's shiny and silvery.
10. T: Esta palabra es "seda." Saben lo que es tela. [= This word is silk. You all know what cloth is.]
11. C: [unintelligible]
12. T: Es tela, pero es bien suavecito y es brillosa. Y con la mano se resbala—el material. [It's cloth, but it's very soft and shiny. You can slide your hand on it—the material.]
13. T: Number four is "pack." Like I'm going to pack a lunch. Or it could be a bag. It could be a backpack, when people go hiking. That's what it is pack.
14. T: Esto es como una bolsa, como empacan una bolsa grande de comida o de lo que sea. [= This is like a bag, like when they pack a large bag of food or whatever.]
15. T: Number five is "neck." El cuello. And number six is "lake." You know what that is. Lago. Number seven is "brick." Ladrillo.
16. T: Number eight is "beak," the mouth of a bird. The beak. El otro es la boca de la, del pajarito. El pico, el piquito. ¿Verdad? El pico. Piquito. [= The next one is the mouth of a bird. The beak, the little beak, right? The beak. Little beak.]

APPENDIX C

Lesson 3

Same teacher as in Excerpt 1 with a reading group in her third grade class. The students are Spanish-English bilingual students, most of them classified as LEP. The teacher has been going over some vocabulary items with these students in preparation for silent reading of a story in their English readers.

Excerpts

1. T: [Points at word "neighborhood" on her chart:] Your *neighborhood.* Who can tell me what that word means? Patricia?
2. C: Like the place where you live?
3. T: Um-hum. It's the area where your house is. Your *neighborhood,* boys and girls, is that area, right close by, where your house is.
4. C: Uh, where it is all the block?
5. T: Uhm-hum. It *usually* means like within a block or so.
6. C: Goes to a block?
7. T: Uh-huh. Within a block or so. And the people who live in your neighborhood are called your what?
8. Cs: Your neighbors!
9. T: Yes, the people who live in your neighborhood are your neighbors. The neighborhood is the area close by your house. OK, let's go over the words again.
[Teacher and students read the list of words again until they get to the word "neighborhood":]
10. T: Neighborhood. Is this a compound word?
11. Cs: Yes. Yeah.
12. T: Made up of what?
13. C: Neighbor!
14. T: And—
15. Cs: Hood!
16. T: Yes!

APPENDIX D

Lesson 4

Teacher with a reading group in a third grade bilingual class. The students are Cantonese-English bilingual students, most of them classified as LEP. They have been going through some new vocabulary items in preparation for completing an assignment in their spelling workbooks.

Excerpts

1. T: Now let's see how you're going to do this. [Page in workbook]
2. T: [Paraphrasing the text:] Now suffixes that tell about what people do can be *-er* or *-or*. What is a suffix?
3. C1: Beautiful?
4. T: This is something we forget all the time. What is a suffix?
5. C2: Part of a word.
6. T: It's a part of a word, but what part of a word?
7. C2: Some part like a "E-R"?
8. T: Yes! Where does a suffix go?
9. C2: Like a, behind a word?
10. T: At the end of a word, right! To change the meaning of a word just a little bit. Now look at the first part. [Reads:] "This woman governs the state." So she's a—
11. Cs: Governor!
12. T: Governor! "O-R" is a suffix. It tells what kind of work a person does. Look at the next one. [Reads:] "This man teaches. He is a—
13. Cs: Teacher!
14. T: Teacher! "E-R" is also a suffix that tells what a person does. All right. Now this says "write the word that belongs on the line." Let's read the words so we know what they are. What are the first two words, John?
15. C4: Sailor, actor.
16. T: Sailor and actor. What does a sailor do?
17. Cs: Sail—on a boat.
18. T: Uh, uh, uh! Hands, hands, hands! What does a sailor do? Lee?
19. C5: Work on a boat.
20. T: Works on a boat. He sails on a boat. He's a sailor. And what does an actor do?
21. C5: An actor is the one who acts.
22. T: In what?
23. C5: In the movie.
24. T: In the movies, or on TV, or in plays. Yes.
25. T: And what are the next two words, Norman? Can you tell me?
26. C6: Inventor.
27. T: Inventor, yes, and—
28. C6: Mayor.
29. T: What does an inventor do? Morris, do you know?
30. C7: I dunno.
31. T: Fong, do you know?
32. C8: They invented up things?
33. T: They make things. New things. An inventor made up the first TV. An inventor made the telephone, the first telephone. An inventor made the first electric light. An inventor invents things. He makes up new things for the first time.
34. T: What does a mayor do?

35. C8: A mayor is the person who own the city?
36. T: He doesn't own the city. The mayor doesn't own the city. He's kind of like the leader of the city. Do we have a mayor?
37. Cs: Yeah.
38. T: Raise your hand. Who is our mayor? [No response.]
39. T: Ooh! You forgot yesterday! Who is our mayor?
40. Cs: Mayor Feinstein!
41. T: Yes! Mayor Feinstein. Is our mayor a man or a woman?
42. Cs: Woman!
43. T: Yes, so a woman can be a mayor. A woman can be a governor. A woman can be a president! All right. The next two.
44. C: Tailor and a collector.
45. T: OK, do you know what a tailor does? May?
46. C9: A tailor is, is someone who makes clothes.
47. T: Yes, a tailor is someone who makes clothes, especially suits and coats. And what about a collector? What does a collector do? Norman?
48. C6: He collects things.
49. T: He collects or gathers and saves things. Collectors sometimes gather and save bottletops, sometimes they gather and save baseball cards. What else can collectors gather together?
50. C6: Stamps.
51. T: Stamps.
52. C6: Money?
53. T: Coins! Lots of people collect coins. All different kinds of money and coins from all over the world. People who collect coins are called coin collectors. All right, the next two? Tong?
54. C: Ranger, butcher.

APPENDIX E

Lesson 5

Teacher with a reading group of 10 LEP students in a third grade Cantonese-English bilingual class. The teacher leads the students in a discussion of the story which the children had just read silently.

Excerpts

1. T: Look on page 42. Where do you suppose they are there?
2. C1: In the, uh, in the park.
3. T: In the park. How many of you have been to Golden Gate Park?
4. Cs: [A few hands up]
5. T: Where is it?
6. Cs: San Francisco.
7. T: It's in San Francisco. Look at that picture there on pages 42 and 43. Do you see—have you ever been to a place where there is a bridge?
8. Cs: Yeah, yes!
9. C2: And you know—and down—uhm—uh, the—uh, uh, 14th Street? [Child gestures as he speaks, arching one of his arm high, the other arm passing under it.]
10. T: Uh, down on East 14th Street? There's a bridge down there?

11. C2: No, uhm, uhm, uh—[He repeats the gesture.]
12. T: Down by the water?
13. C2: Uhm-hmm.
14. T: They call that the es-tu-ary, the estuary. That's where the water comes in—from the bay.
15. C3: They have a baby center there.
16. T: They have a baby center?
17. C4: Yeah, a baby sitter.
18. T: A baby sitter. They have baby sitters!
19. T: Have you ever seen a bridge like this? [Redirects group's attention to the picture in the book:] A wooden bridge! Do you know where there is one like that around here?
20. Cs: I know! I know!
21. C5: At the zoo.
22. T: Yes, at the baby zoo. That's right.
23. C5: And they got one at Laney College.
24. C6: Yeah, it's bigger.
25. T: You know where else there is one? At Golden Gate Park. There's a place called the Japanese Tea Garden.
26. Cs: Yeah, yeah.
27. C6: I been there.
28. T: Did you ever see that wooden bridge?
29. C6: Yeah.
30. T: It's a big one. Goes way up high.
31. C7: I went to San Francisco to Chinatown. And um, on freeway sometime they have a big bridge on them.
32. T: Yes, but the only thing is that on the freeway, those bridges are not made of wood. Those are made of steel and concrete. This one here is made of wood.
33. T: OK, what animal is that on page 43? [A swan]
34. C6: Goose.
35. T: How many say a goose?
36. Cs: [Hands]
37. T: Do you know another animal that looks like a goose?
38. C2: A dock!
39. T: A duck. But this one here has a looo-ong neck! It begins with—sw—[forms initial sounds of the word]—sw—!
40. C4: I know! I know! Uh, uh, a swan!
41. T: A swaaaaan! Yes, a swan. Did you ever hear that poem? Swan swam over the sea. Swim, swan, swim! Swan swam back again. Well swum, swan! Did you ever hear that? That's a good poem. An untwistable tongue-twister poem.

APPENDIX F

Structural Characteristics of Lessons That Worked Well for Language Learning

They were formal lessons with clear boundaries:

- Boundaries marked by changes in location, props
- Beginnings and ends marked by formulaic cues

They were regularly scheduled events:

- Scheduled time for activity
- Scheduled place for activity

Clear lesson format across groups, from day to day—"scripts"

- Clear instructions, lesson phases clearly marked

Clear and fair turn-allocation procedures for student participation

- Lots of turns for each student
- Systematic turn-allocation used at least some of the time
- A variety of response types invited or elicited

Characteristics of Teacher Talk That Works as Input

Clear separation of languages—no alternation or mixing
Comprehension emphasized—focus is on communication:

- Use of demonstration, enactment to convey meaning
- New information presented in context of known information
- Heavy message redundancy

Language used is entirely grammatical—appropriate to activity:

- Simpler structures used, avoidance of complex structures
- Repeated use of same sentence patterns or routines
- Repetitiveness, use of paraphrases for variation

Tailoring of elicitation questions to allow for different levels of participation from students
Richness of language use, going beyond books, playfulness

NOTES

1. Delia Pompa, Coordinator of Bilingual Education, Houston Independent School District (personal communication).
2. L. W. Fillmore and S. Ervin-Tripp, Sources of individual differences in second language learning.
3. We began with 60 subjects, but they dwindled to 43 by the end of the study period.
4. See Wong-Fillmore (1982) for a report of these findings.
5. L. Fillmore, P. Ammon, and B. McLaughlin, Learning English through bilingual instruction.

3

CULTURAL INPUT IN SECOND LANGUAGE LEARNING

Muriel Saville-Troike
University of Illinois at Urbana-Champaign

The choice of the topic for this paper was stimulated by Theodore Schwartz's essay on The Acquisition of Culture, which, in his words:

> was inspired by ignorance—by my sudden and belated realization ... that anthropology had ignored children in culture while developmental psychologists had ignored culture in children. The result is ignorance of the process and content of the child's emerging competence as a member of a culture (1981:4).

The field of applied linguistics has generally ignored *both* cultural process and content in its studies of second language phenomena. It is my intent in this chapter to issue a call similar to Schwartz's for researchers in this discipline: to appeal for them to broaden their scope of inquiry, and especially on the occasion of a book on the theme of "input," to ask for consideration of the *cultural content of input* to second language learners as well as its linguistic form.

Language learning for children is an integral part of their *enculturation* process from three perspectives: (1) language is part of culture, and thus part of the body of knowledge, attitudes, and skills which is transmitted from one generation to the next; (2) language is a primary medium through which other aspects of culture are transmitted; and (3) language is a tool which children may use to explore (and sometimes manipulate) the social environment, and establish their status and role relationships within it. Children learning their first language are learning their native culture;

learning a second language involves learning a second culture to varying degrees—the process of *acculturation.* From another perspective, language learning is also part of a third overlapping process when the learners are 5 or 6 years old and just beginning their experiences with a formal educational instruction—that of *socialization* to the subculture of the school.

Research on first language acquisition has recently begun to relate emerging linguistic forms and functions to emerging cultural schemata (e.g., Heath 1983). In spite of the extensive corpora of materials on second language acquisition that have been collected, however, focus has seldom (if ever) been placed on its cultural content.

In addition to conveying information about the phonological, grammatical, and lexical nature of the English language, input to second language learners in an English-speaking social milieu includes cultural information within which the emergent meaning of the code must be situated and interpreted. New words are encountered along with new cultural artifacts, new verbal routines with new social expectations in role relationships, and new rules for appropriate usage with new cultural values, attitudes, and beliefs. One intent of my research is to situate study of the development of communicative competence within the scope of the development of cultural competence, and to relate input to performance in this broader sense for children acquiring English as a second language in the United States.

The site for the study I am reporting here is a public elementary school which includes a university-owned housing complex in its attendance area. More than one-third of the children enrolled in the school are from families of foreign graduate students or visiting foreign faculty; approximately one-fourth are children of American graduate students; and the remainder are children who live in the immediate vicinity of the school (a relatively low socioeconomic area with mobile homes and detached single-family dwellings).

All limited English speakers in this school receive approximately 30 minutes of pull-out ESL instruction each day; speakers of several languages (including Korean, Japanese, Spanish, Hebrew, and Arabic) receive at least 30 additional minutes each day of pull-out instruction in their native languages. For the remainder of the day at school (a total of 2½ hours for kindergarten, 5 hours for grades 1 to 6), all students receive instruction in "regular" English-medium classrooms.

One of the kindergarten classrooms in the school was the primary target for this study. Three of the children in the kindergarten class spoke no English at all on school entry—one Korean girl (Soo-Mi), one Japanese girl (Akiko), and one Japanese boy (Kazu). These subjects were videotaped weekly during the 1982–1983 school year, beginning on the very first day of the fall semester. Videotaping on each occasion was continuous from the moment children entered the classroom until they left for home, including periods of outdoor play, pull-out ESL and native language instruction, transitions through halls, and occasional "special" experiences. A radio microphone was attached to one of the three children for the duration of each videotaping session, yielding a complete audio record of all verbal input and production for each child at least once a month in addition to weekly visual records and ethnographic field notes.[1] The observations to be reported here to some extent include the cultural content being transmitted to that class as a whole but focus primarily on cultural input to the three children who began school as non-English speakers. In this portion of the study, I will briefly survey the types of cultural input these children were receiving in the earliest stages of learning English as a second language, and discuss the differential sources, channels, and modes of transmission associated with each.

The cultural content of most communicative acts from the kindergarten teacher to all students in the class during the first part of the year was regulatory. Many were explicit verbal directives regarding permitted activities and the schedule, as when she said "Blocks, no. Housekeeping, no" "Time to put away" "Time to sit down." Many were related to safety or hygiene, such as "Not in your mouth," and "Don't hit your friends; hit the ball." Since the kindergarten room was equipped with bathroom facilities, explicit socialization for the entire class also included directives for closing the stall door, lifting the seat (if a boy), sitting down (if a girl), flushing the toilet, and hand washing.

In addition to safety and health considerations, the content of verbal input from the teacher during the first days and weeks of the year emphasized conformity: blocks of the same size are stored together; children should walk in line through the halls, "freeze" when the whistle blows, sit in a chair with feet on the floor, and sit on the floor with legs crossed in front "like an Indian." This last rule was confusing at first to the Asian children in this sample, since they had already learned to sit with their feet bent back beneath them, but they soon mastered the new position.

In listing these rules, I in no way wish to suggest that this class was overregimented in any way; indeed it was typical of a well-run kindergarten class. The atmosphere was relaxed, and the children were very happy. I am only documenting from observations and from transcripts of audio and videotapes what I might well have reported based on several years of my own experience as a kindergarten teacher: most linguistic input to children at the beginning of school is intended to socialize them, to instruct them in appropriate school behaviors.

Input obviously did not depend on language alone, however, since the three young targets of this study understood little or no English at the beginning of the year and the teacher spoke no Korean or Japanese. Yet these children learned the rules promptly and conformed to her directives in almost all respects.

This was probably accomplished in part because the teacher's directions were often performed in a linguistically distinctive fashion by intoning them, and accompanying them with chords on the piano, to emphasize that some new action was called for. Further, the teacher acted out directives and physically led or placed children where they were supposed to be. Meanwhile, the non-English speakers watched English-speaking children closely and imitated their behaviors.

Dramatic proof of the effectiveness of nonverbal communication was provided during a tornado warning and disaster drill which occurred unexpectedly during the very first week of school. Even the non-English speakers in the kindergarten were able to follow the unrehearsed and rather complex evacuation and preparedness procedure, and apparently even enjoyed the event. Like the presence of the video camera, radio microphones, and multiple observers in their classroom, the tornado drill was readily accepted as one of the strange new features of this thing called "school."

It is interesting, if not surprising, to note that verbalizations of rules for appropriate behavior also constituted the content of a fairly large percentage of the earliest productive English from our sample, and were among the first multiword routines. Children were sometimes heard practicing these verbal formulations to themselves. On one occasion, for instance, Kazu recited "Put it away, put it away" to himself as he walked to join the story circle. He then said to Akiko in English, "Put it shelf, put it, put it like this," even though she, too, was a native speaker of Japanese.

Cultural input from other children was more concerned with the social organization of the class—who "friends" are, who has the right to save a place in line, and who can claim objects and territory. "That's mine" was one of the very earliest productive routines we recorded from our subjects, and even the very limited English speakers seemed to understand and respond appropriately to rather complex counterarguments from English-speaking peers. Soo-Mi agreed to let another child play with her Barbie doll, for instance, when threatened with, "Then you not sit by me in the bus."

One of the most interesting developments which occurred was the identification of "same" and "different" languages. Children at first used their native languages indiscriminately, and gradually became aware that they could not be understood by others. Like some adults, the initial response of these kindergarten children to a child who could not understand them was to repeat the utterance at an increased volume. There is some evidence that, as a second stage, the communicative tactic of responding in the appropriate language was adopted by these children as more salient for maintaining interaction than were any intrinsic semantic considerations: in response to Japanese children, some native English-speaking children repeated what to them were meaningless Japanese words; conversely, some speakers of Japanese and other languages responded to English speakers by repeating still meaningless English words or phrases. All three of our subjects then stopped talking at all to other language speakers for a period of at least a month, and one completely abandoned verbal communication with non-Japanese for the rest of the year, although she continued to interact nonverbally with English-speaking children and adults.

Input from other children was inescapably influenced to some extent by the microphones which were attached to our subjects, though the effect was minimal. Formal greetings were sometimes aimed at the mikes, including "How do you do," and children sometimes sang into them or otherwise put on a performance for the benefit of the microphone's unseen audience. Perhaps because of the presence of the video camera, which several children recognized as such, there were a few attempts to dramatize segments of TV programs, and occasional "Scooby Doo" and "Star Wars" sound effects.

In some cases, children found the content of what they had learned in one culture could not be transferred. In her Korean class, for instance, Soo-Mi observed quite aggressive peer challenging by older children, which was taken good-naturedly there. Back in the kindergarten classroom her own similar challenges to peers were interpreted very negatively, and left her friendless for most of the year. The same tears which had elicited comforting hugs and petting from the kindergarten teacher, on the other hand, caused the Korean teacher to become more aloof, and to admonish her with the Korean equivalent of "Don't be a baby." Clearly, there is more for children to sort out in bilingual settings than language alone.

Another example of cultural conflict occurred when, from among the Japanese children in the class, the kindergarten teacher selected Taki (not one of our primary subjects) to bear the most responsibility and be "leader" of the group, since his English was best. He quickly assumed the role of group translator and peer tutor, which included correcting the others' English grammar and pronunciation. Later in the year the Japanese teacher was called into the kindergarten room because of some minor behavior problems with that group. She lectured Kazu (in Japanese) on the nature of *his* responsibility for the whole group since he was the eldest (by about a month). The two teachers' different criteria for selecting a group leader created conflict between the boys, and Kazu and Taki avoided playing together—or even talking to one another—for almost three weeks.

New material artifacts were encountered as part of both socialization to school and acculturation to life in the United States. All the children quickly became familiar with the use of such school paraphernalia as hollow blocks, tray puzzles, easels, earphones, and film-strip projectors. Later, the "housekeeping" corner of the room became a grocery store, including a cash register and play money. Items brought by other children for "Show and Tell" included Star Wars games, E.T. dolls, and other popular American cultural artifacts. Verbal labels for these artifacts rarely appeared in any of the children's productive language except as unstated referents for "That's mine" and "I want that," but the role-play activities they generated carried with them information about American values and social organization— including economic concepts of purchase and trade, and rights and limitations of private ownership.

In contrast to this informal learning, some information about roles and responsibilities in the larger society was transmitted explicitly during "circle time," where the content of more formal class lessons included learning about policemen, mailmen, and firemen. This content also appeared in less traditional contexts, as the relationship of upper- and lowercase letters, for instance, was presented as "big" babysitters taking care of "little" babies.

American customs and traditions were explicitly taught during different seasons of the year, usually through stories, songs, and art projects, as well as through the teacher's simplified explanations of holidays. Some of the concepts transmitted during October must have seemed especially strange and contradictory to children from other cultures: witches are "funny" and "scary" at the same time; people will give you candy if you say "Trick or Treat," but you should not eat any (there was considerable fear of poisoning at that time because of the Tylenol incident). Some seasonal traditions were transmitted entirely as part of child lore and never mentioned by adults, such as pinching anyone who did not wear green on Saint Patrick's Day.

The kindergarten class also included several bilingual children from other parts of the world, and they also shared those cultures with one another to some extent. A girl from Egypt told the other children about seeing Tutankhamen in a "super case," for instance, and a boy from Zambia informed the others that witches would die if you put fire and water on them (thus resolving some of the anxiety that was generated about Halloween).

Transmission of values and attitudes from teacher to children was usually very subtle, but sometimes quite directly conveyed. The children tried very hard to please the kindergarten teacher, and mirrored her attitudes toward objects and events. Praise was plentiful. All art work was "beautiful," as was each new dress or mitten. Children who were working were always "good," and were frequently hugged and patted. As an additional reward, children got to paste stickers on their worksheets when they completed an assignment.

"Work" was probably *the* most highly valued activity. Everyone had to be busy doing "something." There was considerable leeway for choice of what were classified as "work" activities, but the teacher would not accept "nothing" in response when she asked, "What would you like to do?"

Inappropriate behavior, such as attempting to tattle on another child's misdeeds, or talking out of turn during circle time, was usually ignored by the teacher—an action which children correctly perceived as a negative sanction. Stronger sanctions were rarely necessary. And so, bit by bit, the children were readied for first grade.

At the end of the year of observation and recording, I asked the teacher to evaluate how well each of the three subjects had succeeded in learning what she, as an experienced kindergarten teacher, expected children to learn. In retrospect, this provided additional data on what *she* perceived as the content of school socialization.

It is interesting to note that although the teacher had devoted considerable time during the year to teaching knowledge about a variety of subjects and beginning skills for reading and writing, the criteria she used to judge relative readiness for first grade involved only whether rules for appropriate behavior had been learned and whether children had developed the "right attitudes" about school and learning. Whatever content knowledge was acquired during this socialization process was clearly a secondary consideration.

Like linguistic competence, cultural competence is a mentalistic construct which can only be inferred, and it is important to note that the same behaviors which the kindergarten teacher interpreted as meaning "not ready" for school were either interpreted quite differently by the Korean and Japanese teachers or simply were not noticed. In fact, the Japanese student who was judged a complete *failure* by these criteria, and probably would have been destined to repeat the kindergarten year had her family stayed in the United States, was judged the most *precocious* of the children by the Japanese teacher's standards. Indeed, she was already developing considerable competence in reading and writing her native language.

Since all of the subjects for this study returned to their home countries at the end of the school year, there is no way to know for sure how they would have actually succeeded in first grade and above had they remained in this country, but it is very likely that the teacher's perceptions of their "readiness" would have proved to be quite reliable. Research conducted the previous year in the same school (Saville-Troike 1984) included 10 older Asian students in grades 2 through 6, for whom we do have school achievement data from standardized tests administered in English. The children who exhibited the same behaviors and attitudes indicating "readiness" to the kindergarten teacher were indeed the ones who were also most successful at other grade levels.

The findings reported here have been preliminary in nature, but I believe these observations show that the focus for at least some of our studies must be broadened to include the development of cultural competence—even if our interest is merely in the learning of language per se. For those of us particularly concerned with why limited-English-speaking children succeed or fail in our schools, the cultural content of most immediate relevance may be that which is learned in the process of socialization to the subculture of the school.

The context of the school provides a conveniently constrained environment in which to observe the workings of cultural input and intake, where, as we have seen, input ranges from explicit formulations mediated or regulated through language to implicit understandings communicated nonverbally. The controlled nature of the context and the uniqueness of many aspects of the school subculture (which guarantees that they will not have been introduced and mastered elsewhere) create a virtual laboratory for examining relations between input and intake, factors affecting the rate and nature of intake, and of greatest interest to us here, the interaction between language and culture and second language acquisition. Just as Hymes (1966) showed us that we cannot adequately understand linguistic competence without recognizing it as a part of communicative competence, so it is my position that we cannot fully understand, or even satisfactorily study, second language acquisition unless we see it as part of a larger whole—the acquisition of a second culture. We must begin to escape the inherited tyranny of a focus on linguistic form, and even go beyond the limitations of communicative/pragmatic analysis, if we are ever to achieve a truly holistic perspective on the process by which children acquire a second language.

NOTE

1. Kleifgen's chapter (this volume) is based on data collected in the same classroom. She provides additional information on the setting and on the nature of the interaction between the teacher and the limited-English-speaking students.

4

SKILLED VARIATION IN A KINDERGARTEN TEACHER'S USE OF FOREIGNER TALK

Jo Anne Kleifgen
University of Illinois at Urbana-Champaign

Recently, foreigner talk (FT) investigators have moved into the classroom to observe teacher language input to second language students. The classroom studies have concentrated primarily on situations with adult language learners, and on ESL or FL classrooms where language itself is in focus as the subject of instruction (Chaudron 1979; Gaies 1977; Hatch, Shapira, and Wagner-Gough 1978; Henzl 1973, 1975, 1979; Long 1981c; Long and Sato 1983). However, the picture of native speaker (NS) adjustments to nonnative speakers (NNS) is not complete without taking into account teacher language accommodation in regular content area classrooms (cf. Hamayan and Tucker 1980; Schinke 1981; Schinke-Llano 1983; Urzua 1980).

A large body of untapped data exists in elementary classrooms in the United States, where a growing population of limited-English-speaking children spends at least part of the school day with teachers and NS children. The purpose of this chapter is to examine one such classroom by focusing on a kindergarten teacher's input and interactional adjustments to children having varying degrees of proficiency in English. The report will begin with a brief description of the setting and participants. Next there will be an analysis of the teacher's linguistic adjustment in a single instructional event early in the year as she worked simultaneously with four children of differing proficiency in English. A description will then be given of two comparable events which took place over a 6-month period, thus providing diachronic data of the teacher's interactions with two of the same children. Finally, a discussion of the results will conclude the chapter.

SETTING AND PARTICIPANTS

This study formed part of a larger ethnographic investigation in which a regular classroom of a midwestern public elementary school was observed and taped weekly for the duration of 1 year. The school provided a multilingual, multicultural program to a population of children of whom 41 percent came from homes where the mother tongue was not English. Some of their parents were refugees with little formal education; the majority of the parents were graduate students or university faculty members. The kindergarten teacher, the focus of the present study, has been recognized by school administrators and by the community as an experienced and skilled educator. She has worked for several years with second language children but has had no formal training or experience in specialized language instruction. Eleven of the 23 children in her class were speakers of a language other than English. The nationalities represented were Chinese, Egyptian, Indian, Israeli, Japanese, Korean, and Zambian. The physical layout of her classroom consisted of various centers of activity, including the "circle" meeting area, and the housekeeping, game, block-building, art, listening, and seatwork areas.

The lessons chosen for the study met three important criteria: (1) both NNSs and NSs took part to provide contrastive data, (2) the teacher was present to give input, and (3) instruction took place in a small group. This last criterion was applied to assure consistent types of events (cf. Cathcart 1982) and because it has been shown that the quantity and quality of teacher input to students are likely to be greatest in this situation of more personalized instruction (cf. Saville-Troike 1983).

SAMPLING TIMES

October 1982

The first lesson observed, lasting approximately 30 minutes, provided contrastive synchronic data. On October 26, 1982, as part of the daily routine, each child was assigned to one of six centers of activity. The group which was videotaped consisted of four children who were going to learn how to cut and paste witches' masks. Their English proficiency ranged from native to virtually zero. These rankings were based both on teacher judgments and on entry tests administered in August. Three of the children were limited English proficient. The first boy, Kazu, spoke almost no English; one girl,

Fatima, was able to communicate to a limited degree; and another girl, Siti, demonstrated more proficiency than the first two NNSs. The fourth child, Johnny, was a native speaker of English. The teacher joined the group and was present to provide input to all four children.

The transcribed discourse revealed how the teacher skillfully juggled four separate conversations with the children. The verbal exchange consisted of the steps to mask making—from face and features to hair and hat. This instructional process was sprinkled with personalized, informal asides.

The teacher's conversations with the children were compared first for instances of modified input. When grammaticality was examined, 54 (24 percent) of the 225 teacher utterances directed at the NNSs were found to contain deletions of determiner, copula, auxiliary, pronoun, and verb. Larger chunks of language were omitted as well, and often replaced by gestures. For instance, the teacher pointed to Kazu's witch's mask and then toward the children's cubbyholes, and said, "mailbox" (i.e., "Put it in your mailbox."). In a comparison of the four conversations, deletions were found to diminish in frequency according to the increased linguistic proficiency of the children. They were present in 32 utterances directed at Kazu, 19 addressed to Fatima, 3 to Siti, and none to Johnny (NS). (See Table 4-1.)

TABLE 4-1 Frequency and Length of Teacher Utterances* to Children of Varying Levels of Proficiency (October Lesson)

Student†	*Proficiency range*	*% Teacher utterances*	*Teacher MLU*	*Divergent deletions*
S1	Low	40.5	3.18	32
S2	Low–med	27.9	3.37	19
S3	Medium	14.9	4.51	3
S4	High (NS)	16.0	5.27	0

*Total teacher Us = 269 (excluding group-directed Us).
†S1 = Kazu, S2 = Fatima, S3 = Siti, S4 = Johnny.

Likewise, the teacher's utterances were found to vary in length and number according to the linguistic ability of her addressees. On average, her utterances to Kazu, the least proficient child, were the shortest (3.18 mean length of utterance (MLUs)). Utterances directed at Fatima were slightly longer (3.37 MLUs), and her verbal input increased to 4.51 MLUs to Siti and to 5.27 MLUs to Johnny, the NS. Further, it was found that the least proficient of the speakers received the greatest amount of verbal attention from the teacher, with 40.5 percent of her utterances directed at him. The teacher devoted 27.9 percent of her verbal input to Fatima and 14.9 percent to Siti. The total input to Johnny was 16 percent. (See Table 4-1.)

In addition, the lexical input to the NNSs was less varied and supplied in greater quantities to the children according to their descending level of proficiency. Of the total vocabulary items (933) addressed to the children,

37.62 percent were directed to Kazu, 24.75 percent to Fatima, 14.5 percent to Siti, and 23.47 percent to Johnny. A calculation of the type-token ratio showed that while the greatest number of words was directed at the least proficient speaker, input to that child had the least lexical variety. The ratios were .33 for Kazu, .41 for Fatima, .59 for Siti, and .48 for Johnny. (See Table 4-2.) Why the NS received more input and less lexical variety in this lesson than Siti, the most proficient NNS, will be discussed below. Next, a gross analysis was made for functional intent of the teacher's combined utterances to the four children, using a modified form of codings by Dore (1978) and grouped within a broader set of characteristics adapted from Freed (1981). (See Table 4-3.)

TABLE 4-2 Amount and Frequency of Words Directed at Students of Varying Levels of Proficiency (October Lesson)

Student	*% Total items**	*Type/Token*
S1	37.62	.33
S2	24.75	.41
S3	14.50	.59
S4	23.47	.48

*Total vocabulary items = 933.

The analyzed data revealed that the most common functions in use were information exchanges, action directives, and clarifications. Each of these was employed 22 to 23 percent of the time. To achieve the three functions, the teacher made use of expansions, completions, paraphrases, and repetitions. The information-exchange function centered primarily around the task at hand. The teacher requested or shared information regarding mask making through wh- and yes-no type questions, statements about rules and procedures, and descriptions. Inasmuch as the goal of the lesson event was to learn "how-to" create a witch's mask, an equally important communicative function for the teacher was the action directive. This function was achieved either through direct requests for action ("Cut a piece like this") or indirectly through wh- and yes-no questions ("Where does the hat go?" "Would you give us pencil?") and statements of procedures ("You're gonna make her mouth right here."). A third significant input function was clarification. The teacher clarified her own statements or requested clarification of student utterances. During three of every five clarifying functions, the teacher was trying (with ample success) to make sense of what the children were communicating.

Another frequent function of teacher input was organizational devices (16 percent). These included politeness markers, boundary markers, and attention-getting expressions. Evaluative remarks appeared 10 percent of the time and were almost entirely approvals. Many nonverbal cues were given to

TABLE 4-3 Percentages of Teacher Input Functions and Deletions (October Lesson)

*Function**	*Percent utterances*	*Percent deletions*†
Information exchange	22.1	4.00
Action directive	23.7	5.33
Clarification	22.5	8.44
Organizational device	16.1	—
Evaluation	10.0	5.78
Correction	2.0	—
Language instruction	2.0	—
Conversation support	1.2	—
Self-directed speech	0.4	—

*These functions represent a modified version of the categories described by Freed (1981). †Deletions = 23.55% of total input to NNSs.

children that served as evaluations, including smiles, nods, and iconic gestures (e.g., a hand moving from the top of the head upward to indicate pleasure over a tall witch's hat). Perhaps the most surprising element of the data was the almost nonexistent use of the language-instruction function (2 percent). The teacher's concern was not to teach English but to teach a skill through the medium of English. Utterances having syntactic divergences comprised 23.55 percent of the language spoken by the teacher to the NNSs. The deletions were grouped according to the functional categories described above. At no time in the lesson were they used with NNSs in the language-teaching function or in the organizational devices (perhaps because they were short, stock expressions). They did appear distributed among four other functions: clarifications (8.44 percent), evaluations (5.78 percent), action directives (5.33 percent), and information exchanges (4 percent). (See Table 4-3.) Within the four functions, the deletions appeared primarily in yes-no questions, information requests, "how-to" directions, verifications of pupil utterances, repetitions to facilitate student understanding, and praise of pupil accomplishments.

An examination of discourse content revealed that Siti, the most proficient NNS, initiated topics most frequently with the teacher (seven times), Fatima less so (five times), and Kazu initiated the interaction on only one occasion. Exchanges were initiated by the children to describe what they were doing, to ask for materials, to clarify the teacher's directions, and to request the teacher's approval of their progress. In other words, the NNSs who spoke least about the task received the most language input from the teacher. The inverse correlation between the amount of teacher input among the second language children and student-initiated interaction is an indication that the teacher appeared to be providing the amount of assistance necessary for each child to accomplish the instructional goal. That the relative amount of her linguistic input to each child had an instructional aim is suggested by the fact that the teacher provided more input to Johnny, the NS, than to Siti. Siti clearly demonstrated more skill with the scissors and paste than Johnny did, even though her English was more limited. The teacher, for instance, used Siti's work as a model, as illustrated by the following interactions:

S: Have to cut this.
T: You gonna cut em out?
T: (To NNSs) See, Siti's made mouth real scarey. And now she's gonna do eyes.

In contrast, Johnny, being a little heavy-handed with the scissors, was obliged to cut a new circle for the witch's face:

T: Y'have to make another one, Johnny. This is gonna make her face. It's OK. But see, you need to cut this far and stop. Just cut another one.

Thus the NS needed more help and received it with repeated instructions and reassurances.

In spite of the special attention given to Johnny's skill needs, the teacher's sentence structure was more complex in her speech to him, she made no deletions of required forms, and she often selected topics for discussion which were less dependent on the immediate environment. An illustration of such a context-reduced topic is contained in the following exchange, a discussion to establish the identity of Johnny's cousin:

T: Johnny, is your cousin visiting?
J: No. (Inaudible) Mrs. Smith.
T: He's always with Mrs. Smith everyday?
J: No. Mrs. Smith is my cousin.
T: Mrs. Smith's your cousin? Really? How nice. Today I have a box of things for you to take to her.

Data from the first event have thus revealed that in contrast to her speech to the NS, the teacher's language to the NNSs was more context-embedded and was marked by shorter utterances and syntactic divergences. Her input to the NNSs varied in number and length of utterances and number and frequency of lexical items according to the degree of their proficiency in English. The function of the teacher's language with all four children was primarily to accomplish the instructional goal of cutting and pasting, and contained syntactic divergences only when she addressed NNSs.

Two similar events later in the school year (January and April) were examined to determine whether the teacher's varied linguistic accommodations were consistent over time. The teacher interacted with groups of children in which two of the four October subjects, Johnny (the NS) and Kazu, and another NNS, Soo-Mi, were present. The teacher's input to the three children was compared for grammaticality, for length of utterance, and for topic choice.

January 1983

Kazu, the least proficient NNS in the first event, took part in a small group lesson observed 13 weeks later (January 27, 1983). The group activity, lasting approximately 25 minutes, consisted of a pencil-paper exercise matching upper- and lowercase letters. Seven children, four NNSs and three NSs, participated. Since the radio microphone was attached to Kazu, it was possible to capture the teacher's directions to the whole group, her conversations with Kazu, and her interactions with his nearest classmate, Soo-Mi, who arrived on the scene 10 minutes into the exercise and seated herself next to him. In this instructional event the teacher continued to make use of the same accommodation strategies which she had been using before, including divergent structures. By this time the teacher and her pupils had come to know one another more, and this increased familiarity led to greater shared background and perhaps more conversational possibilities. The communication between Kazu and the teacher was compared first with their October exchange and second with the conversation between the teacher and Soo-Mi. Kazu, who had begun the school year with no English, was making progress by January. His improvement in productive English as measured in the mean length of his utterances increased from 1.16 in the first event to 2.64 in the January lesson. Some increase occurred in the teacher's input, as well, from 3.18 to 3.81 MLUs (Table 4-4).

TABLE 4-4 Teacher and Student MLUs in Three Lessons

*Subject**	*October*	*January*	*April*
S1 to T	1.16	2.64	
T to S1	3.18	3.81	
S4 to T	4.17		6.14
T to S4	5.27		5.52
S5 to T		0.00	0.00
T to S5		3.59	3.75

*S1 = Kazu, S4 = Johnny, S5 = Soo-Mi, T = Teacher.

A comparison of the teacher's vocabulary use with Kazu in the two instructional events revealed an increase in lexical variety, with a change in type-token ratio from .33 to .68. Thus she adjusted her language as Kazu's abilities increased.

Soo-Mi, like Kazu, had begun the school year with no English, but she remained in a silent period which was to stretch into spring. Her lack of verbal participation in this January event was no exception. She said nothing. She was, however, able to understand and follow the teacher's instructions and could carry out the letter-matching task. The teacher's language to Soo-Mi measured 3.59 MLUs and contained syntactic divergences. (See Table 4-4.)

One example from the data illustrates the varying degrees of the teacher's language accommodation in the lesson. To explain the task to the children, she used a "baby-sitter" analogy for matching upper- and lowercase letters on a worksheet in their folders. Her instructions to the whole group, using one child's worksheet to demonstrate, were as follows:

These are baby sitters taking care of babies. Draw a line from Q to q. From S to s, and then trace.

The same instructions were simplified when she turned to work individually with Kazu, tracing an imaginary line across his worksheet and saying:

Baby sitter takes care of baby.

She gave individual assistance to Soo-Mi as well, this time simplifying even more, pointing to the letters and saying,

Baby sitter—baby.

A difference in choice of topic was apparent also in the teacher's conversations with the two children. For Soo-Mi all language was related to the immediate environment—the letter-matching task. For Kazu, the teacher began to venture into more context-reduced topics. For example, after using the baby-sitter analogy, she asked him whether he ever had a baby sitter at home:

Kazu, you ever have baby sitter?
You?
Have baby sitter?

To summarize, from the October to January events, the teacher's language use skillfully shifted to more complex, less contextualized structures for the language learner who showed improvement over time, while shorter constructions and more contextualized input occurred in the speech to the child who still would not talk. It remained necessary to match these data against the teacher's instructional language use over time with Johnny, the NS.

April 1983

On April 7, the teacher and 10 children were videotaped as they engaged in an activity centered around the formation of printed letters and sound-symbol correspondence. A large letter chart served as a visual aid for the children, who were copying work into their folders. As in the October and

January lessons, the teacher gave general directions to the group and then worked with each child individually. This time the audio microphone was attached to Johnny, the NS. The presence of Soo-Mi next to him provided further contrastive data. Johnny, who had had trouble handling scissors in October, was showing improvement in the fine-motor skills by April. Although he needed the teacher's assistance with some letter formations ("Start at the top and go down when you make your L"), the teacher acknowledged his efforts, e.g., "That's nice. Good. That A is a little stiff, but that one's real good." Soo-Mi was the academic star in this lesson, successfully carrying out the letter-formation task. The teacher's input to her consisted of initial instructions, but she needed no assistance with a pencil; her talent in fine-motor skills was evident (and even extended to musical skill on the violin). In fact, much of the teacher's input to Soo-Mi took the form of statements of praise for her printing capabilities: "Soo-Mi, beautiful!"

An analysis of the two conversations in this lesson showed first that both Johnny and the teacher were using as before more complex utterances in their speech to each other. In the April event the average length of Johnny's utterances was 6.14. The teacher's utterances to Johnny averaged 5.52. (See Table 4-4.)

Further, as in the October event, the standard syntactic rules of English were preserved throughout the teacher's interaction with Johnny. Contrasted with her input to Johnny, the teacher's utterances to Soo-Mi were simpler (3.75 MLUs) (Table 4-4) and still contained deletions, e.g., "Um, you need pencil." and "(Color the) lamp, Soo-Mi."

Soo-Mi's language production in this lesson did not show a change from the instructional event in January. Consistent with this lack of change, the teacher's complexity of input increased only slightly from 3.59 MLUs in January to 3.75 MLUs in April.

To recapitulate, the teacher's utterances to NNSs across the three instructional events were shown first to be shorter on average than the language addressed to the NS. The teacher also showed skill in maintaining consistency in the differential complexity of her input to both NNSs and NS over the course of the year. Second, grammatical deviations were present in language addressed to children who were very limited in their English proficiency; divergences in the syntax were never made in speaking to the NS. Third, the amount of the teacher's input to each child appeared to be determined primarily by the students' needs in learning a skill; the complexity of her input appeared to be determined largely by the students' linguistic needs.

DISCUSSION

Anyone who has taught young children remembers facing them in the classroom for the first time and thinking, "How can I explain this concept in words they will understand?" Primary school educators all learn to "teach to a given level." This study illustrates how effectively one regular classroom teacher individualized her instructional language. Aware of individual differences in children's motor skill abilities, she devoted more explanation and demonstration time to those who required more assistance from her than others did. The instructional skill of this teacher contrasts with typical teaching patterns found in previous studies. Schinke (1981) and Schinke-Llano (1983), for example, found that teachers interacted more with NSs than with NNSs in middle grade content classrooms. Similarly, Seliger (1977, 1983) described two extremes of learner behavior which affected teacher input. Students who initiated interactions more frequently received more feedback, whereas those who displayed little linguistic initiative received less attention from teachers. Learners in the two groups were called *high-input generators* (HIG) and *low-input generators* (LIG), respectively. That the skilled teacher in this investigation diverged from the apparent norm by attending to the more reticent students demonstrates what might be accomplished through more effective teacher training and staff development.

The study also corroborates the ESL and FL classroom studies conducted by Gaies (1977) and Henzl (1973, 1975, 1979) in which teachers varied their speech adjustments according to the level of the students' competence in the target language. Similarly, the teacher in the present study attended to differences in children's linguistic abilities by varying the complexity of her speech to them. Unlike the language of teachers in previous studies, her language use ranged more widely, from simple, contextualized utterances with less lexical variety and syntactic divergences for limited English proficient speakers to more complex, context-reduced, consistently grammatical structures for the NS. Finally, this study demonstrates that foreigner talk *is* used in the regular-content classroom as a way to achieve successful communication with NNSs. These findings should provide a first step in the generation of hypotheses for larger investigations of instructional input to second language children.

5

TEACHER–PUPIL INTERACTION IN SECOND LANGUAGE DEVELOPMENT

Rod Ellis
Ealing College of Higher Education

This chapter has two aims. The primary aim is to examine the relationship between the interactions that took place between one teacher and two pupils over a 9-month period and the process of second language development of the two children. The secondary aim is a methodological one. I want to argue that qualitative analyses as well as quantitative analyses of input data are essential if we are to increase our understanding of how input affects second language acquisition (SLA).

It has been hypothesized (e.g., Krashen 1982, Long 1983d) that SLA is dependent on the learner's obtaining "comprehensible input." One way that this may be achieved is through the adaptations—formal and interactional—that have been observed to occur in the speech that native speakers address to learners. Another way is through the learner's own use of communication strategies, which serve to help the learner overcome problems of communicating with limited second language (L2) resources. There are now several studies describing "foreigner" or "teacher talk" (e.g., Arthur et al. 1980, Long 1981a, Gaies 1977, Henzl 1979) and several more examining the learner's communication strategies (e.g., Tarone 1977, 1981; Bialystok 1983). These studies are largely taxonomic and quantitative. That is, they provide lists of categories of speech modifications or learner strategies and then count the frequencies of each category. In this way a picture has been built up of what the native speaker and the learner contribute to the task of making the input comprehensible.

One of the problems of this quantitative approach is that "comprehensible input" is not really the result of the *separate* contributions of the native speaker and the learner but of their *joint* endeavors. The speech addressed to learners is the result of an ongoing interaction between learner and native speaker. In this process the interlocutors collaborate in establishing and maintaining a topic. This has been referred to as *negotiation* (e.g., Tarone 1981). At the moment we do not have any effective categories of negotiation and have not been able to accurately count the interpersonal characteristics of negotiation.

One way that has been used to examine the process of negotiation is discourse analysis (e.g., Hatch 1978, Ellis 1980). However, this has been used in qualitative rather than quantitative analyses of representative samples of native speaker-learner discourse. The advantage of discourse analysis is that it has provided us with information about the two-sided nature of the interactions that lead to comprehensible input.

Another problem with the quantitative approach is that it has not yet demonstrated whether there is any relationship between the observed speech modifications/strategies and SLA. The standard approach (e.g., Long 1981a, Scarcella and Higa 1981) is to establish that quantitative differences exist between input addressed to native speakers and input addressed to nonnative speakers and then to hypothesize how these differences are important for SLA. For example, Long (1981a) demonstrates that these differences are more evident in what he calls "interactional" features (e.g., expansions) than in "input" features (e.g., average length of T units) and then suggests that the "interactional" features are more important for SLA than the "input" modifications. However, he does not offer any direct quantitative evidence to support this. Where the research design has been cross-sectional, as in Long's published work, it is not easy to examine the nature of the relationship between interaction and the process of development.[1] It is only possible to hypothesize that the relationship evident at a particular point in time is indicative of the relationship over time.

In order to examine the relationship between the types of interaction that result from native speaker speech adaptations and learner communication strategies on the one hand and SLA on the other, it is useful to ask three separate questions:

1. What are the speech modifications and strategies that occur?

2. Are the speech modifications and strategies developmental? That is, do they change according to the level of the learner's competence?

3. Are the speech modifications and strategies related to the acquisition of new linguistic knowledge and/or the rate of acquisition, and, if so, how?

The first of these questions has been the primary concern of the research referred to above. The second question has received much less attention, but Henzl (1979) has shown that teachers' formal speech adjustments are sensitive to the general level of proficiency of the students being taught. The third question has become the central question in first language acquisition research, and a number of studies have addressed it (e.g., Ellis and Wells 1980, Wells 1981). It has received only speculative attention in SLA research, however.[2]

If we are to show that comprehensible input derived from interaction is important for SLA and how it is important, we need studies that consider questions 2 and 3. It is likely that this will require qualitative analyses based on longitudinal studies of SLA as well as quantitative analyses of cross-sectional data. The study reported in this chapter is an initial attempt to examine questions 2 and 3. It was part of a broader investigation into the relationship between the SLA of two children and their classroom environment. It will make use of both qualitative and quantitative analyses.

METHOD

The two children of the study, brother and sister, were R and T. They were aged 11 and 13, respectively, at the beginning of the study, and both spoke Punjabi as their mother tongue. R was illiterate to begin with and had had very little previous school experience. He was an extroverted child and rapidly made friends with other non-English-speaking children. He found it difficult to concentrate on any single activity for a long period of time and tended to prefer classroom tasks that he could perform easily. T had had more experience of school in Pakistan than her brother and could write a little. She was much quieter and had a greater attention span. She was able to work on classroom tasks for long periods of time without requiring the help of the teacher. Unlike her brother, she tended to make friends only with other Punjabi-speaking girls.

Both R and T were placed in a language unit specially set up to cope with children from overseas who had insufficient English to fit into the normal classroom of a secondary school. They were placed in a reception class which contained only other L2 learners, many of whom spoke Punjabi. English was used as the medium of instruction in the classroom and also served as the medium of communication among pupils with different first languages outside the classroom in the unit. For their first year R and T were almost entirely reliant on this environment for English input, as they received minimal exposure to English in the wider community. The English they were exposed to consisted of both the "interlanguage" of other L2 learners and the standard language of native-speaking teachers.

The main study of their linguistic development was based on data collected from inside the classroom using audio recordings and pencil and paper records. This showed that they acquired English very slowly. By the end of their first school year (i.e., 9 months from the start of the study), for instance, their interrogative utterances were still largely uninverted. There was no evidence of any ability to use the past tense in spontaneous speech, and many of their utterances were propositionally reduced (see Ellis 1982). Their general progress was similar to that reported for Alberto (Schumann 1978b).

The data for the analyses that follow were obtained from a series of "interview" sessions between the two children and their regular class teacher. These took place in an empty room without the researcher being present and lasted approximately 15 minutes each. The teacher was asked to try to elicit speech from the two children. However, no attempt was made to elicit any specific structures. The idea was to "hold a conversation" as far as this was possible. Each session involved the teacher asking questions about pictures with each child separately. The pictures were different in each session, but one set (Learning Development Aids "What's Wrong Cards") was introduced on three separate occasions during the year. In addition to the talk centering around the pictures, there were attempts by the teacher to talk about events he knew the children had participated in and also to ask questions about their family and interests. These were more common in the sessions toward the end of the year. Altogether there were a total of 19 sessions for R and 18 for T.[3] The sessions took place at approximately 2-week intervals over a 9-month period from November to July. Each session was audio-recorded and transcriptions prepared in normal orthography. These were shown to the teacher, who provided contextual information.

Analyses were carried out to investigate (1) to what extent the interactional features of each interview changed over time and (2) what role these features may have played in the children's SLA. These analyses are reported separately below.

THE DEVELOPMENTAL NATURE OF SELECTED INTERACTIONAL FEATURES

In order to investigate to what extent the nature of the teacher-pupil interactions changed over time, three different analyses were carried out. The first analysis considered developments in the teacher's use of a subset of "interactional" features reported on in a study of native-speaker adjustments by Long (1983d). The second analysis concerned the teacher's treatment of the tasks he gave the pupils and also his response to communication breakdown. The third analysis concerned the pupils' contributions to the interactions. It examined their use of a number of communication strategies. Each analysis will be discussed separately.

The Teacher's "Interactional" Adjustments

The interactional features of the teacher's speech that were selected for investigation were a subset of those studied by Long (1983d). A description of these features can be found in Appendix A. Long found significant differences on six measures of the interactional structure of native-speaker speech addressed to nonnative speakers in comparison with native-speaker speech addressed to other native speakers. To examine whether these differences would be reflected developmentally in the teacher-pupil (T-P) conversations, the first 100 turns in two of the early sessions (recordings 3 and 6) and two of the later sessions (recordings 15 and 18) were coded for each occurrence of the six interactional features.

Table 5-1 gives the number of occurrences of each feature and the extent to which the differences between the frequencies in the early and late recordings are significant, based on chi-squared scores. Taking .05 as the level of significance, two of the interactional features in the teacher's speech proved sensitive to both R's and T's level of development. Self-repetitions were *fewer* in the later recordings, whereas expansions were *more numerous.* In addition, the teacher used significantly more confirmation checks in the later sessions when conversing with R but not with T. None of the other features showed a significant difference from one time to the next.

TABLE 5-1 A Comparison of the Interactional Features of the Teacher's Input at Different Times

Feature	R				T			
	n				*n*			
	T1	*T2*	χ^2 *(df = 1)*	*p*	*T1*	*T2*	χ^2 *(df = 1)*	*p*
1. Confirmation checks	3	11	4.57	0.05	3	7	1.60	ns
2. Comprehension checks	4	8	1.60	ns	3	1	1.00	ns
3. Clarification checks	8	10	1.00	ns	7	2	2.78	ns
4. Self-repetitions	17	5	6.55	0.02	10	2	5.33	0.05
5. Other repetitions	12	8	0.80	ns	16	9	1.96	ns
6. Expansions	2	9	4.45	0.05	7	16	4.11	0.05

The Teacher's Treatment of Task and Communication Breakdown

In addition to the comparison of the developmental nature of the six interactional features of the teacher's speech, an analysis of the type of task posed by the teacher's questions and an analysis of the teacher's approach to repairing communication breakdown were carried out. These analyses were based on conversations about five different pictures in the same four sessions as the previous analysis. However, as the length of the conversations varied substantially from session to session and from learner to learner, the scores obtained were weighted to correspond to the equivalent of 20 tasks, where a "task" constituted an initial teacher question followed by whatever talk was required to resolve the demands set up by the question. The features investigated were:

1. Type of task
   a. Questions requiring object identification (e.g., "What's this?")
   b. Questions requiring some comment about the pictures (e.g., "What's the man doing in the picture?" "What's wrong with the picture?")
2. Task establishment
   a. Closed questions (i.e., questions for which the teacher had a preconceived response in mind)
   b. Open questions (i.e., questions for which several possible answers would be acceptable to the teacher)[4]
3. Response to communication breakdown
   a. Teacher accepts (i.e., the teacher accepts a pupil response even though it is clearly not an appropriate response to the task)
   b. Teacher repairs (i.e., the teacher seeks to elicit another response to the task either by repeating his initial question or by reformulating it or requesting clarification)
   c. Teacher supplies (i.e., the teacher gives the solution to the task himself)

The results are shown in Table 5-2. In conversations with both R and T the teacher used far more questions requiring object identification in the early sessions than in the later ones. There were no significant differences involving either task establishment or the teacher's response to communication breakdown.

TABLE 5-2 Comparison of Teacher's Treatment of Task and Response to Communication Breakdown at Different Times

Feature	*R*				*T*			
	T1	*T2*	χ^2	*p*	*T1*	*T2*	χ^2	*p*
1. Type of task								
a. Object identification	22.5	8.5	13.31	0.001	25.8	8.0	28.9	0.001
b. Comment required	17.3	31.5	(df = 1)		14.2	32.0	(df = 1)	
2. Task establishment								
a. Open Qs	6.8	13.2	1.88	ns	7.4	14.2	2.94	ns
b. Closed Qs	32.2	26.8	(df = 1)		32.6	25.3	(df = 1)	
3. Communication breakdown								
a. Accept	9.2	1.4	5.51	ns	6.7	2.2	1.79	ns
b. Repair	22.3	12.3	(df = 2)		12.7	15.7	(df = 2)	
c. Supply	6.9	6.8			7.5	7.9		

The Learners' Communication Strategies

The learners' contributions to the interview conversations were examined in terms of the distinction between "reduction" and "achievement" behavior (Faerch and Kaspar 1980). Reduction behavior was defined as the learner missing a turn by keeping silent, opting out of the task by the use of "no" or "I don't know," etc., topic switching (i.e., ignoring the task nominated by the teacher and substituting some other task in its place), or imitating (i.e., imitating part or the whole of the teacher's previous utterance irrespective of whether this was conversationally appropriate or not). Achievement behavior was defined as using the first language, miming, requesting assistance, or guessing what response the teacher wanted. It was hypothesized that reduction behavior would be more prevalent in the earlier sessions.

For the purposes of this analysis the same two early and two late recordings were examined. The basis was once again the weighted equivalent of 20 tasks in each session (see explanation above).

The results are shown in Table 5-3. R resorted to significantly more reduction-type behavior in the early sessions, but T's behavior did not change. Thus the hypothesis was confirmed for R but not for T.

TABLE 5-3 Comparison of Learners' Communication Behavior at Different Times

Feature	*R*				*T*			
	T1	*T2*	χ^2	*p*	*T1*	*T2*	χ^2	*p*
1. Reduction behavior	22.0	6.1	9.94 (df = 1)	.01	18.9	13.4	0.67 (df = 1)	ns
2. Achievement behavior	16.4	24.7			9.5	9.7		

DISCUSSION

The three analyses reported above were carried out in order to determine whether the T-P interactions changed as the ability of the two learners to use English grew. If, as has been claimed by Long (1983d) and Krashen (1982), SLA requires comprehensible input in order to proceed, it is to be expected that the conversational adjustments made by both the teacher and the learners will vary according to the stage of development of the learners. This is because the amount of adjustment required at an early stage of development will be greater than that required at a later stage (at least on some measures), in order to achieve comprehensible input.[5] The results of the analysis suggest that whereas some of the interactional features in the T-P conversations did change as a result of the learners' increased knowledge of English, other features did not change.

The features that proved developmentally sensitive included both teacher and pupil adjustments. On the teacher's side changes are evident in both "strategies" for avoiding trouble and "tactics" for repairing trouble (Long 1983d). As regards "strategies," the teacher favored identification questions in the early sessions, presumably because they were simpler (Hatch 1978) and also because they served as a means of establishing intersubjectivity. In the later sessions the teacher switched to using more demanding questions. The teacher also used more self-repetition when the two learners possessed little competence in English. This served both to establish a task and to respond to breakdown. Where "tactics" were concerned, the teacher produced more expansions in the later sessions, perhaps because he felt the two children possessed sufficient competence at this stage to benefit from the "task" summaries which the expansions typically provided. On the pupils' side, only R's communicative behavior changed with increased proficiency.

However, many of the features investigated did not change over time. On many of the features Long (1983d) found significant differences between native-speaker/nonnative-speaker conversation and native-speaker/native-speaker conversation; no developmental effects were evident in the T-P conversations. The frequency of comprehension checks, clarification checks, and other repetitions did not change as the learners' competence grew. A number of possible explanations suggest themselves. One is that the results of this study reflect highly idiosyncratic interactional styles which would not be commonly found in a wider population. Another possibility is that the nature of the task affected the results. Show and tell pictures do not constitute a natural communicative task, and this may have restricted the occurrence of specific types of interactional behavior. Another explanation is that some interactional features are only roughly tuned, whereas others are more finely tuned to the individual learner's stage of development. This has the support of mother-talk research (e.g., Ellis and Wells 1980). If the latter explanation is correct, it might be expected that interactional differences will be more evident when the comparison involves stages of development more widely separated than was the case with R and T, who, it will be remembered, did not progress very rapidly in the 9-month period the study covered.

It is also worthwhile drawing attention to the different interaction styles of the two children. Whereas R tried to cope with the communicative pressure posed in the early sessions by topic switching, T was more inclined to simply miss a turn or opt out. R's reduction behavior had almost disappeared by the later sessions, but T continued to give up whenever the going got tough for her. This may partly explain why the teacher used more confirmation checks with R but not with T in the later sessions, as confirmation checks are contingent on the learner's saying something. The point that I particularly wish to draw attention to, however, is that we should not necessarily expect the characteristics of interaction to be determined solely by the need to achieve comprehensible input. They can also be the result of personality. R's greater extroversion may account for why he was prepared to take greater communicative risks at an earlier stage than his sister.

THE ROLE OF INTERACTIONAL FEATURES IN THE CHILDREN'S SLA

Demonstrating that native speakers and learners make adjustments in order to achieve understanding and demonstrating that some of these adjustments change over time in accordance with the learner's knowledge of the L2 are not the same as showing that these adjustments facilitate SLA. To do this we need to show *if* and *how* interactional features contribute to the process by which learners develop a L2.

The SLA literature suggests that there are two ways in which the input may influence the route along which L2 learners pass. (1) The input that results from the interlocutors' attempts to negotiate a shared topic results in specific syntactic forms being modeled more frequently than others. These are processed and acquired by the learner. Thus it is the basic rules of conversation which determine which forms are used frequently and so learned early. This view of the contribution of the input to SLA has been put forward by Hatch (1978). (2) The second way in which the input affects the course of development is through the use of what Wagner-Gough (1975) has called an "incorporation strategy." According to this view, conversations provide the learner with units of different sizes which can be incorporated into sentence structure. Thus the input controls which forms are processed by learners and also provides building blocks which they can use to construct new syntactic patterns, which otherwise lie outside the learner's competence.

In order to examine whether and in what way the T-P interactions contributed to R and T's acquisition of English, the transcripts of the first 10 recordings were examined to identify utterances which featured "new" syntactic knowledge. It cannot be claimed, of course, that these "new" forms were actually in use for the very first time in these contexts, but it was felt that this approach would give an indication of the communicative conditions that appeared to facilitate the *use* of linguistic knowledge which had been recently acquired. As Faerch and Kaspar (1980) point out, the automatization of new items is just as much a part of SLA as their initial internalization. Also it seems a reasonable hypothesis that those conditions that encouraged the use of new items were the same as those that facilitated their assimilation.

Only "creative" speech was considered for this analysis. Imitations of previous teacher utterances were excluded.[6] The "creative" utterances were then analyzed in terms of their syntactic constituents in order to determine both the first instances of two-, three-, and four-constituent utterances and the first instances of new realizations of these utterances. Thus, for instance, it was possible to identify the first occasion in which single-constituent utterances (e.g., a noun phrase) were realized by two words as opposed to one word (e.g., "blue umbrella"—adj. + N) and the first occasion on which two-constituent utterances (e.g., NP + verb) appeared in the speech of the two children.

RESULTS

The pattern of development that emerged was very similar to that reported for the SLA of German by the children of migrant workers in Germany (see Pienemann 1980). In the first two recordings both R and T were restricted to single-constituent utterances. In recording 3 they both produced the first instances of two-word realizations of single-constituent utterances:

R: Black/taes/ (= tyres)
T: No water

and also the first instances of two-constituent utterances:

R: Man going.
T: A man wall.

For the next few sessions both R and T continued to operate with utterances consisting of one or two constituents, but they slowly expanded their syntactical range. The first clear instances of three-constituent utterances occurred in recording 7 for T:

T: This one is bigger.

and recording 8 for R:

R: The boy standing in the door.

T produced four-constituent utterances from recording 8 onward and R from recording 9:

R: Boot is open on car.
T: Boy is hold hand in the bus.

Thus syntactic development of the two children, as evidenced in the recording session, was systematically incremental. Various realizations of first one-, then later two-, three-, and four-constituent utterances were developed.

What contribution did the interactions between each of the two children and the teacher make at the "breakthrough points"? In order to consider this question, selected interactions from the recordings will be analyzed qualitatively to show the role played by negotiation. In the first example R and the teacher are looking at a What's Wrong Card depicting a bicycle with no pedals. The transcript of their conversation is as follows (see Appendix B for an explanation of the transcription conventions followed): R's first two-word utterance concluded this episode.

1	T:	I want you to tell me what you can see in the picture or what's wrong with the picture.	
2			R: A /paik/ (=bike)
3	T:	A cycle, yes. But what's wrong?	
4			R: /ret/ (=red)
5	T:	It's red yes. What's wrong with it?	
6			R: Black
7	T:	Black. Good Black what?	
8			R: Black /taes/ (= tyres)

In this episode the task which the teacher began with in (1) was beyond R. He lacked the linguistic resources both to understand the teacher's demands and to respond to them. His two-word utterance in (8) was the result of a reduction strategy (i.e., topic switching) which the teacher accepted, and of an incorporation strategy based on the teacher's occasional question in (7).[7] Later on in recording 3, R produced another two-constituent utterance consisting of N + V, which again was the result of an incorporation strategy. R appeared to thrive when he was in control of the discourse topic and when he could "lean" on the discourse to help him eke out his meager resources.

T's first two-constituent utterance was in recording 3 also. It also showed how important cooperation between the interlocutors was in the process of building utterances that lay outside or on the edges of the learner's competence. T and the teacher were looking at a What's Wrong Card depicting a man walking through the wall of a room.

1	T:	Do you want to look at the next picture? Yeah? (.3.)	
2			T: Man
3	T:	A man. And do you know what this is? (.4.) A wall.	
4			T: A wall
5	T:	Like that one there. (pointing at picture) A wall.	

6 T: A wall, a wall
7 T: Yes.
Now can you see what the man is doing?
8 T: A man wall
9 T: He's going into the wall.

In this episode the major task that faced the learner was that of encoding the action process represented by the picture. Both R and T, however, were at a stage of development where their linguistic resources limited them to identifying objects. Like Yoshida's (1978) subject, their early vocabulary consisted almost entirely of nouns, and apart from the copula and "have," they used very few verbs. The teacher helped T to get round this problem by breaking the task down into two parts. First, he and T identified the relevant objects in the picture—the man and the wall. Second, the teacher requested T to encode the action process [i.e., in (7)]. T responded with a verbless utterance which juxtaposed the two previously practiced nouns. Her meaning was clear, however, and the teacher was able to conclude the episode with an expansion that provided a well-formed version of T's two-constituent utterance. Thus the success of this episode was the result of (1) the teacher breaking a complex task into parts (i.e., controlling the type of task the learner is faced with), (2) the teacher helping out with vocabulary, and (3) T's use of a juxtaposition strategy involving "man" and "wall."

R's syntactic development also relied heavily on the discourse. His first three-constituent utterance occurred in recording 8:

1 T: What's the boy doing? (.2.)
2 R: The boy (.)
3 T: Yeah, stand
4 R: Standing in the door.
5 T: Standing in the door.
Yes, standing by the door.
By the door.

R responded to the teacher's initial request for action identification by imitating part of the question. The teacher started to supply R with the verb that he required [i.e., in (3)], but R was able to go on and complete the utterance himself in (4). The effect on the tape was of a more or less continuous utterance, with the teacher's prompt occurring at exactly the right moment to aid its completion. From this point onward, R produced plenty of three-constituent utterances.

DISCUSSION

By identifying occasions when "new" grammatical features appear in the speech of the two learners and then examining the discoursal context of these "new" features, it is possible to shed light on how taking part in conversations contributes to SLA. This approach rests on a qualitative analysis of selected interactions. As such, it is not clear whether the discourse processes that appear to contribute to SLA are generalizable. Similar analyses of other learners in other learning situations are needed.

Where the T-P conversations examined in this study are concerned, a number of facilitating characteristics of the discourse can be identified:

1. It appears that "new" rules were most easily practiced when R and T were allowed to initiate the discourse topic. In this way the learners were able to establish intersubjectivity with the teacher without the difficulty of having to comprehend what the teacher wanted them to talk about. For example, in recording 9, R produced a total of seven three-constituent utterances and in each case the discourse showed R to be the initiator. The productive use of "new" L2 forms requires that the learners were given the freedom to establish what and how they will contribute to the discourse. In this way they were able to make the most of the English they already knew and the teacher was able to build on this.

2. Reduction behavior consisting of topic switching enabling the children to replace a teacher-nominated task, which they were not able to handle, with a topic, which they were able to handle. Topic switching which was accepted by the teacher was a device for establishing intersubjectivity.

3. The teacher played an active role in helping R and T to stretch their resources and to build "new" utterance types. One way he did this was by providing "building blocks" which the learners could use as a basis for building "vertical structures" of the type identified by Scollon (1976) in first language acquisition. That is, the children could incorporate part of a previous teacher utterance into one of their own utterances and so achieve a more complex utterance than they could have managed on their own.

4. The teacher also gave feedback on the "new" utterances produced by R and T. He did this principally through expansions which supplied the missing parts of utterances which the learners had struggled to produce and which from a communicative point of view had been successful.

In summary, it was apparent that R and T were most likely to produce "new" forms when they were able to nominate the topic of conversation and when the teacher helped them by supplying crucial chunks of language at the right moment. Perhaps by providing feedback via expansions the teacher helped the learners to assimilate and further develop these "new" forms.

CONCLUSION

It has been argued that comprehensible input is not simply the result of the speech adjustments made by native speakers but the product of interaction involving both the native speaker and the learner. In this interaction the native speaker makes certain formal and discourse adjustments to ensure understanding, while the learner employs certain communication strategies to overcome problems and to maximize existing resources. As Scarcella and Higa (1981) note, it may not be appropriate to talk of input facilitating SLA in terms of *simplification.* In a cross-sectional study they found that child learners received a simpler input than adolescent learners. They then asked why it was that child learners have been observed to learn more slowly than adolescent learners. They hypothesize that it is the *negotiation* that results from the adolescent learners' more active involvement that contributes to their faster development. This involvement is manifest in the strategies they use to obtain native speaker explanations for just those parts they do not understand and the extra work they do in sustaining discourse. Thus, if comprehensible input is a necessary condition for SLA, its provision needs to be understood in terms of the negotiation of mutuality of understanding between interactants rather than in terms of simplified input.

The analysis of the T-P interactions involving R and T lent some support to this viewpoint. The aspect of discourse that proved most sensitive to the children's level of development was the choice of topic. In the early stages topics involving object identification were preferred to topics involving comments about objects. Also the children were more likely to produce "new" linguistic forms if they had sufficient control over the topic to make use of what they already possessed. The teacher's role in the successful exchanges was that of supplying those resources required by the learner to say what she or he wanted to say and of supplying feedback. The *negotiation* apparent in these exchanges was the product of both the search for intersubjectivity and the search for the linguistic forms necessary to establish, maintain, and develop this intersubjectivity.

Because comprehensible input is a negotiated rather than an absolute phenomenon, dependent on the learner's developing communicative proficiency, it may not be possible to specify a finite list of facilitative features. Different features may aid development at different times. For instance, in this study of T-P interactions teacher self-repetitions were more frequent at an early stage of development, and teacher expansions at a later stage. Also the context of activity in which interaction takes place is characterized by a dynamic, utterance-by-utterance adjustment by both partners in the conversation. Both the learner and the native speaker adjust their behavior in the light of the continuous feedback about the success of the discourse with which they provide each other.

This suggests that simply counting native-speaker adjustments will not provide a complete picture of how input is made comprehensible and may, on occasions, be inaccurate. It is for this reason that the focus needs to be placed on how communication is negotiated. This can to some extent be achieved by examining selected interactional features, for, as Long (1983d) has pointed out, features such as confirmation checks involve taking into account the learner's contribution as well as the native speaker's. But the process of negotiation at the moment is probably best understood through qualitative analysis of selected interactions. This raises the question of which interactions to select for analysis. One possible answer—the one followed in this chapter—is to examine those interactions where the learner uses "new" linguistic forms for the first time. This, of course, will require a longitudinal, case-study design.

The study of T-P interaction in this chapter was based on data collected outside the classroom. It is not possible to say, therefore, to what extent the patterns of negotiation that appeared to promote SLA are present in the everyday interactions of the classroom. One obvious constraint is the relative infrequency of one-to-one conversations in the classroom context. If negotiation of the type evident in the successful interview exchanges is the key to acquisition, it is important to discover how and to what extent this takes place in the ordinary classroom.

APPENDIX A

Description of Six Interactional Features in the Teacher's Speech

The following description is closely based on Long (1983d).

1. Confirmation checks, i.e., when the teacher repeats part or whole of learner's immediately preceding utterance and employs a rising intonation (e.g., A house?) or when the teacher repeats the utterance and adds a question tag. They are designed to elicit confirmation that the utterance has been correctly heard or understood.
2. Comprehension checks, i.e., attempts by the teacher to establish that the learner is following what he is saying. Typical realizations are "Right?" "OK?" "Do you follow?"
3. Clarification requests. These differ from confirmation checks in that there is no presupposition that the teacher has understood or heard the learner's previous utterance. They can take the form of questions (e.g., "Sorry?"), statements ("I can't hear."), or imperatives ("Say it again.").
4. Self-repetitions, i.e., when the teacher repeats part or the whole of his preceding utterance and also when the teacher paraphrases part or whole of his preceding utterance.
5. Other repetitions, i.e., when the teacher repeats (but not paraphrases) part or the whole of the learner's preceding utterance without altering the intonation.
6. Expansions, i.e., when the teacher expands a previous learner utterance whether by supplying missing formatives or by adding new semantic information.

APPENDIX B

Notational Convention for Transcripts

1. The teacher's or researcher's utterances are given on the left-hand side of the page.
2. The pupils' utterances are given on the right-hand side of the page.
3. The teachers' utterances are labeled T and the pupils' utterances are labeled by their initials, T or R.
4. Each "utterance" is numbered for ease of reference in the discussions of the transcripts. An "utterance" consists of a single-tone unit except where two-tone units are syntactically joined by means of a subordinator or other linking word or contrastive stress has been used to make what would "normally" be a single-tone unit into more than one.
5. Pauses are indicated in brackets:
   (.) indicates a pause of a second or shorter.
   (.3.) indicates a pause of 3 seconds, etc.
6. Phonetic transcription (IPA) is used when the pupils' pronunciation is markedly different from the teacher's pronunciation and also when it was not possible to identify the English word the pupils were using.
7. Words are underlined in order to show
   Overlapping speech between two speakers
   Very heavily stressed words
8. A limited amount of contextual information is given, where appropriate in brackets.

NOTES

1. Long (this volume) proposes one solution to the problem that cross-sectional research faces in demonstrating a relationship between input features and SLA. He suggests that the role of the input can be assessed indirectly by (a) showing that linguistic/conversational adjustments promote comprehension, (b) showing that comprehensible input promotes acquisition and (c) deducing that linguistic/conversational adjustments promote acquisition.

2. Studies of the role played by motherese in first language acquisition have recognized the need to tackle all three questions listed and have also set about doing so empirically. SLA research in contrast has focused chiefly on the first of the questions, even though there has been tacit acceptance and general discussion of the importance of question 3.

3. In the first recording session the two children were "interviewed" together in order to avoid creating unnecessary tension. T was absent from school on the date of the final recording.

4. Whether a question was coded as "open" or "closed" was determined by the subsequent discourse. That is, if the teacher conducted the subsequent discourse in a way which showed he did not accept the pupil's response to his question, it was coded as "closed." If the pupil's response was of the kind that suggested there was one and only one answer to the question, it was similarly coded. Otherwise the question was coded as "open."

5. Long (personal communication) has pointed out that the absence of significant changes in the teacher's discourse contribution from time 1 to time 2 is not unexpected. He argues that many of the discourse features will continue to reflect adjustment throughout the process of acquisition in order to disambiguate increasingly complex nonnative speaker output. This is an interesting counterargument to the one I am advancing, namely, that the frequency of adjustments will tend to reduce as the learner's proficiency grows. The available evidence from studies of motherese in first language acquisition indicates that at least some discourse features

are developmental (e.g., Ellis and Wells 1980), suggesting that this is also likely to be the case in SLA. It can be hypothesized that those discourse features which have a continued appropriateness throughout development will remain constant, while other features (such as expansions) are finely turned to the learner's level of development. If this is so, the research task is to identify which features are developmental and which ones are not.

6. It was not always easy to distinguish "creative" and "imitated" utterances. Many "creative" utterances had, as one of their components, an imitation of the whole or part of the teacher's preceding utterance. The solution was to accept as "creative" any utterance that was not wholly imitated.

7. An "occasional question" is defined by Brown (1968) as a question that has declarative word order and substitutes the wh- pronoun for the sentence constituent required as a response to the question. Brown hypothesizes that this type of question may aid first language acquisition.

On Adults

6

FOREIGNER TALK IN THE UNIVERSITY CLASSROOM[1]

Marjorie Bingham Wesche and Doreen Ready
University of Ottawa

This study builds upon a recent body of research on the adjustments made by native speakers when communicating with less proficient speakers of their language such as foreigners or young children. Our primary data consist of psychology lectures by two university professors, one native speaker of English and one native speaker of French, to class sections of second language speakers in a regular university course. Directly comparable data from each professor teaching the same lesson to native-speaker students in a different class section of the same course are also analyzed. Thus each professor serves as his or her own control in the comparison of discourse to nonnative and native speakers, allowing us to identify individual differences in speech style as well as shared characteristics of foreigner talk. Furthermore, the subject matter in all four presentations is parallel. This has made possible a more precise analysis than possible in previous research of the interplay between foreigner talk adjustments and particular discourse functions. Evidence of the dynamic role of extralinguistic situational factors, feedback from listeners, and changing content in determining whether adjustments are made, as well as notable differences in personal speech style of the speakers, led us to a consideration of the underlying principles which have been proposed in the literature to characterize foreigner talk.

The study was carried out in the context of a larger project on subject matter language teaching which compared gains in second language proficiency with those of control groups who were of similar proficiency levels and were enrolled in second language courses (Edwards, Wesche, Krashen,

Clément, and Krudenier, forthcoming). In the experimental program, psychology students with high intermediate proficiency in English or French took the second semester of Introduction to Psychology/Introduction à la psychologie in lecture sections of the regular course in which enrollment was limited to second language speakers.[2] Taught by psychology professors for whom the language of instruction was the first language, these groups covered the same material in the same amount of class time as the regular sections. They also took the same final examination, administered in a bilingual format to all students in both the French and English language sections of this course. The psychology professors were aided by language teachers who provided approximately 15 minutes of instruction during each 90-minute biweekly class period. This instruction did not include explicit grammar teaching. Its aim rather was to help students to read and to take lecture notes more efficiently and to clarify any misunderstandings arising from the lectures and the readings. It also provided students with an opportunity to ask questions and to express their ideas in a relaxed atmosphere.[3]

The results of this larger study support recent empirical and theoretical work on second language acquisition (e.g., d'Anglejan 1978, Krashen 1981a, Stern 1981, Swain 1981) which suggests that gains in second language proficiency are best achieved in situations where the second language is used as a vehicle for communication about other subjects rather than itself being the object of study. According to Krashen, "comprehensible input" whose content is understood but which is linguistically somewhat beyond the learner's current proficiency level is a necessary (if not sufficient) condition for successful language acquisition.

Based on the evidence that these students have improved their language proficiency while mastering the subject matter,[4] our hypothesis is that the nature of the professors' presentations of the same course material to L2 speakers and, particularly, any adjustments they make in the presentations to L2 speakers (i.e., their "foreigner talk") may tell us something about the kinds of input required by successful second language learners. Recent research on the nature of foreigner talk has demonstrated that native speakers regularly make both linguistic and conversational adjustments when communicating with nonnative speakers (see Hatch 1983b and Long 1983c for reviews of this work). While native speakers generally maintain grammatical well-formedness in their conversations with less proficient nonnative speakers, they may use syntactically or propositionally less complex speech.[5] Vocabulary range may be restricted and repetition more frequent, more concrete forms may be used, and speech may be "regularized" in certain ways (e.g., via more consistent use of canonical word order and of optional surface constituents (Long 1983c)). Adjustments in intonation, pitch and loudness, pauses, and speech rate have been found at the suprasegmental level of linguistic analysis, and a trend toward clearer enunciation and phonological well-formedness has been noted in a number of studies. Recent studies of the structural characteristics of native speaker–nonnative speaker conversation suggest important adjustments here as well, such as in the selection of content and the amount of "work" done by the native speakers at the discourse level.

Thus the *fact* of modifications by native speakers when communicating with language learners has been well established. Interest has now turned toward establishing the role of these adjustments in communication, formulating a typology of the kinds of adjustments made, and consideration of which ones may relate to the acquisition of various aspects of the second language (e.g., Chaudron 1979; d'Anglejan and Lightbown, this volume). The current study focuses on the first two issues. It first describes characteristics of input to second language speakers in the psychology classes along certain linguistic and extralinguistic parameters which have been used in previous studies in an attempt to identify input factors which may have a role in second language acquisition. It then proceeds to do a finer-grained analysis, with particular attention to individual differences in foreigner talk adjustments based on personal speech style, and on variation of the adjustments made within a given stretch of discourse in relation to topic shifts and other features.

THE STUDY

Data for the Present Study

Data for the comparative study of classroom discourse to first versus second language speakers consisted of videotaped lectures by the French- and English-speaking professors at the beginning of the winter 1983 semester. Each professor was taped presenting parallel lectures to his or her first language and second language classes. Since the English and French language sections followed the same course outline and used the same textbook in translation,[6] it was possible to capture approximately the same overall subject matter in the two English language and two French language lectures, and to carry out certain analyses on the way a particular concept (in this case, "shaping" or "le façonnement") was taught in all four presentations. Videotapes were also made of end-of-semester lectures for longitudinal analysis; they will be reported in a subsequent paper.

For the purposes of this study, the videotapes of the lectures given at the beginning of the semester were transcribed. Housekeeping details at the beginning and end of the lecture periods and any prolonged student-professor dialogues were eliminated from the analyses, leaving approximately an hour of content in each case. From this material, four data sets were derived as follows:

Data Set I: Timed Data Seven 2-minute segments of uninterrupted teacher talk were sampled at regular intervals through the lecture period.

Data Set II: Word Count Data Seven 250-word segments were extracted at regular points from a transcript of each of the lectures, adjusted to the nearest T unit, and did not include sentence fragments.

Data Set III: Theme Excerpts The first 1,000 words of the English L1 and L2 presentations and the entire French L1 and L2 presentations (because of their short length, L1 = 656 words, L2 = 541 words) were used in two analyses.

Data Set IV: Entire Theme Segments The full-length theme segments on "shaping" and "le façonnement" were used in several analyses made from the perspectives of linguistic, discourse, and content characteristics of texts with similar purposes (teaching a given concept) in different situations.

Objectives

Since this study was essentially exploratory in nature in that modifications in discourse to the L2 speakers were expected but their precise form could not be predicted, the following four questions guided the research.

1. Are there systematic deviations from classroom discourse to first language speakers by these professors in parallel presentations to classes composed only of second language speakers?

2. If so, which aspects of the linguistic system are involved? Are there also adjustments at the levels of content selection, discourse structure, and nonverbal behavior? Are these adjustments consistent for varying subject matter? Are they the same for both professors?

3. What do the purposes and functions of the adjustments appear to be?

4. Are there any underlying principles which characterize the kinds of adjustments made by both speakers and across situations?

Analyses comparing each professor's presentations with the L1 and L2 groups were carried out at different levels of the linguistic system. These included the quantitative descriptive analyses reported in Tables 6-1 to 6-8 for which the units of measurement draw particularly on Gaies (1977), Henzl (1973, 1979), Long (1980), and Chaudron (1982). The statistical procedures used were the *t* test for groups using version 650 of the Statistical Package for the Social Sciences (Nie et al. 1975) and applying one-tailed tests of significance based on pooled variance where F values permitted, and the χ^2, incorporating the correction factor for one-way analysis, one degree of freedom (Hatch and Farhady 1980).

In addition to quantitative analyses, features such as the use of discourse markers, vocabulary selection, characteristic syntactic frames, selection and structuring of examples, and the use of contextual and nonverbal support were looked at in a more impressionistic fashion, and are discussed along with the statistical findings.

RESULTS

Suprasegmentals and Phonology

The analyses of speech rate and pause phenomena are reported in Table 6-1. Research indicates that a slower speech rate is frequently a feature of native speaker discourse with nonnative speakers, reflecting clearer enunciation and longer pauses between major constituents (Hatch 1983b). This was not the case for the French-speaking professor, although it should be noted that both her presentations were slower than either of those by the English-speaking professor. On the other hand, there was a significant slowing of speech rate in the L2 presentation of the English-speaking professor.

The pause thresholds of 2 and 5 seconds were determined by native speakers on the basis of the level at which pauses in the data were perceived as unnaturally long hesitations in the flow of speech (2 or more seconds). A qualitative difference between long-hesitation pauses and much longer pauses (5 or more seconds) was made to allow time for nonverbal activity such as when writing on the blackboard. Pauses were measured from high-quality audiotapes by the same observer using a stopwatch. As can be seen from Table 6-1, pauses of 2 or more seconds were a feature in all the discourse presentations. However, significant differences in their use with native and nonnative speakers occurred only between the L1 and L2 presentations of the English-speaking professor. A further analysis involved filled pauses (cf. Jensen 1979), which consisted of verbalized hesitations without semantic significance (for the English-speaking professor, these were the sounds *uh* and *uhm* and for the French speaking professor, *e, hoo,* and *OK*). These pauses occurred in all presentations by both professors. In the case of the English-speaking professor, they tended to occur in bunches in both his L1 and L2 presentations as he appeared to gather his thoughts. In the case of the French-speaking professor, however, there was no discernible pattern. Although there was a significant difference in the use of filled pauses between the L1 and L2 presentations of the French-speaking professor, they still occurred less frequently than they did in the presentations of the English-speaking professor and cannot be described as a notable feature of either her L1 or her L2 discourse. This professor reported trying to avoid these verbalized hesitations; so her greater use of them in the L2 presentation may be a sign of distraction or less control rather than a feature with possible significance in terms of comprehensible input.

The more prominent adjustments made by the English-speaking professor may be related to differences in the style of presentation of the two. The

TABLE 6-1 Suprasegmentals: Speech Rate and Pauses

Data Set I: Seven 2-minute segments from 1-hour lecture

	English-speaking professor to		*L1 vs. L2*	*French-speaking professor to*		*L1 vs. L2*
	L1 students	*L2 students*	χ^2	*L1 students*	*L2 students*	χ^2
Speech rate (total no. of words)	1,883	1,262	122.22†	1,124.2	1,087.8	N.S.
Pauses of 5 or more seconds (number)	0	6	4.16*	3	8	N.S.
Pauses of 2 or more seconds (number)	8	28	10.03†	5	8	N.S.
Average pause length (≥ 2s) (seconds)	2.25	3.25		—	—	
Total pause time (≥ 2s) (seconds)	18	91	47.55†	—	—	
Filled pauses	28	31	N.S.	5	16	4.76*

*$p \leq .05$. †$p \leq .005$.

TABLE 6-2 Vocabulary Analyses

Data Set III: First 1,000 words English theme excerpts, and entire French theme excerpts ("Shaping"/"Le Façonnement")

	English-speaking professor to		*L1 vs. L2*	*French-speaking professor to*		*L1 vs. L2*
	L1 students	*L2 students*	χ^2	*L1 students*	*L2 students*	χ^2
Vocabulary type/token ratio	29.8%	26.6%	N.S.	31%	31%	N.S.
Word-class distribution (numbers)						
1. Nouns	17.3%	17.7%	N.S.	14%	11%	N.S.
2. Verbs	29.6%	31.0%	N.S.	18%	21%	N.S.
3. Adjectives	7.3%	6.5%	N.S.	8%	5%	N.S.
4. Pronouns	12.10%	13.6%	N.S.	26%	26%	N.S.
5. Prepositions	8.4%	8.1%	N.S.	13%	11%	N.S.
6. Indefinite articles	3.5%	3.9%	N.S.	3%	2%	N.S.
7. Definite articles	6.0%	4.9%	N.S.	9%	12%	N.S.
8. Adverbs	7.1%	5.6%	N.S.	4%	4%	N.S.
9. Other	8.7%	8.7%	N.S.	6%	8%	N.S.
Content vocabulary (1–3)	54.2%	55.2%	N.S.	40%	37%	N.S.
Function vocabulary (4–7)	30.0%	30.5%	N.S.	51%	51%	N.S.

TABLE 6-3 Syntactic Analyses: Verbs

Data Set III: First 1,000 words English theme excerpts and entire French theme excerpts ("Shaping"/"Le Façonnement")

	English-speaking professor to		*L1 vs. L2*	*French-speaking professor to*		*L1 vs. L2*
	L1 students	*L2 students*	χ^2	*L1 students*	*L2 students*	χ^2
				(656 words)	(541 words)	
Verbs categories:						
Tensed (nonauxiliary)	47/202 23%	111/219 51%	9.85†	96/138 70%	85/125 68%	N.S.
Auxiliary	59/202 29%	40/219 18%	N.S.	—	—	
Infinitival	96/202 48%	68/219 31%	N.S. §	42/138 30%	40/125 32%	N.S.
Tensed verbs:						
Indicating present time	28/75 37%	96/206 47%	N.S.	80/96 83%	70/85 82%	N.S.
Indicating nonpresent time	47/75 63%	110/206 53%	N.S.	16/96 17%	15/85 18%	N.S.
Tensed be/être forms in:						
Simple present	17*/29* 59%	40†48† 83%	N.S. §	17/20 85%	100% 100%	N.S.
Nonpresent	12/29 41%	8/48† 17%	9.12‡	3/20 15%	—	—
Copula/être forms (excluding auxiliary, including infinitival)	28/143 20%	43/178 24%	N.S.	21¶/138 15%	10/125 8%	N.S.
Other verbs	115/143 80%	135/178 76%	N.S.	117/138 85%	115/125 92%	N.S.
Type/token ratio for verbs	56/143 39%	60/178 34%	N.S.	43/138 31%	36/125 29%	N.S.

*Including 1 auxiliary. †Including 5 auxiliaries. ‡p ≤ .005. § = 3.24, p ≤ .06. ♀Including 1 infinitive.

TABLE 6-4 Syntactic Analyses (Segments): T Units and Clauses (S Nodes)

Data Set II: Seven 250-word segments from 1-hour lecture. (Segment lengths calculated to the nearest T unit)

	English-speaking professor to				*L1 vs. L2*	*French-speaking professor to*				*L1 vs. L2*
	L1 students		*L2 students*			*L1 students*		*L2 students*		
	M	*S.D.*	*M*	*S.D.*	*T*§	*M*	*S.D.*	*M*	*S.D.*	*T*§
T units	12.0	3.51	17.4	3.65	−2.09*	19.0	3.27	19.43	2.37	N.S.
Words per T unit	20.23	6.04	14.90	3.33	2.05*	13.44	2.14	12.93	1.40	N.S.
Clauses (S nodes; tensed verbs)	28.14	4.06	34.00	2.45	−3.27‡	37.14	5.52	38.57	6.29	N.S.
Clauses per T unit	2.02		2.20		N.S.	1.99		1.99		N.S.
Words per clause	9.21	1.54	7.37	.57	2.96†	6.83		6.56		N.S.
Subordinate clauses	14.71	4.07	16.57	3.95	N.S.	18.14	4.34	18.57	4.58	N.S.
Subordinate clause types (percentages):										
Noun	23.85		21							
Adverb	20.30		16.81							
Adjective	8.1		10.90							

*$p \leq .05$. †$p \leq .01$. ‡$p \leq .005$. §Paired *t* tests, pooled variance where F value permits.

TABLE 6-5 Syntactic Analyses (Theme): T Units and Clauses (S Nodes)

Data Set III: First 1,000 words English theme excerpts and entire French theme excerpts (excluding sentence fragments) (French: L1 = 617 words, L2 = 521 words)

	English-speaking professor to				*L1 vs. L2*	*French-speaking professor to*				*L1 vs. L2*
	L1 students		*L2 students*			*L1 students*		*L2 students*		
	M	*S.D.*	*M*	*S.D.*	*T*	*No., %*	*M*	*No., %*	*M*	χ^2
T units	12.25	2.22	15.75	3.10	N.S.‡	43		34		N.S.
Words per T unit	20.58	3.96	15.28	2.30	2.32*		14.3		15.3	N.S.
Clauses (S nodes)	24.75	5.74	32.75	3.59	−2.36*	90		87		N.S.
Clauses per T unit	2.03		2.15		N.S.		2.1		2.6	N.S.
Words per clause	10.25	1.94	7.23	.47	3.04†		6.9		6.0	N.S.
Subordinate clauses	12.50	4.66	17.25	4.79	N.S.	47		53		N.S.
Subordinate clause types (percentages):										
Noun	23.2		28.2			14.4		14.9		
Adverb	20.2		15.3			25.6		31.0		
Adjective	7.1		9.0			12.2		14.9		

*$p \leq .05$. †$p \leq .01$. ‡$p \leq .06$.

TABLE 6-6 Theme Excerpt Characteristics

Data Set IV: Entire theme excerpts ("Shaping"/"Le Façonnement")

	English-speaking professor to			*French-speaking professor to*		
	L1 students	*L2 students*	χ^2	*L1 students*	*L2 students*	χ^2
Total number of words	1,429	1,008	72.38*	656	541	10.86*
Words in sentence fragments	62	62		39	20	
Total number of T units	64	62		43	34	
Total number of S nodes (tensed verbs, including auxiliaries)	144	151		90	87	

*$p \leq .005$.

TABLE 6-7 Communication Devices: Percentages of T Units in Questions, Statements, Imperatives, Quotations

Data Set II: Seven 250-word segments from 1-hour lecture	English-speaking professor to						L1 vs. L2	French-speaking professor to		L1 vs. L2
	L1 students			*L2 students*				*L1 students*	*L2 students*	
	%	*M*	*S.D.*	%	*M*	*S.D.*	*t tests*	%	%	*t tests*
Percentages of T units in:										
Statements	89	12.0	3.46	70	12.14	3.67	N.S.	94	96	N.S.
Questions	6	1.29	1.11	16	2.43	1.51	N.S.*	4	2	N.S.
Imperatives (including let's)	1	.14	.38	12	2.14	.90	−5.42†	2	1	N.S.
Direct quotations	3	.43	.79	2	.29	.49	N.S.			

*p ≤ .06. †p ≤ .005.

TABLE 6-8 Communication Devices: Discourse Characteristics

Data Set IV: Entire theme excerpts ("Shaping"/"Le Façonnement")

	English-speaking professor to					*French-speaking professor to*				
	L1 students		*L2 students*			*L1 students*		*L2 students*		
		%		%	χ^2		%		%	χ^2
Comprehension checks:										
Total number	11		14			2		1		
% of total words	16/1429	1	20/1008	2	N.S.	8/656	1	9/541	2	N.S.
Boundary marker locations:										
Total number	25		30			19		16		
% of total words	33/1429	2	41/1008	4	N.S.	25/656	4	25/541	5	N.S.
Self-repetitions:										
Total number										
Exact	9		4			6		10		
Exact plus rephrasing, equivalence	10		24			12		19		
% of total words:										
Exact	53/1429	4	20/1008	2	N.S.	32/656	5	79/541	15	4.05*
Exact plus rephrasing, equivalence	80/1429	6	206/1008	20	6.5†	98/656	15	169/541	31	4.89*

*$p \leq .05$ †$p \leq .01$.

overall slower rate of discourse of the French-speaking professor has already been cited. A group of professors and language teachers who viewed the videotapes found the enunciation in the French L2 excerpts to be extremely clear. They also noted that the L1 and L2 lectures of the French-speaking professor were similar in content (e.g., the same examples used when developing points) and appeared to follow a tightly organized format, whereas those of the English-speaking professor appeared to be more spontaneous and unplanned. Also, unlike the French-speaking professor whose speech rate remained relatively consistent, the English-speaking professor exhibited a marked variability of rate, including a noticeable tendency to pick up speed as he progressed through a topic and to slow down when introducing a new one.

Vocabulary

Analyses of vocabulary characteristics in the discourse are reported in Table 6-2. These analyses sought to get both at differences in formal characteristics of the lexicon used and at differences in the particular content expressed in the presentations to first versus second language speakers. Thus word-class distributions, as well as content versus function word ratios were compared to determine whether the L1 and L2 presentations differed at these levels. Overall type-token ratios were calculated, based on earlier findings suggesting that native speakers tend to use a more limited lexical set when speaking with language learners (e.g., Henzl 1973, Long 1980). Type-token ratios within content and function word vocabulary were also calculated. Our reasoning was that while overall type-token ratios might not be significantly different owing to an effect of the full use of optional syntactic and discourse markers (as reported by Long 1983c), such an effect might be counterbalanced by a more limited set of content vocabulary in the L2 presentations. However, no significant differences between the L1 and L2 presentations were found for either speaker on any vocabulary measure.

Analyses of particular vocabulary forms suggested, however, that adjustments were indeed made at this level by both speakers in their presentations to the L2 students. For example, the English-speaking professor used significantly more "will"s (19 vs. 2) and "so"s (15 vs. 3) in his L2 presentation and significantly more "would"s in his L1 presentation (40 vs. 2). A closer look at the discourse showed clearly that he avoided using the conditional when speaking to the L2 group, using instead either present or future tense forms. The frequent "so"s in the L2 presentation appeared to serve as discourse connectors, bridging between propositions.

Examples: *would* and *will*

L1: "The management has thought that it *would* be interesting for audiences if. . . ."

L2: "So you are going to be employed by a circus, . . . and what you have to do is . . . "

L1: "How long do you suppose it *would* take you if you waited . . .
L2: "In its natural habitat . . . how often *will* the lion dance? . . . Never . . . "

L1: "You *would* probably say to the circus people . . . "
L2: "And you say, 'sure, I need money so sure, why not?' "

L2 Examples: *so*
"*So* your job is to use shaping . . . "
"*So,* for example, for a lion to dance, what is the first thing . . . "
"*So* your second step is to . . . "
"*So* for step 3, you begin to reinforce . . . "

In the 1982 pilot analyses of parallel data, the same French-speaking professor used "je" significantly more frequently in her presentation to L2 speakers, and "on" significantly more often in the L1 presentation. This was not replicated in 1983, perhaps being tied to particular content. However, it is the impression of native speakers who worked on the French 1983 analyses that the French-speaking professor in general uses relatively more concrete vocabulary in the presentations to L2 speakers and more abstract vocabulary in the L1 presentation. Whether this difference, if real, can be captured in quantitative analyses awaits further work on these and other data from the project. Subsequent analyses might use other units of analysis such as concrete versus abstract nouns, synonyms versus nonsynonyms, or groupings of content words according to domain relationships.

Syntax

Verbs Analyses of some of the characteristics of verbs which other researchers have found to vary from native speaker norms in discourse with nonnative speakers (cf. Long 1980) are reported in Table 6-3. These include the use of finite versus infinitive forms, present versus nonpresent time markings, "*be/être*" forms versus other verbs, and the variety of verbs used. The analyses were based on the "theme" extracts to ensure content similarity.

No significant differences were found between the L1 and L2 presentations by the French-speaking professor on these measures. The analyses revealed significant shifts in usage by the English-speaking professor, however. He used significantly more tensed verbs with the L2 students (51 percent) than with the L1 students (23 percent), and his greater use of infinitive forms with the L1 students (48 percent versus 31 percent) approached significance ($p \leq .06$). Also significantly different was his greater use of nonpresent *be* forms in the presentation to L1 speakers (41 percent versus 17 percent, $p \leq .005$) versus an almost exclusive use of present time with the L2 speakers (83 percent versus 59 percent, $p \leq .06$). The overall difference between the use of present and nonpresent time was not significant, however. But as is indicated above in the analysis of the use of "would" versus "will," a finer-grained analysis would appear necessary to tease out differences in tense usage in these data. It is quite possible—as suggested in other studies—that the present-nonpresent distinction is a critical one at lower proficiency levels, whereas at this relatively high level, more subtle differences are present.

T Units and Clauses (S Nodes) Analyses of characteristics of clauses are reported in Tables 6-4 and 6-5. T units (a principal clause plus all related dependent clauses, Hunt 1970) and S nodes (clauses, identified by a tensed verb, Long 1980) were the units of analysis used to get at the issue of syntactic complexity in the presentations to L2 versus L1 speakers. Analyses were done on the seven 250-word excerpts from the 1-hour lectures and using the theme extracts. The findings were essentially the same for both data sets, indicating that these features remain relatively stable for the two speakers in the L1 and L2 situations between samples of both general lecture content and closely matched content.

No significant differences were found for the French lecturer for the presentations to L1 versus L2 speakers. Significant differences or a strong trend ($p \leq .06$) were found for the English speaker on a number of measures. These included T units (significantly more in the presentation to L2 students), the number of words per T unit (significantly fewer in the presentation to L2 students), the number of clauses (more for the L2 students), and the number of words per clause (fewer for the L2 students). In short, the English-speaking professor used a greater number of shorter clauses, both principal and subordinate, in the presentation to L2 students, representing approximately the same proportion of principal versus subordinate clauses in both presentations. There were no significant differences in the number of clauses per T unit, in the number of subordinate clauses, or in proportions of subordinate clause types in the L2 versus L1 presentations by either professor.

Discourse

Theme Excerpts As a first step in trying to identify adjustments made for L2 speakers at the discourse level, certain overall characteristics of the theme excerpts ("shaping," "le façonnement") were compared for each professor. These analyses, reported in Table 6-6, compare the total number of words devoted to presenting and elaborating on the concept, the number of words in sentence fragments as opposed to the total number of grammatically well-formed T units, and the total number of clauses (S nodes).

Both professors used significantly more words to communicate the concept of "shaping" to the first language speakers. Upon closer examination of the discourse structure, it is apparent that these extra words are not part of the concept presentation but rather go into extra illustrative examples once this has been completed. In fact, the basic presentation is structurally very similar in all four cases, consisting of an explanation of the concept with respect to other known concepts, and an initial illustrative example. Neither professor showed any significant variation between the total number of T units or overall number of clauses, or in the number of words in sentence fragments as opposed to well-formed utterances. The fact that the English professor used considerably more words to put across this concept to both L1 and L2 classes than did the French professor is another indication of their different lecturing styles.

Communication Devices The analysis of the relative proportions of T units in questions, statements, imperatives, and quotations reported in Table 6-7 represents a first attempt at identifying some structural characteristics of the discourse. The use of these devices in what is essentially a one-way communicative situation may be characterized as a kind of "simulated" interaction, in which the professor asks, then answers rhetorical questions and personalizes the content through the use of imperatives and direct quotations.

As indicated in Table 6-7, the French-speaking professor makes no apparent adjustments at this level, consistently using the declarative mode throughout both lectures, with occasional full-sentence comprehension checks in question form in both situations (e.g., "Est-ce que c'est clair?").

The English-speaking professor does adjust his speech to the L2 class at this level, the most striking shift being his increased use of imperatives, which make up 12 percent of the L2 presentation in contrast with 1 percent of the L1 presentation. (Some frequent examples from the transcript include "Imagine that . . . ", "Let's take an example . . . ", and "Suppose that . . . ".) This professor's use of questions, representing 16 percent of the L2 presentation and 6 percent of the L1 presentation, approaches statistical significance ($p \leq .06$)—perhaps not reaching it owing to the considerable variability between segments. Most of these questions are rhetorical. While this professor also verifies student comprehension with questions, they are generally sentence fragments such as "OK?" or "All right?" and so are not included in this analysis.

This analysis again highlights the different lecturing styles of the two professors, which is already in the L1 analyses but which contrasts dramatically in the L2 presentations, that of the English speaker being far more informal and conversational in tone, and more interactive in structure.

Table 6-8 presents comparative analyses of certain communicative devices which have been found to distinguish foreigner talk discourse from native speaker discourse in previous work (cf. Hatch 1983b, Long 1983c). These include *comprehension checks* in which the professor explicitly asks whether students have understood the foregoing, expressed in terms of frequency of occurrence and as a percentage of the total number of words, *boundary markers* between propositions (including "now," "well," and "so" in English, and "donc," "puis," and "bon" in French), and *self-repetitions,* or the use of redundant language forms and semantic content. The last measure includes both the exact repetition of at least two juxtaposed words and rephrased but equivalent content occurring within five consecutive T units.

While the English-speaking professor used explicit comprehension checks more frequently than did the French speaker, neither showed differential usage between their two presentations. Boundary markers between propositions, while prominent in the speech of both professors, again were not significantly different in number or percentage of total words for either in the L1 versus L2 presentations. Nonetheless, as noted above, the use of particular markers (e.g., "so") varied. Of greatest interest in terms of adjustments made for the L2 speakers were the measures of content redundancy: exact repetition, and exact repetition plus equivalence of meaning expressed through rephrasing of the same idea. Both professors used a significantly higher percentage of total words in self-repetitions when presenting the theme to L2 speakers. The English speaker's self-repetitions were characterized by rephrasing the same ideas in his L2 presentations. He often made this explicit by saying "in other words . . . " or by juxtaposing two propositions.

Examples:

L2: "You are going to be employed by a circus. = "It is employment by a circus."

"Take a flag and put it up on the flagpole". = "Put the Canadian flag up on the flagpole."

or at the phrase level:

"to do this . . . " = "to do a dance . . . "

"in its natural habitat . . . " "In terms of its natural behavior" . . .

In addition to the above quantifiable phenomena, the English speaker also frequently used the syntactic frame of *noun clause + copula + relative pronoun + noun clause* to express a kind of hierarchical relationship of equivalence when presenting to L2 speakers. For example:

L2: "What you will find is that "[=]" the rat will press the lever" . . .

The French-speaking professor's L2 presentation is characterized by the use of exact repetition of content vocabulary in different sentence frames.

Examples:

L2: "si je veux enseigner à mon chien *à m'apporter le journal*"

" . . . pour le conditionner *à m'apporter le journal*"

or

"C'est là qu'on a fait appel au principe de *façonnement. Façonnement"* (writes on board). "*Façonnement.* Le terme anglais c'est *shaping.*"

or

"... "*façonner* le comportement ..." = "je veux le *modeler,* le *sculpter graduellement*" ...

Self-repetition such as in the examples noted above was for both professors largely confined to those points in the L2 discourse where new conceptual information and terminology was being presented and initially exemplified, and then was absent in the illustrative and elaborative material that followed the basic presentation. Such repetition was rare for both in the L1 presentations, but where it occurred it was also used for either clarification or emphasis in the presentation of new material.

Nonverbal Behavior

We have not yet had the opportunity to quantitatively analyze features of nonverbal behavior of the two professors. Nonetheless, it is immediately evident to anyone viewing the videotaped lectures that their L1 and L2 presentations differ in this regard. Obvious areas of difference for both are in the use of gesture and of contextual supports such as the blackboard and textbook. As with the analyses at other levels of the communicative system, the differences are not qualitative but rather have to do with the frequency and intensity of use of the various devices.

Both professors spend more time at the blackboard in their L2 presentations, and their use of it for both schematic and representational information is characterized by more frequent use and by greater detail. For example, while both write some new terms on the board in the L1 classes, in the L2 classes, they write more terms as well as the names of persons they refer to. Both label their board drawings more fully for the L2 groups. They write out full words instead of abbreviations, and the English-speaking professor often prints in block letters in the L2 presentations while resorting to cursive scribbles with the L1 students. This professor also used stick figures of animals to illustrate his example in the L2 presentation on shaping, unlike his L1 presentation.

With respect to gestural language, it is the impression of viewers that gestures are used more frequently and in a more exaggerated way in the L2 presentations. Both professors use frequent hand gestures to punctuate the discourse—in a manner that appears somewhat exaggerated and deliberate to first language speakers viewing the tapes but tends not to be noticed by second language viewers. Examples of iconic movements are found in the L2 presentations, as when the English-speaking professor demonstrates how a lion would put its head down and foot forward in the first step of a dance.

It is our impression that exaggerated intonation is also used in the L2 presentations in coordination with the nonverbal behaviors discussed above, to indicate important points.

Clearly, there is much research yet to be done at this level of analysis, which, we are convinced, is an important area in which foreigner talk adjustments are made in this situation.

DISCUSSION AND CONCLUSIONS

The data analysis so far suggests the following conclusions:

1. The most important predictors of the speech characteristics of a native speaker addressing nonnative speakers are the individual characteristics of that person's speech to native speakers rather than any given set of "foreigner talk" discourse characteristics. Individuals differ dramatically in the communicative features they will use in similar situations. Furthermore, the two speakers in this study illustrate dramatically different ranges of variability even within their native-speaker-directed speech, as well as across the L1 and L2 situations. Features which vary include speech rate, syntactic features, discourse features, and nonverbal behavior. Whether this variability can be systematically described when discourse content structure is considered remains to be determined; at least it provides a clear index of individual differences.

2. Notwithstanding the above, both speakers show systematic deviations from native-speaker-directed style when addressing nonnatives in parallel situations and with similar content.

3. Every level of analysis yielded some differences at some point for one or the other speaker, and we are convinced that further analyses would reveal other differences, particularly at the levels of suprasegmentals, phonology and discourse structure, content selection, and nonverbal behavior, as would a more detailed analysis of tense usage and vocabulary.

The fact that no quantitative differences were found for overall vocabulary characteristics in this study, unlike others, may have to do with the proficiency level of the students as well as with the situation. Perhaps a minimum set of vocabulary is essential to get across the subject matter content at the university level. It is also possible that the vocabulary is sufficiently comprehensible to these students not to cause problems because (1) they have a high level of proficiency and (2) they encounter the same vocabulary in the readings and have the opportunity to work on it in the language instruction sessions as well.

One of the perceptions on which the speakers' judgments of their own comprehensibility are based is presumably the proficiency level of the language learner. Our 1982 longitudinal analyses of speech rate and T units by the same English-speaking professor in presentations to L1 and L2 speakers at the beginning and end of the semester support other studies in suggesting this (cf. Hatch 1983b). In our 1982 study, although there was a significant slowing of speech rate in the L2 presentation of the English-speaking professor at the beginning of the semester, there was no significant difference between the L1 and L2 presentations at the end of the semester. The L2 speech rate at the end of the semester was, however, significantly different from the L2 at the beginning of the semester, suggesting that as student comprehension improved, the professor was able to increase his speech rate to one approaching that used with the L1 group. The present data suggest that native speakers are able to make fine adjustments at many levels according to their perception of the effect on comprehensibility to nonnative listeners of such factors as (1) newness and cultural or conceptual difficulty of content, and (2) students' L2 proficiency level according to initial perceptions and as amended through feedback. Furthermore, the differences in the kind and quantity of adjustments made by our two speakers—both of whom were considered by the students to be highly effective teachers—suggest an interaction between the overt propositional logic in the development of argument, or the extent to which discourse is planned, and the speakers' perception of its comprehensibility.

Thus the French-speaking professor, whose highly planned, relatively formal presentations to both classes evolved in a logical manner, closely paralleling the sequence of content in the textbook and outline, made far fewer adjustments in her presentation to the L2 class, yet was easily understood because students knew what to expect. The English speaker in a more spontaneous, less formal, interactive presentation was prone to asides and deviations from the central theme. Perhaps this professor's adjustments at every level of the communicative system were a compensatory attempt to facilitate student understanding where they were less prepared to anticipate succeeding ideas. Of course, native speakers will also vary in their underlying sensitivity to—and even interest in—the comprehensibility of their input to nonnatives. And in addition to these factors, performance data also reflect other constraints such as hurrying at the end of a lecture or distractions which reduce the sensitivity of native speakers to whether their discourse is actually being comprehended.

4. What is the purpose of the adjustments found in foreigner talk? Clearly, these adjustments reflect "language in the service of communication" (Wong-Fillmore, this volume) as speakers attempt to ensure that content is understood. Do the speakers succeed in doing this? We do not yet have quantitative evidence,[7] but there is evidence from the following four sources that they do:

a. These students successfully learned their subject matter as measured by the weekly class quizzes and their final examination marks. This may be partially attributable to their readings.

b. Interaction with the professors and especially with the language teachers when discussing lectures, however, indicates that these students do understand most or all of the lecture content.

c. Students self-report that the lectures are interesting and valuable to them.

d. Nonnatives who have viewed the videotapes impressionistically find the L2 presentations easier to understand than the L1 presentations. (In fact, a number of native speaker viewers have commented that the L2 presentations are not only "easier" to understand but are, for them, patronizing and even mildly insulting.)

As to the possible role of these adjustments in aiding second language acquisition, only the indirect evidence that students in these classes significantly improved their second language performance over time is available as support for the possibility of a causal relationship. Our own observations tempt us to speculate not only about a role but about the possible differential role of specific adjustments in the language-acquisition process—speculations which could form the basis of testable hypotheses in future research. For example, while both exact repetition and paraphrasing may aid communication, might not one expect the latter to provide richer data for the second language acquirer?

5. The particular content being communicated and its place in the overall presentation (new or known, major point versus illustration, beginning or end of lecture) appear to influence whether certain adjustments are made. One critical point is the introduction of a new topic or new terminology. In this situation both speakers use considerably more redundancy in form and content in their presentations to L2 speakers than they do in the L1 presentations or elsewhere in the L2 presentations. Speech rate for the English speaker similarly appeared to vary depending on whether old or new content was being provided but also speeded up toward the end of the lecture in both his presentations. (The latter effect appeared to be due to an attempt to cover all the necessary material in the lecture period rather than related to the L1 versus L2 situation.) In the case of the French speaker, the speech rate was slower during the second half of the lecture after a student intervened and asked her to slow down (i.e., in response to specific feedback about comprehensibility). This slower rate in the later timed segments does not show up in the L1 versus L2 analyses but perhaps would in an analysis of the second part of the L2 lecture compared with the L1 presentation. Thus it is apparent that features of the native speaker discourse to both groups vary through the presentation in response to a variety of textual and situational factors.

6. As for the question of underlying principles which appear to characterize the adjustments made by both speakers and across situations, it must first be noted that far more adjustments were made by one speaker than by the other, including in the matched data where subject matter was controlled. In our view this was due to their differing lecture styles rather than to any differences attributable to their language of presentation (English or French).

Thus even if all the cases of foreigner talk adjustment found in these data conformed to a trend toward, for example, simplification or the use of unmarked forms, such a principle would serve only for post hoc explanation, not for prediction in specific situations. This limitation accepted, to what extent do the adjustment processes reflected in these data conform to explanatory principles proposed elsewhere for foreigner talk?

Simplification Like Ferguson and DeBose (1977), we note that some of the adjustments are in fact in the direction of their concept of "simplification" (conceptual if not necessarily linguistic)—specifically the processes of expansion (clarifying through the use of optional forms) and replacement/rearrangement of material (such as analytic paraphrase). Others, however, are "nonsimplifying" processes in their terms (e.g., clarifying through repetition, or upgrading by making foreigner talk more standard than informal native-speaker norms). Thus simplification per se, or even a more nuanced typology of simplification processes, such as "restrictive" and "elaborative" (Meisel 1977, and as cited by Long 1983b) and "conformative" (Stauble 1978) or the definition of simplification discussed in Long (1983e) does not by itself provide a sufficient explanation of the processes at work.

Well-formedness Well-formedness has frequently been mentioned as a characteristic of foreigner talk (cf. Long 1983c). These data would support this finding, in that the presentations to L2 speakers contain few deviations from standard usage. However, the L1 presentations are also notably well-formed in this situation of relatively planned, formal discourse. Thus this concept does not offer much insight into the adjustments made for L2 speakers.

Explicitness Formal explicitness in the sense of using full underlying forms would appear to come close to characterizing what happens when adjustments are made for L2 speakers. The supplying of optional pronouns, relatives, and discourse markers, the careful nonreduced pronunciation which comes with slower discourse and clearer pausal markings of constituent boundaries, and the greater redundancy of form and content in the L2 presentations all exhibit increased explicitness. This concept does not, however, explain such features as the shorter T units and clauses, the greater use of questions and imperatives, the avoidance of conditionals and the greater use of finite verbs and present tense "be" forms found in the English speaker's foreigner talk.

Regularization Long (1983e) noted that certain opposing tendencies which to some extent are captured in the notions of simplification and explicitness can be accommodated by the concept of "regularization," which he proposed as a possible underlying explanatory principle for deviations from intranative speaker language patterns in both foreigner talk and learners' interlanguage. Regularization refers to the "modification . . . of input . . . in the direction of the minimal set of surface forms needed to communicate the intended message, resulting, among other things, in a preference for unmarked forms (e.g., canonical word order) and the elimination of exceptions . . . and use of a single form for multiple functions" (Long, personal communication). This concept, when applied to the data in this study, could explain the findings at the suprasegmental and phonological levels (standard forms resulting from slower speech rate, better-marked constituent boundaries, more careful enunciation) as well as the shorter clauses and simpler verb constructions found at the syntax level in the English data. The lack of significant differences at the vocabulary level does not support the "minimal set" criterion, nor is there evidence of use of a single form for multiple functions. (However, as noted above, we are looking at post hoc explanation rather than at prediction.) In our view regularization provides an inadequate single explanation for the adjustments taking place because it does not, for example, explain the additional forms used in the L2 presentation (such as the English speaker's "so"), or shifts by this speaker in the direction of more interactive speech (the use of more questions and imperatives), or the redundancy of form and content displayed at the discourse level, or some of the dramatic nonverbal behavior used, for example, to demonstrate animal movements or other specific semantic content.

Redundancy If one concept is to characterize all the findings of this study, it has to go beyond the linguistic code and adjustments made in surface forms of language, to deal as well with semantic and nonverbal adjustments at other levels of communicative behavior. In our view, the concept of redundancy in the sense of Spolsky (1973) and Oller (1973, 1979) would appear to be the best candidate. This refers to the redundancy of form and content within and between the various levels of analysis of the communicative system, used in conjunction with various mechanisms (e.g., pitch, discourse markers such as "bon") to indicate the relative importance of particular content. Redundancy, a characteristic of natural languages, is necessary to permit communication and reduce the possibility of error when there is interference in the communication channel (Spolsky 1973). Even if there is no distortion or noise in the communication channel per se, a less proficient listener's pragmatic expectancy grammar, or ability to hypothesize correctly about what is likely to be said next (Oller 1979) is characterized by gaps and nonstandard rules. It displays, as Spolsky puts it, a lack of richness of "knowledge of probabilities—on all levels, phonological, grammatical, lexical, and semantic—in the language" (1973:170). Like interference in the channel, this incomplete receiving system may result in inadequate comprehension of the meaning behind the incoming signals. In cases of reduced redundancy of information due to interference, less proficient speakers are doubly handicapped. Spolsky observed that nonnatives are unable to function under conditions of reduced redundancy (i.e., native-speaker norms); they need "the full normal redundancy, and at times even that is not enough" (p. 169). By extension, an exaggerated use of redundant information with nonnatives at various levels of the communication system should lead to their increased understanding of the messages behind the language.

In our data, it appears that what the professors are doing in their second language classes is precisely this—exploiting the potential of language and the supporting extralinguistic content to increase the redundancy of the signals through which they communicate their meaning. Thus at the phonological level the full basic or canonical forms are given, supplying more features from which to identify sound clusters and words. Analogously, at higher levels of analysis, the supplying of optional syntactic and discourse markers and the repeated use of certain syntactic frames provide increased formal redundancy. The syntactic features mentioned under "regularization" (above) can be interpreted as providing redundancy in that a minimal (and thus repeated) set of forms and structures is used. At the level of semantic content, exact repetition, the use of synonyms and rephrasing, and explicit signaling of equivalences provide mutually supporting redundancy of both form and content. The use of rhetorical questions and their answers, as well as imperatives which make explicit the role of the listener (e.g., "suppose that" . . .) may also be viewed as a kind of content redundancy. A further example of redundancy between levels of analysis, this time involving nonverbal behavior, is the illustration of verbal content using gestures, the blackboard, or objects in the immediate context.

While redundancy in a general way appears to characterize the changes observed, it does not, as previously noted, help us in predicting where and when and at which levels adjustments in any given stretch of discourse will be made, just as we will never be able to assign an absolute communicative value to a given adjustment or type of adjustment in this highly dynamic and interactive system. This corresponds to Spolsky's (1973) observation that "the principle of redundancy suggests that it will not be possible to demonstrate that any given language item is essential to successful communication, nor to establish the functional load of any given item in communication" (p. 170).

Pragmatic Grammar of Expectancy In our view it is most productive to view the process of adjustments made by proficient speakers of a language when communicating with less proficient speakers using the other side of the redundancy coin, Oller's concept of a pragmatic grammar of expectancy (1973, 1979). The relevant perspective is that of the proficient speaker's ongoing perceptions as the discourse progresses of the nonnative's ability to generate hypotheses about what will be said next—in terms of what has been said already, his or her knowledge of the world, and aspects of the situation such as knowledge of the topic and familiarity with the speaker. The native speaker appears to gear the form and content of the presentation to what he or she thinks the learner's expectancy system will be able to handle.[8] If the content is familiar, or logically follows from what has already been presented, there will be less attempt to lighten the linguistic load. If the native speaker perceives the content to be unfamiliar or conceptually difficult for the nonnative, he or she may regularize the linguistic forms used, as well as provide redundant content to guide and confirm the listener's expectations. The speaker uses comprehension checks and nonverbal feedback from learners, as well as unsolicited feedback to fine-tune adjustments at different points in the discourse. Obviously, some native speakers will misjudge learner competence and not aim at quite the right level at times, and some may use poor strategies (cf. Chaudron 1982). Others, through greater experience or sensitivity, or more helpful feedback, will be more successful. Such input, in Wong-Fillmore's (this volume) words, is "language shaped with learners' needs in mind," and is in fact the stuff of successful communication among native speakers as well as in foreigner talk situations.

This explanation may not satisfy those who seek a predictive model which will generate hypotheses about the form that foreigner talk will take. In our data we are faced with interacting phenomena at different levels of the human communicative system which vary through time as the discourse unfolds. Their occurrence appears to be influenced both by relatively stable factors such as the type of discourse, learner proficiency, and speaker awareness as well as by changing factors such as newness of the content being presented, learner feedback, and environmental distractions. Therefore, it seems to us that a dynamic, interactive concept of this process is needed if we are to even begin to characterize what goes on when meaning is expressed, negotiated, and understood, and language is acquired.

NOTES

1. We wish to thank the following persons for their help with this study: Dr. Henry Edwards and Dr. Marie Gingras, who graciously allowed the videotaping of their classes and who helped along with Bob Courchêne and other project members (see Note 2) in the conceptualization of the research; Mrs. Teresa Drapeau, who transcribed the French tapes and carried out many of the French language analyses; and Mrs. Aline Furness, who patiently typed the final manuscript from a difficult draft. We are also grateful to the students who made it possible.

2. Researchers and teachers in the project included Mrs. Sandra Burger, Mrs. Marie Chrétien, Dr. Richard Clément, Mrs. Linda Dodd-Kelly, Dr. Henry Edwards, Dr. Philip Hauptman, Dr. Stephen Krashen, Dr. Bastian Krudenier, Dr. Marie Gingras, Ms. Suzanne Lalonde, Mrs. Mariette Migneron, Ms. Christine Morel, Mrs. Doreen Ready, and Dr. Marjorie Wesche. Funding was provided by the University of Ottawa, the Ontario Ministry of Colleges and Universities, and the Office of the Secretary of State of Canada. A description of the experiment and its results may be found in H. Edwards, M. Wesche, S. Krashen, R. Clément, and B. Kruidenier, forthcoming.

3. The role of language teachers in this situation is described in S. Burger, M. Chrétien, M. Gingras, P. Hauptman, and M. Migneron, forthcoming.

4. Language-proficiency testing of both L2 classes at the beginning and end of the semester showed significant gains for both groups on tests of receptive language skills (listening comprehension, reading, translation, and cloze). Productive skills were not tested. The gains

shown were approximately equivalent to those of students at similar proficiency levels in well-taught 45-hour courses in English and French as second languages. See Edwards et al. (Note 2) for details.

5. In the context of this study, "foreigner talk" refers to language used by native speakers with second language speakers in a formal situation in which interlocutors are of comparable social status, the aim is transmission of information, and the nonnative speaker has some functional ability in the second language. It does not refer to cases of ungrammatical pidginlike foreigner talk as described by Ferguson (1975). See Long (1983c) for a discussion of the distinction and the conditions under which both kinds of foreigner talk are found.

6. The *Study Guide: Psychology 1200, Psychologie 1600* was prepared by the School of Psychology of the University of Ottawa. It provides a detailed course description, references, description of available audio-visual materials, and other course information. The text (used in a translated version in the French language classes) is E. R. Hilgard, R. L. Atkinson, and B. C. Atkinson. 1979. *Introduction to Psychology.* New York. Harcourt Brace Jovanovitch.

7. A follow-up study on this question is planned, in which listening comprehension tests (audio-visual and audio) will be prepared from parallel L1 and L2 presentations and used to test students over a range of proficiency. We are interested in whether the L2 tape is easier to understand than the L1 tape at each proficiency level, and whether there are thresholds below and above which we find no difference.

8. For other evidence that native speakers tailor their foreigner talk based on evidence of its comprehensibility to nonnatives, see Varonis and Gass (1982).

7

INPUT AND INTERACTION IN THE COMMUNICATIVE LANGUAGE CLASSROOM: A COMPARISON OF TEACHER-FRONTED AND GROUP ACTIVITIES

Teresa Pica and Catherine Doughty
University of Pennsylvania

Many teachers currently are enthusiastic about what has been called the communicative approach to language teaching. This enthusiasm can be seen in lessons which focus on social interaction rather than grammar practice and classroom participation patterns which include small-group work along with the more traditional teacher-fronted format. Despite the widespread acceptance and endorsement in the ESL classroom of these two components of communicative language teaching—socially oriented lessons and small-group interaction—few attempts have been made to provide empirical support for their use.

In a small body of research, it has been shown that when nonnative speakers engage in genuine communication with each other, as opposed to a native-speaker interlocutor, they appear to experience a greater degree of involvement in their negotiation for message meaning (Varonis and Gass 1985b). Furthermore, when students engage independently in group discussion, they have been shown to use their second language for a wider range of rhetorical purposes than in discussion led by their teacher (Long, Adams, McLean, and Castaños 1976). The use of communication tasks and nonnative-speaker group work has thus been supported in a small number of important studies. However, this evidence is not sufficient to support the vast numbers of methods articles, teacher workshops, and instructional materials which promote communicative activities and group tasks.

We felt it appropriate, therefore, to seek additional empirical evidence for use of the communicative approach in the ESL classroom and to examine its possible effects on classroom second language acquisition. Because input and interaction have been identified as critical variables in the acquisition process (Hatch 1983a; Krashen 1981a; Larsen-Freeman 1983b; Long 1980, 1981c, 1983a), we focused our attention on these areas. We aimed first to describe and compare the input and interactional features of communication activities as carried out in small groups vs. teacher-fronted formats, and then to relate our findings to the acquisition of communicative competence in English as a second language.

DATA COLLECTION

Data were collected from three classrooms during two typical ESL communication activities focusing on decision making and values clarification. One activity was teacher-fronted; the other involved students working in groups of four. Each activity was audiotaped. The researchers were not present during the tapings so that data could be collected as unobtrusively as possible.

For the teacher-directed activity, the teachers were asked first to describe a decision-making task involving family planning in the future and then to conduct a discussion of issues with the entire class. After reading, reviewing, and discussing information relevant to the problem posed, the class had to arrive at a consensus and to recommend a solution. The teachers were also asked to note the student with the most distinctive voice and to include the student in the group activity to be recorded. This was to assist the researchers in transcription of the data.

In the small-group task, the teachers were instructed to divide the class randomly into groups of four. Once again, a situation involving a problem was described, and the groups were told to arrive at a solution. This time the problem involved choosing one among six potential recipients for a heart transplant. Each group had to work independently, without interruption from the teacher, and arrive at its own decision. The teacher was asked to record the student with the most distinctive voice.

Our rationale for selecting communicative tasks focusing on decision making was based on their widespread use in current ESL textbooks which profess to follow a communicative approach to language instruction. We did feel, however, that these tasks had a serious shortcoming which could have interfered with our obtaining truly "communicative" data—they were not two-way in design. We were aware of the importance which has been attached to the use of activities with built-in two-way information exchange as a means of promoting second language acquisition in the ESL classroom (Davies 1982, Long 1983a), In such activities, each participant has information which is unknown to fellow participants but is required by them in order to execute a task successfully (Long 1983a). It has been claimed that materials which provide for a two-way information exchange promote optimal conditions for participants to adjust their input to each other's level of comprehension (see also Gass and Varonis, this volume).

The decision-making activities used in the present study, while communicative in emphasis, were nevertheless not two-way in design. Each participant's contribution to the decision, primarily in the form of arguments and opinions, seemed useful in helping other participants arrive at a consensus but was not necessarily required for making the final decision. It was possible, therefore, that the teacher and a few class members would monopolize the conversational interaction in these activities. Such dominance by linguistically more proficient participants (such as the teacher and more fluent NNSs in the classroom) might, for example, cause the bulk of available input to be beyond the current processing capacity of many students in the class and hence incomprehensible to them. On the other hand, input at or below students' current capacity would be limited in its potential for promoting second language acquisition.

We felt that our chosen activities were, however, quite typical of those offered in communication-oriented textbooks used by the classrooms in our study. As Long (1983a) has indicated, two-way information-exchange activities are in fact not to be found in most ESL materials, but in materials designed for improving native speakers' IQ or their skills in solving problems. In view of the widespread use of decision-making tasks rather than genuine two-way information-exchange activities in communicative classroom work, we decided, therefore, to use activities of this kind. Since we did not aim to judge the integrity of communicative classrooms, but rather to describe their input and interactional features, we felt that our chosen tasks were relevant to our research purposes.

SUBJECTS

Subjects for the study included students and teachers from low-intermediate-level ESL classes. Students came from a variety of L1 backgrounds. All of the teachers were native speakers of English with many years of teaching experience. The teachers claimed that they followed a communicative approach to language teaching. Their lessons tended to emphasize group work and functional use of language.

ANALYSIS

In our analysis, it was important to consider both the ESL teacher and the nonnative-speaking students as sources of input to and interaction with each other. Based on the decision-making nature of the tasks, and in keeping with the communicative approach to which our teachers professed adherence, we believed that the language produced by the students in the teacher-fronted task would extend beyond repetition of teacher-produced models and supplying of predictable answers to teacher questions. We believed that the students might offer opinions, initiate arguments, and show agreement and disagreement both with their teacher and with each other. In the group activity, the absence of the teacher as authority and leader would also allow for a variety of rhetorical acts and interpersonal exchanges (as shown by Long et al. 1976). Furthermore, it was possible that students could be affected by utterances not specifically directed toward them. Thus the categories of addressor and addressee were not fixed in our analysis of the data. All native and nonnative speakers in the study had opportunities to function in these roles.

Because of the necessity for decision making attached to the activities chosen for the study, we believed that modifications could be made in the interactional structure of the conversation whenever impasses between addressor and addressee occurred. For example, during communicative exchanges in which addressees had difficulty understanding and addressors sensed this difficulty, addressors could restructure the conversation so as to make their input comprehensible to addressees and thus allow the conversation to continue.

In this restructuring, addressors could, for example, pause and question addressees as to whether they understood, or sensing confusion on the addressees' parts, addressors could simply repeat themselves verbatim or in paraphrase. These same restructuring techniques could be used following utterances of the addressees. Such modifications would give the interlocutors more opportunities to negotiate for message meaning and would allow addressees more time to process message content and thus sort out the confusions it triggered.

Addressees could also restructure the conversation through requests to addressors for clarification or through utterances seeking to confirm whether what they heard was what actually had been said. Repeating their own utterances or those of the addressors might also serve to make the point of the message more understandable. Figure 7-1 depicts aspects of verbal communication between conversational participants and summarizes ways in which conversational interaction can make input more comprehensible.

The features indicated in Figure 7-1 were used in the analysis of data collected for the study. The following analyses were made:

1. *Percentage of grammatical T units per total number of T units.* This was calculated as the number of T units which contained no morphological

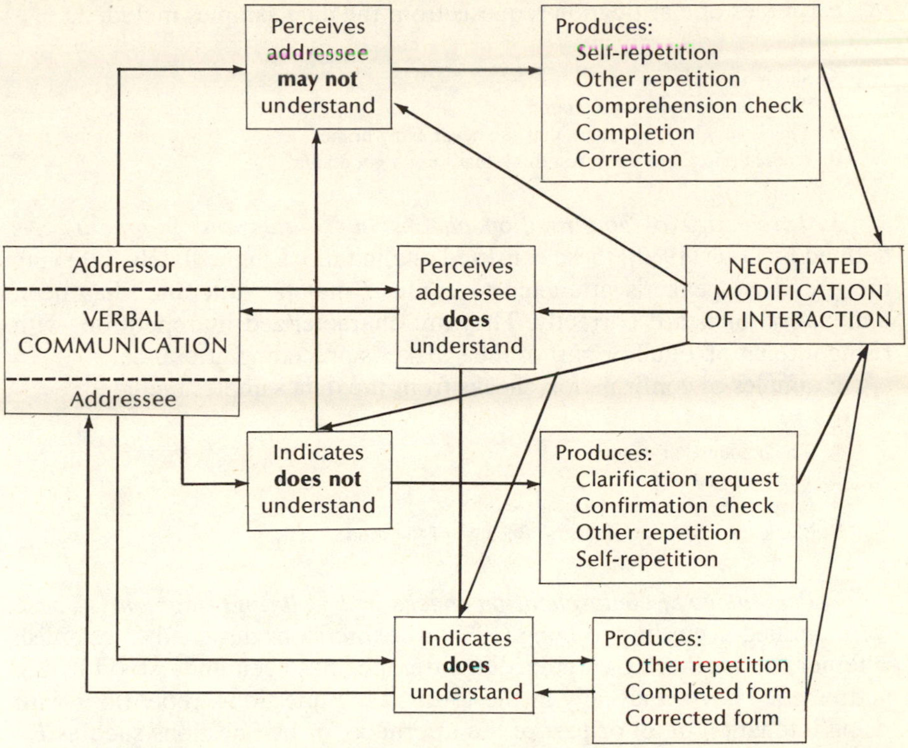

FIGURE 7-1 Negotiated Modification of Conversational Interaction

or syntactical errors divided by the total number of grammatical and ungrammatical T units in each data sample. Fragments and interjections were eliminated from these calculations.

> *T unit:* a main clause and related subordinate clauses and nonclausal structures embedded in it (Hunt 1970).
> *Ungrammatical T unit:* a T unit which contains at least one morphological or syntactical error.
> *Fragment:* nonclausal items such as single-word or phrasal utterances used as initiations or responses as well as false starts and self-repetitions.
> *Interjection:* single lexical responses: yes, no, and OK; and their nonlexical counterparts i.e., um, hmmn, and ah which were not incorporated into T units, phrases, or fragments (e.g., frames were not included in this category).

2. *Percentage of clarification requests in T units and fragments.* As defined by Long (1980), these comprised all expressions designed to elicit clarification of the preceding utterance(s), and consisted of wh-, yes-no, uninverted intonation, and tag questions as well as statements such as *I don't understand* and *Try again.*

Examples of clarification requests from the data samples included:

A: She is on welfare.
B: What do you mean by welfare?
A: This is very bad . . . I think that she never estay home.
B: You're opposed to that? You think that's not a good idea?

3. *Percentage of confirmation checks in T units and fragments.* As defined by Long (1980), these consisted of elicitations immediately following the previous speaker's utterance to confirm that the utterance has been understood or heard correctly. They are characterized by repetition, with rising intonation of all or part of the speaker's preceding utterance.

Examples of confirmation checks from the data samples included:

A: The homemaker woman.
B: The homemaker?
A: Mexican foods have a lot of ulcers.
B: Mexicans have a lot of ulcers? Because of the food?

4. *Percentage of comprehension checks in T units and fragments.* These were defined according to Long (1980) as expressions designed to establish whether the speaker's own preceding utterance has been understood by the addressee. They are usually in the form of tag questions, repetitions with rising intonation of all or part of the utterance, or by questions such as *Do you understand?*

Examples of comprehension checks from the data samples included:

There's no man present, right?
Do you know what I mean?

5. *Percentage of self-repetitions in T units and fragments.* These were realized in the following two forms:

1. Speaker's exact or partial repetition of the same lexical item(s) from own preceding utterance, incorporated into a new utterance, within five speaking turns; repetitions of functors were not included.
2. Speaker's semantic repetition (by synonym substitution, paraphrase, morphological expansion, or work-order change) of the content of own preceding utterance, within five speaking turns.

Three examples of exact repetition from the data samples included:

a. Do you agree with that? Do you agree with that?
b. I think Carlos Whannon is very young, is very, very young.
c. The health is very bad. The health of both the male and female is very bad.

Three examples of semantic repetition from the data samples included:

a. Do you share his feelings? Does anyone else agree with Gustavo?
b. He is more young. He has a lot of life.
c. Maybe there's a cure, something that can improve his sight.

6. *Percentage of other repetitions in T units and fragments.* These were also divided into two groups—

1. Exact or partial repetition of lexical items, within five speaking turns, of the previous speaker's preceding utterance, without the rising intonation characteristic of a confirmation check.
2. Semantic repetition (by synonym substitution, paraphrase, morphological expansion, or word-order change) of the content of the previous speaker's preceding utterance, without the rising intonation characteristic of a confirmation check. Cases of semantic repetition involving morphological expansion differ from correction (see 8) in that the expansion is uttered in the context of a longer utterance; i.e., the repetition does not involve *only* corrected morphological material. These also were scored only if they occurred within five speaking turns.

Examples of exact other repetitions from the data samples included:

A: I think the fourth family.
B: You think the fourth family.
A: I think she has three children.
B: This is the thing. She has three children.

Examples of semantic other repetition from the data samples included:

A: He has a job for many times.
B: Yeah. He's has a job for a long time. He's stable.
A: He doesn't do anything.
B: He no work.
A: Is no normal relation.
B: Yes, it's not normal for two women to raise a child.

7. *Percentage of completions in T units and fragments.* These consisted of utterances by the addressee which interrupted an immediately preceding utterance or occurred immediately after an utterance left incomplete through rising intonation and/or pause. In producing a completion of the addressor's utterance, the addressee supplied a word or phrase appropriate to ending or extending the utterance.

Examples of completions from the data samples included:

A: We have two patients for ______
B: For discussion.
A: Yes, I know . . . but the mental ______

B: Mentality.
A: If she didn't work, then the government
B: help
A: help her.

8. *Percentage of corrections in T units and fragments.* These were defined as utterances (Chun, Day, Chenoweth, and Luppescu 1982) which indicate a response to what is perceived to be a syntactical, morphological, or word-choice error by the speaker in which another item which includes linguistic material not included in the speaker's utterance is supplied. These differ from semantic other repetitions in that the corrected linguistic material is the only new material presented to the speaker.

Examples of corrections from the data samples included:

A: It's illegally for the system
B: It's illegal for the system
A: How much pay the government
B: pays
A: You need more time for herself and for yourself
B: For yourself or himself

9. *Percentage of turns taken by a student selected for individual study.* This consisted of the total number of initiations and responses produced by the individual student, divided by the total number of initiations and responses in each data sample.

10. *Percentage of input directed at a student selected for individual study.* This consisted of the total number of T units, fragments, and interjections produced directly in response to utterances made by the individual student, divided by the total number of T units, fragments, and interjections produced by participants other than this student. This category included conversational features identified in Analyses 2 to 8 above, which were produced by other classroom participants in response to utterances of the individual student.

Interrater reliability checks for 14 of the 15 measures in the above analysis obtained coefficients of .93 or better. Exact self-repetition obtained a coefficient of .88.

RESEARCH QUESTIONS AND HYPOTHESES

In this study we aimed to describe, compare, and contrast the input and interactional features of teacher-fronted and group versions of decision-making, communicative activities. Two research questions formed the focus of the investigation.

1. How do teacher-fronted and group decision-making, communication

activities compare with regard to interactional features of conversation (e.g., self- and other repetitions, confirmation checks, clarification requests, and comprehension checks) which have been claimed to make input comprehensible to nonnative speakers (Long 1980, 1981c, 1983a).

2. What are the contributions of teacher-fronted compared with group decision-making, communication activities to the acquisition of communicative competence (specifically in the areas of linguistic and strategic competence, as defined by Canale and Swain 1980) by the second language learner?

In answering our research questions, we focused our analyses on the input available to and language produced by each class as a whole as well as by one student in each class selected for more detailed study. In the first activity we investigated, the input consisted of all T units, fragments, and interjections from both the ESL teacher (a native English speaker) and other nonnative speakers in the classroom. In the second activity, nonnative input from classmates was the only input source available. Because all input to these students during the activities might have been at the level of exposure, i.e., not negotiated through direct interaction or unattended to by participants, we further examined those utterances directed toward specially selected students, e.g., questions asked of them, answers provided to them, responses to their comments, and utterances of others in their classrooms which contained exact or semantic repetitions of the students' own utterances. The units of analysis in the production area consisted of all T units, fragments, and interjections uttered by the selected student in each of the activities.

Although nonnative input and opportunities for interaction with peers were available to students in each activity, we believed that the teacher's presence or absence would lead to differences in both areas. Thus we suspected that we would find quantitative differences between teacher-fronted and group activities in both the amount of nonnative input available to our students and the amount of talk they produced on an individual basis. We believed that there would be qualitative differences as well. We suspected that even though the students were expected to engage in the decision-making process, the teacher would elicit their responses and follow them up with feedback of some kind. Thus there would be considerably less direct interaction among individual NNS classmates in their teacher's presence than there would be in group work.

Our suspicions that there would be differences in both the input and interactional structure of the conversation in each of the two activities led to the generation of several hypotheses. We reasoned that native speaker utterances from the ESL teacher, which were not available in the group activity, would, of course, increase the amount of grammatical input available in the teacher-fronted decision. However, we also believed that students would produce more grammatical T units in the presence of their teacher than when interacting in their groups. Our reasoning was based on two assumptions:

A1: That the linguistically competent students were likely to dominate student input in the teacher-fronted classroom interaction.

A2: Based on the structure of classroom discourse, in which the teacher elicits student responses and supplies feedback to them, all students, in general, would be likely to monitor their productions in their teacher's presence.

These reasonings motivated the first two hypotheses of our study:

H1: The input in the teacher-fronted activity would be more grammatical than that in the group activity; i.e., there would be more grammatical T units per total T units in the former than in the latter.

H2: Target language productions of students in the teacher-fronted activity would be more grammatical than those of students in the group activity; i.e., there would be more grammatical T units per total T units among students in the former than in the latter activity.

We also believed that the interactional structure of the teacher-fronted and group activities would differ in that the latter would activate more conversational adjustments on the part of the NNS participants in their attempts to understand and be understood by each other. The teacher, more experienced than students in making sense out of interlanguage productions, would be less likely to seek clarification or confirmation of NNS utterances. However, the students, especially, the less linguistically proficient, might be reluctant or embarrassed to indicate their lack of comprehension in front of their teacher or the entire class. Furthermore, the teacher and more fluent students would be more confident than other less proficient participants that they could be understood, hence would be less likely to check their interlocutors' comprehension. In the group situation, participants, sitting in closer, face-to-face view of each other than in the teacher-fronted situation, might notice confusion on the parts of fellow interactants, and thereby feel compelled to check their comprehension. This reasoning led to our third hypothesis:

H3: More clarification requests, confirmation checks, and comprehension checks would occur in the group activity than in the teacher-fronted activity.

We further hypothesized that more other repetitions would be produced in the teacher-fronted activity because of the nature of classroom interaction, which gives the teacher opportunities for providing feedback on students' utterances. We also suspected that there would be more self-repetitions in the teacher-fronted activity because the teacher's presence would create pressure to convey points and adhere to topics in the class's attempts to reach the decision-making goal of the lesson. We had some doubts, therefore, as to whether self- and other repetitions would be used to modify the classroom conversation. We suspected that their purpose in the classroom would be to maintain the goals of the lesson and to conform to classroom conventions.

For both self- and other repetitions, we believed that semantic repetitions would be more prevalent in the teacher-fronted data because of the greater linguistic resources available to the teacher for providing lexical substitutions and morphological expansions of their own students' utterances.

Our thinking on self- and other repetitions led to hypotheses 4 and 5:

H4: More other repetitions would occur in the teacher-fronted than in the group activity. Quantitative differences would be most apparent in the area of semantic other repetitions.

H5: More self-repetitions would occur in the teacher-fronted than in the group activity. This difference would be most apparent in semantic self-repetitions.

We suspected that there would be more correction and completion moves in the teacher-fronted activity than in the group interaction, and that the primary source of these would be the teacher. We believed that, despite the communicative purpose attached to the activity, teachers would feel compelled by virtue of their training and classroom role to assist students in producing accurate messages. Students in the teacher-fronted and group activities, we felt, would be less likely to correct each other because, based on their limited English proficiency (as members of low intermediate classes), they would lack confidence in their ability to correct their classmates' utterances with appropriate forms. This led to hypothesis 6:

H6: More completions and corrections would occur in the teacher-fronted than in the group activity.

Because fewer participants were involved in the group compared with the teacher-fronted activity, we believed that individual students in the group activity, specifically our specially selected participants, would be engaged in more interaction during the group than during the teacher-fronted activity. Our reasonings, together with claims made by Long (1983a) that communication tasks undertaken by students participating in group activities increase the amount of time available to each student for oral language production, led to the following remaining hypotheses:

H7: More turns would be taken by an individual student in the group than in the teacher-fronted activity.

H8: More input would be directed toward an individual student in the group than in the teacher-fronted activity.

H9: A greater quantity of language would be produced by an individual student in the group than in the teacher-fronted activity.

RESULTS

All hypotheses of the study were tested through chi-square analyses on the proportions of input and interactional variables in the teacher-fronted and group communicative tasks. Table 7-1 summarizes the results of our study.

Our results must be viewed with considerable caution in light of the

TABLE 7-1 Summary of Hypotheses, Proportions of Input, and Interactional Variables in Teacher-Fronted and Group Activities, and Results of Chi-Square Analyses ($df = 1, p = 0.05$)

H1: The input in the teacher-fronted activity would be more grammatical than that in the group activity; i.e., there would be more grammatical T units per total T units in the former than in the latter.

Findings: Percentage Grammatical T Units/Total T Units

	Class 1	*Class 2*	*Class 3*	*Mean*
T-F	66	70	63	67
GRP	42	39	16	35

Supported by data. $\chi^2 = 54.0, p < .001$. n(T-F): class 1 = 11, class 2 = 10, class 3 + 13, n(GRP): classes 1, 2, 3 = 4. The n's are the same for all hypotheses tested.

H2: Target language productions of students in the teacher-fronted activity would be more grammatical than those of students in the group activity; i.e., there would be more grammatical T units per total T units among students in the former than in the latter activity.

Findings: Percentage Grammatical T Units/Total T Units Produced by Students

	Class 1	*Class 2*	*Class 3*	*Mean*
T-F	29	44	29	34
GRP	42	39	16	35

Not supported by data. $\chi^2 = 0.15, p < 0.750$, n.s.

H3: More clarification requests, confirmation checks, and comprehension checks would occur in the group activity than in the teacher-fronted activity.

Findings: Percentage Conversational Adjustments/Total T Units and Fragments

	Clarif. reqs.			*Confirm. checks*			*Comp. checks*			*Totals*			
	1	*2*	*3*	*1*	*2*	*3*	*1*	*2*	*3*	*1*	*2*	*3*	*Mean*
T-F	6	5	5	6	4	4	1	1	1	13	10	10	11
GRP	8	2	0	1	0	7	4	0	1	13	2	8	6

Not supported by data. $\chi^2 = 7.0, p < .01$. Result is *opposite* from prediction.

H4: More other repetitions would occur in the teacher-fronted than in the group activity. Quantitative differences would be most apparent in the area of semantic other repetitions.

Findings: Percentage Other Repetitions/Total T Units and Fragments:

	Other reps. exact			*Other reps. semantic*			*Total other reps.*			
	1	*2*	*3*	*1*	*2*	*3*	*1*	*2*	*3*	*Mean*
T-F	14	12	14	10	7	4	24	19	19	22
GRP	14	9	13	3	6	6	17	15	19	16

Partially supported by data. Total other repetitions: $\chi^2 = 4.73, p < .05$. Exact other repetitions: $\chi^2 = 1.37, p < .250$, n.s. Semantic other repetitions: $\chi^2 = 3.55, p < 100$, n.s. However, trend in direction of prediction.

H5: More self-repetitions would occur in the teacher-fronted than in the group activity. This difference would be most apparent in semantic self-repetitions.

Findings: Percentage Self-Repetitions/Total T Units and Fragments:

	Self-reps. exact			*Self-reps. semantic*			*Total self-reps.*			
	1	*2*	*3*	*1*	*2*	*3*	*1*	*2*	*3*	*Mean*
T-F	7	13	8	11	14	10	18	27	18	21
GRP	12	11	6	5	4	4	17	15	10	14

Supported by data. Total self-repetition: $\chi^2 = 6.53$, $p < .025$. Exact self-repetition: $\chi^2 = 0.34$, $p < .900$, n.s. Semantic self-repetition: $\chi^2 = 16.42$, $p < .001$.

H6: More completions and corrections would occur in the teacher-fronted than in the group activity.

Findings: Percentage Completions and Corrections/Total T Units and Fragments:

	Completions			*Corrections*			*Total*			
	1	*2*	*3*	*1*	*2*	*3*	*1*	*2*	*3*	*Mean*
T-F	1	4	0	0	1	2	1	5	2	2
GRP	3	6	1	2	3	0	5	9	0	6

Not supported by data. $\chi^2 = 9.86$, $p < .005$. Result is opposite from prediction.

H7: More turns would be taken by an individual student in the group than in the teacher-fronted activity.

Findings: Percentage Turns by Individual Student/Total Turns:

	Class 1	*Class 2*	*Class 3*	*Mean*
T-F	13	4	15	10
GRP	16	27	27	24

Supported by data. $\chi^2 = 28.6$, $p < .001$.

H8: More input would be directed toward an individual student in the group than in the teacher-fronted activity.

Findings: T Units + Fragments + Interjections Directed at an Individual Student/Total T Units + Fragments + Interjections:

	Class 1	*Class 2*	*Class 3*	*Mean*
T-F	3	3	2	3
GRP	4	18	11	12

Supported by data. $\chi^2 = 40.6$, $p < .001$.

H9: A greater quantity of language would be produced by an individual student in the group than in the teacher-fronted activity.

Findings: T Units + Fragments + Interjections Produced by an Individual Student/Total T Units + Fragments + Interjections:

	Class 1	*Class 2*	*Class 3*	*Mean*
T-F	7	6	12	9
GRP	14	31	21	24

Supported by data. $\chi^2 = 42.9$, $p < .001$.

---

relatively small sample size of the three classrooms. Data collected in four of the seven classrooms which had participated in the study had to be discarded during analysis because of unforeseen difficulties which had arisen during data collection. For example, two teachers sat in on the recording of the small-group interaction, one group of students recorded only their final judgments rather than ongoing arguments, and in one classroom the tape recorder failed to function.

Our research design, in delegating responsibility for data collection to the classroom teachers, enabled us to gather our data as unobtrusively as possible. However, this procedure also presented serious drawbacks to securing the data we needed for hypothesis testing. Our resultant dilemma spoke well to the needs identified by Long (1983b) for training the ESL teacher in classroom research. We noted with particular interest the fact that the three teachers whose classrooms provided us with the data we required for our study had previous training and/or experience in conducting classroom research.

We would also like to exercise caution in making claims about the results of our hypothesis testing in cases where there were differences between overall results and individual classroom analyses. Specifically, in the analyses of hypotheses 2, 3, 4, and 5, several individual classrooms did not follow the overall trend of the findings. Thus our hypothesis 2, that target language productions of students in the teacher-fronted activities would be more grammatical than those among students working in groups, was not supported statistically by the collective data of the three classrooms (χ^2 = 0.15, $p < 0.750$, n.s.). Overall, grammatical T units comprised 34 percent of the total number of T units produced by students in the three teacher-fronted lessons and 35 percent of those in the corresponding group interaction. However, this overall pattern held only for classroom 2 (44 percent in teacher-fronted vs. 39 percent in the group). In classroom 1, students were actually more grammatical in the group than in the teacher-fronted situation (42 percent vs. 29 percent of the total T units). Only in classroom 3 was the percentage of students' T units in the teacher-fronted activity more grammatical than in group work (29 vs. 16 percent).

We also observed tendencies opposite to hypothesis 3, in that significantly more modification of the interaction actually occurred in the teacher-fronted rather than group activity. Clarification checks, confirmation checks, and comprehension checks comprised 11 percent of T units and fragments in the teacher-fronted situations vs. 6 percent of those in the groups ($\chi^2 = 7.0$, $p < .01$). Here, too, there were differences among the individual classrooms. However, unlike the case of hypothesis 2, no individual classroom results supported hypothesis 3. In classrooms 1 and 3, the percentage of conversational adjustments in T units and fragments produced during the teacher-fronted activity was comparable with that used by students working in groups (13 percent in both cases for classroom 1 and 10 percent vs. 8 percent for classroom 3). In classroom 2, the teacher-fronted activity actually offered a greater percentage of conversational adjustments than did the group discussion (10 vs. 2 percent).

As we predicted in hypotheses 4 and 5, overall we found that conversational adjustments such as self- and other repetitions were more abundant in the teacher-fronted than in the group activities ($\chi^2 = 6.53$, $p < .025$ for self-repetition and $\chi^2 = 4.78$, $p < .05$ for other repetition). However, these differences were not always apparent in individual classroom data. In fact, in classrooms 2 and 3, there was little or no difference in percentage of other repetition in T units and fragments in the teacher-fronted and group situations (19 vs. 15 percent for classroom 2 and 19 percent for both teacher-fronted and group situations in classroom 3). In classroom 1, there was little difference in percentage of self-repetition in the two situations. Eighteen percent of the T units and fragments in the teacher-fronted activity and 17 percent of those in group work consisted of self-repetitions.

Our additional prediction in hypotheses 4 and 5, that there would be more semantic repetitions in teacher-fronted data, was supported only for self-repetition (12 percent of the T units and fragments for teacher-fronted vs. 4 percent for group work, $\chi^2 = 16.42$, $p < .001$). With regard to other repetition, our predicted pattern did not hold ($\chi^2 = 3.55$, $p < .100$, n.s.). Because of the considerable discrepancy among teacher-fronted and group semantic other repetitions in classroom 1 (10 percent among the teacher-fronted vs. 3 percent among the group participants), only a trend in the direction of our prediction obtained.

The variation we found among individual classes in testing hypotheses 2 to 5 was not as apparent in our other results. Hypothesis 1, that the input in the teacher-fronted activity would be more grammatical than that in the group situation, was supported by the data. Grammatical T units comprised 67 percent of the total T units in the teacher-fronted lesson, but only 35 percent of those in the group activity ($\chi^2 = 59.0$, $p < .001$). This pattern held for classroom 1 (66 vs. 42 percent), classroom 2 (70 vs. 39 percent), and classroom 3 (63 vs. 16 percent).

Hypothesis 7, that more turns would be taken by an individual student in the group than in the teacher-fronted activity, was also supported ($\chi^2 = 28.6$, $p < .001$). Our individually selected students took 24 percent of the total number of turns in the group interaction, as opposed to 10 percent of the turns in the teacher-fronted activity. This pattern was also exhibited in individual classrooms, particularly in classroom 2, where the student took 27 percent of the turns among group participants compared with 4 percent of the turns in the teacher-student interaction, and in classroom 3, where these percentages were 27 and 15 percent. Only in classroom 1 was this pattern only weakly evident. Our individual student took 16 percent of the group's turns and 13 percent of turns involving teacher and classmates.

Hypothesis 8, that more input would be directed toward an individual student in the group than in the teacher-fronted activity, was also supported in the overall data ($\chi^2 = 40.6$, $p < .001$). Our individually selected students received 12 percent of the total input among group participants, but only 3 percent of the input in the teacher-fronted activity. This pattern held in classrooms 2 and 3 (18 vs. 3 percent and 11 vs. 2 percent, respectively). However, in classroom 1, there was only a slight difference in the input directed toward the student in the group situation (4 percent) vs. that in the teacher-fronted lesson (3 percent).

The data clearly supported hypothesis 9, that a greater quantity of language would be produced by an individual student in the group than in the teacher-fronted activity. Overall, the difference was 24 percent in the group vs. 9 percent in the teacher-fronted situation ($\chi^2 = 42.9$, $p < .001$). In classroom 1, this pattern was 14 percent vs. 7 percent. In classrooms 2 and 3, differences were 31 vs. 6 percent and 21 vs. 12 percent, respectively.

Results of our study led to a rejection of hypothesis 6, as significantly more completions and corrections occurred in group than in teacher-student interaction ($\chi^2 = 9.86$, $p < .005$). Again, there was little variation among the individual classrooms in this pattern. In classroom 1, completions and corrections formed 5 percent of the T units and fragments in group interaction and 1 percent in the teacher-fronted activity. In classroom 2, these features appeared in 9 percent of the group activity but in only 5 percent of the teacher-fronted situation. Classroom 3 exhibited a slight deviation from this pattern (2 percent for teacher-fronted and 0 percent for group). However, we felt that there were too few data for purposes of analysis ($n = 3$ in teacher-fronted and $n = 1$ for group).

DISCUSSION

Results of our study have helped us to identify similarities and differences in the input and interactional features of teacher-fronted vs. group versions of decision-making, communicative activities. In light of these results, we will attempt to discuss the extent to which each version makes input comprehensible to the learner and provides opportunities for the development of communicative competence.

Overall, our analyses can be divided into three broad categories: grammaticality of input, negotiation of input, and amount of input and/or production. We found that more grammatical input was available during teacher-fronted than during group activities. However, the bulk of this grammatical input was produced by the teachers, whereas students' productions were equally ungrammatical in both situations.

Contrary to our predictions, a number of features of negotiation which are claimed to allow for comprehensibility of input—specifically, conversational adjustments such as comprehension and confirmation checks and clarification requests—were more available during the teacher-fronted interaction. However, these features were few in number in both teacher-fronted and group situations. In fact, the teachers in our study made relatively few conversational adjustments compared with native speakers in studies of NS-NNS interaction outside classrooms (see, e.g., Long 1980). This finding regarding teachers' interaction with nonnative speakers has been reported in previous ESL classroom research such as that of Long and Sato (1983) and Pica and Long (1982).

We wish to emphasize, moreover, that the greater or comparable percentages of conversational adjustments in the teacher-fronted activity did not necessarily indicate that all students shared in these interactional modifications. Our claim is based on the finding that more input was directed toward our individually studied students in the group than in the teacher-fronted activity. It was possible, therefore, that conversational adjustments were more abundant in the teacher-fronted activity but served only as a form of exposure to class members who listened while their teacher interacted with others in the classroom. Thus the conversational modifications in the teacher-fronted lessons were not necessarily relevant to individual students' comprehension levels.

We also found that in both the teacher-fronted and group data, the proportions of self- and other repetitions were quite sizable compared with those of the conversational adjustments reviewed above. This first suggested that interactional modifications did indeed occur in our classrooms, especially in the teacher-fronted situation, but that such modifications varied little in terms of discourse strategies. While this may in fact have been the case, we must acknowledge our earlier stated beliefs that self- and other repetitions were products of the classroom situation. We had suspected that self-repetition represented classroom participants' goal orientation and associated feeling of obligation to topic adherence. Other repetition, we had hypothesized, represented feedback moves on interlocutor production. Our initial predictions, together with Long's (1980) claim that native speakers use self- and other repetitions to avoid communication breakdown when speaking with nonnative speakers, suggested to us that self- and other repetitions were used not so much to negotiate meaning but to conform to classroom conventions and ensure completion of task. We feel that, in the future, more stringent repetition categories will have to be developed in order to capture this distinction between classroom-related moves and the negotiated interaction which more closely parallels that which occurs outside the classroom.

Quite unexpectedly, we found that completions and corrections of nonnative-speaking students, generally considered to be the province of the ESL teacher, seemed to be more typical of student group interaction in classrooms 1 and 2. In classroom 3, there appeared to be little of either feature which could be analyzed, and overall these features of negotiation consitute a very small portion of the total input generated.

Finally, we found that individual students appeared to have more opportunities to use the target language in group than in teacher-fronted activities, through either taking more turns or producing more samples of their interlanguage. Such opportunities may have had a positive effect on students' development of linguistic and strategic competence in giving them practice in hypothesizing about interlanguage structures which were still at variable levels of accuracy, or in enhancing their development of second language fluency.

In summary, we feel that as the increased emphasis on a communicative approach to second language teaching has broadened the focus of ESL classroom interaction to include both teacher-fronted and peer-group-oriented tasks, some comments which address the question of how much class time should be devoted to small-group work are in order.

One effect of the communicative approach has been to increase the availability to second language learners of nonnative, potentially ungrammatical samples of target English as produced by their classmates. However, students' production appears to be equally ungrammatical—or grammatical—whether speaking in groups or in the presence of their teacher. It is only the teacher's production which makes the input in a teacher-fronted lesson more grammatical overall. Furthermore, in light of the central role of the teacher in a teacher-fronted lesson, ungrammatical production by students is more likely to be directed at their teacher than at other classroom participants.

Our study has shown that in a teacher-fronted activity, a portion of the teacher's input was negotiated with students. Unfortunately, the group interlocutor necessarily restricted the amount of negotiation time per individual student. Group work, on the other hand, did offer students at least some opportunities to hear grammatical input and to negotiate message meaning, and provided many opportunities for them to practice using the target language and to receive feedback on their communicative effectiveness. We recognize, however, that a steady diet of group activities may restrict the amount of grammatical input available to the classroom learner, leading perhaps to a stabilized nontarget variety (as shown by Plann 1976).

In conclusion, we feel that small-group use of communicative activities can be effective in the ESL classroom but that its benefits may be more limited than had previously been assumed. Thus far, the only obvious advantage to the student engaged in a peer-group task is the opportunity for far more target language practice time than is available in teacher-directed activities. However, one-way communication tasks, such as those we have described, do not appear to facilitate negotiation of message in either situation.

We suspect that we found relatively little negotiation in our teacher-fronted and group data because our decision-making tasks did not guarantee a two-way information exchange among participants in the study. We would like to hypothesize, at this point, that communication activities which are two-way in design will foster a great deal of negotiated modification in the classroom and that perhaps the role of the small-group tasks, when two-way communication is indeed generated, will become crucial to the organization of the ESL classroom. It also seems likely that two-way tasks could be most effective when only two participants are involved. Hence, in the classroom, pair rather than group work on two-way tasks may ultimately be most conducive to negotiated modification of interaction, and hence to second language acquisition. Such predictions, we hope, will be supported through further classroom research.

Section Three

INTERACTION, MODIFICATION, AND NEGOTIATION

On Discourse

8

CHILDREN'S FOREIGNER TALK: PEER TALK IN PLAY CONTEXT

Tuula Hirvonen
University of Jyväskylä

"You don't say *I'm not your friend,* you have to say *no you friend.*" This was one of the answers received when the native English-speaking subjects recorded for this study were asked whether they spoke differently to their English-speaking friends as opposed to children who were learning English. Some children seemed to be very well aware of a need to modify their speech, whereas others either found it less necessary or were unable to reflect on such a question.

Input studies have recently looked at the meaning negotiation process in various types of interactional situations between different interlocutors: between native speakers and nonnative speakers as well as between nonnative speakers. Since age peers may be an important source of input for learners, children's interactions were chosen as the focus of this study. In various studies children have been shown to have the ability to carry on conversations and to use different registers to different speakers (see, e.g., Andersen and Johnson 1973; Shatz and Gelman 1973; Gleason 1973; and Gormly, Chapman, Foot, and Sweeney 1979). There may, however, be differences in this ability.

Speakers of any language differ in their ability to separate language from its communicative function and use it for talking about language itself, e.g., for correction and teaching (Wong-Fillmore 1976, Iwamura 1980, Schachter 1983b). One factor which may account for successful negotiation of meaning may be a heightened metalinguistic sensitivity. It has been suggested (Peal and Lambert 1962, Lambert 1977) that bilinguals may have a higher level of metalinguistic awareness because of their own linguistic experience and that they may be more flexible in their use of language. Because of the potential difference between monolinguals and bilinguals, the study reported on in this chapter investigates interactions between L2 speakers and monolinguals on the one hand and bilinguals on the other. The aim of the study is to look at two broad questions in children's foreigner talk (FT): is there any difference between the language native speakers use to other native speakers as opposed to learners and if so, could any significant differences be found in the language of monolingual and bilingual children in their speech to nonnative speakers?

Eight learners of English, 7 to 10 years old, were recorded in Cardiff, Wales, in conversations with native English-speaking children. The learners came from varying linguistic backgrounds: two speakers of Chinese, Japanese, and Arabic each, one child bilingual in Arabic and Kurdish, and one speaker of Malay. All but one (a Chinese speaker) had spent less than 6 months in Britain at the time of the recordings. Each learner was recorded for 30 to 45 minutes in separate conversations with the monolingual and the bilingual English-speaking age peer. The only language the learner shared with the bilingual child was English. In addition, the monolingual and bilingual children who had been matched with a particular learner were also recorded in conversation with one another. Therefore, the data consist of conversations of 24 dyads of children:

1. Eight monolingual-learner conversations
2. Eight bilingual-learner conversations
3. Eight native speaker–native speaker conversations

One bilingual and one monolingual girl were recorded with two learners, each one with a beginner and a more advanced learner. The children were recorded in their own homes or in their school. They were assigned a task of playing either in a free-play situation (legos, dolls etc.) or in a game instruction situation (explaining a game and playing it). Each dyad was recorded in only one of the situations; the order of the types of interactions and tasks was varied.

The dialogues obtained were coded for sentence level and discourse features. The sentence-level features examined are largely those discussed in other foreigner talk and caretaker speech studies (Long 1981a, Freed 1981, Cross 1978) as either actually or potentially different in simplified and nonsimplified registers. By simplified registers we intend the language used in those situations in which one's interlocutor is considered limited in his or her capacity to understand the language used. The discourse features were drawn from Halliday's (in press) systemic model of discourse and the Bristol

Language Development Projects (e.g., Wells 1975; Wells, Montgomery, and MacLure 1979). In Halliday's model, dialogue is treated as a shared potential and described in terms of the role relationships set up by the speaker for himself or herself and the hearer, and the encoding of these relations in the semantics of language. The dialogue is interpreted as a process of exchange involving two variables: the nature of the commodity that is being exchanged (goods and services or information) and the roles that are defined by the exchange process. In the Bristol study this model has been used in the analysis of L1 acquisition and development up to and including early school age.

The syntax or the input language and the structure of the discourse or the type of interaction have been separated here in order to determine trends in the types of modifications used: are both syntax and interaction modified or only one or the other? (See also Long 1981a and b.)

SENTENCE FEATURES

The sentence-structure variables were chosen to describe the surface complexity and certain textual features of the language the learners were exposed to. We hypothesize that in general foreigner talk would be easier to interpret and in foreigner talk the relations among the linguistic constituents and between the linguistic code and the nonlinguistic environment would be more transparent than in native talk. Also, it was hypothesized that in foreigner talk native speakers would employ various means both to secure their interlocutors' attention and to sustain the conversation.

The variables studied here were the following:

1. Number of clauses per S
2. Number of complex sentences and embedded structures
3. Number of one-word utterances (LUW)
4. Number of one-word subject constituents
5. Number of one-word verbal groups
6. Distribution of surface S types
7. Number of copulas in the total of verbs
8. Number of ungrammatical utterances
9. Number of attention-getting devices
10. Number of vocatives
11. Number of non-present-tense markings
12. Number of utterances with nonimmediate reference
13. Number of stock expressions
14. Number of elliptical structures
15. Number of fragments

These features were used since they were hypothesized to differ between fluent native talk and the type of code where one interlocutor is considered limited in his or her capacity to understand and/or speak the language.

Significant differences were found between FT (mono- and bilingual combined) and NT on 5 of the 15 variables studied. These results are given in Table 8-1.

TABLE 8-1 Distribution of Sentence-level Variables 4, 6, 9, 10, and 12 in Foreigner Talk and Native Talk

Variable	*FT, %*	*NT, %*	χ^2	*df*	*p*
4. Subject constituent*					
Proportion of 1-word subjects	88.5	93.4	14.348	2	$p < .001$
Proportion of 2-word subjects	7.6	4.7			
6. Surface S types†					
Proportions of					
Declaratives	44.0	51.9			
Interrogatives	17.5	13.5	34.372	3	$p < .001$
Imperatives	8.8	5.1			
9. Attention-getting devices† in % of utterances	4.5	1.2	29.753	1	$p < .001$
10. Vocatives† in % of utterances	4.1	1.1	28.146	1	$p < .001$
12. Nonimmediate reference† in % of utterances	12.1	16.9	17.702	1	$p < .01$

*n = 854 (FT) 1007 (NT) †n = 1548 (FT) 1691 (NT)

The distribution of the surface sentence types resembles that found in other studies of modified codes (Long 1981a, Freed 1981). There are fewer declaratives and more questions and more imperatives in foreigner talk than in native talk. The length of the subject constituent is, however, shorter in NT than in FT. This might be explained by the use of pronominal and lexical subjects. It is possible that native speakers use pronominal, and therefore shorter, subjects in NT and resort to more transparent lexical subjects in FT. This cannot be discerned from the data, because the subject constituents were not coded for this feature. There are more vocatives and attention-getting devices in FT, and fewer utterances with nonimmediate reference. These results support the hypothesis: in FT the native speaker needs different kinds of devices to sustain the conversation and FT has a "here and now" quality similar to caretaker speech. The tasks given to the children may have resulted in the nonsignificant difference between NT and FT in the tense marking.

The results show children's ability to modify their speech in accordance with the linguistic proficiency of their interlocutors. Both surface syntax and the function of the utterance and the interactional features differ between NT and FT.

The same variables were tested for differences between mono- and bilingual children in their speech to learners. Four of the variables found to be significantly different between combined FT and NT also attained significance when separate comparisons were made for mono- and bilingual FT speakers (FT1 and FT2). There are two variables that differ between FT1 and FT2 but not between FT and NT. The reason for this may be found in group differences between mono- and bilingual children: the same significant differences were found in their native-talk samples. In Table 8-2 the results of the comparisons between FT1 and FT2 and mono- and bilingual NT (NT1 and NT2) are shown for the variables that differed between them or between combined FT and NT.

There are more one-clause sentences in FT1 than in FT2 (86.6 percent as opposed to 79.4 percent), a higher proportion of one-word utterances (19.5 percent as opposed to 15.4 percent in FT2), fewer statements, more questions, and slightly more commands in FT1. All these differences, with the exception of the frequency of occurrence of commands, are reflected in the NT samples. All the syntactic differences between FT1 and FT2 may then be argued to reflect the group differences between mono- and bilingual children in general rather than their linguistic behavior when talking to learners in particular. The interactional features, on the other hand, do not differ between NT1 and NT2 but are used in FT1 for conversational purposes. There are more attention-getting devices in FT1 (5.8 percent of all utterances contain an attention-getting device in FT1 as opposed to 2.9 percent in FT2) and more vocatives in FT1 (in 7.0 percent of all utterances as opposed to .8 percent in FT2). The proportions of immediate and nonimmediate reference of utterance do not differ significantly between NT1 and NT2 but do between FT1 and FT2 (19.7 percent of utterances in FT1 have a nonimmediate reference as opposed to 9.2 percent in FT2). This is the only variable that shows more modification on the part of the bilingual speaker in the direction of making the interaction both easier to follow and more transparent to the learner. In all the other cases the monolingual children, contrary to the general hypothesis proposed at the beginning, showed more modifications. The same can be seen in the discourse results below.

DISCOURSE

I next turn to an analysis of the conversational structure of these data at the sequence level. Sequences are defined as stretches of conversation which have a topic and purpose in common and which consist of a series of exchanges (Wells 1975). A sequence can be assigned a sequence mode, the dominant purpose of the sequence, and subsequence modes within the main purpose. The sequences used for the analysis are listed below with an example of each type.

TABLE 8-2 Distribution of Sentence-level Variables 1, 3, 4, 6, 9, 10, and 12 in Monolingual and Bilingual Foreigner Talk and Native Talk (n = 8)

Variable	*FT1, %*	*FT2, %*	χ^2	*df*	*p*
1. Number of clauses per S*					
1-clause Ss	86.6	79.4	6.875	1	p < .01
3. LUW†					
1-word utterances	19.5	15.4	11.651	3	p < .01
4. Subject const.‡					
1-word subjects	86.9	90.1	2.630	2	ns
6. Surface S types:					
Declarative	38.0	51.0			
Interrogative	18.7	16.2	27.446	3	p < .001
Imperative	9.6	7.8			
Moodless	33.7	25.1			
9. Attention-getting devices in % of utterances	5.8	2.9	6.729	1	p < .01
10. Vocatives in % of utterances	7.0	.8	35.229	1	p < .001
12. Nonimmediate reference of utterances	14.7	9.2	12.058	2	p < .01

	FT1	FT2
*Number of full clauses	424	394
†Number of utterances	830	718
‡Number of subjects	419	435

Variable	*NT1, %*	*NT2, %*	χ^2	*df*	*p*
1. Number of clauses per S*					
1-clause Ss	84.7	76.5	9.199	1	p < .01
3. LUW†					
1-word utterances	23.1	15.6	24.420	3	p < .001
4. Subject const.‡					
1-word subjects	92.7	94.0	.931	2	ns
6. Surface S types:					
Declarative	45.6	57.6			
Interrogative	16.4	11.0	30.055	3	p < .001
Imperative	4.6	5.6			
Moodless	33.4	25.8			
9. Attention-getting devices in % of utterances	.9	1.6	1.135	1	ns
10. Vocatives in % of utterances	1.1	1.1	.0000	1	ns
12. Nonimmediate reference of utterances	16.4	17.3	1.203	2	ns

	NT1	NT2
*Number of full clauses	430	493
†Number of utterances	799	892
‡Number of subjects	437	570

A. *Control* (influencing the other person's present or future behavior)	1. NS: Mishiko sing a song NS: Yeah NS: Come on then 2. NS: Let's do another one, right? NS: Oh well, is there another one on the back? NS: No NS: Have you got any other games? NS: Yes, but come on
B. *Representational* (exchange of information, discussion)	3. NS: I was going backwards as well! NS: Oh, it doesn't matter
C. *Tutorial* (didactic intent; the NS knows the learner's family and her relationship to the other two girls mentioned here; she seems to be rehearsing the sentence pattern and various types of relations)	4. NS: Is Kyoto your sister? NNS: No NS: Is Yoko your sister? NNS: No, no sister NS: Are Yoko and Kyoto friends? NNS: Yes NS: Are Yoko and Kyoto sisters? NNS: Yes NS: Are you cousins? NNS: No NS: No
D. *Expressive* (an affective, spontaneous response to a situation)	5. NNS: Nice, yes hahhaa yeeees NS: There we are, there we are right ummmm Ooooooh duddud that's right
E. *Play* (play with language, imitations, role play, play routines, etc.)	6. (language play) NS: Hello NNS: Goodbye NS: Thank you NNS: Goodbye NS: Hello, thank you, goodbye NNS: Goodbye NS: Hello 7. (role play) NS: "Do you think plaits'll look nice on her?" NS: "Yes" NS: You said anything NS: "Th . . . they might look nice" "I think they will, coz she's never had plaits before" NS: She said: Mummy, what are plaits? "Mummy, what are plaits?" NS: "Well darling" NS: It's the baby you're talking to now (tone not right) NS: "Darling, see" NS: "Yeah" NS: "Plaits are pretty patterns in your hair."

The subsequence modes are the same as listed above with an additional subsequence mode called procedural, where the channel of communication, checking comprehension, asking for clarification, etc., is of central importance (cf. Varonis and Gass 1985b and Gass and Varonis this volume for a similar construct). For instance, in the following examples the NS first introduces the topic, this utterance being in the procedural mode, and after her original request has to resort to clarifications or repetition on request:

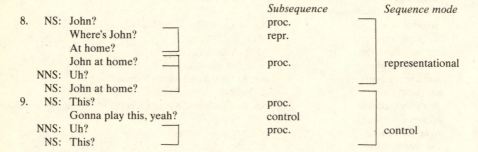

			Subsequence	*Sequence mode*
8.	NS:	John?	proc.	
		Where's John?	repr.	
		At home?		
		John at home?	proc.	representational
	NNS:	Uh?		
	NS:	John at home?		
9.	NS:	This?	proc.	
		Gonna play this, yeah?	control	
	NNS:	Uh?	proc.	control
	NS:	This?		

The breakdown of the types of sequences gives one a fairly good global picture of the types of conversations children were involved in. My hypothesis was that control, tutorial, and procedural sequences and subsequences would have a higher frequency of occurrence in FT. The native speaker may have to take charge and may resort to the use of control mode as a way of sustaining conversation. If there are any tutorial sequences at all, they can be expected to occur in FT. The more aware the native speaker is of his or her role as a foreigner talker, the more he or she can be expected to assume a teaching role. Procedural subsequences reflect the actual negotiation of meaning and the speaker's ability and/or willingness to give metalinguistic information, i.e., to clarify misunderstandings, to give and request clarification, to confirm, etc. (see, e.g., Schachter 1983b). Therefore, it can be expected that these sequences are more frequent in FT. Looking at the distribution of sequences, one finds these, and other, clear differences. The results are given in Table 8-3 for comparisons between FT and NT and between FT1 and FT2.

TABLE 8-3 Distribution of Utterances in the Sequence Modes in FT/NT and FT1/FT2

Sequence mode	*FT,* % (n = 16)	*NT,* % (n = 8)	*FT1,* % (n = 8)	*FT2,* % (n = 8)
Representational	32.7	39.5	36.6	28.0
Control	43.8	33.2	39.0	49.4
Tutorial	1.7	.0	3.2	.0
Expressive	6.7	4.6	7.0	6.3
Play	12.4	19.9	11.7	13.2
Unanalyzable	2.7	2.8	2.6	3.1

$\chi^2 = 93.513$, df = 5, $p < .001$; $\chi^2 = 42.247$, df = 5, $p < .001$

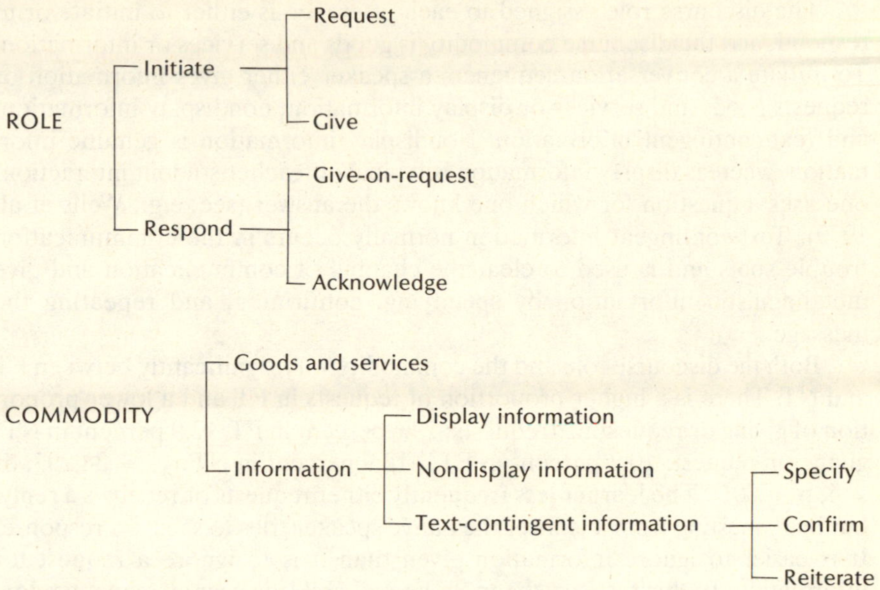

FIGURE 8-1 Discourse Role and Commodity Network

There are more utterances in control sequences and slightly more in expressive sequences in FT. As hypothesized, there are some tutorial sequences in FT and none at all in NT. The fact that there are more utterances in play sequences in NT probably reflects a very real difference between these two types of discourse. The time and space allocated to imaginative play talk in NT is not available in FT, because there are other concerns (the native speaker has to try harder to keep the channel of communication open). The proportions of utterances in various sequence modes do not vary significantly between NT1 and NT2 ($\chi^2 = 6.739$, df $= 4$) but do between FT1 and FT2. All the tutorial sequences occur in FT1 and there are slightly fewer play sequences in FT1. As far as these sequences go, monolingual children seem to adopt the role of a foreigner talker and/or teacher, although the differences are not great. On the other hand, they use considerably fewer control utterances and more representational utterances than the bilingual children. There are more utterances in procedural subsequences in FT1 (15.2 percent as opposed to 13.5 percent in FT2), but the difference is not significant.

It is beyond the scope of this chapter to discuss the exchange structure of the conversations in the different sequences. However, some indication can be given of the types of conversations the children were involved in by referring to the occurrence of the discourse role and commodity, which were noted for each utterance in addition to the sequence type. Figure 8-1 summarizes the choices available to the speakers (Wells et al. 1979).

The discourse role assigned to each utterance is either to initiate or to respond, and the discourse commodity is goods and services or information. To initiate a conversation/sequence, a speaker either gives information or requests goods and services or display information, nondisplay information, and text-contingent information. Nondisplay information is genuine information, whereas display information is typical of teacher-student interaction: one asks a question for which one knows the answer (see, e.g., Wells et al. 1979). Text-contingent information normally occurs in the communication trouble spots and is used to clear the channel of communication and give metalinguistic information by specifying, confirming, and repeating the message.

Both the discourse role and the commodity vary significantly between FT and NT. There is a higher proportion of requests in FT and a lower proportion of giving or requesting (requests: 29.6 percent in FT, 12.9 percent in NT; giving-on-request: 10.2 percent in FT1, 12.9 percent in NT; $\chi^2 = 34.297$, df $= 4$, $p < .001$). The learner less frequently either requests or receives a reply, but by requesting from a learner the native speaker tries to secure a response. It is easier to ignore information given than it is to ignore a request for information. In this respect, the monolingual children seem to show tendencies similar to those found in sentence-level modifications. Monolinguals modify the discourse role significantly more than bilinguals in the direction of observed FT modifications. There are more requests in FT1 (33.6 percent as opposed to 24.9 percent in FT2) and fewer utterances giving information or goods and services (46.5 percent in FT1 as opposed to 54.1 percent in FT2; $\chi^2 = 16.680$, df $= 4$, $p < .01$). However, the same differences can again be found in NT1 and NT2 ($\chi^2 = 18.685$, df $= 4$, $p < .01$).

The proportions of goods and services received or requested are slightly different in FT and NT, and there are significant differences in the occurrence of different types of information. The results for discourse commodity in FT/NT and FT1/FT2 are summarized in Table 8-4. There was no significant difference in this respect between NT1 and NT2 ($\chi^2 = 3.614$, df $= 5$).

TABLE 8-4 Distribution of Discourse Commodity in FT/NT and FT1/FT2

Discourse commodity	*FT, %* (n = 16)	*NT, %* (n = 8)	*FT1, %* (n = 8)	*FT2, %* (n = 8)
Goods and services	12.6	9.8	14.8	10.1
Nondisplay information	77.8	85.0	73.8	82.5
Display information	1.1	.1	2.0	.0
Text-contingent information:				
Specify	1.7	1.1	1.8	1.5
Confirm	1.7	1.6	1.7	1.7
Reiterate	5.1	2.4	5.9	4.2
	100.0	100.0	100.0	100.0
	$\chi^2 = 39.123$ df = 5 p < .001		$\chi^2 = 25.977$ df = 5 p < .01	

The proportion of nondisplay, genuine information is lower in FT and in FT1 when compared with NT and FT2. In FT, and especially in monolingual children's speech, there are more goods and services requested and given-on-request. Therefore, the possibilities for genuine information exchange are fewer. In addition, in FT1 there is more text-contingent information specifying, confirming, or reiterating previous information, i.e., metalinguistic information that may help the learner to acquire the second language. Although both mono- and bilinguals provide this kind of information, there is a tendency for monolinguals to provide more of it, especially as display information in tutorial sequences, as actual language practice.

MONOLINGUAL AND BILINGUAL FOREIGNER TALK

In addition to the FT/NT differences, one of the purposes of the present study was to determine whether monolinguals and bilinguals differed in their approach to communicating with learners. Some differences were found, but not in the hypothesized direction of greater modification on the part of the bilinguals. As was pointed out above, of the variables that differed between FT1 and FT2 the syntactic variables (number of clauses per S; length of utterance and distribution of surface S types) differed also between NT1 and NT2. Therefore, these features do not show foreigner talk modification; rather, they reflect the language of mono- and bilinguals in general. The interactional features (reference and attention-getting devices, including vocatives) and discourse features (see Table 8-4), on the other hand, show that monolingual and bilingual children behave differently in modifying their interaction, since these features do not differ between NT1 and NT2. Monolinguals seem to be more aware of a need to engage the learner's attention, secure a response by requesting rather than giving information or goods and services, and even teach the learner by asking for display information and providing models. It may be that monolingual children react this way because they are faced with a fairly new situation, whereas bilinguals are more familiar with the problems they are presented with and tend to treat the learners more like any other interlocutor. Contrary to my original hypothesis, they may see the learner as an equal rather than as a person who needs special attention. It may also be that bilingual children of this age have experienced situations where the people they converse with have been able to use either one of their languages and the same expectations are carried over to this situation: since they have English in common, at least this language should work. Since they know two languages, they may also expect the other child to be able to do the same.

CONCLUSION

On the basis of the results above we can conclude that children are able to modify their speech when talking to learners. Both sentence-level variables and the discourse structure seem to be modified in foreigner talk in order to make the speech more transparent and to sustain the conversation. In addition, it seems that monolingual and bilingual children behave differently when talking to learners. However, the original hypothesis had to be modified. These results indicate that monolinguals were more inclined than bilinguals to modify the interactional structure when talking to learners. The apparent syntactic modifications may be said to reflect the monolinguals' linguistic behavior in general, not modifications made as a response to the interlocutor's proficiency level. The result hardly means that bilinguals are worse or less skillful foreigner talkers. It may be that they select different ways of engaging learners in conversations, modifying the discourse rather than the surface syntactic structure. For example, the use of reference is modified in FT2 but not in FT1: the bilinguals use more immediate reference when talking to learners. This may indicate the different levels from which the native speaker can select modification strategies: the surface sentence structure where certain interactional characteristics of the discourse are realized, e.g., the use of vocatives, and the discourse structure as a whole (e.g., the use of reference). The bilinguals seem to prefer modifications at the level of discourse, whereas the monolinguals resort more to surface syntax strategies.

On the basis of these data one can say that both groups of children did modify their speech. The discourse features were more consistently modified. My subjective impression of the conversations was that the more the native speaker modified the interaction, the more successful he or she was in engaging the learner, even a virtual beginner, in this particular conversation, and probably would be successful in general in providing the learner with the kind of input he or she requires in order to acquire the L2. If this is the case, we would predict that learners engaged in certain types of conversations would develop differently.

9

TASK VARIATION AND NONNATIVE/NONNATIVE NEGOTIATION OF MEANING[1]

Susan M. Gass and Evangeline Marlos Varonis
University of Michigan

The investigation of nonnative speaker (NNS)-NNS discourse has been receiving attention of late (Doughty and Pica 1984, Long and Porter 1984, Porter 1983, Varonis and Gass 1985b). Since nonnative speakers of a language often spend a great deal of time talking with other NNSs, it seems reasonable to investigate the nature of these interactions. In particular, it is important to discover how these interactions may contribute to the process of second language acquisition.

In an earlier paper (Varonis and Gass 1985b) we introduced a model for the negotiation of meaning between two speakers, focusing specifically but not exclusively on how two NNSs negotiate difficulties in a conversation. In this chapter we extend our research, focusing on how differences in situational and/or social role may influence an interlocutor's behavior as a negotiator of meaning. We are interested in the language demands made on NNSs and the resultant differences in the negotiation of meaning as reflected by different communicative tasks. We focus on two types of interactions involving NNS dyads: (1) an interaction which involves the giving of information from only one participant to the other (this we call a one-way task) and (2) an interaction which involves exchanges of information—that is, exchanges in which both participants have information which must be shared in order to complete a given task, which we call a two-way task.

In this chapter we first review the relevant literature on NS-NNS interactions, including a discussion of the possible roles of comprehensible input and negotiation of meaning in second language acquisition. We then discuss a model we developed (Varonis and Gass 1985b) to describe NNS-NNS "nonunderstanding routines." Finally we present the results of a study we conducted investigating negotiations of meaning in one-way vs. two-way tasks involving NNS-NNS dyads.

Krashen (1980) has argued that in order for L2 acquisition to proceed, learners must be exposed to target language (TL) data which they can access. He calls this "comprehensible input." In other words, the development of interlanguage (IL) occurs by learners being exposed to TL syntax, lexis, phonology, discourse, etc., which is at a more advanced state than their current stage of IL but which is comprehensible to the learner.

Long (1983c, 1983d) distinguishes between modified input and modified interaction. The former has to do with speech directed at the NNS and includes shorter length of T units, fewer embeddings, and greater repetition of nouns and verbs, while the latter involves a modification of the conversational structure itself, including a greater number of confirmation checks, comprehension checks, self- and other repetitions, and so forth. Long (1983d: 138) further suggests that the use of strategies and tactics used by NSs in interactions with NNS "goes some way to making linguistic input comprehensible to the SL acquirer, as evidenced by the fact that without them communication . . . breaks down; with their use conversation is possible and is sustained. NNSs understand and so can take part appropriately." He further argues that input which is not comprehensible to the learner is of no useful purpose for acquisition. The question then is what are the ways that input becomes comprehensible to the learner? If it is not comprehensible, what can the learner do to make it so?

Scarcella and Higa (1981) focused their attention on conversations between NSs and (1) children and (2) adolescents, finding that there was a greater amount of simplified input to children but that the adolescents "worked" harder than the children at maintaining the conversation. Stevick (1976, 1980, 1981) claimed that for there to be successful communication, there must be involvement in the discourse. Active involvement is a necessary aspect of acquisition, since it is through involvement that the input becomes "charged" and "penetrates" deeply. Within this framework it is the hearer who "charges" the input. The adolescents in Scarcella and Higa's study received more "charged" input precisely because they were more involved in keeping the conversation going. The authors thus suggest that the "optimal" input is that input which comes as a result of negotiation work as opposed to that input which is only simplified.

In most conversations (regardless of whether the participants are native or nonnative), discourse progresses in a linear fashion. When the interlocutors share a common background and language, the turn-taking sequence is likely to proceed smoothly. However, not all conversations proceed without interruption. Jefferson (1972) introduced the term "side-sequence" to refer to a break from the main flow of conversation. In this chapter we deal with "negotiations of meaning" which refer specifically to those side sequences that are crucial to the success of the discourse because they let participants maintain as well as possible equal footing in the conversation. Equal footing refers to one interlocutor's ability to respond appropriately to another interlocutor's last utterance. In other words, interlocutors not only take turns when a turn becomes available but do so with full understanding of the preceding turn and its place in the discourse. When one or both interlocutors have "slipped," there is a need to regain their place in a conversation, and negotiation takes place. We refer to these negotiation exchanges as nonunderstanding routines which we operationally define as *those exchanges in which there is some overt indication that understanding between participants has not been complete.* We exclude from this definition exchanges that constitute a misunderstanding which goes unrecognized by interlocutors (cf. Varonis and Gass 1985a for an analysis of misunderstandings in NNS discourse). Below we present examples of nonunderstanding routines or, as we refer to them in this chapter, examples of "unaccepted input."

1. NNS1: My father now is retire.
   NNS2: retire?
   NNS1: yes
   NNS2: oh yeah
2. NNS1: This is your two term?
   NNS2: Pardon me?
   NNS1: Two term, this is this term is t term your two term?

Before turning to the specific study we report on in this chapter, we present a model for the negotiation of meaning which we developed and described in Varonis and Gass (1985b). Our model consists of four primes: (1) a trigger (T), which stimulates or invokes incomplete understanding on the part of the hearer; (2) an indicator (I), which is the hearer's signal that understanding has not been complete; (3) a response (R), which is the original speaker's attempt to clear up the unaccepted input (this is often referred to as a repair); and (4) a reaction to the response (RR), an optional element that signals either the hearer's acceptance or continued difficulty with the speaker's repair. The example in 1 above, which we repeat here, illustrates all these elements.

1. NNS1: My father now is retire—T
   NNS2: retire?—I
   NNS1: yes—R
   NNS2: oh yeah—RR

In Figure 9-1 we diagrammatically represent our model. Utterances described by this model may be viewed as a vertical break in the otherwise horizontal flow of a conversation, as schematized in 3 below.

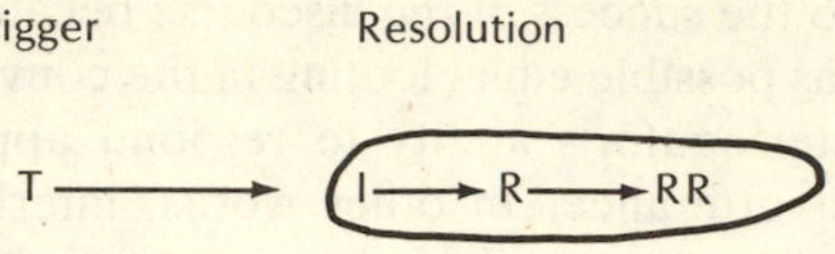

FIGURE 9-1 Proposed Model for "Unaccepted Input" Routines (from Varonis and Gass 1985)

3. NNS1: I'm living in Osaka
   NNS2: Osaka?
   NNS1: yeah
   NNS2: yeah Osaka, Osaka
   NNS1: What do you mean?
   NNS2: Osaka (Japanese word)
   NNS1: oh
   NNS2: I'm not really mean Osaka city. It's near city.
   NNS1: near city?

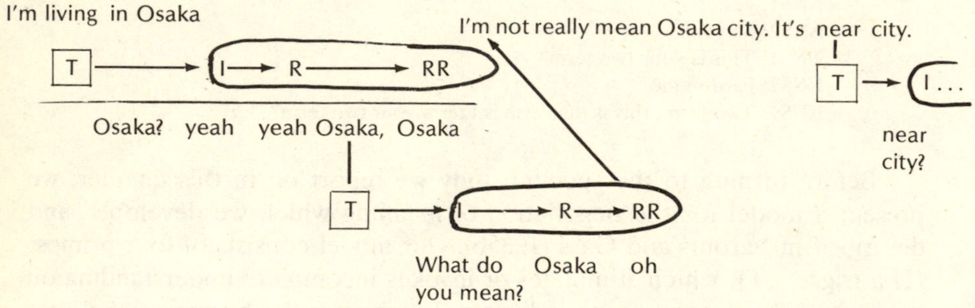

The T initiates a "pushdown" in the conversation, which continues until interlocutors have resolved the difficulty and "pop" back up to the main discourse. While the model was specifically designed to deal with unaccepted input in NNS-NNS discourse, we point out that it is applicable to a wider range of data (cf. Varonis and Gass 1985b for a fuller discussion).

In our earlier work we presented evidence that a greater amount of negotiation work was involved in discourse where both participants were NNSs than in discourse in which only one or none of the participants was a nonnative speaker. We argued that negotiation serves the function of providing the participants with a greater amount of comprehensible input. We further argued that conversations between NNSs allow participants a nonthreatening environment in which to ask for clarification of the other's message if it has not been entirely understood.

METHODOLOGY

In this chapter we continue our investigations into nonnative-nonnative discourse, specifically investigating exchanges in which one or both interlocutors hold information the other needs. Nine nonnative subjects participated in this study. All were intermediate-level students at the English Language Institute of the University of Michigan. There were four female and five male speakers. Four were native Spanish speakers, two were Arabic speakers, one was Korean and two were Japanese. From these nine speakers three dyads and one triad were set up. In each group there were no speakers of the same NL. Each group performed two tasks; we have classified one as a one-way task and the other as a two-way task. Two groups did the one-way task first followed by the two-way task, while the other two groups did the tasks in the reverse order.

In the one-way task one participant was given a picture to describe to an interlocutor without letting the interlocutor see it. The interlocutor's task was to attempt to draw it. After the picture was drawn to the satisfaction of the speaker, the task was repeated with a different picture and with the roles reversed. We should note that by one-way task we differ slightly from Long's use of the term in that there is some exchange between participants. That is, it is not exclusively one-way, as a lecture would be, but information flows *primarily* in one direction.

In the two-way task, group members listened to different tapes of an interview between a detective and two of four robbery suspects. For this part group members were in separate rooms. After completing a worksheet on the suspects' activities and alibis on the night of the robbery, the members of each group came together and exchanged the information they had heard to determine whose alibi did not hold up and hence who had committed the robbery. Each member of a group had information which the other member(s) lacked but needed in order to determine which of the four suspects had committed the robbery. For each task the first 10 minutes of each tape were transcribed and analyzed.

RESULTS

This section is divided into four parts. First, we discuss differences within the one-way task, in other words, the picture tasks. Second, we analyze the results of the two-way task, in other words, the robbery task. Third, we compare the two tasks, and finally, we look at male-female differences.

Before continuing we would like to make one further refinement to the model we have described above. We subdivide indicators into two types: those which we classify as indirect and those which are direct. Direct indicators directly express unaccepted input, leaving no doubt that there has been a lack of understanding. Such indicators are most often, although not always, expressed with a wh-word. See 4 for an example.

4. [Two-way task]
Female: Maid came to seven o'clock
Male: Who?

On the other hand, an indirect indicator is a more gentle means of indicating that comprehension has in some sense been incomplete. Such indicators often realized by echoing a word or phrase of the previous utterance. (See 1 above for an example of an indirect indicator.) A comprehensive list can be found in Varonis and Gass (1985b).

We now turn to an analysis of the data. The values presented in the remainder of this chapter have in some cases been adjusted to compensate for differences in time spent doing a task. In other words, in cases where a particular task did not take the full 10 minutes, values were adjusted accordingly. Furthermore, the results for one speaker in the triad were not calculated, since the role of the participants was a crucial factor in this study and unlike the other participants, her role remained constant for both parts of the one-way task.

One-way Task

The results of the picture tasks were analyzed with respect to three different independent variables, the dependent variable being the number of push-downs initiated, in other words, indicators used, to negotiate meaning. Overall, there were 84 indicators, or an average of 10.50 (S.D. = 12.55) per speaker, for the first picture, and 62 indicators or an average of 7.75 (S.D. = 11.45) for the second. Paired *t* tests yielded a nonsignificant difference. These results are given in Table 9-1.

Describing versus Drawing The lack of significant difference between the two picture tasks is perhaps misleading, since the roles of the participants differed in pictures 1 and 2. That is, at one time an individual received information (i.e., drew a picture) and at another he or she provided information (i.e., described a picture). The large standard deviations for the one-way task reflect the disparity. We have thus subdivided the results for pictures 1 and 2 to account for the effect of describing versus drawing, in other words,

TABLE 9-1 Mean Number of Indicators on One-way and Two-way Tasks

	$\bar{x}$	*S.D.*	
One-way			
Picture 1 n = 8	10.50	12.55	t = .97, ns
Picture 2 n = 8	7.75	11.45	
Two-way			
n = 8	7.63	5.93	
t test one-way vs. two-way, *t* = .91, ns			

giving versus receiving information. These results are given in Table 9-2. The person giving information had a mean of 1.00 indicator (S.D. = 1.16) per trial, while the person receiving information had a mean of 20.00 indicators (S.D. = 11.20) on picture 1 and 1.25 (S.D. = 1.50) and 14.25 (S.D. = 13.82), respectively, on picture 2. Thus, not surprisingly, the person who seeks information is much more likely to attempt to negotiate meaning than the person who holds the information. It is more revealing to look at the kinds of indicators used. We consider direct and indirect indications of nonunderstanding. For the first picture, they are evenly distributed for the describer, with an average of .50 (S.D. = 1.00) for each, while the drawer has more indirect indicators than direct, with averages of 15.50 (S.D. = 11.39) and 4.5 (S.D. = 2.38), respectively.[2] Similarly, in the second picture, the indirect and direct indicators are relatively evenly distributed for the person providing information [.50 (S.D. = 1.00) and .75 (S.D. = .96) respectively], but the person receiving information, the drawer, has more indirect indicators ($\bar{x}$ = 12.25, S.D. = 13.60) than direct ($\bar{x}$ = 2.25, S.D. = .96).

TABLE 9-2 Mean Number of Indicators for One-way Task

	Picture 1		*Picture 2*	
	Information giver (describer) n = 4	*Information receiver (drawer)* n = 4	*Information giver (describer)* n = 4	*Information receiver (drawer)* n = 4
$\bar{x}$	1.00	20.00	1.25	14.25
S.D.	1.16	11.20	1.50	13.82
Direct				
$\bar{x}$	.50	4.50	.50	2.25
S.D.	1.00	2.38	1.00	.96
Indirect				
$\bar{x}$	.50	15.50	.75	12.25
S.D.	1.00	11.39	.96	13.60

While the difference between describer and drawer is in the same direction for both pictures, the degree of difference is smaller for the second picture. The results are graphed in Figure 9-2. In Figure 9-3 are graphed the overall results of direct vs. indirect indicators per picture. As can be seen, there is a small tendency for both direct and indirect indicators to decrease in the second trial.

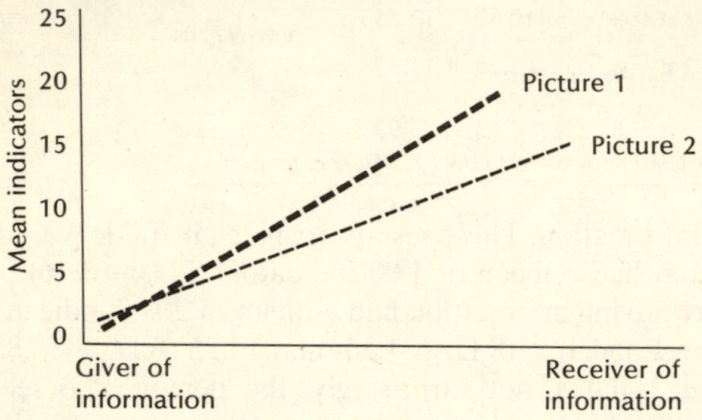

FIGURE 9-2 Mean Number of Indicators for Pictures 1 and 2; Giver vs. Receiver of Information

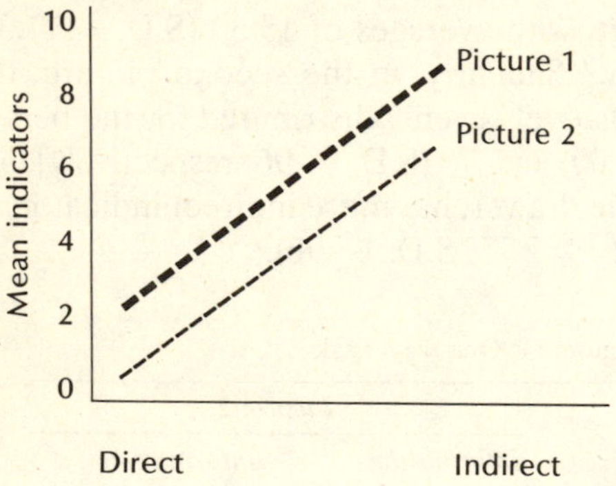

FIGURE 9-3 Mean Number of Direct and Indirect Indicators for Pictures 1 and 2

Two-way Task

Results were analyzed as for the one-way task, with number of indicators being the dependent variable. There were a total of 61 indicators for an average of 7.63 (S.D. = 5.93) per speaker. These results are included in Table 9-1.

Direct versus Indirect In Table 9-3 are the results for the kind of indicators used. As with the one-way tasks, there were more indirect (51, $\bar{x}$ = 5.63, S.D. = 6.16) than direct indicators (10, $\bar{x}$ = 1.25, S.D. = 1.58). The results of a paired t test yield a significant difference ($t = 2.04$, df $= 7$, $p < .05$, one-tail).

TABLE 9-3 Mean Number of Indicators for Two-way Task

	n = 8		
	Direct	*Indirect*	
$\bar{x}$	1.25	5.63	$t = 2.04$, df $= 7$, $p < .05$, one-tail
S.D.	1.58	6.16	

One-way Versus Two-way Tasks

The results for the comparison of the two tasks are given in Table 9-4. A comparison of the number of indicators for the two tasks is not significant (see Table 9-1). Looking at the number of direct versus indirect indicators, we see that there is a slight tendency for the average in both cases to be greater on the one-way task [direct: $\bar{x} = 2.00$, S.D. $= 1.07$ (one-way) vs. $\bar{x} = 1.25$, S.D. $= 1.58$ (two-way) and indirect: $\bar{x} = 7.38$, S.D. $= 5.91$ (one-way) vs. $\bar{x} = 5.88$, S.D. $= 6.38$ (two-way)]. A X^2 yields a nonsignificant result.

TABLE 9-4 A Comparison of Indicators on One-way versus Two-way Tasks

	One-way (n = 8)		*Two-way* (n = 8)	
	Direct	*Indirect*	*Direct*	*Indirect*
$\bar{x}$	2.00	7.38	1.25	5.88
S.D.	1.07	5.91	1.58	6.38

Sex Differences

The final difference we note in this chapter is that of sex differences. It is important to remember that this study was not specifically designed to investigate sex as a variable. However, an interesting finding is the quantity and quality of indicators used by men versus women. Men used more indicators than women across all conditions (men: $\bar{x} = 31.00$, S.D. $= 20.48$ and women: $\bar{x} = 18$, S.D. $= 6.24$). A second point regarding male-female differences has to do with the kind of indicators used. For this we looked at the proportion of direct indicators to the total number of indicators used. On both one-way tasks men had a greater proportion of direct indicators than the women (20 percent male to 17 percent female on the first and 14 percent male to 10 percent female on the second). On the two-way task there was a greater balance (15.9 percent male to 16.6 percent female).

DISCUSSION

In this section we frame our results within the context of nonnative interactions. We noted above that in general on the one-way task there were fewer negotiations on the second drawing than on the first. While this is clearly a trend, the difference is not significant. However, the direction of the difference suggests that task familiarity is an important issue (see Gass and Varonis 1984 for a discussion of the role of familiarity in comprehending NN speech). Because this difference exists for the drawer but not for the describer, it is possible that the drawer of the second picture has a more expanded mental set, having become familiar with the task from the previous trial. Alternatively, there may be greater cooperation between the participants, hence less need for negotiation. Again, this does not compensate for the general need to negotiate.

The second point to consider is the difference noted between the drawer and the describer in terms of who uses more indicators, that is, who initiates the negotiation of meaning. On both the first and second drawing tasks, the drawer had significantly more indicators than the describer. This is not surprising, since it is the drawer who has the most urgent need to ensure that comprehension has taken place. What is perhaps more interesting is the kinds of indicators that were used. While the number of indicators decreased from the first one-way task to the second, there were differences noted in the kinds of indicators used by describer and drawer as a function of time. The former used an equal number of direct and indirect, while the latter used a greater number of indirect indicators to mark unaccepted input. This may be due to the fact that the person who is describing the picture has a more pressing need to gain information in order to respond appropriately. In other words, the describer has a more limited set of expectations of what the drawer can say since the drawer is bound by what the describer has already said. When the drawer's response appears to be outside of the range of the describer's expectations, the describer has the responsibility of bringing the drawer back on track. The most efficient way to accomplish this is by direct questioning. This need to "get back on track" counterbalances the general tendency for speakers to use an indirect means of indicating incomplete understanding.

Long (1983c) found a greater amount of modified interaction in two-way tasks as opposed to one-way tasks. Modified interaction, he predicts, leads to a greater amount of comprehensible input, which in turn leads to greater acquisition. This study indirectly relates to Long's work in that it considers only a subset of what he refers to as modified interaction, that is, overt negotiation of meaning. As mentioned above, we further differ from Long in that what we have been referring to as a one-way task is in a sense less one-way than his one-way, his one way being (1) vicarious narrative, (2) giving instructions, and (3) expressing an opinion. Nonetheless, our results do not support his prediction: there is no significant difference between the number of indicators on one-way tasks and on two-way tasks. A possible explanation to account for this discrepancy concerns shared assumptions. Since we are concerned with areas in which comprehension has either completely or partially broken down, there is less of an opportunity for breakdown in the two-way task since there is greater shared background in that task than there is on the one-way task. That is, there is a shared set of assumptions in the crime task, but not in the one-way task. Further support for this comes from the fact that there is a decrease in number of indicators as a function of shared experience on the one-way task. That is, there is an inverse relationship between instances of indicators and amount of shared background. The greater the shared set of assumptions, the less need for negotiation. Thus the kind of information exchange is *not* the only determining factor of modified interaction. The kind of task interacts with the amount of shared background that the participants bring to the task.

Doughty and Pica (1984) present results from NNS–NNS interactions that support Long's predictions. They prefer to characterize the difference in exchange type as being a difference in *required* versus *optional* information exchange. Nonetheless, there is a methodological issue that must be kept in mind lest we attempt to compare noncomparable results. The task used in the Doughty and Pica study is more similar to our one-way task than to our two-way task, yet it is characterized as a required information exchange. Thus it is not clear how their results compare with Long's or with those of the present study. Furthermore, because our one-way task is less one-way than Long's one-way task, it is not clear how our results compare with his. We suggest that the amount of information exchange required by a given task is a continuous rather than a dichotomous variable. This, of course, makes comparison a complex process.

There is yet another interesting difference between the task type used in various studies which makes comparison an even more complex issue. Various media are used in the tasks. For example, in the study reported on in this chapter the one-way task required subjects to go from linguistic input to pencil-and-paper (drawing) output, while the two-way task involved language input *and* output. On the other hand, the Doughty and Pica task required subjects to go from linguistic input to object-manipulation output. These differences may further complicate the process of comparison and leave us with a murky picture of distinctions between one-way and two-way tasks. Future research in this area must control for input/output medium in addition to considering carefully the amount and type of information exchange.

Looking at differences between male and female participants, we again point out that this study was not designed with that variable in mind. Yet, in analyzing the data, we could not help but note some interesting differences.

In general, men signal unaccepted input more often than women. This suggests that initially women, at least in interactions with men, feel less confident in indicating a lack of understanding. One could, of course, argue that they understood more and did not have a need to negotiate meaning. Within the limits of this study, it is impossible to determine which of these interpretations, or yet another, might be correct. With regard to the kind of indicators used, as we discussed earlier, the amount of shared background might mitigate against the dominant effect of the greater proportion of direct indicators for men.

CONCLUSION

In conclusion, this chapter extends the investigation of the negotiation of meaning that we presented in Varonis and Gass (1985b). Specifically, we found that: (1) interlocutors use more indications of "unaccepted input" when the conversation is focused on a one-way as opposed to two-way flow of information; (2) the *role* of the interlocutor is highly important, with the recipient of information using far more indications of unaccepted input than the giver; (3) the *form* of the indicator is also important, with interlocutors using more indirect than direct means of expressing nonunderstanding; (4) the factors of role and form *interact;* (5) *familiarity* with a particular task (including familiarity with interlocutors) decreases but does not totally compensate for the need to negotiate meaning; and (6) the social variable of *sex* is potentially very important, with women using fewer indications of unaccepted input than men.

Although Crymes and Potter (1981) conclude that native and nonnative participants "did not make very extensive use of questions to pursue understanding," we suggest that interlocutors may pursue understanding by strategies that may or may not take the form of questions. In other words, an indication of nonunderstanding may take a variety of forms. It is the *function* that is crucial. The types of indicators that we have been investigating have the function of initiating pushdowns from the discourse that enable hearers to confirm or reject a hypothesis about the meaning of the linguistic input that they have just received. Candlin (1981) suggests "speaker intent and hearer uptake are two ends of a cline"; when the hearer does not uptake what the speaker intends, the need for negotiation is critical if the conversation is to proceed smoothly, in both linguistic and social terms.

What purpose, then, does negotiation work serve? Following the suggestions of Stevick (1976, 1980, 1981) and Scarcella and Higa (1981), we offer that negotiation is a *positive* variable in interaction because it allows interlocutors to manipulate input. This manipulation is desirable for two reasons: (1) it allows the conversation to proceed with a minimum of confusion; and (2) it allows the nonnative speaker the opportunity to, in Stevick's terms, "charge" the input by actively working on it.

Long (1983a & b) has suggested that input becomes comprehensible through the speech modifications of native speakers addressing nonnatives. We would like to extend that idea by placing more responsibility on the nonnative: a nonnative, whether in interaction with a native or nonnative speaker, may *make* input comprehensible by signaling that it has not been accepted, thus initiating a nonunderstanding routine. Such routines, while interrupting the main flow of discourse, are a very important part of conversations involving nonnatives because they make previously unaccepted input comprehensible, thus facilitating acquisition.

An important area for future investigation is the interaction between comprehensible input and comprehensible output (Swain, this volume). Swain argues that it is not comprehensible input that is necessary for L2 acquisition, but the opportunity for NNSs to make their own speech, or output, comprehensible to interlocutors. We suggest that both, at the very least, facilitate acquisition, and propose that it is precisely NNS-NNS pairs that offer NNSs the greatest opportunity to receive comprehensible input and produce comprehensible output through negotiation.

NOTES

1. We would like to thank Josh Ard, Carolyn Madden, and Orestes Varonis for helpful comments on an earlier version of this chapter. We are also grateful to Ken Guire of the University of Michigan Statistical Research Laboratory for patient discussions on the use of statistics. The order of names does not imply a greater or lesser contribution of the authors. Rather, it reflects our commitment to alternate names on our ongoing research.

2. No statistical analyses are done in those instances where n = 4. Given the small sample size, it is difficult to justify an assumption of normality in order to do a *t*-test analysis. Other measures also seem inappropriate.

10

IS AN "APPROPRIATE RESPONSE" ALWAYS SO APPROPRIATE?

Barbara Hawkins[1]
University of California, Los Angeles

The question of comprehension in foreigner-talk discourse (FTD) is a vital one if we are to understand how foreigner-talk (FT) functions in relation to second language acquisition (SLA). Two suggested functions of FT are that it promotes communication and that it acts as an implicit teaching mode (Hatch 1983a). Presumably, these functions are based on the idea that FT is a simplified register of speech that allows learners to gain entry to native-speaker (NS) speech at their levels of competency; it allows them to *comprehend* speech that would otherwise be beyond their linguistic competency. If we are to find out *how* this comprehension comes about, the first step is to know exactly *what* is comprehended.

In studies that have examined data from FTD, the explicit or implicit assumption in the methodology that has been used to determine comprehension on the part of the nonnative speaker (NNS) has been the criterion of "appropriate response." Comprehension is assumed to have occurred if the learner's response is appropriate in the context of the surrounding discourse. Long (1981c) clearly states the nature of the assumption:

> One assumption is made in this reasoning. It is that one can recognize what is comprehensible input from the learner's perspective. In general, spontaneous NS-NS interaction among educated adults talking informally and at normal speed will be incomprehensible to an elementary level student of English as a second language. Conversely, NS speech addressed to the same learner which is marked by the modifications associated with FTD *and which is responded to*

appropriately by the learner, will be assumed to have been comprehensible input. This does not guarantee, of course, that all of the input is understood, simply that enough of it for the purpose of communication is, which means that the researcher will be operating with some margin of error. (p. 137; emphasis in original)

This chapter examines the "margin of error" by looking at whether or not the assumptions made about comprehension are valid. More specifically, we are asking whether what is determined to be comprehensible input to the learner is truly comprehensible according to the criterion of "appropriate response."

METHOD

Subjects

There were four adult subjects in this study: two native Spanish speakers and two native English speakers. One of the Spanish speakers was male and one was female, and the same was true of the English speakers. The four subjects were paired such that they formed two sets of subjects, each set consisting of one native Spanish speaker and one native English speaker. The women were paired with each other, forming one set, and the men were paired with each other to form the other set. The native English speakers were the native speakers (NSs) for this study, and for all practical purposes were monolingual English speakers. The native Spanish speakers were ESL learners, and were the nonnative speakers (NNSs) for the study. Both NNSs had been living in the United States for an extended period at the time of the data collection. NNS1 had been living in Los Angeles for approximately 4 years and had had 6 weeks of formal English classes at an adult school when she first moved to the United States. These were night classes that met 4 days a week for an hour a day. Other than this meager formal exposure to English, her contact with native English speakers had been very limited. NNS2 had been in the United States for about 2 years, and he had had no formal instruction in English.

Communication Tasks

Both sets of subjects performed four communication tasks designed beforehand by the investigator. The tasks were designed such that both the NNSs and the NSs would be in possession of information needed by their respective partners in order to complete the tasks. In Long's (1980) terms, they were "+ information exchange" tasks. Only the two tasks which appear in the data samples in this paper will be described.

The "Grab Bag" Game For this game, there was a small bag containing various common objects: a key, a plastic knife, a piece of ribbon, a small calendar, an eraser, a playing card, a penny, and a piece of chewing gum. The subjects took turns drawing an item from the bag, being careful not to look in the bag and not to let the other person see the object they had drawn. Once a person had drawn an object, it was the other person's task to discover the identity of the object by asking questions about it. The game proceeded until each person had drawn three objects.

The "Story Telling" Game These games consisted of two "stories" composed of two sets of cartoons without words. The subjects played first with one set and then with the other.

The frames of each cartoon were cut up and individually put on cards. One cartoon had six frames, and the other eight. The cards were then mixed up and put in an envelope. Each player took turns drawing cards until all were gone. Once each player had an equal number of cards, they had to do the following in order to complete the task:

1. Describe the pictures they each had to the other person.
2. Decide the order in which the pictures went, according to each other's descriptions. (These first two steps were completed without seeing each other's pictures.)
3. Expose the cards by putting them out in the order upon which they had agreed in step 2.
4. Discuss and agree upon a final order, using numbers on the back of each card to verify their final decision.
5. Tell—first one subject and then the other—the story contained in the cartoon, while looking at the complete cartoon set and describing each frame in it.

The "Squiggle" Game For this game, there were two sets of squiggles, each set consisting of two identical squiggles. The subjects performed the task twice, once with one set of squiggles and then with the other set. (See Figure 10-1 for copies of the squiggles.)

For the first round, one subject made a picture from the squiggle, being careful not to let the other subject see what he or she was drawing. This person then had to describe the squiggle to his or her partner so that he or she could accurately draw it. When they were finished, the subjects showed their pictures to each other to see how close they had come to duplicating the original picture.

The task was repeated a second time, this time with the roles reversed. That is, the person who had tried to duplicate the picture the first time, this time had to draw a picture and describe it to the other person.

The "Matching Pictures" Game Each player received a chart which was divided into nine squares. Within each square there was a picture. Both subjects had the same pictures, although in different squares. Without looking at each other's charts, each subject had to:

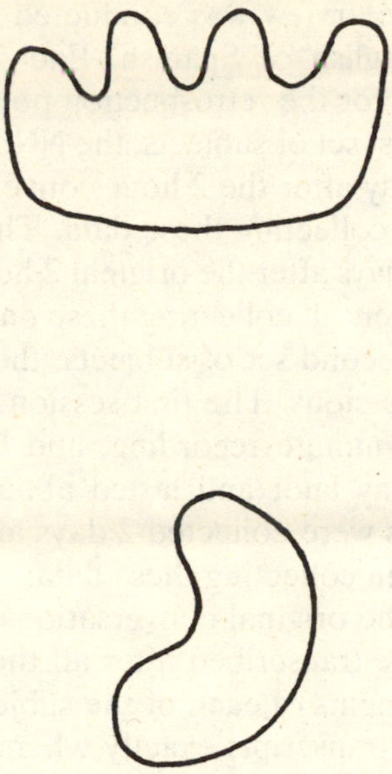

FIGURE 10-1 Squiggles used in the "Squiggle Game"

1. Describe which picture was in which square on his or her own chart.
2. After completing step 1, tell the other person what the other person had in each square.

The results from the squiggle and the matching picture games are not specifically discussed in the next section, although they are included in the analysis of the results.

Procedure

The data for this study include the recordings from (1) a 2-hour conversation between the first set of subjects, (2) a 1 hour and 15 minute conversation between the second set of subjects, and (3) retrospection comments by all subjects about their respective conversations.

The retrospection data were collected from the subjects by a procedure used by McCleary (1980) (cf. also Erickson 1975). The tapes of the original conversations were played back to the subjects and they were asked to "stop the recorder at any time and comment on what you were thinking at that point in the conversation." The investigator also felt free to stop the recorder and ask questions of the subjects if the subjects themselves did not stop the recorder. In the meantime, a second recorder was left on, recording both the conversation and the retrospection comments.

The retrospection interview was conducted in the native languages of each subject, either English or Spanish. Each of the four subjects was interviewed individually for the retrospection portion of the study.

In the case of the first set of subjects, the NNS's retrospection comments were all collected the day after the 2-hour conversation took place. A total of 3 hours was spent in collecting these data. The NS's retrospection comments were collected 2 days after the original 2-hour conversation. Similarly, a total of 3 hours was spent in collecting these data.

In the case of the second set of subjects, the NNS's retrospection data were collected in two sessions. The first session was immediately after the original 1 hour and 15 minute recording, and lasted about 2 hours. The second session was a day later and lasted about another hour. The NS's retrospection comments were collected 2 days after the original recording, and 2 hours were spent in collecting these data.

The recordings of the original conversations and the subsequent retrospection comments were transcribed after all the data had been collected. The retrospection comments of each of the subjects were then transcribed, marking in the original transcripts exactly where each comment occurred. The Spanish comments were then translated into English. The transcription and translation were done by the investigator.

Display of the Data

The data from this study are displayed in numbered charts consisting of seven categories; these categories head columns across the top of the charts. I will use four charts from the study. Since they all follow the same format, I will explain this format with reference to the first chart.

The first category, "transcript excerpt," includes the excerpt from the transcript that is being examined. NNS speech is denoted in three ways: it is indented, it is written in normal script (using lower- and uppercase lettering), and it is marked "NNS." In contrast, NS speech is not indented, is written entirely in uppercase lettering, and is marked "NS." Finally, each excerpt being examined is numbered according to tape number, side of tape and transcript page number.

The second and third categories, "mechanism" and "topic category," display the discourse analysis of the data. For the discourse analysis procedure, the investigator relied heavily on Hatch (1978), Peck (1978), and Hawkins (1981, 1982) for the basic display of the data and for the categorization of topics and mechanisms included in the analysis. From this discourse analysis, the responses being examined are judged for appropriateness.

The fourth category is "appropriate response = comprehension?" ("AR = C?"). This category refers to the research question being addressed in this paper: "Is what is determined to be comprehensible to the learner truly comprehensible input according to the criterion of 'appropriate response'?" Responses are judged to be appropriate according to the analysis performed in the first three columns of the charts. The question of whether these responses signal comprehension or not is answered by reference to the "retrospection" column, the last column on the charts.

The fifth column is headed "benefit." Listed in this column are the features of foreigner talk which may result in benefits to the learner, drawing on Hatch's original list (1983a). The first time a feature is noted, the feature as well as the benefit will appear. Thereafter, only the benefit will appear.

The sixth column is labeled "NNS Strategy/NS Response." Both the strategies and responses have been arrived at based on Tarone's list of communication strategies (1981), the discourse analysis in the first three columns, and the retrospection comments in the last column.

The final column, "retrospection," contains the retrospection comments of the speakers about the particular transcript excerpt being examined. Once again, the NS's comments will be entirely in uppercase lettering, while the NNS's will be in normal lettering. The researcher's comments/questions will take whichever form is in contrast to the subjects, either the NS or the NNS; that is, in representing speaking with the NS, the researcher's comments will be in normal lettering; in representing speaking with the NNS, the researcher's comments will be in uppercase lettering. All of the NNS comments will be *lettered,* and will coincide with letters which appear in the "transcript excerpt" column, marking exactly where the comment occurred. All of the NS comments will be *numbered,* coinciding with the numbers which appear in the "transcript excerpt" column, likewise marking exactly where the comment occurred.

DATA ANALYSIS

The data analysis for this study was performed on the complete set of transcripts for both sets of speakers. Since it is impossible to present the detailed analysis of the complete set of transcripts in this chapter, however, two samples from the transcripts have been chosen to illustrate the method of analysis, one from each set of speakers. The rationale behind the selection of these two samples included three basic guidelines:

1. The samples allow one to see the flow of discourse.
2. The samples highlight the research question.
3. The richness of the retrospection data gives particular insight into the research question.

The samples presented here will include three excerpts; one excerpt is from the first set of speakers, and two closely related excerpts are from the second set of speakers. The data analysis will proceed with reference to numbered charts containing the excerpts, which will be introduced in the order discussed. The excerpts will first be described so as to provide the proper background as to what was occurring in the conversation during the excerpts. The excerpts will then be related to the research question. Following the analysis, there will be a short summary of the findings with respect to the research question and the data presented here for analysis. An expansion of these findings, which will include the results of the complete data analysis, will be presented in the following section.

NS1 and NNS1

The first excerpt is presented in charts 10-1a and 10-1b. Chart 10-1a represents what was happening in the conversation from the NS's point of view. Chart 10-1b represents what was happening from the NNS's point of view. At this point in the conversation, the NS had drawn a plastic knife from the "Grab Bag," and the NNS is trying to guess what it is.

In chart 10-1a, the excerpt begins with the NNS asking the NS for a clue. After the NS tells her that the object is used when eating, the NNS guesses that the object is a spoon. The NS tells her "No," but that she was "close." The NS thinks that the NNS has understood "close," at least in a general way. She proceeds to offer more help, when the NNS tells her that she doesn't know the name of the object. Ignoring this for a moment, the NS gives another clue—the object is used to "cut" with. The NNS persists in telling the NS that she doesn't know the name of the object. The NS listens this time and accepts the NNS's problem. From the retrospection comments, we can see that she thinks that the NNS, although she knew the object was a knife, couldn't think of the name at that moment. Finally, the NS asks the NNS if she "gives up," to which the NNS replies, "Yes." The NS then tells the NNS what she has.

Unbeknownst to the NS, something entirely different has transpired. Turning to chart 1b, we can see that the word "close" was interpreted as "clothes" by the NNS. This makes her think that the item in question was a table cloth, and the rest of the excerpt is her attempt to tell the NS that, although she knows the object is a table cloth, she doesn't know the word for it in English. The NNS interprets the NS's following clues in light of what she is thinking—that the object is a table cloth. When the NS tells her that the object is used to "cut" with, the NNS understands her to ask if she "caught" the clue. So far as she is concerned, the NNS "knew" what the object was several exchanges earlier, and her problem is to get the NS to realize her predicament of not knowing the word in English. The NNS is surprised to find out that the object is a knife, a word she knew all along in English.

Without looking at the retrospection comments, it would appear that there were three appropriate responses that signaled comprehension, when in fact, none of the three signaled comprehension.

NS2 and NNS2

The next two charts—charts 10-2 and 10-3—contain two excerpts. The first one is a long excerpt that centers mostly around the NS trying to explain the word "help" to the NNS. The second excerpt presents another round with the word "help." The subjects are involved in the first "Story Telling" game, and specifically, the NS is trying to describe his pictures to the NNS.

The conversation proceeds fairly well until the NS mentions that one man is looking for another man to "help" him with his car. At this point, the NNS echoes "help" and asks, in Spanish, what it means. The NS asks the NNS if he understands, to which the NNS responds by echoing "help" a second time and by saying "no" to indicate that this is the word that he doesn't understand. The NS understands him to say "car." The NNS says "car, yeah," meaning that the word is understood. He then echoes "help" a third time. Finally, the NS echoes "help" and seems to have identified the problem. The NNS echoes "help" a fourth time, and this time the NS finally engages in what he thinks is a clarification process. Just as he begins, the NNS thinks that he has understood the word and says "up." The NS tells him "no," that the word is not "up," but "help." He repeats the word twice and then continues with his clarification process. In trying to clarify the meaning, the NS circumlocutes by giving an example of when "help" is used. In doing so, he introduces the word "water," which is echoed by the NNS. The NS responds with noises (and gestures), the purpose of which is to demonstrate someone drowning and calling for help. As the excerpt continues in chart 10-3, the NS checks to see that the NNS understands, and when he answers affirmatively, the NS continues with the task at hand.

In the meantime, the NNS is lost, as the retrospection comments show. The problem begins when the NS gives his example to "clarify" the meaning of "help" and starts talking about "water." The NNS did not realize that the NS was giving an example of when "help" is used, and thinks he is continuing to describe his pictures. Because the NNS has his set of pictures to look at, and one of them shows a man looking at a smoking car, he figures that "Help! Help!" must be a way of shouting for water. The result is that the excerpt includes six appropriate responses, only two of which signal comprehension. In addition, the two appropriate responses that do signal comprehension are actually the same response.

The second excerpt in chart 10-3 is closely related to the first and presents more data centering around the word "help." Both subjects have finished describing their pictures, and the NS is reviewing the order in which they go. During the course of the excerpt, the NNS echoes "help" (or "for

TRANSCRIPT EXCERPT	MECHANISM	TOPIC CATEGORY	AR:C?	BENEFIT	NNS STRATEGY/NS RESPONSE	RETROSPECTION
2/1/13 NNS. ... Some word you need. ... (Give it to me.)		TOPIC NOMINATION				
NS. OKAY, UHM, ... YOU, UHM ... —WHEN YOU EAT YOU USE IT. (1)		TOPIC IDENTIFICATION & CONTINUATION				(1) NS. SHE DIDN'T USE THE WORD "CLUE" OR ANYTHING, BUT I KNEW WHAT SHE MEANT
NNS. Uh-hm. ((Yes)) ... Spoon?		TOPIC CONCLUSION; TOPIC NOMINATION (VIA TOPIC CHANGE)				(A) NNS. I understood "clothes"; I thought she meant something made of cloth. So, I was thinking of "table cloth", and I didn't know how to say it.
NS. NO. ... CLOSE!		TOPIC CONCLUSION				
NNS. Close. (A) (2)	FOCUS + PROSODIC SHIFT				ECHO/NO EFFECT	(2) NS. (RE. "CLOSE") I THINK BECAUSE I GAVE HER A POSITIVE RESPONSE, SHE KNEW IT WAS NEARER TO THE RIGHT ANSWER. BUT THE WORD, I'M NOT SURE SHE UNDERSTOOD.
NS. WHAT ELSE DO YOU EAT WITH?		TOPIC NOMINATION				
NNS. ... Yes, but I don't know ...	TOPIC RELEVANT RESPONSE	TOPIC "IDENTIFICATION" AND CONTINUATION	NO.			
NS. AH!						
NNS. —the name ... (use it). (B)						(B) NNS. I was thinking of "table cloth", but I didn't know the word in English.
NS. ... WHEN YOU CUT. (C)		TOPIC NOMINATION		EXTRA VOLUME		(C) NNS. (RE. "CUT") Like if I had "captured" what she said; if I was sure.
NNS. Yes! ... But I don't know //the name ((laugh))//	TOPIC RELEVANT RESPONSE	TOPIC "IDENTIFICATION"; TOPIC CONCLUSION; TOPIC-NOMINATION	NO			
NS. //((laugh))//						
NNS. Yes!		TOPIC CONTINUATION (& CLARIFICATION?)				
NS. YOU DON'T KNOW THE NAME? (3)	REPETITION; MEANING CHECK					(3) NS. I JUST THOUGHT SHE COULDN'T THINK OF THE WORD. SHE KNEW IT WAS A KNIFE, BUT COULDN'T THINK OF IT.
NNS. No.	TOPIC RELEVANT RESPONSE					
NS. OKAY. ... YOU GIVE UP? ((laugh)) (D)		TOPIC CONCLUSION; TOPIC NOMINATION				(D) NNS. (RE. "GIVE UP") I wasn't real sure of the whole sentence, but, yes, I knew what she meant. There are some things it's not necessary to know real, real well. You understand from all the words together. I supposed she was telling me this—she'd take the thing out of the bag and I'd tell her it.
NNS. ((laugh)) Yes.	TOPIC RELEVANT RESPONSE	TOPIC "IDENTIFICATION"	NO			
NS. OKAY. ... IT'S A KNIFE.		TOPIC CONCLUSION TOPIC NOMINATION				
NNS. The knife. (E)	BASIC FOCUS	TOPIC IDENTIFICATION; TOPIC CONTINUATION	YES			(E) RES. WHEN SHE SHOWED YOU THE KNIFE, WHAT DID YOU THINK? NNS. I could never guess that that was what it was. RES. DID YOU KNOW HOW TO SAY "KNIFE" IN ENGLISH? NNS. Yes.

Chart 10-1a

TRANSCRIPT EXCERPT	MECHANISM	TOPIC CATEGORY	AR:C?	BENEFIT	NNS STRATEGY/NS RESPONSE	RETROSPECTION
2/1/13						(1) NS. SHE DIDN'T USE THE WORD "CLUE" OR ANYTHING, BUT I KNEW WHAT SHE MEANT.
NNS. ... Some word you need. ... (Give it to me.)		TOPIC NOMINATION				
NS. OKAY, UHM, ... YOU, UHM... WHEN YOU EAT YOU USE IT. (1)		TOPIC IDENTIFICATION & CONTINUATION.				(A) NNS. I understood "clothes"; I thought she meant something made of cloth. So, I was thinking of "table cloth", and I didn't know how to say it.
NNS. Uh-hm. ((yes))... Spoon?		TOPIC CONCLUSION; TOPIC NOMINATION (VIA TOPIC CHANGE)				
NS. NO. ... CLOSE!		TOPIC CONCLUSION; TOPIC NOMINATION (VIA TOPIC CHANGE)				
NNS. Close. (A) (2)	FOCUS + PROSODIC SHIFT					(2) NS. (RE. "CLOSE") I THINK BECAUSE I GAVE HER A POSITIVE RESPONSE, SHE KNEW IT WAS NEARER TO THE RIGHT ANSWER. BUT THE WORD, I'M NOT SURE SHE UNDERSTOOD.
NS. WHAT ELSE DO YOU EAT WITH?		TOPIC CONTINUATION				
NNS. ... Yes, but I don't know ...	TOPIC RELEVANT RESPONSE	TOPIC NOMINATION (VIA TOPIC CHANGE)	"YES"			
NS. AH!						
NNS. – the name ... (use it). (B)						(B) NNS. I was thinking of "table cloth", but I didn't know the word in English.
NS. ... WHEN YOU CUT. (C)		NS TOPIC CONTINUATION (VIA TOPIC REJECTION)		EXTRA VOLUME		(C) NNS. (RE. "CUT") Like if I had "captured" what she said; if I was sure.
NNS. Yes! ... But I don't know // the name ((laugh))//		NNS TOPIC CONTINUATION (VIA TOPIC REJECTION)	"YES"			
NS. //((laugh))//						
NNS. Yes!						
NS. YOU DON'T KNOW THE NAME? (3)	TOPIC RELEVANT RESPONSE	NNS TOPIC CONTINUATION				(3) NS. I JUST THOUGHT SHE COULDN'T THINK OF THE WORD. SHE KNEW IT WAS A KNIFE, BUT COULDN'T THINK OF IT.
NNS. No.			"YES"			
NS. OKAY. ... YOU GIVE UP? ((laugh)) (D)						(D) NNS. (RE. "GIVE UP") I wasn't real sure of the whole sentence, but, yes, I knew what she meant. There are some things it's not necessary to know real, real well. You understand from all the words together. I supposed she was telling me this—she'd take the thing out of the bag, and I'd tell her it.
NNS. ((laugh)) Yes.			YES			
NS. OKAY. ... IT'S A KNIFE.		TOPIC CONCLUSION; TOPIC NOMINATION				
NNS. The knife. (E)		TOPIC CONTINUATION				(E) RES. WHEN SHE SHOWED YOU THE KNIFE, WHAT DID YOU THINK? NNS. I could never guess that that was what it was. RES. DID YOU KNOW HOW TO SAY "KNIFE" IN ENGLISH? NNS. Yes.

Chart 10-1b

TRANSCRIPT EXCERPT	MECHANISM	TOPIC CATEGORY	AR:C?	BENEFIT	NNS STRATEGY/NS RESPONSE	RETROSPECTION
1/1/16 – 1/1/18						
NS. THAT'S ONE PIC-TURE. ... ANOTHER, ... CAR ... OF MAN... NO BUENO—NO GOOD.	TRANSLATION	TOPIC CONCLUSION; ATTENTION GETTER; TOPIC NOMINATION		EXTRA VOLUME		(A) NNS. The man's car didn't work.
NNS. Uh-huh. ((yes))	TOPIC RELEVANT RESPONSE	TOPIC IDENTIFICATION				(1) RES. Do you think he understood? NS. YEAH.
NS. ...RIGHT? ... UH-HUH-HUH-HUH-HUH. ((Make noise like a car breaking down.))	CONFIRMATION CHECK; NOISES			NOISES		
NNS. YEAH. (A) (1)	TOPIC RELEVANT RESPONSE	TOPIC IDENTIFICATION	YES			(B) NNS. I understood that the man was looking at another man who was leaving in his car. That's what I understood. He said "hat" to me. I don't ((=help?)) know how he showed me.
NS. OKAY. ...MAN ... LOOKS... ((gestures)) —YOU KNOW?	GESTURES.	TOPIC CONCLUSION; TOPIC NOMINATION (VIA TOPIC CHANGE)		GESTURES		
NNS. Uh-huh. ((yes)) ... Look.	TOPIC RELEVANT RESPONSE ATTEMPTED FOCUS	TOPIC "IDENTIFICATION"	NO		ECHO / IGNORED	
NS. —FOR ... ANOTHER MAN ... TO HELP ... FOR HIS CAR. ... YOU UNDERST— (B)		TOPIC CONTINUATION		EXTRA VOLUME		
NNS. Help, ¿Qué es?	FOCUS; "I DON'T KNOW", "WHAT IS?"				ECHO; (2X) "I DON'T KNOW"/ RESULTS "ATTEMPTED" TOPIC CLARIFICATION (VIA MECHANISMS) (2X)	
NS. YOU UNDERSTAND?	MEANING CHECK					
NNS. Help, no.	FOCUS; "I DON'T KNOW"					
NS. CAR?	MEANING CHECK					
NNS. Car, yeah.	FOCUS + PROSODIC SHIFT					(C) RES. DID YOU UNDERSTAND HIS GESTURES AND HIS EXAMPLE OF WHAT "HELP" MEANT?
NS. YEAH, //AUTO//	TRANSLATION					
NNS. //Help.//	BASIC FOCUS	TOPIC CLARIFICATION			ECHO/ RESULTS IN REPETITION	NNS. I thought that—as I looked at the pictures that had the car that was on fire, and from his gestures, I thought that the man was shouting to the other man to give him water to throw on the car. That's what I understood.
NS. ... HELP.	REPETITION					
NNS. ... Help.	BASIC FOCUS				ECHO / RESULTS IN CLARIFICATION	
NS. YOU KNOW, //LIKE—//						
NNS. //Oh, up, yeah.// (C)						
NS. ... NO. NO, ... NO UP.						
NNS. No?						
NS. HELP. ... HELP. ... LIKE, ... UHM, ... "HELP! HELP!" ((shouts)) ... YOU KNOW, AGUA—I MEAN, WATER. (2)	REPETITION (2X) SEMANTIC ADDITION (?) DOWN SHIFT; GENERAL → PARTICULAR; TRANSLATION					(2) RES. Do you think that helped him to understand? NS. A LITTLE BIT; NOT COMPLETELY. I HAD TO SHOW HIM WITH GESTURES AND THINGS.
NNS. Water.	BASIC FOCUS					
NS. YOU KNOW, "BUGLA, BUGLA— ((Noise like someone drowning)) HELP! HELP!" — YOU (THOUGHT)	NOISES			NOISES	ECHO / RESULTS IN CLARIFICATION; (NOISES)	

Chart 10-2

TRANSCRIPT EXCERPT	MECHANISM	TOPIC CATEGORY	AR:C?	BENEFIT	NNS STRATEGY/NS RESPONSE	RETROSPECTION
1/1/16 – 1/1/18, CONTINUED						
NS.— YOU UNDERSTAND?	MEANING CHECK					
NNS. Uh-huh. ((yes))	TOPIC RELEVANT RESPONSE	TOPIC "IDENTIFICATION"	NO			
NS. AND... PERSON... HELP.						(3) RES. Okay, do you think he understood what "help" meant? NS. KIND OF. I MEAN, HE HAD AN IDEA, I THINK. RES. Do you think he got the idea of drowning and all that? NS. YEAH.
NNS. ... Uh-hm. ((yes)) (3)						
NS. HE HELP. ... OKAY, SO ... PERSON ... LOOK ... FOR HELP... FOR-HIS-CAR, ... AND SEES ... ANOTHER ... MAN ... (D) (E)		TOPIC CONTINUATION				(D) NNS. Person, no. It's that, as Steve speaks fast – he speaks very fast –, I didn't manage to understand it, because he — "persona," xxx, person quickly. I didn't manage to hear it.
NNS. Uh-hm. ((yes))	TOPIC RELEVANT RESPONSE	TOPIC "IDENTIFICATION"	NO			
NS. —TO HELP. ..., AND ... HE ASK ... THE MAN ... FOR HELP, ... OKAY? SO NOW, LISTEN. ... CAR ... NO BUENO, ... ((Laugh)) OKAY?	TRANSLATION	TOPIC CONCLUSION; ATTENTION GETTER; TOPIC NOMINATION				(E) NNS. Okay. I didn't know "other". "Other", I now know, but before I didn't know it. And, "help", I didn't know either, but now I know that it's "help" ("ayuda").
NNS. Okay. Carro no bueno.	TOPIC RELEVANT RESPONSE	TOPIC IDENTIFICATION & CONTINUATION	YES			
1/1/22						
NS. ... — NUMBER TWO, ... IS ... THE MAN ... LOOK ... FOR HELP.		TOPIC NOMINATION				
NNS. Uh-huh, ((yes)) for help.	TOPIC RELEVANT RESPONSE; BASIC FOCUS	TOPIC "IDENTIFICATION"	NO		ECHO/RESULTS IN TOPIC CLARIFICATION	(F) RES. DID YOU UNDERSTAND? NNS. Yes, a little, but it was when he was putting his cards in order, and mine also, that I had to — but after I understood, but before, no. RES. DID YOU UNDERSTAND THE WORD, "HELP", HERE? NNS. At that moment, no; I still didn't.
NS. HELP, YOU KNOW. ... "AAH! HELP!" ((shouts softly))				EXTRA VOLUME		
NNS. Uh-huh. ((yes))	TOPIC RELEVANT RESPONSE	TOPIC "IDENTIFICATION"; TOPIC CLARIFICATION	NO			
NS. NO UP. ... HELP.				EXTRA VOLUME		
NNS. Help. (F) (4)	BASIC FOCUS				ECHO/RESULTS IN TOPIC CLARIFICATION	(G) NNS. I still didn't understand "help". RES. YOU REPEATED "FOR HELP". DID YOU THINK "FOR HELP" WAS ONE WORD? NNS. No. I didn't – it was nothing more than repeating it because he was saying it.
NS. YEAH. ... HE ASKED, ... HE ASKED ... A MAN ... FOR ... HELP.						
NNS. ... For help. (G)	BASIC FOCUS				ECHO/NO EFFECT	
NS. YEAH. ... HE ASKED ... THE MAN ... FOR TELEPHONE.		TOPIC CONTINUATION				(4) RES. Do you think he understood "help" by this time? NS. UH-HUH, YEAH.

Chart 10-3

help") three times. The NS tries to clarify it twice, and the third time takes it as being understood by the NNS. As the retrospection comments show, the NNS still did not understand what the word "help" meant. The excerpt presents us with two appropriate responses which in fact do not signal comprehension.

Returning now to summarize the information presented in charts 10-1a, b, 10-2, and 10-3, we find that there were eleven appropriate responses in all. There were no inappropriate responses. Of these eleven responses, there were only two which definitely signaled comprehension (charts 10-2 and 10-3, excerpt 1). There were nine appropriate responses that did not signal comprehension at all (charts 10-1a, b, excerpt 1; charts 10-2 and 10-3, excerpts 1 and 2).

SUMMARY OF RESULTS

For the purpose of summarizing the results, three types of quantification will be presented. (1) The first will include all of the data for which retrospection data were available. (2) The second will be a quantitative analysis showing the proportion of appropriate responses for which there were retrospection data with regard to the total number of appropriate responses in the entire data base. (3) The third and final quantification will be an analysis combining the first and second analyses, showing the relationship of the data for which there were retrospection data to the entire data base.

Quantification of the Portion of Data for Which Retrospection Comments Were Available

The first quantification summarizes the analysis of all the data for which retrospection comments were available in the entire data base. Because it was impossible to present an exhaustive qualitative analysis in this paper, the following is presented as a quantitative summary of the entire qualitative analysis performed on the retrospected data. The results are given in Table 10-1.

TABLE 10-1 Percentage of Appropriate Responses as Related to Comprehension (Data base = all responses for which retrospection data were available)

Subject	*IARs**	*ARs*	*ARs = C?*		*ARs = C*		*ARs ≠ C*	
			no.	%	*no.*	%	*no.*	%
NNS1	4	60	3/60	5	27/60	45	30/60	50
NNS2	3	73	3/73	4	31/73	43	39/73	53
Totals	7	133	6/133	4	58/133	44	69/133	52

*IARs = inappropriate responses

Quantitative Analysis Showing the Proportion of Appropriate Responses for Which There Were Retrospection Data to the Total Number of Responses in the Entire Data Base

It is important to note that the percentages represented in Table 10-1 only account for those responses for which retrospection data were available. In order to clearly show the proportion of those appropriate responses for which retrospection data were available to those for which it was not available, the following analysis was done at the suggestion of Charlene Sato (personal communication). These data are given in Table 10-2.

TABLE 10-2 Percentage of Appropriate Responses for Which Retrospection Data Were Available in Relation to the Total Number of Appropriate Responses (Data base = entire data base)

Subject	*Total number of ARs*	*Number of ARs* without *retrospection data*		*Number of ARs* with *retrospection data*	
		no.	*% of total*	*no.*	*% of total*
NNS1	201	141/201	70	60/201	30
NNS2	190	117/190	62	73/190	38
Totals	391	258/391	66	133/391	34

In order to arrive at the figures in Table 10-2, a discourse analysis was performed on all of the responses in the entire data base, regardless of whether retrospection comments were available or not. (Inappropriate responses were eliminated, since they would not lead one to assume comprehension had occurred.) These totals were then further divided into two categories, showing the proportions of those responses without retrospection data and those with retrospection data.

Quantitative Analysis Showing the Relationship of the Data for Which There Were Retrospection Data to the Entire Data Base

This analysis combines the information from the analyses in Tables 10-1 and 10-2 and is given in Table 10-3. It shows the relation between the retrospected data and the total number of appropriate responses in the entire data base, thus exposing the proportion of appropriate responses in the conversations that we know with certainty did or did not signal comprehension.

If we assume that all the appropriate responses for which there were no retrospection comments did, in fact, signal comprehension, we are still left with a large 18 percent "margin of error," the percentage of appropriate responses that did not signal comprehension in the entire data base. By the same token, we are *certain* that an appropriate response signaled comprehension only 15 percent of the time.

TABLE 10-3 Percentage of Appropriate Responses With and Without Retrospection as They Relate to the Entire Data Base

Subject	*Total ARs*	*ARs = C(?); w/o retro.*		*ARs = C; w/ retro.*		*ARs ≠ C; w/ retro.*	
		no.	%	*no.*	%	*no.*	%
NNS1	201	141/201	70	27/201	13	30/201	15
NNS2	190	117/190	62	31/190	16	39/190	20.5
Totals	391	258/391	66	58/391	15	69/391	18

DISCUSSION OF RESULTS

The data from both conversations examined in this study suggest that the criterion of "appropriate response" as a measure of NNS comprehension in FTD is not completely reliable. As the analyses show, both the NNSs gave many appropriate responses that did not in fact signal comprehension.

The discussion of these results will center around two important issues. The first is that which arises from making decisions about the role of FT in the SLA process. The second is that of the role of the NNS in FTD studies. Although the two issues are closely connected, they will be discussed separately for the sake of clarity.

With respect to the role of FT in the SLA process, the claim that FT makes input comprehensible to the learner certainly does not seem unreasonable. If we wish to show, however, that FT facilitates communication and say that it is an implicit teaching mode which allows the NNS to comprehend speech that would otherwise be beyond his/her linguistic competency, we cannot base our analysis completely on what we judge, from the discourse, to be comprehended by the NNS. The determination of comprehension is, in fact, quite elusive. We cannot make strong claims about *how* FT aids learners in their comprehension if we do not know *what* they comprehend. To do so would run the risk of building our ideas of how FT aids the SLA process based on a faulty decision about what is comprehended.

A suggestion for future research in this regard would be a study which collects retrospection data from a larger number of subjects than this study in order to determine if there is a pattern which exists which would help sift out appropriate responses that do not signal comprehension from those that do. This is to say that the interaction itself might give clues as to when comprehension does and does not occur. Pause length and echoes may very well be signposts which coincide with lack of comprehension.

The second issue is that of the role of the NNS in FTD studies. It seems that input/interaction modification studies impose many of our biases, as

NSs, on learners as to how input is made comprehensible to them. The mere fact that the input/interaction modifications *occur* does not really tell us much about what to do with them. We cannot say that merely because these modifications occur, or that because some types occur more often than others, they are necessarily beneficial (or more beneficial) to the learner. We need to examine more closely what learners' systems are for making sense of the input/interaction they receive; that is, how does the learner handle the input/interaction modifications? *Describing* these modifications is one thing; it is quite another to say *how* they affect the SLA process for the learner.

The first step in dealing with this question is the realization that FT exists only in FTD, i.e., only when there is NS-NNS interaction. FTD studies have taken this into account insofar as it is recognized that an interactional exchange of this type cannot exist in the absence of a NNS. Beyond this recognition, however, the NNS's role in the discourse is almost ignored. Unless NNSs meet with uncooperative NS conversationalists, they can do a lot to force FT from their partners, and their participation accounts, in large measure, for the appearance of the data. In this sense, FT needs to include in its definition not only what NSs *do* when speaking with NNSs—as if FT were an automatic register of speech that is "turned on" under the appropriate circumstances—but also how they *respond, as interlocutors,* in FTD. The fact that a NS uses expansions, for example, says only that; what produces the expansion in the first place is, more likely than not, a conversational signal from the NNS. Unless the expansion is examined in close connection with what prompted it in the first place, as well as its effect, its power for explaining how it works in FTD to aid the learner's comprehension is lost. The more fine-tuned our analyses of FT become in this sense (i.e., in the sense of its close connection with the NNS's end of the conversation), the better our understanding of its role in the SLA process will become.

In terms of future research, this means combining the FTD studies with the "learner strategy" studies (which also must be considered within the realm of FTD; i.e., how they operate in relation to the conversational interaction present in FTD), in order to allow the relationship that exists between the two to come to light. Finally, the use of retrospection data from both the NS and the learner seems invaluable in gaining an "inside view" that will allow us to ascertain more precisely the effect of input/interaction modifications on the SLA process.

In summary, this study indicates two points pertinent to SLA research: (1) comprehension in FTD is an elusive phenomenon that our research needs to pinpoint more exactly, and (2) studies of FT need to consider the NNS's role more closely in FTD, recognizing that FT is the NS's response *as an interlocutor* in conversation with a NNS, and not a phenomenon that exists independently of the NNS.

NOTE

1. I would like to thank the following people for their helpful suggestions and comments on the original version of this paper: Roger Andersen, Evelyn Hatch, Michael Long, Charlene Sato, and John Schumann. Any errors or deficiencies in this study are my own.

On Phonology

11

TASK VARIATION IN INTERLANGUAGE PHONOLOGY

Charlene J. Sato[1]
University of Hawaii at Manoa

Research on phonological aspects of second language acquisition (SLA) has been built in large part upon a foundation of Labovian sociolinguistics. A major goal of such research is to describe and explain systematic variation in linguistic phenomena with reference to such factors as speech situation, discourse topic, and interlocutor roles and relationships.

In the most clearly articulated work in this tradition to date, Tarone (1979, 1982, 1983) posits *speech style* as the locus of variation in interlanguage (IL) development. The principal claim made is that learner speech "varies systematically with elicitation task" in terms of phonological, morphological, and syntactic structure (Tarone 1983: 142) and that this variability must be accounted for by an adequate model of SLA. While earlier studies have provided support for this claim, Tarone (1983) notes the serious need for longitudinal studies with data collected on different communicative tasks which reflect different speech styles, e.g., spontaneous conversation, elicitation, oral reading, and grammaticality judgments. The present study directly addresses this need through a longitudinal analysis of natural speech produced by an adolescent Vietnamese learner of English.

Speech Style, Systematicity, and Attention

In a recent statement of her position, Tarone (1983) argues for the superiority of a "continuum paradigm" over either a "Chomskyian paradigm" (as espoused by Adjémian 1976, 1982) or Krashen's monitor theory (1976, 1981a) in accounting for variable IL speech production. The continuum paradigm Tarone advocates is derived from Labov's (1969b) exposition of the "observer's paradox." She (1983: 152) proposes that IL be viewed as a continuum of styles, style being defined specifically in terms of the "amount of attention paid to language form." The style which occurs when the least attention is paid to speech is called the "vernacular" and exhibits the greatest systematicity (in the sense of internal consistency). Put another way, this least-attended-to style shows the least variability. The style at the other end of the continuum is called "careful style." Data from this style include those obtained under formal circumstances, where speech is being systematically observed, such as experimental task situations and structured interviews with unfamiliar researchers. The careful or "superordinate" style appears to exhibit more variability than the vernacular in that it is more often "permeated" by either target language (TL) or native language (NL) phenomena.

Tarone views learners' shifting along the continuum of styles as a direct function of the amount of attention paid to language form. She claims (1982: 73) that it is necessary to distinguish style shifting from register shifting, the "sociolinguistic ability to speak casually in casual situations, or formally in formal situations," pointing out that learners may very well learn only one register of the TL initially and yet may later manifest systematically different production under changing circumstances. With subsequent acquisition of other registers, a complex interaction between register and style shifting presumably arises.

Tarone notes the methodological correlates of viewing IL as a systematically variable continuum of styles. She points out the necessity of collecting data from as many styles as possible to allow accurate identification of regularities within and among them, and the "relative influence of TL, NL and 'pidgin-like' structures" (1983: 155). Such procedures are crucial, Tarone claims, to the construction of a viable model of the linguistic system underlying IL performance.

Task Variation and IL Development

The relationship between style shifting, or task variation, and IL development toward the TL should be observable, Tarone (1983: 155) suggests, as a movement of a TL structure from appearance in the most careful to the vernacular style. The continuum paradigm predicts "that while TL structures move over time from the careful style to the vernacular, as part of the process of acquisition, those IL structures (i.e., pidginized structures) which spontaneously appear in the vernacular would gradually be replaced by them.

Concretizing styles as communicative tasks (spontaneous conversation, oral reading, a structured interview, elicited intuition statements, elicited imitation, etc.) would not seem to alter the continuum paradigm's predictions. The greatest systematicity should be apparent in the task in which the least attention is paid to language form and, concomitantly, the highest degree of variability should be noted in the task where the most attention is paid to speech, for example, elicited imitation or oral reading. Developmentally speaking, the acquisition of TL forms should take place first in speech produced on more formal tasks and then spread subsequently to the least formal communicative tasks.

Phonological Variables

To date, the particular phonological variables examined with respect to sociolinguistic variation in SL performance seem to have been restricted primarily to segmental phonemes such as /r/ in Japanese and Thai learners of English (Dickerson 1974, Dickerson and Dickerson 1977, Beebe 1980) and /θ/ for Arabic learners of English (Schmidt 1977). It seems reasonable to ask whether learners treat other kinds of phonological phenomena, e.g., consonant clusters, syllable structure, stress, and intonation) differently than they do phonemes. At least one study (Sato 1984) has shown some interaction between segments and syllable structure; specifically, syllable position—initial or final—was seen to affect targetlike production of consonant clusters in English IL.

In general, though, the issue of which particular feature is appropriate to posit as a linguistic variable has not received serious discussion in the SLA literature; researchers have selected features that learners produce inaccurately in the L2. While this practice is understandable, it is also important to broaden the scope of IL phonological analysis by including more than one kind of feature in a study of variation.

A LONGITUDINAL STUDY OF TASK VARIATION IN IL PHONOLOGY

Purpose of the Study

The continuum paradigm offers a means of accounting for the variable phenomenon that is IL speech. It makes explicit claims regarding the continuum nature of IL systems and the systematic variability of IL speech in different situations. The present study provides additional empirical evidence with which the continuum paradigm can be evaluated. It does so through a longitudinal analysis of IL speech from a Vietnamese learner of English. The phonological features examined are word-final consonants and word-final consonant clusters, both of which seem subject to variable production by Vietnamese learners of English. The specific research questions addressed are:

1. To what extent does targetlike production of word-final consonants (Cs) and word-final consonant clusters (CCs) vary with communicative tasks?

2. To what extent is there change over time in the production of word-final Cs and CCs on different communicative tasks?

3. To what extent is task variability in the production of word-final Cs and CCs neutralized by first language transfer?

Method

Subject The subject in this study was Thanh, an adolescent Vietnamese boy who was about 12 years old upon arrival in the United States. He was a boat refugee who, along with a younger brother, was separated from other family members during their departure from South Vietnam and who spent roughly two months in a Malaysian refugee camp before being placed with a white, middle-class foster couple in Philadelphia, Pennsylvania. Since his arrival in the spring of 1981, he has lived with this couple, who have provided a home for other Southeast Asian refugees over the last several years. Their previous foster children, all older teenagers or young adults, have moved out on their own or gone to live with newly arrived family members after a year or two.

Thanh has been enrolled in a local public school in a predominantly black, working- to middle-class community outside Philadelphia. He has never received any ESL instruction, since there are no ESL classes or teachers available in his school.

Although he began attending school a few weeks after arriving in Philadelphia, both Thanh and his teachers report that he remained quiet and uncomprehending for much of the spring 1981 school term. He interacted with other children only minimally. Because of a prolonged teacher strike the following fall, he did not return to school until November 1981, roughly a month after data collection for this study began.

Thanh is literate in Vietnamese and received tutoring in Vietnamese throughout the period of observation. He did not have any English instruction in Vietnam.

Relevant facts about Vietnamese Vietnamese is a monosyllabic tone language (see descriptions by Liễm 1967, Bình and Gage 1975, Thompson 1965). It is labeled monosyllabic because a large proportion of its words consists of single syllables, and tonal because pitch variations signal meaning differences for otherwise homophonous words.

According to Liễm (1967), Vietnamese has 22 consonants, but only eight of them can occur as codas, i.e., syllable-finally. These are /p, t, k, m, ŋ, w/, and /y/. Moreover, these consonants are either unreleased or coarticulated (e.g., /ŋ/with /m/). As for consonant clusters, none occur syllable-finally; and all fourteen possible syllable-initial clusters take only /w/ as a second member.

A tally of the frequency of syllable types in Liễm's (1967) phonemic syllable inventory for Saigon Vietnamese suggests that the major syllable type for Vietnamese is CVD. Of the 4,467 phonemic syllables identified by Liêm, 77 percent end in consonants. Since words are overwhelmingly monosyllabic, the term syllable-final can be roughly equated with word-final in Vietnamese.

From these facts it can be suggested that final consonants in English will be easier for a Vietnamese speaker to produce than final consonant clusters. Also, manner of articulation of final consonants in English might be affected, given the preference in Vietnamese for unreleased and/or coarticulated final consonants.

Data collection The data for this study were collected over 10 months through weekly audiotaping of visits between Thanh and myself, primarily in the home context. The following arrangement had been made with his foster parents: I would provide weekly conversation sessions in exchange for data on his English acquisition. It was agreed that no instruction would be provided, although some help with homework tasks would be given. This condition was maintained throughout the 10-month period of the study.

Thanh's foster mother was present during most of the data-collection sessions, as was his brother Tai. Other occasional participants included his foster father, family friends, and friends of the researcher.

Corpus The data for the analysis consist of speech samples taken at four points during the 10-month period of the study: the first, fourth, seventh, and tenth months. These will be referred to as Times 1, 2, 3, and 4, respectively.

Each time sample contains data from four different communication tasks. At Times 1, 2, and 3, these tasks are (1) free conversation, (2) oral reading of continuous text, and (3) elicited imitation of words and short phrases. At Time 4, the oral reading task is replaced by text recitation, an oral presentation of previously written and rehearsed text. Combining the data from all four tasks, each time sample amounts to roughly 450 to 500 words in running speech.

Analysis All the speech on the tapes for each sample was transcribed using the IPA. For each task, the data were then coded for the following:

1. Word-final consonants in the categories: stops, fricatives, approximants, and nasals
2. Target-final consonants
3. Segment modification processes for single consonants:
   a. Deletion
   b. Feature change
4. Word-final consonant clusters
5. Target-final consonant clusters
6. Segment modification processes for clusters:
   a. Deletion (of the entire cluster)
   b. Reduction (of the cluster)
   c. Feature change (of some member of the cluster or the entire cluster)
   d. Reduction and feature change

The tokens for each of these categories were then tallied and percentages calculated. Observed differences between performance on tasks over time were tested for significance ($\alpha = .05$) using the chi-square test.

Results

Task Variation in Word-Final Consonant Production Each of the four samples will be taken in turn, beginning with Time 1, the results for which are given in Table 11-1. The highest percentage of targetlike final consonants (TFCs) is produced by Thanh in imitation (nearly 79 percent), followed by reading (62 percent) and conversation (52 percent). The differences among these tasks are statistically significant ($\chi^2 = 11.25$, df = 2, $p < .005$). It turns out, further, that this result is primarily due to the significantly higher frequency of TFCs in imitation than in conversation ($\chi^2 = 8.93$, df = 1, $p < .005$). While TFCs were more frequent in imitation than in reading and more frequent in reading than in conversation, neither of these comparisons is statistically significant ($\chi^2 = 3.71$, df = 1, ns and $\chi^2 = 3.40$, df = 1, ns, respectively).

TFCs produced by Thanh at Time 2 are shown in Table 11-2. It can be seen that the relative frequencies of TFCs do not vary significantly with the three tasks ($\chi^2 = 4.11$, df = 2, $p > .10$). However, a comparison of TFCs for conversation (72.41 percent) and reading (61.65 percent) does yield a significant difference ($\chi^2 = 4.48$, df = 1, $p < .05$).

TABLE 11-1 Time 1: Task Variation in Word-final Consonant Production

	Conversation		*Reading*		*Imitation*		*Total*	
	no.	%	*no.*	%	*no.*	%	*no.*	%
Target	104	52.00	128	61.54	33	78.57	265	58.89
Nontarget	96	48.00	80	38.46	9	21.43	185	41.11
Total	200	100.00	208	100.00	42	100.00	450	100.00

(Conv. × Rdg. × Imit., $\chi^2 = 11.25$, df = 2, $p < .005$)
(Conv. × Imit., $\chi^2 = 8.93$, df = 1, $p < .005$)

TABLE 11-2 Time 2: Task Variation in Word-final Consonant Production

	Conversation		*Reading*		*Imitation*		*Total*	
	no.	%	*no.*	%	*no.*	%	*no.*	%
Target	126	72.41	82	61.65	20	64.52	228	67.46
Nontarget	48	27.59	51	38.35	11	35.48	110	32.54
Total	174	100.00	133	100.00	31	100.00	338	100.00

(Conv. × Rdg. × Imit., $\chi^2 = 4.11$, df = 2, n.s.)
(Conv. × Rdg., $\chi^2 = 4.48$, df = 1, $p < .05$)

Table 11-3 shows the results at Time 3. In this case, significant variation in targetlike production is evident with task ($\chi^2 = 7.19$, df = 2, $p < .05$), with the lowest percentage of TFCs occurring in reading (63.7 percent), followed by conversation (73.55 percent) and imitation (79.45 percent). Comparing each pair of tasks separately reveals significant differences in TFCs between conversation and reading ($\chi^2 = 3.97$, df = 1, $p < .05$) and between reading and imitation ($\chi^2 = 4.93$, df = 1, $p < .05$) but not between conversation and imitation ($\chi^2 = .7762$, df = 1, ns).

TABLE 11-3 Time 3: Task Variation in Word-final Consonant Production

	Conversation		*Reading*		*Imitation*		*Total*	
	no.	%	*no.*	%	*no.*	%	*no.*	%
Target	203	73.55	93	63.70	58	79.45	354	71.52
Nontarget	73	26.45	53	36.30	15	20.55	141	28.48
Total	276	100.00	146	100.00	73	100.00	495	100.00

(Conv. × Rdg. × Imit., $\chi^2 = 7.19$, df = 2, $p < .05$)
(Conv. × Rdg., $\chi^2 = 3.97$, df = 1, $p < .05$)
(Rdg. × Imit., $\chi^2 = 4.93$, df = 1, $p < .05$)

Finally, the findings for Time 4 are shown in Table 11-4. Here, performance of TFCs varies only minimally with the three tasks:[2] 69 percent for conversation, 71 percent for recitation, and 73 percent for imitation. The differences are not statistically significant ($\chi^2 = .4228$, df = 2, ns).

At this point, it is helpful to compare targetlike production of FCs by task across all four samples. Results are shown in Table 11-5. Of interest is the fact that targetlike production is highest on imitation tasks at all times

TABLE 11-4 Time 4: Task Variation in Word-final Consonant Production

	Conversation		Reading		Imitation		Total	
	no.	%	*no.*	%	*no.*	%	*no.*	%
Target	251	68.96	114	70.81	40	72.73	405	69.83
Nontarget	113	31.05	47	29.19	15	27.27	175	30.17
Total	364	100.00	161	100.00	55	100.00	580	100.00

(Conv. × Rec. × Imit., χ^2 = .4228, df = 1, n.s.)

except Time 2, where it is highest for conversation. Furthermore, contrary to expectations, more targetlike production occurs in conversation than in reading at both Times 2 and 3.

TABLE 11-5 Targetlike Production of Word-final Consonants by Task

	Sample 1		Sample 2		Sample 3		Sample 4	
Task	*no.*	%	*no.*	%	*no.*	%	*no.*	%
Conversation	104	52.00	126	72.41	203	73.55	251	68.96
Oral reading*	128	61.54	82	61.65	93	63.70	114	70.81
Imitation	33	78.57	20	64.52	58	79.45	40	72.73

*In Sample 4, task is text recitation.

Task Variation in Word-Final Consonant Cluster Production Performance of targetlike final consonant clusters (TFCCs) at Time 1 is shown in Table 11-6. It can be seen that no significant difference obtains in Thanh's production of TFCCs in conversation, reading, and imitation (χ^2 = 3.30, df = 2, ns). It is also important to note that the percentage of TFCCs is quite low on all tasks: 6 percent on conversation, 18 percent on reading, and 13 percent on imitation.

TABLE 11-6 Time 1: Task Variation in Word-final Cluster Production

	Conversation		Reading		Imitation		Total	
	no.	%	*no.*	%	*no.*	%	*no.*	%
Target	3	5.88	8	17.78	4	12.50	15	11.72
Nontarget	48	94.12	37	82.22	28	87.50	113	88.28
Total	51	100.00	45	100.00	32	100.00	128	100.00

(Conv. × Rdg. × Imit., χ^2 = 3.30, df = 2, n.s.)

At Time 2, however, the situation changes, as shown in Table 11-7. Thanh produces significantly different frequencies of TFCCs on different tasks (χ^2 = 13.64, df = 2, $p < .005$). Both reading and imitation yield higher frequencies of target clusters than does conversation—29 and 27 percent as compared with 5 percent—and each comparison achieves statistical significance: reading and conversation (χ^2 = 10.76, df = 1, $p < .005$), and imitation and conversation (χ^2 = 7.03, df = 1, $p < .01$). TFCC production does not differ significantly, however, between reading and imitation (χ^2 = .009, df = 1, ns).

TABLE 11-7 Time 2: Task Variation in Word-final Cluster Production

	Conversation		*Reading*		*Imitation*		*Total*	
	no.	%	*no.*	%	*no.*	%	*no.*	%
Target	4	5.41	13	28.89	7	26.92	24	16.55
Nontarget	70	94.59	32	71.11	19	73.08	121	83.45
Total	74	100.00	45	100.00	26	100.00	145	100.00

(Conv. × Rdg. × Imit., χ^2 = 13.64, df = 2, p < .005)
(Conv. × Rdg., χ^2 = 10.76, df = 1, p < .005)
(Conv. × Imit., χ^2 = 7.03, df = 1, p < .01)

Results at Time 3 are shown in Table 11-8. It can be seen that significantly different frequencies of TFCCs occur in conversation (22 percent), reading (31 percent) and imitation (47 percent) (χ^2 = 9.81, df = 2, p < .01). Comparisons of each pair of tasks reveal that this result derives from the differences between conversation and imitation (χ^2 = 8.57, df = 1, p < .005) and not from the lesser differences in targetlike production between conversation and reading (χ^2 = 1.46, df = 1, ns) or between reading and imitation (χ^2 = 3.39, df = 1, p > .05).

TABLE 11-8 Time 3: Task Variation in Word-final Cluster Production

	Conversation		*Reading*		*Imitation*		*Total*	
	no.	%	*no.*	%	*no.*	%	*no.*	%
Target	18	21.69	31	30.69	25	47.17	74	31.22
Nontarget	65	78.31	70	69.31	28	52.83	163	68.78
Total	83	100.00	101	100.00	53	100.00	237	100.00

(Conv. × Rdg. × Imit., χ^2 = 9.81, df = 2, p < .01)
(Conv. × Imit., χ^2 = 8.57, df = 1, p < .005)

Finally, results for Time 4 are shown in Table 11-9. TFCCs range from a low of 6 percent for recitation, through 15 percent for conversation, to a high of 32 percent for imitation. As at Times 2 and 3, task differences are significant (χ^2 = 9.50, df = 2, p < .01). As for two-task comparisons, significant differences emerge between conversation and recitation (χ^2 = 7.62, df = 1, p < .01) and between recitation and imitation (χ^2 = 7.62, df = 1, p < .01) but not between conversation and imitation (χ^2 = 1.64, df = 1, ns).

Examining the four samples together in Table 11-10 provides an overall picture of Thanh's word-final consonant cluster production over the 10-month period. At Times 1 and 2, TFCC percentages are quite low: 6 and 5 percent, respectively. The highest percentage of TFCCs is for reading in these two samples. In contrast, at Times 3 and 4, the most favorable context for

TABLE 11-9 Time 1: Task Variation in Word-final Cluster Production

	Conversation		*Reading*		*Imitation*		*Total*	
	no.	%	*no.*	%	*no.*	%	*no.*	%
Target	6	14.63	4	6.15	7	31.82	17	13.28
Nontarget	35	85.37	61	93.85	15	68.18	111	86.72
Total	41	100.00	65	100.00	22	100.00	128	100.00

(Conv. × Recit. × Imit., $\chi^2 = 9.50$, df = 2, $p < .01$)
(Conv. × Recit., $\chi^2 = 9.94$, df = 1, $p < .005$)
(Recit. × Imit., $\chi^2 = 7.62$, df = 1, $p < .01$)

TFCCs is imitation, with 47 and 32 percent, respectively. A striking low of 6 percent is observed in the recitation data at Time 4.

TABLE 11-10 Targetlike Production of Word-final Clusters by Task

	Sample 1		*Sample 2*		*Sample 3*		*Sample 4*	
Task	*no.*	%	*no.*	%	*no.*	%	*no.*	%
Conversation	3	5.88	4	5.41	18	21.69	6	14.63
Oral reading*	8	17.78	13	28.89	31	30.69	4	6.15
Imitation	4	12.50	7	26.92	25	47.17	7	31.82

*In Sample 4, task is text recitation.

Task Variation in Word-Final Consonant and Consonant Cluster Production Over Time The developmental findings with respect to variable final consonant and cluster production on different tasks are best introduced in general terms first. The figures for Thanh's total production of final consonants are given in Table 11-11 and those for final clusters in Table 11-12.

Table 11-11 shows that TFC production generally increases over time. It amounts to nearly 59 percent at Time 1, 68 percent at Time 2, 72 percent at Time 3, and 70 percent at Time 4. Overall, the change over time in TFC production from the beginning to the end of the 10-month period amounts to a gain of 10 percent. It should be noted that the percentage at Time 1, 60 percent, was not low to begin with.

TABLE 11-11 Word-final Consonant Production Over Time

	1		*2*		*3*		*4*	
	no.	%	*no.*	%	*no.*	%	*no.*	%
Target	265	58.89	228	67.46	354	71.52	405	69.83
Nontarget	185	41.11	110	32.54	141	28.48	175	30.17
Total	450	100.00	338	100.00	495	100.00	580	100.00

Thanh's production of TFCCs provides an interesting contrast. Table 11-12 shows that TFCC production improves over time through Time 3, but then drops drastically at Time 4. From a low of about 12 percent at Time 1, a high of only 31 percent is achieved at Time 3. In other words, there is an obvious difference in TFC and TFCC production. As illustrated in Figure 11-1,

TABLE 11-12 Word-Final Cluster Production Over Time

	1		*2*		*3*		*4*	
	no.	%	*no.*	%	*no.*	%	*no.*	%
Target	15	11.72	24	16.55	74	31.22	17	13.28
Nontarget	113	88.28	121	83.45	163	68.78	111	86.72
Total	128	100.00	145	100.00	237	100.00	128	100.00

figures for the former are always dramatically higher than those for the latter.

Developmental changes in TFC and TFCC production on different tasks are displayed in Figures 11-2 and 11-3. In the case of final consonants, Figure 11-2 (which may be examined in conjunction with Table 11-5) shows that the relative ranking of the tasks changes from one time to the next. For example, TFC production is lowest (52 percent) on conversation at Time 1 but highest for this task at Time 2 (72 percent), in the middle at Time 3 (74 percent), and lowest again at Time 4 (69 percent). Imitation is the most favorable context for TFC production at Time 1, not so at Time 2, and again the most favorable context at Times 3 and 4. It should also be recalled that significant task differences occur at Times 1 and 3 but not at Times 2 and 4. In other words, TFC production does not vary consistently with task over time.

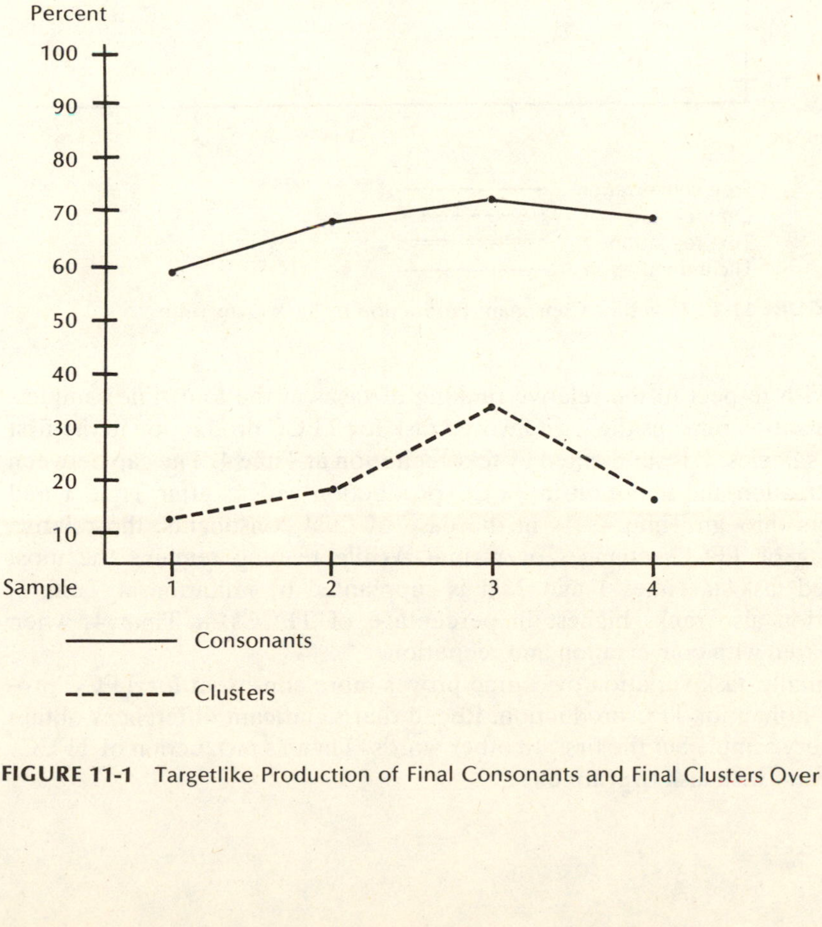

FIGURE 11-1 Targetlike Production of Final Consonants and Final Clusters Over Time

Developmental findings for TFCC production are shown in Figure 11-3, in conjunction with Table 11-10. It is first important to point out that TFCC production never exceeds 50 percent on any task in any time sample. The extremes range from 5.41 percent in conversation at Time 1 to 47.17 percent in imitation at Time 3.

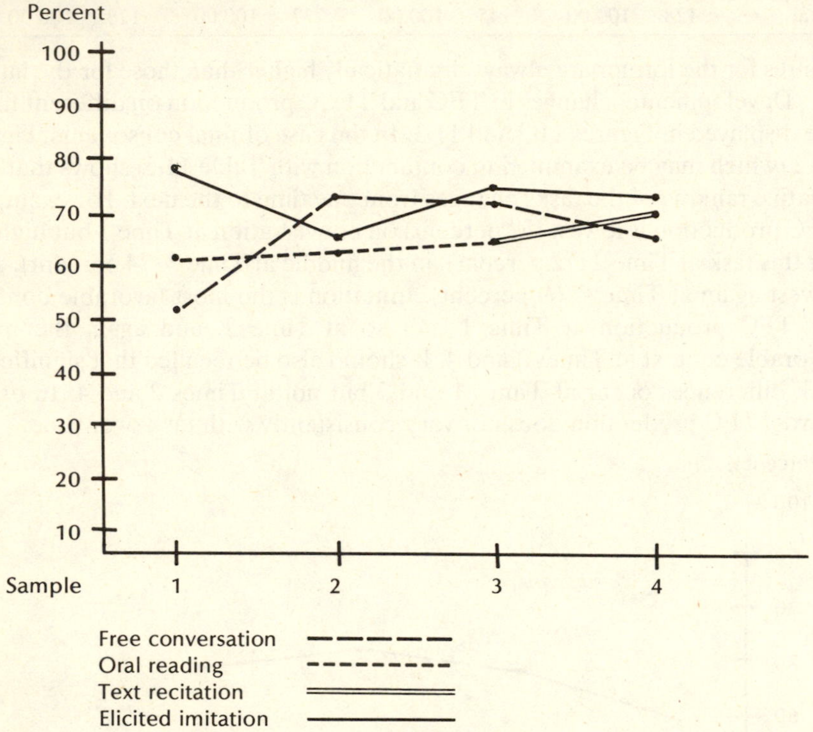

FIGURE 11-2 Targetlike Consonant Production by Task Over Time

With respect to the relative ranking of tasks in the four time samples, conversation remains the least favored task for TFCC production in the first three samples. It is supplanted by text recitation at Time 4. The gap between conversation and imitation in TFCC production widens after Time 1 and persists through Time 4. As in the case of final consonants, the relative ranking of TFCCs changes over time. While reading remains the most favored task at Times 1 and 2, it is supplanted by imitation at Time 3. Imitation also ranks highest in percentage of TFCCs at Time 4, when compared with conversation and recitation.

Finally, task variation over time proves more consistent for TFCC production than for TFC production. Recall that significant differences obtain for every sample but the first. In other words, Thanh's production of TFCCs does vary with task over time.

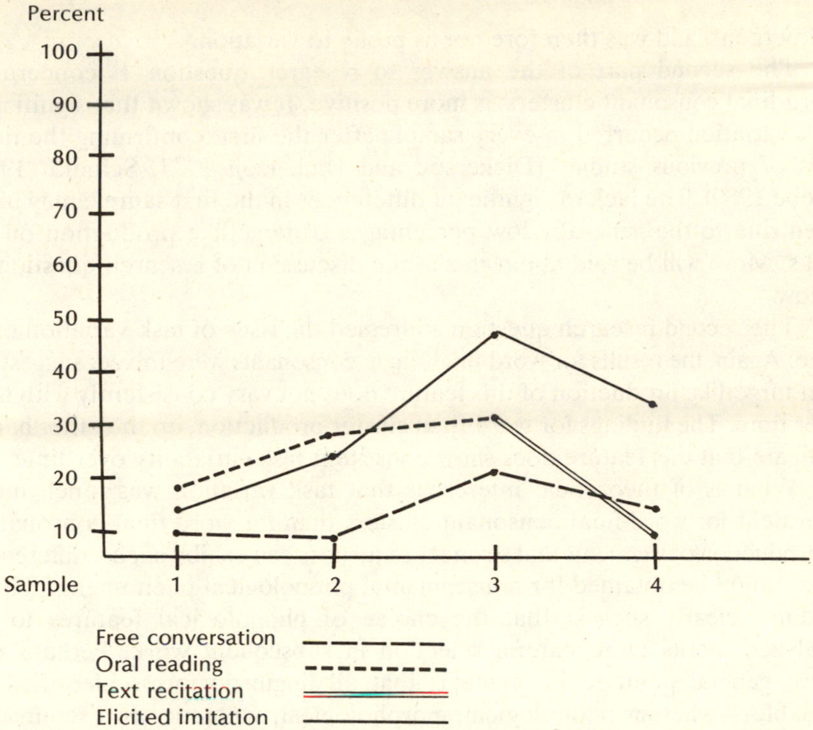

FIGURE 11-3 Targetlike Cluster Production by Task Over Time

Neutralization of Task Variation in Consonant and Cluster Production by First Language Transfer Two findings emerge here. The first is that production of TFCs far exceeds that of TFCCs over the entire period of study. See Figure 11-1 again for this difference. The second finding is the lack of significant differences in TFCC production at Time 1 and a reversal in the subsequent three samples. Refer to Table 11-6 for the relevant percentages at Time 1: about 6 percent TFCCs in conversation, 18 percent in reading, and 13 percent in imitation. Of interest also, as mentioned earlier, is that none of these percentages is very high.

Discussion

The first research question (To what extent does targetlike production of word-final Cs and CCs vary with communicative task?) can be answered in two parts. For word-final single consonants, significant task variation occurred in two samples but not in two others. Thus it must be concluded that task variation is inconsistent for word-final consonants. Perhaps this result is due partly to the fact that targetlike production was high from the very beginning

(59 percent) and was therefore not as prone to variation.

The second part of the answer to research question 1, concerning word-final consonant clusters, is more positive. It was shown that significant task variation occurred in every sample after the first, confirming the findings of previous studies (Dickerson and Dickerson 1977, Schmidt 1977, Beebe 1980). The lack of significant differences in the first sample may have been due to the generally low percentages of targetlike production on all tasks. More will be said about this in the discussion of research question 3, below.

The second research question addressed the issue of task variation over time. Again, the results for word-final single consonants were mixed, suggesting that targetlike production of this feature does not vary consistently with task over time. The findings for word-final cluster production, on the other hand, indicate that this feature does show consistent task variability over time.

What is of theoretical interest is that task variation was much more prevalent for word-final consonant clusters than for word-final consonants. If production of segments and segment sequences can exhibit such a difference, what might be obtained for nonsegmental phonological phenomena? These findings clearly suggest that the choice of phonological features to be analyzed merits more careful selection in subsequent work. Perhaps the more general point to be made is that all linguistic forms identified as variables—whether phonological, morphological, syntactic, or discoursal—cannot be assumed to yield similar patterns, at least with respect to task variability.

The different results obtained for word-final consonants as opposed to clusters must also be examined in light of another well-documented source of phonological variation: the linguistic environment of the segment(s) being analyzed. This is, in fact, the next step in further analysis of the data presented here.

The findings for the third research question (To what extent is task variability in the production of word-final Cs and CCs neutralized by first language transfer?) provide further evidence of first language influence on IL phonological structure. Earlier, it was pointed out that Vietnamese favors the closed syllable and does not allow final consonant clusters. These characteristics of the first language are reflected in the IL: a much greater frequency of targetlike production of final consonants than clusters; and second, a lack of significant task variation in word-final cluster production in the first sample. It seems reasonable to argue that if clusters are extremely difficult for Vietnamese learners of English, in the early stages of acquisition they may not be able to alter their performance very much, whatever the communicative task they are engaged in and however much attention they pay to articulation.

CONCLUSIONS: VARIATION IN IL PHONOLOGY.

The findings of this study raise an important question for the continuum paradigm: is it sufficient to define style solely in terms of the attention paid to language form? Recall that careful style is claimed to result from maximal attention to form and to be most permeable to target and native language structures. In this study, however, a greater incidence of targetlike production of word-final consonants occurred in the "vernacular style"—conversation—than in the "careful style"—reading—in two of the samples. Also, the task of text recitation clearly required a high degree of attention to language form on the part of the learner. Yet the percentage of target word-final cluster production on this task was less than half that for conversation, the "vernacular style," in the last sample. What may be happening here is that such tasks require a great deal of attention, but this attention must be paid, not simply to language form but also to other demands on real-time discourse production: recall and encoding of rhetorical structure, lexical items, clause sequencing, etc. Phonological phenomena such as consonant clusters appear to rank low on this list of demands on the learner. The point here, with respect to the notion of a continuum of styles in IL, is that the definition of style solely in terms of the amount of attention paid to language form appears to be an oversimplification.

Finally, there is also a conceptual problem with the notion of style shifting in relation to register shifting. It may be helpful to characterize style shifting psycholinguistically and register shifting sociolinguistically, as Tarone has done. What seems problematic, however, is that register shifting must also be described ultimately in psycholinguistic terms. That is to say, native speakers engaged in register shifting accomplish such behavior also as a function of differential attention paid to language form. What seems different about second language learners is not this process per se but the fact that they do not have access to the second language norms about which linguistic forms are associated with which social parameters.

Ultimately, research on IL phonology which bases itself on sociolinguistic theory must be reconciled with psycholinguistic accounts of speech production. Further, there must be some evaluation of the continuum paradigm with respect to current applications of markedness theory to IL phonology (e.g., Eckman 1977, 1981a, 1981b), assuming that SLA researchers agree that the same kinds of data are being used in support of both theoretical positions.

To summarize, a longitudinal case study of task variation in IL phonology has been shown to provide limited support for the continuum paradigm. Task variability has been seen to depend partly upon the particular linguistic variable examined; different developmental patterns were identified for English word-final consonants as opposed to word-final consonant clusters. In this case, systematic task variation was demonstrated for word-final clusters but not for word-final single consonants in the English IL of a Vietnamese learner.

NOTES

1. I would like to thank Mike Long for his helpful comments and suggestions.

2. Although one of the cells yields an expected frequency of less than 5, the chi-square test is considered appropriate for these data, following Siegel (1956: 110): "When K (number of categories) is larger than 2 (and thus df is greater than 1), the χ^2 test may be used if fewer than 20 percent of the cells have an expected frequency of less than 5 and if no cell has an expected frequency of less than 1."

12

PHONOLOGICAL ASPECTS OF INPUT IN NS-NNS INTERACTIONS

Jane Zuengler
Indiana University of Pennsylvania

We are witnessing a growing amount of language research which is interaction-based. Those studies focusing on interactions between native speakers (NSs) and nonnative speakers (NNSs), or between several NNSs, are of obvious importance to us for what they contribute to our understanding of second language acquisition and use. Additionally, studies of NS-NNS interactions enable us to simultaneously observe the speech of the NNSs *and* the nature of the target language (TL) input available to them.

To date, however, only a few studies of NS-NNS interactions have looked at phonological aspects of the interlocutors' speech. Such studies include Clyne (1981a) and Katz (1981), each of which focused on NS speech. Both Clyne and Katz conducted descriptive studies of a small number of subjects (four families, in Clyne, and two children, in Katz) and focused on *deviations* from nativeness (i.e., characteristics peculiar to "foreigner talk").

There is an obvious need to conduct more research on the phonology of input, research which is quantitative, and which investigates *normal* (i.e., nondeviant) phonological variation as well as that which deviates in becoming "foreigner talk." Furthermore, we need to have data from phonology with which to test certain claims made by Giles and others in social psychology. In recent years, social psychologists engaged in language research have criticized "traditional" sociolinguistics for being inadequate—more specifically, for largely limiting studies to correlations between linguistic variables and macrolevel, sociodemographic variables such as social class, age, and sex. Social psychologists have argued that a framework for explaining variation in speech performance must also take into account the interlocutors' attitudes, perceptions, and motives—in short, the social psychological dynamics underlying speech behavior. (See, for example, Giles 1977; Giles and Smith 1979; Smith, Giles, and Hewstone 1980; Thakerar, Giles, and Cheshire 1982.) Giles et al. claim that much of the variation that we find in language performance (in both L1 and L2) is due to social psychological "accommodation." That is, commonly when interacting, people make certain modifications in their speech. For one or more social psychological reasons (e.g., attraction to the listener, or suspicion of the listener's motives), speakers may shift their speech toward that of their interlocutor or away from their interlocutor. While most of the research comes from NS-NNS interactions, there is some evidence that a theory such as accommodation can explain the L2 variation found in some NS-NNS interactions (see Beebe and Zuengler 1983).

But, as Beebe and Zuengler (1981) and Trudgill (no date) point out, most of the research which tests accommodation measures linguistic accommodation *impressionistically.* That is, groups of linguistically naive subjects are typically asked to rate the speaker's overall "accent" as "broad" or "narrow." As Trudgill (no date, p. 2) argues, we must have "exact, rather than impressionistic, quantification of linguistic accommodation." Furthermore, if phonological items are in fact sensitive to social psychological motives such as accommodation, we need to determine *which* phonological variables become accommodation markers.

What follows is a report of a subset of results from a study which addresses these needs. First the background to the study will be explained, followed by a description of the method and a discussion of the results.

BACKGROUND TO THE STUDY

The present study is a partial replication of research conducted in Britain by Thakerar, Giles, and Cheshire (1982). Most of the quantitative evidence for speech accommodation theory had been gathered from interactions between interlocutors of relatively equal status, they asserted, and pointed out that research was needed on interactions between people of unequal status. This was particularly important in light of the fact that such interactions are very common (Thakerar, Giles, and Cheshire 1982: 219). They therefore conducted a set of studies designed to look at the effects of *unequal* status on speech, and to determine, in the process, which dimensions of speech are affected the most by "status manipulations"—i.e., which were the clearest dependent variables (Thakerar, Giles, and Cheshire 1982: 220). In the set of studies, status imbalance was induced in several different ways by the researchers.

For example, in one study, dental students who had unequal amounts of training were paired together. They were then asked to discuss several issues which favored the subject with the greater training. In another study, nurses who had differing levels of qualifications were asked to discuss a topic which emphasized their differences. In yet another study, female undergraduates were chosen as subjects, and they were all asked to complete a block-design task, followed by a discussion of it. After that, each member of the pair had to (individually) perform another block-design task. When the pair was finished, only one of the subjects was told that she had done well and that her performance was therefore superior to that of her partner. Thakerar et al. used this as a "manipulation induced to create perceived differences in their status relevant skills" (Thakerar, Giles, and Cheshire 1982, p. 231). Thus status imbalances were established in different ways by the researchers. Several of the studies made explicit inequality of training and experience which the subjects brought with them to the study; in another study, however, status differences were the outcome of the subjects' supposedly differential success at performing a task.

The dependent measures which Thakerar et al. studied included speech rate, standardness of pronunciation, and nonlinguistic, psychological aspects such as competence and acceptance of situation. Primarily, the analyses were subjective; a panel of linguistically naive judges were asked to evaluate the taped samples of speech along gross dimensions of standardness, competence/noncompetence, etc. However, in one of the studies, a more objective analysis was undertaken which involved the phonological variable (t).[1]

All the studies involved an analysis of speech in an "equal status" condition compared with that in an "unequal status" condition. Regardless of the fact that status imbalances were achieved through different methods, all of the studies revealed a common trend: the results indicated that, relative to interlocutors who were of equal status, low-status interlocutors made their speech *more* standard, whereas *high*-status interlocutors made their speech *less* standard. With respect to the phonological variable, (t), low-status subjects were shown to raise their standardness by increasing their production of the standard variant [t], while high-status subjects *decreased* their standardness on (t) by producing a significantly greater proportion of the nonstandard variant [ʔ]. Thakerar et al. suggest that the low-status interlocutors might be concerned about increasing their self-esteem, and also possibly showing respect to their higher-status partner (Thakerar et al. 1982: 240). The high-status interlocutors, on the other hand, had the self-esteem which their partners lacked. Their decrease in standardness may have been motivated by a desire to make their communication understood, and to relax their partner (Thakerar et al. 1982: 241).

Thakerar et al. claim, on the basis of the phonetic analysis of (t), that accommodation theory now has objective linguistic evidence to support it.

The dependent measures, as we pointed out earlier, tended, in most of the studies of accommodation, to be analyses of paralinguistic features such as speech rate, or holistic judgments of, for example, "standardness of pronunciation" by groups of linguistically naive raters. In one of the Thakerar et al. studies, however, tapes of the interlocutors were phonetically analyzed, for production of (t), by a trained linguist, and the analysis showed that the high-status speakers significantly increased their use of the standard variant [t], while the low-status speakers significantly *decreased* theirs. The objective phonetic analysis, which revealed statistically significant results, "afforded speech accommodation theory some linguistic precision for the first time" (Thakerar et al. 1982: 229). However, this evidence must be used with caution. First of all, Thakerar et al. reported analysis of only one variable, the (t). While the evidence of [t]-[ʔ] variation is important, we must be careful about making any claims regarding "objective" phonological evidence for accommodation before we know what effect there is, if any, on other phonological variables in the speaker's speech. Second, Thakerar et al.'s research did not (at least with respect to the study that analyzed phonological variation) include a control group. Consequently, Thakerar et al.'s comparisons are restricted to low-status versus high-status comparisons. That is, one experimental treatment is compared with another. The research design does not enable us to determine whether both experimental treatments (low-status and high-status) had an effect on the speaker's phonology or whether only one treatment affected it. We cannot tell, because we are unable to compare that speech with the speech of a control group.

The present study was undertaken to determine whether *status imbalance* would also affect speech in native-*non*native interactions. Previous research on L1 indicates that there is a continuum of standardness along which a speaker shifts according to such factors as degree of attention to speech and type of task (Labov 1966, 1970)—and, we have seen, relative status in the interaction (Thakerar, Giles, and Cheshire 1982). Research on L2 has shown that some of the same factors (e.g., attention to speech and characteristics of the interlocutor) affecting L1 speakers will cause L2 speakers to shift along a continuum of *correctness* (see, e.g., Beebe 1980, Dickerson 1974, Tarone 1979, 1982). In these respects, then, L1 standardness and L2 correctness appear sensitive to the same variables.

Would unequal status affect speech in NS-NNS interactions as it appeared to affect speech in Thakerar et al.'s NS-NS interactions? That is, would we find NSs shifting in standardness, and NNSs shifting in correctness as a function of their relative status vis-à-vis their interlocutor?

A study was designed to answer these questions. Unequal status pairs were created by drawing on one of Thakerar et al.'s methods (discussed above); the subjects were given a task to perform, and one member of each pair was led to believe she had performed quite successfully, while the partner was led to believe she had not done nearly so well. The inducement was "to create perceived differences in their status relevant skills" (Thakerar, Giles, and Cheshire 1982: 231). Different presumed levels of "expertise" on the task led to status differences (where the task, of course, was concerned). Relative expertise regarding a topic has been shown to affect speech behavior (see Leet-Pellegrini 1980). Since success, or expertise, on a task was claimed to be a "status relevant skill" (Thakerar, Giles, and Cheshire 1982: 231), and since such expertise differences were found to affect the NS subjects' standardness, we will employ a similar means of inducing status differences. For ease of discussion, we will refer to the subject who is led to believe she performed the task well as the relative "expert." This in no way implies that she *is* one, only that, compared with her partner, she appears to have shown a greater degree of expertise on the task which we will explain shortly. Her partner, whom we will lead to believe did *not* perform the task very well, we will henceforth refer to as the relative "nonexpert." For the sake of simplicity, "expert" and "nonexpert" will be used as synonymous with Thakerar et al.'s "high-status" and "low-status," although clearly differences do exist.

If the motivations underlying the shifts in standardness in Thakerar et al.'s NS–NS interactions also occur in NS–NNS interactions, we would expect similar shifts in standardness for the NSs in the present study, regardless of the fact that their interlocutors are NSs or NNSs. As in the Thakerar et al. research, we would expect the high status (i.e., the so-called "expert") NSs to have a sufficient amount of self-esteem and to wish to "relax their partners" (Thakerar, Giles, and Cheshire 1982: 241). Therefore, following the Thakerar et al. results, we would predict that, relative to a control group in which subjects are not informed of their expertise:

1. NSs who are "experts" in NS–NNS pairs will show a *decrease* in L1 standardness.

Again, drawing on Thakerar et al.'s explanation of their results, we would expect the low-status (i.e., the so-called "nonexpert") NSs to be concerned about increasing their self-esteem and showing respect to their higher-status partners (Thakerar, Giles, and Cheshire 1982: 240). We could therefore predict that, relative to a control group in which subjects are not informed of their expertise:

2. NSs who are "nonexperts" in NS–NNS pairs will show an *increase* in L1 standardness.

METHOD

The subjects were 45 NS–NNS pairs. All were female, post high school, and ranged in age from 17 to 36. All of the NNSs spoke Spanish as a first language. The NSs were white, and grew up in the greater New York City area. Insofar as was possible, each NS–NNS pair was matched according to social class. None of the NSs were teachers or TESOL trainees. For purposes of the study, none of the subjects were presently art majors. In all pairs, the interlocutors were strangers to each other.

First, each NS–NNS pair was asked to complete part of a nonverbal task, which was the "Meier Art Test of Aesthetic Perception."[2] The test elicits aesthetic judgments; the subject is asked to rank, from "best" to "worst," a set of four slightly different pictures. The subjects individually judged ten sets of pictures, indicating their decisions by filling in boxes on an answer sheet. After that, each NS–NNS pair was asked to have a 10-minute conversation about the pictures (without looking at their answer sheets). They were told to talk over their choices of "best" and "worst," giving their reasons for making them. The conversation was audiotaped,[3] with the investigator outside the room. This will be referred to as Conversation One.

After the conversation, the subjects completed a second section of the test, again individually. At this point, the pairs were randomly assigned to one of two experimental conditions, or the control group (with 15 pairs assigned to each). Subjects in the two experimental groups were given scores for their performance on the test. This was done to give the subjects a measure of their relative *expertise* in the task. They were told that the scores represented how much they agreed or disagreed with the art experts who put the test together. (It must be emphasized that we set up a supposed expertise imbalance only with respect to expertise in performing the test; we were not implying, or leading the subjects to conclude, that they were relative "art experts" or "art nonexperts.") This investigator made believe she was scoring the subjects' answer sheets; in one experimental group, the NS was told she got a high score of 86 percent, while her NNS partner got a low score of 41 percent on the test. (Hereafter, for ease of discussion, the high scorers will be referred to as "experts" and the low scorers as "nonexperts.") In the other experimental group, the NS got a low score (i.e., was the "nonexpert") and the NNS a high score (i.e., was the "expert"). In the control group, none of the subjects was told how they had done on the test. All pairs were then asked to have a second, 10-minute conversation about the pictures. This will be referred to as Conversation Two. The research design is diagramed in Figure 12-1.

After the second conversation, all subjects filled out a questionnaire. Among other things, the questionnaire asked the subjects to rate how they had performed on the test, relative to their partner (whether they had done better, equal to, or worse than their partner). This was an attempt to find out whether the subjects believed the test scores which they were given earlier in the study.

The data were analyzed by comparing each subject's performance on four phonological variables in Conversations One and Two (i.e., the pretreatment condition and the posttreatment condition). The four variables which were selected as dependent measures were:[4] (dh), whose standard

Conversation 1	Conversation 2	
All subjects uninformed about their task performance	NS = "expert" NNS = "nonexpert"	15 pairs
	NS = "nonexpert" NNS = "expert"	15 pairs
	uninformed (control group)	15 pairs

FIGURE 12-1 The Experimental Design

variant is [ð], the voiced interdental fricative in such words as *these, smooth;* (th), whose standard variant is [θ], the voiceless interdental fricative in *three, tooth;* (r), whose standard variant is [r], the voiced retroflex continuant, which was analyzed in preconsonantal and word-final positions (e.g., in *start, star*); and (oh), whose standard variant is [ɔ], the mid-back rounded vowel in such words as *caught* and *off.* All four were studied by Labov (1966), and each was shown to have socially conditioned standard and nonstandard variants in New York City speech. The proportion of standard variants was related to the particular stylistic context of the speech (see Labov 1966). The analysis of Conversations One and Two consisted of determining whether each variant produced was standard or not. Labov (1966) was consulted as a guide for standard and nonstandard realizations of the variable. In addition, the variants were discussed at length with another linguistically trained, native English speaker prior to the analysis. The total native speaker corpus that was analyzed exceeded 12,000 tokens. Interrater (based on one other rater) and intrarater reliability were determined at an early stage of the data analysis. The interrater reliability figures for (dh), (th), (r), and (oh) were .92, .94, .92, and .83, respectively.[5]

Proportions of standardness were calculated for each subject, on each of the four variables, within Conversation One, and then within Conversation Two. Each proportion consisted of

$$\frac{\text{Number of standard L1 variants produced for the given variable}}{\text{All tokens produced for the given variable}}$$

Thus, for each subject on each variable, there were two standardness proportions, one calculated from Conversation One, and one calculated from Conversation Two. Since both of the hypotheses referred to *direction* of change across the group in question (i.e., Hypothesis 1 predicted a decrease in standardness, while Hypothesis 2 predicted an increase in standardness), the investigator had to decide what constituted a "decrease" and what constituted an "increase" in standardness. That is, for example, if a particular subject had a .85 proportion of standardness on the variable (r) in Conversation One, and a .81 on (r) in Conversation Two, was that to be considered a *decrease* in standardness, or basically *no change?* Since there were no precedents in the literature available to draw upon, a decision was made by this investigator, after consulting with others conversant with linguistics and the particular design of the present study. It was felt, intuitively, that less than a 5 percent difference in proportions did not seem sufficient to be called a *change* in standardness. So, for example, a subject's .85 proportion of standardness on (r) in Conversation One and .81 on (r) in Conversation Two would not be described as a *decrease* in standardness in going from Conversation One to Conversation Two. Nor would, for example, a .46 in Conversation One and a .50 in Conversation Two be called an *increase* in standardness. Therefore, if the subject's standardness, with respect to one of the variables, differed by less than 5 percent from Conversation One to Conversation Two, it was categorized as "no change." If, on the other hand, the standardness proportion in Conversation Two was at least 5 percent higher than that in Conversation One, it was categorized as an "increase" in standardness on that variable, and a "decrease" in standardness if the proportion was at least 5 percent lower.

Two nonparametric tests were chosen, the χ^2 Test for k Independent Samples, and the Fisher Test of Exact Probability. The χ^2 test provides a means of determining whether there was a significant difference among the three groups of NS "experts," NS "nonexperts," and "controls" in terms of a decrease or increase in standardness. The Fisher test, on the other hand, enables us to compare each experimental group *directly* with the "controls." The Fisher test is appropriate when the two groups are independent and the sample size is small.

As explained above, this investigator induced "expertise" in the study—by manipulating the performance scores on the test, leading some of the subjects to be told they had done very well, and their partners not very well. A scale was included on the questionnaire, as we pointed out earlier, that elicited each subject's perception of her performance level (i.e., her expertise). Statistical analyses showed that the subjects in each group *overall* scored their performance as better or worse than their partner's, in accordance with what this investigator led them to believe. That is, the NS "nonexperts," as a group, gave significantly *lower* ratings for their test performance than their NNS partners gave ($t = -6.425$; $df = 28$; $p \leq .0005$); the NS "experts," as a group, gave significantly *higher* ratings for their test performance than their NNS partners gave ($t = 6.66$; $df = 28$; $p \leq .0005$). In the control group, as expected, the ratings by NSs and NNSs on their respective performance were *not* significantly different.

But, in looking at *individual* cases, it was discovered that the subject's *perceived* level of expertise (as measured by the scale) did not always correspond to the *induced* level of expertise. To some extent, cultural factors may have been influencing the subjects' perceptions of their expertise.[6] Since both inducement and perception are relevant with respect to describing expertise in the study, it was decided to group the subjects in two ways—according to *induced* expertise (i.e., following the original research design), and according to *perceived* expertise (elicited by the subject's answer on the questionnaire).

RESULTS

Two sets of results will be discussed with regard to the NSs. One set involves the performance profiles that emerged for the groups in which expertise differences were not salient. The other set of results concerns the outcome of the statistical tests applied to the two hypotheses.

As mentioned previously, the phonological analysis that Thakerar et al. (1982) conducted was not connected to a control group. Consequently, we are unable, from that research, to assess the effect of a particular individual treatment (i.e., being an "expert" or "nonexpert") compared with no treatment at all. The present study, on the other hand, does enable us to compare each experimental treatment directly with a control group. Furthermore, the existence of a control group in itself provides us with important data on the phonology of input available to the NNS when differences between the interlocutors are not made salient.

In addition to the control group, there is a second group within which status differences were not salient. With respect to *perception* of their expertise, a number of subjects answered, on the questionnaire, that their test performance (i.e., their level of expertise) was equal to that of their partner. Thus, according to their stated performance, they did not perceive any clear expertise differences within their particular pair. We will refer to these as perceived "equals."

Figures 12-2, 12-3, 12-4, and 12-5 illustrate performance on each of the four variables by the control group and by the perceived "equals," two groups within which expertise differences were not salient.

Looking at performance on each of the four variables, we note a similar group profile: in the absence of any (felt) experimental treatment, the common tendency is for the largest proportion of subjects (.50 to .74), in both groupings, to remain at the same level of standardness, in going from Conversation One to Conversation Two. A smaller proportion of the groups (.09 to .22) increased in standardness or decreased in standardness (.13 to .20). It should be pointed out that those who remained at the same level of standardness on one variable did not necessarily remain the same on the other three variables [e.g., a particular subject might remain the same on (oh) but increase in standardness on (r) and decrease on (dh)]. There were, however, some subjects who did remain at the same level of standardness on

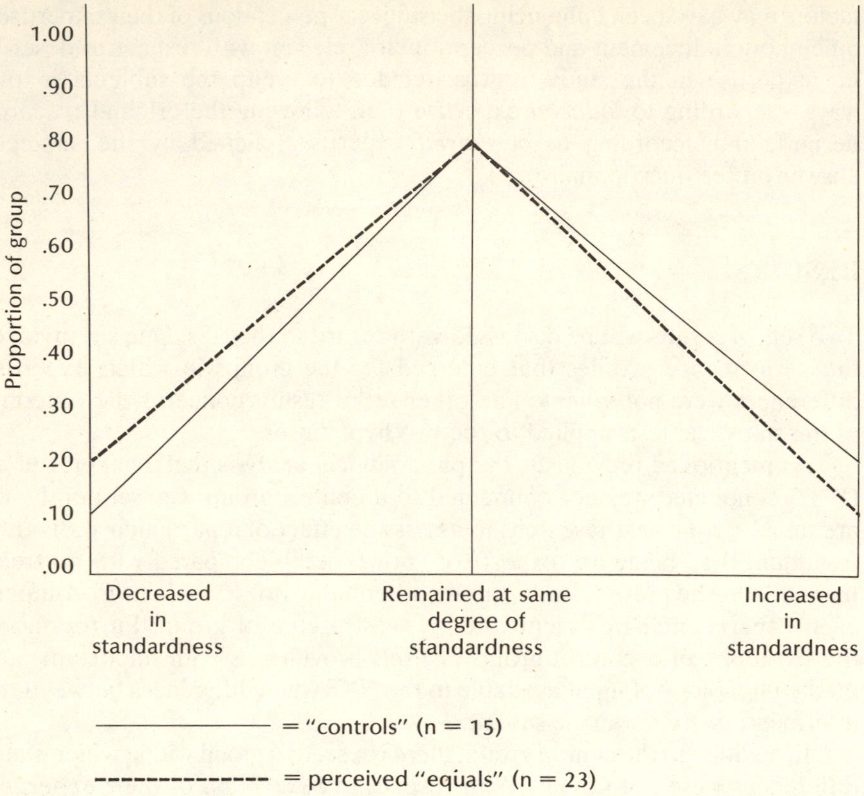

FIGURE 12-2 Performance on (r), Conversation 1 to Conversation 2, When There Are No Clear Expertise Differences

at least three of the four variables. But since the experimental groups also contained such "nonshifters," we cannot conclude that nonshifters were unique to the groups in Figures 12-2 to 12-5.

χ^2 and Fisher tests were done on both induced and perceived groupings. Each of the four variables—(oh), (dh), (th), and (r)—was tested separately. For Hypothesis 1, results of the χ^2 tests on each of the variables showed nonsignificant differences among the groups of subjects. That is, there was no significant difference in the proportion of "experts" who decreased in standardness from Conversation One to Conversation Two. This was true for the induced "experts" as well as for the perceived "experts."

Next, the Fisher test was applied to test Hypothesis 1. Results of this test on each of the four variables also showed nonsignificant differences among the perceived as well as the induced groups. Therefore, we found no statistical support for Hypothesis 1, which had predicted that NS "experts" would decrease in standardness.

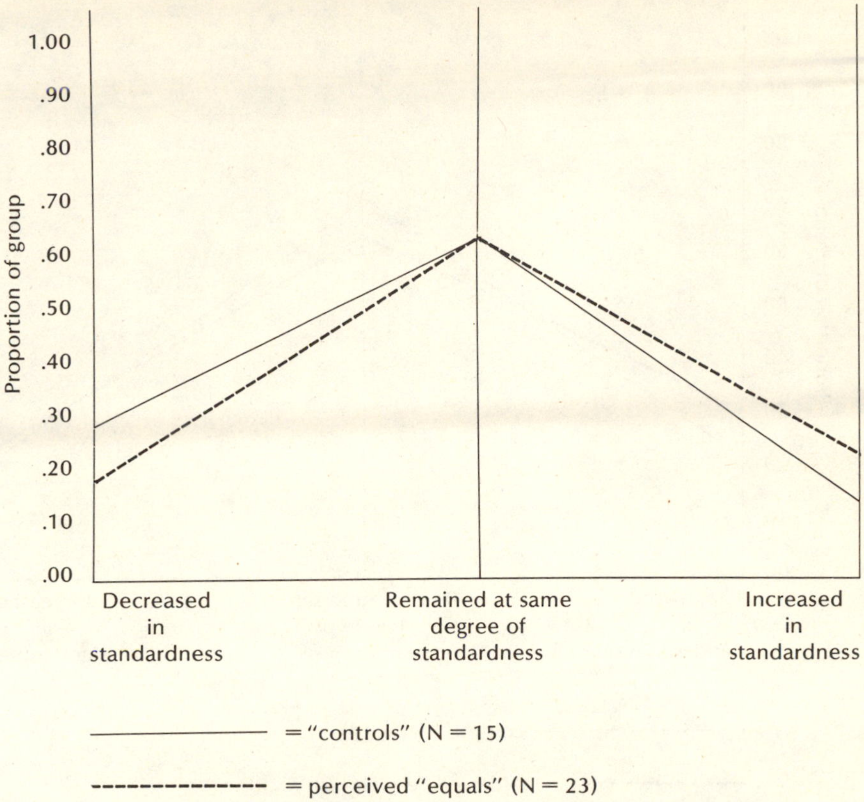

FIGURE 12-3 Performance on (dh), Conversation 1 to Conversation 2, When There Are No Clear Expertise Differences

The χ^2 test of Hypothesis 2, which predicted that NS "nonexperts" would increase in standardness, indicated that the differences were nonsignificant, when comparing all three induced groups with each other, and all three perceived groups with each other. This was true for all four of the variables.

The Fisher test, which, as we pointed out, enabled us to compare each of the "expert" or "nonexpert" groups separately with the control (or "equal") group, resulted in nonsignificant differences for three of the four variables—(r), (dh), and (th). With respect to the (oh), however, we found that there was significance at the .05 level for the perceived "nonexperts." That is, the proportion of perceived "nonexperts" who increased in standardness of (oh) was significantly greater than the proportion of perceived "equals" who increased in standardness of (oh) (exact prob. = .054; cell freqs = 2, 13, 4, 3; marginal freqs = 15, 7, 6, 16; total n = 22). Consequently, there is limited support for Hypothesis 2 with respect to (oh), at least for the "perceived

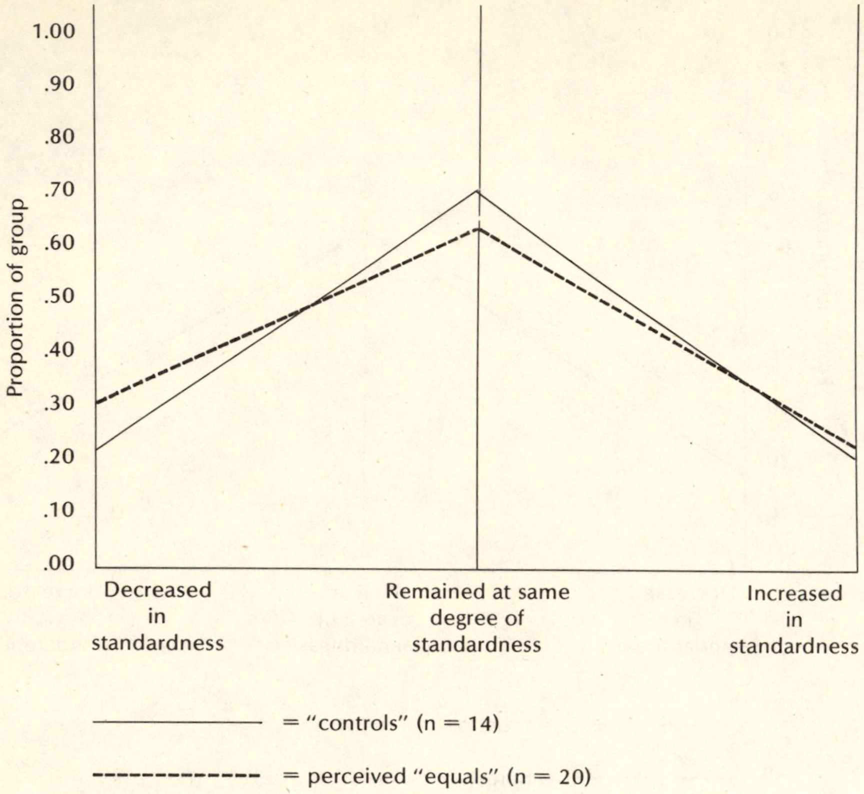

FIGURE 12-4 Performance on (th), Conversation 1 to Conversation 2, When There Are No Clear Expertise Differences

nonexperts."[7] Figure 12-6 illustrates the "perceived nonexperts' " performance on (oh). (Note the differences in proportions increasing in standardness.)

DISCUSSION

With respect to one of the four variables studied, we have found limited support for Hypothesis 2. In terms of performance on (oh), a greater proportion of Ns "nonexperts" increased in standardness, compared with NSs who perceived themselves "equal" to their partner. It must be emphasized that we are referring to "nonexperts" who perceive themselves as such (that is, that they did less well on the task than their partner did, and that they indicated that on the questionnaire). We found that those whose expertise was induced by the investigator did *not* show a significant increase in standardness of (oh). The difference between the induced and perceived

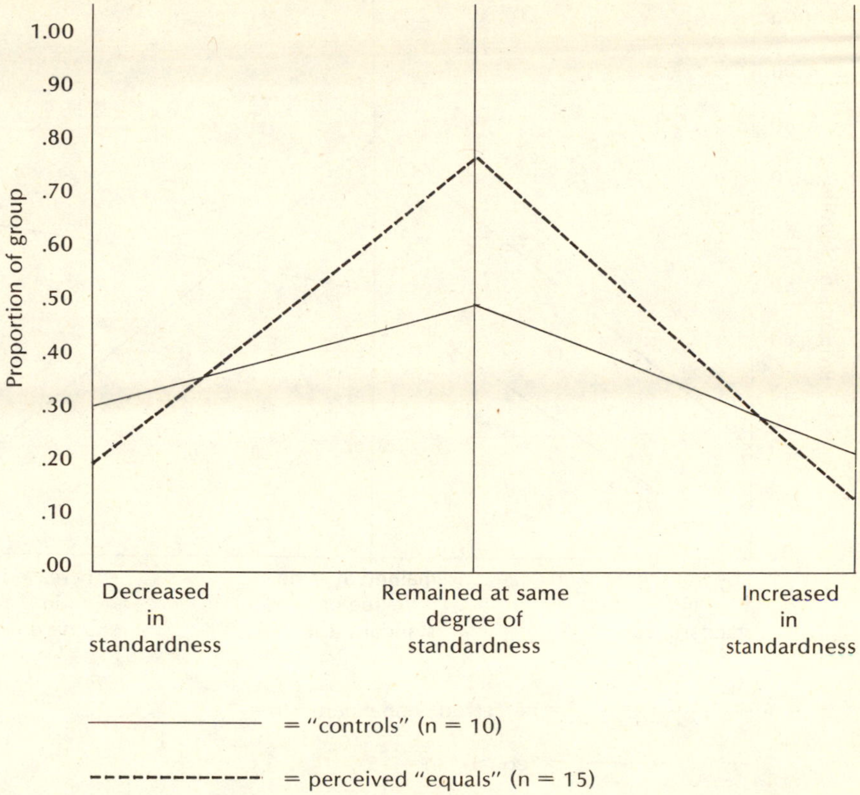

FIGURE 12-5 Performance on (oh), Conversation 1 to Conversation 2, When There Are No Clear Expertise Differences

"nonexperts" is not that surprising; it is quite possible that individual subjects resisted "believing" that their test performance was much lower than that of their partner (even though as a group overall, the "nonexperts'" responses on the questionnaire showed that they rated their test performance significantly *lower* than that of their "expert" partners). They might not have fundamentally accepted their performance as low, or, if they did, it might simply not have affected some of them at all.

But, with respect to performance on (oh) among the *perceived* "nonexperts," we have evidence that corroborates Thakerar et al.'s findings. As in the Thakerar et al. research, NSs in the present study who were low-status in the interaction (i.e., were the "nonexperts"), *increased* their standardness on one phonological variable [here, the (oh)] when interacting with someone who had high status regarding the task. As Thakerar et al. suggest, the motivation for the low-status interlocutors to become more standard may be a need to increase their self-esteem and to show respect to their high-status

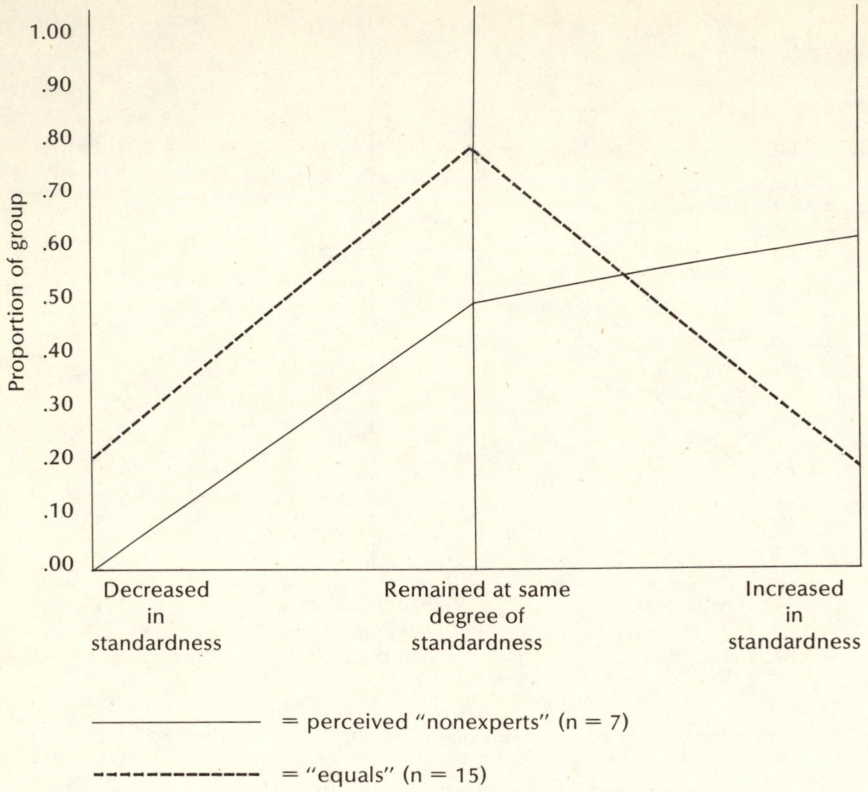

FIGURE 12-6 Performance on (oh), Conversation 1 to Conversation 2, Perceived "Nonexperts" versus "Equals"

partners. The NSs in the present study also wanted to show respect to their higher-status partners, and this was played out in their speech as a shift toward standardness. Whether the NSs were consciously aware of what they were doing, or whether the NNS partners were aware of the shift, and that the NSs were attempting to show respect to them, we do not know. But they are not relevant questions here, for we are talking about motives that operate largely below the level of awareness.

However, we found no statistical support for Hypothesis 2 from the other three variables we analyzed—only for the (oh). Nor did we find any support for a decrease in standardness by "experts" (Hypothesis 1). With respect to performance on the four variables, our "experts" did not act any differently from the controls (or "equals"). Here, our results *do* differ from Thakerar et al.'s (whose "experts" decreased in standardness).

Why did we have significant results on (oh) for "nonexperts" but no significance on (oh) for "experts"? One reason might be that the nonnativeness of the interlocutor becomes a consideration for the NS, when the NS believes she had the *high* status position in the interaction. Having done better than her partner, she can now "afford" to be "sensitive" to her partner's linguistic nonnativeness. We predicted that our "experts" would decrease in standardness, as Thakerar et al.'s had. Their explanation was that since the "experts" had high self-esteem within the interaction (by virtue of the fact that they had higher status than their interlocutors), they would not need to impress their partner (unlike the "nonexperts") but would instead attempt to make what they were saying more comprehensible. The NSs in Thakerar et al.'s research, it must be recalled, were interacting with other NSs. Both interlocutors, as native speakers, presumably had similar linguistic repertoires. Thus comprehensibility of their message *could* be enhanced by a shift away from standardness.

The NSs in the present study, on the other hand, were interacting with *NNS*s. The "experts" may have had the same motivation as Thakerar et al.'s experts (i.e., the desire to make their message more comprehensible to their partner), but becoming *less* standard would not have increased comprehensibility for the NNS interlocutor. Therefore, the nonnativeness of the interlocutor might be one reason why the "experts" in the present study did not become less standard.

Why were there significant results for (oh) but no significance with respect to (r), (dh), or (th)? We can only speculate. Trudgill (no date) suggests that

> during linguistic accommodation generally, it is linguistic features which are relatively high in the speaker's consciousness—markers and stereotypes in Labov's terms—which are subject to modification. (Trudgill, no date: 9)

However, all four of the variables studied—(oh), (dh), (th), and (r)—*are* markers in the Labovian sense; Labov (1966) found evidence that all four are stylistic markers in New York City English. We could argue, nevertheless, that the nonstandard variant of (oh), more than the others, is especially stereotypical of New York City English. The other three variables—the (r), (dh), and (th)—have nonstandard variants which occur in a number of dialects of American English and which are not necessarily pointed out as being peculiarly "New Yorkish." This may account for why only (oh) showed a significant change in this study.

Inclusion of a control group in the present study enabled us to compare experimental treatments with an absence of treatment, rather than limiting ourselves to a comparison of one treatment with another, as in Thakerar's research. Consequently, we were able to determine whether or not the particular treatment had an effect on speech performance. In addition, we were able to compare the control group's (as well as the "equals'") performance on all four of the variables, and see (Figures 12-2 to 12-5) how similar the profiles were. We found that the largest proportions of subjects did *not* shift, either upward *or* downward, on any of the four variables. Only a minority increased or decreased in standardness. Thus, for the majority of subjects to whom expertise differences were not salient, the four sounds did not vary significantly between the two conversations.

CONCLUSION

The results of the present study need to be interpreted with some caution. The significant differences which we found on (oh) between perceived "nonexperts" and "equals"—that is, the limited support we found for Hypothesis 2, were based on small subgroups of subjects. We were comparing 15 "equals" with 7 "perceived nonexperts." Strong claims about performance on (oh) cannot be made until we have more supporting evidence based on a larger number of subjects.

Still, we *can* assert that for the "nonexperts" in this study, lack of expertise (relative to the NNS interlocutor) appears to affect the standardness of one variable, the (oh), of the four that we investigated. Thus the standardness (at least phonologically speaking) of the input available to the NNSs in this study was affected to a certain (albeit limited) extent by relative expertise. As such, the results on (oh) lend partial support to the accommodation framework of Thakerar and Giles. Our evidence from the variable (oh) would indicate that relative expertise *can* exert an influence on standardness, regardless of whether the addressee is native or nonnative.

NOTES

1. In referring to the linguistic variable analyzed in Thakerar et al., as well as the linguistic variables in the present study, we will follow the symbols used by Labov (1966, 1972a). That is, we will use ( ) and [ ]. ( ) will be used to represent a phonological variable which has various phonetic realizations. The actual phonetic realizations exist along a continuum; [ ] will represent a given phonetic realization of the variable. We may illustrate the use of the symbols by reference to the Thakerar et al. study. Thakerar et al. analyzed the subjects' performance on the variable (t). (t) has a number of phonetic realizations. One of them, [t], the voiceless alveolar stop, is the standard English variant. [ʔ], the glottal stop, is a *non*standard variant of (t) in British English. Labov (1972a: 11) pointed out that the use of parentheses reflects a different perspective than that associated with the traditional categories of phoneme and allophone. ( ) indicates a variable; its actual phonetic realizations, denoted by [ ], are sensitive to social factors. As Labov (1972a: 11) explains, this view is "a different approach to the analysis of variation." What is emphasized by the use of ( ) is the fact that the actual phonetic realizations do not occur in free variation but are *socially* patterned.

2. Published by the Bureau of Educational Research and Service, the University of Iowa, Iowa City, 1963. It is based on the research of Norman Charles Meier, the University of Iowa. Available through Stoelting Co., 1350 S. Kostner Avenue, Chicago, Illinois 60623.

3. The tape recorder used was a reel-to-reel, Uher 4400 Report Stereo IC. Two external, standing microphones (one a Uher M517, and one a SONY) were positioned within view of the subjects, to their side. The microphones were placed so that they would be about 12 to 16 inches away from the subjects' mouths. Of course, this distance was impossible to maintain much of the time because the subjects would change posture, gesture, etc., during the course of the conversation. Recordings were made for the most part on Scotch #177 Audio Recording Tape.

4. Originally, (eh) (the vowel in *bad* and *dance*) was included in the analysis. Only a subgroup of contexts for (eh) was considered, following Labov (1966: 51). The result, however, was that the 10-minute conversations produced too few tokens (i.e., less than eight) of (eh) to analyze. Consequently, (eh) was dropped from the analysis.

5. *Intra*rater reliability figures (based on five randomly selected conversations) were as follows: (dh), .97; (th), 1.00; (r), .97; and (oh), .91. Later in the analysis, a third rater analyzed a random sample of the tapes. Both outside raters were native speakers of English (one raised in Manhattan, one in New Jersey near New York City), were linguistically trained, and rated the transcripts blindly. Interrater reliability with the third rater was (dh), .80; (th), .87; (r), .76; and (oh), .73. The lower figures with this rater, relative to the earlier rater, were felt to be due to the differences in preparation time spent with the rater. The earlier rater and the investigator spent at least 6 hours jointly listening to sounds on practice conversations, discussing at length which variants were perceived, and whether the variant should be judged standard or not. Consequently, a basic agreement about the range of "acceptable" variants was reached prior to the reliability tests. In contrast, the third rater and the investigator discussed the criteria of analysis for only 1 1/2 hours, and much of that time was also spent in discussing *NNS* tokens as well as ensuring that the rater could operate the playback equipment.

6. For example, of the 15 NS subjects who were told they got a high score on the test, and that their partner got a low score, 73 percent (11/15) rated their performance as better than their partner's. However, among the 15 *NNS* subjects who were told they got a high score on the test, and that their partner got a low score, only 47 percent (7/15) rated their performance as better than their partner's. This difference between NS and NNS subjects could be due to the influence, on the NNS subjects, of a Hispanic culture which downplays social differences (Anna Doran, personal communication; Kagan 1977).

7. For the induced "nonexperts," the results were nonsignificant.

13

PROSODIC DOMAINS IN FOREIGNER TALK DISCOURSE[1]

Peter Avery, Susan Ehrlich
University of Toronto
Carlos Yorio
Lehman College, City University of New York

Recent work in second language acquisition research has focused on the nature and role of input to the second language learner rather than on the nature of the output produced by the second language learner. While input studies are ultimately concerned with the role of input in the second language acquisition process, preliminary work has attempted to characterize the nature of input. In considering the relationship between input and output in the second language acquisition process, it is first necessary to identify the characteristics of input; i.e., is it different from the language addressed to native speakers and if so, is this difference qualitative or quantitative?

Many input studies have dealt with the modifications made by native speakers (NS) when addressing nonnative speakers (NNS), describing input primarily from an interactional, syntactic, and/or lexical point of view. The study described here examines the phonology of native speakers' speech to nonnative speakers [foreigner talk (FT)].

A review of the literature reveals that few studies of FT deal exclusively with its phonology. Researchers studying other aspects of FT comment in a rather impressionistic way on the phonology, mentioning its clearer articulation, slower rate of speech, higher pitch, and extra heavy stress (Ferguson 1975, Freed 1980, Chaudron 1982). More systematic studies have been conducted in the area of segmental phonology (Henzl 1973, 1979; Kazasis 1969). These studies have claimed that the phonology of FT preserves underlying contrasts which may be obscured in NS–NS interactions through the application of low-level phonetic rules. They have contributed to our understanding of the phonology of FT in that they have revealed the existence of phonological adjustment[2] in the speech of NSs when addressing NNSs. However, a limitation of these studies lies in their failure to consider discourse factors which may influence the specific points at which phonological adjustment occurs. In fact, Kazasis states that adjustment occurs "sporadically" throughout the discourse, the implication being that its placement is arbitrary in some sense. Henzl, on the other hand, reports that FT can be characterized by the absence of reduction phenomena, the implication here being that adjustment occurs throughout the discourse.

In this chapter we depart from previous studies of the phonology of FT in that we examine the phonology within a discourse framework. In addition, we employ a model of phonological representation which allows for a unified treatment of both segmental and suprasegmental processes. We provide evidence that the phonological analysis must make reference to the discourse function of linguistic material if true insight into the nature of phonological adjustment is to be gained. In comparing FT with NS–NS interactions, we shall conclude that from a phonological point of view adjustment is not restricted to FT. Rather, the adjustment reflects universal strategies of discourse production.

THE STUDY

Eight pairs of speakers (four NS–NNS and four NS–NS) participated in a problem-solving activity which required one of the speakers to instruct the other in the drawing of simple objects. In the case of the NS–NNS pairs, it was always the native speaker who gave the instructions. The interactions were taped and later transcribed. The duration of the task was 20 to 30 minutes, and all but two pairs completed the task.[3]

Subjects were matched for sex and controls were established for native language of the NNSs (Japanese), dialect of the NSs (southern Ontario), educational background (all university students), age (between 20 and 30), and experience of NSs in dealing with NNSs (no previous ESL teaching experience). The nonnative speakers came from an intensive English language program at the University of Toronto. Two had been placed in a low-intermediate class and two in a high-intermediate class.[4]

Subjects participated in a "warm-up" task in order to give the NSs an opportunity to assess the proficiency of the NNSs. After this "warm-up" task, one subject (the NS in the NS–NNS dyads) was given a sheet of paper divided into 16 squares in which the objects had been drawn (see Figure 13-1). The other subject was given a sheet of paper which had 16 squares but was otherwise blank. The subject with the completed sheet was then told to instruct his or her partner in the drawing of the objects. All subject pairs understood the instructions clearly and performed the task as directed.

FIGURE 13-1 Diagram Used in the Experiment

DISCOURSE FRAMEWORK

The highly specific nature of the problem-solving task yielded a tightly structured discourse unit allowing us to make direct comparisons across speakers. Following Linde and Labov (1975) and Linde (1979), we see this discourse unit as a "pseudo-narrative" in that it corresponds with the basic structure of a narrative while reporting nonoccurring events.

In Linde's study of the descriptions of apartment layouts, she found that speakers consistently described their apartments in the form of a tour through the apartment. Speakers transformed the spatial configuration of their apartments into a temporal sequence analogous to the temporal sequence of events within a narrative. The discourse unit produced by our task can also be seen as the transformation of a spatial configuration (the diagram) into a temporal sequence (a tour through the diagram).[5] Our task departs from Linde's in that the speaker does not merely describe the objects on the tour but must ensure that the listener is able to replicate them.

For the purposes of our analysis, we invoke a distinction made in discourse studies (Grimes 1972; Hopper 1979; Dry 1983) of narrative between linguistic material which serves to propel the narrative through time on what is termed the main time axis (the foreground) and linguistic material which is off the main time axis because it is either nontemporal or describes events on a time axis other than the main time axis (the background). Rather than employing the terms foreground and background, which are subject to some controversy regarding their exact definition (Reinhart 1982), we distinguish between *core* linguistic material which is directly involved in the execution of the task and serves to move the task toward its completion along the main temporal axis of the discourse and *noncore* linguistic material which is not directly related to the task and is thus off the main temporal axis. This noncore material, rather than creating new points on the main temporal axis (which is the function of core material), serves to expand previously established points.

Core propositions in our study contain new linguistic material corresponding to the semantic criteria in 1.

1 a. Orientation of object on the page, e.g., *Starting in the upper left-hand corner.*
  b. Identification of object, e.g., *I have a picture of a tulip.*
  c. Orientation of object within individual square, e.g., *It's right in the middle.*
  d. Description of object, e.g., *You know, it's got sort of a round bottom with a jagged top.*

All this information is directly involved in moving the task to its completion. In all cases the ordering of the material remains constant, with specific formal markers signaling the move from one point in the discourse to another (i.e., okay, now, next, so).

Noncore propositions contain linguistic material corresponding to the functional criteria listed in 2.

2 Repetitions
  a. Self-initiated, e.g., But it starts at *the bottom left-hand corner* and it goes diagonally halfway towards the right-hand top. . . . so start it at *the bottom left-hand corner.*
  b. Other-initiated, e.g., NS: And right in the middle of the cup is a capital letter V.
     NNS: Pardon me.
     NS: Right in the middle of the cup. . . . there's a capital letter V.

  Expansions
  a. Self-initiated, e.g., yeah and they go on a V/like the shape of a V/one side of a V/they're on a slant.
  b. Other-initiated, e.g., NS: Five portholes in the hull
     NNS: Five . . . ?
     NS: Little windows, round windows, in the boat part.

  Responses
  a. Confirmations

b. Denials
c. Echoes, e.g., NNS: Circle windows?
NS: Yes, circle windows.

Metastatements
a. Internal, e.g., I'm just describing to you sort of what they basically look like, you know.
b. External, e.g., I wish I could remember my science from high school.

Repetitions are defined as the reiteration of lexical items, which in most cases also involves the reiteration of syntactic constructions. Expansions are defined as restatements and/or paraphrases of the core information as well as information that may not have been previously mentioned in the discourse but is inferrable from the previous discourse (Prince 1981, Brown and Yule 1983).[6] Responses include confirmations and denials which involve yes-no answers, and echoes, which serve to confirm or deny through repetition. Metastatements are commentaries either on the nature of the task (internal) or on the nature of the situation (external).

The core/noncore distinction outlined here is crucial to our analysis, as it is core propositions which are phonologically adjusted within the discourse. The only noncore propositions which show evidence of phonological adjustment are those repetitions and expansions which are other-initiated and, not surprisingly, almost exclusively limited to the NS–NNS interactions.[7] These other-initiated repetitions and expansions can be regarded as equivalent to core propositions in that from the perspective of the interlocutors, they constitute new linguistic material.

PHONOLOGICAL FRAMEWORK

Most descriptions of the phonology of FT have listed its characteristics without elucidating the interdependence of the observed phenomena. For example, Tarone (1980) in reviewing the input literature compiles the following list of phonological characteristics (as adapted from Hatch 1979a):

3 Slow rate—clearer articulation (little "sandhi variation")
Final stops are released and voiced final stops more heavily voiced
Some glottal stops used before words beginning with vowels
Fewer reduced vowels and fewer contractions
Longer pauses
Extra volume and exaggerated intonation (from Tarone 1980: 423)

Our goal is to provide a model of phonological representation within which these characteristics receive a unified treatment. More specifically, we wish to show that there exist clear links between pretheoretical notions such as "clearer articulation" and "exaggerated intonation" and that these segmental and suprasegmental modifications which have been said to characterize FT are related in a nontrivial fashion. It would be desirable if the clustering of properties listed in 3 followed from deeper principles of phonological organization.

Recent approaches to phonology have incorporated the notion of metrical structure into phonological representation (Liberman and Prince 1977, Selkirk 1978). Rather than viewing an utterance as merely a linearly ordered string of segments with syntactic bracketings, metrical phonology represents utterances in hierarchically organized tree structures which, though read off the syntax, are not necessarily isomorphic with it. Selkirk (1978) proposes a theory of prosodic domains in which she motivates three phonological domains beyond the level of the word that are relevant to the application of phonological rules: the phonological phrase (ϕ), the intonational phrase (I), and the utterance (ʊ). These domains are organized into binary-branching hierarchically arranged tree structures on which prominence relations are defined by labeling nodes on the tree as strong (s) or weak (w). One principle of this theory is that a node can only be strong relative to a sister node which is weak, and two sister nodes cannot both be labeled strong or weak. Consider the trees in 4.

4

a.

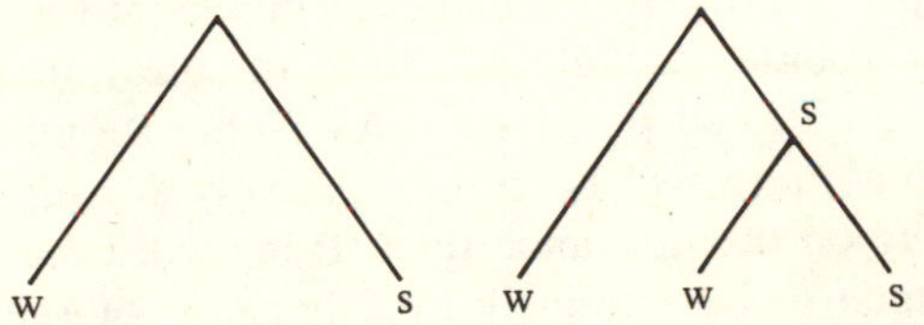

b.

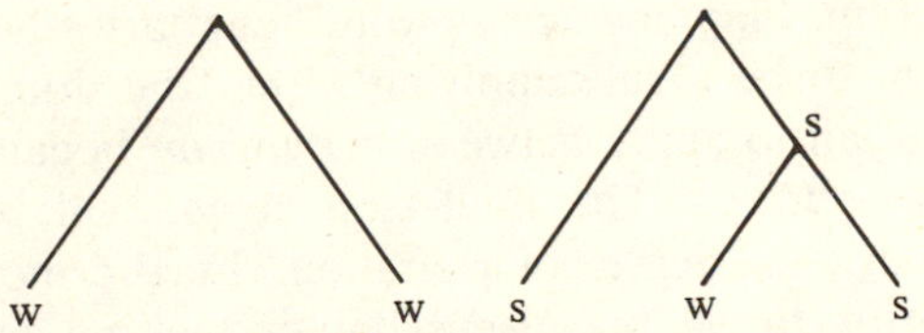

In 4a, the trees are well-formed as all pairs of sister nodes are labeled weak-strong while those in 4b are ill-formed because prominence relations are not defined on sister nodes.

The phonological phrase takes as its input words in syntactic combination and defines prominence relations among them. The intonational phrase takes phonological phrases as its input and defines prominence relations among them. The intonational phrases are organized in a similar fashion at the highest level of structure, the utterance. Within the theory of prosodic domains, phonological rules are defined as applying within a particular domain.

5 John got on the bus.

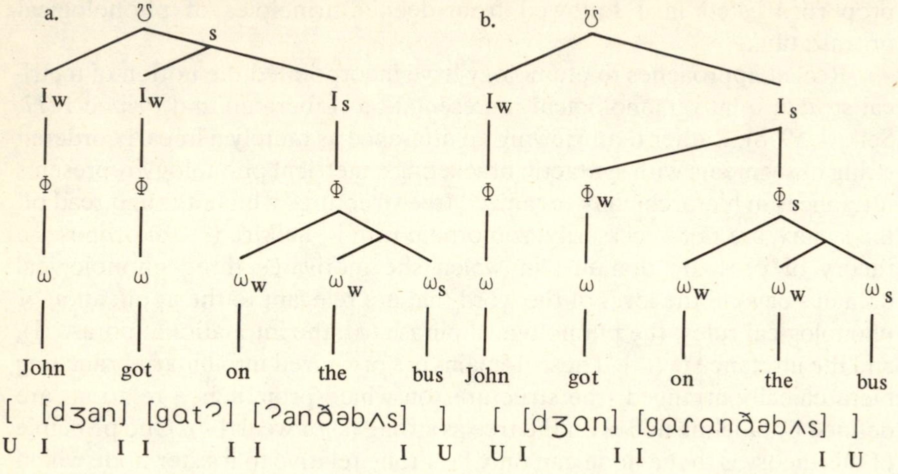

Consider the different parsings available, at the level of the intonational phrase, for a sentence such as 5. In 5a the utterance (ʊ) consists of three separate intonational phrases (I). As each *I* represents a stress group, this predicts that there will be three relatively strong stresses, with the main stress falling on the utterance final strong word *bus.* We would thus expect this utterance to be relatively loud because of the three stresses and the vowel in *bus* to be lengthened to accommodate the other two stressed syllables. However, this parsing has other consequences apart from stress and intonation. Flapping across word boundaries, which Nespor and Vogel (1982) claim to be a rule applying within the domain of the intonational phrase, will fail to apply between *got* and *on* because they are in separate intonational phrases. The final stop in *got* will be either glottalized or released with some degree of aspiration.[8] Furthermore, a glottal stop will be inserted prior to *on* because syllables lacking onsets cannot occur in intonational phrase-initial position.[9]

In 5b, where there are two intonational phrases, flapping will occur between *got* and *on* and there will be no glottal stop prior to *on.* There will be no main stress on *got,* as the verb no longer constitutes its own intonational phrase. The stress on *bus* will be weakened relative to 5a because there are now only two main stresses within the utterance.

In 5c, where the entire utterance is taken as a single intonational phrase, nasal assimilation will occur between the final *n* of *John* and the initial velar of *got,* yielding [dʒ aŋ] rather than [dʒ an].[10] This assimilation was blocked in 5a and 5b because the subject NP was in a separate intonational phrase. This sentence will have only one main stress (on *bus*)

c.

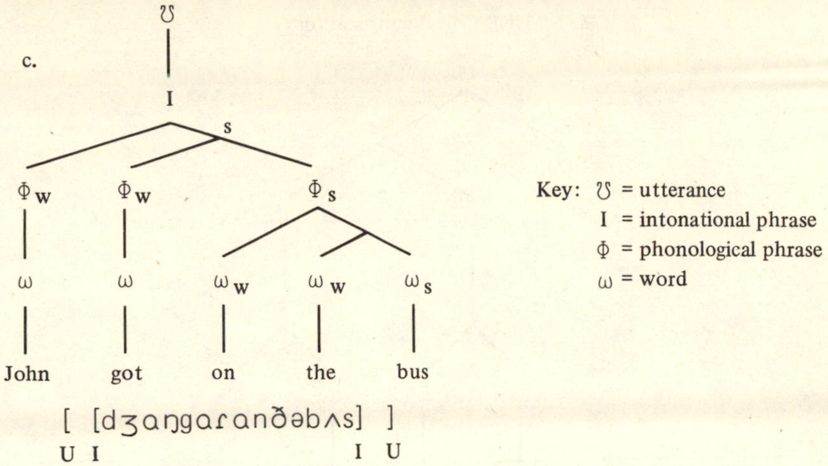

which will be relatively weak in comparison with 5a and 5b.

Consider the difference in the surface phonetic forms of 5a and 5c. The lexical items in 5a are almost identical to their representation in the lexicon, while the lexical items in 5c evidence a departure from this lexical representation which is quite striking. We have shown that the absence of low-level phonetic phenomena in 5a and the presence of these phenomena in 5c are the result of the speaker's use of variable intonational phrasing. The chunking of utterances into many intonational phrases renders the utterance transparent with respect to the lexical representation. Thus such utterances will show phonological features which have been said to characterize FT, as in 3. The utterance in 5c, on the other hand, is opaque with respect to the lexical representation of the individual words as sandhi processes have applied and altered the segmental makeup of the utterance.

We define phonological adjustment as the maximal utilization of intonational phrases within an utterance. Thus utterances such as 5a will be included under this definition whereas utterances such as 5b and 5c will not.

ANALYSIS

Let us now consider the data in light of the discourse and phonological frameworks outlined above. Examples 6 and 7 illustrate the way in which core and noncore information are treated in NS–NNS interactions.

Example 6 constitutes core information as it serves to identify the object being described. An utterance of only four words has been broken into two intonational phrases. This renders the utterance lexically transparent as contraction is blocked from applying between *there* and *is,* a marked form of

6 NS-NNS/Core/Identification

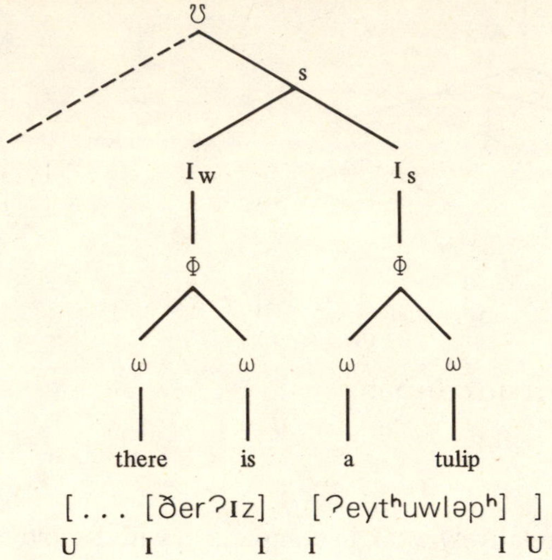

7 NS/NNS/Non-core/Internal Metastatement

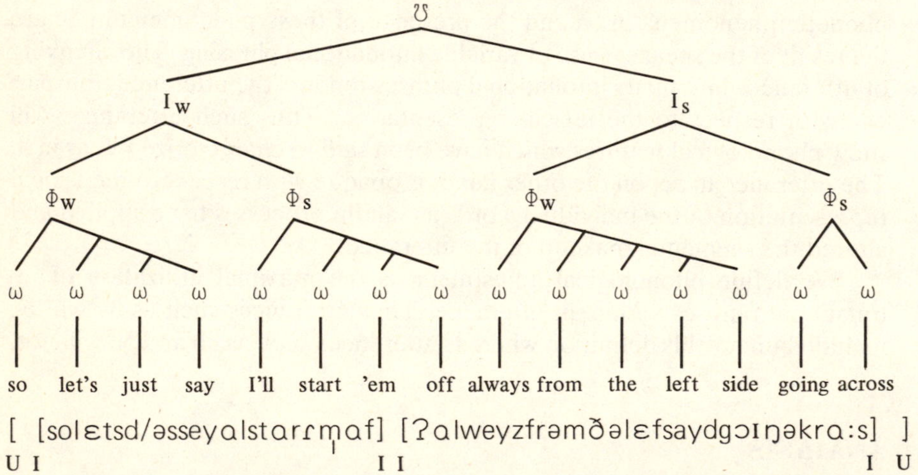

the indefinite determiner occurs, and there is vowel lengthening and heavy release on the final stop in the word *tulip.* The blocking of contraction between *there* and *is* is related to the intonational phrase-final position of *is,* and the citation form of the determiner *a* is related to its intonational phrase-initial position. Furthermore, heavy release of final stops, as mentioned previously, occurs in utterance-final position.

Contrast 6 with 7, a typical noncore task-related (internal) metastatement occurring in an NS-NNS interaction. Here, the utterance also consists of two intonational phrases but these two intonational phrases each dominate two phonological phrases. These phonological phrases are much more complex than those in 6, as they consist of several words. The correctness of the proposed phrasing is evidenced by a pitch fall on *off* and the occurrence of a glottal stop prior to *always.* Notice that the two intonational phrases do not correspond to the syntactic bracketing of the utterance. The intonational phrase break splits a VP between its verb and the PP it dominates (*from the left side*). Notice that contraction, consonant cluster reduction, and vowel reduction occur freely within each intonational phrase. These low-level phonetic processes result in a surface form which is opaque with respect to the lexical representation of the individual words. This exemplifies what we have termed unadjusted speech.

A similar contrast between core and noncore information (within an NS-NNS interaction) can be seen in examples 8a and 8b.

8. a. NS-NNS/Core/Orientation

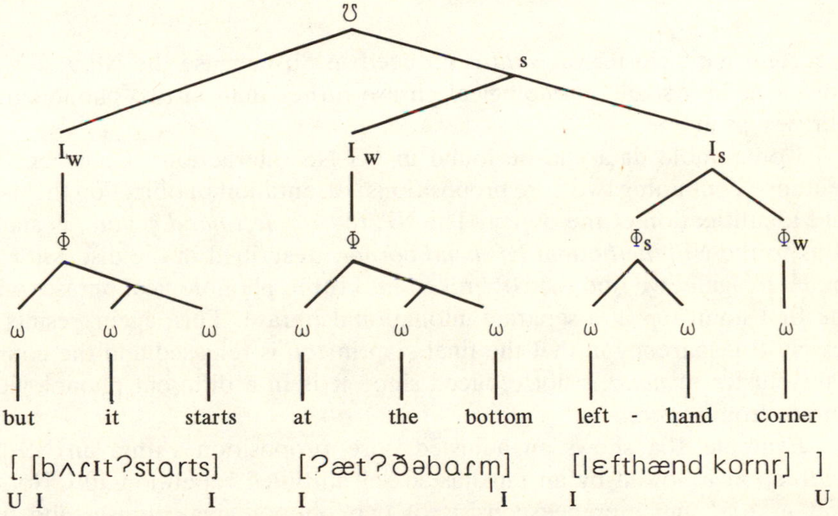

In 8a we find a core proposition which orients the object being described on the page. The utterance is broken into three separate intonational phases, the final two serving to break up a complex noun phrase (*bottom left-hand corner*). This means that there are three pitch falls, one at the end of each intonational phrase. This gives the utterance a rather exaggerated intonation. The core proposition exemplified in 8a was subsequently repeated by the speaker, and this self-initiated repetition is unadjusted. Notice the difference between the two occurrences of *at.* In 8a, we have a glottal stop prior to the word-initial vowel, but in 8b, the glottal stop does not occur. Furthermore,

8 b. NS-NNS/Non-core/Self-initiated repetition

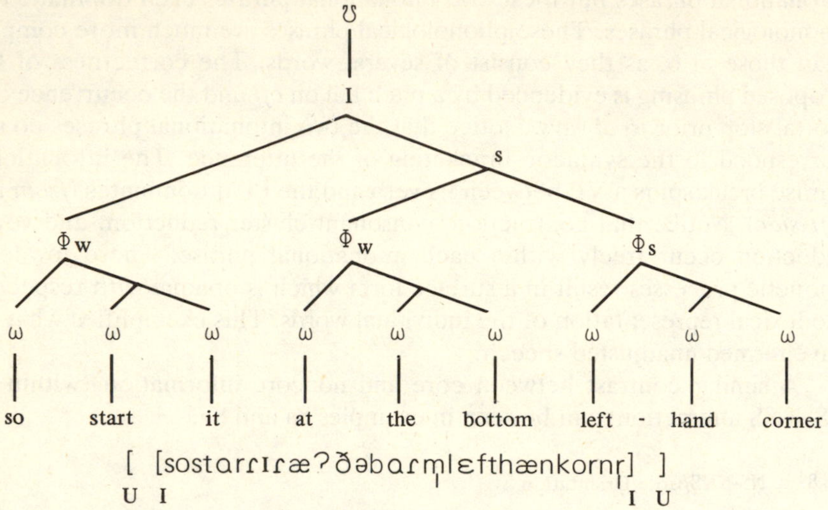

the consonant cluster of *hand* is reduced in 8b because the NP, *left-hand corner,* is in a single phonological phrase rather than in two phonological phrases, as in 8a.

Comparable data can be found in NS–NS interactions. Consider 9, a sentence containing two core propositions: orientation of object on the page and identification of the object. The NP, *the top left-hand square,* is analogous to the NP, *the bottom left-hand corner,* described in the discussion of 8a. Here again, we find the NP broken into three phonological phrases with the first noun *top* in a separate intonational phrase. This, again, results in lexical transparency in that the final stop in *top* is released and the consonant cluster in *hand* is not reduced since it is in a different phonological phrase from *square.*

Example 10a shows an adjusted core proposition within an NS–NS interaction followed by an unadjusted self-initiated repetition 10b. Notice that in 10a, the utterance consists of two phonological phrases and two intonational phrases, whereas the self-initiated repetition 10b is a single phonological phrase. The utterance is spoken at a faster rate in 10b than in 10a as a result of this phrasing.

DISCUSSION

Our finding is that phonological adjustment, at least in the specific type of discourse generated by our task, does not occur throughout the discourse but is limited to specific points in the discourse. And these points in the

9 NS-NS/Core/Orientation-Identification

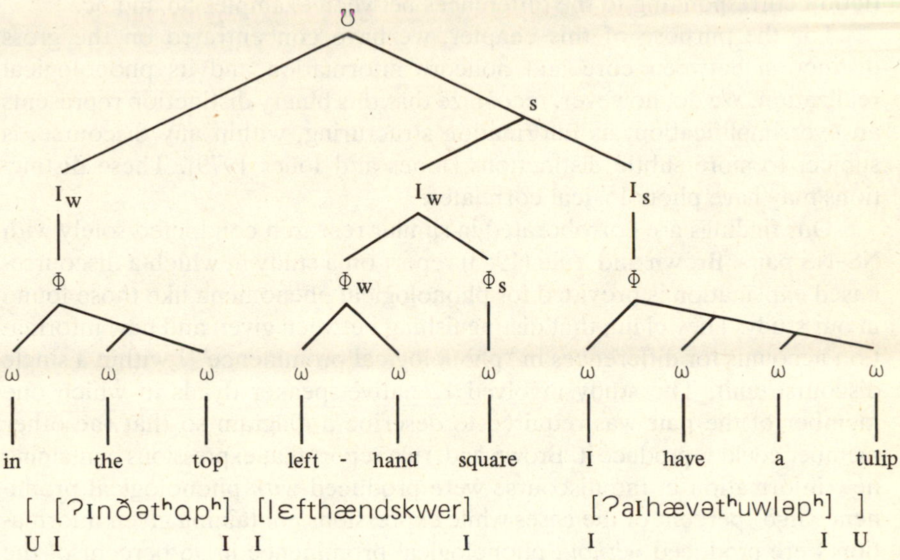

10 a. NS-NS/Core description b. NS-NS/Non-core/Self-initiated repetition

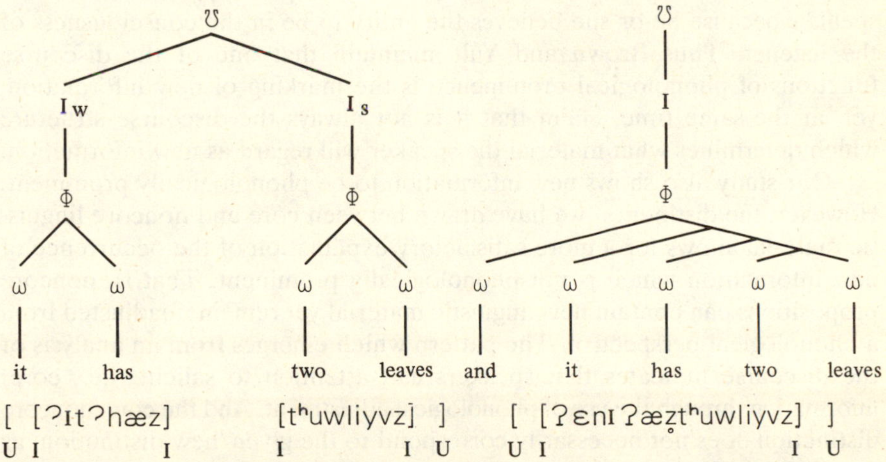

discourse are predictable by appealing to the discourse function of the linguistic material. We have said that phonological adjustment is restricted to core information within the discourse. Furthermore, this phonological adjustment occurs in the core in both NS–NNS and NS–NS interactions. Noncore information does not evidence phonological adjustment as we have defined it. However, within the noncore, there may be phonological differentiation corresponding to the differences between examples 5b and 5c.

For the purpose of this chapter, we have concentrated on the gross distinction between core and noncore information and its phonological realization. We do, however, recognize that this binary distinction represents an oversimplification, as information structuring, within any discourse, is subject to more subtle distinctions (Jones and Jones 1979). These distinctions may have phonological correlates.

Our findings are corroborated in similar research conducted solely with NS–NS pairs. Brown and Yule (1983) report on a study in which a discourse-based explanation is provided for phonological phenomena like those found in our study. They claim that distinguishing between given and new information accounts for differences in "phonological prominence"[11] within a single discourse unit. The study involved 12 native-speaker dyads in which one member of the pair was required to describe a diagram so that the other member could reproduce it. Brown and Yule report that expressions containing new information in the discourse were produced *with* phonological prominence in 87 percent of the cases while expressions containing given information were produced *without* phonological prominence in 98 percent of the cases. While it seems that given information is produced without phonological prominence, it is not the case that new information is always phonologically prominent. Brown and Yule speculate that an entity which is introduced into the discourse for the first time can be treated as given information by the speaker because he or she believes the entity to be in the consciousness of the listener. Thus Brown and Yule maintain that one of the discourse functions of phonological prominence is the marking of new information, yet, at the same time, claim that it is not always the discourse structure which determines what material the speaker will regard as new information.

Our study also shows new information to be phonologically prominent. However, the distinction we have drawn between core and noncore linguistic material allows for a more satisfactory explanation of the occurrence of new information which is not phonologically prominent. That is, noncore propositions can contain new linguistic material yet remain unadjusted from a phonological perspective. The pattern which emerges from an analysis of the discourse indicates that speakers call attention to salient (i.e., core) information through the use of phonological adjustment. And the core/noncore distinction does not necessarily correspond to the given/new distinction, as new information is not always considered to be salient by the speaker. Consider example 7 above. This is a discourse-initial utterance containing new information. As the material in this utterance is not directly involved in the execution of the task but is rather a comment about the execution of the task, we predict that it will be phonologically unadjusted, and this is the correct prediction.

It is important to note that the study reported on by Brown and Yule involved native speakers. Phonological prominence was shown to be an integral aspect of NS–NS discourse, at least in the discourse unit generated by their task. This is consistent with our finding that phonological adjustment is not restricted to NS–NNS interactions but occurs as well in the NS–NS interactions.

As our examples show, core propositions are subject to phonological adjustment in both NS–NNS and NS–NS interactions. What we have not discussed is the possibility that quantitative differences exist between the two types of interactions. Consider the difference between 8 and the final intonational phrase in 9. In the NS–NNS interaction, four words have been broken into two intonational phrases, while in a comparable proposition in the NS–NS interaction only one intonational phrase is used. Such differences in phrasing may suggest that the NS–NNS interactions are characterized by the chunking of information into smaller units. However, as we have seen, such chunking is not restricted to the NS–NNS interactions. In fact, even examples similar to those in 6 can be found in the NS–NS speech as in 10.

CONCLUSION

While we have not conducted a systematic quantitative study of the phonological phenomena under discussion, we have provided evidence that such a study must consider phonological adjustment as a discourse function. A quantitative study, which merely counts segmental modifications without regard for their place in the discourse, fails to reveal the functional nature of phonological adjustment. Furthermore, segmental modification, itself, cannot be viewed as a dependent variable, as it is not independent of prosodic structure. We would argue that quantitative studies must take prosodic domains as their dependent variables, as segmental modification is merely a manifestation of prosodic structure.

To conclude, we should first note that our phonological analysis, which unites segmental and suprasegmental phenomena, allows for insights into the nature of phonological adjustment. The interdependence of notions such as clearer articulation, slower speech, and extra heavy stress and vowel reduction, contraction, and consonant cluster reduction follow naturally from a metrical model of phonological representation.

Second, we have found that phonological adjustment is a property of both NS–NNS and NS–NS discourse. Furthermore, the type of information which is adjusted in the NS–NNS interactions is identical to the type of information which is adjusted in the NS–NS interactions. The information which is not adjusted is also identical in both interactions. This suggests that the *presence* of adjustment is not a function of the nonnativeness of the interlocutor.

What, then, are the distinctive characteristics of the phonology of FT?

We have suggested that there is a tendency for smaller intonational domains in the NS-NNS discourse. While these may be more pervasive in the NS-NNS discourse, they are not exclusive to it, as they also occur in the NS-NS discourse. Our study did not focus on possible quantitative differences between the two types of interactions; however, further research could be conducted along the lines developed in this chapter. What our study does reveal is that the phonology of FT is not qualitatively different from the phonology of NS-NS interactions, at least in the discourse generated by our task. Rather than viewing phonological adjustment as a function of FT, we claim that this adjustment reflects universal strategies of discourse production. That is, all discourse, be it caretaker speech or NS-NS, contains information differentiation, and in spoken discourse this differentiation has phonological realizations.

NOTES

1. We would like to thank the Department of Linguistics, University of Toronto, for its support during the writing of this chapter. The research was also supported by doctoral fellowships from the Connaught Foundation and Social Sciences and Humanities Research Council of Canada to the first and second authors, respectively.

2. We provide a more precise definition of phonological adjustment in the following section of the chapter. We will continue to use the term in anticipation of this definition.

3. One of the pairs not completing the task consisted of native speakers.

4. Placement is based on a standardized listening test and an informal assessment of writing and speaking ability.

5. Evidence for this claim can be adduced from speaker's consistent use of temporal deictics (*now, then,* etc.) to indicate the move from one point in the discourse to another.

6. The core propositions are repeated and expanded upon in all the interactions; however, the number of repetitions and expansions of the core information is higher in the NS-NNS interactions. The discourse produced in the NS-NS interactions progresses relatively smoothly through the core information with fewer interruptions and/or digressions to cause movement off the main time axis of the discourse.

7. This is consistent with Long's (1983a) claim that a distinctive feature of foreigner talk is the presence of frequent negotiations for meaning. Other-initiated repetitions and expansions are attempts by the nonnative speaker to "negotiate" the conversation.

8. The precise conditions under which word-final stops are glottalized or released are not clear. Our data show that stops are released when stressed and in utterance-final position. However, as Selkirk (1982) has pointed out, releasing of labials is more likely than releasing of alveolars in any position.

9. Again, the precise conditions under which glottal stops are inserted are not clearly understood. However, what is clear is that glottal stops will always be inserted in intonational phrase-initial position. Other conditions exist under which glottal stops will be inserted before word-initial vowels, i.e., when a syllable receives stress. For some discussion of syllable structure in English, see Kahn (1976).

10. It is also possible that the final nasal is deleted in this position and that nasalization occurs only on the vowel.

11. Brown and Yule (1983) use the term "phonological prominence" to refer to the syllables within a single expression which receive tonic accent, tonic accent being identified in

terms of intonational peaks. The term is not strictly equivalent to our term "phonological adjustment." They discuss phonological prominence in terms of intrasentential phenomena: specifically the structure of given/new information within an expression. We, on the other hand, are concerned with intersentential phenomena and therefore can consider entire expressions as produced without phonological adjustment. It is not clear that an entire expression could be produced without phonological prominence, as presumably every expression would contain at least one intonational peak in Brown and Yule's framework.

The reason we even attempt to equate the two terms "phonological adjustment" and "phonological prominence" is their respective functional roles within a discourse. Both are viewed as a means of differentiating information.

Section Four

INPUT, INTAKE, AND OUTPUT

On the Relationship between Input and Output

14

COMMUNICATIVE COMPETENCE: SOME ROLES OF COMPREHENSIBLE INPUT AND COMPREHENSIBLE OUTPUT IN ITS DEVELOPMENT[1]

Merrill Swain
The Ontario Institute for Studies in Education

The role of input is, without a doubt, of critical importance in understanding the what and why of second language acquisition. To this end, we are seeing an increasing number of studies which focus on fine-grained analyses of the nature of foreigner talk, teacher talk, and learner talk, as well as on the variables intervening between input and intake. The data base for the majority of these studies is input to learners of English as a second or foreign language, and input to adults.

The focus of this chapter, and the data base employed, are considerably different. Rather than focusing on a microanalysis of learner input in specific interactional events, attention will be paid to the input-output relationships at the level of language proficiency *traits,* specifically the traits of grammatical, discourse, and sociolinguistic competence. The data come from children whose first language is English and who are learning French as a second language in the school setting of a French immersion program. Compared with ESL learners, these children make infrequent use of the target language outside of the school setting. Thus the second language input to these students is largely that of native-speaker teacher talk and nonnative peer talk, as well as, of course, experience with literacy activities. Within a theoretical framework that incorporates traits and contexts of language use, the structure of the immersion students' output, that is, the structure of their language proficiency, can be seen to relate rather directly to the nature of the input received. However, aspects of the immersion students' second language proficiency cannot be totally accounted for on the basis of the input received.

This chapter, then, will consider the second language proficiency exhibited by these French immersion students, relating their output at a macro level to their language learning environment. Of the conclusions I will draw, one that I think is fundamental to our understanding of the role of input in second language acquisition is that although comprehensible input (Krashen 1981b, 1982) may be essential to the acquisition of a second language, it is not enough to ensure that the outcome will be nativelike performance. In fact, I will argue that while comprehensible input and the concomitant emphasis on interaction in which meaning is negotiated (e.g., Long 1983a; Varonis and Gass, 1985b) is essential, its impact on grammatical development has been overstated. The role of these interactional exchanges in second language acquisition may have as much to do with "comprehensible output" as it has to do with comprehensible input.

The data I will be drawing on in this chapter come from one study undertaken within the context of a large-scale research project concerned with the development of bilingual proficiency.[2] The overall aim of the research is to explore the influences of social, educational, and individual variables on the processes and outcomes of second language learning. The specific goal of the study I will be discussing here was to determine the extent to which certain components of language proficiency represented in our theoretical framework as linguistic traits were empirically distinguishable and were differentially manifested in oral and written tasks. Other studies currently underway as part of the same large-scale research program will compare the structure of language proficiency of French immersion students with that of other learners who have learned their second language under considerably different conditions. Thus, although of theoretical interest, the research program has been designed to have direct bearing on language policy issues in schools through the identification of strengths and weaknesses in certain aspects of the students' language proficiency.

The basic theoretical framework within which the study was carried out is diagramed in Figure 14-1. The framework incorporates as traits several components of communicative competence proposed by Canale and Swain (1980)—grammatical, discourse, and sociolinguistic; and incorporates as methods, oral- and literacy-based tasks. For each cell in the matrix of traits by methods shown in Figure 14-1, a test and relevant scoring procedures were developed. The details of the tests, scoring procedures, and reliability indices are described elsewhere (Allen et al. 1982, 1983). Here, I will confine myself to a brief trait-by-trait description of the tests and main features of the scoring procedures utilized. The scoring breakdown has theoretical interest in that it pinpoints which aspects of language competence are being assessed in each test.

Traits / Methods	*Grammar*	*Discourse*	*Sociolinguistic*
Oral production	Structured interview	Film retelling and argumentation	Requests Suggestions Complaints
Multiple choice	45 items	29 items	28 items
Written production	←—— ←——	2 narratives 2 letters ——→	2 notes } directives

FIGURE 14-1

The trait of grammatical competence was operationalized as rules of morphology and syntax, with a major focus on verbs and prepositions. The oral production task consists of a structured interview which embeds 36 standardized questions in a conversation. The topics are concrete and familiar, designed to focus the student's attention on communication rather than on the second language code. The standardized questions are designed to elicit a range of verb forms and prepositions in French, as well as responses that were sufficiently elaborated to score for syntactic accuracy. Grammatical scoring, then, was based on the student's ability to use certain grammatical forms accurately in the context of particular questions.

The grammatical multiple-choice test consists of 45 items assessing knowledge of aspects of syntax and morphology similar to those elicited in the interview situation.

In the grammatical written production tasks the student is presented with four situations and asked to write a short text about each. The four topics were designed to bias for the use of the past and present tenses through two narrations, and future and conditional tenses through two letters of request. Grammatical errors were tallied for each of four categories: syntactic errors, preposition errors, homophonous verb errors, and non-homophonous verb errors. The error counts were translated into accuracy scores by considering them, in the case of syntactic errors, relative to the number of finite verbs produced; in the case of prepositions, relative to the number of obligatory contexts for prepositions; and in the case of verb errors, relative to the number of verb forms produced.

Before moving on to a description of the tasks and scoring procedures used in measuring the discourse and sociolinguistic traits, it is useful to examine the results obtained by the grade 6 immersion students who took the grammar tests relative to native speakers of French also in grade 6. The results reported in this chapter are based on a subsample of 69 French immersion students who were administered the entire battery of oral production, multiple-choice, and written production tests. These immersion students have been in a program in which they were taught entirely in French in kindergarten and grade 1, about 80 percent in French in grades 2 through 4, about 60 percent in French in grade 5, and about 50 percent in French in grade 6—the year they were tested. The comparison group of native French speakers consists of 10 grade 6 students who likewise were administered the entire test battery. The native speakers of French were in a unilingual French school in Montreal.

The results for the grammatical oral production, multiple-choice, and written production tasks are shown in Tables 14-1, 14-2, and 14-3, respectively. The essential point to note in these tables is that with the exception of correct use of homophonous verb forms, the native speakers score significantly higher ($p < .01$) than the immersion students, indicating clearly that, although the immersion students are doing quite well, they have not acquired nativelike abilities in the grammatical domain.

TABLE 14-1 Grammatical Oral Production—Percentage Correct

	Immersion students		*Native speakers*		*Comparisons*	
	Mean	*S.D.*	*Mean*	*S.D.*	*t*	*sig of t*
Syntax	81.3	13.1	96.5	6.8	3.60	.01
Prepositions	80.5	12.1	100.0	0.0	—	—
Verbs	57.0	18.1	96.4	5.1	6.79	.01
Total	73.2	8.6	96.9	4.0	8.56	.01

TABLE 14-2 Grammatical Multiple-Choice—Percentage Correct

Immersion students		*Native speakers*		*Comparisons*	
Mean	*S.D.*	*Mean*	*S.D.*	*t*	*sig of t*
60.7	4.41	81.3	4.40	6.20	.01

TABLE 14-3 Grammatical Written Production—Percentage Correct

	Immersion students		*Native speakers*		*Comparisons*	
	Mean	*S.D.*	*Mean*	*S.D.*	*t*	*sig of t*
Syntax	75.5	12.1	93.6	6.9	4.60	.01
Prepositions	78.8	10.5	96.0	6.3	5.01	.01
Nonhom vb	85.5	7.2	95.9	4.6	4.49	.01
Hom vb	78.5	9.0	79.1	10.3	.20	ns
Total	70.9	8.7	85.0	8.5	4.82	.01

The second trait measured, that of discourse competence, was defined as the ability to produce and recognize coherent and cohesive text. The discourse oral production task is designed to elicit narrative and argumentation. The students are shown a short nonverbal film, *The Mole and the Bulldozer*, chosen for its appropriateness to the age group of the students being tested, and for its provocative content which illustrates the conflict between modern technology and the preservation of nature. The day following the film's showing, students are taken individually from class and asked to tell the story of the film. A series of pictures of key events is placed in front of the child to minimize the burden on memory. Following the narration, the student is asked to role-play the mole and try to convince the bulldozers not to change the route of a road, using all the arguments he or she can think of.

Scoring of the story-retelling task was based on four categories: (1) setting the scene, (2) identification, (3) logical sequence of events, and (4) time orientation. Under the category of "setting the scene," the student's establishment of the idyllic habitat and lifestyle of the mole was assessed. This was important for the coherence of the story, as it was this idyllic atmosphere that was at risk throughout. Under the category of "identification," the student was rated for the explicitness and clarity with which key characters, objects, and locations were introduced into the narrative. Because the student had been given to understand that the interviewer had not seen the movie, it was incumbent on the student to name the characters, objects, and locations. Under the category "logical sequence of events," a rating was given for the logical coherence with which the events of the story were narrated. Thus it was important to explain how the mole knew the bulldozers were coming and would endanger his garden, and what the various steps were that the mole took to ensure the safety of his property. And finally, under the category of "time orientation," a rating was given for the coherent use of verb tenses, temporal conjunctions, adverbials, and other elements that clarified the temporal relationship between the events of the story. Each of these categories was rated on a scale of 1 (low) to 5 (high). The role-playing situation was also rated on a scale of 1 (low) to 5 (high) for the extent to which logical arguments were presented to support the mole's case that the road should not be straightened. And finally a global score of 1 (low) to 5 (high) was obtained representing the raters' subjective integration of scene setting, identification, logic, time sequence, and argument.

The multiple-choice test of discourse competence consists of 29 items primarily measuring coherence. Each item is a short passage of 2 to 5 sentences. One sentence is omitted from the passage, and the task is to select the appropriate completion from a set of three alternatives. The criterion for selection is primarily the logical coherence of the passage. Intersentential cohesive devices are explicitly incorporated in some items as a basis for choice. An example is given below:

Le premier voyage en ballon dirigible a eu lieu en France en 1783. ____________________.
Cependant ça a été un grand événement pour les français.

a. Il n'a duré que 8 minutes.
b. Il avait été bien planifié.
c. Il était rempli d'air chaud.

The written discourse production tasks were the same ones used in the grammatical production tasks, two compositions involving narrative discourse and two letters involving suasion. Scoring for discourse involved six categories: (1) basic task fulfillment, (2) identification, (3) time orientation, (4) anaphora, (5) logical connection, and (6) punctuation. The assessment of "basic task fulfillment" involved rating how well the written work fulfilled the basic semantic requirements of the discourse task. To qualify as narratives, for example, the compositions needed to include a series of events. To qualify as suasion, the letters had to contain a request with at least one supporting argument. The category of "identification" was similar to that for the oral production task in which an assessment was made of whether new characters, objects, and locations were sufficiently identified, or whether too much prior knowledge on the part of the reader was assumed. The category of "time orientation" was also similar to that used in the oral production task, assessing how adequately events or situations were located in time and, where relevant, whether the temporal relationship between events or situations was clear. Under the category of "anaphora," the use of anaphoric reference to already identified characters, objects, or locations through the use of subject pronouns, possessive adjectives, and articles was assessed. The category of "logical connection" assessed the logical relationship between segments of the text: whether there were non sequiturs, semantically obscure or fragmentary incidents, or logically missing steps in the argument or sequence of events. The final category, that of "punctuation," was rated as an indication of the information structure of a text. Ratings were based on the extent to which punctuation clarified the information structure of the text by indicating boundaries of information units. Each of these categories was rated on a five-point scale of 0 (low) to 2 (high), i.e., (0, 0.5, 1, 1.5, 2).

Following the detailed scoring, the raters who had scored six discourse categories independently assigned a global discourse score by first sorting the written tasks into three categories of below average, average, and above average, and then rating them as relatively high or low within each of these three categories. This resulted in a six-point scale. The criteria for assigning a global score were not closely specified; the scorers were simply asked to keep in mind the general criterion of coherent discourse.

The discourse results are shown in Tables 14-4, 14-5, and 14-6 for oral production, multiple-choice, and written production tasks, respectively. On the separate aspects of discourse which were rated, examination of the comparisons between the immersion and native-speaker students reveals only two significant differences: in the case of oral production, native speakers are rated significantly higher than immersion students on time orientation (p < .01); and in the case of written production, native speakers are rated significantly lower than immersion students on punctuation (p < .01). The nonsignificant trend revealed by these comparisons, but indicated in the comparison of total discourse scores, is that native speakers generally perform better than the immersion students on the oral story retelling task but do not differ in their performance on the written production tasks. The only indication to the contrary is that the global score for the written production tasks shown in Table 14-6 reveals a significant difference (p < .05) between the mean scores obtained by the two groups in favor of the native speakers.

TABLE 14-4 Discourse Oral Production Ratings on a Scale from 1 (low) to 5 (high)

	Immersion students		*Native speakers*		*Comparisons*	
	Mean	*S.D.*	*Mean*	*S.D.*	*t*	*sig of t*
Scene	3.0	1.16	3.5	.85	1.43	ns
Ident.	3.2	1.07	3.9	1.37	1.89	ns
Logic	2.9	1.29	2.9	1.37	.04	ns
Time	3.5	1.18	4.5	.71	2.54	.01
Arg.	2.9	1.55	3.4	1.26	1.06	ns
Total	3.1	.79	3.6	.79	2.10	.05
Global	2.9	.88	3.6	1.04	2.16	.05

TABLE 14-5 Discourse Multiple-Choice Percentage Correct

Immersion students		*Native speakers*		*Comparisons*	
Mean	*S.D.*	*Mean*	*S.D.*	*t*	*sig of t*
66.6	3.78	71.0	2.84	1.03	ns

TABLE 14-6 Discourse Written Production Ratings on a Scale from 0 (low) to 2 (high)

	Immersion students		*Native speakers*		*Comparisons*	
	Mean	*S.D.*	*Mean*	*S.D.*	*t*	*sig of t*
Basic	1.7	.28	1.8	.30	1.61	ns
Ident.	1.3	.31	1.2	.25	− .58	ns
Time	1.5	.30	1.4	.38	− .47	ns
Anaph.	1.7	.24	1.6	.33	− .98	ns
Logic	1.5	.30	1.6	.35	1.34	ns
Punct.	1.6	.41	1.2	.54	−2.67	.01
Total	1.5	.19	1.5	.24	− .72	ns
Global	3.3	1.04	4.1	1.42	2.22	.05

There would seem to be two possible interpretations for the different results obtained by a comparison of the *total* written discourse scores from those obtained by a comparison of the *global* written discourse scores (Table 14-6). It may indicate that the raters were able to detect qualitative differences in the written discourse of native speakers and immersion students that were not captured in the detailed component scores, or it may be that the raters did not stay strictly within the bounds of discourse in making their global ratings. For example, if the raters inadvertently attended to grammatical aspects, which, as has been seen, are clearly better in the native-speaking sample, they may have rated the native speakers better for the wrong reason.

At this point, then, it can be seen that differences between the native and nonnative groups depend on the trait being measured. For grammar, the difference is large regardless of method; for discourse, the difference is small regardless of method. These results suggest that the grammatical trait is distinguishable from the discourse trait.

The third trait measured, that of sociolinguistic competence, was defined as the ability to produce and recognize socially appropriate language within a given sociocultural context. The oral production sociolinguistic test consists of presenting a series of 12 situations using slides and audio accompaniment describing the situation. Each situation is a particular combination of one of three functions—request, suggestion, or complaint; of one of two levels of formality—high or low; and of one of two settings—in school or out of school. The test begins with the tester explaining to the student being tested how different registers of speech may be used in different situations and illustrates this with an example. The student then watches a set of three slides and listens to the synchronized description. With the showing of the last slide, the student responds in the most appropriate way as if addressing the person shown in the slide. For example, one set of slides shows two children in the school library who are the same age as the student being tested. The student hears a description, in French, that says, "You're in the library to study. But there are two persons at the next table who are speaking loudly, and are bothering you. You decide to ask them to make less noise. What would you say if the two persons were friends of yours?" To change the level of formality, another set of slides shows two adults in the library, and the final question is "What would you say if the two persons were adults that you don't know?"

The objective of the scoring was to determine the extent to which students could vary their language use appropriately in response to the social demands of the different situations. In other words, the scores were to indicate the student's ability to use linguistic markers of formal register in formal situations and to refrain from using them in informal situations. Thus, for each situation, a student's response was scored for the presence (= 1) or absence (= 0) of six markers of formal register. The six formal features were: (1) the use of an initial politeness marker such as *pardon* or *madame* in the utterance opening; (2) the use of *vous* as a form of address; (3) the use of question forms with *est-ce que* or inversion; (4) the use of the conditional verb form; (5) the inclusion of formal vocabulary and/or the use of additional explanatory information; and (6) the use of concluding politeness markers such as *s'il vous plaît.* A student's score on a particular marker in a particular situation was taken as the difference between use of the marker in the formal variant of the situation and use in the informal variant. A good sociolinguistic score was thus a relatively high difference score, and a poor sociolinguistic score was a relatively low or negative difference score.

The multiple-choice test of sociolinguistic competence consists of 28 items designed to test the ability of a student to recognize the appropriateness of an utterance with respect to its sociocultural context. The items describe a specific sociocultural situation and the student is asked to select the best of three possible ways to express a given idea in that situation. The items are designed to include both written and spoken language use in varying degrees of formality, and include the identification of certain written styles such as those used in proverbs, in publications such as journals, encyclopedias, and magazines, and in public notices. Before the test is started, the distinction between oral and written language is drawn to the students' attention, and the students are told that the register of the responses, not their grammaticality, is the important consideration. Each item is scored according to the degree of appropriateness based on native-speaker responses, with values ranging from 0 to 3 points. Two examples are given below:

1. A l'école, dans la cour de récréation, dite par une élève à son ami
   a. Pourrais-je te voir un instant?
   b. Est-ce que je pourrais te parler quelques minutes?
   c. Je peux te parler une minute?
2. Devant l'hôtel de ville, écrit sur un panneau public
   a. Prière de ne pas passer sur le gazon.
   b. Ne pas passer sur le gazon.
   c. Vous ne devez pas passer sur le gazon.

The sociolinguistic written production tasks focus on two extremes of directive. The students wrote two letters requesting a favor of a higher-status, unfamiliar adult. In addition, the students wrote two notes in which they assumed the role of a familiar adult (mother, teacher) imposing authority by means of a brief informal note to get action from the student who is at fault in some way (has left room untidy, homework undone).

As with the sociolinguistic oral production tasks, the scoring of the sociolinguistic written production tasks was designed to capture the student's ability to use formal sociolinguistic markers of politeness that were appropriate in the context of the letters, and to abstain from using such markers in the context of the notes. Thus each letter and note were scored for the presence or absence of several formal markers: (1) the use of conditional verb forms; (2) the use of modal verbs, and/or *est-ce que,* inverted and indirect question forms, and/or the use of idiomatic polite expressions (e.g., *ayez l'obligeance de*); (3) the use of *vous* as a form of address; and (4) the use of formal closings (e.g., *merci à l'avance, merci de votre collaboration*). As with the sociolinguistic oral task, a difference score was calculated between the use of each marker in the formal contexts and its use in the informal contexts.

The sociolinguistic scores are shown in Tables 14-7, 14-8, and 14-9 for the oral production, multiple-choice, and written production tasks, respectively. The results suggest that overall, native speakers perform significantly better on the sociolinguistic tasks than the immersion students. Excluding for the moment the use of *vous* as a polite form of address, the only discernible pattern in the results is that in those categories of sociolinguistic performance where formulaic politeness terms are possible, immersion students tend to perform as well as native speakers, whereas in those categories where grammatical knowledge inevitably plays a role in the production of the appropriate form, immersion students' performance is inferior to that of native speakers. This is especially obvious in the use of the conditional where immersion students perform relatively poorly on both written and oral tasks. This result is not particularly surprising in light of the grammatical results reviewed earlier. As Tables 14-1 and 14-3 indicate, immersion students are relatively weak in verb morphology. Here, then, appears to be a good example of the dependence of some aspects of sociolinguistic performance on grammatical knowledge.

The underuse of *vous* as a polite marker in formal contexts by immersion students as indicated in both Tables 14-7 and 14-9 can be linked directly to the input the students have received. Teachers address the students as *tu,* and students address each other as *tu.* The use of *vous* in the classroom setting is likely to be reserved for addressing groups of students, thus signaling its use as a plural form, or as a means of signaling annoyance on the part of the teacher. There are thus few opportunities in the classroom for the students to observe the use of *vous* as a politeness marker used in differential status situations.

TABLE 14-7 Sociolinguistic Oral Production Difference Scores, Formal-Informal Use

	Immersion students		*Native speakers*		*Comparisons*	
	Mean	*S.D.*	*Mean*	*S.D.*	*t*	*sig of t*
Intro	.522	.263	.400	.263	−1.37	ns
Vous	.300	.220	.800	.132	6.97	.01
Quest	.117	.180	.417	.180	4.96	.01
Cond	.042	.150	.267	.210	4.22	.01
Other	.102	.167	.517	.183	7.25	.01
Finale	.095	.203	.200	.258	1.49	ns
Total	1.170	.530	2.600	.570	7.94	.01

The picture which emerges from these results, then, is one of a group of language learners who, although they have in some respects reached a high level of target language proficiency, are still appreciably different in their use of some aspects of the language from native speakers. This appears to be particularly evident in those aspects of communicative performance which demand the use of grammatical knowledge. These results are consistent with those we have found with grade 9 immersion students using a completely different set of tests (Lapkin, Swain, and Cummins 1983).

TABLE 14-8 Sociolinguistic Multiple-Choice, Percentage Correct

Immersion students		*Native speakers*		*Comparisons*	
Mean	*S.D.*	*Mean*	*S.D.*	*t*	*sig of t*
35.29	6.13	40.50	10.10	2.29	.05

Krashen (1981b) has argued that learners "acquire structure by understanding messages and not focusing on the form of input, by 'going for meaning'." (p. 54). According to Krashen, this comprehensible input "delivered in a low (affective) filter situation is the only 'causative variable' in second language acquisition." (p. 57). Comprehensible input I take to mean language directed to the learner that contains some new element in it but that is nevertheless understood by the learner because of linguistic, paralinguistic, or situational cues, or world knowledge backup. It is different in nature, I think, from what Schachter (1984) has referred to as negative input. Negative input is feedback to the learner which indicates that his or her output has been unsuccessful in some way. Negative input includes, for example, explicit corrections, confirmation checks, and clarification checks. There is no reason to assume that negative input necessarily includes some new linguistic element in it for the learner. It may, for example, consist of a simple "What?" in response to a learner utterance. As such it is basically information given to learners telling them to revise their output in some way because their current message has not been understood.

TABLE 14-9 Sociolinguistic Written Production Difference Scores, Formal-Informal Use

	Immersion students		*Native speakers*		*Comparisons*	
	Mean	*S.D.*	*Mean*	*S.D.*	*t*	*sig of t*
Cond	.195	.335	.700	.350	4.43	.01
MQP	.645	.365	.750	.355	.85	ns
Vous	.230	.350	1.000	.000	—	—
Closing	.405	.455	.650	.410	1.60	ns
Total	1.480	.840	3.100	.667	5.83	.01

The hypothesis that comprehensible input is the *only* causal variable in second language acquisition seems to me to be called into question by the immersion data just presented in that immersion students do receive considerable comprehensible input. Indeed, the immersion students in the study reported on here have been receiving comprehensible input in the target language for almost 7 years.

One might question, then, whether the immersion students have, in fact, been receiving comprehensible target language input. The evidence that they have, however, seems compelling. The evidence comes from their performance on tests of subject matter achievement. For years now, in a number of French immersion programs across Canada, immersion students have been tested for achievement in such subjects as mathematics, science, history, and geography, for which the language of instruction has been French, and their performance has been compared with that of students enrolled in the regular English program who are taught the same subject matter content in their first language. In virtually all the comparisons, the French immersion students have obtained achievement scores equivalent to those obtained by students in the regular English program (Swain and Lapkin 1982). Furthermore, on tests of listening comprehension in French, the immersion students perform as well as native speakers of French by grade 6 (Swain, Lapkin, and Andrew 1981). This strongly suggests that the immersion students understood what they were being taught, that they focused on meaning. Yet, as we have seen, after 7 years of this comprehensible input, the target system has not been fully acquired.

This is not to say that the immersion students' input is not limited in some ways. We have already seen that there are few opportunities in the classroom for the students to observe the use of *vous* as a politeness marker in differential status situations. I suspect also that the content of everyday teaching provides little opportunity for the use of some grammatically realized functions of language. The use of the conditional may be a case in point. But until data are collected pertaining to the language actually used by immersion teachers, nothing further can be said on this point. It is our intention to collect such immersion teacher talk data next year.

Another way in which the immersion students' input may be limited is by virtue of peer input. The students hear their peers speaking as they do. But as I will point out below, in the later grades of school, students are likely to hear more teacher talk than peer talk. And my own informal observations indicate that most peer-peer interaction that is not teacher-directed is likely to occur in English rather than in French at this grade level.

Given these possible limitations in input, the fact still remains that these immersion students have received comprehensible input in the target language for 7 years. Perhaps what this implies is that the notion of comprehensible input needs refinement. Long (1983a), Varonis and Gass (1985b), and others have suggested that it is not input per se that is important to second language acquisition but input that occurs in interaction where meaning is negotiated. Under these conditions, linguistic input is simplified and the contributions made by the learner are paraphrased and expanded, thereby making the input more comprehensible. Given, then, that comprehensible input is the causal variable in second language acquisition (Krashen 1981b), the assumption is that second language acquisition results from these specific interactional, meaning-negotiated conversational turns.

If this is the case, then, we may have part of the explanation for the immersion students' less than nativelike linguistic performance. In the context of an immersion class, especially in the later grade levels, and as in any first language classroom where teachers perceive their primary role as one of imparting subject-matter knowledge, the teachers talk and the students listen. As Long (1983a) has indicated in the context of language classes, there are relatively few exchanges in classroom discourse motivated by a two-way exchange of information where both participants—teacher and student—enter the exchanges as conversational equals. This is equally true of content classes, and immersion classrooms are no exception.

Immersion students, then, have—relative to "street learners" of the target language—little opportunity to engage in two-way, negotiated meaning exchanges in the classroom. Under these circumstances, the interaction input hypothesis would predict that second language acquisition would be limited. This prediction is consistent with the immersion students' performance if it is confined to grammatical acquisition. Confining this prediction to grammatical acquisition is compatible with what appears to be an assumption underlying the input interaction hypothesis—that second language acquisition is equivalent to grammatical acquisition. As has been indicated by the theoretical framework of linguistic proficiency used in this study, however, we consider second language acquisition to be more than grammatical acquisition, and to include at least the acquisition of discourse and sociolinguistic competence as well, in both oral and written modes. From this perspective, the relative paucity of two-way, meaning-negotiated exchanges does not appear to have impeded the acquisition of discourse competence. Indeed, it seems likely that the diet of comprehensible, noninteractive, extended discourse received by the immersion students may account—at least in part—for their strong performance in this domain relative to native speakers. In short, what the immersion data suggest is that comprehensible input will contribute differentially to second language acquisition depending on the nature of that input and the aspect of second language acquisition one is concerned with.

As I have suggested, the interaction input hypothesis is consistent with the prediction that immersion students will be somewhat limited in their grammatical development relative to native speakers because of their relatively limited opportunity to engage in such interaction. Although this provides a theoretically motivated and intuitively appealing explanation, I have several doubts about its adequacy. The doubts relate to two interrelated assumptions: (1) the assumption that it is the exchanges, themselves, in which meaning is negotiated that are facilitative to grammatical acquisition as a result of comprehensible input, and (2) the assumption that the key facilitator is input rather than output.

The first assumption, that the exchanges themselves are facilitative to grammatical acquisition, rests on the possibility that a learner can pay attention to meaning and form simultaneously. However, this seems unlikely. It seems much more likely that it is only when the substance of the message is understood that the learner can pay attention to the means of expression—the form of the message being conveyed. As Cross (1978), examining the role of input in first language acquisition, stated:

> By matching the child's semantic intentions and ongoing cognitions, (the mother's) speech may free the child to concentrate on the formal aspects of her expressions and thus acquire syntax efficiently. (p. 214)

In other words, it would seem that negotiating meaning—coming to a communicative consensus—is a necessary first step to grammatical acquisition. It paves the way for future exchanges, where, because the message is understood, the learner is free to pay attention to form. Thus comprehensible input is crucial to grammatical acquisition, *not* because the focus is on meaning, *or* because a two-way exchange is occurring, but because by being understood—by its match with the learner's ongoing intentions and cognitions—it permits the learner to focus on form. But this would appear to be the sort of comprehensible input that immersion students do, in large part, receive.

What, then, is missing? I would like to suggest that what is missing is output. Krashen (1981b) suggests that the only role of output is that of generating comprehensible input. But I think there are roles for output in second language acquisition that are independent of comprehensible input. A grade 9 immersion student told me about what happens when he uses French. He said, "I understand everything anyone says to me, and I can hear in my head how I should sound when I talk, but it never comes out that way." (Immersion student, personal communication, November 1980.) In other words, one function of output is that it provides the opportunity for meaningful use of one's linguistic resources. Smith (1978, 1982) has argued that one learns to read by reading, and to write by writing. Similarly, it can be argued that one learns to speak by speaking. And one-to-one conversational exchanges provide an excellent opportunity for this to occur. Even better, though, are those interactions where there has been a communicative breakdown—where the learner has received some negative input—and the learner is pushed to use alternate means to get across his or her message. In order for native-speaker competence to be achieved, however, the meaning of "negotiating meaning" needs to be extended beyond the usual sense of simply "getting one's message across." Simply getting one's message across can and does occur with grammatically deviant forms and sociolinguistically inappropriate language. Negotiating meaning needs to incorporate the notion of being pushed toward the delivery of a message that is not only conveyed, but that is conveyed precisely, coherently, and appropriately. Being "pushed" in output, it seems to me, is a concept parallel to that of the i + 1 of comprehensible input. Indeed, one might call this the "comprehensible output" hypothesis.

There are at least two additional roles in second language acquisition that might be attributed to output other than that of "contextualized" and "pushed" language use.[3] One, as Schachter (1984) has suggested, is the opportunity it provides to test out hypotheses—to try out means of expression and see if they work. A second function is that using the language, as opposed to simply comprehending the language, may force the learner to move from semantic processing to syntactic processing. As Krashen (1982) has suggested:

> In many cases, we do not utilize syntax in understanding—we often get the message with a combination of vocabulary, or lexical information plus extra-linguistic information (p. 66).

Thus it is possible to comprehend input—to get the message—without a syntactic analysis of that input.[4] This could explain the phenomenon of individuals who can understand a language and yet can only produce limited utterances in it. They have just never gotten to a syntactic analysis of the language because there has been no demand on them to produce the language. The claim, then, is that producing the target language may be the trigger that forces the learner to pay attention to the means of expression needed in order to successfully convey his or her own intended meaning.

The argument, then, is that immersion students do not demonstrate native-speaker productive competence, *not* because their comprehensible input is limited but because their comprehensible output is limited. It is limited in two ways. First, the students are simply not given—especially in later grades—adequate opportunities to use the target language in the classroom context. Second, they are not being "pushed" in their output. That is to say, the immersion students have developed, in the early grades, strategies for getting their meaning across which are adequate for the situation they find themselves in: they are understood by their teachers and peers. There appears to be little social or cognitive pressure to produce language that reflects more appropriately or precisely their intended meaning: there is no push to be more comprehensible than they already are. That is, there is no push for them to analyze further the grammar of the target language because their current output appears to succeed in conveying their intended message. In other words, although the immersion students do receive comprehensible input, they no longer receive much negative input.

This discussion has so far referred primarily to the acquisition of spoken language. However, much of the experience these immersion students have had with French has been literacy-based. The primary task of early education is the development of reading and writing skills, and early immersion education is no different, except that it occurs in the students' second language.

The results already presented relate not only to spoken language but to language which makes use of literacy skills as well. However, performances across tasks within traits are not directly comparable in any way. Thus the results presented so far cannot address the issue of the relationship between spoken and written language. For this, we need to rely on factor-analytic analyses.

The factor analyses carried out to date have involved only the total or global scores for each trait by method cell. The correlations among the scores of the nine cells for the 69 students in the immersion sample only are presented in Table 14-10. Inspection of this table shows that the simplest interpretation of the correlations in terms of the three traits and three methods is not possible. If the only causes of correlations were shared trait and method, tests that shared neither would not correlate, or at least they would not correlate as highly as tests that shared a common trait, a common method, or both. Yet some pairs of tests that share neither trait nor method do correlate more highly, such as grammatical multiple-choice and discourse written production (.47).

TABLE 14-10 Correlations Among Overall Cell Scores

	GO	*GM*	*GW*	*DO*	*DM*	*DW*	*SO*	*SM*
GM	.180							
GW	.286	.600						
DO	.160	.100	.074					
DM	.240	.432	.432	.245				
DW	.178	.467	.496	.261	.460			
SO	.139	.073	.175	.103	.085	.023		
SM	.268	.314	.417	.295	.260	.326	.171	
SW	−.067	.198	.170	.219	.344	.530	−.038	.109

Several hypotheses concerning the structure underlying the correlations among the nine scores were tested using confirmatory factor analyses (LISREL). One very acceptable solution was found ($\chi^2 = 14.13$, df = 21, p = .864) and is shown in Table 14-11. It is a two-factor solution with a general factor and a method factor. The method factor reflects the school experience of the students with the target language—one that highlights written rather than oral language—and is most strongly represented by the written discourse task. It is to be noted that the written discourse task, as indicated in Table 14-6, is the one in which native speakers and immersion students performed most similarly. It also represents the sort of task which all students have had considerable experience with in school. That immersion students do as well as native speakers may reflect, then, their comprehensible output in this domain of language use. These results also indicate that there is no strong relationship between performance on the literacy-based tasks and performance on the oral tasks, except that captured by the global proficiency factor.

TABLE 14-11 Confirmatory Factor Analysis—LISREL

	Factor 1 general	*Factor 2 written*	*Uniqueness*
GO	.53	—	.72
GM	.49	.55	.47
GW	.68	.39	.38
DO	.30	—	.91
DM	.41	.42	.65
DW	.20	.66	.52
SO	.23	—	.95
SM	.47	.24	.72
SW	−.03	.49	.76

$\chi^2 = 14.13$, df = 21, p = .864.

These results do not show the validity of the three postulated traits. However, it has already been shown that in the wider context of immersion students *plus* native speakers, at least two of the three traits—grammar and discourse—are distinct.[5] The fact that these two traits do not emerge in the factor analysis is probably due largely to the homogeneity of the immersion sample. In the wider sample, the native speakers have had considerably different experiences from the immersion students, but among the immersion students the main experience for all the students is in the same sort of immersion classroom. There are not major opportunities for some students to acquire certain aspects of language proficiency, and others to acquire different aspects. What is in common for these students is their literacy-based experience as revealed by the structure of their target language proficiency. The fact that no strong relationship is shown between their written and oral performance can be interpreted within the context of the previous discussion: whatever knowledge they have of the language that is literacy-based is only weakly demonstrated in their oral performance because in general, they have had limited opportunity to use and practice their speaking skills in communicative exchanges that require a precise and appropriate reflection of meaning, whereas they have had considerable practice in doing so in written tasks.

To summarize and conclude, the results of a series of tests administered to grade 6 French immersion students indicate that, in spite of 7 years of comprehensible input in the target language, their grammatical performance is not equivalent to that of native speakers. Immersion students, however, perform similarly to native speakers on those aspects of discourse and sociolinguistic competence which do not rely heavily on grammar for their realization. In addition, results from the immersion data reveal a structure of proficiency reflective of their school-based language-learning situation: one which emphasizes written rather than spoken language.

The findings are compatible with an explanation of grammatical acquisition resulting in part through conversational exchanges in which meaning is negotiated. It was suggested, however, that these sorts of exchanges, although a prerequisite to acquisition, are not themselves the source of acquisition derived from comprehensible input. Rather they are the source of acquisition derived from comprehensible output: output that extends the linguistic repertoire of the learner as he or she attempts to create precisely and appropriately the meaning desired. Comprehensible output, it was argued, is a necessary mechanism of acquisition independent of the role of comprehensible input. Its role is, at minimum, to provide opportunities for contextualized, meaningful use, to test out hypotheses about the target language, and to move the learner from a purely semantic analysis of the language to a syntactic analysis of it. Comprehensible output is, unfortunately, generally missing in typical classroom settings, language classrooms and immersion classrooms being no exceptions.

NOTES

1. I wish to express my gratitude to Patrick Allen, Jim Cummins, Birgit Harley, Eric Kellerman, Sharon Lapkin, Jacquelyn Schachter, and Nina Spada for taking time from their busy schedules to read an earlier draft of this chapter and discuss it with me. I would also like to thank those who worked so long and arduously preparing the test materials, collecting the data, and scoring so carefully and meticulously the vast quantities of data gathered: Suzanne Bertrand, Christian Ducharme, José Lopes, Françoise Pelletier, Greta Shamash, and Mireille Tremblay. Thanks also go to Mary Lou King, who kept the data files organized and systematic, and to Jud Burtis and Gila Hanna, who were invaluable in providing statistical advice and interpretation.

2. The Development of Bilingual Proficiency Project is funded by a grant (no. 431-79-0003) from the Social Sciences and Humanities Research Council of Canada to Merrill Swain, Patrick Allen, Jim Cummins, and Raymond Mougeon.

3. Roger Andersen (personal communication, March 7, 1984) has suggested another possible function of output. "My argument is that if the learner has some sort of expectation to have to *use* the L2 in clearly definable ways, that future use of the language can cause the learner to perceive aspects of the input very differently from what his/her perception would be if there is no clear, definable, future expected *use* of the language."

4. Gary Cziko suggests (personal communication, January 17, 1984) that "you can make a stronger case for the importance of output in second language acquisition by considering the notion of a fuzzy, open, non-deterministic syntactic parsing strategy that can be used for *comprehending* discourse but would be inadequate in *producing* it." (See Clark and Clark 1977 and van Dijk and Kintsch 1983, especially pages 28–31.) It may not be just that only semantic processing is required for comprehension but that in addition any syntactic processing involved in comprehension might be very different from the closed logical system of rules required to *produce* a grammatical utterance.

5. That evidence for a distinction between grammatical and discourse competence was found by the fact that the French immersion students lagged further behind the native speakers

in grammatical competence than in discourse competence, yet the factor analysis failed to reveal a similar distinction, may be an example of one of the problems of using a correlational approach to investigate models of communicative competence (Cziko 1984). Cziko suggests (personal communication, January 17, 1984) that "what you found may be similar to Examples 6 or 7 on Table 2 where norm-referenced (or correlational) interpretation might suggest a common factor underlying two dimensions of communicative competence while a criterion-referenced interpretation might suggest separate factors."

On Quantity and Quality of Input

15

THE USE OF THE TARGET LANGUAGE IN CONTEXT AND SECOND LANGUAGE PROFICIENCY[1]

Richard R. Day
University of Hawaii—Manoa

Second language acquisition research has identified a variety of factors which are claimed to affect the proficiency levels attained by language learners. Among these factors is the use of the target language, both in the classroom and away from or outside the classroom. It is widely assumed that the use of the target language is one of the crucial variables in the successful acquisition of the target language—the more often students use or practice the second or foreign language, the more likely they are to learn it.

There have been a number of articles which discuss the importance of second language learners using the target language away from the classroom. For example, Rubin (1975) claims that the good language learner practices the target language. Stern (1983: 411) believes that good language learners "seek communicative contact with target language learners and the target language community . . . (and) become actively involved as participants in authentic language use."

Bialystok (1978), in a study of Canadian high school students learning French, found that "functional practice" helped to account for her subjects' performance in French. Bialystok defines functional practice as attempts by the learner to have additional exposure in using French in order to increase communicative competence. She claims that when the target language is used for communication, the learner's proficiency, including formal aspects of the language, improves. This results in an increase in performance on classroom tasks (1978:230).

Seliger (1977) posits an interaction continuum of second language learners, with one end characterizing students who seek out opportunities to use the target language, who practice by initiating interactions in the target language. The opposite end of the interaction continuum finds students who experience difficulty in functioning in natural language settings and tend to avoid interacting in the target language. In his study of ESL students, he claims first that ESL students who generated significantly more English input in the ESL classroom than other ESL students were more proficient in English; and second, that these same students—the high-input generators of English—tended to score higher on certain questions which measured the use of English outside the classroom than did the low-input generators of English.

Motivated by Seliger's investigation, we conducted an investigation into the relationship between the classroom participation of ESL students and second language proficiency (Day 1984), and use of the target language outside the classroom and proficiency in the target language. This chapter is concerned with that part of the investigation which dealt with the use of English by nonnative speakers in context—away from the classroom—and its relationship with proficiency in English. The specific hypothesis we examine here is that the use of English outside the classroom as reported by our subjects is significantly related to the scores they obtained on two measures of ESL proficiency.

This chapter is organized as follows. The next section provides information on the methodology of the investigation, in which we present information on the subjects, the questionnaire used to gather information about their use of English away from the ESL classroom, and the two measures of English proficiency. Next the results are presented, followed by a discussion. We then consider related studies which show conflicting findings. The paper concludes with a consideration of the study's limitations and the implications of the findings for second language acquisition.

METHODOLOGY

The Subjects

The subjects were 58 adults, ranging in age from 19 to 39; 43 (74 percent) were between the ages of 19 and 27. There were 38 females and 20 males. All but one of the 58 subjects were from Asia, with 51 (88 percent) from Japan. The length of residence in Hawaii as measured at the beginning of the investigation varied, from 2 weeks (two subjects) to 5 years (one subject). Thirty-three (57 percent) had lived in the United States for 6 months or less, with 23 (40 percent) having lived in the United States for 3 months or less.

All were enrolled in an intensive ESL program at the University of Hawaii. At the time of our investigation, the program had nine levels of instruction, ranging from a beginning course, level 1, to a course for advanced students, level 9. The 58 subjects were enrolled in levels 4 through 8. Placement in a given level for new students was done by scores on the Hawaii Auding Test, a multiple-choice listening comprehension test. Subsequent placement was determined by the success students had completing the class in which they were enrolled. Each class was scheduled to meet for 4 hours each afternoon, Monday through Friday, for 8 weeks.

The ESL program was aimed at developing skills in conversational English. There was little emphasis, if any, on reading and writing.

The Language Contact Profile

The subjects' use of English away from the classroom was measured by the Language Contact Profile, or LCP, given in Appendix A. The LCP is a modified version of one used by Seliger (1977). It is a self-report questionnaire, designed to elicit information on each subject's linguistic background, the amount of current use of the subject's native language or other languages besides English, the amount of current use of English, and the degree of motivation to learn English. The subjects were asked information about the amount of time they spent with English speakers, watching television, reading, and so on.

The LCP was pilot-tested on 53 nonnative speakers of English who were enrolled in five ESL classes at the University of Hawaii. The 53 were chosen because they were similar to our subjects in English proficiency, age, and cultural backgrounds. The pilot group of subjects took about 20 minutes to complete the LCP, and the format did not seem to cause them any difficulties. An item analysis did not reveal any problems; so it was considered appropriate for our 58 subjects.

The LCP was administered twice to the subjects, during the second week and during the last week of instruction; the results of both administrations are reported in this chapter. For some classes, the teacher incorporated the LCP into the lesson for the day, going over each item with the subjects to make sure they understood it. For other classes, investigators from the research project handed out the LCP directly to the students, who were expected to complete it outside of class. The investigators made themselves available to these students to answer any questions they had about the LCP.

The completed LCPs were collected and reviewed for accuracy. When necessary, the investigators checked with the subjects to ascertain the reliability of some of their responses. We then scored each LCP, using the procedure in Appendix B. The total number of points awarded for each language—native and English—were then totaled separately. This report treats only English scores.

Measures of English Proficiency

Information on the subjects' proficiency in English was obtained by two measures, the Bachman-Palmer Oral Interview and a cloze test. The Bachman-Palmer Oral Interview (BP) was used to measure the subjects' communicative proficiency in English. An adaptation of the Foreign Service Institute procedure, the BP took about 25 to 30 minutes for two interviewers to administer to one subject. One of the interviewers assumed a formal role and the other, first a neutral and then an informal, role.

At the end of the session, the two interviewers rated the subject individually for grammatical, pragmatic, and sociolinguistic competence. The grammatical component included range and accuracy of morphology and syntax. Pragmatic competence refers to the ability to express and comprehend messages and measured vocabulary, coherence, and organization. In scoring, we followed Bachman's recommendation that the scores on the grammar and pragmatics sections be combined. The sociolinguistic component included a judgment of register, nativeness, and cultural reference. In addition to the scores on the individual components, an overall BP score was figured by summing the results of the individual components. The BP was given during the fifth and sixth weeks of instruction to 26 of the 58 subjects. Each interview was tape-recorded, with the subject's permission.

Before the BP was administered, the five project investigators who administered the BP listened to taped interviews also provided by Bachman and Palmer, and practiced rating the interviews using score sheets provided by Bachman and Palmer. These same five researchers next practiced interviewing a number of beginning, intermediate, and advanced ESL students, none of whom was enrolled in the same ESL program as our 58 subjects.

The five interviewers later scored three randomly selected tapes of the 26 interviews in order to establish interscorer reliability. A reliability of more than 85 percent was achieved for total scores for all three tapes.

Since the BP took the form of an oral interview, we decided that we needed information on our subjects' formal knowledge of English. In order to obtain that information, we constructed a 28-item cloze test in which every fifth word was left out. After it was pilot-tested and revised (see Appendix C), we gave it to a group of subjects similar to our 58 for validation. It was then administered, by class, to our subjects during the sixth week of instruction. It was scored using the exact word method.

RESULTS

The results of the two measures of English proficiency and the preLCP and postLCP are shown in Table 15-1. Because of occasional absentees during the course of our research, the sample size varies for the different measures. Table 15-1 gives the means, standard deviations, and minimum and maximum scores for the entire sample.

TABLE 15-1 Means, Standard Deviations, and Minimums and Maximums for Language Contact Profile, Bachman-Palmer Oral Interview, and Cloze Test Results

Measure	*N*	*Mean*	*S.D.*	*Minimum*	*Maximum*
PreLCP	58	14.7	6.27	3.7	33
PostLCP	46	14.3	6.88	4.0	32
Bachman-Palmer	26				
Grammar		4.9	1.71	2.0	8.5
Pragmatics		6.5	1.95	3.0	9.5
Grammar + Prag.		11.4	3.54	5.0	19.0
Sociolinguistics		3.0	1.81	0.0	7.0
Total		14.4	4.95	7.0	25.0
Cloze	46	9.5	2.85	4.0	17.0

In order to discover if there were any support for the hypothesis that the use of English away from the classroom is significantly related to scores on the two measures of English proficiency, we ran Pearson product moment correlations on the LCP scores and the scores on the Bachman-Palmer and the cloze test. None of the correlations was significant at the .05 level or less. The results of these analyses are presented in Tables 15-2 and 15-3.

TABLE 15-2 Pearson Product Moment Correlations Between Language Contact Profilie and Bachman-Palmer Oral Interview Results

		Bachman-Palmer				
	N	*Grammar*	*Pragmatics*	*Grm + Prg*	*Sociolx*	*Total*
PreLCP	26	0.17251 ns	0.30631 ns	0.25462 ns	0.09268 ns	0.21627 ns
PostLCP	21	0.03783 ns	0.14674 ns	0.10278 ns	0.25749 ns	0.17384 ns

From other analyses done on the data (see Day 1984), we learned that the class which the students were in was significantly related to scores on the BP and the cloze test. Because of this, we ran a multiple regression analysis on the fluency scores with the LCP results, holding class level constant. Again, as with the results of the Pearson product correlations, there were no significant relationships.

TABLE 15-3 Pearson Product Moment Correlations*

	N	*Cloze test*
PreLCP	46	0.18272 ns
PostLCP	42	0.08691 ns

*Between language contact profile and cloze test results

DISCUSSION

From Tables 15-2 and 15-3, we learn that scores on the LCP, both pre and post, are not significantly related to scores on either the BP or the cloze test. This means that there is no support for the hypothesis that the use of English away from the classroom as perceived by the students themselves is significantly related to scores on these two measures of English proficiency.

Further, the results of multiple regression analyses of the same data with the class level of the subjects held constant provide no support for the hypothesis, since there were no significant relationships. As a result, we must reject the hypothesis. For our subjects, their reported use of English in context, away from the ESL classroom, did not predict English proficiency.

It is important to point out one result which might indicate a trend. From Table 15-2 we see that the score on the sociolinguistic subsection of the BP does not correlate significantly with results from either the preLCP or the postLCP. Note, however, the increase in correlation coefficient from preLCP (0.09268) to postLCP (0.25749). It might be that the time factor between the two administrations of the LCP (approximately 6 weeks) was not sufficient to result in a positive, significant correlation. Given the trend indicated by this result, we might expect a longitudinal study to uncover a relationship between ESL students' use of the target language away from their classroom and their sociolinguistic competence.[2]

It could be that using the total LCP scores in the analyses might obscure significant patterns of use as measured by the various individual questions on the LCP. If the LCP data were analyzed by individual questions, rather than a total score, we might discover that living with a native speaker of English, for example, might be an important variable in predicting scores on the Bachman-Palmer or the cloze test.

Because of this possibility, two additional analyses were performed using an item analysis of the LCP. The first, a correlation matrix with all of the variables entered, including individual results from the LCP, revealed no statistically significant patterns. Next, an exploratory regression analysis, stepwise technique, was performed. We used a version called Maximum R-Square, considered superior to the stepwise technique because it does not settle on a single model; rather, it tries to find the best one-variable model, the best two-variable model, and so on.

The results of this analysis, performed on both the cloze text and the Bachman-Palmer Oral Interview, do not indicate that any single question or group of questions on the LCP significantly predict results on the two measures of English proficiency. With the Bachman-Palmer results, the amount of time spent watching English television (question 14), friends in Hawaii with whom English was spoken (question 19), and the average number of daily hours listening to radio, cassettes, tapes, or records in English (question 18) were part of models ranging from one to seven variables. With the cloze results, only watching English television (question 14) appeared in models with one to seven variables with any regularity.

Thus it would appear as though there are no particular variables, with the possible exception of amount of time spent watching television in English, that consistently appear in any of the stepwise regression models. From this, we find no support for the hypothesis that the use of English outside the classroom is a factor in scores on the two measures of English proficiency used in the investigation.

The lack of support for the hypothesis might be surprising, even counterintuitive, given the widespread notion that it is easier to learn a second or foreign language if the learner seeks out opportunities to use the target language, thereby generating or being exposed to target language input. As noted above, this claim has been advanced by, among others, Bialystok (1978). Bialystok's work, however, might not be relevant to the investigation reported here, since the two situations are not obviously comparable. In one, there were Canadian teenagers learning French in high school—a language they could use on a daily basis in their home environment. In the other, Asian adults in Hawaii were studying English as a second language; these adults were in Hawaii only for a relatively short time, and all planned to return to their home countries, where their future use of English was questionable.

There is research, though, from comparable settings which, on the surface at least, apparently provides support for the notion that the use of English by ESL learners outside the classroom is a factor in learning the language. We mentioned previously Seliger's investigation (1977), in which he claims to have found a significant relationship between ESL students' use of the target language away from the classroom and their scores on measures of English proficiency.

There are, however, difficulties with Seliger's study. Seliger himself notes that the small number of subjects (six) might have influenced his findings. In addition, I illustrate elsewhere (Day 1984) that Seliger's data could be reasonably interpreted in such a way that there was no significant relationship between second language performance and use of the target language outside the classroom.

Another study claiming to provide evidence between English proficiency and use of English outside the classroom by ESL students was done by Monshi-Tousi, Hosseine-Fatemi, and Oller (1980). The English proficiency of 55 Iranian college students studying in the United States was measured by two cloze tests and two dictations. Their use of English was gathered by a 21-item questionnaire in order to determine what factors might have contributed to their proficiency.

Using a stepwise procedure, Monshi-Tousi et al. found two significant predictors of proficiency: the number of American friends, which accounted for 35 percent of the total variance, and the number of credit hours earned up to the time of testing, which explained an additional 16 percent of the variance. Also a factor was the length of time the subjects had been in the United States.

It would be difficult, however, to conclude from their study that the level of proficiency attained by the 55 subjects was significantly related to use of English outside the classroom. Simply having an American roommate can hardly be construed as representing the use of English away from the ESL classroom. For example, Monshi-Tousi et al. did not report a significance between English proficiency and the question which asked how often the subjects saw their American roommates. Yet if the use of English outside the classroom had been important, we would expect the degree to which the subjects interacted with their English-speaking roommates to be a significant factor.

Evidence rather different from the studies discussed so far comes from a study by Willerman (1979). She administered a self-report questionnaire which measured the subject's social and living arrangements to 133 students studying in a 15-week intensive ESL program in the United States. The responses were correlated with scores on the CELT (Comprehensive English Language Test).

Willerman found that, after the effects of initial CELT scores were partialed out, there were significant negative correlations between improvement in English and single marital status, reports of frequent use of English away from the classroom, a greater number of roommates, and a greater number of American friends. These findings are questionable, though, since they involved the use of the CELT, which, so far as we know, is a test which has not been subjected to normal validity or reliability procedures.

Furthermore, with the exception of Bialystok's work, all the studies discussed in this chapter relied crucially on the use of reports by the subjects. The difficulties in using self-report data in language studies have been well documented in the literature (e.g., Oller and Perkins 1978). Thus any study which uses such data must be regarded as suspect. The ideal research situation would involve observing second language learners as they interact outside the classroom, in addition to using a questionnaire to supplement the data.

Another difficulty with the study might lie in the LCP itself. The LCP might not have been sensitive enough to gather the appropriate information about the encounters the ESL students had with native speakers of English or other nonnative speakers of English. A different instrument, for example, might discover crucial situations in which ESL students interact in the target language.

Finally, the LCP only measured the quantitative use of the target language. It did not attempt to assess any qualitative aspects of the use of English. We learned that a subject might have spent 3 or 4 hours a day with an English-speaking roommate, but we did not learn anything about the nature of their linguistic interaction, if any. The LCP was not designed to provide information about the actual use of language between the ESL subjects and native speakers of English.

CONCLUSION

We have found that the results of an investigation into the use of English in context—away from the classroom—as reported by ESL students show that their use of English outside the classroom is not significantly related to their proficiency in English. Further, we learned that evidence purporting to support the claim that the level attained by ESL students is related to their use of English outside the classroom is mixed and questionable.

What this suggests to me is that the matter is still open to question. Based on the available evidence, it is not clear if the use of English away from the classroom is a factor in the successful acquisition of English by ESL students. One of the keys to resolving this crucial aspect of second language acquisition may be found not in looking at how often ESL students interact with native speakers of English but in examining the nature of such interactions. We should investigate, in addition to the quantitative use of the target language in social settings, the qualitative use of the target language. Such research should also be conducted on a long-range basis. Until such research is done, the issue of the importance of the use of the target language away from an instructional setting in the acquisition process will remain unsettled.

NOTES

1. I would like to thank Christine Joffres, Ann E. Chun, Earl Nakahara, Beth Ruze, Kerry O'Sullivan, Ermile Hargrove, and Braxton Grizzard for their help in planning the study and gathering the data. I would also like to thank Dennis Imada, Kris Ito, Pinky Kobayashi, Marsha Nakasone, and Marshall Palmer for allowing us to come into their ESL classrooms, and Craig Chaudron and Mike Long for their helpful suggestions.

2. We must also note, that the correlation coefficients in the grammar and pragmatics sections of the BP decreased from the first to the second administration of the LCP, from

0.17251 to 0.03783, and from 0.30631 to 0.16764, respectively. We do not know if these results mean that over a longer period of time we could expect a continued pattern of less and less positive relationship between these sections of the BP and the LCP.

APPENDIX A The Language Contact Profile: Questionnaire

1. Name ______________________________ 2. Sex: Male/Female
3. NICE level ______________________________ 4. Age __________
5. Native country ______________________________
6. What is your native language(s)? ______________________________
7. Do you speak other languages? Yes/No. If yes, what are they? ______________

____

8. How long have you been in the US? (Include all visits.)

   ________ years ________ months

9. Where have you studied English? For how long?

a. Elementary school	yes____	no____	____years	____months	____weeks
b. Junior high school	yes____	no____	____years	____months	____weeks
c. Senior high school	yes____	no____	____years	____months	____weeks
d. University/College	yes____	no____	____years	____months	____weeks
e. NICE, HELP, (in Hawaii)			____years	____months	____weeks
f. Other	yes____	no____	____years	____months	____weeks

10. Do you live with anyone who speaks your *native language*? Yes/No. If yes, how many *hours* do you spend with them each day? (Circle one.)

    0 ½ 1 1½ 2 2½ 3 3½ 4 4½

    5 5½ 6 6½ 7 7½ 8 8½ 9 over 9

11. Do you live with anyone who speaks *only English*? Yes/No. If yes, how many *hours* do you spend with them each day? (Circle one.)

    0 ½ 1 1½ 2 2½ 3 3½ 4 4½

    5 5½ 6 6½ 7 7½ 8 8½ 9 over 9

12. Do you live with anyone who is not a native speaker of English and who does not speak your native language? Yes/No. If yes, how many *hours* do you spend with them each day? (Circle one.)

    0 ½ 1 1½ 2 2½ 3 3½ 4 4½

    5 5½ 6 6½ 7 7½ 8 8½ 9 over 9

13. Circle the average number of *hours* each day you watch television in a language other than English.

    0 ½ 1 1½ 2 2½ 3 3½ 4 4½

    5 5½ 6 6½ 7 7½ 8 8½ 9

14. Circle the average number of *hours* each day you watch television in *English.*

    0 ½ 1 1½ 2 2½ 3 3½ 4 4½

    5 5½ 6 6½ 7 7½ 8 8½ 9

15. Are newspapers, magazines, or books available in your *native language*? Yes/No. If yes, circle the average number of *hours* you spend reading them each day.

    0 ½ 1 1½ 2 2½ 3 3½ 4 4½

    5 5½ 6 6½ 7 7½ 8 8½ 9

16. Circle the average number of *hours* each day you read newspapers, books, or magazines in *English.*

0 ½ 1 1½ 2 2½ 3 3½ 4 4½

5 5½ 6 6½ 7 7½ 8 8½ 9

17. Circle the average number of *hours* each day you listen to radio, cassettes, tapes, or records in your *native language.*

0 ½ 1 1½ 2 2½ 3 3½ 4 4½

5 5½ 6 6½ 7 7½ 8 8½ 9

18. Circle the average number of *hours* each day you listen to radio, cassettes, tapes, or records in *English.*

0 ½ 1 1½ 2 2½ 3 3½ 4 4½

5 5½ 6 6½ 7 7½ 8 8½ 9

19. List the three friends in Hawaii that you see the most each day.

	Name of Friend	Language Used	Time Each Day
a.	______	______	______
b.	______	______	______
c.	______	______	______

20. List the three *English-speaking Americans* that you speak English with the most. What is their relationship to you? (For example: teacher, friend, neighbor, bus driver.) How much time do you spend with them *each day*?

	Name of American	Relationship	Time Talking
a.	______	______	______
b.	______	______	______
c.	______	______	______

21. Do you spend time trying to improve your English outside of NICE? Yes/No. If yes, list the activities that you do outside the classroom that help you learn English. (For example: watching TV, reading, writing, speaking with friends, going to movies/parties.) Also, list how often you do each activity. (For example: one hour a day; two times a week; once a month.)

	Activity	Frequency
a.	______	______
b.	______	______
c.	______	______
d.	______	______
e.	______	______
f.	______	______
g.	______	______

22. When you have homework in English do you
    a. do it as soon as you can?
    b. do it if you find time?
    c. do it at the last possible moment?
    d. do it but turn it in late?
    e. other (explain) ______

23. If you have a choice between reading in your native language or reading in English, you
    a. prefer native language
    b. prefer English
    c. have no preference

THANKS FOR HELPING US WITH OUR STUDY.

APPENDIX B Language Contact Profile: Scoring Procedures

Omit 1–7.

8. Score the exact number of years and months.
9. a. Score the time spent studying in the U.S.A.
   b. Score the time spent studying elsewhere.
10. a. Yes = 1; no = 0
    b. Score the time reported (e.g., 2 hours = 2)
11. a. Yes = 1; no = 0
    b. Score the time reported
12. a. Yes = 1; no = 0
    b. Score the time reported

13–18. Score one-half of the time reported (e.g., 2 hours = 1)

19. Score one point for each English-speaking friend. (Disregard ESL teacher if named.)
20. Score one point for each person naamed, but do not count ESL teacher.
21. Score one point for each activity listed.
22. a = 3   b = 2   c = 1   d = 0
23. b = 2   c = 1   a = 0

Directions: Please read the following passage and fill in the blanks. You will have 20 minutes to work. (*Hints*: Read the passage completely and try to write something in every blank. Guessing is OK.) Good luck!

Unit No. 4 — CLOCKS, CLOCKS, CLOCKS

One clock doesn't make any sound. Yet, it wakes people ________ the morning. This clock ________ off light. The light ________ people wake up. Some ________ it the Light Clock!

________ clock gets people up ________ faster. This clock gives ________ one who is sleeping ________ little shock of electricity. ________ could be called the ________ Clock!

One clock really ________ the time. It calls ________ the time. This clock ________, "five o'clock" or "two ________," or whatever the time ________ be. It's the Talking ________!

People have to look ________ to see most clocks. ________ is not so with ________ clock in New York. ________ look down. They see ________ clock under their feet. ________ the Sidewalk Clock!

How ________ you like to have ________ Ring Clock! It really ________ ring. It is called ________ Ring Clock because you ________ put it around your ________.

16

REQUESTS FOR SPECIFIC LANGUAGE INPUT: DIFFERENCES BETWEEN OLDER AND YOUNGER ADULT LANGUAGE LEARNERS

Cheryl Brown
Brigham Young University

Anyone who has dealt with language learners has recognized that all input does not have the same impact on the learner. Some aspects of the input can be traced almost immediately and directly into the output. This has been shown, for example, in the studies of Carey (1981), who found that certain lexical items can be found in the output of a child after the child has heard them only once. Other things do not impact so easily or so directly. We have all experienced this phenomenon in our adult acquisition of vocabulary. We learn a new word and discover that it is everywhere. Rationally, we assume that the item has been there all along and that we, for some unknown reasons, have not previously felt its impact sufficiently to learn it. We therefore recognize that all input that is available to the learner does not have the same impact on him or her.

The input that is actually incorporated by the learner has been called "intake." According to Hatch (1983a), Krashen has likened the entire process to the "casting of a net" into the sea of input. Anything the learner draws in becomes intake.

This fishing analogy, if extended, can help us understand the worth of studying specific requests for input. A specific request for input—that is, a question about some particular aspect of the language or communication—is tantamount not to the learner "casting a net" but to the learner letting down a carefully baited and lured hook with the hope of catching some particular thing. What the learner finds important to "catch" is of interest. This is especially true of requests for input made in the classroom because there we can assume that the learners at least recognize that the purpose of the expedition is to "fish." The learners know they are "in the boat."

And so we come to the main question which this chapter is designed to answer: what specific requests do language learners make for input? This is coupled to a second question: are there any differences between the specific requests that older (here defined as over 55 years of age) and younger (here defined as older than 18 and younger than 25) adult language learners make? This second question gives perspective to the first because there are such obvious differences in the success of these two groups. If it can be shown that there are differences between the specific requests for input that these two groups of learners make, it might be possible to determine what some of the language learning processes are which contribute to the difference in success of the two groups.

The data derived for use in this study were taken from data gathered as part of a larger study of the distinguishing characteristics of the older adult language learner (Brown 1983). Two groups of learners supplied the data which were used in this study of specific requests for input. Group 1 consisted of 18 subjects (8 couples and one pair of women assigned as partners for the duration of the language study). The subjects were in an 8-week intensive Spanish program used for training missionaries for the Church of Jesus Christ of Latter-day Saints. The subjects ranged in age from 55 to 75, with the median age being 63.6. The subjects were chosen strictly by availability. They were all of the senior missionaries learning Spanish who started their language learning program at the Missionary Training Center (hereafter abbreviated MTC) in the 3-month period from October 1, 1981, to January 1, 1982. The subjects varied in several areas, such as previous experience with language, amount and recency of education, geographical origin previous to the mission, and area of assignment for the mission. They were all highly motivated, as evidenced by the facts that their missions were completely voluntary, that they accepted the assignment to go wherever they were asked, and that they were willing to pay their own costs for the 18 months of their mission experience.

Group 2 consisted of 18 young subjects (10F, 8M) who were chosen because they matched the group 1 subjects in sex and, as nearly as possible, in previous experience with languages, including Spanish. All the other varying factors mentioned above were considered in the matching process. However, sex and previous language experience were the factors considered most crucial to this study; so they were the prime matching factors. The subjects in group 2 ranged in age from 19 to 23, with the median age for the group being 20.9. These subjects were chosen from among the many young missionaries learning Spanish who started their language program at the

MTC during the same time period that the senior missionaries started their program. Like the older subjects, these learners had volunteered for the service, had accepted assignments to go wherever they were asked, and were paying (or family or friends were paying for them) their own costs for the term of their mission experience.

The language program that both groups of subjects participated in was originally designed to be as similar as possible. The program uses an eclectic approach currently consisting of oral translation both from Spanish to English and from English to Spanish and of traditional kinds of grammar drills. Another aspect of the program, however, is aimed at communicative competence in the work the missionaries will be doing. This part of the program involves a great many role plays and interactive kinds of activities. It also involves committing to memory prepared dialogues that the missionaries use to teach once they are in the language area. Both groups also participate in a special speaking program. This program consists of each missionary using the target language for absolutely everything he or she possibly can. The course for both groups involves 6 hours of classes during the day and a somewhat less intense study and review period for 2 hours in the evening.

Although the entire language program was originally designed to be similar for both older and younger missionaries, the older missionaries have always had difficulty and do not generally reach the point in the program where they are learning the dialogues. They do participate in the role plays and other activities, however.

The classes for the younger learners were generally composed of from eight to ten persons. The classes for the older learners were smaller, usually consisting of four learners or fewer. This was a result of the smaller number of older learners entering training at any one time and also of the fact that the older learners felt so much pressure when they studied in groups.

Two kinds of data were used to look at the specific requests for input that the learners made. The first kind consisted of requests which the learners made in language learning journals that they were asked to keep. The learners were given notebooks to use as language learning journals and were asked to write in them their thoughts and feelings about language learning. The specific instructions for the journal can be found in the Appendix.

The contents of the journals were analyzed extensively as part of the larger study. Two of the analyses done for that study are important to the issue of input. In the first, the journals were analyzed for the topics they encompassed. Since the general journal instructions had not been specific about what to write except that it should apply to language learning, it was assumed that any topic mentioned was part of what the learner perceived to be a factor in language learning. For example, if a learner wrote, "I spent two hours today memorizing one dialogue," it would be assumed that he or she saw memorization as a language learning factor. It would also be assumed that he or she saw time as a factor and that the material memorized—the dialogue—was also seen as an influence. The journals were analyzed for factors which previous studies had shown to be possible factors in language learning, although new factors were added as persistent reference to them in the journals showed them to be important to the learners. A journal statement would be analyzed as being about a particular factor if it in any way matched the definition which had been written for the factor, such as the following definition for "input":

any reference to input desired; to amount of input given; to type, complexity, or meaningfulness of input.

The analysis of all the journals resulted in a list of 76 factors which learners considered important. (The detailed description of how the analysis was done, how objectivity was checked, how the 76 factors were arrived at, and what they were can be found in Brown 1983.)

The factor of most interest to this current study was the one defined above entitled "input." Any time that the learners referred to any input they wanted, to the amount or type of input received, or to the complexity or meaningfulness of the input, it was counted as a mention of this factor. In order to minimize the bias that might be produced because different learners wrote different amounts in their journals, a score for each factor was calculated for each learner based on the number of times per thousand words the learner mentioned the factor. The individual learner scores were then used to calculate a mean number of times per thousand words that each group mentioned the factor. This calculation produced a median of 0.48 mentions of input per thousand words for the older learners and 2.19 mentions of input per thousand words for the younger learners. In other words, the younger learners talked about input as part of the language learning process more than four times as much as the older learners. Although it is impossible to state the exact reason why such a difference should appear, it seems to be an indication of the relative importance that the two groups give to the factor.

In the second analysis made for the larger study which also bears on this study, all of the 76 factors were ranked by the number of times per thousand words each group mentioned the factor. When this was done, the differences in ranking for the older and younger groups were examined to see what differences in focus could be found. This examination showed that "input" was the third most different in ranking for the two groups. Only "memory aids," which the younger learners rank higher and "assignments," which the older learners rank higher, are more different in the two rankings than "input" (see Table 16-1).

The difference in focus on input and the realization of its role in language learning is part of a picture which became very clear when all analyses were considered together. Brown (1983) shows the older learner to be "outward focused, depending on external factors to make the learning

TABLE 16-1 Factors/Abilities Differing by at Least 10 in the Ranking of Older and Younger Learners*

Higher on the ranking of the older learners		*Higher on the ranking of the younger learners*	
Factor	*Diff*	*Factor*	*Diff*
Assignments	30.5	Memory aids	41.5
Visuals	25.0	Input	30.0
Age	23.5	Thinking in the L2	23.5
Feedback	22.0	Depth of processing	20.0
Teacher attitudes	20.0	Learning strategies	18.0
Marriage	17.5	Memory	18.0
Teacher activities	17.0	Monitor	16.5
Activity—read/writing	16.0	Interference	15.0
Media	15.5	Efforts and goals	14.5
Activity—vocabulary	14.5	Environment	14.0
Variety	14.0	Language variability	14.0
Language play	14.0	Speaking	13.5
Activity—nonlinguistic	12.5	Materials	12.0
Teacher attitudes	12.5	Self-concept	12.0
Spiritual aspects	12.5	Organization	11.5
Activity—grammar	12.0	Health	11.0
Auditory discrimination	12.0	Measurements/tests	11.0
Anxiety	11.0	Ped attitude: gen learn	10.5

*Taken from Brown 1983

possible or easier" and the younger learner to be "more responsible for his or her own learning, a learner who is internally figuring out how to handle the information coming in" (p. 170). In other words, the larger study showed that overall, the younger learners were much more aware than the older learners that input was a part of language learning worth mentioning.

This finding was further substantiated when, for the purposes of the smaller study reported here, the journal data were reanalyzed to see more exactly what the learners were saying about input. First, the mentions of input were divided into two categories: those dealing with the amount of input and those dealing with the kind of input.

There were definite quantitative differences in the learners' focus on the amount of input they were receiving. Older adults discussed the amount of input an average of 0.51 times per thousand words while younger adults discussed amount an average of 1.61 times per thousand words. A *t* test yielded significance ($t = 2.044$, df = 31, $p < .05$). More than the older learners, then, the younger learners seem to focus on the amount of input that they want to have or that they feel expected to take in. How this greater realization of the amount of input around them affects the language learning process deserves further investigation.

There was no quantitative difference, however, in discussion of the kind of input coming in. A *t* test run on the number of times per thousand words each group mentioned kind of input was not significant (t = .824). In other words, in their language learning journals, older learners and younger learners discuss the kind of input they are receiving about equal amounts. These discussions usually center on materials and lesson content.

However, there are qualitative differences in the writing of the two groups about the kind of input they are receiving. Over 28.2 percent of the writing of the older group requested changes in the kind of input they were receiving. The kinds of changes requested ranged from simple desires to have more examples on a particular page in the textbook to having the teachers present the entire course content in a different order. Only 2.7 percent of the writing by the younger group requested changes.

The second kind of data used to examine the learners' requests for input came from participant observation which was also part of the larger study. The observations took place for a total of 44 hours in the classrooms and other activities and areas where the subjects were. Field notes for the observations were kept and later transcribed. Eleven of the observation sessions were also audio-recorded and transcribed.

Some adjustments had to be made in the field notes that could be used for some portions of this smaller study in order to have the amount of notes and the kinds of observations they detailed be as nearly equal as possible for any quantitative data reported. Therefore, only similar observations—those made at basically the same point in training, the same time of day, and the same field-note method (taped or not)—for the matched pairs of subjects were selected. This selection resulted in the use of data taken from nine pairs of matched subjects in 12.75 hours of observation as recorded in 179.25 pages of field notes.

All requests in the classroom were then extracted from the field notes. These requests came principally in the form of questions, but some statements were taken as requests if they had the illocutionary force of a directive to give information. These were statements such as "We don't understand when you're supposed to use SER."

A count to see if older learners differed from younger learners in the total number of requests made revealed that each of the senior missionaries asked an average of 10.39 questions per hour while each of the younger missionaries asked an average of 2.81 questions. This difference was significant (t = 2.64, df = 16, $p < .05$). However, when all of the questions asked by anyone during the class period in the matched classes were counted and means calculated, the mean for the senior missionary classes was 20.52 questions per hour and the mean for the young missionary classes was 16.63 questions per hour. This figure was not significant (t = .602). It appears that class size may be a more important factor in the number of requests for input than is the age of the learner.

For another way of looking at the differences in the requests of the two groups, the requests extracted from the field notes were then categorized according to what they were a request for. The requests fell into seven categories.

Grammar: used for any questions about grammatical structure (e.g., Do you need to add a "u" in *dormir* when you form the imperfect?)

Vocabulary: used for any requests or questions about the meaning of a *word* expressed either as a question about what a Spanish word meant or about how to translate an English word into Spanish (e.g., What's "mess"?)

Pronunciation: used for any requests or questions about how to say a word, how a particular spelling was pronounced (e.g., ¿Convenío or convenio?)

Repetition: used for several kinds of requests or questions including asking to have something repeated (e.g., What was the question again?), expressing lack of comprehension (e.g., I can't understand what you're saying there), asking for confirmation of something said—as if saying, "Is this right?" (e.g., This table?), and using rising intonation on a word or phrase when there are no other cues as to whether the student was checking grammar, vocabulary, pronunciation, or a mixture of any of them (e.g., Uhh, do we understand death?)

Procedures: used when the students were asking for clarification of classroom procedure, exercise instructions, etc. (e.g., You want us to make a sentence with *estar?*) or when they were telling the teacher what kinds of things they wanted to do or to study

Other content: used for questions or requests not directly related to the language learning or missionary task (e.g., Where are you from?)

Miscellaneous: used for all requests for how to say entire phrases when it is impossible to tell whether the request is for grammar, vocabulary, pronunciation, of any mixture of these three (e.g., How do you say, "I am dead"?) and also used for all requests which could not fit any of the categories above (e.g., How do you spell it?)

In order to minimize the effects of researcher subjectivity, the questions were categorized by two raters using the descriptions above as a guide. A third rater categorized all questions (approximately 15 percent of the total) on which the first two raters did not agree. If two of the three raters agreed on the categorization for a question, the request was placed in the category. This "consensus" categorization resulted in all of the questions except five being categorized. It was decided to place these five questions in the "miscellaneous" category since it was used, as stated above, "for all requests which could not fit any of the other categories." The total counts for the matched individual older and younger learners on the various categories are given in Table 16-2.

TABLE 16-2 Kind of Input Requested by Matched Individuals

	Gram	*Vocab*	*Pron*	*Repet*	*Proced*	*Oth Cont*	*Misc*
Older	21.00	11.66*	1.00	47.33	11.00	0.00	2.50
Younger	6.33	6.00	0.00	9.00	1.00	2.00	2.00

*Figures showing "partial" questions (e.g. = .66) are the result of calculations to equalize the data into terms of questions per hour.

After the data were counted, several categories were dropped. This was necessary if all the cells were to be of an acceptable size for a chi-square to be performed. As a result, only the categories of "grammar," "vocabulary," "repetition," and "procedures" were used.

The observed chi-square for the kinds of requests made by the matched individuals was 3.956. This is nonsignificant, suggesting that there is no difference between the kinds of requests that the older learners are making and those that the younger learners are making.

Once again, however, a visual scan of the data suggested that there might be a difference in the kinds of requests which were being made overall in the classes in which the matched learners were engaged. Therefore, all of the questions from those classes were categorized into the seven categories discussed above. That categorization yielded the results shown in Table 16-3.

TABLE 16-3 Kind of Input Requested in Classes of Matched Individuals

	Gram	*Vocab*	*Pron*	*Repet*	*Proced*	*Oth Cont*	*Misc*
Older	40.32	22.67	1.00	93.00	22.67	0.67	5.33
Younger	20.33	30.00	2.70	64.33	13.33	7.00	14.00

Once again, "pronunciation," and "other content," were eliminated because of low counts, and the chi-square was performed using the remaining categories.

The observed chi for the kinds of questions by the group was 13.973 ($p < .01$). This suggests that, even if individuals themselves are not making different requests for input, the input being requested in the environment is different for older and younger adult learners. As can be seen from Table 16-3, the major differences come in the categories of "vocabulary," "repetition," and "miscellaneous." The younger adult learners ask disproportionately more about vocabulary than the older learners, and the older learners ask disproportionately more to have entire phrases repeated. Also, there were more of the requests of the younger learners which were not echo questions but which were not easily classified as grammar, vocabulary, or pronunciation.

What do these differences mean? First, they show a greater interest on the part of the younger learners in vocabulary. Possibly this focus on words is what spells the difference in the success of the learners. This idea would require further exploration.

Second, the results show a difference in the way the two groups of learners request specific information. It is clear that the younger learners can separate out particular vocabulary items that they wish to know, making very specific requests for very specific items. With the older learners, it is different. They do not ask about particular vocabulary items as much; they ask for global repetition. This high number of requests by the older learners which fit in the repetition category might be an indication of their inability as input seekers to make it clear exactly what they want. Two factors suggest caution in accepting this interpretation, however. First, the older learners *do* make requests about specific grammatical items and, second, the younger learners do make global requests as shown by the figures in the "miscellaneous" category. These questions differ from the "repetition" category only in that they are not repetitions of what has been said before, not direct expressions of lack of comprehension. Further research should be undertaken to be sure if the seeming difference in the way requests are made—particularly or globally—is real.

In summary, then, the studies reported here suggest four major differences in older and younger language learners as input seekers:

1. The older learners do not seem to focus on the input in language learning as much as the younger learners.

2. While the younger learners are more concerned about the amount of input they are responsible for, the older learners are more concerned about changing the kind of input they get.

3. While the older learners seem to make more individual requests for specific input, the total number of requests per class per hour is not significantly different for the two groups.

4. The younger learners make significantly more requests than older learners for the input of specific vocabulary items.

These four differences might be part of the reason that there is such a great difference in the success of the two groups. However, the study reported here is not extensive enough to prove in any way that the differences in the input requests of the two groups of learners definitely *are* the cause of the differential success of the two groups. Nevertheless, this research should serve to direct attention to possible areas of productive study if we hope to help learners take from the sea of input that which will be of optimal value.

APPENDIX
JOURNAL INSTRUCTIONS

This journal has two purposes. The first is to help you with your language learning. As you write about what you think and feel as a language learner, you will understand yourself and your experience better.

The second purpose is to increase the overall knowledge about language learning so that learning can be increased. You will be asked to leave your language learning journal when you leave the MTC. However, your journal will not be read by teachers at the MTC. It will be read by researchers interested in language learning.

Your identity and the identity of others you may write about will be unknown (unless you wish it otherwise) to anyone except the researchers.

You will be given 15 minutes a day to write. Please write as if this were your personal journal about your language learning experience.

On Comprehension

17

A METHOD FOR EXAMINING THE INPUT/INTAKE DISTINCTION[1]

Craig Chaudron
University of Hawaii-Manoa

There have been several approaches to investigating the relationship between target language (TL) input and second language learners' acquisition. Of interest in these approaches, of course, is the way in which the phonological, lexical, syntactic, and pragmatic features of the target language are perceived, understood, and subsequently assimilated into the learner's developing grammar. This is the process of the intake of input forms, a process dependent both on characteristics of the input and on aspects of the learner's competence. The present study is concerned with the ways in which this process can be investigated in order to determine the characteristics of input that have the greatest influence on learners' TL acquisition. Some researchers (e.g., Wagner-Gough and Hatch 1975, Larsen-Freeman 1976b, Long 1981c) have argued that the structure and variability of forms and functions in TL input to the learner is related to the acquisition of those forms either due to relative frequency, or through modifications that render the input meaningful to the learner. Yet very little research has explored the connection between input and intake, a distinction first noted by Corder (1967: 165).

RELATIONS BETWEEN INPUT AND INTAKE

Early studies of the relationship between input and intake compared the rank orders of the frequency of occurrence of morpheme target forms in native speakers' speech with learners' rank orders of accuracy. Larsen-Freeman (1976a) compared the morpheme order ranking in language teachers' classroom speech with the accuracy of L2 learners on a speaking task (Bilingual Syntax Measure). She found a significant relationship supporting her previous finding of a significant correlation between the learners' orders and the average NS ranking[2] from Brown's (1973) L1 studies (Larsen-Freeman 1976b). Additionally, Long (1981c) found that Krashen's proposed natural morpheme order correlated significantly with the ranking of accurate morpheme production by nonnative speakers (NNS) in conversations with native speakers (NS), as well as with the ranking of *frequencies* of NS's morpheme input in those same conversations.

These findings for frequency suggest a plausible relationship between input and acquisition. Yet the relationship is distant, in that the measures are not specifically of input to the same learners in these studies, and further, the correlations with production could be spurious, in that the frequency of need to produce the TL morphemes could have been an intervening variable (among others) in the learners' acquisition of them. However, given the "right" amount of exposure and the necessity to use certain forms, L2 learners should gradually assimilate the more frequent target structures into their grammars.

In addition to possible effects of frequency, several theorists of L2 acquisition have stressed the importance of modifications of input, input that is rendered comprehensible through simplification, negotiation, or redundancy, and so on. Modification permits learners to be able to segment and assimilate the structures at the "edge" of their developing grammars (cf. Krashen 1982, 1983; Schachter 1983a; Scarcella and Higa 1981; and Long 1983d). Several chapters in this volume point out the complex interactions between the input, negotiated or otherwise, and both universal and specific qualities of the learners' developing grammars. In order to obtain a clear picture of the processes learners engage in to assimilate this input, I suggest that we need to adopt research methods that are appropriate for investigating the different stages of learners' intake process.[3]

I am here especially interested in the early stages of intake, that is, those stages involving learners' initial perception and segmenting of the input. I suggest that for learners to acquire a new form by means of comprehensible, simplified, or negotiated input, they must first perceive the form and encode it, before perhaps trying to employ it. Thus the measures I will concentrate on will be those that determine learners' immediate perception of the input, rather than their developed grammars as seen in measures of free production. I will specifically illustrate one such measure that researchers could make use of, placing it within a more general categorization of measures of responses to input. This is a listening cloze procedure that was investigated in a test-development project in 1983.

MEASURES OF RESPONSES TO INPUT

Figure 17-1 shows various measures of learners' responses to target language input, where the concern is primarily with aural input. Each of these measures could be used to investigate a learner's reactions to specific variables in input, thereby obtaining information about how the learner was processing the input. Yet these measures differ in the degree to which they allow intervening variables, such as conscious knowledge or performance constraints, to influence the learner's response. The major differences lie primarily along two dimensions: (1) a production dimension (the horizontal axis), which represents the amount of encoding or recoding of the input by the learner into other forms, whether motor responses or language, and (2) the comprehension dimension (the vertical axis), that is, the level of grammatical abstraction from the input that is required of the learner.

These dimensions have implications for both the time involved and the stages of intake processing. Briefly, along both dimensions, toward the right on production and toward the bottom on comprehension, more time is required for the task. The more time available, the more opportunity the learner has to engage knowledge sources that are more complex than the automatic routines that would be used for immediate perception of the input. Thus, on the production dimension, nonverbal responses involve simply a match between the input and some preset image or expectancy in short-term memory. Oral responses also involve such a match but additionally require further recoding to a productive mode, so that there is some potential for interference from inappropriately automatized production routines (e.g., articulatory performance). The actual perceptual competence of the listener would thus be obscured. Likewise, written responses normally require another step in recoding, and potential further confounding, through an aural representation to a graphic one.

In a similar manner, the comprehension dimension suggests that the tasks toward the bottom require more time, in that they involve greater access to and processing of the input in long-term memory, in which are stored the more complex rule systems the learner will have accumulated regarding the target language. That is, gradually greater amounts of semantic and syntactic integration of the input are required in order to provide an appropriate response.

By displaying the various response measures in this way (Figure 17-1), I am suggesting that we need to select an appropriate measure, depending on the scope of the investigation. We must take into account whether we are

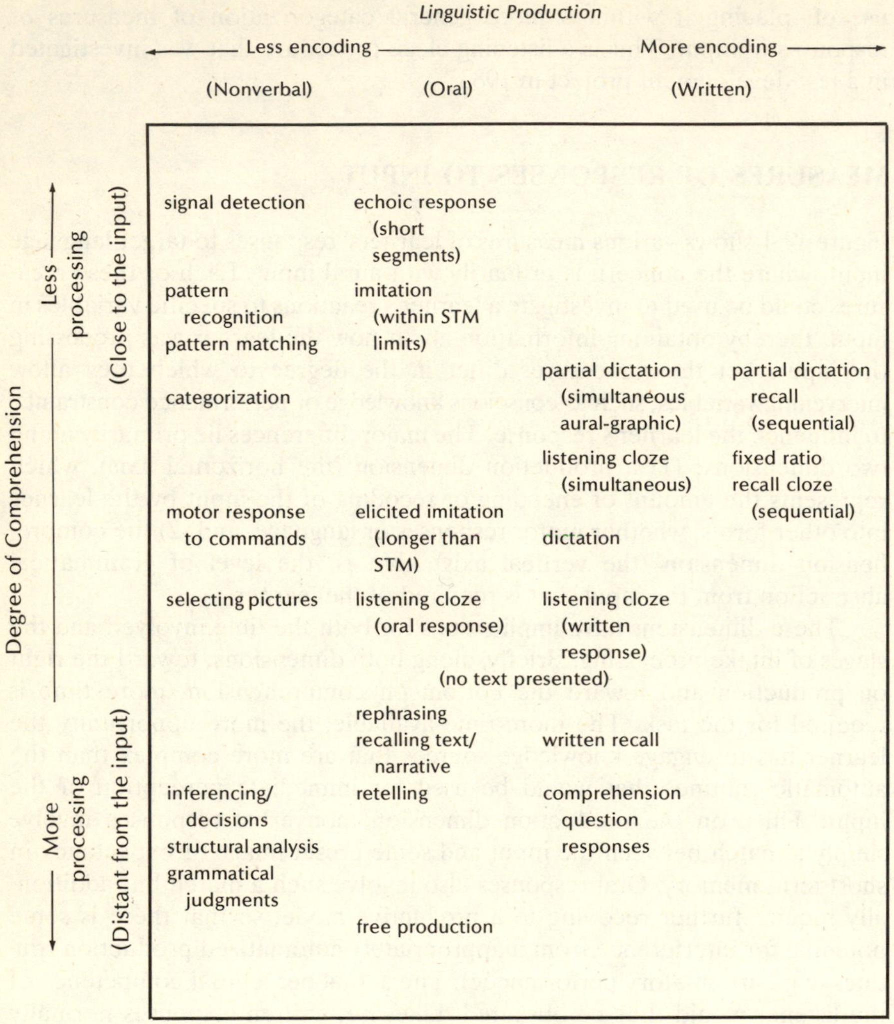

FIGURE 17-1 Dimensions of Tasks Responding to Input

exploring the effects of input on immediate perception (the upper portions of the comprehension scale), or on comprehension alone, or on free production following some processing of the input. As others have suggested (e.g., Bialystok 1979, 1982), learners vary with respect to the amount of target language knowledge they have acquired, as well as the automaticity or immediateness of accessibility of that knowledge. Since the different response measures allow different degrees of access to knowledge, comparisons of learners' responses on different measures should reveal their degree of accessibility, the amount of language knowledge, and possibly third, the qualitative differences in their knowledge representations.

Since the interest in this study is on the early stages of perception of input, I will illustrate these measures briefly with a measure that has been used previously (perhaps too little) in second language acquisition research, namely, elicited imitation (cf. Naiman 1974; Swain, Dumas, and Naiman 1974; Markman, Spilka, and Tucker 1975; and Gallimore and Tharp 1982). I will then describe more extensively a second group of measures that have been developed primarily as measures of L2 proficiency, rather than as tools for analysis of intake processing, namely, listening cloze and dictation. Let us consider first the elicited imitation. This task has to be constructed so that it surpasses the learner's short-term memory capacity (cf. Massaro 1975, Glanzer 1982), in order to ensure that some grammatical processing is taking place, and not simply rote repetition. (However, a measure of rote repetition might be useful if, for example, one were investigating the earliest stages of acquisition of phonology.) Naiman's research (1974) with this procedure showed indeed that learners performed better on the nonlinguistic production task involving picture choices than on the elicited-imitation production task. Nevertheless, the elicited imitation does appear to be a technique that can reveal the state of learners' knowledge relative to specific target language rules, if the items to be imitated are appropriately designed and controlled.

Second, let us consider listening cloze and dictation measures, indicated on the right side of the horizontal dimension around the midlevel. The writing production task of filling in clozed items in a passage while listening to a text has been used occasionally (Smith and Rafiqzad 1979; Henning, Gary, and Gary 1981), and is an obvious approach to exploring the degree of perception and processing of target forms in aurally presented material. Several different procedures are possible, depending on whether or not the written passage is presented and whether it is presented simultaneously or sequentially following the aural text. Just as with elicited imitation, the written response formats like dictation and listening cloze have been employed more as measures of general proficiency, yet it was of interest in the study reported here to explore their potential as measures for localizing and specifying the processing of input as intake. The fact is that with elicited imitation and with listening cloze procedures, we have the potential to select particular features of the input for examination. Because of the time constraints on the responses, there is less potential for more complex knowledge or learners' inferences to interfere with their responses. They can also be used with continuous natural texts. For this reason, the present study undertakes to test the reliability and validity of two listening-comprehension measures that could be employed with naturalistic spoken texts, in this case, videotaped lectures on scientific topics.

PREVIOUS STUDIES OF LISTENING CLOZE AND DICTATION

Various listening cloze and partial dictation and recall measures have been validated relative to other more discrete-point measures and to some oral production measures. (See Chaudron, in preparation, for a fuller discussion of these studies.)

Testing procedures such as sentence recall (Harris 1969), listening cloze (Gregory-Panopoulos 1966; Oakeshott-Taylor 1979; and see Bowen 1976, and discussion in Oller 1979 and Oller and Perkins 1980), listening recall (Henning et al. 1981), and dictation and partial dictation (Oller 1971, 1979; Johansson 1973; Oller and Streiff 1975; Savignon 1982) have been employed, showing high reliabilities or validity measures, such as high correlations with standard tests of listening comprehension. While these studies have been concerned with global proficiency on the part of the learners, it also makes some sense to consider whether a listening cloze test can be used to determine the "listenability" or "comprehensibility" of the aurally presented material. This was the intent in several L1 studies (DeVito 1965, and Theobald and Alexander 1977) which attempted to judge teachers' comprehensibility. Wilcox (1978) and Smith and Rafiqzad (1979) adopted such a procedure to test comprehensibility of various accents of English, with not entirely clear results, however. If listening cloze and dictation procedures not only discriminate between more and less proficient L2 learners in a global way, and thereby are validated as measures of listening skill, but also establish comprehensibility for a given group of learners, it should be possible to consider the differences in difficulty of specific items in such tests as indications of their degree of comprehensibility. That is, the degree to which the items, as input, are perceived and processed in the initial stages of intake could be determined. Further, since cloze procedures, and especially partial dictation, allow for selective deletion of items, specific input rules or features might be manipulated by the researcher. The question is whether different procedures or deletion patterns result in equivalent reliabilities or difficulties.

In selecting two such measures for this study, it was deemed useful to develop a listening measure that could be used by researchers as readily as the cloze based on oral or written texts. One consequence of this intent is that the true listening cloze as Gregory-Panopoulos (1966) has developed it, in which items are deleted and replaced by a tone, and in which subjects are not supplied the surrounding text for their responses, is a less desirable alternative, because of the difficulty of making such an edited tape. Also, as suggested in Figure 17-1, this type of listening cloze requires much greater grammatical and pragmatic analysis on the part of the listener. Therefore, two procedures involving recall of recently heard text were focused on: a fixed-ration recall cloze and a partial dictation recall.

For the fixed-ratio recall cloze items, a deletion rate of every fifth word was maintained, giving three to five response words per targeted interruption, the same rate used by Gregory-Panopoulos (1966) and DeVito (1965). The partial dictation recall measure required the listeners to fill in sequences of blanks representing two or three consecutively clozed words. The sentences in Example 1 illustrate these two conditions.

Example 1:
Fixed-Ratio Cloze Recall
The glass ______ the heat so that ______ cannot be reradiated.

Partial Dictation Recall
The ______ ______ the heat so that it cannot be reradiated.

The reasons for the choice of sequential recall rather than simultaneous aural-graphic presentation will be explained below.

The research questions were:

1. Would these procedures produce reliable and valid measures of listening skill?
2. Is either procedure more reliable or valid?

In the event that these procedures proved reliable and valid, they should then be helpful as measures of learners' initial stages of processing input, especially insofar as the time allowed for the response is limited. And if the more flexible partial dictation were especially reliable and valid, specific input items could be examined in more detail.

METHOD[4]

Subjects

The subject population was comprised of the second- and third-quarter adult students at two technical academic preparation English Language Centers in the People's Republic of China. This population, consisting of highly trained scientists and professionals, was expected to be able to follow the more technical aspects of the videotaped minilectures developed for this study. The total number of subjects completing the listening tests was 215. The distribution of subjects into conditions at each English Language Center is shown in Table 17-1.[5]

TABLE 17-1 Number of Subjects in Each Condition

	Condition 1, note taking	*Condition 2, partial dictation*	*Condition 3, fixed ratio*	*Total*
Center 1	39	43	43	125
Center 2	31	32	27	90

Materials

Two university lectures by the same professor on scientific topics were videotaped in the fall quarter of 1982. It was believed that using real lecture material and presenting it on videotape as a listening test would provide a close approximation to the natural listening task required for academic purposes. Segments of these lectures were selected for scripting and editing, thereby obtaining self-contained minilectures for testing sessions.

The minilecture topics were "Solar Energy" and "Models of Disease." After pilot testing of the material and procedures, the two lectures were edited onto a 1-hour SONY UC-60 videotape. There were a number of parts to the tape. First, for each condition there were practice exercises using short segments from the lecture. These were followed by an uninterrupted playing of the first minilecture (approximately 10 minutes). Next on the tape was the same minilecture, this time with intermittent interruptions. At the interruption, of 20 seconds each, the subjects were to turn a page in their answer booklets and write in what they recalled from what was just said in the segment. The context was provided with deletions by either fixed ratio or sequences of two to three blanks. Following the 20 seconds, the lecture continued. Sixteen interruptions throughout the lecture were in four groups of four interruptions each. The groups were spaced at about 1- to 1½-minute intervals throughout the minilecture, while the four interruptions within each group occurred at the end of almost every second or third sentence. In this way, a sample of all the minilecture language and content was being tested. The second minilecture, approximately 13 minutes, followed a similar format: one practice exercise, an uninterrupted playing, followed by the interrupted test playing.

Corresponding to each minilecture were a set of instructions, response booklets for each condition, and a 12-item comprehension quiz covering the lecture content. The response booklets for the fixed-ratio recall cloze and partial dictation recall conditions contained transcripts of the one or two spoken sentences immediately preceding the interruption pauses with only one page in the booklet per interruption. The subjects were prevented from reading the sentences until the interruption. Unlike the studies of Smith and Rafiqzad (1979) and Johansson (1973), where the listeners had the text before them while listening and thus could benefit from the simultaneous presentation of the material in two modalities, this procedure requires the subjects to recall what they have heard, with the clozed text serving as a prompting cue. The cloze recall procedure belongs in the upper part of the right side of Figure 17-1, because only a little processing is allowed to take place. However, as in the standard elicited imitation, it was assumed that the subjects' short-term memory limits were surpassed, so that some amount of grammatical processing of the utterances was likely. In pilot testing, native speakers were generally able to recall the items tested.

Following completion of the lecture and cloze recall tasks, the summary comprehension quiz over the entire lecture segment required the listeners to identify whether or not (yes or no) statements on the quiz were identical to statements made in the lecture. This quiz therefore served as a motivation for the subjects to listen carefully to the lectures.

Design

At the first minilecture presentation, the 215 subjects were distributed randomly into the three listening conditions and stayed in their condition for both minilectures, which were presented about 4 or 5 days apart. Since the two English Language Centers were composed of slightly different populations, the centers have been considered separately in this analysis. Item analysis, test reliability, and intertest correlations on the listening measures and comprehension quizzes are the measures used here to ascertain the appropriateness and validity of these tests.

Procedure

To maintain anonymity, the subjects were given identification numbers to keep for the two sessions. In their native language, they were given instructions on how to follow the test procedures. Next, they did two practice exercises for the first minilecture (only one practice exercise was used for the second minilecture). To facilitate their understanding of the main ideas, they were first shown an uninterrupted segment of the lecture. It had previously been found that, without such an initial opportunity to understand the material, subjects from this population tended to score very low on cloze tests (J. D. Brown, personal communication). The same segment was then replayed, this time with the intermittent interruptions. Following listening, the subjects completed the true/false comprehension questions.

Scoring and Analysis

The first minilecture (Solar Energy) consisted of 55 clozed items in the fixed-ratio and partial dictation recall, while the second was slightly longer, with 58 items.[6] All subjects' cloze responses were written out on coding forms and rated by four independent judges. The following coding system was applied:

0 Blank
1 Incorrect word

3 Phonologically close and semantically plausible word
4 Exact word, allowing for understandable misspellings and slight changes in morphology

An additional code, 2, was given for exact word responses in the partial dictation recall condition which were shifted over one or two blanks from the correct location. Only the exact score results are shown here.

RESULTS

Lecture and Quiz Scores

The important results obtained thus far pertain to the average item difficulty for the quiz and exact cloze lecture scores of the two experimental condition groups, and the subtest reliabilities and intercorrelations, as calculated using TESTAT.[7] The average item difficulties on the quizzes and the cloze lectures are shown in Table 17-2.

TABLE 17-2 Item Difficulties

	Center 1				
Subtest	*Number of items*	*Mean*	*S.D.*	*s^2*	*Diff*
Condition 2 (partial dictation):					
Quiz 1	12	8.67	1.86	3.5	.72
Quiz 2	12	8.74	1.46	2.1	.73
Lecture 1	55	19.05	5.87	34.5	.35
Lecture 2	55	24.7	7.23	52.3	.45
Condition 3 (fixed-ratio cloze):					
Quiz 1	12	8.42	1.54	2.4	.70
Quiz 2	12	8.56	1.78	3.2	.71
Lecture 1	55	21.74	5.36	28.7	.40
Lecture 2	58	31.05	5.86	34.3	.53

	Center 2				
Subtest	*Number of items*	*Mean*	*S.D.*	*s^2*	*Diff*
Condition 2 (partial dictation):					
Quiz 1	12	7.19	1.61	2.6	.60
Quiz 2	12	7.16	1.79	3.2	.60
Lecture 1	55	13.56	7.46	55.7	.25
Lecture 2	55	14.56	8.09	65.4	.26
Condition 3 (fixed-ratio cloze):					
Quiz 1	12	7.37	1.66	2.8	.61
Quiz 2	12	7.11	1.95	3.8	.59
Lecture 1	55	17.22	6.75	45.6	.31
Lecture 2	58	19.74	7.99	63.8	.34

The subtest reliabilities (internal consistency as determined by Cronbach's alpha) are shown in Table 17-3.[8]

TABLE 17-3 Subtest Reliabilities*

	Center 1	*Center 2*
Condition 2 (partial dictation):		
Quiz 1	.40	.07
Quiz 2	.11	.31
Lecture 1	.77	.88
Lecture 2	.83	.89
Condition 3 (fixed ratio):		
Quiz 1	.24	.10
Quiz 2	.37	.44
Lecture 1	.67	.82
Lecture 2	.74	.86

*Internal consistency calculated with Cronbach's alpha.

Table 17-4 displays the subtest intercorrelations between all quizzes and lecture scores for the two cloze conditions.

TABLE 17-4 Subtest Intercorrelations

	Center 1			*Center 2*		
	Quiz 2	*Lect. 1*	*Lect. 2*	*Quiz 2*	*Lect. 1*	*Lect. 2*
Condition 2 (partial dictation):						
Quiz 1	.23	.10	.43†	.34	.13	.43*
Quiz 2		.12	.43†		.00	.32
Lecture 1			.59‡			.65‡
		(n = 43)			(n = 32)	
Condition 3 (fixed ratio):						
Quiz 1	.28	.13	.27	.23	.24	.19
Quiz 2		.20	.57‡		.33	.46*
Lecture 1			.67‡			.74‡
		(n = 43)			(n = 27)	

*$p < .01$ (one-tailed) †$p < .005$ (one-tailed) ‡$p < .001$ (one-tailed)

DISCUSSION

Quizzes

The item difficulties in Table 17-2 for the two quizzes indicate that they were too easy for students in both centers (total difficulties ranging from .59 to .73), and the internal reliability measures in Table 17-4 were very low (alpha ranged from .07 to .44). This poor outcome could be attributable in part to the small number of items on these quizzes, and to the fact that the subjects had heard the lectures twice. Thus, the quizzes only served to focus attention on the main ideas of the lectures.

Reliability of Lectures

The reliability measures of the experimental conditions on the two lectures at both centers were high (alpha ranged from .67 to .89), as seen in Table 17-3. There was a slight trend for lecture 2 to have higher reliability, which might be explained by the subjects' increased familiarity with the two procedures. It should also be noted that the partial dictation recall was consistently more reliable internally than the fixed-ratio procedure.

Subtest Intercorrelations

In order to show the stability of these procedures across different material, it was of interest to determine the extent to which the two lecture scores correlated, as a measure of alternative form reliability for the cloze recall conditions. While the intercorrelations with the quizzes were low, the partial dictation recall and fixed-ratio intercorrelations between the first and second lectures were high (significant at $p < .001$), more so at center 2 (see Table 17-4). The fixed-ratio condition had slightly higher intercorrelations than the partial dictation recall (.67 and .74 versus .59 and .64, respectively).

Applications in Testing Listenability

Since it appears that both procedures are reliable, with the partial dictation slightly better internally, and the fixed-ratio recall cloze slightly better in equivalent form reliability, the application of interest is whether or not specific items in the lectures were perceived with consistently greater or lesser difficulty. This is to say, would a lexical item in a specific context be equivalently difficult in both listening procedures, and would different items and contexts be consistently ordered in difficulty across groups of listeners? If either proves to be the case, then it is plausible that these procedures are measuring differential ability to process different input items. A tentative answer to this question can be made by comparing how well the different groups succeeded with sets of items that were the same across conditions.

In lectures 1 and 2 there were 12 and 13 clozed items, respectively, which were identical for the two experimental listening conditions. For these items, the mean difficulty across subject groups (in the two language centers and the two conditions) showed considerable variation, but a comparison across groups of the *rank order of difficulty* of these items within each group indicates the extent to which the items in context are more, or less, perceivable.

After first assigning ranks to the items within groups, based on their mean difficulty scores (Table 17-5), rank-order correlations were calculated (Kendall's tau for tied ranks, and Kendall's coefficient of concordance, as described in Hays 1973). The rank-order correlations are shown in Table 17-6.

It can be seen in Table 17-6 that the rank orders of difficulty of the items are significantly correlated with one another in all cases, at least at the .05 level. Kendall's coefficient of concordance and average r is also high across the four groups for both lecture item sets. There is thus a monotonic trend in the two sets of items, regardless of the specific procedure used in recall.

These results increase the plausibility of using these procedures to selectively study items in input, since the partial dictation procedure, for example, allows the researcher to sample various sequences of items. An important caveat for such an approach is in order, however. Besides the fact that these results deserve further analysis and validation with independent listening measures, it should be borne in mind that the assumption for internal reliability indices, namely, that each item should contribute equally to the total test, discriminating equally between upper and lower proficiency groups, is not congruent with a test whose purpose is to find both those items that are very easy, thus part of the learner's grammar, and those that are very difficult, that is, far beyond the learner's ability to process. This expectation in the latter type of test implies that the variance among items will always be greater than desired for standard test evaluation. But we are not in fact interested in using this type of elicitation procedure to *discriminate between individuals at all.* Rather, we would want to find a relatively homogeneous group of individuals (or equate them somehow in terms of their developing grammars, background knowledge, attitudes, etc.) and test the perceptual differences *among the items.* Thus, traditional approaches to test development may not be so useful. What has been illustrated here is merely the fact that the outcome for particular items can be consistent across groups and types of procedure and moreover that the procedures themselves produce similar results in alternative forms (as seen in Table 17-4).

CONCLUSION

The results of this test-development project suggest that reasonably high reliabilities can be obtained with measures of listeners' precise recall of audiovisually presented target language. The partial dictation recall measure, which is more interesting for the purpose of investigating specific input targets, was more difficult and had somewhat lower test-retest correlations than the fixed-ratio cloze, although it showed a higher internal reliability

TABLE 17-5 Mean Item Difficulties and Rank in Groups*

	Lecture 1							
	Condition 2				*Condition 3*			
	Center 1		*Center 2*		*Center 1*		*Center 2*	
Item	$\bar{X}$	*Rank*	$\bar{X}$	*Rank*	$\bar{X}$	*Rank*	$\bar{X}$	*Rank*
House	.98	1	.91	1	.91	1	.89	1
Cool	.86	2	.63	2	.81	2	.59	3
Will	.33	5	.28	3	.63	3	.81	2
Is	.21	8	.13	5	.56	4	.33	4
Available	.63	3	.13	5	.42	6	.07	10.5
This	.44	4	.13	5	.23	9	.11	8.5
Tree	.30	6	.06	9	.49	5	.19	6.5
Insulates	.23	7	.09	7.5	.26	8	.30	5
It	.07	9	.00	11.5	.28	7	.19	6.5
Take	.00	11.5	.09	7.5	.14	10	.11	8.5
Of	.05	10	.03	10	.05	11	.07	10.5
Bounces	.00	11.5	.00	11.5	.00	12	.00	12

	Lecture 2							
	Condition 2				*Condition 3*			
	Center 1		*Center 2*		*Center 1*		*Center 2*	
Item	$\bar{X}$	*Rank*	$\bar{X}$	*Rank*	$\bar{X}$	*Rank*	$\bar{X}$	*Rank*
Period	.86	2	.66	2	.95	1.5	.70	1
Five	.93	1	.69	1	.86	4	.56	3
In	.79	3	.31	5.5	.95	1.5	.63	2
Health	.77	4	.44	3	.93	3	.44	4
Symptoms	.58	5	.34	4	.70	5	.33	5
Hazard	.56	6	.31	5.5	.56	6	.19	8.5
Really	.23	11	.16	8.5	.31	7	.30	6
Physician	.37	7	.06	11.5	.30	8.5	.15	10.5
That	.30	9.5	.19	7	.23	11	.15	10.5
Least	.30	9.5	.13	10	.30	8.5	.07	13
System	.02	13	.16	8.5	.02	13	.26	7
Respect	.33	8	.03	13	.26	10	.11	12
Social	.21	12	.06	11.5	.12	12	.19	8.5

*Example cloze items from lecture 2:

Condition 2 (partial dictation): I don't wind up going to see a __(physician)__ __(when)__ I don't feel in a state of disease, when I do not __(present)__ __(symptoms)__ .

Condition 3 (fixed ratio): I don't wind up going to see a __(physician)__ when I don't feel __(in)__ a state of disease, __(when)__ I do not present __(symptoms)__ .

TABLE 17-6 Item Rank-Order Correlations Between Groups
(Kendall's tau for tied ranks)

Lecture 1 (N = 12)	*Center 1*		*Center 2*	
	Condition 2	*Condition 3*	*Condition 2*	*Condition 3*
Center 1:				
Condition 2	—	.63†	.66†	.44*
Condition 3		—	.67†	.65†
Center 2:				
Condition 2			—	.58†
Coefficient of concordance across all groups: W = .81 (average r = .74)				

Lecture 2 (N = 13)	*Center 1*		*Center 2*	
	Condition 2	*Condition 3*	*Condition 2*	*Condition 3*
Center 1:				
Condition 2	—	.77‡	.60†	.51†
Condition 3		—	.60†	.46*
Center 2:				
Condition 2			—	.65‡
Coefficient of concordance errors across all groups: W = .82 (average r = .77)				

*p <.05 †p < .01 ‡p < .001

(Cronbach's alpha, seen in Table 17-3). The rank orders of difficulty for items that were the same across conditions proved to be significantly intercorrelated as well.

Since the lecture comprehension quizzes appeared inadequately reliable, it remains to test the concurrent validity of these two procedures with respect to other measures of listening comprehension. However, if it can be confirmed that these measures are related to learners' natural processing of target language, and they are not simply meaningless mimicry, applications are possible in two related directions. On the one hand, we have a method for investigating differences in learners' intake of naturally contextualized input. Similarly, on the other hand, to the extent that we can determine the grammatical constraints on items that are isolated by means of these listening procedures, and independently determine the particular states of target language knowledge attained by learners, we can use such measures to compare the influence of the learners' knowledge on their processing of specific forms in input.

NOTES

1. The process of developing this research involved many individuals over a long period of time. It is impossible to detail the invaluable contributions and advice offered by the people named here. Without them, this study would not have been possible. Nevertheless, the author takes full responsibility for any inadequacies in this study.

The Office of Instructional Development, UCLA, supported it with a minigrant. Initial motivation and support came from Leland McCleary, Larry Miller, and especially Russ Campbell. For expert production of the materials, I thank especially Donna Brinton. I am also indebted to Alan Friedman, Pat Ryan, Lois Precup, Greg Orr, Brian Lynch, Thom Hudson, Wang Ying-long, Zhou Fu-qiu, Jiang Ming-shan, Noreen Webb, Jim Brown, Earl Rand, Frances Hinofotis, the staff and students of the English Language Centers in the People's Republic of China, and Eleanor Hoops. For the data analysis, I especially thank Debra Jonas, and Laura Miccoli, Joseph Nidue, Chang Li, David McGirt, Agnes Chen, and Patricia Liu.

2. The input in this case comes from the parents of the children.

3. For example, Krashen (1983) has proposed a hypothesis-testing model (a clarification of his input hypothesis), in which the learners test input against a hypothesized rule in their interlanguage grammar, and adopt the rule if the input matches the hypothesis. Krashen claims that this can happen only if the rule is one "stage" advanced [designated as $t(i + 1)$] of the learners' current internalized rule system [designated as $t(i)$]. Since Krashen has proposed here that these rules do not have to be real target language rules, but only "transitional" learners' rules, to test his proposal requires a methodology that can identify both the rule the learner is hypothesizing and the rule the learner perceives in the input. As yet, we have not refined an appropriate methodology for this. I am indebted to Mike Long for focusing my attention on this point.

4. The description of the method and results of this study is necessarily abridged. See Chaudron (in preparation) for details.

5. Condition 1, note taking, was intended as a control on the experimental procedures, and it will not be discussed further here.

6. Because of an error in test preparation, the second lecture for the partial dictation recall condition contained only 55 items.

7. TESTAT is a test-analysis program written in FORTRAN by D. J. Veldman, and revised by Earl Rand (October 1975). The output includes total scores by subject, and various test and subtest measures of item difficulty, reliability, and intercorrelations.

8. It is usually considered that measures of internal reliability, such as alpha, are not appropriate with cloze tests, owing to the interdependence of the items. However, this listening procedure, requiring isolated cases of immediate recall, allowed little time for the listener to reflect over the larger context. In this sense, each item independently samples the learner's ability to recall it in its context, just as other proficiency tests sample grammatical knowledge in different contexts. While the debatable nature of alpha in this case is recognized, the results are provided for the reader to interpret according to his or her choice. Equivalent form reliability, also used here, is not subject to the same critique.

On Speech Acts

18

DEGREE OF APPROXIMATION: NONNATIVE REACTIONS TO NATIVE SPEECH ACT BEHAVIOR[1]

Elite Olshtain
Tel Aviv University

Shoshana Blum-Kulka
University of Jerusalem

How long do you have to live in a target speech community in order to learn to react to speech behavior as a native would?

In recent years, the emphasis on communicative competence as a goal in second and foreign language learning has highlighted the importance of cross-cultural differences in interactional styles. To become, eventually, a competent second language user, one needs to acquire sociocultural rules of appropriacy, as well as grammatical competence. Lack of sociocultural competence, even when grammatical competence is there, may result in communicative failure. As researchers, we are therefore urged by practitioners to find out more about the acquisition process of sociocultural rules by learners participating in different learning situations.

This chapter aims to demonstrate how reaction to native speech act behavior by nonnatives may serve as a useful indication of their degree of acculturation to the target speech community. In our study, we found that there seems to be an increasing approximation of native response patterns, as a function of the nonnatives' length of stay in the target speech community. The process of approximation discussed in this chapter relates to the receptive and sociocultural aspects of language learning. In order to gain better insight into the process, we developed acceptability (judgment) tests which were given to native speakers of Hebrew and learners of Hebrew at various stages of their stay in Israel. We found that there seems to be an increasing similarity between native and nonnative acceptability judgments as a function of the nonnatives' length of stay in the target speech community.

APPROXIMATION OF SPEECH ACT RESPONSE PATTERNS AND ACCULTURATION

This chapter aims to link the approximation of speech act behavior with the acculturation process of the learner to the target speech community. Such an acculturation process is defined here in Schumann's (1978b) terms, namely, the social and psychological integration of the learner within the target language group. According to Schumann, a learner can be placed on a continuum ranging from social and psychological distance to social and psychological proximity with speakers of the target language. Schumann claims that the level of acculturation, or the position of the learner on this continuum, controls his or her acquisition of the second language.

Evidence to support Schumann's view of acculturation and second language acquisition comes from a variety of studies (for example, Schumann 1975, 1976, 1978b, 1981, 1984, Stauble 1978, 1984) which have focused mostly on syntactic and morphological features of the learners' output in the target language.[2] In this chapter, we suggest looking at the learner's acceptance of the target sociocultural rules regardless of grammatical competence. We maintain that appropriate reaction to speech act behavior rather than linguistic output is a good indication of the internalization of such rules, regardless of grammar errors which that output may contain.[3]

The various studies linking grammatical features as indicators of language acquisition with the process of acculturation, and specifically the Heidelberg project (1975), seem to show that the learner acquires syntax mostly during the first 2 or 3 years after arrival in the target community. Later syntactic development depends on social and psychological factors. In our study, we found that after 10 years of stay in the target community, learners (immigrants) behave like native speakers in terms of their acceptability of target speech act behavior. Looking at their linguistic output, we may find grammatical deviance even after response to speech act has become very nativelike. This leads us to believe that speech act behavior might serve as a useful indicator of acculturation related to length of stay in the target community irrespective and independently of grammatical competence. Furthermore, on the basis of the data which we have collected in various speech act studies, we have reason to believe that as acculturation continues, the speakers might even adopt target speech act behavior norms into their first language.

In view of what has been said so far, this chapter will discuss speech act behavior from the receiver's point of view, focusing on two speech acts—requests and apologies. We intend to show that by using a judgment test of speech act behavior, one can compare preferences for linguistic realizations of native speakers and nonnative speakers who are on various points of the native approximation continuum. Future research will have to compare these levels of approximation with independent measures of social and psychological distance on the one hand, and with measures of linguistic competence on the other, in order to evaluate the relationship between these three aspects.

REQUESTS AND APOLOGIES

Acceptability of speech act behavior in the study focuses on two different speech acts—requests and apologies, which were chosen on the basis of a series of earlier studies covering a wide scope of subtopics (Blum-Kulka 1982; Blum-Kulka, Danet, and Gerson 1983; Cohen and Olshtain 1981; Olshtain and Cohen 1983). Based on our earlier findings, we felt that these two speech acts exhibit interesting cultural and linguistic differences across languages and might therefore be suitable for research related to the learning process.

Requests express the speaker's expectation toward some prospective action (verbal or nonverbal) by the hearer. Thus, as suggested by Brown and Levinson (1978), all types of requests impinge upon the private territory of the hearer. All languages seem to provide their speakers with a wide variety of direct and indirect strategies for making requests; this variation is motivated, universally, according to Brown and Levinson, by the need to minimize the impingement, or threat to face, involved in requesting behavior. Another phenomenon observed about requests (Searle 1975, Labov and Fanshel 1977) is the seemingly systematic relationship between pragmatic preconditions necessary for the performance of the act and its linguistic realizations. This relationship is observable in verbal patterns referred to as "conventional indirect speech acts," which provide speakers across languages with linguistically fixed utterances that "count" habitually as requests (such as "could you . . . ").

The realization patterns for requests seem to consist of at least three basic categories, two of which can be defined using linguistic and pragmalinguistic[4] formal criteria. Together, these three categories form a scale of directness which seems to be shared by all languages. The first category consists of the direct, linguistically marked ways for making requests (such as imperatives and performatives). The second category, which is the most difficult one to compare across languages, consists of those indirect strategies which are conventionally used for requesting in a given language, such as "could you" or "would you" in English. The third category consists of the open-ended set of indirect hints, such as "It is cold in here" used as a request to close the window.

The act of apologizing is rather different from the act of requesting, since it is called for *after* some behavior or action has resulted in the violation of social norms (or just before such an infraction is about to happen). When an action or an utterance (or the lack of either) results in the fact that one or more persons perceive themselves as deserving an apology, the culpable person(s) is (are) expected to apologize. The speaker, therefore, intends to placate the hearer and to restore thereby his or her own social status (Edmondson and House 1981). According to Searle (1979) a person who apologizes for doing A expresses regret at having committed an aggressive act. It is therefore clear that here there is no threat to the hearer's face; on the contrary, apologies by their very nature are hearer-supportive acts which threaten the speaker's face.

In terms of verbal patterns, in the case of apologies, we are concerned, on the one hand, with formulaic (performative) routines ("I'm sorry") and, on the other hand, with an open-ended variety of possible utterances, which by their propositional content express notions associated with the speech act of apology, used in addition to or instead of the formulaic expressions.

These basic categories for analyzing apologies and requests can serve as a basis for setting up cross-linguistically comparable speech act sets for each of the two speech acts. Thus, comparing apologies across languages, it would be interesting to note the nature of the formulaic routine expressions in each, as well as the relative role in language use of the basic notions of apologizing. For requests such a comparison should yield the language-specific variations in the group of direct and conventionally indirect strategies, as well as the major types of context-bound open-ended sets of indirect ones.

In our attempt to compare learners of a language with the native speakers of that language, our main objective is to establish patterns of use related to social constraints, i.e., to discover the preferences of the two groups of speakers across socially varied situations, thus establishing "what needs to be learned" when moving from one language to the other. In order to do that, suitable data-collection tools need to be developed. When focusing on speech act production (from the speaker's point of view) we have used the discourse completion test originally developed by Blum-Kulka (1982) and used extensively in a current research project aimed at the study of cross-cultural patterns of speech act realizations also dealing with requests and apologies in six different languages.[5] The study reported here, since it focuses on response patterns to speech act behavior from the hearer's point of view, suggested the development of a judgment test as a tool for data collection.

THE STUDY

Theoretical Framework

The development of the acceptability (judgment) test and specifically the selection and phrasing of the items included in the test were based on Brown and Levinson's (1978) model of politeness phenomena, mentioned earlier. The underlying assumption of this model is that a speaker faced with the wish to perform an act which might threaten the hearer's face (such as a request) has a series of options to go through, and at each juncture of this option-taking path, he or she makes a decision.

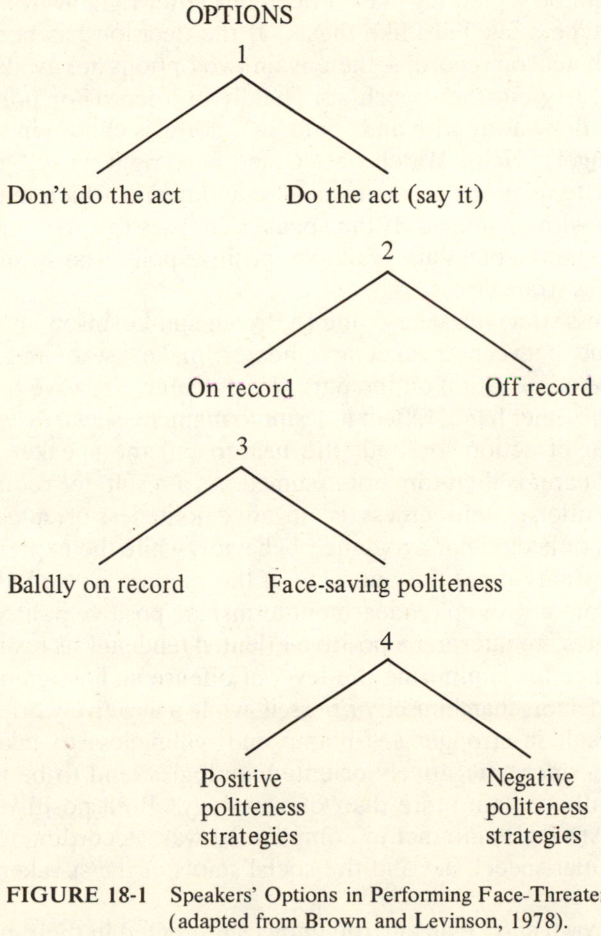

FIGURE 18-1 Speakers' Options in Performing Face-Threatening Speech Acts (adapted from Brown and Levinson, 1978).

The first option which the speaker faces, according to Brown and Levinson, is the choice as to whether to perform the speech act or not. Such a decision, at the individual level, is probably determined by the way in which the speaker assesses the social situation. For instance, if a department head needs to have a letter typed immediately but the only secretary available in the office is one who usually does not do the typing, he or she may decide to type the letter by himself or herself and not perform the speech act of requesting. On the other hand, at this first juncture of option taking, the decision may be to perform the act (in spite of the special situation), and here again two options are available—this speech act can be performed "off record" or "on record." If the speaker decides to choose the "off record" route, the request is made by dropping some hint and hoping that the secretary would perceive it as a request and offer to help. Such an "off record" request might be something like, "I need this letter right away and it takes me hours to type a few lines like these." If the decision has been to carry out the speech act "on record"—then again two options are available: we may choose to carry out the speech act "baldly on record" or politely. Politeness is usually done away with and "bald on record" is chosen in cases of urgency and danger: "Help! Watch out! Come here right away!" or in cases of close intimate relations between speaker and hearer which make it possible to do away with politeness. If the speaker chooses to carry out the request politely, two new choices are available: positive politeness strategies or negative politeness strategies.

Positive politeness strategies, according to Brown and Levinson, emphasize common ground between speaker and hearer, make use of in-group markers, presuppose cooperation on the part of the hearer. Negative politeness strategies, on the other hand, reflect a desire to maintain social distance, unhindered freedom of action for both the hearer and the speaker, and cooperation of the hearer is therefore not assumed. As a result, for requests, for example, conventional indirectness is negative-politeness-oriented, as well as other means of hedging or avoidance behavior, while the expression of optimistic assumptions about the outcome of the request, as well as the establishment of common ground (endearment terms) are positive-politeness-oriented. For apologies, we interpret a positive-oriented tendency as resulting in speakers' preference for minimizing the level of offense and assigning responsibility to other factors than himself or herself, while a negatively oriented approach would result in stronger self-blame and willingness to take on responsibility. Furthermore, negatively oriented apologies tend to be more intensified and usually contain more than one strategy.[6] Both positive and negative politeness strategies interact in complicated ways according to the nature of the particular speech act and the social status of the speaker and the hearer.

According to Brown and Levinson, the choices presented in their model represent different ways of achieving communicative ends available to members of all societies, and the model can therefore be viewed as pancultural in nature. Yet, preferences for certain decisions and choices made along the way are probably culture-dependent. Thus, there might be cultural differences as to when certain speech acts are performed depending on social factors relevant to the specific situations. Furthermore, there may be cultural preferences concerning the choices made between positive and negative politeness strategies. Although both types of strategies are available in all cultures, societies which tend to minimize social distance will show a preference for positive politeness strategies, while societies that place a high value on respect for private "space" will show preference for negative politeness. This model allows us to make useful comparisons across cultures.

From our findings in other studies (Blum-Kulka, Danet, and Gerson 1983), we have come to believe that speakers of Hebrew, when compared with other languages (at least American English), often prefer "bald on record" performance of speech acts—the more direct and unmitigated form which seriously encroaches on the hearer's territory. Furthermore, Israeli culture seems to be in general more positive-politeness-oriented, and in comparison with other languages, Hebrew speakers seem to prefer positive politeness strategies to negative politeness ones, although they often use negative strategies as well. Accordingly, when we focus on the hearer's receptive end, we find that Hebrew speakers are more tolerant to a variety of strategies for the performing of a speech act, generally focusing more on the positive-politeness end of the continuum.

Research Methodology

In order to incorporate Brown and Levinson's model and, at the same time, ensure cross-cultural comparability, we developed a judgment test consisting of eight items: four request situations and four apology situations (see Appendix). For each situation we presented respondents with six different choices, and for each choice they had to react by choosing from one to three on an evaluation scale of most appropriate, more or less appropriate, and not appropriate. Thus, number 1 could indicate levels of agreement on the acceptability of the items while number 3 indicated rejection of it.

For each situation on the judgment test, there were therefore six different realizations: two were marked as P (positively oriented), two were marked as N (negatively oriented), one was marked as D (bald on record—direct), and one was a distractor.[7] All the choices presented in the test had been taken from earlier discourse completion tests and were therefore speakers' produced—elicited—data.

The following request situation is an example of the items on the judgment test:

Situation 1. Asking for a Loan
Ruth, a friend of yours at the university, comes up to you after class and tells you that she has finally found an apartment to rent. The only problem is that she has to pay $200 immediately and at present she only has $100. She turns to you and says:

a. How about lending me some money? (P)
b. So, do me a favor and lend me the money. (P)
c. Do you want to lend me the money? (distractor)
d. I'd appreciate it if you could lend me the money. (N)
e. Could you possibly lend me the money? (N)
f. Lend me the money, please. (D)

The social variables of power and distance were supplied as part of the description of the situation. Respondents, native speakers, and learners at different stages of their stay in Israel were asked to rate each of the six realizations on a scale of appropriateness from one to three.

Population

The test was administered in two versions: English and Hebrew. The English version was administered to 172 native speakers of English. The Hebrew version was administered to 160 native speakers of Hebrew and 124 nonnative speakers. All the subjects were students at the Hebrew University. The data base for the analysis reported is derived from the following:

1. Ratings of the utterances on request situation on the test. English version (172 × 6).
2. Ratings of two request situations. Hebrew version (364 × 12).
3. Ratings of two utterances on apology situation 8. (364 × 2).

Culture-Dependent Response Patterns

Research Question 1 To what extent do acceptability judgments of native speakers in a given situation reflect preferences for either positive or negative politeness strategies or direct, bald on record choices?

Our first research question relates to levels of agreement exhibited by native speakers in terms of strategy preferences in a given situation. If indeed such response patterns indicate culture-dependent choices, they should reveal systematic acceptability of certain types of strategies, as well as systematic rejection of other types, across the same situations. The results of the English questionnaires show that this is indeed the case (at least for American English); in all four request situations, native speakers of American English indicated a definite preference for conventionally indirect N-oriented strategies and rejected informal, P-oriented, and direct options. This trend becomes evident from the distribution of ratings for judging different ways of asking for a loan from a friend, as shown in Table 18-1.

TABLE 18-1 Levels of Agreement

Distribution of Ratings to Situation 1 "Asking for a Loan"
English Version (n = 172)

Strategy			*Most appropriate*	*More or less appropriate*	*Not appropriate*
			1 %	2 %	3 %
1a	P_2	How about lending me the money?	7.4	39.5	53.1
1b	P_2	So, do me a favor and lend me the money.	1.9	24.7	73.5
1c	X	Do you want to lend me the money?	6.6	49.4	44
1d	N_1	I'd appreciate it if you could lend me the money.	60.1	36.3	3.6
1e	N_2	Could you possibly lend me the money?	84.8	12.3	2.9
1f	D	Lend me the money, please.	5.4	40.4	54.2

P = positive politeness strategy X = distractor N = negative politeness strategy
D = direct—bald on record

The results presented in Table 18-1 indicate *high levels of agreement* (above 50 percent) among informants with regard to five out of six options presented on the test. The options judged as *highly acceptable* by the majority of American-English speakers represent negative-politeness-oriented indirect strategies:

Sentence 1 d:
I'd appreciate it if you could lend me the money. (N—conventionally indirect—60 percent acceptability).

Sentence 1 e:
Could you possibly lend me the money? (N—hedging, less assuming 85 percent acceptability.)

The level of agreement exhibited by these answers with respect to negative politeness strategies as found suitable for this situation by American-English speakers is further reinforced when we examine the clear rejection by the same respondents, of the positive-oriented options:

Sentence 1 a:
How about lending me the money? (P) 53 percent rejection.

Sentence 1 b:
So, do me a favor and lend me the money. (Strong P) 73 percent rejection. Furthermore, Americans rejected the *direct* option for this situation.

Sentence 1 c:
Lend me the money, please (D) 54 percent rejection.

Responses derived from American-English speakers seem to indicate, therefore, a clear preference for negatively oriented choices, as compared with clear rejection of positive options, in the situation of asking for a loan from a friend.

Cross-Cultural Variance

Research Question 2 To what extent do judgments concerning strategy preferences differ across speech communities relative to the same situation, thus reflecting cross-cultural differences in interactional styles with respect to bald on record, and positive or negative politeness strategies?

Following Brown and Levinson's model, cross-cultural differences in interactional styles might be manifested by culture-dependent preferences for certain types of strategies in the same social situation across two cultures. A comparison of response patterns of American-English speakers and native Hebrew speakers in judging requests for a loan indicates that the two cultures indeed differ in interactional styles.

TABLE 18-2 Cross-Cultural Variance—Asking for a Loan

		English (n = 172)				*Hebrew (n = 150)*		
		1	2	3		1	2	3
Sentence	*Strategy*	%	%	%		%	%	%
S1a	P_1	7.4	39.5	[53.1]	≠	[60.4]	28.9	10.7
S1f	D	5.4	40.4	[54.2]	≠	32.5	45.6	21.9
S1d	N_1	[60.1]	36.3	3.6	=	[71.9]	20	8.1
S1e	N_2	[84.8]	12.3	29	≠	41.9	39	19.5
S1b	P_2	1.9	24.7	[73.5]	=	4.4	21.5	[74.1]

As the results in Table 18-2 indicate, American speakers, when asked for a loan by a friend, seem to expect formal conventional negative-politeness-oriented indirectness only (S1d and S1e), and show no tolerance for either the direct approach or for intimate, informal, positive politeness forms. Israelis, on the other hand, do accept the nonformal positive politeness approach (S1a-P1) but reject, as do Americans, the strong presumptuous positive-oriented option (S1b-P2). Some Israelis (32 percent acceptance and only 22 percent rejection) even regard the bald on record, direct version (S1c) as appropriate. It is interesting to note, however, that Israelis are equally tolerant toward a conventional indirect N strategy (S1d-N1) in this situation. What becomes evident when looking at these results is the fact that certain norms of appropriateness are *shared* across cultures, while others *are not.* The difference between the two cultures exhibited here relates to choices made along the positive-negative politeness continuum. American judgments show preference for N-type strategies while Israelis show acceptance of both N and P types.

The following diagram illustrates how we can plot option preferences for P and N tendencies in requesting behavior, along the continuum.

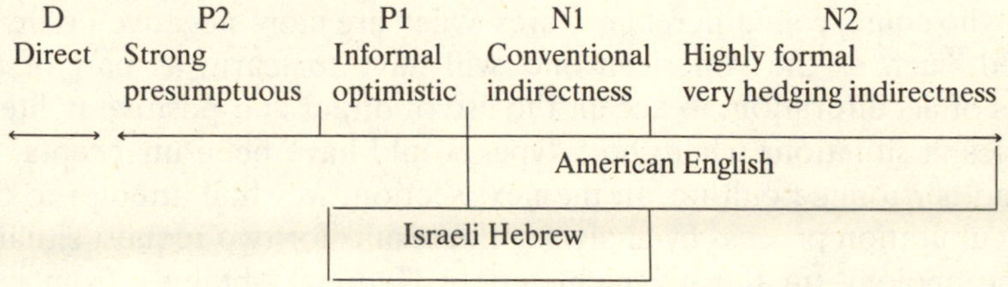

The strong presumptuous P-oriented option is placed at one end of the continuum while the highly formal, exaggerated N-oriented version is at the other end. In the center of the continuum, we find the informal, optimistic P-oriented option and the conventional indirect one. The direct option is placed outside this continuum since it serves as an alternative choice to both positive and negative politeness (see Figure 18-1).

When comparing Hebrew speakers with American-English speakers for situation 1, asking for a loan from a friend, we find that both groups share acceptability of negative-oriented conventional forms (N1) but differ with respect to more formal and hedging N forms. The latter (N2) are acceptable to American but rejected by Israelis, while the informal optimistic (P1) option is accepted by Israelis but rejected by Americans. The strong presumptuous version (P2) is equally rejected by Israelis and Americans.

The diagram shows Israeli culture as being more positive- than negative-politeness-oriented. This is in line with results from another study, based on 477 request tokens in Hebrew, obtained via ethnographic methods (Blum-Kulka, Danet, and Gerson 1983). The results showed a wide variance in types of request strategies used; the main predictors of this variance were the goals of the request and, surprisingly, *not* the social dimensions of relative power and distance.[8] The ethnographic study also revealed a high level of directness: the proportion of direct strategies in the whole sample reached 51 percent (conventionally indirect strategies comprised 35 percent and off-record strategies 14 percent). It should be borne in mind that the judgment test results reflect native speakers' *expectations* as to appropriate linguistic behavior in different situations and do not necessarily coincide with actual use. Hence the level of directness found through ethnographic methods is not the same as the one shown in ratings on the judgment test.

The results from both studies show the trend charted on the diagram; according to this trend, Israeli culture seems to be direct and positive-politeness-oriented. Since social distance is never assessed as very great in

Israeli culture (as predicted by Brown and Levinson for all positive-politeness-oriented societies), speakers can afford either to abstain from paying tribute to social distance, or to minimize it by verbal means. The process of abstaining from face-redressing action will result in bald on record directness, while the minimization will be expressed by positive-politeness strategies.

From the results discussed so far, it follows that learners of Hebrew in Israel, who come from different cultures which are more negative-politeness-oriented, such as the American one, will have to learn, as part of their process of acculturation, to accept the use of direct and positive politeness strategies in situations where both types would have been unacceptable in their mother tongue culture. In the next section, we shall attempt to trace this acculturation process by analyzing the results for two request situations and one apology (in the judgment test in Hebrew) obtained from native speakers and learners at various lengths of stay in the country.

The Process of Approximation to Target Language Acceptability Norms

Research Question 3 To what extent do the ratings of nonnative speakers on the judgment test reveal gradual assimilation to target culture acceptability norms, depending on their length of stay in the target community?

We have addressed the issue presented in question 3 by comparing the ratings given by three groups of nonnative speakers of various lengths of stay in the target speech community with those of native speakers. Four groups of respondents participated, therefore, in this study:

Group A: Learners who had spent less than 2 years in the country by the time they filled out the questionnaires (36).
Group B: Nonnative speakers who had lived in the country for 2 to 10 years (44).
Group C: Nonnative speakers who had lived in Israel for over 10 years (44).
Group D: Native speakers of Hebrew (160).

The results presented here are based on a comparative analysis of the ratings of each of the nonnative groups with the native speakers' group, on two request situations presented in the judgment test: asking for a loan from a friend and asking for a ride from an acquaintance.

Learners (less than 2 years) Compared with Native Speakers In order to establish whether there is a significant difference between interactional styles of learners in their initial period of stay in the target speech community and target language speakers, we compared the acceptability patterns for group A (learners less than 2 years) and group D (native speakers). Our hypothesis was that differences would be most pronounced with respect to positive politeness and direct strategies. The results of this comparison (as presented in Table 18-3) bear out our expectations only partially.

TABLE 18-3 Interlanguage Variance Distribution of Ratings of Learners (Less Than 2 Years) and Native Speakers (Hebrew Questionnaire)*

	Learners (n = 36)			*Native Ss (n = 160)*			
Sentence	*1* %	*2* %	*3* %	*1* %	*2* %	*3* %	*Significance* (chi-square test)
A. Asking for a loan: S1a (P1) Say, could you lend me 100IS until next week?	47	26	27	[60]	29	11	$p < 0.05$
S1c (D) Lend me the money, please.	20	43	37	32	46	22	n.s.
S1d (N1) Could you lend me 100IS until next week?	[64]	22	14	[72]	20	8	n.s.
S1e (N2) Do you think that you could lend me 100IS until next week?	22	45	33	41	39	20	$p < 0.05$
S1b (P2) You can lend me 100IS until next week, right?	3	29	[68]	4	22	[74]	n.s.
B. Asking for a ride: S2d (P1) Is it possible perhaps to go to town with you?	[51]	43	6	[80]	17	3	$p < .005$
S2e (D) I hope you can take me back to town with you. †	6	41	[53]	[16]	*50*	34	n.s.
S2c (N1) Are you going to town by any chance?	[67]	22	11	[61]	31	8	n.s.
S2a (N2) Excuse me. I wanted to ask you if you have room for me, by any chance, in your car?	37	43	20	26	30	44	$p < 0.05$
S1f (P2) Say, do you think I can join you going back to town?	18	44	*38*	35	48	17	$p < 0.01$

*The sentences were translated into English; percentages were rounded off.
† The sentence loses some of its directness in translation.

The results presented in Table 18-3 indicate:

1. *Differences in ratings of acceptability of the informal, optimistic (P1) strategy (S1a and S2d).* In asking for a loan, this strategy is accepted by fewer learners than native speakers (47 versus 60 percent, respectively). This tendency is repeated in the situation of asking for a ride (51 versus 80 percent). Although learners tend to accept rather than reject this strategy (contrary to our initial expectations), the difference between the actual ratings of the two groups is statistically significant for both situations, when calculated for a chi-square test with S1a, $\chi^2 = 8.94$, $p < .05$, df = 2 and S2d, $\chi^2 = 14.45$, $p < .005$.

2. *Differences in preferences for the direct (D) strategy (S1f and S2e).* Here we find a difference between the two request situations: in asking for a loan, fewer learners accept directness than native speakers (20 versus 32

percent) and more reject it (37 versus 22 percent), but this difference does not prove to be statistically significant on a chi-square. On the other hand, in asking for a ride, learners show a clear tendency toward rejecting this option (53 percent), while 50 percent of the native speakers are undecided and judge it as more or less acceptable (2 on the scale of acceptability). It seems, therefore, that rating patterns exhibited by learners with respect to positively oriented strategies (P1) and direct options (D) differ less from native patterns than the cross-cultural data indicated when we compared English and Hebrew speakers. English speakers (in English) had rejected these two strategies with high levels of agreement. Approximately half the population of respondents living in the country up to 2 years accept the (P1) positive, optimistic option and seem hesitant about rejecting the direct strategy. It might be the case that this tendency points to the beginning process of approximation already within the first 2 years of stay in the target speech community.[9]

3. *Negative conventional strategies.* With regard to negatively oriented strategies of the conventional indirect type (N1) for the two request situations (S1d and S2c), the results show no significant difference between the groups, as might have been expected on the basis of the cross-cultural comparison for the "loan" situation given in Table 18-2. This type of indirectness proves to be equally appropriate for learners of varying cultural backgrounds and for native speakers, thus reinforcing its universal potential for requesting behavior.

4. *Negative hedging indirectness.* The extreme negatively oriented strategy (N2), which we had placed on the end of the positive-negative politeness continuum, brings about different native speakers' reactions across the two situations. In asking for a loan, the trend is toward acceptability (41 percent) while in asking for a ride, the trend is toward rejecting this option (44 percent), but neither case shows high levels of agreement either for learners or for native speakers, although the distribution patterns are somewhat different and even statistically significant (S1e, $\chi^2 = 10.56$, $p < .005$, df $= 2$; S2a, $\chi^2 = 20.40$, $p < .001$, df $= 2$).

5. *Presumptuous positive politeness.* The other extreme option on the positive-negative politeness continuum, the strong presumptuous oriented strategy (P2), is treated with similar decisiveness by both groups in the first situation: all respondents find it definitely inappropriate (68 percent learners and 74 percent native speakers reject it). In the "ride" situation, the pattern is, however, less clear; the ratings for neither group show high levels of agreement on either acceptance or rejection, though more learners (38 percent) than native speakers (17 percent) agree to reject this strategy. It should be noted that the P and N choices provided on the judgment test represent sentences of equal grammatical complexity in Hebrew; hence the learners' agreement on N1 strategies and their hesitance on accepting P choices *cannot* be attributed to their level of grammatical competence.

The results presented so far show that in their initial period of stay in the target speech community, learners' acceptability norms toward requesting behavior differ in some cases significantly from those of native speakers. It follows that in order to assimilate target language acceptability norms in these instances (learn what to expect from native speakers) learners will have to change some of their response patterns. At the same time, however, they should continue to maintain patterns which they share with native speakers.

In terms of the two situations which have been analyzed in this chapter, the process of assimilation to native speakers' range of acceptability and rejection will require learners to do the following: (1) develop more tolerance for positive-oriented politeness, (2) learn not to absolutely reject direct strategies, and (3) maintain their acceptance of conventionally indirect negative-politeness forms.

Nonnative Speakers (after 10 years) Compared with Native Speakers In the preceding paragraphs, we analyzed the comparison of ratings for groups A and D. In this section, we shall analyze the comparison of group C and group D in order to answer the question as to whether learners eventually reach acceptability norms similar to those exhibited by native speakers. In our case the nonnative speakers have been living in the country for over 10 years.

On the basis of the strategy ratings of group C versus group D, as given in Table 18-4, we find that generally speaking, response patterns of nonnative speakers (over 10 years) become *similar* to native speakers' responses. This seems to indicate that the nonnatives have acquired nativelike behavior with respect to "knowing what kind of interactional style to expect from native speakers."

The following points emerge from the comparison presented in Table 18-4:

1. *Higher acceptance of informal optimistic (P1) strategy.* Nonnative speakers develop a higher level of tolerance for the Hebrew, presumably culture-specific, type of positive politeness. Thus, with respect to the two request situations analyzed here, the initial difference between nonnative and native speakers regarding P1-oriented strategies disappears. The difference between ratings of groups C and D for the P1 sentences (S1a and S2d) becomes statistically nonsignificant on a chi-square test.

2. *Less rejection of D strategies.* Nonnative speakers react to the direct strategies in both request situations very much like native speakers. This means that nonnatives have learned to reject this strategy less than they had originally done and thus the distribution patterns have become very similar (S1c and S2e) to native speakers' reactions.

3. *Maintenance of the conventionally indirect (N1) strategy.* Nonnative speakers tend to maintain their tolerance for conventional indirectness (N1), although in both request situations they have deviated somewhat from the native norms—in situation 1, "loan," acceptability ratings have dropped somewhat while in situation 2, "ride," they have increased, in both cases causing statistical significance (S1d, $\chi^2 = 10.66$, $p < .005$; S2c, $\chi^2 = 5.68$, $p < .05$), although levels of acceptability (ratings of 1 on the scale) have not changed considerably.

TABLE 18-4 Interlanguage Variance: Distribution of Ratings of Nonnative Speakers (Over 10 Years) and Native Speakers (Hebrew Questionnaire)*

Sentence	*Nonnative Ss (n = 44)*			*Native Ss (n = 160)*			*Significance* (chi-square test)
	1 %	*2* %	*3* %	*1* %	*2* %	*3* %	
A. Asking for a loan: S1a (P1) Say, could you lend me 100IS until next week?	57	32	11	60	29	11	n.s.
S1c (D) Lend me the money, please.	43	37	18	32	46	22	n.s.
S1d (N1) Could you lend me 100IS until next week?	55	43	2	72	20	8	p < 0.01
S1e (N2) Do you think that you could lend me 100IS until next week?	36	34	30	41	39	20	n.s.
S1b (P2) You can lend me 100IS until next week, right?	5	43	52	4	22	74	p < 0.01
B. Asking for a ride: S2d (P1) Is it possible perhaps to go to town with you?	86	14	0	80	17	3	n.s.
S2e (D) I hope you can take me back to town with you.†	13	48	39	16	50	34	n.s.
S2c (N1) Are you going to town by any chance?	78	23	0	61	31	8	p < 0.05
S2a (N2) Excuse me, I wanted to ask you if you have room for me, by any chance, in your car?	39	32	29	26	30	44	n.s.
S2f (P2) Say, do you think I can join you going back to town?	23	43	34	35	48	17	p < 0.05

*The sentences were translated into English; percentages were rounded off.
†The sentence loses some of its directness in translation.

4. *Negative hedging indirectness.* Both groups C and D react to the extreme negatively oriented strategy (N2) in more similar patterns than they did originally, but the levels of agreement are still rather low.

5. *Presumptuous positive politeness (P2).* Both groups still tend to reject this strategy, although the slight changes on the acceptability scale cause significance in statistical terms (S1b, $\chi^2 = 8.51$, $p < .01$; S2f, $\chi^2 = 6.59$, $p < .05$).

The main point that emerges from the above analysis is that after 10 years, nonnative speakers tend to exhibit almost nativelike tolerance for positive politeness strategies while continuing to maintain their tolerance for conventional indirectness. Thus the overall range of strategies thought appropriate in both request situations becomes similar for native and nonnative speakers.

What Is the Nature of "Change over Time" with Respect to Nonnative Acceptability Patterns? Research Question 4 Is there a gradual approximation sequence dependent on the length of stay within the target speech community?

In order to trace the development over time, we have looked at the acceptability ratings of the four groups of nonnative speakers as compared with native speakers (Table 18-3, 18-4, and 18-5[10]). Our discussions of the

TABLE 18-5 Interlanguage Variance: Distribution of Ratings of Nonnative Speakers (Between 2 and 10 Years) and Native Speakers

	Learners (2–10 years) (n = 44)			*Native Ss (n = 160)*			
Sentence	*1* %	*2* %	*3* %	*1* %	*2* %	*3* %	*Significance* (chi-square test)
A. Asking for a loan: S1a (P1) Say, could you lend me 100IS until next week?	57	16	27	[60]	29	11	$p < 0.01$
S1c (D) Lend me the money, please.	25	39	36	32	46	22	n.s.
S1d (N1) Could you lend me 100IS until next week?	50	39	11	[72]	20	8	$p < 0.01$
S1e (N2) Do you think that you could lend me 100IS until next week?	20	40	40	41	39	20	$p < 0.01$
S1b (P2) You can lend me 100IS until next week, right?	2	23	75	4	22	74	n.s.
B. Asking for a ride: S2d (P1) Is it possible perhaps to go to town with you?	77	14	9	[80]	17	3	n.s.
S2e (D) I hope you can take me back to town with you.	7	55	38	16	50	34	n.s.
S2c (N1) Are you going to town by any chance?	61	34	5	[61]	31	8	n.s.
S2a (N2) Excuse me, I wanted to ask you if you have room for me, by any chance, in your car?	41	48	11	26	30	44	$p < 0.01$
S2f (P2) Say, do you think I can join you going back to town?	34	44	22	35	48	17	n.s.

results will relate only to the strategy types that were shown as being treated differentially by group A (learners—less than 2 years) compared with native speakers. The following patterns emerge from this analysis:

Pattern A: Increase in Tolerance for Positive Politeness—As Change over Time (High-Acceptability Ratings Only)

		Learners less than 2 years	Nonnatives 2–10 years	Nonnatives more than 10 years	Native speakers
S1a	(P1)	47%	56%	57%	61%
S2d	(P1)	51%	77%	86%	80%

As the figures show, the proportion of nonnatives rating P1 as highly acceptable rises steadily over time. The gradual change or approximation is particularly obvious in situation 2, "asking for a ride." The same pattern of gradual increase in tolerance for positive politeness emerges in apology situation 8. This situation entails respondents reacting to someone who has bumped into them at the supermarket. The informal, positively oriented strategy here is a brief "I'm sorry" containing no verbal intensifiers. We find the results showing the same gradual increase in acceptability:

		Learners less than 2 years	Nonnatives 2-10 years	Nonnatives more than 10 years	Native speakers
S8a	(P1)	55%	64%	93%	95%

Pattern B: Less Rejection of Directness—As Change over Time (Rejection Ratings Only)

		Learners less than 2 years	Nonnatives 2-10 years	Nonnatives more than 10 years	Native speakers
S1c	(D)	37%	36%	18%	22%
S2e	(D)	53%	34%	39%	34%

There is a steady drop in the proportion of nonnative speakers rejecting the direct strategies and thus indicating a higher level of tolerance for the target culture level of directness in interaction.

A similar drop in rejection becomes evident in apology situation 8. The D strategy takes the form of "This can happen, madam, it's not so terrible," (expressed as an apology for bumping into someone). This type of apology expresses speakers' wishes to minimize the level of violation and relieving themselves from all responsibility. The figures below represent rejection rates of this strategy (D):

		Learners less than 2 years	Nonnatives 2-10 years	Nonnatives more than 10 years	Native speakers
S8e	(D)	62%	40%	31%	32%

Pattern C: Maintenance of Shared Strategies—No Change over Time Conventionally indirect forms are highly acceptable to at least 50% of the respondents for request situations at all points in time:

		Learners less than 2 years	Nonnatives 2-10 years	Nonnatives more than 10 years	Native speakers
S1d	(N1)	64%	50%	55%	72%
S2c	(N1)	68%	61%	78%	62%

This occurs at the same time that they continue to maintain the universal forms shared by their original and new culture.

SUMMARY AND DISCUSSION

It has been shown repeatedly in the literature that second language learners fail to achieve native communicative competence even at a rather advanced stage of learning (or acquisition in the natural setting). This phenomenon has been demonstrated with regard to speech-act performance and sociolinguistic competence in general (Blum-Kulka 1982, Thomas 1983, Swain this volume).

The study reported here follows this line of research in concentrating on the development of communicative competence, particularly with regard to speech acts, yet it differs from the previous studies on two accounts:

1. This study centers around the *receptive* rather than the productive aspect of communication.

2. This study focuses on *length of stay* in the target speech community rather than on length of learning period (or overall competence in L2).

In spite of the limited scope of this study, some of the findings might be useful for future research in this area. Thus the use of the judgment test has proved to be helpful in establishing culturally shared norms regarding the type of strategy thought appropriate by native speakers in a given situation, as well as exhibiting variability across situations. Some of these norms were found to be shared cross-culturally, while others were culture-specific.

With regard to learners, the findings seem to indicate the following:

1. The response patterns of second language speakers to the judgment test change over time as the function of the speakers' length of stay in the target speech community.

2. Changes over time of nonnatives' response patterns reflect a process of approximation of target language norms: on the one hand they develop tolerance for new interactional styles, and on the other hand they maintain features shared by the two cultures.

Previous research in productive speech act behavior has shown (House and Kasper 1981, Blum-Kulka 1982, Cohen and Olshtain 1981) that learners at advanced stages of linguistic competence still deviate from native speech realization patterns. The present study seems to indicate a different trend—irrespective of the level of linguistic competence, learners may reach native-like speech-act acceptability patterns as a function of the length of stay in the target community.

The above two types of findings raise a number of basic questions regarding the relationship between linguistic competence and the process of acculturation:

1. Is it the case that there might be a significant difference between

receptive and productive interlanguage speech-act behavior which might result in nativelike receptive patterns?

2. Is it the case that the linguistic level of competence and the social-cultural level of competence do not necessarily correlate?

Our study opens a new avenue of investigation with regard to question 2. We think that future research should investigate the interrelations holding between the two types of competence at different levels of interlanguage, taking into account length of stay in the target speech community.

NOTES

1. The research has been supported by the Fund for Basic Research administered by the Israeli Academy of Science and Humanities. We are grateful to Andrew Cohen, Eric Kellerman, Michael Sharwood Smith, and Larry Selinker for their comments.

2. Schumann (1984) discusses relative clauses and negation as features which serve as indicators of the level of second language acquisition. Stauble (1984) concentrates on the English verb phrases morphology in the speech of 12 learners exhibiting different degrees of negation development.

3. People who live in a country other than their original homeland may often exhibit fossilized grammatical forms yet be viewed by their environment as acting socially and culturally in an appropriate manner. We suggest that they have acquired the receptive sociolinguistic rules of speaking although their productive competence is not fully nativelike. An illustration of this phenomenon in the speech of one adult nonnative speaker of Hebrew, living in Israel over 15 years, is given here:

a. In a mock attempt to get rid of a fly—"Lexi zvuv" (Go away fly). Wrong grammatically, since "zvuv" is masculine in Hebrew, here addressed as feminine.

b. Over the telephone to a colleague asked to prepare a lecture—"hazman doxek" (literally, time is pressing). The phrase is grammatically correct, but register-wise, too formal for the occasion.

c. In the garden, talking to another adult—"mutar li lakaxat kise." (Literally, is it permissible for me to take a chair?) Again, the phrase is grammatically correct, its deviation having to do with speech act patterns, the conventional idiomatic pattern being—"ěsar lakaxat kise" (is it possible to?). This last deviation from native use might cause a breakdown in communication. It is easily interpreted as having an ironic overtone, as is often the case with deviation from conventionality in speech act patterns. (Compare—"Can you pass me the salt?" with "Are you able to pass the salt?") Actually here it was simply a case of transfer from the English, "May I . . . " pattern.

4. The term "pragmalinguistic" refers to the mapping of pragmatic force onto the linguistic form, thus relating contextual criteria with linguistic ones.

5. A research project aimed at the study of cross-cultural patterns of speech act realization (CCSARP), currently underway, uses discourse completion tests as the basic data-collection instrument. The project focuses at this stage on two speech acts (requests and apologies) in the following languages: American English (Wolfson and Rintell), British English (Thomas), Australian English (Ventola), Danish (Kasper and Faerch), German (House and Vollmer), Canadian French (Weitzman) and Hebrew (Blum-Kulka and Olshtain). (This project is described in Blum-Kulka and Olshtain 1984.)

6. Examples of positive- and negative-oriented apologies:

"I'm sorry." (P)

"I'm terribly sorry. It is my fault. I really don't know how it happened." (N)

7. The utterances were marked as "positively oriented," "negatively oriented," or "bald on record" on the basis of quantitative analysis by the researchers. The utterances were then presented to two groups of judges (advanced students in discourse analysis, familiar with Brown and Levinson's model), who independently confirmed the categorization.

8. This finding comes from a multiple regression analysis which looked at personal and social variables that account for variance of levels of directness. The strongest predictor of the level of directness was found to be the goal of the request while status differences between participants accounted for only 2 percent of the variance, and degree of familiarity did not even enter the equation (Blum-Kulka, Danet, and Gerson 1983).

9. The learners in our study came from a variety of linguistic backgrounds (including Arabic, Slavic, Romance languages, and English). Yet it seems reasonable to assume similar norms of acceptability at least for the European cultures and the American one. The ratings which we received for learners of less than 2 years might therefore be interpreted as indicating an ongoing process of cultural assimilation as early as within the first 2 years of stay.

10. We have chosen not to provide a full analysis of Table 18-5 within the chapter but rather to select the strategies which show differential responses during the initial period of stay in the target community. Table 18-5 is provided for reference.

APPENDIX Questionnaire (Translated from Hebrew)

Each of the following situations describes an event which might have easily taken place in reality. The situation is followed by six different sentences. Please rate each sentence on a scale as being: 1 = appropriate, 2 = more or less appropriate, and 3 = not appropriate, for the particular situation.

Situation 1

A friend of yours at the university comes up to you after class and tells you that she has finally found an apartment to rent. The only problem is that she has to pay $200 immediately and at present she has only $100. She turns to you and says:

______ a. Say, could you lend me 100IS until next week?

______ b. You can lend me 100IS until next week, right?

______ c. Lend me the money, please.

______ d. Could you lend me 100IS until next week?

______ e. Do you think that you could lend me 100IS until next week?

______ f. Maybe you have a little money to give me so that I could take the apartment?

Situation 2

At the end of a party which took place in a suburb, an acquaintance who knows that you live in town and that you have a car comes up to you and says:

______ a. Excuse me, I wanted to ask you if you have room for me, by any chance, in your car?

______ b. Maybe you can give me a lift to town?

______ c. Are you going to town by any chance?

______ d. Is it possible perhaps to go to town with you?

______ e. I hope you can take me back to town with you.

______ f. Say, do you think I can join you going back to town?

Situation 3

You are in an unfamiliar part of town and unintentionally you park your car in a "no parking" area. As you get out of your car, a policeman comes up to you and says:

______ a. Move your car, please.

______ b. You'd better move your car from here immediately, do you hear me?

______ c. It's necessary to move the car from here.

______ d. Could you move the car from here, please?

______ e. You'd better move; otherwise you'll get a ticket.

______ f. Madam/sir, you have to move the car from here.

Situation 4

You're a member of a research group. Many people are missing from a meeting and it is necessary for someone to notify them about the next meeting. Your boss turns to you and says:

______ a. Notify those who are missing, OK?

______ b. Perhaps you could notify those who didn't come?

______ c. Could you please notify the others about our next meeting?

______ d. How about getting in touch with the people who were absent?

______ e. I'd appreciate it if you could notify the people who were absent.

______ f. You will notify the people who were absent.

Situation 5
You arranged to meet a friend to get some notes for an exam. You waited for an hour and a half and she did not show up. You call and she says to you:

______ a. I'm really sorry. I don't know what happened to me. I'll get it to you right away.
______ b. Oh, my, I forgot all about it. I'll get it to you as soon as I can.
______ c. I apologize.
______ d. I waited for you and you didn't show up. Maybe we got mixed up.
______ e. I'm afraid I forgot about the meeting. When can I bring it to you?
______ f. I was terribly busy and couldn't come. What can I do about it?

Situation 6
You're trying to park your car in a parking lot and suddenly another car backs into your car. The driver gets out and says:

______ a. I'm terribly sorry but I wasn't careful enough.
______ b. I'm very sorry, I should have been more careful. I'll give you my address.
______ c. I'm very sorry. It is my fault. I didn't look carefully.
______ d. Don't worry, I'll pay for the damage.
______ e. It's my fault and my insurance will pay for it. What can be done about it? What's happened, happened.
______ f. OK, what happened—happened. My insurance will pay.

Situation 7
In a discussion at work, you were offended by something that one of your colleagues said. She comes up to you afterward and says:

______ a. I'm sorry, I didn't mean it personally.
______ b. I'm sorry but what I said was the truth.
______ c. I'm terribly sorry that I said something which could have been interpreted as a personal offense. I did not mean to insult you. I'm very sorry that you understood what I said in this manner.
______ d. It is a shame that you misunderstood me. I didn't mean to insult you.
______ e. I couldn't possibly have said something bad to you. I'm sorry that this is how you interpreted what I said.
______ f. I meant exactly what I said.

Situation 8
You're at the supermarket. Another customer bumps into you with a shopping cart. You turn around and that person says:

______ a. I'm sorry.
______ b. Forgive me, I didn't mean this to happen.
______ c. I'm terribly sorry. Please forgive me. I was thinking about something else and I wasn't careful.
______ d. Sorry!
______ e. This can happen, madam, it wasn't intentional.
______ f. Excuse me, madam, you were in the way.

On Grammatical Acquisition

19

GRAMMARS IN SEARCH OF INPUT AND INTAKE

Helmut Zobl
Université de Moncton

In seeking a theoretical solution to the input-intake relationship and to the status of each in the attainment of nativelike ability, the investigator must invoke a third component—the data universe, the potentially infinite number of forms generable by the rules of the grammar.[1] A learner's final-state grammar not only has to predict the input data which make up the learner's experience with the target language; it must also have the capacity to predict a potentially infinite number of forms which were not encountered in the input. Input to the learner will always amount to only a minute slice of the data universe. Nonetheless, this slice mediates between the data universe and the developing grammar, and it must contain the means which make possible the projective power of the final-state grammar. The issue sketched is one facet of what is commonly referred to as the "projection problem" (Peters 1972:192).

The projective capacity of the final-state grammar is a matter of grammatical knowledge as it has been defined within the homogeneous competence model (Chomsky 1965). But input also plays a crucial role at an abstract performance level: it shapes rule output strength. Differences in rule output strength are a key discriminator of varieties and subvarieties of a language. Differences in rule output strength, or variable rule application, distinguish speech communities on the basis of the frequency with which a linguistic variable regularly occurs in the speech of their members. A problem which has engaged theoreticians of patterned variation (e.g., Labov 1969a, Bickerton 1971, Cedergren and Sankoff 1974, and Fasold 1978) is how members of a speech community "learn" to bring their rule output into an approximate frequential line with that of other members. It certainly cannot be the case that speakers extract this information directly from the input data. In Bickerton's caricature of this position, speakers would continually have to monitor and compare frequencies in the input and their own output—an absurd probability. It is beyond the scope of this chapter to enter into this theoretical debate. What is germane to the theme of the chapter is the fact that, for the task of fixing the rule output strength of a certain feature, any trivial notion of learning from the input will simply not do.

In both cases we have considered—grammatical knowledge and rule output knowledge—we have to account for ultimate states of knowledge attainment which surpass the input data but are, in some sense, made possible by them. This seeming paradox can be resolved if we recognize that input possesses an abstract structure and that it is not merely "raw data," as was suggested at one time (Dulay and Burt 1978:85).[2] Specifically, I propose that markedness conditions represent the abstract structuring principles of the input. The markedness conditions of concern to us here are categories or rules that enter into implicational relations (e.g., dual implies plural) and oppositions which, in certain contexts, are neutralized in favor of one of the contrasting terms (e.g., in French, the gender contrast with third person plural pronouns *ils* and *elles* is neutralized in favor of *ils* whenever the deictic referent or the antecedent is not exclusively feminine). It is worth noting that the marked vs. unmarked values defined by these procedures have in common an opposition between, respectively, what is more restricted and specific, on the one hand, and what is distributionally more frequent and general, on the other.

The markedness conditions characterizing a set of input data make possible two kinds of acquisition of linguistic knowledge which allow the grammar to overcome the data limitations: (1) acquisition via markedness implications and (2) acquisition via correlations between markedness values of different but related parameters. Both acquisition procedures are projection procedures in the sense that they permit the learner to arrive at a knowledge of properties of the target language that are not represented in a set of input data.

In Zobl 1983 I argue that a projection model of acquisition is indicated once we take into account the disparity between the input data available to the learner and the ultimate state of knowledge attainment, as well as such empirical conditions on language learnability as the relatively short time span in which acquisition is accomplished (cf. Pinker 1979). Put in its simplest formulation, a projection model of acquisition claims that, in acquiring knowledge about target attributes w, x, y, present in a set of input data, a learner also comes to have knowledge about one or several attributes that were not part of the input data set. Figure 19-1 schematically represents the projection procedure.

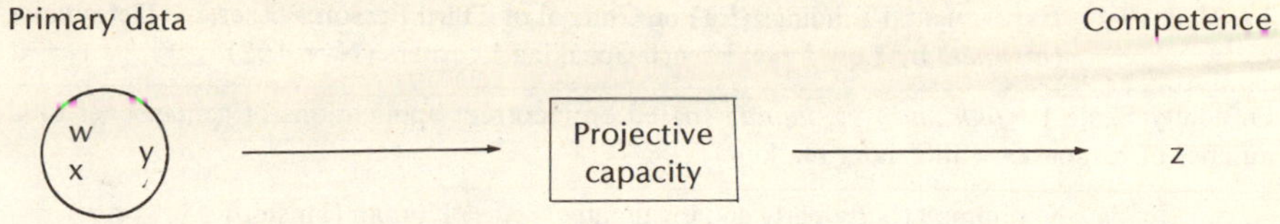

FIGURE 19-1 Projection Model (Adapted from Zobl 1983)

The two projection procedures I propose above—acquisition via markedness implications and acquisition via correlations between markedness values of related but different parameters—are two substantive hypotheses about the manner in which a learner can overcome the limitations of the input data. As such, both proposed procedures are to be looked upon as a contribution to the question of the learnability of natural languages.

The following sections of this chapter are given over to a presentation and discussion of some findings from two experiments with manipulated input. While the findings are not conclusive, they support the claims I have put forward concerning the role of markedness conditions in enabling the grammar of the learner to project beyond the input data.

TWO EXPERIMENTS WITH MANIPULATED INPUT

The Background

In 1981, I conducted an experimental study (Experiment 1, henceforth E1) which investigated patterns of variation in the control of the English possessive determiner rule for the third person singular forms *his* and *her* (Zobl, 1984). The population for the study was composed of 162 French-speaking learners. two findings from E1 are pertinent for the design of the input experiment (see Table 19-1).

Table 19-1 displays two scales of difficulty. The first scale, which is based on 84 speakers whose rate of supplying of gender-marked tokens was ≥ 83 percent, states that an implicational relation obtains in acquiring categorical control of the third person possessive determiner rule. Any learner who exhibits categorical control of the rule governing gender marking with possessed kinship entities (e.g., *his mother, her father*) will also have categorical control of the rule with possessed inanimate entities (e.g., *her hand, his car, her doll*). The converse relationship does not obtain; thus it is possible for a learner to show categorical control of the rule with possessed inanimate entities while still producing immature forms in the kinship domain. Although the study probed for control of the English rule in three semantic domains, kinship, body parts, and inanimate entities, no appreciable differences were

TABLE 19-1 Experimental Findings (E1) on Control of Third Person Possessive Determiner (*his, her*) by Low-Level French-Speaking Learners (N = 162)

Difficulty Scale I: *nonhuman* vs. *human* (based on incorrect applications of gender over total number of responses with gender marking)

Nonhuman (body parts and inanimates)	Human (kinship)
$\frac{156}{1961} = 8.0$	$\frac{166}{778} = 21.3$

Order of difficulty: *human* > *nonhuman*

Scalability: *human* ⊃ *nonhuman* (criterion for inclusion in implicational scale was 83% suppliance in human and nonhuman domains)

Conform: 80 speakers
Violate: 4 speakers

$$R = 1 - \frac{4}{80 \times 2} = 97.5$$

Difficulty Scale II: *his* vs. *her* (incorrect applications of gender on determiners requiring *his* or *her*)

Masculine	Feminine
$\frac{63}{1326} = 4.8$	$\frac{259}{1493} = 17.3$

Order of difficulty: *her* > *his*

found between body parts and inanimate entities. For the purpose of the input experiments these two domains were collapsed into a *nonhuman* domain, and this was opposed to a *human* domain, which comprised the kinship terms.

The second scale of difficulty that emerged from the study reveals that, of the two gender-marked forms, *his* and *her,* the latter is the more difficult; that is, learners will overgeneralize *his* at the expense of *her.* Similar findings indicating that it is the masculine pronominal form which is overgeneralized are reported in Tarone, Frauenfelder, and Selinker's (1976) study of anglophone children learning French.

Is there independent linguistic evidence suggesting that the two difficulty scales reflect a contrast in markedness between *human-nonhuman* and *her-his?* Let us consider, first, the differential difficulty posed by the masculine form, *his,* and the feminine form, *her.* In English, nouns showing a formally marked gender opposition (e.g., *host-hostess, lion-lioness, poet-poetess*) do not enjoy equal distributional privileges. A phrase such as *a group of young poets* can refer to a group of male and female poets; in contrast, *a group of young poetesses* can only refer to a group of female poets. Thus, whenever the sex is not known or is irrelevant, it is the masculine form which neutralizes the sex distinction (Clark and Clark 1977:524). Similarly, anaphoric reference to the indefinite pronouns *everybody* and *everyone* is traditionally carried out with the masculine form *his.*[3] In French, as we noted earlier, the gender opposition between *ils* and *elles* is also neutralized in favor of the masculine form. These considerations suggest that forms denoting female gender are marked vis-à-vis forms denoting male gender.

Turning now to the first difficulty scale, *human > nonhuman,* the notion of marked vs. unmarked contexts will allow us to arrive at a markedness determination. Gruber (1976) notes that nouns referring to human and inanimate entities both share the feature *concrete* but that human nouns also are marked for the features *animate* and *human.* These three features form an implicational hierarchy: *human* $\supset$ *animate* $\supset$ *concrete.* Thus nouns referring to human entities are marked, i.e., more specific vis-à-vis nouns referring to inanimate entities. For our purposes, we can look on human nouns as a marked context and inanimate nouns as an unmarked context. Now, work on linguistic markedness (Greenberg 1963) has demonstrated that marked contexts are less favorable to the marking of grammatical or semantic distinctions. Plural, a marked context vis-à-vis singular, frequently neutralizes distinctions made in singular contexts. Hence, in English the gender distinction we find with third person singular pronouns is neutralized in the plural. Looked at in this way, inanimate nouns provide a more favorable, i.e., unmarked context for the formal elaboration of the gender distinction.[4]

The Design of the Input Experiments

In 1982 (Experiment 2; henceforth E2) and in 1983 (Experiment 3; henceforth E3), low-level, adult French-speaking ESL learners were randomly assigned to two groups, a *human* data group and a *nonhuman* data group.[5] Both groups were given a pre- and posttest which consisted of a series of 15 pictures about which the investigator posed 20 oral questions designed to elicit responses containing *his* and *her* with human and nonhuman entities. For example, one picture showed a man giving a ring to a woman. The accompanying question was "For whom, do you think, did the man buy a ring?" The expected response was " . . . for his wife/girlfriend/fiancee." Informants were instructed to write their answers to these questions as quickly and unreflectingly as possible.

Immediately after the pretest there followed an intensive exposure session. Using a different set of eight pictures, the investigator posed similar questions which the informants answered orally. The crucial feature of the experimental design resided in the kinds of pictures used and the questions asked during the exposure phase. The questions directed at the *human* data group elicited only answers in which the determiners *his* and *her* marked possession of human entities, while the questions directed at the *nonhuman* data group elicited responses containing *his* and *her* with nonhuman entities. At no time during the exposure phase, which lasted approximately 15 minutes, did the investigator engage in any overt instruction or explanation. When an informant volunteered an answer containing an incorrect determiner choice, the investigator repeated or paraphrased the answer with the correct determiner form supplied. The answers of the informants and the positive examples of the investigator thus provided the input data to each group in the exposure session. It is important to emphasize that in the exposure session the frequency with which *his* and *her* were elicited by the investigator's questions was strictly controlled.

After the intensive exposure session, and before the posttest was administered, informants were invited to ask each other questions about any aspect of the pictures that had been employed in the input session. The purpose of this brief question-and-answer game was to divert attention away from what had been the focus of the input session and to reduce any short-term retention benefits. The input experiments E2 and E3 were carried out in small groups not exceeding 10 informants, and the average length of an experimental session was 60 to 65 minutes. Needless to say, the purpose of the input experiments was not disclosed to the informants.

E2 was carried out in 1982 and E3 a year later. Since the number of informants available for E2 was relatively small (N = 18) and the findings were only suggestive of tendencies (albeit they conformed to the predictions; see below), it was deemed desirable to repeat the experiment with another population. The experimental procedure for E3 was unchanged, although as the reader will discover, a number of additional measures were employed in the analysis of the data. In reporting on the findings from the two input experiments, I have decided not to pool the data. First, the one discrepant finding to emerge from E3 would have become obscured if the data had been pooled. Second, if the two experiments are kept separate, E3 acquires the character of a replication study, and this was the spirit in which it was undertaken. As such, the finding of constant effects across both experiments strengthens the case I am making for the role of markedness conditions in (1) permitting the learning device to project beyond the available input and (2) selectively influencing the intake filter and rule output.

Hypotheses and Findings

On the basis of the findings from E1, two hypotheses were formulated regarding the effect of the two types of input data on performance with the possessive determiner rule:

1. Since control of the rule with human entities entails control of the rule with nonhuman entities, any knowledge benefits accruing from exposure to input data from the human domain should also project to the nonexperienced, nonhuman domain.

2. Since control of the rule with nonhuman entities does not entail control of the rule with human entities, any knowledge benefits accruing

from exposure to input data from the nonhuman domain should not project to the nonexperienced, human domain.

What intake tendencies are observable in both experiments when intake is defined operationally as changes in a learner's rule output after the exposure session? We turn now to a presentation of the findings. First, however, I present the pre- and posttest scores of both input data groups from Es 2 and 3 (Table 19-2). Their preexposure performance, as judged by the percentage of error, is highly similar. This allows one to interpret the changes in their rule output after the exposure session with greater confidence.

TABLE 19-2 Error Frequencies on Pre- and Posttests

		Human domain	*Nonhuman domain*
a. Experiment 2 (1982)			
Nonhuman data	Pretest	19/101 = 18.8	9/56 = 16.1
group (N = 18)	Posttest	17/100 = 17.0	9/58 = 15.5
Human data	Pretest	21/106 = 19.8	9/56 = 16.1
group (N = 18)	Posttest	15/116 = 12.9	4/66 = 6.1
b. Experiment 3 (1983)			
Nonhuman data	Pretest	21/ 95 = 22.1	9/58 = 15.5
group (N = 21)	Posttest	13/ 96 = 13.5	7/65 = 10.8
Human data	Pretest	24/94 = 25.5	8/65 = 12.3
group (N = 19)	Posttest	18/110 = 16.4	4/72 = 5.5

Changes in the organization of the possessive determiner rule In E2, the group exposed to the unmarked, nonhuman data exhibited a numerically larger incidence of rule simplifications on the posttest than the *human* data group (Table 19-3*a*). It would thus appear that the unmarked input data encouraged unmarking, or simplifying, tendencies in the organization of the determiner rule. In E3 (Table 19-3*b*) there is only a negligible difference on this score between the two experimental groups, what difference there is being consistent with the finding of the previous year. The chief difference between the groups resides in the far greater rule stability displayed by the group exposed to the unmarked data. This group made far less use of the input data for effecting some reorganization of their preexposure determiner rules, suggesting that there was less intake overall. The unmarking effect noted in E2 and the stability that was observed in E3 take on a special significance when they are seen in conjunction with the second major finding.

Changes in rule output strength[6] In E2 the *human* data group exceeded the *nonhuman* group in gains made in upping the output of third person forms. This information can be gleaned from the number of new contexts on the posttest in which a third person form was supplied (39 vs. 27) and from a comparison of the total output gains on the pre- and posttest (+20 vs. +1; see Table 19-4*a*). The findings from E3 (Table 19-4*b*) are fully consistent with those of E2. First, the *human* data group supplied more third person forms in new contexts (46 vs. 37). Second, the total output gains of the *human* group

TABLE 19-3 Main Effects of Exposure on Rule Organization

	Human data group	*Nonhuman data group*
a. Experiment 2 (1982)		
Complexification* (i.e., marking changes)	6	5
Simplification† (i.e., unmarking changes)	7	13
b. Experiment 3 (1983)		
Complexification	8	7
Simplification	7	8
Stability (i.e., no changes)	4	9

*Complexification was defined as introducing a gender-marked form for the first time, introducing the gender opposition for the first time, restricting the scope of an existing overgeneralization, and reorganizing the possessive determiner rule from one that betrays evidence of influence from the French rule to a different system.

†Simplification was defined as introducing an overgeneralization where none had existed before; expanding the scope of an existing overgeneralization, loss of gender-marked forms and their replacement by *your,* the article or determiner omission, and loss of the gender opposition.

in the number of third person forms supplied again exceeded the gains of the *nonhuman* group (+23 vs. +9). The greater gains on the part of the *human* group in upping its rule output of third person forms after the exposure session is thus a very solid finding.

The analysis of the data from E3 considered two additional facets of the pre- and postexposure rule output strength: frequency of article usage and avoidance of third person forms. At this point a brief digression is necessary, however, so that the reader will be in a better position to assess the implications of the differences between the two groups.

The analysis of the data from E1 permitted a reasonably accurate reconstruction of the developmental stages involved in acquiring the third person singular possessive determiner rule (for a full analysis, see Zobl, 1984). A feature analysis of this rule reveals that it comprises several subcomponents. All possessive determiners share the semantic feature "definite," this being the most general meaning component. More specific, but still more general than gender, is the feature "person," in this case third person. Gender is the most specific feature of the meaning components that make up the third person singular rule. In English, for example, gender is only marked in the third person singular. This general-to-specific cumulative complexity underlies the developmental progression observable in E1. The English rule is built up from the bottom, so to speak. Learners with no knowledge of the English rule almost invariably use the definite article or omit the determiner. A very common intermediate form before third person marking appears is *your. Your* is more complex than the article, since it does

TABLE 19-4 Changes in Rule Output Strength

		Human data group	*Nonhuman data group*
		a. Experiment 2 (1982)	
New contexts:			
Human domain		21	15
Nonhuman domain		18	12
Total		39	27
Total output gains:			
Human domain	Pretest	106	101
	Posttest	116	100
Nonhuman domain	Pretest	56	56
	Posttest	66	58
		+ 20	+ 1
		b. Experiment 3 (1983)	
New contexts:			
Human domain		30	17
Nonhuman domain		16	20
Total		46	37
Total output gains:			
Human domain	Pretest	94	95
	Posttest	110	96
Nonhuman domain	Pretest	65	57
	Posttest	72	65
		+ 23	+ 9
		c. Experiment 3 (1983)	
Frequency of article usage:			
Human domain	Pretest	23	15
	Posttest	15	15
Nonhuman domain	Pretest	42	43
	Posttest	25	35
		− 25	− 8
Frequency of avoidance:*			
Pretest		80	69
Posttest		58	77
		− 22	+ 8
		(= −20.7)	(= + 11.5)

*Avoidance was taken to include pretest—determiner omission, article, *your*; posttest—determiner omission, *your,* article, and no response on an item that was incorrect on pretest.

contain the feature "person," though its use clearly indicates that the learner has not yet attained the necessary level of specificity with regard to person number. For a learner who is sorting out "person," the choice of *your* is well motivated since it is invariable with regard to the most specific feature, gender. Let us now turn to the two new aspects of rule output strength that were additionally considered in the analysis of E3, frequency of article usage and avoidance of third person forms (Table 19-4*c*).

Complementing the larger output of gender-marked, third person forms among the *human* data group there is also a larger reduction in article usage (−25 vs. −8 percent). The second aspect investigated, avoidance, involved a pre- and postexposure comparison of both groups on the use of immature forms and determiner omission. The *human* data group significantly reduced the frequency of avoidance, whereas the *nonhuman* data group actually showed an increase in avoidance (−20.7 vs. +11.5 percent).

Taking all four measures together (i.e., total output, new contexts, article usage, avoidance), we notice a consistent interlocking pattern in both input experiments—the *human* group's exposure to the marked input data led to a striking rise in rule output strength; in contrast, the *nonhuman* data group's exposure to the unmarked data resulted in lower gains, and on one measure, it actually diminished rule output strength.[7]

Interactive effects of the two markedness conditions Yet another robust finding which emerges from both experiments concerns an interaction between the two markedness conditions, *human* vs. *nonhuman* and *her* vs. *his.* As mentioned earlier, independent linguistic evidence as well as the findings of E1 point to [+*human*] as the marked and [−*human*] as the unmarked term. Similarly, *her* is the marked term and *his* the unmarked term of the gender opposition. For the two markedness parameters the correlations between the markedness values are:

Marked: [+*human*] ~ *her*
Unmarked: [−*human*] ~ *his*

Both experiments provide evidence that the matching markedness values interact in intake.

In both E2 and E3 a quantitative tendency can be found after exposure for the *human* group to be more prone to overgeneralize *her;* the *nonhuman* data group, on the other hand, is more prone to overgeneralize *his.* Information on these contrary tendencies can be inferred from a number of measures contained in Table 19-5*a* and *b.* Thus we find in E2 (Table 19-5*a*) that the *nonhuman* data group has the highest percentage of *his* overgeneralizations (45.5 percent) and the *human* data group the highest percentage of *her* overgeneralizations (33.3 percent) on the measure "errors in new contexts." The same measure in E3 (Table 19-5*b*) reveals a comparable degree of *his* overgeneralizations by both groups (21.7 percent by the *human* group and 20.0 percent by the *nonhuman* group). However, on a number of other measures the contrasting tendency reappears. If we examine the pre- and postexposure differential, we see that the *nonhuman* group improved considerably more on *his* contexts in the human domain; conversely, the *human* group improved more on *her* contexts in the nonhuman domain. On the measure "targeted corrections," the *nonhuman* data group performed best on *his* contexts in the human domain and the *human* group performed best on *her* contexts in the nonhuman domain. The most striking difference between the two groups in E3 is displayed in Table 19-5*c*. For each of the markedness values of the two parameters under study I calculated the error frequency on the pre- and posttest. On the pretest, both groups have the same dominant hierarchy of difficulty: *human > nonhuman;* on the posttest, the *human* data group's hierarchy of difficulty remains unchanged, but the *nonhuman* group's dominant hierarchy of difficulty has switched to the other markedness parameter so that *her* contexts have now become the most difficult, regardless of the semantic domain. This switch in the dimension of difficulty shows clearly that, after the exposure, the *nonhuman* data group has a more marked tendency to overgeneralize *his* in contexts requiring *her*.

Type of data exposure and knowledge benefits The final finding to be presented bears on the question of whether the type of input data each group encountered during the intensive exposure session led to differences in "knowledge" benefits. I use the term to refer to knowledge at the level of competence, not performance, since I have already presented findings indicating that there are clear differences with regard to rule output. I should also make it clear that I use the term with a great deal of reservation, as all the measures employed in the analysis of the data (e.g., targeted corrections, errors in new contexts, posttest gains) only offer an oblique view of this knowledge state.

As I stated earlier, the input experiments were designed with the aim of testing two hypotheses: (1) that knowledge benefits resulting from exposure to examples from the marked, human domain would project to the nonexperienced, unmarked domain, and (2) that knowledge benefits resulting from exposure to the unmarked, nonhuman domain would not project to the marked domain. The data from E2 fully support both hypotheses. The measure "preexposure/postexposure differential" (Table 19-6*a*) indicates not only that the *human* data group surpassed the *nonhuman* group in that domain for which they had received input but also that they surpassed the *nonhuman* group in the domain for which they had received no input. Clearly, then, knowledge benefits resulting from exposure to the marked domain were projected to the unmarked, nonexperienced domain. In contrast, the *nonhuman* group made only negligible gains in both domains and actually improved less on that domain in which they had received input. The measure "targeted corrections" similarly favors the *human* data group. E3 diverges from that of the previous year in one important respect. As in the previous year, the *human* data group surpasses the *nonhuman* group in the unmarked, nonhuman domain (Table 19-6*b*); but unlike the previous year, the *nonhuman* group shows some striking gains in the human domain. This becomes apparent when one considers "targeted corrections" and "errors in new contexts." On the latter measure, the *human* data group performed better only in the nonhuman domain. Thus, with regard to the question of whether exposure to unmarked data permits the projection of knowledge

TABLE 19-5 Interactive Effects Between [± *human*] and *his/her*

		Human data group	*Nonhuman data group*
		a. Experiment 2 (1982)	
Errors in new contexts:*			
Human domain	*His*	1/9 = 11.1	5/11 = 45.5
	Her	4/12 = 33.3	1/4 = 25.0
Nonhuman domain	*His*	2/7 = 28.6	1/4 = 25.0
	Her	2/11 = 18.2	0/8 = 0.0
		b. Experiment 3 (1983)	
Errors in new contexts:*			
Human domain	*His*	1/7 = 14.3	0/6 = 0.0
	Her	5/23 = 21.7	0/11 = 0.0
Nonhuman domain	*His*	0/7 = 0.0	0/5 = 0.0
	Her	0/9 = 0.0	3/15 = 20.0
Pre/postexposure differential:			
Human domain	*His*	+ 4.8	+ 9.2
	Her	+12.2	+11.8
Nonhuman domain	*His*	(+ 6.3)†	(+12.5)
	Her	+ 6.5	+ 2.5
Targeted corrections (minus to plus/total minuses on pretest):			
Human domain	*His*	2/7 = 28.6	4/8 = 50.0
	Her	4/17 = 23.5	1/13 = 7.7
Nonhuman domain	*His*	0/1 = 0.0	1/2 = 50.0
	Her	4/7 = 57.0	2/7 = 28.6
		c. Experiment 3 (1983)	
Dominant hierarchy of difficulty:			
Pretest			
Human domain	*His*	7/38 = 18.4	8/43 = 18.5
	Her	17/56 = 30.4	13/52 = 25.0
Nonhuman domain	*His*	1/16 = 6.3	2/16 = 12.5
	Her	7/49 = 14.3	7/41 = 17.1
		Human > nonhuman	*Human > nonhuman*
Posttest			
Human domain	*His*	6/44 = 13.6	4/43 = 9.3
	Her	12/66 = 18.2	7/42 = 13.2
Nonhuman domain	*His*	0/21 = 0.0	0/17 = 0.0
	Her	4/51 = 7.8	7/48 = 14.6
		Human > nonhuman	*Her > his*

*The tabulations were done differently for the two studies. In Table 19-5*a*, the frequencies refer to the number of times *his* or *her* were applied incorrectly. Thus, for the *human* data group, 1/9 means that *his* was used incorrectly once in a context demanding *her*. In Table 19-5*b*, the tabulation gives the error frequencies occurring in a particular context. For the *human* data group, 1/7 means that in contexts requiring *his*, one error occurred.

†Bracketed percentages are based on only one token.

benefits to the marked domain, the findings over the two years remain inconclusive. The constant finding is that knowledge benefits derived from exposure to marked data do project to the unmarked domain. The first of our two hypotheses is consequently supported by both studies. Yet another constant finding to emerge from both studies—one which did not form part of the original predictions—is that the unmarked data exposure received by the *nonhuman* group does not translate into any notable knowledge benefits in their input domain.

TABLE 19-6 Data Exposure and Knowledge Benefits

		Human data group	*Nonhuman data group*
a. Experiment 2 (1982)			
Pre-/postexposure differential:			
Human domain		+ 6.9	+ 1.8
Nonhuman domain		+10.0	+ .6
Targeted corrections:			
Human domain		13/21 = 62.0	8/19 = 42.1
Nonhuman domain		4/9 = 44.4	4/9 = 44.4
b. Experiment 3 (1983)			
Pre-/post exposure differential:			
Human domain	*His*	+ 4.8	+ 9.2
	Her	+12.2	+11.8
Nonhuman domain	*His*	(+ 6.3)	(+12.5)
	Her	+ 6.5	+ 2.5
Targeted corrections:			
Human domain	*His*	2/7 = 28.6	4/8 = 50.0
	Her	4/17 = 23.5	1/13 = 7.7
Nonhuman domain	*His*	0/1 = 0.0	1/2 = 50.0
	Her	4/7 = 57.0	2/7 = 28.6
Errors in new contexts:			
Human domain	*His*	1/7 = 14.3	0/6 = 0.0
	Her	5/23 = 21.7	0/11 = 0.0
Nonhuman domain	*His*	0/7 = 0.0	0/5 = 0.0
	Her	0/9 = 0.0	3/15 = 20.0

DISCUSSION

Given the relatively brief duration of the intensive exposure session (15 minutes) and the closely matched performance of both groups on the preexposure test, the differences that were found are striking. I should also stress once more that, to the extent it was possible, all variables were controlled, especially frequency. The only experimental variable which differed was the semantic domain membership of the input examples.

There are two findings which relate in a straightforward manner to the markedness implication *human* ⊃ *nonhuman.* In both input studies, the *human* data group increased its rule output of third person (i.e., gender-marked) forms significantly after the exposure. The *nonhuman* group's rule output stagnated and in one case actually diminished. Recall, now, the theoretical issue dealt with briefly in the introduction; namely, short of keeping a running score on frequencies in the input, how do speakers succeed in synchronizing their rule output strength with the frequential norms of their speech community? Suppose that speakers, or learners, who already possess a variation-sensitive rule at the level of competence, find evidence in the input that a rule applies in a marked context. Without any further evidence from the input they could assume that the rule also applies in the implied, unmarked context. Thus, evidence from the marked context would suffice to raise the rule output in both contexts. Consider, now, the case of a speaker who finds evidence in the input that the rule applies in an unmarked context. Without further evidence it would not be possible to assume that the rule applies in the implying, marked context. This is exactly what we find with the *nonhuman* data group. In both input experiments this group increased its gender-marked output somewhat in the nonhuman domain; in the human domain rule output strength remains unchanged.

The same theoretical argument applies when we consider the intake effects at the level of grammatical knowledge. Knowledge increments gained in the marked domain should be automatically generalizable to the less difficult, unmarked domain.[8] This is indeed the case when one considers the findings on the *human* data group. In both studies the group improved not only in their own input domain but also in that domain for which they had received no input data. As we noted earlier, the findings on the *nonhuman* group are inconclusive. Contrary to the prediction that knowledge increments acquired in the less difficult, unmarked domain would not be generalizable to the marked domain; and contrary to the findings of E2, which supported the hypothesis, we find that in E3 the *nonhuman* data group did appear to generalize the benefits of input from the unmarked domain to the nonexperienced marked domain.

It will be recalled that a constant finding for the *nonhuman* group concerned its failure to match the improvement of the *human* data group in the nonhuman domain, even though this was the domain from which its input examples were drawn. Here we are faced with the paradoxical finding that direct, domain-specific experience proved to be less successful than indirect, non-domain-specific experience. The implicational relationship *human* $\supset$ *nonhuman* does not account for this paradoxical finding. I believe an explanation must be sought elsewhere. The explanation I shall propose will also account for the larger incidence of rule simplifications that was found among the speakers making up the *nonhuman* group.

The input to the *nonhuman* group contained only unmarked data. Thus far we have encountered two findings which indicate that these unmarked input data appear to have had an unmarking effect on the preexposure determiner rules of the group's members: a higher incidence of rule simplifications and a tendency to overgeneralize *his.* (Recall that *his* is the unmarked term of the gender opposition.) The opposite effect was noted with the *human* data group: a higher incidence of rule complexifications and a tendency to overgeneralize *her*. Marked data thus appear to promote marking changes while unmarked data appear to promote unmarking changes. Given the preexposure performance of the *nonhuman* data group, it is not difficult to see that unmarked data do not serve its needs. The group already possesses an advanced degree of control of the possessive determiner rule in the nonhuman domain. In view of the unmarking effects of unmarked input data, it can be argued that once grammars reach a certain level of complexity such that their rules begin to predict to unmarked structures with some regularity, marked data become necessary if progress on unmarked structures is not to stagnate. The *human* data group received marked input and, as we have seen, not only did knowledge benefits derived therefrom project to the nonexperienced domain, but it turns out that projected knowledge based on marked data was more powerful, in a sense, than direct, domain-specific experience.

The final aspect I wish to discuss concerns yet another constant finding from both experiments, namely, the interaction between matching markedness values of related markedness parameters. It will be recalled that exposure to the marked domain correlated with a tendency to overgeneralize *her* whereas exposure to the unmarked domain correlated with a tendency to overgeneralize *his*. These correlations suggest that exposure to the unmarked value [−*human*] sensitizes the input filter to the correlated markedness value *his;* conversely, exposure to the marked value [+*human*] sensitizes the input filter to the marked value *her*. Thus intaking of marked data from one markedness parameter promotes intake of marked data from another, related markedness parameter. The net effect would be that acquisition along one parameter entails acquisition along another parameter. If we extrapolate this finding from the experimental situation to a naturalistic acquisition context, we can see that correlational projections translate into a significant reduction in the amount of input a grammar requires to attain the final-state predictive capacity.

CONCLUSION

The theoretical issue addressed in this chapter is the oft-noted disparity between a learner's experience with language data and the ultimate knowledge states which characterize native or, in the case of L2 acquisition, nativelike competence with respect to grammatical knowledge and variable rule output knowledge. The thesis advanced in this chapter is that markedness conditions constitute the abstract structuring principles of input. They are abstract because they relate the input data to the whole, the data universe, and they provide the abstract routes whereby a grammar can project to the data universe. Two substantive projection procedures were proposed and empirical support for each of them was adduced: projection via markedness implications and projection via matching markedness values of related markedness parameters. Thus markedness conditions in the input data may well provide the crucial and necessary shortcuts which make possible the ultimate states of knowledge in spite of the limitations of the input data from an experiential point of view. If the two proposed projection procedures are supported by future research, we will have taken an important step in our efforts to provide an accounting of language learnability.

NOTES

1. An earlier version of this chapter reporting on only part of the data presented here was given at the 17th Annual TESOL Convention, Toronto, March 15-20, 1983.

2. Significantly, Dulay and Burt do not deal with markedness in their discussion of input factors and acquisition.

3. Admittedly, a change is taking place with respect to the use of *his* for anaphoric reference to indefinite pronouns and noun phrases containing the quantifiers *each* and *every,* as in *each person. Their* has become the preferred form in spoken language.

4. Another markedness framework, based on perceptual complexity, makes a similar prediction. Grosu's (1972) "dichotomous behaviour principle" states that "complexity arises when two sets of cues assign contradictory values to a stimulus in terms of some parameter" (p. 2). Universally, it would seem that gender marking on possessive markers can be determined by the gender of the possessed entity or the gender of the possessor. The data analysis in E1 revealed that a number of learners used the natural sex of the possessed human entity in marking gender on the possessive determiners, e.g., *The boy saw her mother. This rule is formally analogous to the one that exists in French, although only natural gender, and not grammatical gender, can serve as input to the rule. Thus, with possessed human entities, a conflict in natural sex between the possessor and the entity possessed would give rise to contradictory values. Such a conflict would not arise with possessed inanimate entities, since they have no natural gender.

5. E2 included a *mixed* data group as well. This group is disregarded here.

6. Since the elicitation context does not vary, the changes in rule output strength have nothing to do with stylistically conditioned variable output; we are, instead, dealing with inherent variability.

7. The formal simplifications in the possessive determiner rule which we noted in the previous section thus appear to have a concomitant in the weaker output of gender-marked, third person forms.

8. The asymmetry in the generalizability of knowledge with which we are concerned has also been the subject of investigation in L1 acquisition research using prototype theory (for an overview, see de Villiers 1980, especially p. 35). For L2 acquisition, Gass (1982) has drawn on Keenan and Comrie's (1977) NP Accessibility Hierarchy for relativizing on NP functions to test the directionality of generalizability in an experiment with manipulated input.

20

IF AT FIRST YOU DO SUCCEED . . . [1]

Eric Kellerman
University of Nijmegen

This chapter is a first attempt to deal with the concept of U-shaped behavioral development as it applies to second language learning, and in particular as it applies to the acquisition of L2s typologically similar to the L1, in this case English and German as acquired by Dutch speakers. The term "U-shaped behavior" is used here to describe systematic linguistic behavior over time as realized in three distinct stages. The first stage is characterized by performance on the part of learners (child or adult, L1 or L2) in some limited linguistic domain, which is error-free, that is, accords with the target norm (i.e., the adult language or the L2). The second stage is characterized by performance which is now deviant in terms of the target, and hence differs from performance in stage 1. The third stage marks a return to performance which matches the norm, as was also the case in stage 1. U-shaped behavior thus refers to this tripartite sequence, where, in stage 2, acquirers seem, to use Karmiloff-Smith's phrase, "to go beyond success" (Karmiloff-Smith 1984).[2] This tripartite sequence is shown in diagrammatic form in Fig. 20-1.

U-SHAPED BEHAVIOR IN FIRST LANGUAGE ACQUISITION

Let us begin with a well-known example. Ervin (1964) reports how children, having apparently mastered English irregular past-tense morphology (came, went, broke), proceed to partially supplant these forms with regularized, and thus deviant, past forms (comed, goed, breaked). These new forms are

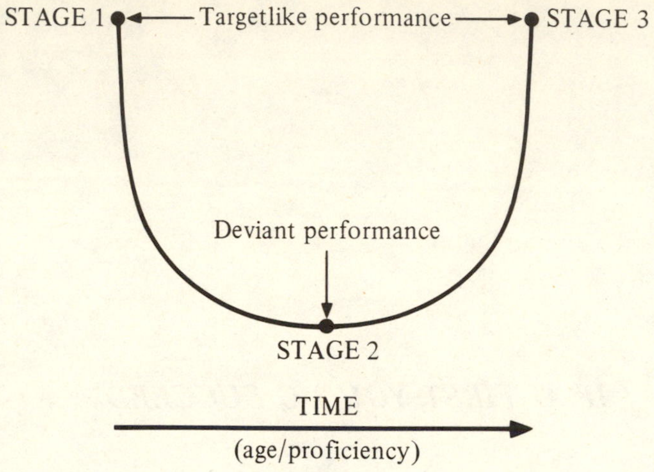

FIGURE 20-1 U-Shaped Behavior

themselves supplanted by the irregular forms already evident in stage 1, and finally disappear. It has been argued that the appearance of deviant forms should not be seen as attrition in linguistic competence, but as a "cognitive advance" (Strauss and Stein 1978), compatible with the notion that the learner has indeed gone "beyond success." Research on U-shaped behavior has been conducted by Bowerman (on causative and "reversative" verbs, Bowerman 1982) and particularly by Karmiloff-Smith (especially 1984). I shall provide two related examples from the work of the latter since they are relevant to the data from second language acquisition I shall present below. In her study of the language development of French children aged between 3 and 11, Karmiloff-Smith notes that after apparently having accepted that a single linguistic form can have more than one semantic function (stage 1) children may in certain circumstances insist on an isomorphism between form and meaning. At stage 1, the successful stage, Karmiloff-Smith claims that these functions will have been treated as if they were expressed by separate (though superficially identical) forms, but as the child develops linguistically, so he or she proceeds as if the relationship were indeed one form to many functions. This is stage 2. The result of this discovery is that children tend to differentiate between the meanings they have teased out from the single form, at the same time creating new and distinct (but linguistically related) surface forms. Karmiloff-Smith shows how French children initially postpose color adjectives correctly, e.g., *la voiture jaune* (the yellow car), but at stage 2 distinguish between the descriptor and determiner functions of these adjectives, as dictated by the requirements of the relevant discourse. Thus *la voiture jaune* is now used to refer to the yellowness of the car, but a new construction with preposed adjective +

partitive, *la jaune de voiture,* is used when it is important to contrast the yellow car with an array of cars of different colors. This nontarget form later disappears, indicating the arrival of stage 3.

A second example from Karmiloff-Smith of a stage of differentiation made by the child but not required by the adult grammar concerns *le/la même* (the same). In French, *le/la même* can mean both "the same one" and "of the same kind," just as "same" can in English. Initially Karmiloff-Smith's subjects used *le/la même* to cover both the "strict identity" and the "same kind" meanings. Subsequently, however, *le/la même* occasionally began to be used primarily for the sense of "strict identity" and a new ungrammatical form arose, *un/une de même,* to indicate "of the same kind" (*j'ai une même de vaches chez moi*). At stage 3, all the redundant markers and forms of questionable grammaticality gradually disappear.

U-SHAPED BEHAVIOR IN SECOND LANGUAGE ACQUISITION

There has been no explicit discussion of U-shaped development that I am aware of in the second language acquisition literature. One recent study that does apparently report on such phenomena (without using the term "U"), is Huebner (1983). In his study of a Hmong learner of English, he refers to "backtracking" in the acquisition of the function of the definite article. That is to say, his informant used *da* (the) ungrammatically more frequently halfway through the study than in the initial stages. Another study dealing with developmental data that could be described as U-shaped is Wode, Bahns, Bedey, and Frank (1978), who discuss the initial appearance of correct "premature forms" like feet, sheep, and fish (cf. the Ervin study above) which then give way to regularized plural forms. Also clearly relevant to U-shaped phenomena are those studies dealing with chunk learning, where the learner correctly and appropriately produces a number of utterances, which, from the observer's point of view, exhibit a level of grammatical complexity that is clearly beyond the learner's proficiency as evidenced by his output in toto. Such chunks represent the outcome of holistic learning, as indicated by the appearance at later stages of less complex related structures that are more productive (see, e.g., Wong-Fillmore 1976, Hakuta 1982). The real issue that has yet to be settled is whether these success formulas are themselves analyzed in stage 2 or whether they simply atrophy with the independent development of interim grammars (see Krashen and Scarcella 1978, Peters 1983 for discussion of these points).

CROSS-LINGUISTIC INFLUENCE AND U-SHAPED BEHAVIOR

The three cases of U-shaped behavior illustrated below concern adolescent and adult Dutch learners of typologically close foreign languages (English and German) in instructional settings. The data derive from cross-sectional experimental studies. Furthermore the data demonstrate the critical role played by cross-linguistic influence in the manifestation of U-shaped behavior. The three studies deal respectively with (1) the transitive/intransitive verb break, (2) the linguistic marking of hypotheticalness in the protasis of conditional sentences, and (3) the acceptability of L1-like idiomatic expressions in the L2.

U-Shaped Behavior and the Transitive/Intransitive Distinction

Kellerman (1979) reported on learners' acceptances of the translations of intransitive *breken* (to break) in the Dutch sentence *het kopje brak* (the cup broke), as compared with their acceptance of translations of transitive *breken in hij brak zijn been* (he broke his leg). The learners in question were arranged in eight groups according to the number of years they had studied English, and ranged in age from 13 to 23+. From the age of roughly 18, all subjects were full-time university students of English. If one plots performance on one sentence against the other for each group (Fig. 20-2), it is clear that up to the age of 17 there is no appreciable difference in performance for the transitive and intransitive meanings. At 18, the last year at school, there is a marked change. Groups now start treating the two *breaks* differently, with only the transitive *break* being accepted fairly close to optimum level. There is a clear drop in performance for intransitive *break,* bottoming out among the 20-year-old group and rising again for the most advanced group. The problem is how to explain the fact that the more advanced groups appear to perform less well than the remaining groups. It is my contention that this U-shaped curve for intransitive *break* demonstrates the development of sensitivity to a pragmatic distinction (implicitly known) between the causative and noncausative meanings of a single verb. The oddness of intransitive *break* for the more advanced Dutch learners is due to its lack of a specific animate agent in the test sentence. *Break* is seen primarily as a causative verb—cups as a rule do not break by themselves, and there must be an overt agent somewhere, even if it is not mentioned in the same clause (cf. *the cup broke* with *John squeezed the cup until it broke*—further tests show that once it is embedded in contexts of the latter type, learners have no problem in accepting intransitive break, whatever their proficiency level. See Kellerman 1983). Sensitivity to this pragmatic distinction between causative and noncausative meaning is thus developmental as well as task-related. These data, like those reported by Karmiloff-Smith, provide insights into how learners seize upon and manipulate what appear to be important functional distinctions and attempt to give them distinct surface forms (or reject forms where these distinctions are not made). The motivation for doing so must be internally generated and cannot be related to the form of the L2 input. Younger learners, who have had less instruction and are less sophisticated metalinguistically, seem to be unconcerned about these distinctions. This means that their judgments and translations give the impression of being superior to those of more proficient learners. Researchers unfortunate enough to sample data only at stage 1 (or stage 3) would get the false impression that a final state of acquisition had been reached (and maintained) from the earlier time of sampling.

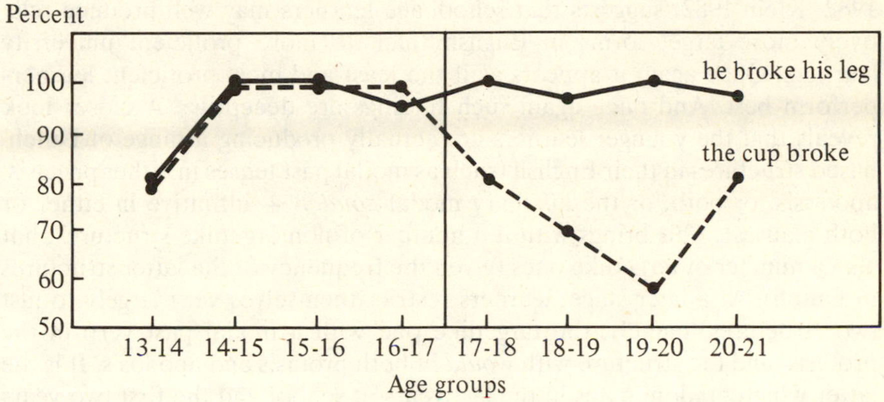

FIGURE 20-2 Performance on Transitive/Intransitive *Break*

U-Shaped Behavior and Hypothetical Conditionals

The second case concerns the structure of conditionals in Dutch and English produced by Dutch learners. Dutch allows a modal auxiliary + infinitive in both protasis (the if-clause) and apodosis (the consequent clause), i.e., structures of the type:

als het zou regenen, zouden wij thuis blijven
if it would rain would we house remain

and also (modal) past verb forms in either or both clauses:

als hij kwam, zouden wij uitgaan
if he came would we go out

identical to the standard English target. There seem to be subtle meaning differences between these various structures having to do with the potentialis/

irrealis distinction, the past tense in nonpast hypotheticals being counterfactual, the modal auxiliary signifying either hypothetical or counterfactual, depending on context. A characteristic and persistent "error" made by Dutch learners is to produce sentences of the kind **if it would rain, we would go out* (but only rarely of the kind **if it rained, we went out* or **if it would rain, we went out,* the translations of which are possible Dutch structures). The interesting question is why this should be so, given that there is a highly frequent Dutch analog of the target English structure. Our research (Kellerman and Wekker 1982, Klein 1982) suggests that school-age learners may well produce relatively more target forms in English than do more proficient university learners. Once again it appears as if the least and most proficient learners perform best. And once again such findings are deceptive. A closer look reveals that the younger learners are actually producing a range of Dutch-based structures in their English (such as modal past tenses in either protasis, apodosis, or both, or the auxiliary modal *zouden* + infinitive in either or both clauses). This brings with it a number of nontargetlike structures, but also a number of targetlike ones (given the frequency of the latter structures in Dutch). At a later stage, learners restrict themselves very largely to just two structures, namely, the targetlike one with a modal past verb in the protasis, and the structure with *would* in both protasis and apodosis. It is the latter which predominates in the last years at school and the first two years of college, and in some speakers it is never eradicated. As in our previous case, stage 2 goes beyond success. The high incidence of conditional sentences with *would* in both clauses relates not to the sensitization of the learner to the notion of hypotheticalness but to the realization that what is morphologically a past tense does not have prototypical past tense meaning in counterfactual sentences, thus the apparent desire in stage 2 to mark the distinction by formal means. Dutch provides a means of expressing hypotheticalness via a salient free morpheme equivalent in meaning to English *would.* At the same time the availability of this free morpheme allows the learner to circumvent the ambiguity of the past tense in English. The subtle irrealis meaning of the past tense in Dutch is thus sacrificed to the overt expression of hypotheticalness in English, as it may also be in Dutch, where even in strongly irrealis contexts, *would* equivalents in both protasis and apodosis are perfectly permissible. It is relevant to note here that, in Dutch, in preposed apodoses, there is a tendency not to use the past tense and to favor the modal auxiliary, as is borne out by corpus data and acceptability judgments. This may be due to the momentary ambiguity of the past tense in the absence of a specific marker of conditionality like *if* or its Dutch equivalent *als* (Comrie 1983). The structure of Dutch, plus the strong formal similarities between Dutch and English, permit advanced Dutch learners to make a distinction in Dutch which is clearly important to them, even though it is not required by the target language. An alternative hypothesis, particularly relevant to the language situation in the Netherlands, where English exerts a pervasive influence through the media (no foreign language films or television programs are ever dubbed), is that learners are exposed outside classroom time to forms of American English which do permit *would* in the protasis, i.e., through the media and via the lyrics of the indubitably popular pop and folk songs. In other words, learners are just responding to the presence of *would* in the input, where its salience is no doubt enhanced by the existence of a parallel presence in Dutch. This argument raises a number of questions. First, just how frequent is the double *would* conditional in American English, and second, why should it be more salient than the standard (target) form, since this too has an analog in Dutch? But the most critical argument against the presence of American *would* in the protasis being significant is the fact that Dutch learners of French chronically use the conditional tense in the *si* clauses of hypotheticals where French requires an imperfect. It would be very difficult to argue that this was due to the influence of nonstandard varieties of French in the input (unless we accord some special role to "junky" input from other learners, which argument is circular in any case).

U-Shaped Behavior and Idiomatic Expressions

My third case concerns Dutch learners of German at university level, and their treatment of German idiomatic expressions. Jordens (1977) showed that second year learners tended to reject Dutch-like idiomatic expressions in German (whether correct or not) while first year learners were relatively accepting. Third year learners showed signs of being able to distinguish those expressions that were possible in German from those that were specific to Dutch. Jordens' stage 2 would seem to indicate that the learner becomes sensitive to the mismatch between the literal and figurative meanings of the idiomatic expressions; the more semantically opaque the expression, the more likely its translation equivalent is to be rejected in the L2. Presumably at stage 1 learners do not concern themselves with this problem, working on the reasonable assumption that as German and Dutch are particularly close, they probably share idioms as well. In the three cases above we may distinguish a stage 1 where L1 structure appears to serve as a source of predictions about the form of the L2, leading to positive transfer. In stage 2, the L1 declines as a source of predictions, with the resultant errors. Finally, in stage 3, learners theoretically acquire native speaker levels of competence in the linguistic subdomains involved. In each case we may say that stage 1 represents a relexification phase (plus a number of the relevant local grammatical rules). Learners at this stage do not appear to be sensitive to the fact that such abstract semantic notions as hypotheticalness, causality, and metaphor are not given unique formal representations in their own language. For stage 1 learners, since these notions are handled in a particular way in Dutch, they will be thus handled in the same way in the L2. If learners at stage 2 lose confidence, so to speak, in this early assumption, this may lead to a concern that these notions should be explicitly expressed in the L2. Where Dutch, the L1, does not provide the basis for doing this, compensatory means must be found in the L2, and hence the change in the interim systems and the corresponding dip in performance described above. This is what makes the study of typologically related languages and how they are learned so worthwhile—we need to know why learners become dissatisfied with the possibilities of formal expression their own language offers them.

IS THERE A ROLE FOR INPUT IN STAGE 2?

Stage 1 is to be seen as a phase in which the learner's output is successful from both a linguistic and a situational point of view. This is true for first language as it is for second language acquisition where appropriate chunks are produced deriving either from the L2 or generated out of the L1. However, in stage 2, the learner now sets about to reorganize his or her mental representations of these structures into a system within the relevant linguistic subdomain. As Karmiloff-Smith states: "children . . . ignore or violate external reality in pursuit of the organising whole." This may result in the explicit marking of semantically important distinctions in surface form, which in fact leads to utterances which now become deviant. French children no longer accept the fact that one form can cover more than one function and will instead seek to mark these differing functions in their output, even though there may be nothing in the input constraining them to do so. Exactly the same may hold for Dutch learners. The pragmatic oddness of an isolated sentence like *the cup broke* forces stage 2 learners to seek less exceptionable ways of saying the same thing in English; the ambiguity of the past tense in Dutch encourages learners to mark hypotheticalness overtly; Dutch learners react against Dutch-like German idioms, while their less proficient peers are happy to accept them. Deviant stage 2 behavior cannot be related to the specific form of the output learners receive, since the systems the learners appear to develop are not present in the input. To adapt a quote from Karmiloff-Smith (1984):

> Although . . . negative feedback may play some role at Stage One, the behavior of Stage Two learners shows that . . . learners go beyond success to reorganise and understand the implicit information carried in the earlier correct forms. It is the positive feedback from a success criterion that generates subsequent reorganisation.

The questions that now need to be asked are "Under what linguistic conditions will U-shaped phenomena arise and why? And what is it that triggers off the change from stage 1 to stage 2, and the change from stage 2 to stage 3?" To put this in more specific terms, why is it that learners move from a phase of transfer from the L1, when there is no negative evidence from the L2 environment to motivate them to do so, to a phase where their performance (in the widest sense of the word) does not tally wholly with either the L1 or the L2, and then on to a further phase where they do indeed (begin to) perform in accordance with the L2 input they are receiving? The answer will probably have something to do with the kind of teaching they are exposed to and the number of years they have been studying, but the exact nature of the mechanisms responsible for these changes must for the moment remain a mystery.

NOTES

1. I am very grateful to Melissa Bowerman and Christiane von Stutterheim for their comments on an earlier version of this chapter, and to Clive Perdue for his astute comment on the version presented here. This chapter was also given at the Second Language Research Forum, University of Southern California, Los Angeles, November 1983.

2. Despite their superficial similarity, U-shaped behavior and "backsliding" or "variable behavior" are not terminological variants. While in itself a purely descriptive term with no magical properties, U-shaped behavior is used by researchers in developmental psychology to refer to performance curves consisting of clearly defined, stable, systematic, and long-term phases (cf. the introduction to Strauss 1982). What such curves mean for a theory of development is of course the interesting question. Thus while "backsliding" is generally used to refer to unstable oscillation between later-acquired (often targetlike) forms and earlier (nontarget) ones, due to any number of triggering causes, U-shaped performance, as it is generally discussed in the literature, deals with movement through time from a targetlike phase to a nontargetlike one, and then back again, and represents changes in competence (Sharwood Smith and Kellerman, forthcoming). If one must draw the parallel, it would be more appropriate to call such behavior "forwardsliding."

21

THE ROLE OF INTAKE IN THE DETERMINATION OF LEARNERS' COMPETENCE

Juana M. Liceras
University of Ottawa

A main concern in second language acquisition research is to determine the role of intake and its relationship to input. It has repeatedly been argued, on the one hand, that learners do not assimilate all the language data they are exposed to and, on the other, that their interlanguage contains rules and constructions which do not occur in L2 input. In order to explain these facts, it is necessary to determine the cognitive capacities that intervene at the level of intake and the role they play in the organization of the data which form an interlanguage grammar. In other words, what is the role of intake in the determination of learners' competence?

Determination of learners' competence requires a sophisticated analysis of interlanguage output that can only be undertaken within the framework of a coherent theoretical model. I am going to propose that a model of "homogeneous competence" can in fact account for interlanguage variability, provided that we have an adequate theoretical framework for determining both the nature of and the relationship between variability and permeability in interlanguage systems.

Chomsky makes a distinction between language and the grammar of a language, "Note that the central concept throughout is 'grammar,' not 'language.' The latter is derivative, at a higher level of abstraction from actual neural mechanisms" (Chomsky 1981:4). Paraphrasing Chomsky's distinction, a "nonnative grammar" would reflect learners' competence, while an "interlanguage" would include, in addition to the nonnative grammar itself, production and comprehension mechanisms, social and pragmatic factors, etc.

It is argued in this chapter that determination of learners' competence through the analysis of interlanguage output requires making such a distinction. Thus, while the description and prediction of systematic variability in second language data would fit into a model of interlanguage, it is nonetheless a model of nonnative grammar that should account for nonnative intuitions.

According to this distinction, variability reflects a variable interlanguage output that is due to the different mechanisms involved in speech production in different communicative situations. Permeability, on the other hand, as a component of the speakers' cognitive linguistic capacity, accounts for nonnatives' variable intuitions. Variable intuitions result from the fact that there may be rules of parameters of core grammar that will be fixed in a variety of ways or not fixed at all. Nonnative grammars are extremely permeable owing to a combination of different factors such as (1) lack of exposure to the crucial data that would provide evidence for a particular rule or parameter and (2) the mastering of a whole system of knowledge—the native language and other languages—that will somehow shape learners' choices. In this chapter it is suggested that issues of markedness may also play a role at the level of intake so that there may be a relationship between markedness and permeability.

To determine the role of intake, I analyze various constructions in the Spanish interlanguage of English speakers at three different levels of proficiency. I begin with a discussion of permeability and variability in order to delimit the methodological framework of the study. I then outline the relevant input data and examine the role that several cognitive capacities may play at the level of intake. This is followed by a brief description of the experimental tasks used to elicit the interlanguage data. In the final sections of the chapter I analyze and discuss the interlanguage output in order to propose:

1. That the role of intake mediates the relationship between input and output at each different level of proficiency, and that similar outputs do not necessarily reflect the same underlying competence.

2. That while variability of intuitions is determined by the relationship between input and intake, the different degrees of variability reflected in the two experimental tasks are a function, not of the intake but rather of the various mechanisms involved in carrying out the tasks.

PERMEABILITY AND VARIABILITY IN INTERLANGUAGE

One of the aims of linguistic theory is to construct a model of grammar that specifies what a speaker-hearer actually knows about his or her language and the principles that underlie that knowledge. That model of grammar does not prescribe the character or functioning of a model of speech production or of a perceptual model, which have to be defined within a model of language use. However, a grammar which expresses the speaker-hearer's knowledge of the language must be incorporated as a basic component in the model of language use (Chomsky 1965, 1975, 1981).

This distinction also holds if the study of interlanguage systems is conceived of as the specification of the speakers' knowledge of those systems rather than the characterization of the mechanisms that account for the ways in which that knowledge is used. In fact, as Adjémian (1982) maintains, there is no theoretical justification to avoid dealing with an ideal speaker-hearer of a given interlanguage. Nor is one justified in arguing, as Selinker, Swain, and Dumas (1975) and Frauenfelder and Porquier (1979) do, against the appropriateness of Chomsky's term "competence" because it cannot account for the knowledge of a speaker who is neither native nor ideal. As in the case of a native speaker, a nonnative speaker has competence, albeit a nonnative competence, which reflects his or her knowledge of the interlanguage. In fact, if any degree of idealization is accepted at all, it can apply to both native and nonnative speakers. If linguistic theory can provide the framework for investigating the properties of native grammars, it should also be applicable to L2 learners' grammars.

It is with an idealized model in mind that Adjémian (1976) proposes that interlanguage systems should be viewed as natural languages with some specific characteristics, permeability being the one that allows the penetration of L1 rules and the overgeneralization and distortion of L2 rules in those systems. Thus permeability is conceived of as being a property of interlanguage systems but not of all language systems.

Arditty and Perdue (1979) argue that there is a contradiction in simultaneously maintaining on the one hand that, as natural languages, interlanguages have a system of rules and are subject to the same general constraints as all languages and on the other hand that interlanguages are different by virtue of their specific characteristics. According to them, the characteristics that Adjémian considers to be specific to interlanguage systems are found in all natural languages because native speakers can also find themselves in situations in which their system may be penetrated by alien rules or their own rules may be distorted. Adjémian (1982) rejects their position by maintaining that permeability, backsliding, fossilization, etc., are part of the abstract properties of the grammar of interlanguages. According to him, the examples of permeability, backsliding, and fossilization given by Arditty and Perdue are not to be interpreted as reflecting the knowledge that native speakers have of their language (competence) but, rather, as sociologically motivated (they involve other dialects, language contact, bilingualism). In other words, they will occur when a performance act requires the interaction of grammar and another component. Adjémian argues that given that interlanguage speakers cannot avoid permeability, backsliding, etc., when they speak their interlanguage, those characteristics have to be specific to the nonnative grammar rather than the result of a communicative situation. This implies that it is not native grammar theory but nonnative grammar theory that accounts for permeability and other possible properties of interlanguage grammars.

Two different issues are involved in the above discussion: first, the question of whether native grammar theory and nonnative grammar theory are different and second, the question of whether both native and nonnative grammars may share some abstract properties.

The first issue has had a long history in second language acquisition research. The traditional dispute over the existence of transfer in second language learning versus the total identification of L1 and L2 learning is still alive, and it implies two different positions concerning the nature of a nonnative grammar. New developments in linguistic theory provide tools for identifying areas of potential transfer (Gass and Selinker 1983). However, on the basis of new developments in linguistic theory with respect to the role of positive and negative evidence in language acquisition (Baker 1979, Chomsky 1981), it is also suggested that only positive evidence from L2 may be involved in the acquisition of a second language (Mazurkevich 1984).

One can take the position that rejects a total identification of L1 and L2 learning, and consequently maintain that native and nonnative grammar theory are different, and still argue that permeability is an abstract property of both native and nonnative grammars. Adjémian's labeling of the native output discussed by Arditty and Perdue (1979) as being socially motivated does not answer the question of whether that output reflects or is the result of a permeable grammar. As in the case of interlanguage speakers, bilinguals or dialect speakers may not be able to avoid permeability when they speak one of their languages or dialects. If this is the case, permeability can be defined as the abstract property of *all* grammars that accounts for speakers' variable intuitions. Permeability, rather than resulting in a violation of the internal systematicity of the nonnative system by allowing the presence of L1 rules and overgeneralizations of its own rules—as in Adjémian (1982)—should be seen as a reflection of the nature of grammars. It is a consequence of the fact that universal grammar contains a system of rules which present parametric variation.[1] However, this does not imply that no difference exists between native and nonnative grammars, any more than it means that permeability has to be defined as a specific characteristic of interlanguages; in fact, it is probably the case—as I have suggested before (Liceras 1981)—that what is specific to nonnative grammars is not their permeability per se but the actual areas of the grammar which are permeable and the form that permeability may take. In other words, permeability—and probably other characteristics that have been posited as specific to nonnative grammars—may be found in any language system. This is because there will always be parameters of core grammar that are fixed in a variety of ways or not fixed at all. In fact, languages provide empirical evidence for the existence of cases in which native speakers have different intuitions or cannot decide with respect to a given rule. Solan (1981) argues that children learning a language may not always be exposed to the crucial data which would allow them to fix a particular parameter or to decide as to the correct primitives in terms of which rule should be formed. For example, children learning English may never decide as to whether the number agreement rule between subjects and verbs should apply as in 1 or in 2

1 Are the police after you

2 Is the police after you

For almost the full range of English data there is no conflict between morphological and semantic factors in the application of this agreement rule. However, when conflict exists—as in the case of collective nouns—it may be difficult or even impossible to decide, mainly because of the small number of this type of noun.

By the same token, second language learners may not be able to decide whether it is the complementizer *que* or a wh-phrase—3 versus 4—that appears in Spanish nonoblique relativization.[2] In other words, they may not be aware of the fact that in Spanish nonoblique restrictive relativization, the neuter strategy (the use of the complementizer *que*) is not optional but obligatory.

3 Ese es el piloto francés *que* (yo) conocí ayer
That is the French pilot that I met yesterday

4 *Ese es el piloto francés *quien/el que/el cual* (yo) conocí ayer
That is the French pilot who/m I met yesterday

Depending on the language, this parameter may be fixed as optional (both the complementizer *que* (*that*) as in 3 and a relative pronoun as in 4 are possible) or as obligatory. In the latter case, only 3 occurs.

Native speakers of English have fixed the above parameter as optional because both 3 and 4 are possible in English. What remains to be determined is the crucial data that will lead them to fix this parameter as obligatory when learning Spanish. A nonnative grammar must reflect the ways in which second language learners fix the various parameters, the degree and contexts which favor one parameter over another, etc. In this chapter it is proposed that the cognitive capacities that intervene at the level of intake contribute to determine such crucial data, so that learners may select data which do not lead them to fix a given parameter. When this happens, learners' intuitions will vary around the possible alternatives that universal grammar offers for the fixing of a given parameter. The existence of these alternatives in combination with the mechanisms involved in fixing parameters constitute the basis of a permeable grammar which yields variable intuitions. Thus variable intuitions should be taken into consideration in determining learners' competence.

This does not imply, however, that a model of "homogeneous competence" cannot acount for interlanguage variability. On the contrary, it can provide the adequate theoretical framework for explaining how the variability of interlanguage data reflects an underlying competence which is filtered out or remolded by the actual mechanisms involved in the realization of different tasks. What the interlanguage reflects is a variable competence, namely, a grammar that is permeable, and permeability remains constant not only across tasks but also within a given task. With respect to the same rules, some tasks will reflect permeability to different degrees than others. However, the output of all tasks should reflect the same competence; that is, it should reflect which parameters are not fixed and what type of parametric variation is favored by different performance mechanisms.

INPUT-INTAKE-OUTPUT: COMPLEMENTIZER STRUCTURES IN THE SPANISH INTERLANGUAGE OF ENGLISH SPEAKERS

Following Corder's (1973) distinction between input and intake, Frauenfelder and Porquier (1979) made the first systematic attempt to define intake within a coherent model of second language acquisition. However, because of the theoretical framework of this study, the terms input, intake, and output cannot be used as in Frauenfelder and Porquier. First, Frauenfelder and Porquier present a diachronic model while I have taken a synchronic approach. Rather than trying to account for the process of acquisition, I attempt to determine what is acquired and why acquisition occurs on the basis of the cognitive capacities and linguistic structures that intervene in the construction of the interlanguage grammar at a given stage. Second, all three terms, input, intake, output, are used within the framework outlined, which deals with language knowledge rather than language use. Naturalistic versus institutional settings, implicit versus explicit distinctions, or styles such as formal versus informal are not taken into consideration. The input is defined as the linguistic data to which the learner is exposed. It consists of second language data and data from the L1 and other languages that may be brought in through translation, comparison, etc.[3]

The cognitive capacities that may play a role at the level of intake are:

1. Attained linguistic knowledge: the grammatical knowledge of the native language and of any other language(s) familiar to the learner.

2. Metalinguistic abilities: the learner's capacities to reflect on language

and to perceive (perhaps surface) regularities in incoming linguistic data.

The theory of markedness which imposes preference structures upon the properties of universal grammar may also play a role at the level of intake.

The output consists of the interlanguage data produced by the learner.

Input

The relevant input data in this study are the following syntactic processes and lexical items:

Lexical items:

1. Complementizer. *Que* is the Spanish wh- complementizer. It occurs in all tensed subordinate clauses as well as in relatives as shown in 5 and 11.

5 Pedro dice que tiene frío
Pedro says that (he) is cold

2. Relative pronouns. *Quien,* which is [+human]; el que and el cual which are [±human]. All three occur in oblique relativization as shown in 6.

6 Juan es el hombre [con quien/con el que/con el cual] yo salgo[4]
Juan is the man with whom I am going out

Syntactic processes:

1. wh-movement. This is the transformation that applies, among other constructions, to the deep structure of relative clauses as in 7, yielding 8,

7 Ese es el piloto francés [$_{\bar{S}}$ $_{COMP}$ [$_S$ (yo) conocí [wh]]]

8 Ese s el piloto francés[$_{\bar{S}}$ wh$_i$ $_{COMP}$ [$_S$ (yo) conocí [t$_i$]]]

That is the French pilot who/m I met

"t" is the trace of the moved constituent. If a wh pronoun such as *el que, el cual,* or *quien* (who/m) is present, the result is ungrammatical in Spanish, as shown in 4 above.[5]

In order to account for the presence of the complementizer *que* or *that*—see 3 above—Jaeggli (1980) proposed that it is not a wh phrase but the empty category PRO that is moved to COMP as shown in 9 and 10.

9 Ese es el piloto francés [$_{\bar{S}}$ $_{COMP}$ [$_S$ (yo) conocí [PRO]]]

10 Ese es el piloto francés [$_{\bar{S}}$ PRO$_i$ $_{COMP}$ [$_S$ (yo) conocí [t$_i$]]]

Since the complementizer is lexicalized as *que* (or *that*), both PRO and the complementizer are present as a unit. Thus the final result—as shown in 11—is *que* with the feature [+ pronoun].[6]

11 . . . piloto francés [que + PRO]
COMP

English and Spanish differ in that Spanish cannot have a relative pronoun in nonoblique nonrestrictive relativization, as shown in 3 above and 12 below,

12a Pedro es el profesor [que/*quien/*el cual/*el que] vive aquí
Pedro is the professor [that/who] lives here

12b Ese es el piloto francés [que/*quien/*el cual/*el que/*Ø] conocí ayer
That is the French pilot [that/who/m/Ø] I met yesterday

12c Canadá no es el país [que/*el cual/*el que/*Ø] era
Canada is not the country [that/?which/Ø] it used to be

As shown in 12, modern Spanish requires the obligatory presence of complementizer *que* in nonoblique relativization.

2. Preposition stranding. Spanish does not have the relexicalization rule that applies in English to deep structures such as 13a to yield 13b, as shown below.[7]

13a	the woman Peter lives with						
	the woman [		[Peter	[	[lives]	[with	[wh]]]]
		$\overline{S}$ COMP	S	VP	V	PP	NP

13b	the woman [		[Peter	[	[lives with]	[wh]]]]
		$\overline{S}$ COMP	S	VP		NP

The wh in 13b may be extracted and moved to COMP because the preposition forms a lexical unit with the verb. This language-specific rule does not apply in Spanish. Consequently, sentences such as 14 are not possible.

14 * . . . la mujer que Pedro vive con
the woman that Peter lives with

Intake

The cognitive capacities that may play a role at this level are composed of the following linguistic data:

Attained Linguistic Knowledge This includes knowledge of the English rules which permit wh-movement and PRO-movement in nonoblique relativization, as well as preposition stranding. Some of the subjects in this study also know French, Italian, or Portuguese, which behave like Spanish with respect to wh/PRO movement and preposition stranding.

Metalinguistic Abilities Learners are able to relate nonoblique restrictive relatives to other syntactic phenomena in the target language, in their first language, and in other languages they may be familiar with. For example, learners may relate the optional use of *que* in nonrestrictive relatives—as in 15—to restrictive relatives—as in 12—without inferring its obligatory use as in 12; they may also restrict the use of *el que* to free relatives where it is treated as the sequence of determiner + complementizer rather than as a lexical unit (a relative pronoun), as in the case of restrictive relativization—16 versus 17 below.[8]

15 Esa mujer, [que/quien/la cual/la que] vive con Pedro, es amiga mía
That woman, [*that/who] lives with Pedro is a friend of mine

16 Juan es *el que* lo resolvió
Juan is the that it solved
"Juan is the one who solved it"

17 Juan es el profesor con *el que* vamos a visitar la exposición
Juan is the profesor with whom (we) are going to visit the exhibit

Owing to the surface structure similarity between cleft constructions and restrictive relatives, learners may also assume that the use of *quien* and *el que* in cleft constructions such as 18 is possible in restrictive relatives.[9]

18 Fue María [la que/quien/*que] lo hizo
It was Mary who did it

I have proposed that the theory of markedness may also play a role at this level. Let us assume that extractions are allowed by universal grammar as indicated in Figure 21-1, so that different languages may extract from all or some phrases. Native speakers of English fix the parameter that allows extraction from prepositional phrases (PP) as in 13, because they get empirical evidence of the existence of the relexicalization rule. This phenomenon of preposition stranding which results from extracting a wh-phrase out of a prepositional phrase has been considered highly marked in the literature (see Allen 1977, Chomsky 1977, Hornstein and Weinberg 1981, Van Riemskijk 1978). Provided that this is the case, it may be hypothesized (Muñoz-Liceras 1983) that this process will seldom occur in the Spanish nonnative grammar, the assumption being that learners should easily detect the lack of a relexicalization rule in Spanish, the target language, that would allow extraction of wh-phrases out of prepositional phrases as shown in 13.

In the case of PRO-movement, a native speaker of English has fixed the parameter as optional, as shown in Figure 21-2. Hirschbühler and Rivero (1981) propose that the obligatory use of PRO-movement in Spanish restric-

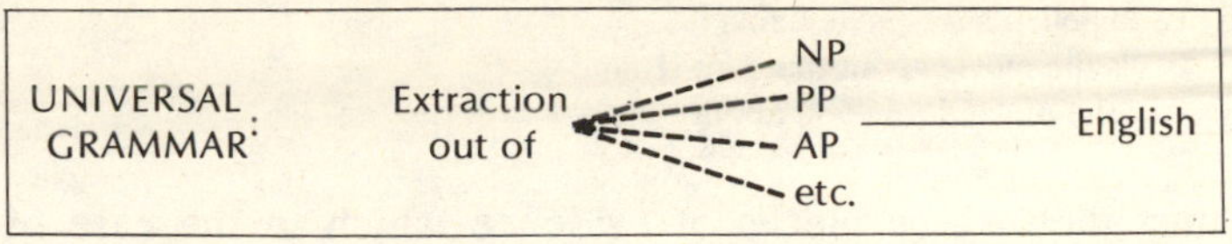

FIGURE 21-1 Parameter Allowing Extractions Out of Phrases

tive relativization represents the marked fixing of this parameter.[10] In the case of my subjects, this would imply that, unlike with preposition stranding, they will not be equipped to easily detect the lack of optional application of PRO-movement in Spanish.

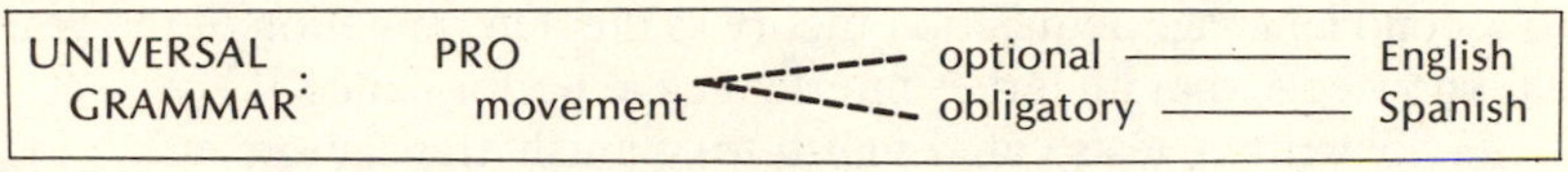

FIGURE 21-2 Parameter Allowing PRO-movement in Nonoblique Restrictive Relativization

In fact, while nothing in the input data would provide evidence of a relexicalization rule in Spanish, several constructions closely related to restrictive relatives offer evidence for relative pronouns, as shown in 15, 16, 17, and 18 above. Furthermore, the very nature of the phenomenon offers conflicting evidence given that the complementizer *que* may be perceived as one of the various Spanish relative pronouns.

Besides the fact that the complementizer in restrictive relatives may be perceived as different from the one in tensed subordinate clauses (in Jaeggli's analysis the former has the feature [+ pronoun]), there are three specific factors that may lead to the assumption that it really is a relative pronoun. First, unlike English *that,* Spanish *que* shares the initial morpheme with relative pronouns *qu*ien, el *que*, etc. Second, there is an interrogative pronoun, *qué,* in 19, whose only phonetic difference from complementizer *que* is the fact that it is tonic.

19 ¿*Qué* hace usted?
What are you doing?

Third, Spanish *que* can appear after prepositions in oblique restrictive relatives such as 20,

20 Es la película *de que* te hablé
(it) is the movie about that you (I) told
It is the movie I told you about

Thus, these three pieces of evidence which in the case of English lead speakers to perceive *that* as different from relative pronouns do not exist in Spanish. In fact, in spite of markedness considerations, the very nature of the phenomenon and the target language, Spanish, seem to form a conspiracy to prevent the existence of an obligatory *que* in nonoblique restrictive relatives in the interlanguage grammar.

Output

The Study The results reported here are a partial sample of a large study carried out in 1981/82 to investigate the relevance of linguistic theory to second language acquisition theory in the determination of the grammatical knowledge that underlies interlanguage performance.[11]

Two written tests, an English-to-Spanish translation task (T) and a grammaticality judgments task (J) were administered to 50 subjects: 45 regular, full-time native English-speaking students who were taking Spanish at two Canadian universities, and five native Spanish speakers. The subjects were chosen as follows: (1) Group I: Beginners. This group includes 15 beginning students who had not been formally taught how to use the Spanish constructions under study. They had been studying Spanish for seven months. (2) Groups II and III: Intermediate and Advanced. Fifteen intermediate and 15 advanced students comprised these groups. They had been given specific instruction on relative clauses. Group IV: Control. The five native speakers in the group were from Spain and had all been in Canada for less than 2 years. They all had university degrees and had studied English in Spain. The subjects in the nonnative group had had formal instruction in French that ranged from 3 to 11 years. Eight subjects in group I, 4 in group II, and 7 in III had studied Italian. Portuguese had been studied by one subject in groups I and II and two subjects in group III.

The translation text contained 50 items (sentences or short paragraphs) which included instances of the various constructions under study. The test items were taken from two American novels and a sociology textbook. Two native speakers of English were enlisted to ensure that despite the use of short or incomplete passages, the sentences sounded natural. The Spanish word was supplied for those lexical items whose Spanish equivalent was unlikely to be familiar to the learners. In addition, subjects were told to leave a blank if they could not translate a given word, but to try to translate the rest of the sentence. This enabled even the beginners to perform the task: they were able to give the translation in spite of missing a word or two.

The grammaticality judgments test was made up of 50 items, 16 of which contained correct samples of the structures being tested. The order of presentation of the different constructions was randomized. The subjects were asked to identify any errors and to correct them if necessary. An effort was made to ensure that the items sounded meaningful even in their incorrect form and that they were interpreted as intended. This was done by having them translate each item in the judgment task into English.

The vocabulary was elementary enough to ensure that beginning students could understand the meanings of all the sentences.

The Results: Preposition Stranding This construction was judged grammatical by almost half the subjects in group I (Table 21-1) in the case of the J task, and the same group also produced some stranded prepositions in the translation task. It is interesting to note that learners with a low-level proficiency—those in group I—accepted and produced some stranded prepositions. Group I learners had not been taught how to form relative clauses. However, they had been taught how to form questions and had both formulated and been exposed to many questions which could never involve stranded prepositions. This does not seem to have provided enough evidence concerning the fixing of this parameter in Spanish. Group I learners' production may be a reflection of variable intuitions in relation to extraction from PP. These learners may not have been exposed to enough crucial data to decide whether extractions from PP are possible in Spanish. Thus their intuitions may lead them to accept stranded prepositions in some situations and to reject them in others.

The results in the case of the intermediate and the advanced groups (see Table 21-1) parallel my previous findings from written compositions, judgments and translations in which I concluded that nonnative learners include no marked structures in their Spanish nonnative grammar (Liceras 1981). An advanced student in the 1981 study, when asked why she had not accepted those constructions, answered that she would never strand a preposition when learning another language, because she had been taught that those constructions were not "proper" English. Another native speaker of English who said that she would never preposition strand in another language had the impression that such constructions were very peculiar, a "kind of idiom." These opinions may reflect native speakers' intuitions about marked constructions, though they may simply reflect learners' perceptions of language distance as defined by Kellerman (1979). It may also be argued that normative usage is responsible for the results, since written English shows many fewer cases of preposition stranding than spoken English. Nonetheless, the subjects in this study used preposition stranding systematically in their English translations of the J task.

For those who produced and accepted stranded prepositions in group I there is a noticeable difference between the number of cases that are accepted and those that are produced (Table 21-1, judgments versus translation).[12]

TABLE 21-1 Percentage and Number of Subjects Per Group Who Accepted and Produced "Preposition Stranding" Constructions

	Group I (N = 15)		*Group II* (N = 15)		*Group III* (N = 15)		*Group IV* (N = 5)	
Judgments:								
Item 40 (hablaba de/speak about)	.40	6/15	.07	1/15	—		—	
Item 45 (trabajas para/work for)	.47	7/15	.20	3/15	.20	3/15	—	
Total	.43	13/30	.13	4/30	.10	3/30	.0	0/10
Translation:								
Item 10 (hear about)	.40	6/15	—		—		—	
Item 30 (told us about)	.07	1/15	—		—		—	
Item 31 (sleep with)	.20	3/15	.07	1/15	.07	1/15	—	
Item 17 (paid for)	.20	3/15	—		—		—	
Item 35 (talk about)	.13	2/15	—		—		—	
Total	.20	15/75	.01	1/75	.01	1/75	.0	0/25

Nonoblique Restrictive Relatives As indicated above, the use of *que* is obligatory in Spanish nonoblique restrictive relativization. If this obligatoriness represents the marked condition, as Hirschbühler and Rivero (1981) propose, it should be a source of variable intuitions; that is, the interlanguage output would show instances of the unmarked condition: the optional use of the complementizer or of a relative pronoun as in English.

As shown in Table 21-2, *que* occurs at a high rate in subject (SU), direct object (DO), and nominal predicate (Nom. Pred.) position for the translation task, and there is no difference in frequency or pattern among the three groups of learners. However, the grammaticality judgments task shows that PRO-movement (use of *que*) applies at a lower rate. Tables 21-3 and 21-4 show the actual rates of production and acceptance of noun phrases. *Quien* is produced or left unchanged in both SU and Nom. Pred. position. Comparing the results from the J task with those from the T task (Table 21-4), it becomes clear that noun phrases (both *quien* and *el cual*) are less likely to be produced in translation than to be left unchanged, and this is so even though the T task includes three *who* noun phrases as stimuli and two *which* noun phrases versus two *that* complementizers. Indeed, seven out of the eight instances of *quien* produced by the beginners group correspond to cases in which the stimulus was *who,* and five out of the seven *quien* are translations from *who* by the advanced group. Only one *quien* out of four instances in the case of the intermediate group corresponds to English *who.* The other three translate *that.* In other words, the stimulus may provoke

TABLE 21-2 Proportion of *Que* in Obligatory Contexts

	Group I (N = 15)		*Group II* (N = 15)		*Group III* (N = 15)		*Group IV* (N = 5)	
Judgment:								
SU	.38	23/60	.63	38/60	.58	35/60	.95	19/20
DO	.53	16/30	.77	23/30	.93	28/30	.100	10/10
Nom. Pred.	.37	11/30	.54	16/30	.63	19/30	.100	10/10
Translation:								
SU	.86	90/105	.80	84/105	.80	84/105	.86	30/35
DO	.93	14/15	.87	13/15	.86	13/15	.100	5/5
Nom. Pred.	.97	29/30	.100	30/30	.93	28/30	.100	10/10

some instances of noun phrases, but this is a minor effect, as shown in Table 21-5.[13]

The fact that few noun phrases are produced by all three groups might lead to the conclusion that the nonnative grammar, like native Spanish grammar, applies PRO-movement in nonoblique relativization, as I concluded in a small-scale study (Liceras 1981). However, the J task shows that no definite judgment is given with respect to the obligatoriness of *que*. In fact, there was no difference among the three groups in the production of noun phrases and there is no difference between groups I and III with respect to the acceptance of noun phrases. This seems to indicate that more exposure to Spanish does not lead to a nativelike fixing of the parameter. This may be due to the optional application of PRO-movement in English and to the conflicting evidence from Spanish discussed above. Even if *que* is perceived as a relative pronoun and is in fact a relative pronoun in the interlanguage grammar, it is not the only one that appears in nonoblique restrictive relativization. The results may also indicate that this somehow hidden property of modern romance syntax is not easy to detect.[14]

The fact that more exposure to Spanish does not lead to a greater rejection of noun phrases represents an interesting pattern because it indicates that similar output in the case of the various groups may reflect different competence. In the case of group I learners, their knowledge of English and one or two romance languages plus their overall exposure to Spanish leads them to the realization that *que* is the complementizer, and they use it in relative constructions. For group II, formal exposure to relative clauses makes them aware of the fact that noun phrases are not used in Spanish nonoblique restrictive relativization. Grammatical explanations together with negative evidence in the form of classroom exercises that are corrected should also play some role. Nonetheless, variable intuitions persist.

TABLE 21-3 Noun Phrases in Nonoblique Relativization. Judgments

	Group I (N = 15)		Group II (N = 15)		Group III (N = 15)		Group IV (N = 5)	
SU:								
quien	.22	(13/60)	.15	(9/60)	.20	(12/60)	.0	(0/20)
el que	.02	(1/60)	.0	(0/60)	.0	(0/60)	.0	(0/20)
el cual	.38	(23/60)	.17	(10/60)	.22	(13/60)	.05	(1/20)
Total	.47	(37/60)	.32	(19/60)	.41	(25/60)	.05	(1/20)
DO:								
quien	.0	(0/30)	.0	(0/30)	.0	(0/30)	.0	(0/10)
el que	.0	(0/30)	.07	(2/30)	.0	(0/30)	.0	(0/10)
el cual	.0	(0/30)	.0	(0/30)	.03	(1/30)	.0	(0/10)
Total	.0	(0/30)	.07	(2/30)	.03	(1/30)	.0	(0/10)
Nom. Pred.:								
quien	.43	(13/30)	.23	(7/30)	.20	(6/30)	.0	(0/10)
el que	.0	(0/30)	.0	(0/30)	.0	(0/30)	.0	(0/10)
el cual	.0	(0/30)	.0	(0/30)	.03	(1/30)	.0	(0/10)
Total	.43	(13/30)	.23	(7/30)	.23	(7/30)	.0	(0/10)

TABLE 21-4 Noun Phrases in Nonoblique Relativization. Translation

	Group I (N = 15)		Group II (N = 15)		Group III (N = 15)		Group IV (N = 5)	
SU:								
quien	.08	(8/105)	.04	(4/105)	.7	(07/105)	.0	(0/35)
el que	.01	(1/105)	.05	(5/105)	.4	(04/105)	.0	(0/35)
el cual	.06	(6/105)	.07	(7/105)	.8	(08/105)	.06	(2/35)
Total	.15	(15/105)	.16	(16/105)	.19	(19/105)	.06	(2/35)
DO:								
quien	.02	(1/45)	.0	(0/45)	.13	(6/45)	.0	(0/15)
el que	.0	(0/45)	.04	(2/45)	.0	(0/45)	.0	(0/15)
el cual	.0	(0/45)	.0	(0/45)	.04	(2/45)	.0	(0/15)
Total	.02	(1/45)	.04	(2/45)	.17	(8/45)	.0	(0/15)
Nom. Pred.:								
quien	.03	(1/30)	.0	(0/30)	.0	(0/30)	.0	(0/10)
el que	.0	(0/30)	.0	(0/30)	.0	(0/30)	.0	(0/10)
el cual	.0	(0/30)	.0	(0/30)	.0	(0/30)	.0	(0/10)
Total	.03	(1/30)	.0	(0/30)	.0	(0/30)	.0	(0/10)

In fact, group II learners have already had conflicting evidence in the form of nonrestrictive relatives since, as indicated in 15, both *que* and a relative pronoun are allowed in these constructions. For group III, more exposure to Spanish will offer conflicting evidence in the form of free relatives, nonrestrictive relatives, and clefts—11 versus 15, 16, and 18 above. While the results from groups II and III may indicate a degree of knowledge of the obligatory application of PRO-movement in Spanish, the results for group I indicate some knowledge of the general rule which allows the use of PRO-movement in nonoblique relativization in English and romance languages (it should be recalled that group I had not been formally taught how to form Spanish relative clauses).

TABLE 21-5 Noun Phrases in Subject Relativization. Translation

Stimulus	Answers	Groups I	II	III	IV
Test item 1	que	15	14	11	4
"that"	quien	—	1	2	—
	el cual	—	—	2	—
Test item 42	que	15	10	12	3
"that"	quien	—	2	—	—
	el cual	—	—	1	—
Test item 2	que	13	12	15	5
"who"	quien	2	—	—	—
	el que	—	1	—	—
Test item 21	que	11	14	12	5
"who"	quien	3	—	3	—
	el cual	1	—	—	—
	el que	—	1	—	—
Test item 25	que	13	11	12	5
"who"	quien	2	1	2	—
	el cual	—	—	1	—
	el que	—	1	—	—
Test item 22	que	11	10	10	3
"which"	quien	1	—	—	—
	el cual	3	5	2	2
	el que	—	—	3	—
Test item 40	que	12	13	12	5
"which"	quien	—	—	—	—
	el cual	2	1	2	—
	el que	1	1	1	—

In summary, the results for PRO-movement indicate that permeability (variable intuitions concerning the optional versus obligatory use of *que*) will be visible at the production level: the Spanish interlanguage of English speakers will contain noun phrases in nonoblique restrictive relativization even if—as in the translation task—they are not abundant.

CONCLUSIONS

Determination of learners' competence is a complex task which has to be undertaken within the framework of a sophisticated model of grammar. In the same way that linguistic theory aims to construct a model of native grammar, it can also specify what a nonnative speaker knows about his or her interlanguage and the principles that underlie that knowledge. In fact, if grammatical theory is defined as characterization of knowledge, determining learners' competence and constructing a model of nonnative grammar become closely related and somehow overlapping tasks.

In this chapter, I have proposed a model of nonnative grammar which relates the notion of permeability to the fact that some parameters of core grammar may be fixed in a variety of ways or not fixed at all, thus resulting in learners' variable intuitions. To determine learners' competence within this framework it is necessary to differentiate the variable intuitions of their permeable grammar from task-bounded variability.

The advantages of this model are:

1. It differentiates nonnative grammar from interlanguage and, likewise, variable intuitions from variability. This makes it possible to explain why, on the one hand, the two syntactic processes have a remarkably different status in the nonnative grammar and, on the other, that each syntactic process shows a clear within-group, across-task consistency. For example, only group I accepts and produces stranded prepositions but they do so in both tasks, although more so in the J task. There is a similar pattern for all three groups in the case of production and acceptance of noun phrases in nonoblique restrictive relativization.

The two syntactic processes are different in status because variable intuitions related to extracting from PP (preposition stranding) do not occur in the grammar of learners who have been taught how to form relative clauses. However, variable intuitions occur at all levels in the case of the obligatory use of *que.* In spite of their different status, the pattern of variability that differentiates the two tasks remains constant. The model accounts for this, since it permits the status of a given process in the nonnative grammar to be determined in relation to, but to be differentiated from, its realization in the interlanguage.

2. It proposes a system of general rules containing a set of parameters that may or may not be fixed, thus offering a basis for comparing syntactic processes in learners' native and target languages, as well as in other natural languages, and making it possible to predict how intuitions may vary.

I have proposed that variable intuitions reflect the permeability of the nonnative system and are explained by the relationship between input and intake. In the case of preposition stranding, nothing in the input data leads learners to fix the parameter that allows extraction from PP. However, group I learners may not have been exposed to enough or to crucial data. As I mentioned above, they knew how to form questions, but there may not be an obvious relationship between extractions in questions and in relativization at this stage in the nonnative grammar.

A similar degree of acceptance of noun phrases as relativizers in the case of groups I and III indicates that learners continue to have variable intuitions with respect to the optional/obligatory use of the complementizer *que.* This indicates that positive evidence from Spanish and formal instruction does not lead to fixing this parameter as obligatory. The special status of PRO-movement in the nonnative grammar is not surprising in view of the nature of the phenomenon and the conflicting surface evidence offered by Spanish. It is not clear whether *que* is perceived as a relative pronoun or as a complementizer. Even in this second case, it may be different from the complementizer *que* (*that*) in tensed subordinate clauses, since, as Jaeggli indicates, it seems to have the feature [+pronoun]. We may be facing a case of wh-movement where different relative pronouns, *que* among them, alternate, none of them being unique in its relationship to nonoblique restrictive relativization. If the interlanguage grammar does not have a PRO-movement rule that follows from the avoid pronoun principle as proposed by Jaeggli (1980), there may not be any relationship between the obligatory use of *que*, the dropping of subject pronouns, and other specific properties of languages such as Spanish.[15] A similar situation may be reflected in the lack of relation between extraction out of PP in questions and relativization mentioned before. These may be rather relevant facts because a nonnative grammar may differ from a native grammar precisely in that syntactic processes and/or clusters of properties are not related in similar ways or not related at all in the nonnative grammar. This would greatly contribute to nonnative grammar's being most sensitive to permeability.

A further piece of evidence concerning the complexity involved in the determination of learners' competence is the fact that similar outputs by learners at different levels may not reflect the same underlying competence. More sophisticated testing, comparison of outputs obtained from different learning situations (classroom versus "naturalistic" settings), and more control over input are mandatory if we are to provide accurate interpretations of interlanguage data. The results of this study provide a number of suggestions for further research.

One thing appears to be obvious: eliciting data through different tests will contribute to determining learners' "homogeneous" competence. All tests should contribute to determine whether or not variable intuitions, or a given rule, are present in the nonnative grammar of learners at a given level of proficiency. However, the presence of any given rule or variable intuition will not necessarily be reflected to the same degree in each test.

In spite of the different status of preposition stranding and obligatory use of *que* in the nonnative grammars of learners at different proficiency levels, the same relationship is maintained between the production of relative pronouns and stranded prepositions in the T task and their acceptance in the J task. The difference between the number of relative pronouns and stranded prepositions in both tasks indicates that the interlanguage output reflects a task-bounded variability.

To conclude, I have argued that attained linguistic knowledge, metalinguistic abilities, and issues of markedness may play a role at the level of intake and have to be considered to account for the relationship between input and output at different levels of proficiency. I have also argued that similar outputs in the case of different groups do not necessarily reflect the same competence. Nonetheless, different tasks performed by a given group of learners should reflect the same competence even when the production mechanisms involved in performing each task affect the output in a quantitative way. This task-bounded variability should be differentiated from the variable intuitions reflected in a given task. The different cognitive capacities that play a role at the level of intake are responsible for the specific ways in which the permeability of nonnative grammars gives way to those variable intuitions.

NOTES

1. Universal grammar is considered an element of biological endowment which contains the genetic principles common to human species. Languages select from among those principles to fix parameters in a number of permitted ways, thus determining a particular grammar (a "core grammar"). This setting of parameters is triggered by experience in combination with available genetic principles. Children learning a language will have to fix the parameter(s) which correspond to that language when they receive enough empirical evidence (see Chomsky 1981, Lightfoot 1982).

2. Nonoblique relativization refers to relativized positions where no preposition occurs. Oblique relativization refers to relative clauses involving prepositional phrases.

3. The L1 data, and data from other languages that are considered to be part of the input, are those that are presented in the classroom or by some interlocutor, book, etc., through comparison or translation. It does not refer to learners' knowledge.

4. In the case of *el cual* there are some stylistic differences and restrictions depending on the type of preposition. There may also be stylistic differences in the choice of *quien* over *el que* (see Plann 1980). Nonetheless, there are many contexts in which a native speaker cannot decide upon which one to choose. In the present study, there was a definite preference for *el que* on the part of the control group.

5. Relative pronouns are possible in direct object position involving [+animate] objects, provided that preposition *a* is inserted.

6. There have been different analyses to account for the presence of the complementizer *que/that* in nonoblique restrictive relatives. For instance, Chomsky and Lasnik (1977) and Rivero (1979) proposed that the wh was moved to COMP and further deleted. PRO-movement seems a better alternative because, as Jaeggli (1980) points out, it captures the intuition that the complementizer in relative constructions is in fact slightly different from the *que/that* in tensed subordinate sentences such as 5. I have avoided all the technicalities concerning the internal structure of COMP. For an account of the rule that yields 10 see Jaeggli (1980), p. 269.

7. This relexicalization rule has been proposed by Hornstein and Weinberg (1981).

8. See Rivero (1982).

9. There seem to be dialectal differences within the Spanish-speaking population. For an analysis of the status of these constructions in native and nonnative systems see Muñoz-Liceras (1984).

10. For a discussion of this proposal, see Muñoz-Liceras (1983).

11. See Muñoz-Liceras (1983) for a full report on the study.

12. The cases of preposition stranding produced by groups II and III were produced by two students whose overall performance corresponds to that of students in group I.

13. No *who* or *whom* stimulus occurs in the case of the DO, but the advanced group produce the largest number of noun phrases in this position. It may be that these learners were attempting to formulate oblique relative DOs, as in (a), but omitted the preposition.

(a) . . . ese chico francés [*a* quien *a*l que *a*l cual] conocí ayer

Indeed, they did produce this construction in several instances. It may also be that the advanced learners are more familiar with the lexical items in question and use them with human antecedents in nonoblique relativization.

14. A further complication comes from the fact that French has the complementizers *que* and *qui,* this second one in subject position. See Adjémian and Liceras (1984) and Muñoz-Liceras (1983) for an analysis of the acquisition of French and Spanish relatives.

15. Unlike English and French, Spanish and Italian drop subject pronouns and do not need dummy subjects such as *it* or *il* in sentences such as (a):

(a) *it* is necessary
il est necessaire
∅ es necesario

Languages such as Spanish and Italian share a number of properties related to what Chomsky (1981) refers to as the Pro-drop parameter. It may be the case that a nonnative grammar contains one or two but not all of those properties.

Section Five

METHODOLOGY AND THEORY

22

INPUT AND SECOND LANGUAGE ACQUISITION THEORY

Michael H. Long
University of Hawaii-Manoa

While much descriptive work remains to be done, a good deal is already known about linguistic and conversational adjustments to nonnative speakers. (For review, see Hatch 1983b, Long 1983c.) Consequently some researchers have begun to study the *effects* of different kinds of input and conversational experience on second language (SL) development. This research will ultimately help determine the scope of learner and environmental[1] contributions to second language acquisition (SLA) and hence will be influential in shaping SLA theory. Its findings will also have implications for a number of applied concerns, such as bilingual and immersion education, syllabus design, teaching methodology, and the preparation of simplified reading materials.

One approach to investigating the effects of environmental variation is correlational. Environmental features are measured at time 1, and relationships sought between these measures and SL proficiency at time 1, SL proficiency at time 2, or proficiency gain scores from time 1 to time 2. While this approach has obvious merit, a problem is that it is very time-consuming to obtain a large enough sample of the environmental features, and difficult to control for environmental effects before and after the sample is taken. Thus, in an early study, Snow and Hoefnagel-Höhle (1982) found no consistent relationships between current Dutch achievement scores or Dutch SL gain scores of American children in Holland and (1) the quantity of Dutch they heard inside the classroom, (2) the percentage of all classroom speech which was specifically directed to them, and (3) the quantity of classroom speech directed to them. The researchers note, however, that their study concerned a very small sample of children (n = 6) of differing ages and proficiency levels, and a very small sample of classroom speech (30 minutes). Further, there was no control over the amount of Dutch the children heard outside school during the 5-month period of the study, and no assurance that the classroom speech addressed to them, though modified, was comprehensible.

All these problems could, of course, be handled through use of a miniature artificial language, as suggested by McLaughlin (1982) or through use of a true experimental design in a foreign language setting. To my knowledge, however, no such studies have yet been conducted where the focus was on global characteristics of the linguistic or conversational environment.[2]

Fortunately, demonstrating *direct* relationships between environmental features and interlanguage development is not the only possible approach to this line of research. An alternative, *indirect* approach, breaks the task down into three steps:

Step 1: Show that (a) linguistic/conversational adjustments promote (b) comprehension of input.
Step 2: Show that (b) comprehensible input promotes (c) acquisition.
Step 3: Deduce that (a) linguistic/conversational adjustments promote (c) acquisition.

Satisfactory evidence of the a → b and b → c relationships would allow the linguistic environment to be posited as an indirect causal variable in SLA. (The relationship would be indirect because of the intervening "comprehension" variable.)

The literature on normal and abnormal first and second language acquisition provides considerable evidence of a (b) comprehensible input → (c) acquisition relationship. (For review, see Krashen 1980, 1982; Long 1981a, 1983a.) Unfortunately, there has been very little SL research on the effects of (a) linguistic/conversational adjustments on (b) comprehension. Some work has been done, however, and the initial results are encouraging.

As part of a larger study, Johnson (1981) found that 46 intermediate/advanced Iranian students of English were able to recall more events from an adapted (linguistically "simplified and paraphrased") version of an American short story they had read than from an unadapted version, although the cultural origin of a text was generally more important for recall than was linguistic adaption. In a second study involving reading, Blau (1982) compared the comprehension scores of 85 Spanish-speaking college students and of 111 Spanish-speaking eighth graders on three versions of the same reading passages, in which content and vocabulary was held constant. Version 1 was written in the short, simple sentence style common in basal readers:

Disease germs may be present in food. Cook food for a long enough time. This will kill any disease germs . . .

Version 2 contained complex sentences, and so fewer and longer sentences than version 1. It also retained explicit surface clues to underlying meaning relationships, e.g., by not deleting optional relative pronouns and by retaining subjects and finite verbs in subordinate clauses:

If you cook food for a long enough time, you will kill any disease germs that may be present . . .

Version 3 also employed longer, complex sentences. It differed from version 2 in that it also deleted optional relative pronouns and any form of "be" that followed them, as well as surface subjects in subordinate clauses, and used nonfinite verbs in subordinate clauses:

Cooking food for a long enough time will kill any disease germs possibly present. . . .

While differences did not reach statistical significance at the .05 level, comprehension scores of both groups of subjects were generally highest on version 2. In other words, of two types of adjustments, that which resulted in greater explicitness/redundancy, while retaining syntactic complexity, tended to facilitate comprehension most.[3]

In another study, this time of aural comprehension, Chaudron (1983a) scripted five lecturettes on different topics such that each lecturette contained a paired set of subtopics which were mentioned twice and later reinstated. The (sub)topics were each encoded in one of five different ways:

1. *Repeated noun* (The beer . . . the beer tastes terrific.)
2. *Simple noun* (The beer tastes terrific.)
3. *Rhetorical question* (What about the beer? It tastes terrific.)
4. *If-clause* (If you can afford the beer, it tastes terrific.)
5. *Synonym* (The brew tastes terrific.)

The order of occurrence of the topic-reinstatement devices, and the textual distance between second and reinstated mentions were control variables. The lecturettes were played to 135 adult ESL students in two conditions: *recognition only* (n = 60), who heard each lecturette and then answered 12 recognition questions, and *recall-recognition* (n = 75), who did the same as the recognition-only group but also completed four short cloze items (two on the reinstatements and two distractors) during brief interruptions of the lecturettes.

Chaudron found that *recognition* scores were significantly higher for repeated noun than for simple noun for the recognition-only group. *Recall* scores were significantly higher for repeated noun than for if-clause and synonym, and scores for simple noun were superior to those for synonyms for the recall-recognition group. Aggregating scores across the various proficiency levels represented in the sample, the overall pattern for recall scores was 1 through 5 above. If we assume that "simple noun" was equivalent to *un*adjusted (native speaker/native speaker) speech in this research, then all three studies find that at least some kinds of adjustments promote comprehension by nonnative speakers. There is also a suggestion of an effect for proficiency level, with adjustments being more beneficial for students of lower proficiency in Chaudron's study.

Chaudron suggests that the *redundancy* of repeated noun probably made it the most successful reinstatement device overall, at least in its effect on immediate language intake. Support for this interpretation is provided by a more recent small-scale study of the effect of exact repetition of complete sentences on comprehensibility, as measured by the ability to take dictation (Cervantes 1983). Cervantes randomly assigned 16 "intermediate" ESL students enrolled in a remedial writing course for nonnative speakers at the University of Hawaii to one of two groups. A listening passage divided into 26 sequences, each roughly 15 syllables in length, was recorded and played to the subjects under one of two conditions. One group heard each sequence once, followed by 30 seconds for transcription. The other group heard each sequence twice, followed by 30 seconds for transcription. The group receiving exact repetition of each sequence scored significantly higher on two measures of comprehension of the passage, i.e., number of correct (lexical and grammatical) morphemes transcribed, and a scorer-rated index of equivalence of meaning for each phrasal unit in the dictation.

While these initial studies have provided evidence consistent with a causal adjustment → comprehension relationship, there is clearly a need for additional research. In particular, there has been no work to date on the effects on NNS comprehension of global foreigner talk (FT) adjustments to spoken discourse. To this end, a study was conducted to determine the relative comprehensibility of two versions of a lecturette, scripted to control for content: one version intended for a native speaker (NS) audience, the other adjusted for nonnative speakers (NNSs).

A STUDY OF THE EFFECTS OF SPEECH ADJUSTMENTS ON NONNATIVE SPEAKER COMPREHENSION OF A LECTURETTE[4]

Hypotheses

It was hypothesized that:

1. Comprehension of a lecturette would be higher among NNSs hearing a version adjusted for a NNS audience than among students hearing an

unadjusted version intended for a NS audience, as measured by scores on a multiple-choice test on the lecturette's content.

2. Perceived comprehension of the same lecturette would also be higher among the NNSs hearing the adjusted version, as expressed by a self-report measure.

Subjects

Subjects for this study were 34 foreign students at the University of Hawaii at Manoa in the spring semester, 1983. All were NNSs of English and came from a variety of (mostly oriental) first language backgrounds. Their English proficiency, tested at the beginning of the semester, was fairly homogeneous and could be described as "intermediate," ranging from about 450 to approximately 520 on the TOEFL (Test of English as a Foreign Language). While simultaneously enrolled in one or more content courses in their regular academic programs at the university, each was also taking ELI 70, a listening-comprehension course meeting for 5 hours per week, at the time they participated in the study. Subjects had previously had varying amounts of formal ESL instruction in the United States and in their own countries, and an average of a little over 4 years of informal exposure to English. They ranged in age from 18 to 40, with the majority in their late teens or early twenties.

Treatment

Two versions of a lecturette on Mexico were prepared, using information found in a variety of reference books and current affairs magazines. The first version was written in an informal, but "academic," spoken style, intended for an audience of university undergraduates who were NSs of English. The script included such typical performance phenomena as run-on sentences, pause fillers, stress marking, and parenthetical remarks (asides). It began like this:

> OK So today I'm gonna be talking about the United States' southern neighbor—Mexico. We'll be looking briefly at three things: the geography, the political system and the economy. First, the geography.

The lecturette contained 1,702 words. It was recorded by a female NS of Standard American English, and lasted 12 minutes and 15 seconds.

A second version of the lecturette was then scripted, using as nearly identical propositional content as possible, and with the information presented in the same order, but this time designed for an audience of university undergraduates who were NNSs of English. This "foreigner talk" version again included typical performance phenomena, but it was also modified in a variety of other ways well-attested in the descriptive literature as characterizing speech adjusted for NNSs. It was, for example, longer (2,140) words and syntactically slightly less complex (as measured by average length of T units in words and average number of S nodes per T unit), and it contained many rephrasings and restatements. It was also recorded more slowly (by the same female speaker), lasting 16 minutes and 45 seconds, with the slightly clearer articulation that typically accompanies slower speech. In keeping with previous findings to this effect (see Long 1983a, for review), there were no ungrammaticalities in the foreigner talk version, which began like this:

OK So today I'm going to talk about *Mexico,* the country south of the United States. I'll talk a little about three things: the *geography* of Mexico, the Mexican *political* system and the Mexican *economy.* First, the *geography.*

A post hoc analysis of the NS and FT versions of the lecturette showed that they differed in the following ways:

	NS	FT
Number of words	1702	2140
Number of T units	114	166
Average length of T units in words	14.93	12.89
Average number of S nodes per T unit	1.94	1.68
Duration of lecturette (minutes and seconds)	12.15	16.45
Average rate of delivery (words per minute)	138.90	127.80

The female American NS who recorded both versions of the lecturette made every effort to sound "natural" on the tapes. Nevertheless, linguistically sophisticated listeners—although not necessarily nonnative listeners of the proficiency level used in this study—would quickly recognize that she was reading aloud from a script in each case. The slight loss in generalizability resulting from this procedure is inevitable in studies of this sort, given the need to control for propositional content and sequence of information, and the impossibility of obtaining two spontaneous lectures with either of these features. Any artificiality discernible to the NNSs from the reading aloud procedure itself was, at least, present in both conditions in the study.

Measures

A 20-item multiple-choice test was prepared on the factual content of the lecturette. Each item consisted of a stem—either a question or a statement to be completed—followed by four possible answers, of which one was correct and three were distractors, e.g.:

4. The true population of Mexico City in 1980 was
   a. ten million
   b. a quarter of a million
   c. twenty million

The items tested comprehension only of information contained in the lecture, and the sequence of questions paralleled the order in which the relevant information was presented by the lecturer.

Following the 20 test items, there appeared one more question, numbered 21, but not actually part of the test. Data from this item were used to test the study's second hypothesis:

21. What percentage of this lecture do you think you understood? Indicate the amount by putting a cross: "X" on the scale below:

	0%	10	20	30	40	50	60	70	80	90	100%	
NOTHING	ı	ı	ı	ı	ı	ı	ı	ı	ı	ı	ı	EVERYTHING

Procedures

The 34 subjects were randomly assigned to one of two conditions: FT (n = 17) or NS (n = 17). Each group was told they would shortly be hearing a short lecture on Mexico and that they would only hear it once. They were given 3 minutes to read the questions, and were told they should answer them during the lecture as far as possible and finish any unanswered ones in a further 3-minute period after the tape had ended. They were told to guess the answers to any questions they could not handle, and that while wrong answers would not be penalized, unanswered questions would obviously be counted as wrong. One group then heard the NS version of the tape; the other group heard the FT version. The two parts of the study were run in separate rooms. Subjects were unaware of the purpose of the research or that the two groups were hearing different versions of the lecturette. Subjects answered item 21 at the very end of the testing session, after completing their answers to the 20 questions on the lecturette.

Analyses

Two *t* tests for independent samples were used to determine whether there were any differences in (1) subjects' comprehension scores, and (2) subjects' self-reported perceived comprehension of the lecturette, due to the version (NS or FT) they had heard. Reliability of the test instrument was calculated using the Kuder-Richardson 21 formula.

Results

Means, standard deviations, and Ns for each group on the 20-item comprehension test are shown in Table 22-1. The results of the *t* test indicated that the average comprehension score of the FT group was significantly higher than the average for the group hearing the NS version of the lecturette (t = 4.86, df = 32, $p < .0005$). Means, standard deviations, and Ns for each group on the self-rated perceived comprehension scale are shown in Table 22-2. The results of the *t* test indicated that the average perceived comprehension score of the FT group was, again, significantly higher than the average for the group hearing the NS version of the lecturette (t = 1.74, df = 32, $p < .05$). The obtained KR 21 reliability coefficients for the test were very low: .26 for the NS group, and .16 for the FT group.

TABLE 22-1 Means, Standard Deviations, and Ns for FT and NS Groups' Comprehension Scores

	n	$\bar{x}$	s
FT group	17	13.18	1.97
NS group	17	9.88	1.99

$t = 4.86$, df = 32, $p < .0005$.

TABLE 22-2 Means, Standard Deviations, and Ns for FT and NS Groups' Perceived Comprehension Scores

	n	$\bar{x}$	s
FT group	17	69.06	10.34
NS group	17	59.94	18.95

$t = 1.74$, df = 32, $p < .05$.

Discussion

The results presented in Table 22-1 are consistent with the hypothesis that one or more of the speech adjustments NSs make when addressing NNSs facilitates NNS comprehension. It is not necessarily the case, of course, that *all* the adjustments noted in this and other studies have that effect. It might be, for example that the presence of one or more adjustments, such as repetition or use of a slow rate of delivery, preempt the effect of other modifications. Alternatively, some adjustments, such as repetition and use of a slow pace, may aid NNS comprehension, while other modifications may have no beneficial effect at all. Further research is needed to tease out the relative contributions of different kinds and combinations of adjustments.[5]

The results shown in Table 22-2 support the hypothesis that NNSs perceive their own comprehension to be higher when faced with spoken discourse adjusted for NNSs than when confronted with speech intended for a NS audience. Once again, however, it is not necessarily justified to assume that *all* the adjustments NSs make have this effect on NNSs' perceived comprehension.

The low KR 21 coefficients obtained on the NS and FT versions of the test used in this study are obviously disturbing. An item analysis revealed few poor items, however, with 12 out of 20 having discrimination indexes of between .25 and .75. The low reliability coefficients are more probably due to other factors. First, the test was rather short, having only 20 items, of which the first two were intentionally easy but produced zero discriminatory power as a result. Second, while global listening comprehension ability was obviously being tapped in the study, the test involved did not address language per se but rather knowledge of factual information about Mexico obtained from the lecturette. The information asked for was a sampling of the informational domains in the lecturette, and (with the exception of the first two) the items were of approximately equal difficulty. We are dealing, therefore, with something approximating a criterion-referenced test, in which subjects were revealing whether or not they knew certain information, rather than with the usual norm-referenced measure, in which students of different language proficiency introduce considerable variability into test results by competing with each other. As is well known by now, it is unwise to assess the reliability of criterion-referenced tests by the normal reliability measures appropriate for norm-referenced tests (see, e.g., Popham and Husek 1969). Lastly, the fact that the sample in this study was quite homogeneous in terms of ESL proficiency would in any case predict little variability in the results within groups, and hence, low internal reliability coefficients. In this regard, note the very small standard deviations in Table 22-1.

Notwithstanding these caveats, it was felt desirable to conduct a replication study using a slightly longer test, with minor changes to three of the weaker items, and using a larger pool of subjects. This would not only help address the concerns about instrumentation but would generally help determine the robustness of the results of the initial study.

REPLICATION STUDY[6]

Hypotheses and Method

The basic hypotheses tested in the replication study were the same as those in the first study. First, comprehension scores were expected to be higher in the FT than in the NS group. Perceived comprehension was also expected to be higher in the FT condition. In addition, however, it was predicted that there would be an interaction effect between comprehension scores and SL proficiency, such that the comprehension-facilitating effect of the speech adjustments would be stronger for students of lower proficiency. To enable this hypothesis to be tested, a somewhat wider SL proficiency range was sampled in the second study, with subjects being drawn from ELI 70 classes, as before, but also from a number of ELI 80 classes. The latter offer training in listening comprehension at a more advanced level, with students ranging from "intermediate" to "upper intermediate" proficiency, i.e., from about 520 to 570 on the TOEFL, compared with approximately 450 to 520 in the ELI 70 classes. A field-test version of the TOEFL listening test administered within a week of the replication study found ELI 80 students to be significantly more advanced on this subtest: ELI 80 students $\bar{x} = 44.84$, $s = 8.68$; ELI 70 students $\bar{x} = 35.29$, $s = 8.30$; $t = 6.69$, $p < .0005$.

The method used in the replication study, conducted with a different sample of 106 students in the fall semester, 1983, was almost identical to that employed in the initial study. The only differences were as follows: First, the three items on the original tests having weakest discrimination indices were modified, and four new items added, to give a total of 24 items instead of the original 20. Second, students were allowed 5 minutes instead of 3 in the original study to read through the 24 questions before hearing the tape. All other aspects of the two studies were identical. Three *t* tests for independent samples were used to determine whether there were differences in the comprehension scores of the FT and NS groups at the ELI 70 level, the ELI 80 level, and across both groups combined. The same was done for perceived comprehension scores. Finally, to confirm these findings and to test for a treatment x proficiency interaction effect, a two-way ANOVA was run on the comprehension scores only. Kuder-Richardson 21 reliability coefficients were calculated for both versions of the test.

Results

Means, standard deviations, and Ns for each group on the 24-item comprehension test are shown in Table 22-3. The results of the *t* tests confirmed the findings of the first study, indicating that the average comprehension scores of all three FT groups were significantly higher than average scores for the NS groups: for ELI 70 students: $t = 4.23$, $df = 56$, $p < .0005$; for ELI 80 students: $t = 4.74$, $df = 56$, $p < .0005$; and for both groups combined: $t = 6.12$, $df = 104$, $p < .0005$.

Means, standard deviations, and Ns for each group on the self-rated perceived comprehension scale are shown in Table 22-4. The results of the *t* tests indicated that the average perceived comprehension scores of the FT

TABLE 22-3 Means, Standard Deviations, and Ns for FT and NS Groups' Comprehension Scores (Replication Study)

		n	$\bar{x}$	s
ELI 70*	FT group	24	15.42	3.96
	NS group	24	11.46	2.30
ELI 80†	FT group	29	16.28	2.10
	NS group	29	13.14	2.88
ELI 70	FT group	53	15.89	3.08
+ 80‡	NS group	53	12.38	2.82

*t = 4.23, df = 46, p < .0005. †t = 4.74, df = 56, p < .0005. ‡t = 6.12, df = 104, p < .0005.

groups were significantly higher than the average for the groups hearing the NS version of the lecturette: for ELI 70 students: t = 6.78, df = 46, p < .0005; for ELI 80 students: t = 2.53, df = 56, p < .01; and for both groups combined: t = 5.99, df = 104, p < .0005. Again, these results confirm the findings of the first study.

TABLE 22-4 Means, Standard Deviations, and Ns for FT and NS Groups' Perceived Comprehension Scores (Replication Study)

		n	$\bar{x}$	s
ELI 70*	FT group	24	73.15	13.31
	NS group	24	44.63	15.73
ELI 80†	FT group	29	69.86	14.84
	NS group	29	59.41	16.54
ELI 70	FT group	53	71.34	14.13
+ 80‡	NS group	53	52.72	17.67

*t = 6.78, df = 46, p < .0005. †t = 2.53, df = 56, p < .01. ‡t = 5.99, df = 104, p < .0005.

The results of the two-way ANOVA of the comprehension scores confirmed the t test findings on these data. As shown in Table 22-5, there was a significant main effect for (FT or NS) version of the lecturette (F = 38.75, df = 1/102, p < .01), and also a significant main effect for (ELI 80 or ELI 70) proficiency level (F = 5.02, df = 1/102, p < .05), with the higher-proficiency (ELI 80) students scoring higher than the lower-proficiency (ELI 70) students. Contrary to the third hypothesis, however, there was no significant interaction effect for lecturette version x proficiency level.

Finally, the KR 21 reliability coefficients obtained for the two versions of the test were a little higher than in the original study but still very low: .45 for the FT group, and .26 for the NS group.

TABLE 22-5 ANOVA for Comprehension Scores Related to Lecture Type and Proficiency Level (Replication Study)

Source	*SS*	*df*	*MS*	*F*
Between groups:				
Lecture type (A)	326.38	1	326.38	38.75*
Proficiency level (B)	42.33	1	42.33	5.02†
A × B	4.42	1	4.42	0.52
Within groups	859.03	102	8.42	
Total	1232.16	105		

*$p < .01$. †$p < .05$.

Discussion

The replication provided strong support for the findings of the original study with respect to hypotheses 1 and 2. Comprehension of the lecturette was again significantly higher among students hearing a (FT) version adjusted for a NNS audience than among students hearing an unadjusted version intended for NSs. Perceived comprehension of the same lecturette was again also higher among the NNSs hearing the adjusted version. Both studies, that is, provide clear evidence consistent with the hypothesis that speech modifications for nonnative listeners result in greater NNS comprehension.

The failure to find a significant lecturette version x proficiency interaction was probably due to the relative proximity of the two groups (ELI 70 and 80) in terms of their ESL ability. The interaction observed was in the predicted direction, however, suggesting that this part of the research warrants replication with a group of students of lower ESL proficiency. As mentioned earlier, such research might also consider systematic rotation of different kinds and combinations of adjustments. The aim would be to determine just which ones contribute, and to what degree, to the facilitating effect of *global* adjustments observed in these studies.

As noted above, the new KR 21 reliability coefficients for the revised form of the comprehension test were an improvement on those obtained in the first study, but still disappointing. Probable reasons for their continuing to be low have already been offered and will not be repeated here.

Conclusion

The two studies reported above provide evidence of a causal relationship between linguistic and conversational adjustments of the kinds NSs make to nonnatives under certain conditions and the comprehensibility of what they say to their nonnative listeners. If one accepts that there is already substantial evidence of a second causal relationship between comprehensible input and SLA, then one can deduce the existence of an *indirect causal relationship between linguistic and conversational adjustments and SLA.*

THE STATUS OF THE LINGUISTIC ENVIRONMENT IN SLA THEORY

Despite the large number of empirical studies of input to SL acquirers and of NS-NNS and NNS-NNS conversation in recent years, very few claims have been made about the linguistic environment in SLA theory. Of some 15 to 20 so-called theories, models, metaphors, and perspectives in the current literature, few make any reference to environmental contributions at all, later versions of Krashen's monitor theory (e.g., Krashen 1982) being the most obvious exception. Instead, they tend to attribute most, or sometimes exclusive, importance to factors internal to the learner, such as attitude and motivation (Gardner 1978), or to social-psychological variables, such as sociocultural factors (Brown 1980) and acculturation (Schumann 1978a)

Such "theories" attempt to account for SLA without reference to other factors which many would agree have been shown to play a role in the acquisition process: age, first language background, transfer, markedness—and the linguistic environment. In a sense, therefore, they are demonstrably inadequate, or wrong. Arguably, however, it would be a mistake to ignore them, given what the history of other sciences has shown about the process of theory construction.[7]

While the exact terms they use may differ, most writers on science and scientific method distinguish two basic approaches to scientific inquiry. Reynolds (1971) calls them two "strategies" for developing a scientific body of knowledge: (a) "research-then-theory," and (b) "theory-then-research."

(a) *Research-then-theory* Adoption of this strategy, according to Reynolds (1971: 140), involves the researcher in four activities:

1. Select a phenomenon and list all its characteristics.
2. Measure all the characteristics in as many and as varied situations as possible.
3. Analyze the resulting data by looking for systematic patterns.
4. Formalize significant patterns as theoretical statements (the laws of nature).

Reynolds claims that the experience of various disciplines suggests that two conditions must be met if research-then-theory is to be an efficient strategy for theory building. First, there need to be a relatively small number of variables to measure—this to make step 3 feasible. Second, there must only be a few significant patterns found in the data—to facilitate steps 3 and 4. Most social situations, he points out, fail to meet either of these conditions. On the contrary, as shown by the SLA literature, there are usually almost as many variables as there are researchers investigating them, and not a few, but a large number of intricate direct and indirect causal relationships at work in different settings.

(b) *Theory-then-research* This strategy, according to Reynolds (1971: 144), involves the researcher in five activities:

1. Develop an explicit theory in axiomatic or causal process form.

2. Derive a testable prediction from the theory.

3. Conduct research to test the prediction.

4. If the prediction is disconfirmed, modify the theory and test a new prediction (or abandon the theory altogether).

5. If the research findings confirm the prediction, test a new one.

Note that, rather than assume, as does the research-then-theory strategy, that the scientist's role is to "discover" existing laws of nature one by one, the theory-then-research strategy requires the scientist to start by "inventing" an interim solution to the problem (what John Lamandella calls "our current best shot") and then, recognizing that it is probably false, seeking to demonstrate this (by testing the theory's *weakest* areas).

Both strategies have strengths and limitations. Researchers working with the research-then-theory strategy are less likely to be "wrong" at any time, for the simple reason that any theoretical claims they make are limited to the empirical evidence at hand. For the very same reason, however, those claims are always limited in scope, and so are less interesting than claims arising out of the theory-then-research strategy. They may also turn out to be irrelevant for (SLA) theory in the long run since, even if true, the phenomena they concern may themselves ultimately turn out to be irrelevant.

The theory-then-research strategy has the advantage of providing an approximate answer until the "final truth" is known, perhaps because it is less "bound by data." It is also, Reynolds claims, the strategy which has been associated with paradigm shifts in other sciences—with "scientific revolutions." On the negative side, however, there is the problem of scientists' knowing when to abandon rather than simply to modify a theory they have invested time in developing, and of some individual scientists' not being willing to do so when that time comes.[8]

In addition to reflecting different conceptions of science and of scientific method, as well, perhaps, as different personality types among researchers, adoption of one or other of the two strategies has implications for the *forms* of theory that will be produced. The research-then-theory strategy commits the researcher to what is known as the *set-of-laws* form, i.e., a set of independent statements, each embodying something that is known about some phenomena as a result of repeated observation of the same behavioral pattern. This is because the claims emanating from use of this strategy always and only arise from empirical observation. They are really no more (or less) than generalizations about relationships among variables to which no counterexamples have been found, hence the term "set-of-*laws*." To test such relationships, researchers have at some time had to predict, i.e., hypothesize about, what would be observed when those variables were manipulated, and they must always have been correct in their prediction. Note, however, that this means, in turn, that any variable, or concept, about which statements are now made in the theory must have been operationalizable (and operationalized). Otherwise, the claims could not have been tested empirically. It is, after all, the requirement that claims be testable against data that is one of the most basic differences between hypotheses and theories. (Theories must be verifiable, too, of course, but not every part of them need be, as will discussed below.) Hence, no theory in the set-of-laws form may contain a hypothetical construct, such as, in SLA theory, "i" or "i + 1" (Krashen 1980).

The theory-then-research strategy, likewise, is linked to certain *forms* of theory, of which only one will be mentioned here: *causal-process* form. Causal-process theories consist of (1) sets of definitions of theoretical concepts and constructs, together with operational definitions of some (but not necessarily all) of them, (2) sets of existence statements, and (3) sets of (deterministic and/or probabilistic) causal statements, which together specify not only *when* or *that* a process (such as SLA) will occur, but *how*. In order to provide this sense of *understanding* (the *how*) of the process they purport to explain, statements in causal-process theories are not independent (as they are in set-of-laws form) but are interrelated. This in turn means that hypothetical *constructs* (such as "i" and "i + 1") *are* permitted in such theories. While the statement containing such a construct cannot itself be tested directly, because the construct is unoperationalized and so is untestable in the real world, a related statement can be tested. If this statement survives the test, the related statement containing the construct receives indirect support.

The theory-then-research strategy and the related causal-process form of theory allow for more efficient research. This is because the theory governing the research at any point in time tells the investigator which the relevant data are, which is the crucial experiment to run. A causal-process theory also has the advantage that it offers an *explanation* of a process, although often invoking a "mechanism" (Atkinson 1982) which is not directly observable in order to do so. A set-of-laws theory simply reports what is known about a process at any moment.

In the case of some "theories" of SLA which ignore the research findings of other investigators, the theorist making such claims is operating with a theory-then-research strategy, and has posited a particular set of variables as those of relevance to understanding acquisition. The only way of refuting such a theory is to disprove it on its own terms. A way of "removing it from the competition" is to show that a second theory accounts for more data or accounts for the same data more economically.

It is also often the case that the research findings which are seemingly being ignored are the product of the research-then-theory strategy. Much of the research on input, for example, is clearly of this type, being descriptive and (occasionally) correlational, as we have seen. When this is so, it is also quite possible that, while true, these findings may be irrelevant in *fact,* not to mention irrelevant from the perspective of the researcher who has adopted the theory-then-research strategy. In other words, it is not enough for researchers to work at establishing "laws" of SLA, and then expect existing causal-process theories to be modified by their developers to take account of the "new data." Rather, the onus is on the researcher with the new "law" (in practice, rarely more than a generalization in SLA research to date) to *explain* his or her findings—and this means abandoning a preference for the research-then-theory strategy and developing a causal-process theory.

Most researchers of the linguistic environment in SLA are currently working with a research-then-theory strategy, and few seem ready to shift gears as yet. The main focus of research continues to be the *description* of speech adjustments to NNSs. Tentative generalizations are beginning to be drawn—on the basis of groups of completed studies—about such issues as which kinds of NSs adjust, which features are adjusted, when, where, triggered by what, and for what purpose (see, e.g., Long 1983c, Varonis and Gass 1982). People are looking at the data first, and working upward toward theoretical claims.

Given the limited state of knowledge in this area, as in so many others in SLA, it is an attitude that for some seems not only defensible but desirable. I take it to be, for example, the attitude Hatch (1979b) advocates when she urges researchers to build low-level or interlevel constructs before leaping to the whole picture, to put order, in other words, into one piece of the SLA puzzle at a time. It is, however, no more than an attitude, as I hope to have shown, and a strategy with certain well-known limitations.

NOTES

1. By "environmental contributions" is meant any linguistic or conversational experiences which serve to permit, facilitate, delay, or preempt language acquisition. Variables might include, for example, the amount of target language exposure learners receive, whether or not that exposure is to speech or conversation adjusted to their level of comprehension, and variation in the frequency and/or saliency of particular items in the input. Thus, one way of viewing formal language instruction is as the manipulation of frequency and saliency in input.

2. For use of a true experimental factorial design to study specific "within input" differences (the effect on acquisition of frequency of exposure to marked and unmarked forms), see Zobl (this volume).

3. This result supports an earlier claim (Long 1981a) to the effect that NS adjustments of the interactional structure of discourse are more important in promoting NNS comprehension than NS choice among linguistic forms in the input itself.

4. I would like to acknowledge useful discussions with Jan Hulstijn, Kenneth Hyltenstam, and Manfred Pienemann of methodological issues in conducting this type of study. For their enthusiastic cooperation throughout the study itself, I am indebted to Charles Mason, director of the University of Hawaii at Manoa's English Language Institute, and to the three ELI 70 instructors: Bill Beers, Ann Gleason, and Andy Harper. Special thanks are due Deborah Gordon for recording the lecturettes, and to Anne Ogama, Bill Riopel, and Michael Strong for their help with data collection.

5. An excellent model for such research can be found in the work of Sue Gass and Litsa

Varonis at the University of Michigan on the relative contribution of various factors to the comprehensibility of nonnative speaker speech (see, e.g., Gass and Varonis 1984).

6. For their support in conducting the second study, I am again indebted to Charles Mason, ELI director, and to the following ELI instructors and staff: Jason Alter, Peter Halpern, Andy Harper, Dave Rickard, Bill Riopel, and Joel Wiskin. I thank Graham Crookes and Charlie Sato for their help with data collection.

7. The following is based chiefly on my reading of P. D. Reynolds' book, *A Primer in Theory Construction* (Reynolds 1971). Other treatments of these and related issues include Blalock (1969), Cummins (1983), Harré (1972), Lakatos and Musgrave (1970), Mitroff and Kilman (1978), and Stinchcombe (1978). Discussions in the SLA literature include Candlin (1983), Larsen-Freeman (1983a), Schumann (1983), and Schachter (1983b). I thank Evelyn Hatch, Barbara Hawkins, and Charlie Sato for helpful (albeit critical) comments while I was writing this section.

8. Perhaps the following analogy is helpful. Conducting research to understand SLA is like trying to make a picture by assembling the pieces of a jigsaw puzzle, but when you have reason to suspect that the pieces in view have been mixed with pieces from other puzzles, too. (Some work considered part of the SL acquisition literature, for example, may really be relevant to understanding aspects of SL performance only.) You are faced, then, with two problems: trying to decide what the final picture looks like, and not knowing which the relevant pieces are. How to proceed?

Noticing that most pieces you can see are either light blue or dark green, one way is to work with pieces of just those colors, believing that they should fit together somehow, and to ignore pieces of different colors, as well as how the pieces you are working on might eventually fit into the whole picture. Gradually, small sections begin to take shape, and it looks as if you have assembled parts of a beach scene, with blue sky and green sea. You are still not sure, however, that the small segments of completed sky and sea really come from the same picture. This is the "research-then-theory" strategy.

Another way is to start by looking at the pieces in view, and to guess that the final picture will be a rural landscape, with blue sky and green fields. Starting work on (say) the fields, you put to one side any pieces whose shape or color have no obvious relevance to assembling a picture of a field. You assume that they are from another puzzle. This is the "theory-then-research" strategy. The projection it allows as to what the final picture is supposed to look like determines which pieces you select as relevant to work on (only those which could help build a picture of a rural landscape).

When the person working with the other strategy tells you that he or she has put together some pieces which show a green wave breaking on a shore, you are unimpressed because you think he or she is working (albeit successfully) on part of a different picture. Also, you think you know, from the outset, what the final picture will look like, whereas he or she is admittedly very vague about that. On the other hand, you are sometimes worried that you may be ignoring relevant parts of the puzzle, even though you cannot see how they could fit in, and even though the person working on those parts cannot tell you, either. The biggest frustration, or the magic of the exercise, depending how you look at it, is that neither of you will know who was right until one of you solves the puzzle.

23

FROM INPUT TO INTAKE: ON ARGUMENTATION IN SECOND LANGUAGE ACQUISITION

Michael Sharwood Smith
University of Utrecht

The key question to be addressed in this chapter is to what extent we allow multiple causation to enter into theoretical explanations of how input becomes intake, and how we may avoid trivializing the explanations by so doing. The tendency nowadays is to produce different, competing explanations for learner performance data as a fallback position when a monolithic (or "singular") explanation cannot be found. Illustration for this problem will be taken from a range of projects at Utrecht University which have investigated the complex behavior of adverbs in the interlanguage of Dutch (and other) learners of English. In essence, this constitutes a plea for a stronger theoretical underpinning for projects looking into the way in which second language acquirers interpret or ignore input for the purpose of developing a grammar or grammars of the target language.[1] Since ever-increasing amounts of data will never produce explanations of their own accord, it would seem eminently advisable to strengthen the theoretical framework that determines in advance how the results of a given investigation will be explained.

THEORETICAL BACKGROUND

If one were to characterize the dominant assumption in the field at the moment, it would be as follows:

> Acquirers of a second or other language process the linguistic input they are exposed to in such a way as to allow cognitive mechanisms the primary role in dictating what is and is not converted into stable mental representations of the target system, and ascribing a secondary (though not necessarily trivial) role to the environment.

This basic line conceals a number of important disagreements among scholars, one of those being the degree to which first or "other-than-target" language knowledge affects the way input becomes intake. One view, the creative construction view (see Dulay, Burt, and Krashen 1983 for a recent version), essentially minimizes the contribution of anything other than target language input provided in more or less naturalistic conditions. It is fairly well established that this view is supported first and foremost by evidence from "natural order" studies, indicating a relatively fixed order of morphemes in the development of target language ability by speakers of widely differing language backgrounds (cf. Dulay, Burt, and Krashen 1983). Not much convincing evidence is yet available where more complex areas of the grammar are concerned, even assuming the reliability of the findings for the grammatical morphemes: in either case, there are not infrequent appeals to "interference" or "transfer" as a partial and secondary explanation of the data (see, for example, Hakuta 1974, Butterworth and Hatch 1978, Anderson 1978, etc.). Occasionally investigators touch on the possibility of two apparently competing explanations actually being one, for example, viewing language transfer as a special case of overgeneralization (cf. Taylor 1976, for example) or of there being an *interaction* between different processes (cf. Hakuta 1974, Jordens 1977). For example, mother tongue influence has been viewed as a distractor or delaying factor (see Wode 1976). It is not usually the case that experiments are deliberately designed to investigate the interaction between different cognitive processes posited as part of a fully fledged theory of language acquisition. This is hardly surprising, since there exists no such theory in second or first language acquisition studies that seems able to yield ready-made and testable hypotheses about interaction. The closest one can get to a useful theory—in this specific sense of "useful"—which has tested over the last decade, is Krashen's model, based primarily as it first was on the distinction between *acquisition* and *learning.* This particular model has proved to be difficult to test (cf. Hulstijn 1982, for example), and testing by Krashen and his associates has led to a considerable downgrading of the monitor and the associated concept of *learned* knowledge such that the distinction is no longer as interesting as it used to be: (1) only some people "monitor" (in Krashen's sense),

(2) the scope for monitoring is very limited (to easy rules), and (3) it is not certain even then if monitoring actually takes place even when the learner is capable of employing learned knowledge. The concept of conscious learning is now discussed mainly in a teaching context where it is pointed out what factors are *not* relevant in second language development (see discussion in Dulay, Burt, and Krashen 1983). It might be argued that the transfer/overgeneralization distinction as discussed in Selinker's interlanguage model (Selinker 1972) provided a framework for the investigation of multiple causation. In fact, it has been more often used to categorize observed errors in different ways (into, for example, transfer errors, overgeneralization errors, and ambiguous errors; cf. Dulay and Burt 1974). Without elaborating the models it has been possible only to talk informally about how these processes posited in the theoretical framework might interact, and it is precisely that which makes multiple causation interesting. This means that those approaches that make claims about interaction and have a model to explain those interactions are more promising than those that do not.

THE UNRULY ADVERB

Adverbial placement is a hornet's nest for the linguist. Jackendoff speaks of the "unruly adverb" (Jackendoff 1972): for linguist and acquirer alike, there are a number of problems involved, in particular how to isolate the more *syntactic,* and the more *lexical* aspects of adverbial usage. Learners, like linguists, although in a different way, have to work out those positions in the sentence which can admit adverbials *in principle,* and they have to subcategorize each adverbial in their lexicon for the positions in which that particular adverbial can fit and under what circumstances. For example, adverbials, i.e., single-word or phrasal adverbs, may be placed in sentence-initial position but not, say, between a preposition and a following noun:[2]

1. *Clearly* he had fallen under the table.
2. He had fallen under [the clearly table].

The prepositional phrase (*under the table*) cannot be interrupted by an adverbial, but the verb complex (*had fallen*) can:

3. He [had *clearly* fallen] under the table.

The learner has nevertheless to know that *clearly* in this particular sense cannot be placed in front of the prepositional phrase:

4. * He had fallen *clearly* under the table.

Again, there are *canonical* or more usual positions for adverbials, and *marked* positions, i.e., positions which indicate some degree of focus or emphasis or positions which are filled when something in the context forces the adverb out of its normal position. One example of the latter situation is what is sometimes called heavy NP shift or "end weight" (cf. Quirk Greenbaum, Leech, and Svartvik 1972: 965). Although it is usually unacceptable in English to interrupt a transitive verb/direct object sequence, as in:

5. * He [stroked *tenderly* his girl friend].

When the object NP is "heavily" modified, either by a long string of pre- or postmodifiers or by a following relative clause, this unacceptable position becomes acceptable:

6. He stroked tenderly the girl *he had been so terribly rude to.*

7. He stroked tenderly the *never-to-be-forgotten* girl *of his nocturnal imaginings.*

These restrictions are not typical of languages like Finnish or Polish, where the word order is freer or of languages where the word order is at least as restricted as English, like Dutch and German.

THE PREAUXILIARY POSITION

There have been a number of Utrecht-based investigations into adverbial placement at various levels of proficiency ranging from early secondary school to late university levels. A variety of adverbials are involved, and in the case of one investigation, a cross-linguistic project, a variety of languages, i.e., Finnish, French, Polish, German, and Dutch, all being acquired in formal classroom environments (cf. S. Kellerman 1982, Bourgonje 1983).[3] An interesting type of error that occurs particularly in advanced Dutch learners is the placement of adverbials in the preauxiliary position. Examples of this taken from the written Dutch English error corpus (WDEEC) are listed in Table 23-1.

The pre-aux position is chosen in these spontaneous written composition data[4] and in some of the experimental data (see van de Weide 1982, Breveld and Geeman 1983, S. Kellerman 1982, Bourgonje 1983). The interesting aspect here is the fact that this is not a Dutch position chosen by Dutch learners. In other words, this deviant pattern is a candidate for explanations based on common or universal processes in the acquisition of English. For example, where Dutch learners may well produce 8, the literal translation, i.e., 9, is either marked, odd, or unacceptable:

8. ? She *always* can begin.
9.* Zij *altijd* kan beginnen. } Subj + Adv + Aux + main verb

PRE-AUX POSITION IN ENGLISH

Before considering alternative hypotheses to explain this trend in Dutch-English interlanguage, assuming for the moment it is a real trend, it is useful

TABLE 23-1 Examples of Pre-aux Adverbials in Dutch-English Interlanguage*

IL	*NL*
simply because I *hardly* had written in English	... I had *hardly* written
children *also* are the first victims	... are *also* the first victims
this *especially* is the case when ...	... this is *especially* the case
so that the undergraduates *too* would think that ...	... would *also* think ... would think ... *too.*
discover everything that *possibly* could be discovered	... could *possibly* be
their quarrels *usually* are caused by	... are *usually* caused ...
the students *each time* will have to consult their dictionaries	... will have to ... *each time.*
The question whether we *still* must consider the results	... we *must still*
because they *never* have learned to think	... have *never* learned
if this happens, most shops *surely* will be closed	... will *surely* be
the brush with which the star was painted *never* was lifted from the shield	... was *never* lifted

*These examples come from the *Written Dutch-English Error Corpus* and are taken from the 1976 sample. They were judged (by native speaker instructors) as incorrect or inappropriate in context.

Native speakers will note that by manipulating the IL examples, i.e., introducing stress and/or hesitation, these (IL) utterances can be made to sound normal. It is instructive in this regard to consider the Jacobson (1975) corpus analysis where pre-aux adverbs are indeed in the less preferred position in Modern English (see discussion elsewhere in this chapter; see also note 8).

to consider the facts in English. The closest we can get to a picture of how English works is to look at Sven Jacobson's corpus data, there being no neat rule or set of rules to account for the system involved (Jacobson 1975). Jacobson, it should be noted, has probably done more research into English adverbials than anyone else reported in the literature. Jacobson's data are drawn from a number of sources and are not necessarily a completely faithful picture of the input for the subjects in question, although there is little reason to think that it could have differed in significant ways. This might conceivably have been true if learners relied primarily on certain types of American newspaper English where there is a greater incidence of pre-aux adverbs. Even then, there is no sense in which pre-aux is the *dominant* English position for adverbials as a whole. Table 23-2 gives some samples taken from Jacobson (1975).

EXPLANATIONS

Assuming, for the sake of the argument, that this Dutch learner preference for pre-aux position *is* well established, the problem in a nutshell is this: why have Dutch learners opted a position which is "input-oblique" (cf. Sharwood Smith and Kellerman forthcoming) and also "L1-oblique"? They seem to have ignored both the input and their mother tongue knowledge. Explanations for present purpose may be grouped into those

TABLE 23-2 Pre-aux Versus Other Preverbal Placement in Modern (American) English

Examples taken from Table 23-1	*Number occurring in corpus*	*Pre-aux %*
surely	108	12.96
usually	605	10.25
still (= "*not* no longer")	1269	8.43
never	2301	6.98
possibly	97	3.09

Note the low frequency of *never* in pre-aux position despite idiomatic phrases such as "you never can tell." These American data are taken from Jacobson 1975.

supporting the creative construction hypothesis in its best-known form (CCH) and what may be called the *cross-linguistic hypothesis* (CLH) which extends the notion of creative construction to incorporate the recruitment of other tongue knowledge (in a manner to be determined by the theory).

CCH EXPLANATIONS

Although the CCH position is supported mainly via natural order evidence, it is not clear whether a natural order exists for all structures or whether order of acquisition is automatically of any great theoretical interest. If, however, we look at systematic deviance, and not just the way that target structures first establish themselves in performance (see Sharwood Smith and Kellerman forthcoming for the dangers involved in this approach), "developmental errors" (cf. Dulay and Burt 1974) may occur which defy explanations based on mother tongue influence, and which may be attested among learners with different language backgrounds (see, for example, evidence of such deviance in Anderson 1978, Bakker 1983). We may briefly list a set of arguments for the CCH:

1. Pre-aux position in Dutch main clauses is not permitted except where adverb is fronted to first position (e.g., "*often* can she hear you"). Hence a large range of IL sentences produced by Dutch learners has no equivalent in L1 (see example 8).

2. Pre-aux position *is* completely acceptable for some adverbs and acceptable but not canonical for some others. Hence there is evidence in the L2 input that pre-aux position can take adverbs. Deviance may be ascribed to a generalization of correct, or marked but *salient* pre-aux placement.[5]

3. Evidence for deviant pre-aux placement may be found in the English of non-Dutch learners (cf. S. Kellerman 1982, Bourgonje 1983).

4. Learners may avoid breaking up the aux-main verb complex (e.g., *may come, may have come, would have been coming*). This suggests a

structure-external-to-internal development of IL reminiscent of the negation literature (cf. Wode 1982 and also Clahsen 1980 on adverbials). Adverbs come at major syntactic breaks in sentence structure (see Keyser 1968); there may be an implicational hierarchy of development of permissible breaks for adverbs followed by all learners of English as a second/foreign language.

CLH EXPLANATIONS

Turning now to cross-linguistic explanations, it might seem at first sight, that is, in view of argument 1 (above), that there is little room for anything approaching a contrastive-analysis-hypothesis-based explanation. However, two arguments may be made in defense of indirect transfer, namely, arguments 5 and 6 (below).

5. Whereas Dutch main clauses typically disallow pre-aux adverbs (following the subject, in other words), it is the standard position in *subordinate* clauses and there are fairly well-established claims in the linguistic literature that Dutch, like German, displays its basic word order in the subordinate (SOV) configuration rather than in the main clause (one explanation entails main clause word order involving a movement of the verb out of its canonical final position into the derived, second position in the sentence).[6] In other words, L1 canonical orderings will be more likely to affect (form a model for) IL grammars than *derived* word order.

If argument 5 seems shaky thus formulated, it gains credibility if we consider some diachronic evidence from Jacobson 1981. Here the change from Old English, an SOV language like Dutch, into Modern English, an SOV language,[7] apparently implies an increasing preference for post-aux over pre-aux position. This might suggest, following a line of argumentation in the style of Zobl (e.g., Zobl 1980b) that the synchronic influence between SOV Dutch and SVO English in the developing bilingual may produce associated SOV/SVO effects also found in the synchronic development of English. If English is treated in some sense as an SOV language, under the influence of L1 Dutch, one of the results should be a *reduced* preference for post-aux placement and an *increased* preference[8] for the pre-aux position. Dutch and English are presumably close enough typologically to trigger such cross-linguistic correspondences in IL grammars. A careful examination of the linguistic consequences of *pre* versus *post* aux placement is of course necessary to explain why L2 English should be ignored or distorted in this way, and the diachronic linguistic literature may be illuminating here (see Jacobson 1981 for discussion). Argument 6 has to do with the status of modal verbs in Dutch and English:

6. What in native English are modal *auxiliaries* may not have the same status in learner (IL) grammars of Dutch and German learners, where modal verbs have more *main-verb* characteristics. Again Dutch is more like English in an earlier stage of (diachronic) development (cf. Lightfoot 1979a and b; 1982: 159). Hence in placing the adverb prior to the modal, learners may be treating English modals less as *aux* and more as main verbs, which (in L2 + L2) permit adverbs more regularly. The double status of *have* in English (aux and MV) may of course contribute to this confusion. Hence overgeneralized pre-aux placement may reflect an immature analysis of the target verb system. The form this immaturity takes or, at the very least, the extent to which it occurs, is influenced by cross-linguistic comparisons between L1 and L2 verb systems that the Dutch (or German) learner makes.[8]

INTERACTIONS

It may easily be appreciated that once the ban on cross-linguistic influence between grammars is lifted, all the arguments listed above may be put forward as part of a broader explanation based on different factors interacting cumulatively to produce a more or less "intense" effect as the case may be (see related discussion on language attrition in Sharwood Smith 1983a). In particular, the creation of (mental) grammars to organize second language input may, for every learner whatever mother or other tongues are involved, and at a given stage of development, open up a set of optional routes. The learners' psychotypology (in Kellerman's sense: Kellerman 1983), i.e., their personal assessment of the relationships pertaining between the target language and other known languages, will be one important factor in determining which of those routes will be followed. Put another way, the input from *outside,* the primary linguistic data, will be interpreted by the acquisition device together with input from *inside,* that is, the various structural templates provided by the mother or other tongue. The degree to which this takes place will depend in part on the perceived distance between the various (mature or partially mature) language systems already constructed by the learner for other languages. This, it should be emphasized, is something radically different from interference phenomena during the act of speech (or recognition) (see Sharwood Smith 1983b for further discussion) whereby the learner falls back on previous linguistic knowledge to cope with a given problem of communication at a given moment in time.

CONCLUSION

To sum up the main argument, what is needed is not more data, or *just* more data, but a richer theoretical base. Such a base, it is argued, has to accept the interaction of separate processes in the construction of L2 (IL) grammars as a fact of life, rather than seek for the one valid process or be satisfied with partial or alternative explanations. It also seems particularly unreasonable to give L2 input the unique role in explanations of intake and to deny internal input from other tongues. In any case, it is better to think of the acquisitional process as a consequence of a *conspiracy* of factors and deal with it in the following manner; i.e., by starting with three principal assumptions:

CONSPIRACY PRINCIPLES

1. Always assume a conspiracy: there is always more than one cause.
2. Some causes are more equal than others; there must be leading conspirators and hangers-on.
3. The theory, not the raw data, determines the identity and the status of those conspirators.

NOTES

1. It is important to distinguish input to the *comprehension* system where the listener/reader employs a whole network of linguistic and nonlinguistic knowledge sources, and input to the language acquisition, i.e., "grammar constructing" device, which will *not* be coextensive with the first type of input (cf. Sharwood Smith 1981).

2. Jackendoff identifies three basic surface positions in English: initial position, final position without intervening pause, and the position between subject and main verb (Jackendoff 1972: 49).

3. A joint paper specifically on trends in the cross-linguistic project is in preparation.

4. The WDEEC has been extracted from a corpus of written compositions (both in-class tests and home assignments): a study of the written compositions (Pankhurst and Sharwood Smith 1978) suggests that different kinds of learners basically adopt the same focus on communication and rely largely on their intuitions when writing essays irrespective of the fact that form (correctness) is paid attention to by the instructors and that (sometimes) they have ready access to reference books.

5. There may be a link between the stressed status of some pre-aux adverbs, the consequent salience of this position for the learner, in spoken English, and the *relatively* high frequency (compared with other styles of American or British English) of pre-aux adverbs in recent American newspaper style. Unless the emphatic placement of adverbials is taken into account in acceptability judgment tests for learners or native speakers (where canonical or unemphatic positions are being investigated), the results may be skewed in favor of pre-aux placement and may not reflect the picture presented by the corpus data. Subjects need to be trained to consider only the unstressed positions.

6. See de Haan 1976 and McCawley 1982 for alternative analyses which still posit SOV as the basic order in Dutch and German.

7. Care should be taken to distinguish surface word order typology which typically focuses on main clauses, and analyses based on some notion of deep word order. Surface word order analyses which reflect main clause word order configurations would not be relevant here.

8. These comparisons may or may not be performed at a level of conscious awareness.

24

INPUT: CHOOSING THE RIGHT STUFF[1]

Leslie M. Beebe
Teachers College
Columbia University

It is the contention of this chapter that studies of input in second language acquisition (SLA) must view nonnative speakers (NNSs) not simply as passive recipients of comprehensible or incomprehensible input from native speakers (NSs) but as active participants in choosing the target language models they prefer and thus acquiring "the right stuff" according to their values. In other words, this chapter views NNSs as having "input preferences" (or "model preferences") in the sense that they consciously or unconsciously choose to attend to some target language models rather than others. They do not simply acquire a language; they adopt a variety or varieties of that language. Second, input studies must report the complex of social-psychological variables that shape the NNS's preference for acquiring and using certain models over others in addition to reporting on traditional aspects of input, such as form, frequency, content, saliency, or comprehensibility. Finally, studies must interpret apparent model preferences in terms of existing or new social-psychological theories.

This chapter attempts to accomplish several purposes: (1) to create a fuller taxonomy of input preferences than the one suggested in Dulay, Burt, and Krashen (1982), i.e., peers over teachers, peers over parents, own social group over other social group; (2) to cite literature to demonstrate that exactly the opposite model preferences have also been documented; and (3) to propose an initial list of social-psychological theories and situational contexts that mediate model preferences in an attempt to sort out some regular principles which govern NNSs' preferences for some target language models over others.

Input preferences are viewed as marked or unmarked choices. The unmarked category is the more frequent, basic, or expected situation which tends to be the norm. The marked category is a secondary type of preference which is most likely to exist as an additional category, but not so likely to stand alone as the norm in a society at large or in an interpersonal interaction.

MODEL PREFERENCES: THE UNMARKED CHOICE

Table 24-1 gives us an overview of the most frequent claims in the literature regarding model preferences by either nonnative speakers learning a second language or native speakers adopting a second dialect.[2]

Peers over Teachers

Perhaps the most frequent claim about model preferences is for peers over teachers (see Dulay, Burt, and Krashen 1982). Labov (1972b) gives extensive evidence that his black subjects took as their model the Black English Vernacular (BEV) of their peer groups (the Jets, Thunderbirds, Cobras, and Aces) rather than the Standard English that is used and advocated by most teachers and administrators in a school setting and would be taught in ESL classes. Stewart (1964, discussed also in Dale 1976) reports that of the many black dialects of English in Washington, D.C., the lowest-status variety, or basilect, is used consistently only by small children. By the age of 7 or 8, however, children begin to shift toward a more prestigious variety. Stewart's claim is that the children are not influenced by school language (e.g., teachers' language) but by peer groups. It is a social rule that boys who want to join the older age group must modify their speech in this way. Milon (1975) describes a case of second language acquisition where a 7-year-old Japanese boy who immigrated to Hawaii learned the Hawaii Creole English dialect of his peers rather than the Standard English of his teachers. Milon claims that receptive knowledge of a teacher's language is acquired, but if children acquire productive competence, it is only at a later age. Milon's data are important because he also demonstrates that current peers assume influence rapidly over former peers. The Japanese child first acquired the Hawaii Creole English of his peers in the low-income, welfare-dominated neighborhood where he lived. However, when he moved to a middle-class neighborhood where his peers spoke Standard English, he was found to be using Standard English after 1 year.

TABLE 24-1 Target Language Model Preferences

Unmarked choice	*Marked choice*
Peers over teachers:	Teachers/parents/adults/own ethnic group over peers:
Labov (1972b) black gangs' BEV over SE	Labov (1972b) lames
Stewart (1964) black children	Wolfram (1973) lames
Milon (1975) Japanese child, HCE and SE of peers	Subjective reaction tests
Wolfram (1973) Puerto Ricans' BEV	LaFerriere (1979) own ethnic Chinese group over Irish peers
Peers over parents:	
Hewitt (1982) British black youths of Caribbean origin	
L1 loss in second- and third- generation immigrants	
Labov (1972b) New Jersey middle-class white children	
Stewart (1964) black children learning BEV in Washington, D.C.	
Poplack (1978) Puerto Ricans learning BEV despite low contact	
Own social group over other social group:	Other social group over own social group:
Labov (1972b) black gangs' BEV	Wolfram (1973)
Fishman (1966) language loyalty	Reinstein and Hoffman (1972)
LaFerriere (1979) ethnic stratification in Boston	Poplack (1978)
Beebe (1981) Chinese Thai ethnic identity markers	Hewitt (1982) white using black creole
Hewitt (1982) black adolescents	
Benton (1964) Maori child	
Friends over nonfriends:	Nonfriends over friends:
Poplack (1978) Puerto Rican 6th graders	Poplack (1978) nonreciprocal friendship
Milroy (1980) social networks in Belfast	Labov (1972a) influence despite hostility
Labov (1972b) black gangs	
Hewitt (1982) white using black creole of friends	
High-contact over low-contact:	Low-contact over high-contact:
Wolfram (1973) Puerto Rican adolescents	Poplack (1978) Puerto Ricans learning BEV over SE
Reinstein and Hoffman (1972) Puerto Rican 4th graders	
Taylor, Meynard, and Rheault (1977) French Canadian university students	
Higher-prestige over lower-prestige:	Lower-prestige over higher-prestige:
French preference for English over "American" language	Labov (1972b) black gangs
Subjective reaction tests	Poplack (1978) Puerto Ricans' BEV
Labov (1972b) lames	Wolfram (1973) Puerto Ricans' BEV
Day (1980) SE over Hawaii Creole	

Peers over Parents

The literature also claims a general preference for peers over parents. This preference is evident in second- and third-generation immigrants who acquire the language of their peers rather than the language of their parents. They may acquire both languages, but if only one is acquired in the host country, it is virtually always the language of their peers, not their parents' native language. Hewitt (1982) cites interviews with black British adolescents of Caribbean origin who discuss their parents' objections (particularly mothers') to their using creole. One of his informants explicitly states that his mother considers creole a bad influence socially and educationally; however, he says he likes to use creole because:

> I feel black and I'm proud of it, to speak like that. That's why when I speak it, I feel better than when I'm talking like now. (p. 220)

Labov (1972b) found that middle-class New Jersey children of New York City-born parents did not drop postvocalic /r/ as did their parents, but rather pronounced /r/ as did their peer group. Beebe (unpublished data) found that 20 Puerto Rican third-grade children in a bilingual school on the edge of New York City reported a preference for English over Spanish, regardless of enrollment in a bilingual or a monolingual program. The accuracy of self-report preferences can be challenged, but it is nevertheless interesting that the stated preference was never for the home language. Poplack (1978) found that Puerto Rican children adopted the language of their peers over the language of their parents (or the school). Her data were particularly interesting, however, in that unlike Wolfram, who found a correlation between extent of contact with blacks and adoption of BEV variants, Poplack found that despite very low contact with blacks in school or in the neighborhood, Puerto Rican children displayed significant BEV influence. Analysis of the speech of one mother for each peer group indicated that the children were not using mothers as models.

Own Social Group over Other Social Group

Another set of model preferences is for ingroup over outgroup—i.e., for one's own social group over some other social group. Labov (1972b) demonstrates the importance of sounding black for black adolescents, despite societal pressure to conform to the standard English of white middle-class society. LaFerriere (1979) illustrates phonological stratification along ethnic group lines in Boston's Italian, Irish, and Jewish communities. Hewitt's black adolescent subject, C.A., explicitly indicates his preference for his own ethnic group's speech over a standard dialect, saying:

> I just kind of feel that as a black I should speak it . . . say I'm walking the street and a black man goes to me, "Dread, d'you have the time?" if I turn round and say, "No. Sorry, I haven't got the time," I'm gonna sound funny. So I go, "No, man, mi na got de time. Sorry Dread." (1982, p. 220)

Benton describes a Maori child's explicit statement to a teacher concerning preference for own ethnic group: "Maoris say, 'Who's your name?' so that's what I say" (1964, p. 93, cited in Richards 1974: 75).

There may be a hierarchy of preferences. For example, ethnic group may outweigh peer group in some instances. LaFerriere (1979) found that a 15-year-old Chinese high school girl did not use a stigmatized variant that her two close friends who were Irish used, despite the fact that all three grew up together and had similar class backgrounds and the same college aspirations. LaFerriere hypothesizes that ethnic group has a relatively greater influence than peer group when the two conflict.

Friends over Nonfriends

Another category of model preference is for friends over nonfriends. Poplack (1978) studied the self-reported friendship patterns of Puerto Rican sixth-grade children. Several Puerto Ricans named a black student, John, as one of their best friends, although he did not name them in return. This reported friendship is seen as one of the explanations for the prevalence of BEV variants in the Puerto Rican boys' speech. Milroy's study of social networks (1980) provides data from adults in Belfast, Ireland, to support this type of model preference. Adults conformed more closely to vernacular norms if they belonged to a local community network, and the degree of conformity was correlated to the level of integration into the network. Milroy's work with adults confirms the findings of Labov (1972b) with black adolescent gangs, which are, of course, friendship networks.

High-Contact over Low-Contact Group

Wolfram (1973) emphasized the importance of extent of contact, claiming that Puerto Ricans who had a high level of contact with black speakers displayed greater use of BEV variants than those who had a low level of contact. Reinstein and Hoffman (1972) studied 30 Puerto Rican fourth graders and found that those who interacted with blacks adopted features of black speech and were more similar to blacks on Gross' pronunciation test than to Puerto Ricans who did not interact with blacks. Taylor, Meynard, and Rheault (1977) studied 246 French Canadian university students and found a correlation between proficiency and extent of personal contact with English Canadians.

Higher-Prestige Group over Lower-Prestige Group

In general, we might say that model preferences are for a higher-prestige group than one's own rather than a lower-prestige group, if one adopts the features of another group or class. Thus, we might expect NNSs to adopt the

English of target language (TL) speakers who are of their own prestige level or a higher level. In fact, upper-middle-class ESL students frequently admit to rejecting TL dialects they consider stigmatized or lower than their own. Eisenstein (1982) found that adult ESL learners develop an early sensitivity to dialects. In France, where British English has greater prestige than American Standard English, an experienced American ESL teacher, who had received positive evaluations in previous positions, was dismayed to find that 25 French businessmen complained loudly about her speaking "American" and not "English." Then, one by one, all of them dropped her class within the space of a month (personal communication). Although second language learners frequently break the unwritten sociolinguistic rules of the TL, it is much less common that they unwittingly acquire nonstandard dialects or dialects of much lower socioeconomic status. This may be due to extent of contact, but most likely prestige level is also a factor.

MODEL PREFERENCES: THE MARKED CHOICE

Although there seems to be a fair amount of evidence for model preferences such as peers over teachers, peers over parents, current peers over former peers, ingroup over outgroup, higher-prestige over lower-prestige group, high-contact over low-contact group, friends over nonfriends, there also exists evidence for just the opposite preferences. In this section, I shall briefly summarize some of the support for the less common, i.e., marked, preferences. I shall argue that the marked choice is just as principled and systematic as the unmarked choice. Both kinds of model preferences are governed by at least two types of factors: (1) internal feelings and motivations, and (2) external social and situational factors.

Parents and Teachers over Peers

Whereas evidence was previously presented to illustrate a preference for peers over teachers and parents and for own social group over other social group, Labov (1972b) and Wolfram (1973) discuss at length the "lames"—the black adolescents who do well in school, who are not gang members, who listen to their mothers, and who learn the Standard English of their teachers and the white mainstream society. Lames do not find primary influence in the black peer groups, and demonstrate that parents' and teachers' values can be preferred over peers' values. It seems that lames look to adults over peers and follow rules of the other ethnic group rather than their own in some instances. Lames have higher reading achievement than peer-group members, greater use of educated phonological markers (e.g., [r]), and lower use of stigmatized variants like final [t]/[d] deletion (Labov 1972b).

Whereas black peer group members shift to white standard norms of [t]/[d] deletion when they become adults, lames start out following the norm for adults and whites. Thus age is one of the social factors that affects model preferences. Most of the research showing peer preference is related to children ages 9 to 18 who are most subject to peer influence or to young children in grades K to 6 who display striking attitude shifts (e.g., Day 1980, Hamayan and Tucker 1980, Poplack 1978). Sex is also reported to be a factor which affects model preferences. Some suggest that males, more than females, are influenced by peer groups (see Labov 1972a, Stewart 1964, Dale 1976, Milroy 1980, Trudgill 1972).

Other Ethnic Group over Own Ethnic Group

Several studies have documented the preference for another ethnic group over one's own as a speech model. Wolfram (1973), Reinstein and Hoffman (1972), and Poplack (1978), while illustrating unmarked choices of peers over parents and teachers, also demonstrated that bilingual Puerto Rican adolescents and preadolescents make the marked choice for another ethnic group (blacks) rather than their own. Wolfram concluded that contact was the reason, whereas Poplack argued that her Puerto Rican subjects had almost no contact with blacks and that the covert prestige of blacks was the explanation. On the other hand, they may have made a choice for an ethnic/racial group which seemed more similar to their own than the white mainstream group did. Hewitt (1982) documented the use of black creole by white adolescents and demonstrated that marked preferences exist for the other ethnic group over one's own ethnic group. The study also showed that preferences conflict. Steve, a white adolescent creole user, used creole because all his friends were black. When he got to be 15, there were more opportunities to have contact with white boys, and he switched back to standard British English under pressure from a black friend who had said "Well, you sound stupid, a white person speaking patois" (p. 228). In the case of Steve, the marked choice of other race over own race was outweighed by the choice of friends over nonfriends. Age, too, played a factor, since Steve at age 17 said his own black creole use represented an immature stage of his life.

Nonfriends over Friends

Poplack's (1978) Puerto Rican subjects acquired the Black English of speakers whom they considered to be friends but who did not reciprocally consider them friends. Admittedly, in some sense, there was still a choice for friends in that the subjects felt friendship toward the children they named as friends.

However, we seem to be dealing more properly with prestige and feelings of identification rather than friendship, since friendship is normally thought of as reciprocal. In this sense, the children made the marked choice for nonfriends over friends. Moreover, it has also been observed (Labov 1972a) that even a group which shows open hostility toward another group often adopts many linguistic features of that group. Labov makes reference to cases observed on the Lower East Side of Manhattan in New York City and in the Highland Park section of Detroit where blacks exerted considerable influence on the speech of whites although the two groups were engaged in open conflict. And in the white, Irish, working-class community of Inwood at the northern tip of Manhattan, where hostility toward blacks was expressed and where contact was presumably low, it was found that patterns of merger in front vowels reflected not those of the white community in Manhattan at large, but rather those of the Black English Vernacular.

CONCLUSION

In conclusion, it is argued that when we study the question of what input becomes intake in SLA, we must study the feelings or motivations behind preference for or rejection of various target models and the social and situational factors that shape preferences. (The interaction of such factors is schematized in Figure 24-1.) Evidence has been given that learners actively (though not necessarily consciously) choose what input models to attend to, and that, therefore, we must understand the motivational dynamics behind their choices. Moreover, as has been shown, second language model preferences cannot be categorically claimed for peers over teachers, peers over parents, or own social group over other social group, as in Dulay, Burt, and Krashen (1982), because the opposite preferences exist, and the decision between the two depends upon many variables. (See Tables 24-2 and 24-3.)

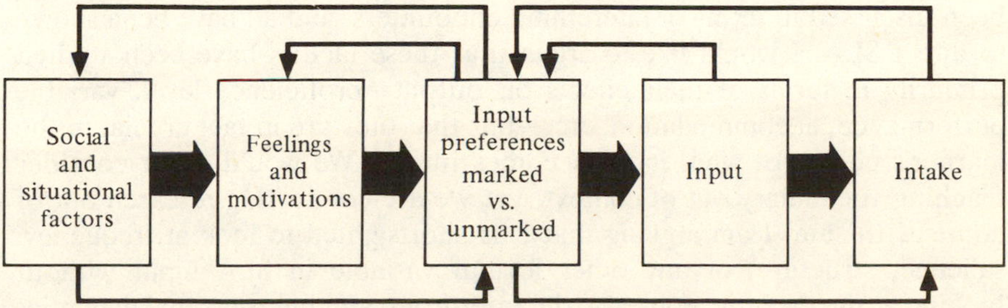

FIGURE 24-1 Factors Shaping Input Preferences and Ultimate Intake

The argument for studying motivations is also based on the notion that second language acquisition involves an intergroup encounter; it requires learners to go outside their own group boundaries—linguistically and also culturally in the majority of ESL situations. Therefore, theories that deal with intergroup dynamics, ethnic group identification, reference groups, and ethnic boundary maintenance are highly relevant to the field of second language acquisition.

TABLE 24-2 Feelings and Motivations Affecting Input Preferences

Group identity theories: membership
Solidarity (Milroy 1982)
Ethnocentrism (Gardner and Lambert 1972)
Ethnic group affiliation (Gatbonton-Segalowitz 1975)
Loyalty (Fishman 1966)
Social identity theory (Tajfel 1974, 1978)
Ethnolinguistic identity theory (Giles, Bourhis, and Taylor 1977; Beebe and Giles 1984)
Intergroup theory (Giles and Byrne 1982)
Reference group theory (Weber 1964, Merton 1968, Lamy 1979)
Speech accommodation theory (Giles and colleagues)
Similarity attraction (Byrne 1969)
Social exchange (Homans 1961)
Causal attribution (Kelly 1967, Jones and Davis 1965)
Intergroup distinctiveness (Tajfel 1974, 1978)
Psychological Reactance theory (Brehm 1972, Ryan 1979)
Motivational orientation (Gardner and Lambert 1972)
Instrumental
Integrative

Solidarity (Milroy 1982), ethnocentrism (Gardner and Lambert 1972), feelings of identification (Gatbonton-Segalowitz 1975, Goldstein 1984), loyalty (Fishman 1966), social identity theory (Tajfel 1974, 1978), ethnolinguistic identity theory (Giles, Bourhis, and Taylor 1977; Beebe and Giles 1984), and intergroup dynamics (Giles and Byrne 1982) are diverse concepts and theories, but they have one thing in common: the concept of membership. All have been discussed in terms of interethnic encounters, and all have been shown to affect SLA. I would like to argue that these factors have been studied primarily in terms of their effects on output—proficiency level, variable performance, accommodation, etc.—but that they are in fact crucial in the learner's choice of what input becomes intake. We would never consider teaching vocabulary out of context; yet we are conducting research out of context. In sum, I am arguing that it is shortsighted to look at frequency, salience, structure, or any other formal variable in SLA input without looking at the essential context—the intergroup and interpersonal dynamics that constitute the affective domain.

Milroy (1982) makes a plea for sociolinguistics to incorporate into one model both the status-oriented and the solidarity-oriented functions of lan-

TABLE 24-3 Social and Situational Factors Affecting Input Preferences

Age:
Peers vs. teachers/parents/adults
Labov (1972b) black gangs
Stewart (1964) blacks
Wolfram (1973) Puerto Ricans
Standard vs. vernacular
Day (1980)
Own social group vs. other social group
Hewitt (1982) white's black creole ended at 17 years
Sex:
Peers vs. teachers/parents/adults
Trudgill (1972)
Milroy (1980)
Labov (1972b)
Stewart (1964)
Dominance (Gaies 1982, Schumann 1978a)
Ethnolinguistic vitality (Giles and Byrne 1982):
Status
Demographics
Institutional support
Societal values and prestige norms (Labov 1966, 1972a, 1972b)
Amount of contact (Wolfram 1973)
Ethnic mix in peer group (Parkin 1977)
Emergent vs. stabilized bilingualism (Parkin 1977)
Attention to speech (Labov 1970, Tarone 1979)
Additive vs. subtractive environment (Gardner and Lambert 1972)

guage variation. Beebe (1983a, 1983b) has attempted to integrate both these functions into her proposed sociolinguistic paradigm of SLA. Both status and solidarity are important for the study of input preferences. We must attempt to determine whether the second language learner's personal values are primarily status-oriented or solidarity-oriented and what situational variables affect orientation. I would like to hypothesize that preference for higher-prestige models and teacher models is most likely status-oriented, whereas preference for peer models, friends, and own ethnic group models is solidarity-oriented. Whether status or solidarity takes priority is a function of personal values which are, in turn, highly affected by social and situational context.

NOTES

1. I would like to express my appreciation to Martha Cummings and Lynn Broquist, doctoral students at Columbia University Teachers College, whose bibliographical research and comments were extremely helpful.

2. The review of the literature in Dulay, Burt, and Krashen (1982) on model preferences

was useful as a starting point for the taxonomy and list of references which appear in Table 24-1. Also very helpful was the review of the literature done by Lynn Goldstein, a doctoral student at Columbia University Teachers College, in a dissertation prospectus in preparation (1984) on the role of contact vs. feelings of ethnic identification in second language acquisition.

25

SOME INPUT CONSIDERATIONS FOR WORD ORDER IN FRENCH L1 AND L2 ACQUISITION

Patsy M. Lightbown
Concordia University

Alison d'Anglejan
Université de Montréal

Like other important issues—such as the role of L1 transfer in L2 acquisition—input has had its ups and downs as a focus of research, and there have been extreme views regarding its role. At one extreme is the view that "what goes in comes out." It is this view which continues to dominate much second language teaching in which the language is presented in graduated bits for cumulative consumption. At the other extreme is a view which treats input factors as irrelevant. A number of things may contribute to this view. One is the fact that learners produce "creative" language (including so-called errors) which could not have been copied from the input. In addition, L1 researchers have not consistently found positive correlations between frequency of occurrence in the input and order of acquisition. These facts, together with a resurgence of interest in Chomsky's view of language and language acquisition, have led some researchers to consider that for both L2 and L1 development, acquisition is "triggered" by input but is also, in some sense, independent of input. (See Cook, 1985, for a review of this view in L2 research.)

It is perhaps significant that this conference on language input should be held now at the University of Michigan, just as there was a conference held in the same place a few years ago on transfer—a sign that, for input as for transfer, researchers are leaving simplistic and extreme views behind and looking instead at questions such as *when, how,* and *in what aspects* language acquisition is influenced by input factors.

The present study was motivated by our intuition that some aspects of the acquisition of French which might be claimed to confirm certain hypothetical universals of language acquisition could as easily be shown to support a hypothesis that the observed output phenomena reflect input phenomena. The similarity between input and output may not always be apparent, because comparisons are often made on the basis of descriptions obtained from grammar books or introspection rather than from observations of the language which learners are actually exposed to. In this chapter, we wish to report on some observations about word-order phenomena in three aspects of French: interrogation, negation, and the canonical status of subject-verb-object (SVO).

The corpora for analysis were samples of informal speech in which language learners of French and native speakers interacted. There is a corpus from two 2-year-old L1 children's spontaneous interaction with their mothers, play interactions with two 7-year-old L2 learners and an adult native speaker, and interviews with two L2 adults. (For more information on the child studies see Lightbown 1977, 1980. For further details of the adult study, see below and Painchaud, d'Anglejan, and Vincent 1982.)

INTERROGATION

It is a well-documented fact that learners of English—L1 and L2—pass through a period in which they use declarative word order for interrogative sentences. Learners of French L1 and L2 have also been observed to use uninverted word order (accompanied by rising intonation in yes/no questions) to formulate questions. It is at first reasonable to assume that these learners have overgeneralized declarative word order. On the basis of a comparison with data from English and German, one might claim that this aspect of French L2 interlanguage is based on an operating principle such as that proposed by Slobin (1973) to avoid the rearrangement of linguistic units. However, as we will demonstrate below, careful study of the input which learners of French actually receive, as distinct from that which some grammarians, linguists, and native speakers would lead us to believe they receive, reveals that input cannot be discounted as the most parsimonious explanation for the learners' use of this form.

There are, to simplify a bit, three ways of forming questions in French: (1) the inversion of subject and verb or subject and auxiliary[1] for both yes/no and information-eliciting questions:

Veux-tu prendre un taxi?
(want-you to-take a taxi)[2]
Allez-vous au cinéma?

(go-you to-the movie)
Pourquoi vient-il si tard?
(why comes-he so late?)

(2) the use of declarative word order, with rising intonation for yes/no questions:

Tu veux prendre un taxi?
(you want to-take a taxi)

or with a preposed question word for information-eliciting questions:

Pourquoi tu veux faire ça?
(why you want to-do that)

(3) placing the question formula *est-ce que* (literally, "*is it that?*") before the subject—auxiliary or verb unit:

Est-ce que tu viens avec nous?
(*question* you come with us)
Quand est-ce que sa mère viendra?
(when *question* his/her mother will-come)

It should be noted that when *est-ce que* is used, the principal constituents of the sentence (subject-auxiliary or subject-verb) are not rearranged.

In her study of question forms produced by four French L1 3-year-olds, Redard (1976) documents the prevalence of declarative forms, showing the virtual nonoccurrence of any form other than the declarative forms in the children's speech. Redard notes that it is not surprising to find no incidence of the use of *est-ce que* in the children's speech, since that form is rarely used by adults and only in specific situations such as in telephone conversations, in front of an audience, or in *conversations with nonnative speakers* (p. 104). She states, on the basis of observations and recordings of everyday conversations among adult native speakers, that the only form used for yes/no questions in conversations is declarative word order with rising intonation. As additional confirmation of her observations, she notes a study by Behnstedt (1973), who reported that 90 percent of the questions in a vast sample drawn from various regions of France were uninverted yes/no questions with rising intonation.

In his quantitative study of the use of interrogatives in "everyday spoken French" in selected contemporary French plays, Terry (1970) reported that uninverted questions accounted for 62.18 percent of all questions in a corpus of 4365 items (see Table 25-1). Furthermore, when yes/no questions were considered separately, the dominance of uninverted questions was even more pronounced (85.54 percent) and the *est-ce-que* form, which most grammars imply is the common form in colloquial French, accounted for no more than 3.22 percent of yes/no questions tabulated. As can be seen from Table 25-1, inverted questions forms were significantly represented in information-eliciting questions (52.11 percent) only.

TABLE 25-1 Distribution of Question Forms in Corpus Analyzed in Terry (1970: 83)

Question types	% of total
All questions (N = 4365):	
Inverted	23.87
Popular forms (uninverted)	62.18
Est-ce que	13.95
Yes-no questions (N = 3016):	
Inverted	11.24
Intonation change (uninverted)	85.54
Est-ce que	3.22
Information-eliciting questions (N = 1349):	
Inverted	52.11
Incomplete syntactic transformation (uninverted)	9.93
Est-ce que	37.96

In the speech addressed to child learners of French L2 and in the speech which they produce, there is a virtual absence of inverted forms—even in information-eliciting questions. Lightbown (1980) reported that the children in her study used inversion only in a few rote-learned questions or, even less frequently, in sentences with *be* or a modal, such inversion being consistent with rules for inversion in English, their native language. The adult interlocutor who interacted with these learners rarely used inversion for forming questions: "The exceptions, as in the children's speech, were units such as *où est* ______ and *est-ce que* ______. The other cases include a small number of sentences in the passé composé, e.g., 'as-tu terminé?' (have you finished) where the auxiliary inversion leaves the salient full verb in its postsubject position (. . . you finished?). Overwhelmingly, for both yes/no and Q-word (information-eliciting) questions in the native speaker's speech, declarative word order was left unchanged or *est-ce que* was added to form the questions." (p. 168)

Pourqoi il fait ça?
(why he does that?)
Comment tu prononces ton nom?
(how you pronounce your name?)
Où est-ce qu'il est?
(where is-it that he is?)

In order to gain some information about the input that adult L2 learners of French receive, we analyzed transcripts of interviews with two Indo-Chinese immigrants in Montreal. The transcriptions were part of a corpus gathered in 1981 to provide information about the French L2 performance of 36 immigrants at two times: (1) as they entered the final week of a 900-hour intensive FSL program, and (2) 6 months later (see Painchaud, d'Anglejan, and Vincent 1982). The half-hour interviews, focusing on the subjects' experiences before and after arriving in Montreal, were conducted by an anthropological linguist who was experienced in natural speech elicitation techniques.

The results of the analysis of the interviewer's questions to the adult immigrant subjects are shown in Table 25-2. These data are of interest from several points of view. A first point, of anecdotal interest, is the high proportion of yes/no questions (79 percent) addressed to these nonnative speakers, in spite of the fact that it was agreed in advance with the interviewer that she should try to ask information-eliciting questions in order to obtain a good sample of the subjects' interlanguage. This figure is even higher than the 69 percent reported by Terry as the proportion of yes/no questions in his corpus and approaches the 90 percent figure found in the Behnstedt (1973) study cited above. Second, these data confirm the very rare occurrence of inverted question forms in the input addressed to language learners. The few which did occur were almost all more or less formulaic, such as "Quel âge avez-vous?" Third, the data confirm Redard's observation that the *est-ce que* form, infrequently used in face-to-face interactions between native speakers, is used quite frequently in interactions with foreigners. In the first interview, two-thirds (66.4 percent) and in the second interview nearly half (48 percent) of the questions were formed with *est-ce que*. This high-frequency usage can be explained within a discourse-analysis framework: The native speakers appear to be using *est-ce que* as a clear device for alerting the nonnative speakers to the fact that a question is about to be asked. Using what can probably be considered a preposed *free-form* rather than a sentence-internal rearrangement of elements would seem to reflect a general type of simplification which is widely observed in both L2 interlanguage and in "foreigner talk" (Wode 1978). It is striking, however, that, according to Redard, *est-ce que* is not used in addressing children. This difference between caretaker speech and foreigner talk will be an interesting area for future investigation.

The importance of the above findings is emphasized when we examine what grammarians have to say about French question forms. We selected at random some grammar books from our shelves—pedagogical, descriptive, and prescriptive grammars which L2 learners and teachers frequently consult. We found such definitions as the following from David (1976):

> A sentence is in the interrogative when one forms a question. The pronoun (subject) is placed after the verb or one places at the beginning of the affirmative sentence an interrogative expression (est-ce que).

TABLE 25-2 Distribution of Native Speaker's Question Forms in Interviews with Two Adult Speakers of French L2

	Subject 1		Subject 2			
	*Interview**		*Interview**			
Question forms	*A*	*B*	*A*	*B*	*Total*	%
All questions (N = 400):						
Inverted	3	1	0	0	4	1
Uninverted	27	47	32	63	169	42
Est-ce que	53	42	70	62	227	57
	83	90	102	125	400	
Yes/no questions (N = 317):						
Inverted	0	1	0	0	1	—
Uninverted	19	39	31	58	147	46
Est-ce que	40	29	55	45	169	53
	59	69	86	103	317	
Information questions (N = 83):						
Inverted	3	0	0	0	3	4
Uninverted	8	8	1	5	22	26
Est-ce que	13	13	15	17	58	70
	24	21	16	22	83	

*Interview A was conducted at the end of the 7-month period of intensive instruction; interview B took place 6 months later.

Viendrez-vous?
(will-come you)
Est-ce que vous viendrez?
(Question you will-come)
(p. 51, our translation)

No mention is made of the declarative form with rising intonation. However, in another section of the book dealing with registers, the following form appears in a quiz in which readers are to identify the register to which it belongs:

Beatrice est au courant de la liaison avec Karine?
(Beatrice is aware of the relationship with Karine?)

Surprisingly, the correct response is "literary" register—the highest of the four alternatives proposed.

More pertinent information is provided by Grévisse's *Bon Usage* (1975) under the heading "La proposition interrogative":

The direct question is characterized either simply by intonation: in principle it ends on a rising note: the voice rises progressively until the accented word which calls for the response: *Tu pars déjà?* or by a change in construction *Pars-tu déjà?*—or by the use of *est-ce que* and intonation *Est-ce que tu pars déjà?* (p. 139, our translation).

A fuller discussion of subject placement in questions is provided in a later section where, after describing the inverted question, the author discusses the word-order variations which occur in information word questions:

> one frequently hears in everyday usage, direct questions with *neither subject inversion nor rising intonation*[3] at the end
>
> Quel âge vous avez?
> (what age you have? = how old are you?)
> Où vous travaillez?
> (where you work)
> p. 147, our translation).

Grévisse also deals with the *est-ce que* form, but although he provides more reliable information regarding French question forms than do other authors of prescriptive grammars, he still provides no information regarding their relative frequency in the language.

Valdman (1975) observed that French L2 learners receiving formal instruction in the absence of informal contact with the language also used uninverted question forms even though, he says, their teacher never did. However, it may be that he was considering the formal instructional portion of teacher-student interaction and not the interpersonal or nondidactic classroom input which these students received. It would be interesting to have more information about the total input the students received and whether in fact their total input did contain only questions with inversion. It would also be important to have quantitative information about the number of the students' so-called inverted questions which were formed with *est-ce que,* which as has been pointed out, may be considered a preposed free form, as it does not alter the SVO word order in the body of the sentence.

As we have seen from the frequency data provided by Terry and the subjects from the Lightbown, Redard, as well as the Painchaud, d'Anglejan corpora, the various question forms are by no means evenly distributed in the everyday spoken French to which learners might be exposed or in the speech directed specifically to them by native speakers. Since uninverted forms and questions with *est-ce que* massively predominate over inverted forms in all quantitative studies we have examined, it is not surprising to find that declarative questions predominate in the early interlanguage of French L2 learners. The point we must stress here is that we could not have reached this conclusion on the basis of French textbooks, the formal descriptions of French commonly provided by linguists or grammarians, or even on native speakers' intuitions about their use of inversion, an intuition which is influenced by exposure to the written language and by formal language instruction. For example, the adult native speaker who interacted with the French L2 children in the Lightbown (1980) study was astonished at the results of the analysis, which showed the virtual absence of inversion in her information-eliciting questions. And the native speaker in the adult L2 study, fully prepared to ask open-ended questions, produced few question-word questions (21 percent over all), and her yes/no questions were virtually all *est-ce que* questions or declarative forms with rising intonation.

It is worthwhile to consider briefly some of the assumptions made about the relationship between *English* learner language and the input which English L1 and L2 learners are exposed to. While there are some discourse contexts in which English does permit declarative word order in yes/no questions (Vander Brook, Schlue, and Campbell 1977) subject-auxiliary inversion is generally assumed to be obligatory. Furthermore, uninverted *wh* questions are usually unacceptable to speakers of standard English. Nevertheless, there is input from English which could also be perceived by learners as evidence that uninverted word order is permitted.

It was noted in the Lightbown study of child L2 French that some sentences which do have inversion can *appear not to* because of rapid speech and sentence stress. For example,

As-*tu fini?*
(have-you finished?)
Veux-*tu venir?*
(want-you to-come?)

Similarly, in English, uninverted word order in questions might be explained by the learners' perception of questions as having declarative form because the auxiliary—particularly *do*—is unstressed in most affirmative interrogatives, thus difficult to hear in ordinary rapid speech. For example,

(Do) you have any blue ones?
What time (do) they get home?

In fact, native speakers sometimes delete the sentence-initial *do* in yes/no questions, even though, when asked to repeat or speak more slowly, they will always include it. Brown (1968) in an L1 study and Ravem (1974) in his L2 study have both pointed out the importance of looking for "strong" evidence of noninversion, for example,

What you can show me?

where the uninverted subject and auxiliary are both clearly present, as well as looking at "weak" evidence, for example,

Where you put the puzzles?

where absence or deletion of the auxiliary is as good a description as noninversion. The clearest examples of noninversion are questions where *do* is inserted but not inverted. For example,

Why you do have that one?

The reduced or deleted *do* in the input may not account for, but may contribute to, the late acquisition of *do* relative to other auxiliaries. Its low semantic weight—its role as a bearer of grammatical rather than informational content—no doubt contributes to it as well. However, one would expect to find differences between literate and nonliterate, tutored and nontutored learners with respect to their perceptions of such input. Once the sentence-initial auxiliary is discovered, learners sometimes over "do" it. Most teachers and researchers are aware of the phenomenon of students placing an auxiliary in sentence-initial position, leaving the rest of the sentence intact (exactly parallel to placing *est-ce que* before a French declarative to form a question. For example,

Do you are fixing my boots?
Do you can come?

Other auxiliaries also occur in this way:

Is this is my ice cream?

Thus some cases of apparent inversion in English learner language may reflect the learner's use of a sentence-initial question marker rather than actual inversion. In summary, there is substantial evidence from French and some evidence from English that the appearance and persistence of uninverted questions in interlanguage could be at least partially explained by the actual or perceived input learners are exposed to.

One very relevant issue about which we cannot provide information at the present time is the actual use of *est-ce que* questions by French L2 *learners.* In particular, we would want to know whether it is used by formally instructed learners more frequently than by those exposed only or principally to informal speech data. On the one hand, *est-ce que* has a number of characteristics which would encourage its use: sentence-initial position, nonvariant free form, and high frequency in input addressed to nonnative speakers. Unfortunately, our own data do not provide a sufficient number of questions by learners to permit an answer to this question. A number of studies have shown that, in teacher-centered classes, students rarely *ask* questions (e.g., White and Lightbown 1984). And it is difficult to elicit a substantial corpus of spontaneous questions from second language learners (see Bailey, Eisenstein, and Madden 1976 and Abbott 1980 for some suggestions).

NEGATION

In the formal and/or written language, French has a double particle construction for the negative (Dahl 1979). The first particle *ne* (or *n'* before vowel) precedes the finite verb and any clitic object pronouns which precede it, and the second particle *pas* follows the finite verb.

Il *n'*est *pas* au bureau.
(he NEG is NEG at the office).

Je *ne* l'ai *pas* vu aujourd'hui.
(I NEG him have NEG seen today).

Elle *ne* vient *pas* avec nous.
(She NEG comes NEG with us).

Je *ne* veux *pas* manger.
(I NEG want NEG to eat).

In informal spoken French, the first particle is rarely heard: it is often deleted altogether, and even if the speaker produces it, it is such a reduced form that it is virtually inaudible in speech produced at a normal rate. Thus, oral input to L2 learners outside formal instructional settings consists of sentences such as

Il est pas au bureau.
(he is NEG at-the office).
Elle vient pas avec nous.
(she comes NEG with us).

Previous research indicates that French learners—both L1 (see Moreau and Richelle 1981) and L2 (Trévise, 1984)—show a preference for the informal (*pas* without *ne*) negation. The only exceptions appear to be L2 learners who (1) have received some formal instruction in which, in slow formal speech, the *ne* is made salient; (2) are literate and have noted the *ne*-verb-*pas* form in the written language; or (3) are Spanish speakers whose preverbal *no* negation may predispose them to discover the presence of preverbal *ne* and use it with higher frequency than that observed for other L2 learners or for L1.

In the research by Painchaud, d'Anglejan, and Vincent cited above, a study of sentence negation showed that the 36 subjects overwhelmingly used targetlike negative constructions, including a surprisingly high frequency of use of the *ne*. This observation itself may make a good case for the influence of input. As the authors suggest, the high frequency of *ne* is probably explainable by the fact that the learners had spent considerable time in a formal instructional setting. The proportional frequency of *ne* actually diminished over the 6-month period between the first and second interviews, that is, during the period of less instruction or no instruction, and varying degrees of contact with native speakers. This change after a 6-month period may reflect more targetlike use of informal verb-*pas* negative construction or may simply be due to a faster speech rate in which the *ne,* though "intended" by the speaker, is virtually imperceptible to the hearer.

In input to L1 learners and child L2 learners in the Lightbown corpus, we found *ne* rare in the adult interlocutor's speech. The L1 learners never used *ne.* The L2 learners used it only in two memorized expressions: *je ne sais pas* and *je ne veux pas.* Thus, in the following discussion of the word order in sentence negation, we take for granted the absence of *ne* in most of the language which learners actually hear outside an instructional setting.

Looking only at sentences in the informal register cited above, one could argue that informal French provides evidence to learners that (informal) French is a language with postverbal negation. In sentences with only one verbal element, this is literally true. On the other hand, from the point of view of aural input, there is another important factor. In sentences with two verbal elements (Aux + Vb), French could appear to the learner at an early stage in the acquisition of French (particularly the child or the nonliterate noninstructed learner) to have preverbal negation in the sense that the negative particle *pas* occurs before the salient or stressed verbal element, that is, before the nonfinite lexical verb—participle or infinitive.

Je l'ai *pas vu* aujourd'hui.
(I him-have NEG seen today)
Je veux *pas manger.*
(I want NEG eat)

This is even more important when one takes sentence stress into account. The beginning of the sentence is often reduced, certainly unstressed, and can give the learner considerable evidence for preverbal negation. In sentences with copula or a single verbal element, the negator—while postverbal—precedes stressed sentence complements.

Il est *pas au bureau.*
(he is NEG at-the office)
Elle vient *pas avec nous.*
(she comes NEG with us)
Je veux *pas ce camion.*
(I want NEG this truck)

It is impossible, thus, to characterize informal spoken French as having *either* preverbal *or* postverbal negation. When sentence stress, rapid speech, and deletion or ellipsis phenomena are taken into account, one finds evidence for both preverbal and postverbal negation.

Given this conflicting (preverbal/postverbal) input, what do learners produce? Anyone familiar with L1 French (or with the earliest stages of L2 interlanguage) will find that such forms as

pas camion
(NEG truck)
pas comme ça
(NEG like that)
pas manger
(NEG eat)

sound very familiar. They are also the stereotypes of both foreigner talk and pidgin French. That they also appear to belong to a group of hypothetical universals "Neg X" forms is also apparent (Wode 1981). Thus, one might expect a high frequency of Neg-X constructions in French interlanguage.

In the Painchaud, d'Anglejan, and Vincent study, only those negative sentences which included a verb were analyzed; thus that report does not include a count of Neg-X or X-Neg utterances where X is a unit with no verb, e.g., "pas comme ça." For word order, as also reported above for the use of *ne,* the accuracy rate was very high. When all acceptable forms are combined, more than 91 percent of the learners' negative constructions were correct (actually, targetlike) at both the first and second interviews. Nevertheless, virtually all the nonstandard forms in both interviews were some variant of Neg-verb (see Table 25-3), usually *pas*-verb.

Turning to the findings for L1 and L2 children, it is possible to note some similarities and to add some further details. Here too, the word order used for negative sentences by both L1 and L2 learners conformed overwhelmingly to the model provided by informal French. So-called Neg-X utterances were confined to elliptical utterances in which the negative element preceded, for example, a noun phrase or locative expression, or where *pas* immediately preceded the verb in a sentence with no subject expressed.[4] Furthermore, when the negative particle *pas* preceded the verb, it conformed to the input in that it almost always occurred before nonfinite verb forms, e.g., "pas attrapé fleur" (NEG caught[5] participle flower). When *pas* followed the verb, the verb was most often a conjugated (finite) verb, e.g., "roule pas" (rolls NEG).

The adult learners' speech has not yet been analyzed in a way that makes it possible to quantify the placement of *pas* after (or before) finite (or nonfinite) verbs for both "standard" and "nonstandard" forms. Some examples in the text of the Painchaud et al. report suggest that there were nonconforming utterances, e.g., "je parlé pas bien le français" (I spoken NEG well the French).[6] However, as can be seen in Table 25-4, the nonstandard forms which, as noted above, were almost all of the form NEG-verb,

TABLE 25-3 Frequency of Negative Forms in Learners' Speech (N = 36) in Two Interviews

	*Interview A**			*Interview B**		
Forms	*F*		%	*F*		%
Standard:						
V – *pas*	149		22.5	402		35.7
Ne – V – *pas*	348		52.5	421		37.3
Aux – *pas* – V	12		2	41		3.6
Ne – aux – *pas* – V	96		14.5	154		13.6
Total		605	91.5		1018	91.2
Nonstandard:						
Pas – V	18		3	60		5
Ne – *pas* – V	12		2	25		2
Aux – V – *pas*	2		.5	2		0
Non – V	1		0	0		0
V – *non*	1		0	0		0
Ne – V	23		3	21		1.8
Total		57	8.5		108	8.8
TOTAL		662	100		1126	100

Adapted from Painchaud et al., Table 22.
*Interview A was conducted at the end of the 7-month period of intensive instruction; interview B took place 6 months later.

were far more likely to occur with nonfinite verbs than were the standard forms. It will be interesting to examine other data from noninstructed learners to see whether there is evidence that this tendency to conform to the input—*pas* before nonfinite verbs and *after* finite verbs—goes beyond our child subjects.

TABLE 25-4 Frequency of Nonfinite Verbs, Used with Standard and Nonstandard Negation

	Interview			
	A		*B*	
Forms	*F*	%	*F*	%
Standard	19/605	3.1	26/1018	2.5
Nonstandard	30/57	52.6	71/108	65.7
Total	49/662	7.4	97/1126	8.6

Adapted from Painchaud et al., Table 23.

SVO ORDER

Finally, a brief remark regarding SVO word order—another facet of French which could easily give rise to inappropriate inferences with regard to the origins of interlanguage phenomena. Language typologies (e.g., Comrie 1981) include French among SVO word order language while pointing out certain violations which are part of standard grammar. These include clitic placement of object pronouns and subject-verb or subject auxiliary inversion in questions. However, such formal descriptions tend to overlook the most striking violation of SVO found extensively in spoken French. This is the phenomenon known as dislocation, possibly reflecting pragmatic word order, which produces sentences such as the following:

Elle part demain, sa soeur.
(she leaves tomorrow, her/his sister)
Je l'ai remis sur l'étagère, ton livre.
(I it-have put-back on the shelf, your book)

As these examples from Calvé (1982) show, dislocation usually involves the displacement of one of the constituents of the sentences, usually a noun, either to the front or to the end of the sentences, and its substitution within the sentences by a pleonastic pronoun. There are other possibilities, however, and in a recent paper, Trévise (in press) proposed at least 24 plausible versions of the sentence "Jean aime les pommes," varying the use of pronouns (e.g., Il les aime Jean, les pommes (he likes, John, the apples)). Calvé provides an interesting discussion of the dislocation phenomenon which, he states, seems to totally defy the word order of written French as well as that which is reported in formal descriptions of the language. More importantly, he points out that it is not restricted to Québecois French or to so-called "français populaire" and cites a variety of studies (e.g., Bally 1909, Blinkenberg 1928, Larsson 1979, Calvé 1978) which have clearly demonstrated the universality and high frequency of the phenomenon in spoken French. Ironically simple SVO order may prove to be at least as frequent in interrogatives as in declaratives. What is clear is that classroom-instructed learners, exposed to formal instructional language and the written language may be unaware of the existence of this variation in word order in informal spoken French.

Observations regarding the development of word order in French by learners whose L1 represents a different word order typology must be made in light of the fact that spoken French provides copious examples of VOS, VS, and OSV orders. One cannot conclude that variable word order in the interlanguage is based simply on transfer. Learners may be predisposed to expect a particular word order—or range of word orders—because of their L1. Finding some examples of such word order in the French input may make such forms persist in interlanguage. A similar phenomenon has been observed in the acquisition of English sentence negation by Spanish speakers—where there appears to be an interaction between L1 features, target language features, and possibly universal developmental stages or strategies. Such an interaction contributes to the development of certain interlanguage phenomena (see Schumann 1979, Zobl 1980a, b).

There are various potential hypotheses about the role of this phenomenon in foreigner talk. Input research has shown that native speakers and caretakers have some tendency to simplify their speech in addressing language learners (Long 1981a, and papers in Snow and Ferguson 1977), but it is not clear whether dislocation and topicalization should be considered simplification or complexification. On the one hand, the disruption of SVO or the use of different word orders rather than one dominant one might be considered a kind of complexity; on the other hand, the added redundancy and emphasis on important semantic units might be seen to simplify the learner's task of extracting meaning. At a minimum, it is necessary to observe and describe accurately the word order patterns used by French native speakers in addressing children and nonnative speakers.

In Lightbown (1977) it was noted that sentences with dislocation were fairly infrequent in L1 caretaker speech overall, but their importance may be greater than their simple frequency implies if, because of their unusual stress or emphasis on meaning, they are more likely to be attended to or more easily comprehended. We have not yet analyzed data on input to French L2 learners in terms of dislocation.

CONCLUSIONS

The observations in this chapter were not presented to make a case for the view that L2 interlanguage is merely a copy—or a reduced copy—of the input learners are exposed to. This is clearly not the case. Many researchers have examined aspects of learner language which clearly reflect other powerful influences in the L2 acquisition process. What we do propose here is in fact quite simple:

First, while it is important to examine a broad range of L1-L2 interlanguages, the interlanguages *must* be examined *together with* accurate information about the *input* language if we are to make appropriate inferences about how the L1 and L2 interact in determining the patterns found in the interlanguage.

Our second point follows from this: although certain evidence from French interlanguage resembles evidence reported for other languages, we question whether it can be used as straightforward confirmatory evidence for some proposed language universals or for transfer from certain L1s when the model for the French L2 interlanguage form is predominant in the input. In a more general sense, we are asking whether the same surface phenomena in different interlanguages must be assumed to reflect the same underlying processes.

Third, we have tried to point out that the input which learners actually receive may be radically different from that which textbooks and grammarians would have us believe they receive *and* from that which native speakers believe they produce.

Fourth, and finally, we wish to join others who suggest that language acquisition is shaped by multiple interacting and overlapping processes—input, transfer, instruction, universals, cognitive and pragmatic strategies—and that it is misleading to attribute interlanguage phenomena to only one process when *many* are clearly involved.

NOTES

1. In fact, it is incorrect to refer to "subject-auxiliary" or "subject-verb" inversion without further specifying that noun and pronoun subjects are governed by different rules. Briefly, pronouns, but not nouns, can be inverted. If inversion is to be used with nouns, a pronoun must be added, for example, Jean, vient-il ce soir? (John comes-he tonight). See Zobl (1979) for discussion of how this distinction between nouns and pronouns appears to influence English L2 acquisition by francophones.

2. In these and all subsequent examples, a word-for-word translation will be provided in parentheses. Hyphens are used where they occur in the original French sentence and in instances where bound morphemes in French are translated by free forms in English.

3. Note that, in fact, in French as in English, information-eliciting questions do not ordinarily have rising intonation.

4. In the case of one child L1 learner, *pas* sometimes appeared sentence-initially—in sentences with inverted subject-verb, e.g., "pas dodo la poupée" (NEG sleep the doll) and, more rarely, where the subject was present and, in fact, repeated after the verb: "pas la poupée dodo la poupée" (NEG the doll sleep the doll). See Lightbown (1977) for discussion of this child's global verb forms such as "dodo."

5. The form /atrapé/ is the phonetic realization of several different finite and nonfinite forms of the verb *attraper:* past participle, infinitive, second person plural, and second person formal. It is, in some dialects, also homophonous with the imperfect.

6. See note 5 for discussion of the homophonous verb forms.

Section Six

A LOOK AT THE PAST, PRESENT, AND FUTURE

26

STATE OF THE ART ON INPUT IN SECOND LANGUAGE ACQUISITION

Diane Larsen-Freeman
School for International Training

This volume on input in second language acquisition comes at a propitious time. Although research focusing on input in second language acquisition (SLA) was begun less than a decade ago, much work has been done in the intervening years; it is a good time, therefore, to take stock and to see what we have learned. It is also fitting that this area of our field be subject to the same scrutiny as other phenomena, long recognized to play major roles in the process of SLA (e.g., transfer; see Gass and Selinker 1983).

It was not so long ago that I heralded the new interest in input, hoping that we would be afforded a perspective on SLA that we had previously been denied (Larsen-Freeman 1979, 1980). Like all good ideas that are only obvious in hindsight, it was hard to believe that researchers had virtually ignored input prior to that time. Most of our efforts in the 1970s went into describing syntactic forms in learners' speech and arguing about whether they were due to mother tongue interference or not.

Through these endeavors, many important insights into the process of SLA were obtained. But by focusing solely on learner speech or output, researchers began to realize that they were overlooking a major piece of the puzzle. Hatch and Wagner-Gough (1976) were among the first to call our attention to the fact that if we wanted to say anything interesting about learner output, we would have to look at the target language input with which the learner had to work. And thus the leftmost box of our now famous tripartite schema [input] → [black box] → [output] became a legitimate, indeed essential, domain for SLA research to address. Since that time, a lot of valuable work on the nature of input has been done, and I would like to review this. But first, let me digress to offer a further rationale for our work on input in SLA.

Much of the work of the seventies which I just described was motivated by the question of whether L1 = L2; i.e., are the two acquisition processes identical, or at least similar, not necessarily in their product, but in the way they occur? The other major research undertaking at this time was motivated by the differential success question: why wasn't it possible for all learners to reach native-speaker proficiency in their L2? Why were some learners more successful than others? (For discussion of these questions, see Hatch 1977.) While the first question focused on the process or *learning,* the second question focused on the *learner.*

Although both of these questions are valid and indeed still motivate a great deal of research in the field, I believe that they should not be addressed independently as they have been. I think it will not be the case that we will come to some understanding of the SLA process and then introduce learner variables and calculate their effect on the process. Likewise, I think we cannot fully understand what influences the learner apart from his or her engagement in the process of learning. For this reason, I see input studies as having an especially important function. They are at the intersection in our field where these two streams of research must come together. In studies of target language input, both *learning* and *learner* must be considered.

In earlier studies of the SLA process, all one really needed to know was the learner's L1. In input studies, the more we know about the learner—not only his or her L1, but also his or her age, socioeconomic status, target language proficiency, sex, opportunities for interaction with TL speakers, conditions under which the learning took place, etc.—the more we will know about the nature of the input the learner is likely to receive. Thus input studies provide a natural synthesis of foci on the learner and learning.

My charge was to offer a state-of-the-art summary of the chapters in this volume. In order to do this, let me review what was known about input prior to the publication of this volume. I have divided the studies that were conducted into three areas, which I believe will also accommodate most of the chapters included here:

1. Studies which explore some aspect of the link between input and output.

2. Studies which characterize native-speaker-nonnative-speaker (NS-NNS) interactions.

3. Studies which characterize NNS-NNS interactions.

What is known about each?

1. Studies which are concerned with the quantitative or some qualitative aspect of input and its link to output.

Researchers in the area of input quantity (Rubin 1975; Seliger 1977; Bialystok 1978; Snow and Hoefnagel-Höhle 1982; Chesterfield, Barrows-Chesterfield, Hayes-Latimer, and Chávez 1983) have entertained the prospect that learners who have the opportunity to use the TL the most or to receive the most TL input will be those who exhibit the greatest proficiency. Almost all of these researchers adduced evidence in support of the hypothesis (Snow and Hoefnagel-Höhle being the exceptions), with Seliger perhaps making the most explicit statement about input. He found that "ESL students who generate significantly more English input" both inside and outside ESL classrooms were more proficient than the so-called low-input generators.

Research in the area of input quality has been conducted by Perkins and Larsen-Freeman (1975); Wagner-Gough and Hatch (1975); Larsen-Freeman (1976a, 1976b); Gaskill, Campbell, and Vander Brook (1977); Anderson (1977); Butoyi (1978); Plann (1979); Long (1980, 1981a and c); Hamayan and Tucker (1980); Vander Brook, Schlue and Campbell (1980); Snow, Van Eeden, and Muysken (1981); Lightbown (1980, 1983); and Long and Sato (1983). These researchers have examined some quality or qualities of the input (e.g., perceptual saliency, frequency of occurrence in native-speaker speech, syntactic complexity, semantic complexity, instructional sequence) to see if that quality or those qualities would account for learners' output. The most recurring [although not unchallenged; see Lightbown (1983) and Long and Sato (1983)] finding is that there is a positive correlation between the frequency of a particular form in the native-speaker input and the order with which learners produce it in the output (Larsen-Freeman 1976a, 1976b; Anderson 1977; Butoyi 1978; Plann 1979; Lightbown 1980; Hamayan and Tucker 1980; Long 1980, 1981a).

2. The second major area comprises studies which characterize NS–NNS interactions (usually with the aim of identifying modifications which NSs make during these exchanges).

Following Long, I will divide this area into modifications NSs make to the linguistic input (foreigner talk or FT) and those they make to the interactional structure [foreigner talk discourse (FTD)]. Researchers who have contributed to these areas are Ferguson (1975); Wagner-Gough and Hatch (1975); Meisel (1977); Katz (1977); Hatch, Shapira, and Wagner-Gough (1978); Peck (1978); Arthur, Weiner, Culver, Lee, and Thomas (1980); Freed (1980, 1981); Long (1980, 1981c); Clyne (1981b); Scarcella and Higa (1981, 1982).

Research of this sort has also been conducted in the classroom; hence it is sometimes referred to as "teacher talk" (TT), by Allwright (1975); Long, Adams, McLean, and Castaños (1976); Wong-Fillmore (1976); Gaies (1977); Henzl (1973, 1979); Long (1981a); Snow and Hoefnagel-Höhle (1982); Chaudron (1979, 1983b); and Long and Sato (1983). For my summary of this research area, I am especially indebted to Hatch (1983b) and Long (1983d). Linguistic *form* modifications include the following:

Input to NNSs is shorter and less complicated and is produced at a slower rate than speech between adult NSs. This input tends to be more regular, canonical word order is adhered to, and there is a high proportion of unmarked patterns. There are fewer false starts and there is less repair. High-frequency vocabulary is used—more restricted vocabulary as measured by type-token ratios. There is a limited use of pronouns, presumably in the belief that references should be as unambiguous as possible.

There are more questions. Question tags and alternative questions occur more frequently. There is less preverb modification, presumably so new information can be highlighted at the end of an utterance, where it is more salient. The input is higher-pitched, it shows more intonation variation in pitch, and it is louder in volume. It contains fewer reduced vowels and fewer contractions.

Of course, not all NS-NNS interactions manifest all these features—and, in fact, Varonis and Gass (1982) have been exploring just when it is that FT is likely to be used by native speakers.

The second part of this second area has to do with modifications that are made to the interactional structure of NS-NNS discourse. Research concerning how topics are nominated tells us that there is a preference for questions in topic-initiating moves in FTD. There is also the use of stress or a pause before topics to make them more salient. Topics are generally treated simply and briefly. Topics are more restricted also, most dealing with the "here and now." Native speakers employ tactics and strategies (Long's terms) such as self and other repetitions, comprehension checks, expansions, clarification requests, and confirmation checks. Sometimes "decomposition" occurs where intended meaning is broken down into manageable parts.

Apparently the task that is being performed in the conversation, when there is one, makes a difference. More modification of the interaction is claimed to take place where the conversation requires an exchange of information than when information is just transmitted one-way from sender to receiver.

Long also notes that it is not the use of these strategies which distinguishes FTD from NS conversation, but rather their higher frequency in FTD.

3. The third and final area of research I will summarize is that which deals with NNS interaction.

Compared with the second category, this area has been relatively little explored. Researchers who have done so are Plann (1976); Long, Adams, McClean, and Castaños (1976); Harley and Swain (1977); Larsen-Freeman (1982); and Varonis and Gass (1985). From their efforts we know that NNS input may be responsible for the development of so-called classroom dialects in immersion programs (Harley and Swain for French immersion in Canada, Plann for Spanish immersion in the United States). On the other hand, there has also been research which points to benefits NNSs might derive from engaging in TL conversation with their peers. In one study (Long, Adams,

McLean, and Castaños) it was found that NNS interaction involved a greater number and variety of rhetorical acts than NS-NNS interactions where the NS is the teacher. Findings from other research (Varonis and Gass) suggest that since communication breakdowns are more frequent between NNSs, such speakers gain practice in negotiating to restore meaning—they can't rely on a NS skilled in FT to intervene and resolve the breakdown for them. Finally, another researcher (Larsen-Freeman) has claimed that peer input is valuable, since it is often more accessible to other NNSs than NS speech.

Using the three-category framework I have just proposed, I will now attempt to show how the chapters in this volume add to or challenge the brief summaries of previously published research I have given.

One chapter in this volume appears to contradict findings from previous studies which have investigated the relationship between quantity of input and language proficiency. The direct challenge comes from Day's study of 58 ESL students and their self-reported use of English outside the classroom. Using two measures of the subjects' English proficiency, an oral interview and a cloze test, Day rejected the hypothesis that the use of English outside the classroom is significantly related to ESL proficiency. As Day says, the issue of input quantity and its relation to language proficiency is still open to question. The study reported on by Swain also seems to have some bearing on the quantity of input issue. Swain examined the output of French immersion students in light of the traits of grammatical, discourse, and sociolinguistic competence. Although the subjects of her study presumably have received abundant comprehensible input (7 years' worth), they have still not fully acquired the target language. At least in terms of grammatical competence, no quantity of comprehensible input may be enough. Swain concludes, therefore, that comprehensible *output* is a necessary mechanism of SLA, independent of the role of comprehensible input. Swain's chapter appears to be particularly provocative in light of Krashen's claim that comprehensible input "delivered in a low (affective) filter situation is the only 'causative variable' in second language acquisition" (Krashen 1981b:57, quoted in Swain).

There are several chapters in this volume which relate to input quality. While there appear to be no direct challenges to extant findings, the authors of two chapters leave us a little less self-assured about the nature of what it is we have been calling target language input. In their chapter, Lightbown and d'Anglejan caution against our relying on grammar book descriptions of the NS input in order to account for learners' interlanguage. The way grammarians describe the TL may be quite different from the way NSs actually use it. Thus forms in the learners' IL may just as well be due to naturally occurring NS input as to some other cause such as linguistic universals. Their warning is reminiscent of the findings with regard to uninverted questions in English by Vander Brook, Schlue, and Campbell (1980). Lightbown and d'Anglejan further warn us not to be satisfied with simplistic explanations such as "what goes in comes out" in our zeal for looking to the input for all the answers. Underscoring this theme, Beebe in her chapter reminds us that learners are active participants in choosing the target language models they prefer. We must not assume that all of the varieties of TL available to the learner constitute input; NNSs have certain input preferences to which they attend more than others, Beebe contends.

Consistent with the theme of learner autonomy is the chapter by Brown. Her study supports Peck's (1980) contention that input differences may account for the differential success between younger and older learners. What's more, Brown observes that it is the learners themselves who are responsible for the differences in the input they receive due to the specific in-class requests that they make.

Also in this category, we should place the chapter by Saville-Troike. She urges SLA researchers to broaden their inquiry beyond looking at linguistic form in the input to looking at the cultural content of the input as well. Saville-Troike argues that especially for children L2 learners, the study of the development of communicative competence should really be situated within the scope of the development of cultural competence.

The final two chapters which belong in the first category are those by Kellerman and Zobl. Both of these chapters echo the cautionary note mentioned earlier in Lightbown's and d'Anglejan's and again in Beebe's chapter that it is overly simplistic to assume that "what goes in comes out." In fact, the paradox with which we are presented in Kellerman's chapter is how/why at a certain stage learners can apparently overrule or ignore the target input to which they are exposed. Moreover, learners produce forms contrary to the input they are receiving. The so-called U-shaped phenomenon is an intriguing one which again demonstrates that the learner is clearly not a passive absorber of all NS input.

Zobl in his chapter underscores this by proposing that not all the forms of an IL are encountered in the input to which a learner is exposed. Learners must therefore possess the ability to project from what they do know to what they don't know without necessarily experiencing confirmatory data in the input. Zobl believes that it is the markedness conditions in the input which the learner can draw upon to make his or her projections "in spite of the limitations of the input data from an experiential point of view." Zobl's casting the learner in such an active role should do much to dispel the notion that the learner is merely a passive recipient of NS input.

In the second area, the one dealing with NS-NNS interaction, there have been additions and refinements.

In his chapter Long offers evidence to empirically validate the intuitively appealing notion that foreigner talk modification (both linguistic and interactional) facilitates comprehension. Long then presents his case for FT modification being an indirect causal variable of SLA. Long reasons that it is indirect since his study proves that modification increases comprehension and he believes the literature supports the notion that increased comprehension causes acquisition. Thus his contention that FT modification is a causal variable of SLA is arrived at by deduction.

The next paper in this category I would like to consider is Hirvonen's. She looked at both linguistic modification and discourse or interaction modification among child NS-NNS interlocutors. The hypothesis that bilingual NSs would be better FT users than monolingual, owing to the former's heightened sensitivity, was not borne out. All the children did use FT to some extent, however; and confirming Long's (1981) observation, Hirvonen found that it was discourse or interaction modification which especially characterized the difference between talk among NSs and FT. As for linguistic modifications, the differences which Hirvonen found to exist could be argued to reflect style differences among NSs rather than adjustment of their linguistic behavior when talking to NNSs.

This last finding is also reported in the chapter by Wesche and Ready. After investigating a number of different linguistic modifications in their study of TT in a university classroom, these researchers observe that the adjustments the professors make appear to be rather individual. Furthermore, the modifications that they make appear to be constantly changing because of extralinguistic situational factors, feedback from listeners, and the changing content of their lectures. Wesche and Ready conclude that no single principle may account for the dynamic changes that the professors make. It may be more apt to say that speakers play to their audience's expectancy grammar.

The other two chapters in this volume having to do with teacher talk also attest to the dynamic quality of the adjustments that teachers make. Kleifgen, like Henzl earlier, shows that a teacher's formal adjustments are sensitive to the general level of proficiency of the students being taught. The complexity of the teacher's input appears to be determined largely by the students' linguistic needs—not only synchronically, but diachronically as well—with the teacher increasing the complexity of her input as her students' proficiency increases.

And in his chapter in this volume, Ellis makes a number of similar observations to those of Wesche and Ready. Although Ellis writes about negotiated TT rather than unidirectional lectures as do Wesche and Ready, authors of both chapters see TT as a negotiated, rather than an absolute, phenomenon which is constantly being adjusted. Both suggest that simply counting the number of native speaker adjustments will not provide a complete picture of how input is made comprehensible. Ellis, in particular, recommends that researchers conduct qualitative research of selected interaction in order to see just what contribution TT makes.

Wong-Fillmore and her associates have chosen to do just this. What they discovered in their qualitative study of individual differences in second language learning is that only certain teachers are able to organize their classes and use language in instructional events in such a way as to promote the language learning of their limited English proficiency students. Wong-Fillmore reports on a number of characteristics that appear to differentiate lessons that facilitate language learning from those that do not.

Besides dealing with NS-NNS interaction, the next two chapters belonging to this category have in common the fact that they deal with phonology, an oft-neglected area of study in SLA.

Zuengler's findings show that in addition to modifying their input to NNS, NSs also heed social factors (in this case status imbalance), and thus FT exhibits some of the normal sociolinguistic variation of any NS discourse. Not all the hypothesized variation occurred (only the standardness of one out of a possible four variables was affected), however, leaving Zuengler to speculate that the demands that FT places on the NS may override the NS's normal inclination to nonstandardness.

The other chapter in this category is one by Avery, Ehrlich, and Yorio. These researchers investigated the phonological modifications made by NSs to other NSs and by NSs to NNSs. What they found is that phonological adjustments occur differentially according to the discourse function of the linguistic material. It is in core propositions that phonological adjustments take place. Avery, Ehrlich, and Yorio agree with Wesche and Ready, and Ellis. A simple enumeration of phonological adjustments would not be revealing and in fact here would obscure their very interesting finding that the phonological adjustments have a discourse function to fulfill. These researchers also offer further support for Long's contention that the difference between NS-NS speech and NS-NNS speech is a quantitative, not a qualitative, one.

The third major research area summarized above was aimed at characterizing NNS-NNS interaction. I feel that neither of the chapters in this volume seriously challenges the prevailing research findings. They do, however, add to our knowledge of what differences exist in this kind of interaction compared with NS-NS exchanges. They also clarify what benefits are derivable to NNSs from their engagement in conversations with other NNSs. Clearly, more work in this area is particularly desirable, especially given the enthusiasm for small-group work in L2 teaching today.

Pica and Doughty investigated the differences between teachers talking to L2 students versus the students talking among themselves. Altogether they subjected nine hypotheses to empirical tests. In general, the results were not too encouraging for those seeking to justify the use of small groups. Among other findings, Pica and Doughty discovered that the students' opportunity to hear grammatical input only really occurred when the teacher directed such input to the class; students did not, however, produce more grammatical samples of the TL in the presence of the teacher. They also report that there was very little negotiation in both teacher-fronted and group data. They attribute this finding, however, to the fact that neither exchange allowed for a genuine two-way exchange of information.

The other chapter in this category is the one by Gass and Varonis. It appears that the type of task, the role of the interlocutor, task familiarity, and the sex of the interlocutor all play a part in how unaccepted input is indicated. Gass and Varonis assert that indications of unacceptable input are a positive aspect of NNS interaction because they require that NNSs gain practice in manipulating their output (recall Swain's introduction of the notion of comprehensible output) in order to restore comprehensibility.

Finally, this volume contains several chapters that constitute a category unto themselves, and which don't fit into one of the areas I have already discussed. The authors of these chapters have taken on the difficult task of helping us to refine our research methodology or of helping us clarify some theoretical issues. This category may be original with this volume; I am not aware of previously published work dealing with methodology in input studies.

The first chapter in this category is the one by Chaudron. Chaudron proffers partial dictation and fixed-ratio cloze tests as tools which we can use to get a better close-up view of what goes on between input and intake. Since the tools are designed so that subjects will respond to each with what they immediately recall of what they have perceived from the input, researchers should be able to investigate L2 learners' preliminary intake through the use of these tests.

Hawkins' contribution lies in warning us of the need to be more circumspect before making judgments about NNS comprehension. It seemed reasonable to assume that a NNS had comprehended an utterance when he or she responded appropriately. Hawkins shows us, however, that a learner's appropriate responses need not be reliable in this regard. NNSs can give signals that they understand the FT they are receiving, when in fact they don't understand. If we are going to construct theories on the basis of comprehensible input, then we'd better rethink the way we verify that the input has been comprehended.

Sharwood Smith warns us about another pitfall in conducting (or offering a theoretical explanation for the results of) research on input: that of expecting a simple explanation for the complex process of SLA. If, Sharwood Smith argues, we put all of our hopes on TL input as providing us with the key to understanding the SLA process, then our focus will be unduly limited. Rather, we should acknowledge that SLA has multiple causes. The target language input is crucial, to be sure, but so is the effect of the mother tongue or knowledge of other tongues that the learner possesses.

In their chapter, Olshtain and Blum-Kulka contend that learners' productive grammatical (linguistic) competence and their ability to make acceptability judgments on speech acts progress at different rates and that the latter ability is a function of the length of stay in the target community. This chapter seems to support Swain's acceptance of the independence of the various traits: grammatical, sociolinguistic, and discourse. Also, Olshtain and Blum-Kulka's work seems to add further evidence to Swain's observation that sheer quantity of input/interaction may cause sociolinguistic competence to progress but may only allow grammatical competence to progress up to a certain point.

The two remaining chapters I have to discuss have in common a reminder that learners do not assimilate all the input data to which they are exposed and that learners' variable performance across tasks must be taken into account.

In her chapter Liceras points out that attained linguistic knowledge, metalinguistic abilities, and issues of markedness all play a role in accounting for the fact that what goes in doesn't necessarily come out. Liceras also makes an important distinction between task-bound variability and learners' variable intuitions. The former acknowledges the fact that different tasks make different demands of learners; the latter represents the fact that the rules of the TL may not yet be fixed or may be fixed in a variety of ways. When we talk about differences due to task, we will have to bear this distinction in mind.

And it seems fitting to conclude by calling attention to Sato's chapter, in which it appears even this phenomenon of task variation is not simple and straightforward. Certain phonological features in Sato's subject's interlanguage varied from task to task; others didn't. In any case, Sato feels that the subject's paying differing degrees of attention to his or her speech (Tarone 1983) is not sufficient to explain the variation Sato found between tasks. Sato goes on to caution us against assuming that all linguistic forms (e.g., phonological features or morphemes) subject to task variation pattern in the same way.

After my brief review of the chapters in this volume, I would now like to make three general observations stimulated in my thinking by my reading of this volume.

First, if we ever believed it was possible before, we certainly must now reject the notion that we can account for SLA with the simple linear model of [input] → [black box] → [output]. We have read chapters here which remind us that learner output is not isomorphic with NS input, that learners do not assimilate all of the NS forms to which they are introduced. We must ascertain, therefore, just what exactly is the intake in SLA and what its relationship is to the input (chapters by Liceras, Sharwood Smith, and Chaudron). We must do so all the while recognizing that there are probably many factors in the input which we have not even or have just begun to examine (Saville-Troike; Zuengler; and Avery, Ehrlich, and Yorio) and that we cannot rely on anything but empirical descriptions of the nature of the TL input as it is actually used by NSs (Lightbown and d'Anglejan).

We have also read chapters here by Swain and Olshtain and Blum-Kulka advising us to broaden our definition of learner output: to look beyond the influence of the input on the learner's grammatical competence (to include at least sociolinguistic competence as well) and to further investigate the value of the learner's producing comprehensible output (Swain, Day, and Gass and Varonis). We have also been warned against generalizing learner output with regard to a particular linguistic feature to all other instances of a similar feature (Sato), and against accepting appropriate output as proof that the input to learners was comprehensible (Hawkins).

And we have considered a number of chapters suggesting that the middle ground—the black box or mind of the learner—does not operate in a predictably simple fashion either: Chapters by Beebe and Brown indicate that learners can do a great deal to fashion their own input and by signaling when the input is unacceptable (Gass and Varonis) can help to create their own comprehensible input. Then, too, chapters by Kellerman and Zobl emphasize learner autonomy from mimicking TL input. Not only do learners sometimes ignore forms in the input, they also produce IL forms for which they have received no examples in the input.

Clearly the learner does receive *dynamic,* customized input (chapters by Ellis, Kleifgen, Wesche and Ready, Hirvonen, Pica and Doughty, and Long, and Wong-Fillmore) but equally clearly, the learner cannot be seen to be a passive recipient of such—not merely a black box waiting to be spoon-fed NS input.

Second, we must review the hypotheses being promulgated pertinent to the role of input in SLA and subject them to continued rigorous empirical tests. I don't know anyone who would seriously question the claim that comprehensible input is necessary for SLA, but is it *the* causal variable as Krashen has suggested? Swain's macrostudy and a study reported on recently by Celce-Murcia (1983) would seem to suggest otherwise.

Is it then that there is "an indirect causal relationship between linguistic and conversational adjustments and SLA" (Long, this volume)? As Long himself points out, it would be highly desirable to have direct tests of his step 3: "linguistic/conversational adjustments promote acquisition" rather than relying on deduction.

Or is it that the real advantage in participating in a conversation is that the learner is actively engaged in comprehending and using the TL in a meaningful way? In so doing, the learner gains comprehensible input but also has the opportunity to rehearse the target language and thereby gain access to more comprehensible input and native speaker feedback.

What we really need at this point is some qualitative research (Ellis) to better understand the relationship between input, learner interaction, and learner output. Day seems to concur when he concludes that a crucial aspect of SLA may be found not in looking at how often ESL students interact with NS of English, but at the nature of such interaction.

Strong (1983) recently put it this way:

What these findings appear to imply is not so much that faster learners receive more exposure to English from English speakers, but rather a greater ability on the part of those faster learners to make active use of the input they do get.

How the faster learners do this should occupy our attention now.

Third, and finally, if there was any doubt before, it should be put to rest: input studies are very worthy of our attention. Focusing on the input will not provide us with all the answers to SLA, but it will do much to illuminate our understanding by focusing attention on the interface between learner and learning.

A preliminary research agenda suggested by the topics in this volume would include (in addition to the ones I have already outlined and those proposed by chapter authors) at least:

- Clarity on how intake is derived from input (Sharwood Smith, Chaudron, Liceras)
- More accurate descriptions of the TL input (Lightbown and d'Anglejan, Beebe)
- An examination of sources of input in addition to that received by NNSs through conversation with NSs (Wesche and Ready)
- Features of FT in addition to syntactic modifications (Avery, Erhlich, and Yorio; Zuengler)
- Features of TT and their relationship to language-learning success (Pica and Doughty, Ellis, Kleifgen, Wong-Fillmore)
- Looking at learner achievement beyond grammatical competence and its relation to the input (Swain, Olshtain and Blum-Kulka)
- A study of the input/output relationship when learners are performing different tasks (Sato, Liceras, Ellis, Gass and Varonis)
- Studies of input where the TL is other than English (Swain, Lightbown and d'Anglejan, Sharwood Smith, Wesche and Ready)
- Further studies of NNS–NNS interactions (Pica and Doughty, Gass and Varonis)
- How it is that learners ignore certain input forms and produce others beyond that which they receive evidence for in the input (Kellerman, Zobl)

Rather than despairing at how little we do know, let us be heartened by how much progress we have made in such a short time. Let us be cheered by all these exciting questions awaiting our attention. Input should rightfully take its place as a phenomenon which plays a major role in SLA and as a worthy area for much future investigation.

REFERENCES

Abbott, G. 1980. Teaching the learner to ask for information. *TESOL Quarterly.* 14. 5-16.

Adjémian, C. 1976. On the nature of interlanguage systems. *Language Learning.* 26.297-320.

Adjémian, C. 1982. La spècificité de l'interlangage et l'idéalisation des langues secondes. In J. Guéron and S. Sowley (eds.). *Grammaire transformationelle: théorie et méthodologies.* Vincennes. Université de Paris VIII.

Adjémian, C., and J. Liceras. 1984. Accounting for adult acquisition of relative clauses: universal grammar, L1 and structuring the intake. In F. Eckman, L. Bell, and D. Nelson (eds.). *Universals of Second Language Acquisition.* Rowley, Mass. Newbury House.

Alderson, J. C. 1979. The cloze procedure and proficiency in English as a foreign language. *TESOL Quarterly.* 13.219-227.

Alderson, J. C. 1980. Native and nonnative speaker performance on cloze tests. *Language Learning.* 30.59-76.

Allen, C. L. 1977. Topics in diachronic English syntax. Ph. D. dissertation. University of Massachusetts. Amherst.

Allen, J. P. B., E. Bialystok, J. Cummins, R. Mougeon, and M. Swain. 1982. The development of bilingual proficiency: interim report on the first year of research. Toronto. The Ontario Institute for Studies in Education.

Allen, J. P. B., J. Cummins, R. Mougeon, and M. Swain. 1983. The development of bilingual proficiency: second year report. Toronto. The Ontario Institute for Studies in Education.

Allwright, R. L. 1975. Problems in the study of the language teacher's treatment of learner error. In M. K. Burt and H. C. Dulay (eds.). *On TESOL '75.* Washington, D.C. TESOL.

Andersen, E. S., and C. E. Johnson. 1973. Modifications in the speech of an eight-year-old as a reflection of age of listener. *Stanford Occasional Papers in Linguistics.* 3.149-160.

Andersen, R. W. 1983. *Pidginization and Creolization as Language Acquisition.* Rowley, Mass. Newbury House.

Anderson, J. 1977. A comparison of the order of difficulty in English sentential complements between native speakers of Spanish and native speakers of Persian. Paper presented at the Second Language Acquisition Forum. 1977.

Anderson, J. I. 1978. Order of difficulty in adult second language acquisition. In W. C. Ritchie (ed.). *Research in Second Language Acquisition.* New York. Academic Press.

Ardittty, J., and C. Perdue. 1979. Variabilité et connaissance en langue étrangère. *Encrages.* Numéro spécial de linguistique appliquée. Vincennes. Université de Paris VIII.32-43.

Arthur, B., R. Weiner, M. Culver, Y. Lee, and D. Thomas. 1980. The register of impersonal discourse to foreigners: verbal adjustments to foreign accent. In D. Larsen-Freeman (ed.). *Discourse Analysis in Second Language Research.* Rowley, Mass. Newbury House.

Atkinson, M. 1982. *Explanations in the Study of Child Language Development.* Cambridge. Cambridge University Press.

Bachman, L. F. 1982. The trait structure of cloze test scores. *TESOL Quarterly.* 16.61-70.

Bachman, L. F. 1983. Performance on different item types in cloze passages with fixed-ratio and random deletions. Paper delivered at the Seventeenth Annual TESOL Convention. Toronto, March 18.

Bachman, L. R., and A. S. Palmer. 1982. The construct validation of some components of communicative proficiency. *TESOL Quarterly.* 16.449-465.

Bailey, N., M. Eisenstein, and C. Madden. 1976. The development of Wh-questions in adult second language learners. In J. F. Fanselow and R. Crymes (eds.). *On TESOL '76,* Washington, D.C. TESOL.

Baker, C. L. 1979. Remarks on complementizers, filters, and learnability. Paper presented at the Sloan Foundation Workshop on criteria of adequacy for a theory of language. Stanford University.

Bakker, C. 1983. *The economy principle in the production of sentential verb complements by Dutch learners of English.* Unpublished M.A. dissertation, English Department, University of Utrecht.

Bally, C. 1909. *Traité de stylistique française.* Paris. Klincksieck.

Barker, L. L. 1971. *Listening Behavior.* Englewood Cliffs, N.J. Prentice-Hall.

Beebe, L. M. 1980. Sociolinguistic variation and style shifting in second language acquisition. *Language Learning.* 30.433-477.

Beebe, L. M. 1981. Social and situational factors affecting the communicative strategy of dialect code-switching. *International Journal of the Sociology of Language.* 32. 139-149.

Beebe, L. M. 1983a. Applying L1 theories to L2 data: how far can we go? Paper presented at the Seventeenth Annual TESOL Convention. Toronto, March, 1983.

Beebe, L. M. 1983b. A new sociolinguistic paradigm for second language research. Paper presented at the Seventeenth Annual TESOL Convention, Toronto, Canada, March.

Beebe, L. M., and H. Giles. 1984. Speech accommodation theories: a discussion in terms of second language acquisition. *International Journal of the Sociology of Language.* 46. 5-32.

Beebe, L. M., and J. Zuengler. 1981. A word before the final vows. Review of H. Giles and R. N. St. Clair (eds.). Language and social psychology. *Contemporary Psychology.* 20.4.279-280.

Beebe, L. M., and J. Zuengler. 1983. Accommodation theory: an explanation for style shifting in second language dialects. In N. Wolfson and E. Judd (eds.). *Sociolinguistics and Language Acquisition.* Rowley, Mass. Newbury House.

Behnstedt, P. 1973. Viens-tu? Est-ce que tu viens? Tu viens? Formen und Strukturen des direkten Fragesatzes im Französischen. Tübingen. Gunter Narr Verlag.

Benton, R. 1964. *Research into the English Language Difficulties of Maori School Children, 1963-1964.* Wellington, New Zealand. Maori Education Foundation.

Bialystok, E. 1978. Language skills and the learners: the classroom perspective. In C. Blatchford and J. Schachter (eds.). *On TESOL '78.* Washington, D.C. TESOL.

Bialystok, E. 1979. Explicit and implicit judgments of L2 grammaticality. *Language Learning.* 29.81-103.

Bialystok, E. 1982. On the relationship between knowing and using linguistic form. *Applied Linguistics.* III.181-206.

Bialystok, E. 1983. Some factors in the selection and implementation of communication strategies. In C. Faerch and G. Kaspar (eds.). *Strategies in Interlanguage Communication.* London. Longman.

Bickerton, D. 1971. Inherent variability and variable rules. *Foundations of Language.* 7.715-762.

Bình, Du'o'ng-Thanh, and W. Gage. 1975. *Vietnamese-English Phrasebook with Useful Word List (for English Speakers).* Washington, D.C. Center for Applied Linguistics.

Blalock, H. M., Jr. 1969. *Theory Construction: From Verbal to Mathematical Formulations.* Englewood Cliffs, N.J. Prentice-Hall.

Blau, E. K. 1982. The effect of syntax on readability for ESL students in Puerto Rico. *TESOL Quarterly,* 16.4.517-528.

Blinkenberg, A. 1928. *L'ordre des mots en français moderne.* Copenhagen. A. F. Host & Son.

Blum-Kulka, S. 1982. Learning to say what you mean in a second language: a study of the speech act performance of Hebrew second language learners. *Applied Linguistics.* 3.1. 29-59.

Blum-Kulka, S., B. Danet, and R. Gerson. 1983. The language of requesting in Israeli society. Paper presented at the Language and Social Psychology Conference, Bristol.

Blum-Kulka, S., and E. Olshtain. 1984. Requests and apologies: a cross cultural study of speech act realization patterns. *Applied Linguistics.* 5.3. 196-213

Bourgonje, B. 1983. Adverbial placement in EFL: report of a cross-linguistic project. Paper given at the LARS 83 conference, University of Utrecht. October 1983.

Bowen, J. D. 1976. Current research on an integrative test of English grammar. *RELC Journal.* 7.30-37.

Bowerman, M. 1982. Starting to talk worse: clues to language acquisition from children's late speech errors. In S. Strauss (ed.). *U-Shaped Behavioral Growth.* New York. Academic Press.

Brehm, J. W. 1972. *Responses to Loss of Freedom: A Theory of Psychological Reactance.* Morristown, N.J. General Learning Press.

Breveld, J., and M. Van Geeman. 1983. The influence of Dutch as a mother tongue on adverbial placement in English as a foreign language. Unpublished M.A. term paper. English department, University of Utrecht.

Brown, C. 1983. The distinguishing characteristics of the older adult second language learner. Unpublished Ph.D. dissertation. Los Angeles, California. UCLA.

Brown, G., and G. Yule. 1983. *Discourse Analysis.* Cambridge. Cambridge University Press.

Brown, H. D. 1980. The optimal distance model of second language acquisition. *TESOL Quarterly.* 14.2.157-164.

Brown, P., and S. Levinson. 1978. Universals of language usage: politeness phenomena. In E. Goody (ed.). *Questions and Politeness.* Cambridge. Cambridge University Press.

Brown, R. 1968. The development of WH questions in child speech. *Journal of Verbal Learning and Verbal Behaviour.* 7.279-290.

Brown, R. 1973. *A First Language.* Cambridge, Massachusetts: Harvard University Press.

Burger, S., M. Chrétien, M. Gingras, P. Hauptman, and M. Migneron. Forthcoming. Le rôle du professeur de langue dans un cours à contenu académique. *Canadian Modern Language Review.*

Butoyi, C. A. 1978. The accuracy order of sentential complements by ESL learners. Unpublished M.A. in TESL thesis. UCLA.

Butterworth, G., and E. Hatch. 1978. A Spanish-speaking adolescent's acquisition of English syntax. In E. M. Hatch (ed.). *Second Language Acquisition.* Rowley, Mass. Newbury House.

Byrne, D. 1969. Attitudes and attraction. *Advances in Experimental Social Psychology.* 4. 35-89.

Calvé, P. 1978. Dislocation in French: a functional study. Unpublished doctoral dissertation. Georgetown University.

Calvé, P. 1982. Un trait du français parlé authentique: La dislocation. *Bulletin of the Canadian Association of Applied Linguistics.* 4. 25-44.

Canale, M., and M. Swain. 1980. Theoretical bases of communicative approaches to second language teaching and testing. *Applied Linguistics.* 1(1).1-47.

Candlin, C. 1981. Discoursal patterning and the equalizing of interpretive opportunity. In L. Smith (ed.). *English for Cross-Cultural Communication.* New York. St. Martin's Press.

Candlin, C. N. 1983. Three into one must go: integrating input, interaction and inference in the study of L2 discourse. Plenary address, 5th Los Angeles Second Language Research Forum. Los Angeles. University of Southern California, November 11-13.

Carey, S. 1981. The child as word learner. In M. Halle, J. Bresnan, and G. Miller (eds.). *Linguistic Theory and Psychological Reality.* Cambridge, Mass. MIT Press.

Cathcart, R. 1982. Will the real data please stand out. Paper presented at the TESOL colloquium on classroom research. Honolulu, Hawaii.

Cedergren, H., and D. Sankoff. 1974. Variable rules: performance as a statistical reflection of competence. *Language.* 50.333–355.

Celce-Murcia, M. 1983. A case study that raises some questions about learning a second language through immersion. Paper presented at the Fifth Second Language Acquisition Research Forum. Los Angeles. UCLA.

Cervantes, R. 1983. "Say it again Sam": the effect of repetition on dictation scores. Term paper, ESL 670. Honolulu. University of Hawaii at Manoa.

Chaudron, C. 1979. Complexity of teacher speech and vocabulary explanation/elaboration. Paper presented at the Thirteenth Annual TESOL Convention. Boston, Mass.

Chaudron, C. 1982. Vocabulary elaboration in teachers' speech to L2 learners. *Studies in Second Language Acquisition.* 4.2.170–180.

Chaudron, C. 1983a. Simplification of input: topic reinstatements and their effects on L2 learners' recognition and recall. *TESOL Quarterly.* 17.3.437–458.

Chaudron, C. 1983b. Foreigner talk in the classroom—an aid to learning? In H. Seliger and M. Long (eds.). *Classroom Oriented Research in Second Language Acquisition.* Rowley, Mass. Newbury House.

Chaudron, C. In preparation. A test of two second language listening comprehension procedures. University of Hawaii at Manoa, Honolulu.

Chesterfield, R., K. Barrows-Chesterfield, K. Hayes-Latimer, and R. Chávez. 1983. The influence of teachers and peers on second language acquisition in bilingual preschool programs. *TESOL Quarterly.* 17.401–420.

Chomsky, N. 1965. *Aspects of the Theory of Syntax.* Cambridge, Mass. MIT Press.

Chomsky, N. 1975. *Reflections on Language.* New York. Pantheon.

Chomsky, N. 1977. On wh-movement. In P. Culicover, T. Wasow, and A. Akmajian (eds.). *Formal Syntax.* New York. Academic Press.

Chomsky, N. 1981. *Lectures on Government and Binding.* Dordrecht. Foris.

Chomsky, N., and H. Lasnik. 1977. Filters and control. *Linguistic Inquiry.* 8.425–504.

Chun, A., R. Day, N. A. Chenoweth, and S. Luppescu. 1982. Types of errors corrected in native-nonnative conversations. *TESOL Quarterly.* 16.4.537–548.

Clahsen, H. 1980. Psycholinguistics of L2 Acquisition. In S. Felix (ed.). *Second Language Development.* Tübingen. Narr.

Clark, H., and E. Clark. 1977. *Psychology and Language: An Introduction to Psycholinguistics.* New York. Harcourt Brace Jovanovich.

Clyne, M. G. 1981a. 'Foreigner talk' as the name of a simplified register. *International Journal of the Sociology of Language.* 28.69–80.

Clyne, M. (ed.). 1981b. *International Journal of the Sociology of Language.* 28. Special Issue on Foreigner Talk.

Cohen, A. D., and E. Olshtain. 1981. Developing a measure of socio-cultural competence: the case of apology. *Language Learning.* 31.1.113–134.

Cohen, A., and M. Swain. 1976. Bilingual education: the "immersion" model in the North American context. *TESOL Quarterly.* 10.1.45–53.

Comrie, B. 1981. *Language Universals and Linguistic Typology.* Chicago. University of Chicago Press.

Comrie, B. 1983. Conditionals: a typology. Paper given at the Conditionals Conference. Stanford University. December.

Cook, V. J. 1985. Universal grammar and second language learning. *Applied Linguistics.* 6.1.2-18
Corder, S. P. 1967. The significance of learners' errors. *IRAL.* 5.161-170.
Corder, S. P. 1973. The elicitation of interlanguage. In *Errata: Papers in Error Analysis.* Lund. CWK Greerup.
Cross, T. G. 1978. Mothers' speech and its association with rate of linguistic development in young children. In N. Waterson and C. Snow (eds.). *The Development of Communication.* New York. John Wiley & Sons.
Crymes, R., and W. Potter. 1981. Questions in the negotiation for understanding. In L. Smith (ed.). *English for Cross-Cultural Communication.* New York. St Martin's Press.
Cummins, R. 1983. *The Nature of Psychological Explanation.* Cambridge, Mass. MIT Press.
Cziko, G. A. 1982. Improving the psychometric, criterion-referenced, and practical qualities of integrative language tests. *TESOL Quarterly.* 16.367-379.
Cziko, G. 1984. Some problems with empirically-based models of communicative competence. *Applied Linguistics.* 5(1).23-38.
Dahl, O. 1979. Typology of sentence negation. *Linguistics.* 17.79-106.
Dale, P. S. 1976. *Language Development: Structure and Function.* New York. Holt, Rinehart, and Winston.
d'Anglejan, A. 1978. Language learning in and out of classrooms. In J. Richards (ed.). *Understanding Second and Foreign Language Learning.* Rowley, Mass. Newbury House. 218-236.
Darnell, D. K. 1970. Clozentropy: a procedure for testing English language proficiency of foreign students. *Speech Monographs.* 37.36-46.
David, J. 1976. *Grammaire structurale.* Dorval, Québec. Editions de l'Etoile Polaire.
Davies, N. 1982. Training fluency: an essential factor in language acquisition and use. *RELC Journal.* 13.1.1-13.
Day, R. R. 1980. The development of linguistic attitudes and preferences. *TESOL Quarterly.* 14. 27-37.
Day, R. R. 1984. Student participation in the ESL classroom or Some imperfections in practice. *Language Learning.* 34.3.69-102
De Haan, G. 1976. Regelordening en domainformuleringen op transformaties. In G. Koefoed and A. Evers (eds.). *Lijnen van taaltheoretisch onderzoek.* Groningen. Tjeenk Willink.
de Villiers, J. 1980. The process of rule learning in child speech: a new look. In K. Nelson (ed.). *Children's Language,* vol. 2. New York. Gardner Press. 1-44.
DeVito, J. A. 1965. Comprehension factors in oral and written discourse of skilled communicators. *Speech Monographs.* 32.124-128.
Dickerson, L. 1974. Internal and external patterning of phonological variability in the speech of Japanese learners of English. Ph.D. dissertation. University of Illinois.
Dickerson, L., and W. Dickerson. 1977. Interlanguage phonology: current research and future directions. In S. P. Corder and E. Roulet (eds.). *The Notions of Simplification, Interlanguages and Pidgins and Their Relation to Second Language Pedagogy.* Neuchâtel: Faculté des Lettres. 18-30.
Dore, J. 1978. Variation in preschool children's conversational performances. In K. E. Nelson (ed.). *Children's Language.* vol. 1. New York. Gardner Press. 397-444.
Doughty, C., and T. Pica. 1984. Small group work in the ESL classroom: does it facilitate language acquisition? Paper presented at TESOL 1984. Houston.
Dry, Helen. 1983. The Movement of Narrative Time. *Journal of Literary Semantics.* 12.19-53.
Dulay, H., and M. Burt. 1974. You can't learn without goofing. In J. C. Richards (ed.). *Error Analysis,* London. Longman.
Dulay, H., and M. Burt. 1978. Some remarks on creativity in language acquisition. In W. C. Ritchie (ed.). *Second Language Acquisition Research.* New York. Academic Press.
Dulay, H., and M. Burt. 1980. The relative proficiency of limited proficient students. In J. E.

Alatis (ed.). *Georgetown University Round Table on Languages and Linguistics 1980.* Washington, D.C. Georgetown University Press, 181-200.
Dulay, H., M. Burt, and S. Krashen. 1982. *Language Two.* New York. Oxford University Press.
Duncan, S. E., and DeAvila, E. A. 1979. Bilingualism and Cognition: some recent findings. NABE Journal, 4.1.15-50.
Eckman, F. 1977. Markedness and the contrastive analysis hypothesis. *Language Learning.* 27.315-330.
Eckman, F. 1981a. On the naturalness of interlanguage phonological rules. *Language Learning.* 31.195-216.
Eckman, F. 1981b. On predicting phonological difficulty in second language acquisition. *Studies in Second Language Acquisition.* 4.18-30.
Edmondson, W., and S. House. 1981. *Let's Talk and Talk about It.* Munich. Urban & Schwarzenberg.
Edwards, A. D., and V. J. Furlong. 1978. *The Language of Teaching.* London. Heinemann.
Edwards, H., M. Wesche, S. Krashen, R. Clément, and B. Krudenier. Forthcoming. Second language acquisition through subject-matter learning: a study of sheltered psychology classes at the University of Ottawa. *Canadian Modern Language Review.*
Eisenstein, M. 1982. A study of social variation in adult second language acquisition. *Language Learning.* 32.367-391.
Ellis, R. 1980. Classroom interaction and its relation to second language learning. *RELC Journal.* 11.2.29-48.
Ellis, R. 1982. The origins of interlanguage. *Applied Linguistics.* 3.3.207-223.
Ellis, R., and G. Wells. 1980. Enabling factors in adult-child discourse. *First Language.* 1.46-62.
Enkvist, N. E., and V. Kohonen. 1977. Cloze testing, some theoretical and practical aspects. In A. Zettersten (ed.). *Papers on English Language Testing in Scandinavia. Anglica et Americana 1.* University of Copenhagen, Project in Error Analysis, Interlanguage Studies, and Contrastive Linguistics.
Erickson, F. 1975. Gatekeeping and the melting pot: interaction in counseling encounters. *Harvard Educational Review.* 45.1.44-70.
Ervin, S. 1964. Imitation and structural change in children's language. In E. Lenneberg (ed.). *New Directions in the Study of Language.* Cambridge, Mass. MIT Press.
Evans, G., and K. Haastrup. 1976. Experiments with cloze procedure. *English Language Teaching Journal.* 31.35-41.
Faerch, C., and G. Kaspar. 1980. Processes in foreign language learning and communication. *Interlanguage Studies Bulletin.* 5.1.47-118.
Farhady, H. 1979. The disjunctive fallacy between discrete-point and integrative tests. *TESOL Quarterly.* 13.347-357.
Farhady, H. 1982. Measures of language proficiency from the learner's perspective. *TESOL Quarterly.* 16.43-59.
Fasold, R. 1978. Language variation and linguistic competence. In D. Sankoff (ed.). *Linguistic Variation: Models and Methods.* New York. Academic Press.
Ferguson, C. 1971. Absence of copula and the notion of simplicity: a study of normal speech, baby talk, foreigner talk and pidgins. In D. Hymes (ed.). *Pidgnization and Creolization of Languages.* New York. Cambridge University Press.
Ferguson, C. 1975. Towards a characterization of English foreigner talk. *Anthropological Linguistics.* 17.1-14.
Ferguson, C., and C. DeBose. 1977. Simplified registers, broken language and pidginization. In A. Valdman (ed.). *Pidgin and Creole Linguistics.* Bloomington. Indiana University Press.
Fishman, J. 1966. *Language Loyalty in the United States: The Maintenance and Perpetuation of Non-English Mother Tongues by American Ethnic and Religious Groups.* The Hague. Mouton and Co.
Frauenfelder, U., and R. Porquier. 1979. Les voies d'apprentissage en langue étrangère. *Working Papers on Bilingualism.* Toronto. OISE.17-38-64.

Freed, B. F. 1980. Talking to foreigners versus talking to children: similarities and differences. In R. Scarcella and S. Krashen (eds.). *Research in Second Language Acquisition,* Rowley, Mass. Newbury House.

Freed, B. F. 1981. Foreigner talk, baby talk, native talk. *International Journal of the Sociology of Language. 18.*19–39.

Gaies, S. 1977. The nature of linguistic input in formal second language learning: linguistic and communicative strategies in ESL teachers' classroom language. In H. D. Brown, Yorio, C. A., and R. H. Crymes (eds.). *On TESOL '77.* Washington, D.C. TESOL.

Gaies, S. J. 1982. Modification of discourse between native and non-native speaker peers. Paper presented at TESOL Conference. Honolulu, Hawaii, May 1982.

Gaies, S. J., H. L. Gradman, and B. Spolsky. 1977. Toward the measurement of functional proficiency: contextualization of the noise test. *TESOL Quarterly.* 11.51–57.

Gallimore, R., and R. G. Tharp. 1981. The interpretation of elicited sentence imitation in a standardized context. *Language Learning.* 31.369-392.

Gardner, R. C. 1978. Social psychological aspects of second language acquisition. In H. Giles and R. N. St. Clair (eds.). *Language and Social Psychology.* Baltimore. University Park Press.

Gardner, R. C., and W. E. Lambert. 1972. *Attitudes and Motivation in Second Language Learning.* Rowley, Mass. Newbury House.

Gaskill, W., C. Campbell, and S. Vander Brook. 1977. Some aspects of foreigner talk. In C. A. Henning (ed.). *Proceedings of the Los Angeles Second Language Research Forum.* Los Angeles. UCLA.

Gass, S. 1982. From theory to practice. In M. Hines and W. Rutherford (eds.). *On TESOL '81.* Washington, D.C. TESOL. 129–139.

Gass, S., and L. Selinker (eds.). 1983. *Language Transfer in Language Learning.* Rowley, Mass. Newbury House.

Gass, S., and E. Marlos Varonis. 1984. The effect of familiarity on the comprehensibility of nonnative speech. *Language Learning.* 34.1.65–89.

Gass, S., and E. Marlos Varonis. 1985. Variation in native speaker speech modification to non-native speakers. *Studies in Second Language Acquisition.* 7.1.37–57.

Gatbonton-Segalowitz, E. 1975. Systematic variations in second language speech: a sociolinguistic study. Unpublished Ph.D. dissertation. McGill University.

Giles, H. 1977. The social context of speech: a social psychological perspective. *ITL: A Review of Applied Linguistics.* 35.27–42.

Giles, H., R. Y. Bourhis, and D. M. Taylor. 1977. Towards a theory of language and ethnic relations. In H. Giles (ed.). *Language, Ethnicity and Intergroup Relations.* London. Academic Press.

Giles, H., and J. L. Byrne. 1982. An intergroup approach to second language acquisition. *Journal of Multilingual and Multicultural Development.* 3.17–41.

Giles, H., and P. Smith. 1979. Accommodation theory: optimal levels of convergence. In H. Giles and R. N. St. Clair (eds.). *Language and Social Psychology.* Baltimore. University Park Press.

Glanzer, M. 1982. Short-term memory. In C. R. Puff (ed.). *Handbook of Research Methods in Human Memory and Cognition.* New York. Academic Press.

Gleason, J. B. 1973. Code switching in children's language. In T. E. Moore (ed.). *Cognitive Development and the Acquisition of Language.* New York. Academic Press.

Goldstein, L. 1984. Non-native speakers' use of linguistic variants of New York City English dialects. Ed.D. dissertation prospectus, in preparation, Teachers College, Columbia University.

Gormly, C. M. R., A. J. Chapman, H. C. Foot, and C. A. Sweeney. 1979. Accommodation in children's mixed-age social interaction. Paper presented in the symposium on Conversation and Interpersonal Interaction at BPS Social Psychological Section. International Conference on Social Psychology and Language. Bristol.

Greenberg, J. 1963. Some universals of grammar with particular reference to the order of meaningful elements. In J. Greenberg (ed.). *Universals of Language.* Cambridge, Mass. MIT Press.

Gregory-Panopoulos, J. F. 1966. An experimental application of 'cloze' procedure as a diagnostic test of listening comprehension among foreign students. Ph.D. dissertation. University of Southern California, Los Angeles.

Grévisse, M. 1975. *Le bon usage.* Gembloux. Editions J. Duculot, 10ème édition.

Grimes, J. 1972. *The Thread of Discourse.* The Hague. Mouton.

Grosu, A. 1972. The strategic content of island constraints. *Working Papers in Linguistics No. 13.* Department of Linguistics, Ohio State University.

Gruber, J. 1976. *Lexical Structures in Syntax and Semantics.* Amsterdam. North-Holland.

Hakuta, K. 1974. Prefabricated patterns and the emergence of structure in second language acquisition. *Language Learning.* 24.287-297.

Hakuta, K. 1981. Grammar in the minds of adults, children and linguists. In S. Felix and H. Wode (eds.). *Language Development at the Crossroads.* Tübingen. Narr.

Hakuta, K. 1982. The second language learner in the context of the study of language acquisition. Paper presented at the Society for Research in Child Development Conference on Bilingualism and Childhood Development. New York University, June.

Halliday, M. A. K. In press. Language as code and language as behavior: a systemic-functional interpretation of the nature and ontogenesis of dialogue. In M. A. K. Halliday, S. M. Lamb, and A. Makkai (eds.). *The Semiotics of Culture and Language.* Buffalo. The Press at Twin Willows.

Hamayan, E. V., and G. R. Tucker. 1980. Language input in the bilingual classroom and its relationship to second language achievement. *TESOL Quarterly.* 14.453-468.

Harley, B., and M. Swain. 1977. An analysis of verb form and function in the speech of French immersion pupils. *Working Papers on Bilingualism.* 14:33-46.

Harré, R. 1972. *The Philosophies of Science. An Introductory Survey.* London. Oxford University Press.

Harris, D. P. 1969. Report on an experimental group-administered memory span test. *TESOL Quarterly.* 4.203-213.

Hatch, E. 1977. An historical overview of second language acquisition research. In C. A. Henning (ed.). *Proceedings of the Los Angeles Second Language Research Forum.* Los Angeles. UCLA.

Hatch, E. 1978. Discourse analysis and second-language acquisition. In E. Hatch (ed.). *Second Language Acquisition: A Book of Readings.* Rowley, Mass. Newbury House.

Hatch, E. 1979a. Interaction, input and communication strategies. Paper presented at the First Nordic Symposium on Interlanguage, Helsinki.

Hatch, E. M. 1979b. Apply with caution. *Studies in Second Language Acquisition.* 2.1.123-143.

Hatch, E. 1983a. Simplified input and second language acquisition. In R. Andersen (ed.). *Pidginization, Creolization as Language Acquisition.* Rowley, Mass. Newbury House.

Hatch, E. 1983b. *Psycholinguistics: A Second Language Perspective.* Rowley, Mass. Newbury House.

Hatch, E., and H. Farhady. 1980. *Research Design and Statistics for Applied Linguistics,* Rowley, Mass. Newbury House.

Hatch, E., R. Shapira, and J. Wagner-Gough. 1978. Foreigner talk discourse. *ITL: Review of Applied Linguistics.* 39-60.

Hatch, E., and J. (Wagner-) Gough. 1976. Explaining sequence and variation in second language acquisition. In H. D. Brown (ed.). *Papers in Second Language Acquisition.* Special Issue No. 4, *Language Learning.*

Hawkins, B. 1981. Papiamentu: a study in non-native use. Unpublished 250K paper, UCLA.

Hawkins, B. 1982. Comprehension in foreigner-talk discourse: an observational study. Unpublished M.A. thesis in TESL. UCLA.

Hays, W. L. 1973. *Statistics for the Social Sciences. 2d ed.* New York. Holt, Rinehart and Winston.
Heath, S. 1983. *Ways with Words.* Cambridge. Cambridge University Press.
Heidelberger Forschungsprojekt "Pidgin-Deutsch" 1975. *Sprache and Kommunikation auslandischer Arbeiter, Analysen, Berichte, Materialen.* Monographien Linguistik and Kommunikationswissenschaft, 20, Kronberg/TS. Scriptor Verlag.
Henning, G., N. Gary, and J. O. Gary. 1981. Listening recall—a listening comprehension test for low proficiency learners. Paper presented at AILA, Lund. August 9, 1981.
Henzl, V. M. 1973. Linguistic register of foreign language instruction. *Language Learning.* 23. 207-222.
Henzl, V. M. 1975. Speech of foreign language teachers: a sociolinguistic register analysis. Paper presented at the 4th International Congress of AILA. Stuttgart, August.
Henzl, V. M. 1979. Foreign talk in the classroom. *International Review of Applied Linguistics.* 17.159-167.
Hewitt, R. 1982. White adolescent creole users and the politics of friendship. *Journal of Multilingual and Multicultural Development.* 3.217-232.
Hirschbühler, P., and M. Rivero. 1981. Catalan restrictive relatives: core and periphery. *Language.* 57.591-625.
Homans, G. C. 1961. *Social Behavior: Its Elementary Forms.* New York. Harcourt, Brace, and World.
Hopper, P. J. 1979. Aspect and foregrounding in discourse. In T. Givon (ed.). *Syntax and Semantics* 12. New York. Academic Press.
Hornstein, N., and A. Weinberg. 1981. Case theory and preposition stranding. *Linguistic Inquiry.* 12.55-92.
House, J., and G. Kasper, 1981. Politeness markers in English and German. In F. Coulmas (ed.). *Conversational Routine.* The Hague. Mouton.
Huebner, T. 1983. *A Longitudinal Analysis: The Acquisition of English.* Ann Arbor, Mich. Karoma Press.
Hulstijn, J. 1982. Monitor use by second language learners. Unpublished Ph.D. dissertation, University of Amsterdam.
Hunt, K. 1970. Syntactic maturity in school children and adults. *Monographs for the Society for Research in Child Development.* 35 (Serial No. 134).
Hymes, D. 1966. On communicative competence. Paper presented at the Research Planning Conference on Language Development among Disadvantaged Children, Yeshiva University.
Iwamura, S. G. 1980. *The Verbal Games of Pre-School Children.* London. Croom Helm.
Jackendoff, R. 1972. *Semantic Interpretation in Generative Grammar,* Cambridge, Mass. MIT Press.
Jackson, P. 1968. *Life in Classrooms.* New York. Holt, Rinehart and Winston.
Jacobson, S. 1975. Factors influencing the placement of English adverbs in relation to auxiliaries. Stockholm. Almquist and Wiksell.
Jacobson, S. 1981. *Preverbal Adverbs and Auxiliaries,* Stockholm. Almquist and Wiksell.
Jaeggli, O. 1980. On some phonologically-null elements in syntax. Ph.D. dissertation. Cambridge, Mass. MIT. (Published as *Topics in Romance Syntax.* Dordrecht. Foris Publications. 1981.)
Jefferson, G. 1972. Side sequences. In D. Sudnow (ed.). *Studies in Social Interaction.* New York. Free Press.
Jensen, L. 1979. Encoding of interlanguage: a preliminary investigation. M.Sc. dissertation. University of Edinburgh.
Johansson, S. 1973. Partial dictation as a test of foreign language proficiency. Swedish-English contrastive studies. Report No. 3. Department of English. Lund University. Lund, Sweden.
Johnson, P. 1981. Effects on reading comprehension of language complexity and cultural background of a text. *TESOL Quarterly.* 15.2.169-181.

Jones, E. E., and K. E. Davis. 1965. From acts to dispositions: the attribution process in perception. In L. Berkowitz (ed.). *Advances in Social Psychology II.* London. Academic Press.

Jones, L., and L. K. Jones. 1979. Multiple Levels of Information in Discourse. In Linda Jones (ed.). *Discourse Studies in Mesoamerican Languages.* SIL Publications in Linguistics. 58.1.

Jordens, P. 1977. Rules, grammatical intuitions, and strategies in foreign language learning. *Interlanguage Studies Bulletin.* 2.5–76.

Kagan, S. 1977. Social motives and behaviors of Mexican-American and Anglo-American children. In J. L. Martinez, Jr. (ed.). *Chicano Psychology.* New York. Academic Press.

Kahn, D. 1976. *Syllable Based Generalizations in English Phonology.* Indiana University Linguistics Club.

Karmiloff-Smith, A. 1984. Children's problem solving. In M. Lamb, A. Brown, and B. Rogoff (eds.). *Advances in Developmental Psychology.* vol. III. Hillsdale, N.J. Erlbaum.

Katz, J. 1977. Foreigner talk input in child second language acquisition: its form and function over time. In C. A. Henning (ed.). *Proceedings of the Los Angeles Second Language Research Forum.* Los Angeles. UCLA.

Katz, J. T. 1981. Children's second-language acquisition: the role of foreigner talk in child-child interaction. *International Journal of the Sociology of Language.* 28.53–68.

Kazazis, K. 1969. Distorted Modern Greek Phonology for Foreigners. *Glossa.* 3:198–209.

Keenan, E., and B. Comrie. 1977. Noun phrase accessibility and universal grammar. *Linguistic Inquiry.* 8.63–99.

Kellerman, E. 1979. The problem with difficulty. *Interlanguage Studies Bulletin,* 4.27–48.

Kellerman, E. 1983. Now you see it, now you don't. In S. Gass and L. Selinker (eds.). *Language Transfer in Language Learning.* Rowley, Mass. Newbury House.

Kellerman, E., and H. Wekker. 1982. On the acquisition of conditional syntax by Dutch learners of English. Paper given at the International Conference of Contrastive Projects. University of Jyväskylä, Finland. June.

Kellerman, S. 1982. Adverbial placement in English as a foreign language—a progress report. Unpublished ms. University of Utrecht.

Kelly, H. H. 1967. Attribution theory in social psychology. *Nebraska Symposium on Motivation.* 14.192–241.

Keyser, S. J. 1968. Review of Sven Jacobson, Adverbial positions in English, *Language* 44. 357-374.

Klein, A. 1982. Once a plus/plusser, always a plus/plusser? On conditionals. Unpublished term paper. English Department, University of Utrecht. The Netherlands.

Krashen, S. 1976. Formal and informal linguistic environments in language learning and language acquisition. *TESOL Quarterly.* 10.157–168.

Krashen, S. D. 1980. The input hypothesis. In J. E. Alatis (ed.). *Current Issues in Bilingual Education.* Washington, D.C. Georgetown University Press.

Krashen, S. 1981a. *Second Language Acquisition and Second Language Learning.* Oxford. Pergamon.

Krashen, S. D. 1981b. The "fundamental pedagogical principle" in second language teaching. *Studia Linguistica.* 35:50–70.

Krashen, S. 1981c. Bilingual education and second language acquisition theory. In California State Department of Education. *Schooling and Language Minority Students: A Theoretical Framework.* Los Angeles. Evaluation and Dissemination and Assessment Center.

Krashen, S. 1982. *Principles and Practice in Second Language Acquisition.* Oxford. Pergamon.

Krashen, S. D. 1983. Newmark's 'ignorance hypothesis' and current second language acquisition theory. In S. Gass and L. Selinker (eds.). *Language Transfer and Language Learning.* Rowley, Mass. Newbury House.

Krashen, S., and R. Scarcella. 1978. On routines and patterns in language acquisition and performance. *Language Learning.* 28.151-167.

Labov, W. 1966. *The Social Stratification of English in New York City.* Washington, D.C. Center for Applied Linguistics.

Labov, W. 1969a. Contraction, deletion and inherent variability of the English copula. *Language.* 45.715-762.

Labov, W. 1969b. The study of language in its social context. *Studium Generale.* 23.30-87.

Labov, W. 1972a. *Sociolinguistic Patterns.* Philadelphia. University of Pennsylvania Press.

Labov, W. 1972b. *Language in the Inner City: Studies in the Black English Vernacular.* Philadelphia. University of Pennsylvania Press.

Labov, W., and D. Fanshel. 1977. *Therapeutic Discourse.* New York. Academic Press.

LaFerriere, M. 1979. Ethnicity in phonological variation and change. *Language.* 55.603-617.

Lakatos, I., and A. Musgrave (eds.). 1970. *Criticism and the Growth of Knowledge.* Cambridge. Cambridge University Press.

Lambert, W. E. 1977. The effects of bilingualism on the individual: cognitive and sociocultural consequences. In P. Hornby (ed.). *Bilingualism: Psychological, Social and Educational Implications.* New York. Academic Press.

Lambert, W. E. 1984. An overview of issues in immersion education. *Studies on Immersion Education: A Collection for United States Educators.* Sacramento, Calif. California State Department of Education.

Lamy, P. 1979. Language and ethnolinguistic identity: the bilingualism question. *International Journal of the Sociology of Language.* 20.23-36.

Lapkin, S., M. Swain, and J. Cummins. 1983. Final Report on the Development of French Language Evaluation Units for Saskatchewan. Toronto: OISE. (ms.)

Larsen-Freeman, D. E. 1976a. ESL teacher speech as input to the ESL learner. *Workpapers in Teaching English as a Second Language.* 10. Los Angeles. University of California at Los Angeles. 45-49.

Larsen-Freeman, D. E. 1976b. An explanation for the morpheme acquisition order of second language learners. *Language Learning.* 26.125-134.

Larsen-Freeman, D. 1979. The importance of input in second language acquisition. Paper presented at LSA winter meeting, Los Angeles. Published in Andersen 1983.

Larsen-Freeman, D. 1980. Introduction to *Discourse Analysis in Second Language Research.* Rowley, Mass. Newbury House.

Larsen-Freeman, D. 1982. Negotiated input and classroom interaction. Paper presented at the Fifteenth Annual TESOL Convention. Honolulu, Hawaii.

Larsen-Freeman, D. 1983a. Second language acquisition: getting the whole picture. In K. Bailey, M. H. Long, and S. Peck (eds.). *Second Language Acquisition Studies.* Rowley, Mass. Newbury House.

Larsen-Freeman, D. 1983b. The importance of input in second language acquisition. In R. Andersen (ed). *Pidginization and Creolization as Language Acquisition.* Rowley, Mass. Newbury House.

Larsson, E. 1979. *La dislocation en français. Etude de syntaxe générative.* Etudes romanes de Lund 28. Lund. CWK Gleerup.

Leet-Pellegrini, H. M. 1980. Conversational dominance as a function of gender and expertise. In H. Giles, W. P. Robinson, and P. Smith (eds.). *Language: Social Psychological Perspectives.* Elmsford, N.Y. Pergamon.

Legaretta. D. 1977. Language choice in bilingual classrooms. *TESOL Quarterly.* 11.1.9-16.

Legaretta, D. 1979. The effects of program models on language acquisition by Spanish speaking children. *TESOL Quarterly.* 13.4.521-534.

Liberman, M., and A. Prince. 1977. On stress and linguistic rhythm. *Linguistic Inquiry.* 8.249-336.

Liceras, J. 1981. Markedness and permeability in interlanguage systems. *Working Papers in Linguistics.* 2. University of Toronto.

Liêm, Nguyen-Dang. 1967. Phonemic syllable repertory in Vietnamese. Papers in South East Asian Linguistics No. 1, 11-18 (Tables 5-24). Linguistic Circle of Canberra Publications, Series A, No. 9.

Lightbown, P. M. 1977. Consistency and variation in the acquisition of French. Unpublished Ph.D. dissertation. Columbia University.

Lightbown, P. M. 1980. The acquisition and use of questions by French L2 learners. In Felix, S. (ed.). *Second Language Development: Trends and Issues.* Tübingen. Narr.

Lightbown, P. 1983. Exploring relationships between developmental and instructional sequences in L_2 acquisition. In H. Selinger and M. Long (eds.). *Classroom Oriented Research in Second Language Acquisition,* Rowley, Mass. Newbury House.

Lightfoot, D. W. 1979a. *Principles of Diachronic Syntax.* Cambridge. Cambridge University Press.

Lightfoot, D. W. 1979b. Review of C. J. Austin (ed.). Mechanisms of syntactic change. *Language* 55.381.

Lightfoot, D. 1982. *The Language Lottery.* Cambridge, Mass. MIT Press.

Linde, C. 1979. Focus of attention and the choice of pronouns in discourse. In Talmy Givon (ed.). *Syntax and Semantics* 12. New York. Academic Press.

Linde, C., and W. Labov. 1975. Spatial networks as a site for the study of language and thought. *Language:* 51:924-939.

Long, M. 1980. Input, interaction and second language acquisition. Ph.D. dissertation. UCLA.

Long, M. 1981a. Input, interaction and second language acquisition. In H. Winitz (ed.). *Native Language and Foreign Language Acquisition.* 379. New York. Annals of the New York Academy of Sciences.

Long, M. 1981b. Variation in linguistic input for second language acquisition. Paper presented at the European-North American Workshop on Cross-Linguistic Second Language Acquisition Research. Lake Arrowhead, Calif.

Long, M. 1981c. Questions in foreigner talk discourse. *Language Learning.* 31.1.135-158.

Long, M. 1983a. Native speakers/non-native speaker conversation in the second language classroom. In M. Clarke and J. Handscombe (eds.). *On TESOL '82: Pacific Perspectives on Language Learning and Teaching.* Washington, D.C. TESOL.

Long, M. 1983b. Training the second language teacher as a classroom researcher. Paper presented at the 34th Annual Round Table on Languages and Linguistics: Applied Linguistics and the Preparation of Second Language Teachers: Toward a Rationale. Washington, D.C. Georgetown University.

Long, M. 1983c. Linguistic and conversational adjustments to non-native speakers. *Studies in Second Language Acquisition.* 5.2. 177-193.

Long, M. 1983d. Native speaker/non-native speaker conversation and the negotiation of comprehensible input. *Applied Linguistics.* 4.2. 126-141.

Long, M. 1983e. Foreigner talk and early interlanguage: a cross-linguistic study. Unpublished paper.

Long, M., L. Adams, M. McLean, and F. Castaños. 1976. Doing things with words—verbal interaction in lockstep and small group classroom situations. In J. Fanselow and R. Crymes (eds.). *On TESOL '76,* Washington, D.C. TESOL.

Long, M., and P. Porter. 1984. Group work, interlanguage talk and classroom second language acquisition. Paper presented at TESOL 1984, Houston.

Long, M., and C. Sato. 1983. Classroom foreigner talk discourse: forms and functions of teachers' questions. In H. W. Seliger and M. H. Long (eds.). *Classroom Oriented Research in Language Acquisition.* Rowley, Mass. Newbury House.

Lowenstamm, J. 1981. On the maximal cluster approach to syllable structure. *Linguistic Inquiry.* 12:575-604.

Madsen, H. S. 1979. An indirect measure of listening comprehension. *Modern Language Journal.* 63.429-435.

Markman, B. R., I. V. Spilka, and G. R. Tucker. 1975. The use of elicited imitation in search of an interim French grammar. *Language Learning.* 25.31-41.

Martin, T. 1982. Introspection and the listening process. M.A. in TESL thesis, Department of English–ESL. UCLA.

Massaro, D. W. 1975. Preperceptual images, processing time, and perceptual units in speech perception. In D. W. Massaro (ed.). *Understanding Language: An Information-Processing Analysis of Speech Perception, Reading, and Psycholinguistics.* New York. Academic Press.

Mazurkevich, I. 1984. Dative questions and markedness. In F. Eckman, L. Bell, and D. Nelson (eds.). *Universals of Second Language Acquisition.* Rowley, Mass. Newbury House.

McCawley, J. D. 1982. *Thirty Million Theories of Grammar.* London. Croom Helm.

McCleary, L. 1980. Tuning in on the monitor and listening to the critic. Unpublished 262K paper, UCLA.

McLaughlin, B. 1982. On the use of miniature artificial languages in second language acquisition research. *Applied Psycholinguistics.* 1.4.357-369.

Meisel, J. 1977. Linguistic simplification: a study of immigrant workers' speech and foreigner talk. In S. Corder and E. Roulet (eds.). *Actes du 5ème Colleque de Linguistique Appliquée de Neuchatel.* Paris. AIMAV/Didier.

Merton, R. K. 1968. *Social Theory and Social Structure.* New York. Free Press.

Milon, J. P. 1975. Dialect in the TESOL program: if you never you better. In M. Burt and H. Dulay (eds.). *On TESOL '75: New Directions in Second Language, Learning, Teaching, and Bilingual Education.* Washington, D.C. TESOL.

Milroy, L. 1980. *Language and Social Networks.* Oxford. B. Blackwell.

Milroy, L. 1982. Language and group identity. *Journal of Multilingual and Multicultural Development.* 3.207-216.

Mitroff, I. I., and R. H. Kilman. 1978. *Methodological Approaches to Social Science.* San Francisco. Jossey-Bass.

Monshi-Tousi, M., A. Hosseine-Fatemi, and J. W. Oller, Jr. 1980. English proficiency and factors in its attainment: a case study of Iranians in the United States. *TESOL Quarterly.* 14:365-372.

Moreau, M.-L., and M. Richelle. 1981. *L'acquisition du langage.* Bruxelles: Mardaga.

Muñoz-Liceras, J. 1983. Markedness, contrastive analysis and the acquisition of Spanish as a second language. Ph.D. dissertation. University of Toronto, Toronto.

Muñoz-Liceras, J. 1984. Variation and interlanguage: accounting for the acquisition of Spanish cleft constructions. Paper presented at the 7th World Congress of Applied Linguistics. Brussels, Belgium.

Murdock, B. B., Jr. 1982. Recognition memory. In C. R. Puff (ed.). *Handbook of Research Methods in Human Memory and Cognition.* New York. Academic Press.

Naiman, N. 1974. The use of elicited imitation in second language acquisition research. *Working Papers on Bilingualism.* 2.1-37.

Nespor, M., and I. Vogel. 1982. Prosodic domains of external Sandhi rules. In H. van der Hulst and N. Smith (eds.). *The Structure of Phonological Representations.* Dordrecht: Foris Publications.

Nichols, R. G. 1948. Factors in listening comprehension. *Speech Monographs.* 15.154-163.

Nie, N., H. Hull, J. Jenkins, K. Steinbrenner, and D. Bent. 1975. *Statistical Package for the Social Sciences. 2d ed.* New York. McGraw-Hill.

Oakeshott-Taylor, J. 1979. Cloze procedure and foreign language listening skills. *IRAL.* 17.150-158.

Ochs, E. 1980. Talking to children in Western Samoa. ms.

Oller, J. W., Jr. 1971. Dictation as a device for testing foreign-language proficiency. *English Language Teaching.* 25.254-259.

Oller, J. 1973. Pragmatic language testing. *Language Sciences.* December 1973.

Oller, J. W., Jr. 1979. *Language Tests at School: A Pragmatic Approach.* London. Longman.

Oller, J. W., Jr., and K. Perkins. 1978. Language proficiency as a source of variance in self-reported affective variables. In J. W. Oller, Jr., and K. Perkins (eds.). *Language in Education: Testing the Tests.* Rowley, Mass. Newbury House.

Oller, J. W., Jr., and K. Perkins (eds.). 1980. *Research in Language Testing.* Rowley, Mass. Newbury House.

Oller, J. W., Jr., and V. Streiff. 1975. Dictation: a test of grammar based expectancies. In R. L. Jones and B. Spolsky (eds.). *Testing Language Proficiency.* Washington, D.C. Center for Applied Linguistics. 71–88.

Olshtain, E., and A. Cohen. 1983. Apology: a speech act set. In N. Wolfson and E. Judd (eds.). *Sociolinguistics and Language Acquisition.* Rowley, Mass. Newbury House.

Otto, S. A. 1979. Listening for note-taking in EST. *TESOL Quarterly.* 13.319–328.

Painchaud, G., A. d'Anglejan, and D. Vincent. 1982. Acquisition du français par un groupe d'immigrants asiatiques. Université de Montréal. Rapport de Recherche, Faculté des Sciences de l'Education, 1982.

Pankhurst, J. N., and M. A. Sharwood Smith. 1978. The developmental history of a written assignment: a study in language learning and communicative strategies. Paper given at the 5th AILA Congress, Montreal.

Parkin, D. 1977. Emergent and stabilized multilingualism. In H. Giles (ed.). *Language, Ethnicity, and Intergroup Relations.* London. Academic Press.

Peal, E., and W. E. Lambert. 1962. The relation of bilingualism to intelligence. *Psychological Monographs.* 76. Whole no. 546.

Peck, Sabrina. 1978. Child-child discourse in second language acquisition. In E. Hatch (ed.). *Second Language Acquisition: A Book of Readings.* Rowley, Mass. Newbury House.

Peck, S. 1980. Language play in child second language acquisition. In D. Larsen-Freeman (ed.). *Discourse Analysis in Second Language Research.* Rowley, Mass. Newbury House.

Perkins, K., and D. Larsen-Freeman. 1975. The effect of formal language instruction on the order of morpheme acquisition. *Language Learning.* 25:237–243.

Peters, A. 1983. *The Units of Language Acquisition.* Cambridge, England. Cambridge University Press.

Peters, S. 1972. The projection problem: how is a grammar to be selected? In S. Peters (ed.). *Goals of Linguistic Theory.* Englewood Cliffs, N.J. Prentice-Hall.

Pica, T., and M. Long. 1982. The classroom linguistic and conversational performance of experienced and inexperienced teachers. Paper presented at the 16th Annual TESOL Convention. Honolulu, Hawaii.

Pienemann, M. 1980. The second language acquisition of immigrant children. In S. Felix (ed.). *Second Language Development: Trends and Issues.* Tübingen. Narr.

Pinker, S. 1979. Formal models of language learning. *Cognition.* 7.217–283.

Plann, S. 1976. The Spanish immersion program: towards native-like proficiency in a classroom dialect? Master's thesis. UCLA.

Plann, S. 1979. Morphological problems in the acquisition of Spanish in an immersion classroom. In R. W. Andersen (ed.). *The Acquisition and Use of Spanish and English as First and Second Languages.* Washington, D.C. TESOL.

Plann, S. 1980. *Relative Clauses without Overt Antecedents and Related Constructions.* University of California Press.

Popham, W. J., and T. R. Husek. 1969. Implications of criterion-referenced measurement. *Journal of Educational Measurement.* 6.1.1–9.

Poplack, S. 1978. Dialect acquisition among Puerto Rican bilinguals. *Language in Society.* 7. 89–103.

Porter, D. 1978. Cloze procedure and equivalence. *Language Learning.* 28.333–341.

Porter, P. 1983. Variations in the conversations of adult learners of English as a function of the proficiency level of the participants. Ph.D. dissertation. Stanford University.

Prince, Ellen. 1981. Toward a taxonomy of given-new information. In P. Cole (ed.). *Radical Pragmatics.* New York. Academic Press.

Quirk, R., S. Greenbaum, G. Leech, and J. Svartvik. 1972. *A Grammar of Contemporary English.* London. Longman.

Ravem, R. 1974. The development of Wh questions in first and second language learners. In J. Richards (ed.). *Error Analysis.* London. Longman.

Redard, F. 1976. Etude des formes interrogatives en français chez les enfants de trois ans. *Etudes de Linguistique Appliquée.* 21.98–110.

Reinhart, T. 1982. Principles of Gestalt perception in the temporal organization of narrative texts. Paper presented at Synopsis No. 4, Tel Aviv.

Reinstein, S., and J. Hoffman. 1972. Dialect interaction between Black and Puerto Rican children in New York City: implications for the language arts. *Elementary English.* 49. 190–196.

Reynolds, P. D. 1971. *A Primer in Theory Construction.* Indianapolis. Bobbs-Merrill.

Richards, J. C. 1974. Social factors, interlanguage and language learning. In J. C. Richards (ed.). *Error Analysis: Perspectives on Second Language Acquisition.* London. Longman.

Rivero, M. 1979. That-relatives and deletion in COMP in Spanish. In J. T. Jensen (ed.). *Cahiers Linguistics d'Ottawa.* 9. Proceedings of the 10th Annual Meeting of the North Eastern Linguistic Society.

Rivero, M. 1982. Las relativas restrictivas con *que. Nueva revista de filología hispánica.* 31. 195–234.

Rubin, J. 1975. What the "good language learner" can teach us. *TESOL Quarterly.* 9:41–51.

Ruhlen, M. 1975. *A Guide to the Languages of the World.* Stanford. Stanford University Language Universals Project.

Ryan, E. B. 1979. Why do low-prestige language varieties persist? In H. Giles and R. N. St. Clair (eds.). *Language and Social Psychology.* Baltimore. University Park Press.

Sato, C. 1984. Phonological processes in second language acquisition: another look at interlanguage syllable structure. *Language Learning.* 34.4.43–57.

Savignon, S. J. 1982. Dictation as a measure of communicative competence in French as a second language. *Language Learning.* 32.33–51.

Saville-Troike, M. 1983. "It's easy to English": new research findings on children's second language acquisition. Paper presented at the State Convention of Illinois TESOL/BE, Springfield, Ill. April.

Saville-Troike, M. 1984. What *really* matters in second language learning for academic achievement? *TESOL Quarterly.* 18.2.199–219.

Scarcella, R., and C. Higa. 1981. Input, negotiation and age differences in second language acquisition. *Language Learning.* 31.2.409–437.

Scarcella, R., and C. Higa. 1982. Input and age difference in second language acquisition. In S. Krashen, R. Scarcella, and M. Long. (eds.). *Child-Adult Differences in Second Language Acquisition.* Rowley, Mass. Newbury House.

Schachter, J. 1983a. Nutritional needs of language learners. In M. A. Clarke and J. Handscombe (eds.). *On TESOL '82: Pacific Perspectives on Language Learning and Teaching.* Washington, D.C. TESOL.

Schachter, J. 1983b. Three approaches to the study of input. Paper presented at the Xth University of Michigan Conference on Applied Linguistics, Input in Second Language Acquisition. Ann Arbor, Mich.

Schachter, J. 1984. A universal input condition. In W. Rutherford (ed.). *Universals and Second Language Acquisition.* Amsterdam. John Benjamins.

Schinke, L. 1981. English foreigner talk in content classrooms. Ph.D. dissertation, Northwestern University.

Schinke-Llano, L. 1983. Foreigner talk in content classrooms. In H. W. Seliger and M. H. Long (eds.). *Classroom Oriented Research in Language Acquisition.* Rowley, Mass. Newbury House.

Schmidt, R. 1977. Sociolinguistic variation and language transfer in phonology. *Working Papers in Bilingualism.* 12.79-95.

Schumann, J. H. 1975. Affective factors and the problem of age in second language acquisition. *Language Learning.* 25.2.209-235.

Schumann, J. H. 1976. Social distance as a factor in second language acquisition. *Language Learning.* 26.2. 391-408.

Schumann, J. H. 1978a. The acculturation model for second-language acquisition. In R. C. Gingras (ed.). *Second Language Acquisition and Foreign Language Teaching.* Arlington, Va. Center for Applied Linguistics.

Schumann, J. 1978b. *The Pidginization Process: A Model for Second Language Acquisition.* Rowley, Mass. Newbury House.

Schumann, J. 1979. The acquisition of English negation by speakers of Spanish: a review of the literature. In R. W. Andersen (ed.). *The Acquisition and Use of Spanish and English as First and Second Languages.* Washington, D.C. TESOL.

Schumann, J. H. 1981. Reaction to Gilbert's discussion in R. Andersen. *New Dimensions in Second Language Acquisition Research.* Rowley, Mass. Newbury House.

Schumann, J. H. 1983. Art and science in second language acquisition research. In M. A. Clarke and J. Handscombe (eds.). *On TESOL '82: Pacific Perspectives on Language Learning and Teaching.* Washington, D.C. TESOL.

Schumann, J. H. 1984. Non-syntactic speech in the Spanish-English basilang. In R. Andersen (ed.) *Second Languages: A Cross-Linguistic Perspective.* Rowley, Mass.: Newbury House.

Schwartz, T. 1981. The acquisition of culture. *Ethos.* 9.1.4-17.

Scollon, R. 1976. *Conversations with a One Year Old.* Honolulu. University of Hawaii.

Searle, J., 1975. Indirect speech acts. In P. Cole and J. Morgan (eds.). *Syntax and Semantics.* vol. 3. *Speech Acts.* New York. Academic Press.

Searle, J., 1979. *Expression and Meaning.* Cambridge. Cambridge University Press.

Seliger, H. W. 1977. Does practice make perfect?: a study of interaction patterns and L2 competence. *Language Learning.* 27.2.263-278.

Seliger, H. W. 1983. Learner interaction in the classroom and its effect on language acquisition. In H. W. Seliger and M. H. Long (eds.). *Classroom Oriented Research in Second Language Acquisition.* Rowley, Mass. Newbury House.

Selinker, L. 1972. Interlanguage. *IRAL.* 10.209-231.

Selinker, L., M. Swain, and G. Dumas. 1975. The interlanguage hypothesis extended to children. *Language Learning.* 25.139-151.

Selkirk, E. 1978. *On Prosodic Structure and Its Relation to Syntactic Structure.* Indiana Unlversity Linguistic Club.

Selkirk, E. 1982. The syllable. In H. van der Hulst and N. Smith (eds.). *The Structure of Phonological Representations. Part II.* Dordrecht. Foris.

Sharwood Smith, M.A. 1981. On interpreting language input. Paper given at the BAAL Seminar on interpretation of strategies in language learning. Lancaster, 1981.

Sharwood Smith, M.A. 1983a. On first language loss in the second language acquirer: problems of transfer. In S. Gass and L. Selinker (eds.). *Language Transfer in Language Learning.* Rowley, Mass. Newbury House.

Sharwood Smith, M.A. 1983b. Crosslinguistic aspects of second language acquisition. *Applied Linguistics.* 3.192-199.

Sharwood Smith, M., and E. Kellerman. Forthcoming. The interpretation of language output. In H. Dechert and M. Raupach (eds.). *Transfer in Production.* Norwood, N.J. Ablex Publishing Corporation.

Shatz, M., and R. Gelman. 1973. The development of communication skills: modifications in the speech of young children as a function of listener. *Monographs of the Society for Research in Child Development.* 152.38.5.

Siegel, S. 1956. *Nonparametric Statistics for the Behavioral Sciences.* New York. McGraw-Hill.

Slobin, D. 1973. Cognitive prerequisites for the development of grammar. In C. A. Ferguson and D. I. Slobin (eds.). *Studies of Child Language Development.* New York. Holt, Rinehart and Winston.

Smith, F. 1978. *Reading without Nonsense.* New York. Teachers' College Press.

Smith, F. 1982. *Writing and the Writer.* New York. Holt, Rinehart and Winston.

Smith, P., M. H. Giles, and M. Hewstone. 1980. Sociolinguistics: A social psychological perspective. In R. N. St. Clair and H. Giles (eds.). *The Social and Psychological Contexts of Language.* Hillsdale, NJ. Lawrence Erlbaum Associates.

Smith, L. E., and K. Rafiqzad. 1979. English for cross-cultural communication: the question of intelligibility. *TESOL Quarterly.* 13.371-380.

Snow, C. 1972. Mother's speech to children learning language. *Child Development.* 43.549-565.

Snow, C., and C. Ferguson. (eds.). 1977. *Talking to Children.* New York. Cambridge University Press.

Snow, C. E., R. Van Eeden, and P. Muysken. 1981. The interactional origins of foreigner talk. *International Journal of the Sociology of Language.* 28:83-93.

Snow, C. E., and M. Hoefnagel-Höhle. 1982. School-age second language learners' access to simplified linguistic input. *Language Learning.* 32.2. 411-430.

Solan, L. 1981. Fixing parameters: language acquisition and variation. In J. Pustejousky and V. Burke (eds.). Markedness and learnability. *University of Massachusetts Occasional Papers in Linguistics.* 6.

Spolsky, B. 1973. What does it mean to know a language; or how do you get someone to perform his competence? In J. Oller and J. Richards (eds.). *Focus on the Learner.* Rowley, Mass. Newbury House.

Stauble, A. 1978. The process of decreolization: a model for second language development. *Language Learning.* 28.29-54.

Stauble, A. M. 1984. A comparison of a Spanish-English and a Japanese-English second language continuum: negation and verb morphology. In R. Andersen (ed.) *Second Languages: A Cross Linguistic Perspective.* Presented at the European-North American Conference.

Stern, H. 1981. Communicative language teaching and learning: toward a synthesis. In H. Altman and J. Alatis (eds.). *The Second Language Classroom: Directions for the 1980s.* New York. Oxford University Press.

Stern, H. H. 1983. *Fundamental Concepts of Language Teaching.* London. Oxford University Press.

Stevick, E. 1976. *Memory, Meaning and Method.* Rowley, Mass. Newbury House.

Stevick, E. 1980. *Teaching Languages: A Way and Ways.* Rowley, Mass. Newbury House.

Stevick, E. 1981. The Levertov machine. In R. Scarcella and S. Krashen (eds.). *Research in Second Language Acquisition.* Rowley, Mass. Newbury House.

Stewart, W. A. 1964. Urban Negro speech: sociolinguistic factors affecting English teaching. In R. W. Shuy (ed.). *Social Dialects and Language Learning.* Champaign, Ill. National Council of Teachers of English.

Stinchcombe, J. 1978. *Constructing Social Theories.* Englewood Cliffs, N.J. Prentice-Hall.

Strauss, S. (ed.). 1982. *U-Shaped Behavioral Growth.* New York. Academic Press.

Strauss, S., and D. Stein. 1978. U-shaped curves in language acquisition and the learning of physical concepts. *Die Neueren Sprachen.* 3.326-340.

Strong, M. 1983. Social styles and the second language acquisition of Spanish-speaking kindergartners. *TESOL Quarterly.* 17:241-258.

Swain, M. 1981. Target language use in the wider environment as a factor in its acquisition. In R. Anderson (ed.). *New Dimensions in Second Language Acquisition Research.* Rowley, Mass. Newbury House.

Swain, M., G. Dumas, and N. Naiman. 1974. Alternatives to spontaneous speech: elicited translation and imitation as indicators of second language competence. *Working Papers on Bilingualism.* 3.68-79.

Swain, M., and S. Lapkin. 1982. Evaluating Bilingual Education: A Canadian Case Study. Clevedon, England: Multilingual Matters, 1982.

Swain, M., S. Lapkin, and C. M. Andrew. 1981. Early French immersion later on. *Journal of Multilingual and Multicultural Development.* 2.1-23.

Tajfel, H. 1974. Social identity and intergroup behavior. *Social Science Information.* 13. 65-93.

Tajfel, H. 1978. Social categorization, social identity and social comparison. In H. Tajfel (ed.). *Differentiation between Social Groups: Studies in the Social Psychology of Intergroup Relations.* London. Academic Press.

Tarone, E. 1977. Conscious communication strategies in interlanguage: a progress report. In H. Brown, C. Yorio, and R. Crymes (eds.). *On TESOL '77.* Washington, D.C. TESOL.

Tarone, E. 1979. Interlanguage as chameleon. *Language Learning.* 29.181-191.

Tarone, E. 1980. Communication strategies, foreigner talk and repair in interlanguage. *Language Learning.* 30.417-431.

Tarone, E. 1981. Some thoughts on the notion of communication strategy. *TESOL Quarterly.* 15.3.285-295.

Tarone, E. 1982. Systematicity and attention in interlanguage. *Language Learning.* 32.69-84.

Tarone, E. 1983. On the variability of interlanguage systems. *Applied Linguistics.* 4.142-163.

Tarone, E., U. Frauenfelder, and L. Selinker. 1976. Systematicity/variability and stability/instability in interlanguage systems. In H. D. Brown (ed.). *Papers in Second Language Acquisition* (Language Learning Special Issue No. 4). 93-134.

Taylor, B. P. 1976. The use of overgeneralisation and transfer learning strategies by elementary and intermediate students of ESL. *Language Learning.* 25.1.73-92.

Taylor, D. M., R. Meynard, and E. Rheault. 1977. Threat to ethnic identity and second-language learning. In H. Giles (ed.). *Language, Ethnicity and Intergroup Relations.* London. Academic Press.

Terry, R. M. 1970. *Contemporary French interrogative structures.* Montréal: Editions Cosmos.

Thakerar, J. N., H. Giles, and J. Cheshire. 1982. Psychological and linguistic parameters of speech accommodation theory. In C. Fraser and K. R. Scherer (eds.). *Advances in the Social Psychology of Language.* Cambridge. Cambridge University Press.

Theobald, J. T., and J. E. Alexander. 1977. An auditory cloze procedure for assessing the difficulty level of teacher instructional talk in the intermediate grades. *Elementary School Journal.* 77.389-394.

Thomas, J. 1983. Cross-cultural pragmatic failure. *Applied Linguistics.* 4.2.91-112.

Thompson, L. 1965. *A Vietnamese Grammar.* Seattle. University of Washington Press.

Tikunoff, W. J. 1983. *An Emerging Description of Successful Bilingual Instruction: An Executive Summary of Part 1 of the SBIF Descriptive Study.* San Francisco, Calif. Far West Laboratory for Educational Research and Development.

Trévise, A. 1984. Adult Spanish speakers and the acquisition of French negation forms. In R. W. Andersen (ed.). *Second Language Acquisition: A Cross-Linguistic Perspective.* Rowley, Mass. Newbury House.

Trévise, A. In press. Is it transferable, topicalization? In E. Kellerman and M. Sharwood Smith (eds.). *Cross-Linguistic Influence in Second Language Acquisition.* Oxford. Pergamon.

Trudgill, P. 1972. Sex, covert prestige and linguistic change in the urban British English of Norwich. *Language in Society.* 1.179-195.

Trudgill, P. No date. Linguistic accommodation: sociolinguistic observations on a sociopsychological theory. Unpublished ms.

Urzua, C. 1980. Language input to young second language learners. Paper presented at the Los Angeles Second Language Acquisition Research Forum. UCLA. March.

Valdman, A. 1975. Error analysis and pedagogical ordering. In S. Pit Corder and E. Roulet (eds.). *Theoretical Models in Applied Linguistics.* vol. 5. Brussels. AIMAV.

Vander Brook, S., K. Schlue, and C. Campbell. 1977. Discourse and second language acquisition of yes/no questions. In H. D. Brown, C. Yorio, and R. Crymes (eds.). *On TESOL '77, Teaching and Learning English as a Second Language: Trends in Research and Practice.* Washington, D.C. TESOL.

Vander Brook, S., K. Schlue, and C. Campbell. 1980. Discourse and second language acquisition of yes/no questions. In D. Larsen-Freeman (ed.). *Discourse Analysis in Second Language Research,* Rowley, Mass. Newbury House.

Van de Weide, M. 1982. Preference and deviations in adverbial placement by advanced Dutch learners of EFL: a performance analysis. Unpublished M.A. term paper. English Department, University of Utrecht.

van Dijk, T. A., and W. Kintsch. 1983. *Strategies of Discourse Comprehension.* New York. Academic Press.

Van Riemskijk, H. 1978. A case study in syntactic markedness. Lisse. The Peter de Ridder Press.

Varonis, E. Marlos, and S. Gass. 1982. The comprehensibility of non-native speech. *Studies in Second Language Acquisition.* 4.2.114-136.

Varonis, E. Marlos, and S. Gass. 1985a. Miscommunication in NS/NNS interactions. *Language in Society. 14.*2.

Varonis, E. Marlos, and S. Gass. 1985b. Non-native/non-native conversations: a model for negotiation of meaning. *Applied Linguistics.* 6.1.71-90.

Wagner-Gough, J. 1975. Comparative studies in second language learning. *CAL-ERIC/CLL Series on Languages and Linguistics.* 26.

Wagner-Gough, J., and E. Hatch. 1975. The importance of input data in second language acquisition studies. *Language Learning.* 25.297-307.

Weber, M. 1964. *The Theory of Social and Economic Organization.* New York. Free Press.

Wells, C. G. 1975. *Coding Manual for the Description of Child Speech.* University of Bristol School of Education.

Wells, G. 1981. *Learning through Interaction.* Cambridge. Cambridge University Press.

Wells, C. G., M. Montgomery, and M. MacLure. 1979. Adult-child discourse: outline of a model of analysis. *Journal of Pragmatics.* 3.337-380.

White, J., and P. M. Lightbown. 1984. Asking and answering in ESL classes. *Canadian Modern Language Review.* 40. 228-244.

Wilcox, G. K. 1978. The effect of accent on listening comprehension: a Singapore study. *English Language Teaching Journal.* 32.118-127.

Willerman, B. S. 1979. Effects of nonclassroom environment on ESL performance. Paper presented at the Thirteenth Annual TESOL Convention, Boston.

Wode, H. 1976. Developmental sequences in naturalistic L2 acquisition. *Working Papers on Bilingualism.* 11.1-31.

Wode, H. 1978. Free vs. bound morphemes in three types of language acquisition. *Interlanguage Studies Bulletin. Utrecht.* 3.6-22.

Wode, H. 1981. Language acquisitional universals: a unified view of language acquisition. In H. Winitz (ed.). *Native Language and Foreign Language Acquisition.* Annals of the New York Academy of Sciences. vol. 379.218-234.

Wode, H. 1982. *Learning a Second Language,* Tübingen. Narr.

Wode, H., J. Bahns, H. Bedey, and W. Frank. 1978. Developmental sequence: an alternative approach to morpheme order. *Language Learning.* 3.175-185.

Wolfram, W. A. 1973. *Sociolinguistic Aspects of Assimilation: Puerto Rican English in New York City.* Washington, D.C. Center for Applied Linguistics.

Wong-Fillmore, L. 1976. The second time around: cognitive and social strategies in second language acquisition. Unpublished Ph.D. dissertation. Stanford.

Wong-Fillmore, L. 1982. Instructional language as linguistic input: second language learning in classrooms. In L. C. Wilkinson (ed.). *Communicating in the Classroom.* New York. Academic Press.

Wong-Fillmore, L., P. Ammon, M. S. Ammon, K. DeLucchi, J. Jensen, B. McLaughlin, and M. Strong. 1983. *Learning Language through Bilingual Instruction: Second Year Report.* Submitted to the National Institute of Education. Berkeley, Calif. University of California.

Yoshida, M. 1978. The acquisition of English vocabulary by a Japanese-speaking child. In E. Hatch (ed.). *Second Language Acquisition.* Rowley, Mass. Newbury House.

Zobl, H. 1979. Nominal and pronominal interrogation in the the speech of adult francophone ESL learners: some insights into the workings of transfer. *SPEAQ Journal.* 3. 69–93.

Zobl, H. 1980a. Developmental and transfer errors: their common bases and (possibly) differential effects on subsequent learning. *TESOL Quarterly.* 14. 469–479.

Zobl, H. 1980b. The formal and developmental selectivity of L1 influence on L2 acquisition. *Language Learning.* 30.43–57.

Zobl, H. 1983. Markedness and the projection problem. *Language Learning.* 33.293–313.

Zobl, H. 1984. The wave model of linguistic change and interlanguage systems. *Studies in Second Language Acquisition.* 6.2.160–185